The first 40 Presidents of Queens' College, Cambridge

Their lives and times

Jonathan H. Dowson

Grosvenor House
Publishing Limited

This book is published by
Grosvenor House Publishing Ltd
Link House
140 The Broadway, Tolworth, Surrey, KT6 7HT.
www.grosvenorhousepublishing.co.uk

A CIP record for this book
is available from the British Library

ISBN 978-1-83975-889-8

Preface

History not only helps us to understand the ever-changing present, but also to navigate our future. The focus of the present account is the lives- and their contexts- of the first 40 Presidents of Queens' College, Cambridge, from the early fifteenth century to March, 2021.

There have been several histories of Queens', most notably those of William George Searle and John Twigg. Searle was a fellow of Queens' during 1854-58, before becoming vicar of Oakington, Cambridgeshire. He published 'The History of the Queens' College of St Margaret and St Bernard in the University of Cambridge' in two volumes; Volume 1 in 1867 and Volume 2 in 1871. As the College website notes:

'The two published volumes were an antiquarian-style history strictly chronological, authorities carefully referenced and with many original documents transcribed and published for the first time'. However, the project was never completed and the account ends in 1662. Twigg's 'A History of Queens' College, Cambridge, 1448-1986' was published in 1987, and is:

'more a social history than a chronological story. Chapters are arranged by topic, rather than period...It is written to the standards of modern professional historians'. It provides 'an extraordinary variety of information', with 29 chapters and 19 appendices. Another history of the College was published in 1899 by Joseph Henry Gray, a fellow of Queens' for over 50 years, entitled 'The Queens' College of St Margaret and St Bernard in the University of Cambridge'. Although Gray notes:

'Mr. Searle has been my chief guide as far as his work extends viz, to 1662, and a very large proportion of my materials has been derived from him', nevertheless, his book has been considered to have:

'some value for documentary events in the 19th century which were within living memory when this work was written'.

While there are no other substantial histories of Queens', many extensive and detailed accounts of aspects of the College's history have been included in the College's annual 'Record', and on the College website, in particular by the Reverend Dr Jonathan Holmes, fellow and former Dean of Chapel, and Dr Robin Walker, fellow and former Junior Bursar and Estate Bursar. Also, there is a short account of the foundation of the College, and its buildings, by John Willis Clark, academic and antiquarian, in 1898. The College's collection of paintings, made available online by the charity 'Art UK', (online: Discover Artworks-Art UK. Queens' College, Cambridge), contains portraits of 20 of the first 40 Presidents.

The two main histories have the College as the focus, while the present account considers the institution through the lives and times of each of the 40 Presidents, in chronological order, and attempts to collate a range of related events for which information is available.

Most of us, including most readers of history, are interested in biography, which brings a structure to a variety of related past events. When I practised medicine, I used to reflect that an uninteresting life-history does not exist, and I have certainly found this to be true for the Presidents of Queens'. I hope that this account can sustain the interest, not only of a member of the College, but also of a reader who is interested in the interactions between the academic community and the social, scientific and political life in Britain, over the last five and a half centuries.

Jonathan Dowson. March 2021.

Jonathan Hudson Dowson. M.A., M.D., (Cantab.), D.P.M., PhD, (Edin.), F.R.C.Psych.

Jonathan Hudson Dowson was born in Leeds in 1942, the only child of John Heaton Dowson, woollen manufacturer, and Margot Blanche Hudson, teacher. He was educated at The Leys School Cambridge, Queens' College Cambridge, and St Thomas' Medical School London. He was married to Lynn Susan Dothie in December 1965. He moved to Edinburgh in 1967 for postgraduate training in psychiatry at the Royal Edinburgh Hospital, obtaining the Edinburgh University Diploma in Psychological Medicine in 1969. He became a Fellow of the Royal College of Psychiatrists in 1972. He was a Lecturer in Anatomy, Edinburgh University, during 1969-72, while carrying out research in neurohistochemistry at the Medical Research Council's Brain Metabolism Unit. He proceeded PhD at Edinburgh in 1972. Subsequently, he was a Lecturer in Psychiatry, University of Edinburgh and, during 1975-77, Consultant Psychiatrist with the Wessex Health Authority, based at Swindon, Wiltshire. In 1977 he was appointed as Honorary Consultant Psychiatrist and University Lecturer in Psychiatry at Cambridge University, based at Addenbrooke's Hospital. He proceeded MD at Cambridge in 1985 and became Director of Studies for Clinical Medicine for Queens'. His research interests have included neuronal lipopigment in the aging and dementing brain, personality disorders and adult attention-deficit disorders. He retired in 2009. He and Lynn have three children and six grandchildren. He is a Grand Officer of the Freemasons' United Grand Lodge of England, a Liveryman of the Worshipful Company of Horners and, since 1985, a Fellow-Commoner of Queens' College, Cambridge.

Cover.

A page of a 12th century volume: 'Miscellanea Theologica MSS' in the Old Library, Jesus College, Cambridge. Photographed by the author. The inscription at the top of the page shows that it was once owned by the first President of Queens':

'Lib magri Andree Doket

rectoris sci Botulfi Cantabr.' (...Andrew Doket...rector... Botolph's Cambridge).

The further inscription reads:

'Liber Thomae Cave

Quicquid erit, superanda omnis fortuna ferando est'

(The second line is a quotation from Virgil's Aeneid- the first word can also be spelt as quidquid- which translates as:

'Our fate, whatever it be, is to be overcome by our patience under it'). By permission of the Master and Fellows of Jesus College, Cambridge.

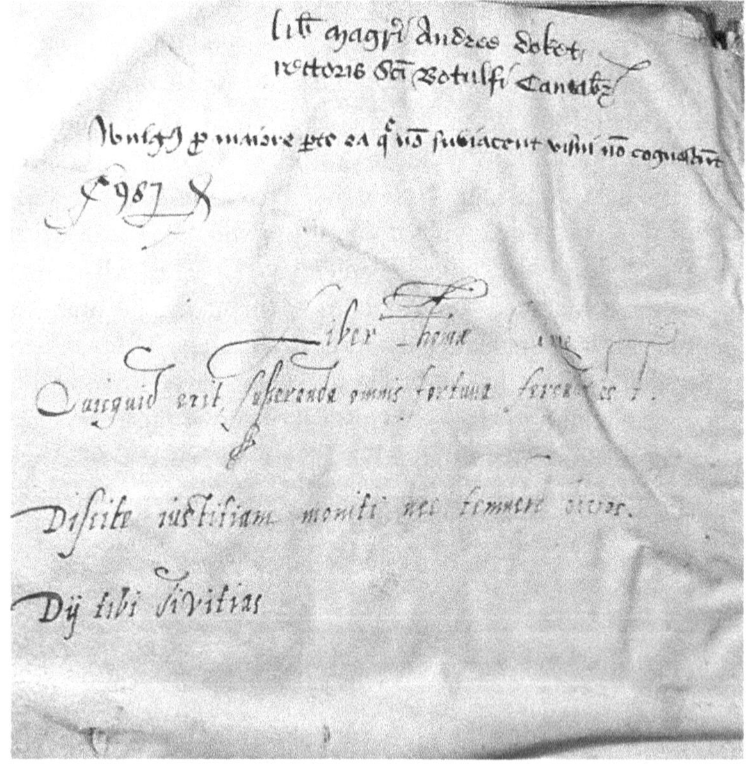

A drawing by the antiquary William Cole, (1714-82), of the gravestone of the first President of Queens'. This was in the original chapel of the College, but is no longer extant. (The Cole Manuscripts are in the British Library, Add MS 5803, folios 10v-19; Add MS 5808, folios 120v-123v). Photographed by the author.

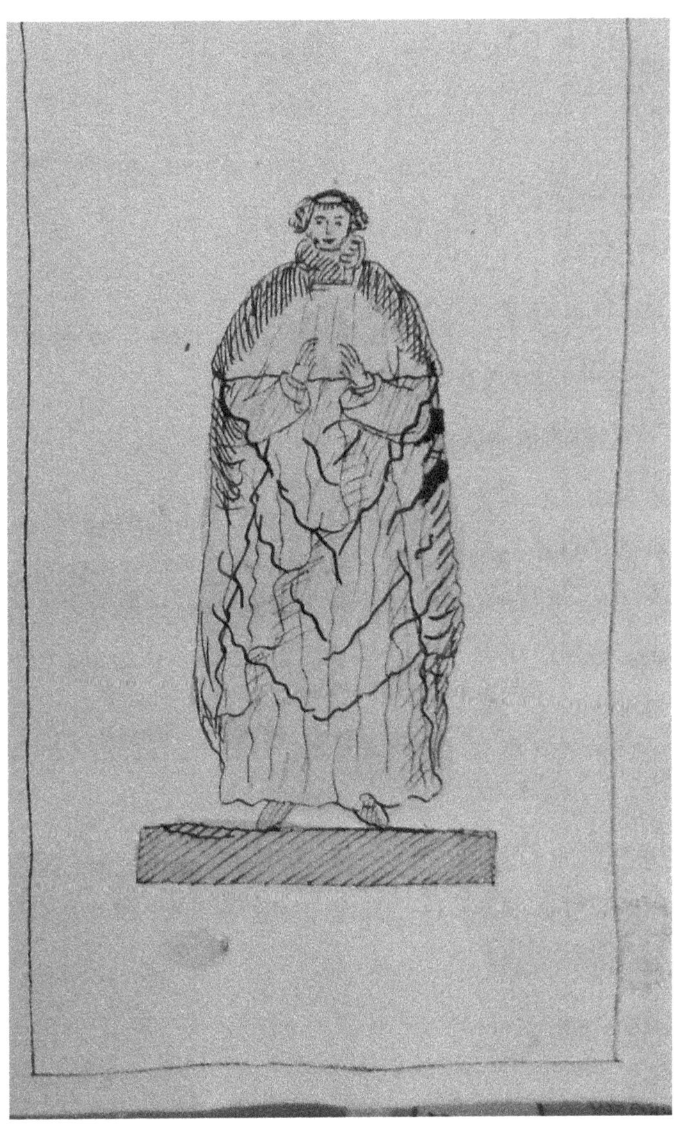

Queens' College, Cambridge. Produced by David Loggan, c1685, published in 'Cantabrigia Illustrata', 1690. David Loggan's work provides the oldest views of the colleges.

Foreword

Looking ahead: the future of the College seen in October 2021 by the 40th President.

Queens' continues to be committed to providing transformational intellectual opportunities to students and is thought of as one of the most friendly, supportive, inclusive and diverse academic settings in both Cambridge and Oxford.

In this generation-defining moment, we continue to live in a world of 'unusual uncertainty' that requires us to pull even more from a dwindling reservoir of resiliance. Yet, due to the agility and responsiveness of many members of our commumity, several good things are happening that bode well not just for the immediate period ahead but also for the longer-term.

There are several areas where important progress is being made: from open competitive and inclusive transition processes for key decision-makers in College to exciting opportunities to bring new intellectual capabilities to Queens'; and from enhanced donor-supported capacity to alleviate what otherwise would be crushing financial and welfare burdens on students and Fellows, to the launch of an exciting project to convert Owlstone Croft from what is commonly (and erroneously) viewed as a secondary residence site, to a dynamic part of Queens' that contributes materially to our intellectual vibrancy and curiosity.

Throughout all this, we are doing more to expand access and patrticipation. This is a particularly critical effort at a time when the great 'unequalising' effects of the virus risk undoing years of gains in reducing the inequality of educational opportunity.

None of this would be possible without the considerable help we get from our alumni, donors and friends. This support has been critical, and especially so at a time when major sources of funding are severely damaged (such as room rents and conference income) and we continuously risk the 'urgent and important' crowding out important strategic efforts.

As has been crystal clear from lots of of feedback to the donor-supported 'Covid Student Support Fund', alumni involvement has been instrumental in illustrating and reinforcing a critical message that serves as an important anchor to navigate better this difficult period of solidarity, emphasizing that we are all in this together, and that we will manage through it together.

Dr Mohamed A. El-Erian.

Contents

CHAPTER 1

Andrew Doket (Dokett, Ducket, Duckett, Dukett, Dogket, Dogett). President 1448-84.

Summary.

Andrew Doket was the first President of Queens' College, Cambridge, which was founded at Doket's instigation by Henry VI's Queen, Margaret of Anjou, in 1448. At this time, Doket was rector of St Botolph's Church in Cambridge and the Principal and owner of a lodging house for students, the St Bernard's Hostel. Doket would need formidable diplomatic skills to guide his new College though the years of imminent national turmoil known as the 'Wars of the Roses', which involved a:

'breakdown in the structure of politics and society, exacerbated by Henry VI's inability to govern'. Colleges whose foundations were associated with the 'Lancastrian' regime of Henry VI were vulnerable after his overthrow by the 'Yorkist' Edward IV in 1461. However, the new King did not show hostility to Queens', although support was withdrawn from Henry VI's linked foundations of Eton College and King's College, Cambridge.

In 1464, Edward married Elizabeth Woodville, despite her previous Lancastrian connections and her status as a commoner. She promoted the College's interests and, in 1475, the first Statutes for the College were issued, in which the Queen was named as the foundress.

In the 1460s and 70s, Doket took up four church appointments in other parts of the country, including Chancellor of Lichfield Cathedral.

Edward died in 1483, and his brother seized the throne as Richard III. Both before and after his accession, Richard was a generous benefactor of the College and, in 1484, his Queen, Anne, was named as both patroness and yet another royal foundress. But, after a further two years of civil war, Richard was defeated at the battle of Bosworth, to be succeeded by Henry VII, whose regime proceeded to deprive the College of Richard's generous endowments. Henry and his Queen Elizabeth, (the daughter of Elizabeth Woodville), did not show any obvious interest in the College.

Doket died in 1484 and was buried in the crypt of the College chapel, (the present Memorial Library). He is represented by a stone carving as part of the keystone of the outer arch of the main Queens' College gateway:

'Dokett had been spared to govern his foundation during the most critical period of its existance. Its prosperity was largely, perhaps almost wholly, due to his personal exertions and to the wisdom wherewith he had shaped its course through the stormy years of war and revolution. He had commenced with four Fellows: the number of Fellows was now seventeen; the buildings were practically completed, and the College was not inadequately endowed'.

Timeline.

c1410. Estimated date of birth.

1422. Accession of Henry VI.

1444. Appointed rector of St Botolph's Church, Cambridge.

1445. Henry VI marries Margaret of Anjou, who is aged 15.

1446. The College of 'Sancti Bernardi' (St Bernard) is founded by a charter of Henry VI. Doket is named as President.

1447. A second charter of Henry VI refounds St Bernard's College on a new site, which is part of the present site of Queens' College.

1448. The College of St Bernard is dissolved, refounded and renamed, by a charter of Queen Margaret, as:
'Reginale Collegium Sancte Margarete et Sancti Bernadi' (The Queen's College of St Margaret and St Bernard). Doket is named as President. (The Queen's charter of the 15th of April followed a charter of King Henry dated the 30th March, granting his Queen licence to found a college).

1450. The College's Old Court completed, except for the north-west corner.
1454. The College chapel consecrated.
1455. The Wars of the Roses begin.
c1460. Estimated date of the construction of the riverside building, now part of the President's Lodge and the oldest college building on the river.
1461. Henry VI is deposed. Accession of Edward IV.
1464. Edward IV marries Elizabeth Woodville, (Wydville, Wydeville, Widvile).
1465. Queen Elizabeth named as patroness of the College.
1467. Prebendary of Ryton at Lichfield Cathedral.
1468. Visit of Queen Elizabeth to the College.
1470. Henry VI restored to the throne. Resigns as rector of St Botolph's Church. Chancellor of Lichfield Cathedral.
1471. Edward IV restored to the throne. Death (probable murder) of Henry VI in the Tower of London.
1475. The first Statutes for the College are given by Queen Elizabeth, who is referred to as the foundress.
1477. Endowment made to the College by Richard, Duke of Gloucester.
1483. Death of Edward IV. Accession of Richard of Gloucester as Richard III.
1484. Second endowment by Richard. Death of Andrew Doket.
1485. Death of Richard III. Accession of Henry VII.

Priest with formidable diplomatic skills, who was responsible for the foundation of Queens' College in 1448. Foundation President for 36 years.

Foundation of 'The Queen's College of St Margaret and St Bernard', 1448:

The first of two charters relating to foundation of the: 'Reginale Collegium Sancte Margarete et Sancti Bernardi in universitate Cantebr.' ('The Queen's College of St Margaret and St Bernard'...), now held in the Cambridge University Library, was signed at

Westminster, 'Per ipsum regem...' (through the King himself) on 'tricesimo die Martii anno regni nostri vicesimo sexto' (the thirtieth day of March in the twenty-sixth year of our reign, ie 1448).[2] It was issued on behalf of King Henry VI and granted to his Queen, Margaret of Anjou, the lands of St Bernard's College and licence to found a new college. Andrew Doket (Andream Doket) was named as the first President.[2] A second charter, issued on 15th April on behalf of the Queen, just repeats the King's charter with only minor variations and additions, but can be considered to mark the foundation of Queens' College.

(Of the various spellings of 'Doket', it seems appropriate to select the one in the foundation charters as the default).

Doket's early years:

We know little about Doket's early life, although it has been claimed that he may have descended from the Ducketts of Grayrigg Hall, near Kendal, Westmorland, perhaps being the second son of Sir Richard Duckett (d1448).[3] But it has also been suggested that he was related to, and perhaps the brother of, John Doket, who served as a diplomat to Edward IV before becoming private chaplain to Richard III and, subsequently, provost of King's under Henry VII.[1] (John Doket came from Sherbourne in Dorset and was a nephew of Thomas Bourchier, Archbishop of Canterbury). There were another two 'Dokets' at Queens' during the 1480s: Robert, a commoner in 1485, and William, a fellow in 1484-85, but although 'Doket' was an uncommon surname, there is no evidence of their having any relationship to Andrew.

It has been claimed that Doket was, variously: 'formally a friar' (ie a member of a religious order),[4] 'a Carmelite friar',[5] and: 'a friar of the Franciscan order'.[6] However, William Cole, (antiquary, 1714-82), considers such claims to be unlikely:

'Most of ye authors, who mention him of late suppose him to be a Minorite or Franciscan Fryar, & ye Author of ye History of ye Antiquities of ye English Franciscans, to reconcile his being a Secular, as being Rector of a Parish, & holding other Preferments, against ye rules of that order, supposes him to have been made a

Suffragan Bishop, & that he held his Benefices to maintain his Dignity. But I think it w[d] be much more reasonable to imagine, that he never was of that Order, seeing we have no authority to support that opinion'.[7] However, Doket and the College were admitted into a confraternity, (ie an association involving lay people), with the Franciscans,[3] and William Searle, a fellow of Queens' during 1854-58, in his history of Queens' published in 1867, reproduces the contents of the corresponding: 'deed of fraternization' with the Franciscans of Cambridge, drawn up in 1479.[2]

Doket became vicar of St Botolph's Church, Cambridge, at some time between 1432 and 1439, when the living was in the gift of Corpus Christi College. (The church was built in about 1350, and contains the only medieval Rood Screen in the parish churches of Cambridge. Although the paintings on the screen's panels date from the late 19th century, the screen was installed in about 1460, during Doket's lifetime). In 1439, Doket initiated a judicial process in which Barnwell Priory, which acted as rector of St Botolph's, was summoned by the Bishop of Ely for neglect in maintaining the buildings. The Priory's rights as rector were subsequently renounced and Doket was appointed as rector on the 21st October 1444, but with the right of presentation remaining with Corpus Christi College.[3] His tenure at St Botolph's was marked by subsequent structural improvements.[8]

In the 1440s, he was also Principal and owner of St Bernard's Hostel, which was one of the many lodging houses for Cambridge students. Most undergraduates at that time lived in hostels, which were under the control of the University, while the colleges catered mainly for graduate students reading for higher degrees.[1] Doket may have founded the hostel, as there is no record of it before his time. The facilities included a hall, gallery and chapel, which are mentioned in the bursar's book of Queens' in 1504-05.[9] (The chapel was demolished in 1530, at a time when the hostels generally ceased to have an independent existence).[9] The Hostel's site is now the New Court of Corpus Christi College, near the present gateway. Doket remained its Principal while President of Queens', and was responsible for altering and enlarging its buildings, as shown in a memorandum by John Botwright, Master of Corpus Christi College, in 1456, related to the erection of a new bakehouse for his College, near the Hostel. It was to be:

'as long as the middle house lately built by Master Andrew Doket, and as high under the eaves as the upper part of the windows, which lately, to our detriment, have been placed in S. Bernard's Hostel'.[9] The first four fellows of Queen's College were probably lodged in St Bernard's Hostel, until the new buildings were ready.

Doket owned other property and, in 1449, gave a house in Milne Street (now Queens' Lane) to Henry VI for the building of King's College.[1]

The first stage in Doket's project to establish a college began with a charter issued on behalf of Henry VI, dated the 3rd December 1446, which founded a College (as translated):

'....for a president and four fellows, more or less, according to the increase or decrease of their means, in the university of Cambridge by the name of St Bernard's college'.[2] The society, as constituted by this charter, consisted of Andrew Doket (Andream Doket), President, with John Lawe (Johannem Lawe), Andrew Forkelowe (Alexandrum Forkelowe), Thomas Haywode (Thomam Haywode) and John Carewey (Johannem Carewey), clerks (clericos), the first fellows. (The original document has been lost, but the contents are known from the charter of the second foundation of St Bernard's College).[2]

The site which was proposed for the College was not developed for this purpose and is now part of St Catharine's College. This was because Doket procured a more favourable site near the river, which was given to the King in a deed dated the 1st August, 1447, as the first step to refound the College. The College then returned the foundation charter to the King's Chancery, with a petition that it be cancelled and the College be refounded on the new site, which was next to a house of Carmelite friars. Two of Doket's wealthy parishioners, Richard Andrew and John Morris, were particularly involved in obtaining the land for both the first cramped site and the eventual riverside location and, in the years leading to the foundation of Queens', Doket's undoubted tact and skill in the art of persuasion seem to have been directed to his friends and neighbours. It was the large property and garden of John Morris (except the house itself- see below), which formed the core of the new site.[8]

In 1424, Richard Andrew was one of the two Cambridge burgesses representing the town in parliament. In his will, his surname is given as Andrew alias Spycer, indicating his trade. In August 1446, John Aldreth, another burgess, together with John Lawe and Thomas Forkelowe, ('clerks', ie members of the clergy, two of the original fellows of the College), acquired two tenements in the parish of St Botolph, which were then conveyed to Richard Andrew.[1] An adjoining tenement was acquired by Andrew in October and the three properties made an almost rectangular plot, extending from Milne Street (the present Queens' Lane) to the High Street (the present Trumpington Street), set back behind a row of houses on the north side of Smallbridges Street (the present Silver Street). The charter of 3rd December 1446, which founded St Bernard's College on this site, was made possible after the plot had been made over to the King by: 'Ricardi Andrewe burgensis ville Cantabrigie'.[2] Although Doket was soon negotiating for a larger site, it seems that Andrew did not lose interest in the college project, as he was a witness for two contracts for carpentry work for the first court on the future riverside site and, when he died in 1459, the President and fellows received eighty marks and tenements in St Peter's and St Botolph's parishes, for the maintenance of a bible clerk in the College, on condition that there should be an annual commemoration in St Botolph's church for the souls of himself, his wife, friends, parents and other benefactors. Also, he directed that the congregation should include the President and fellows of Queens' and the Mayor and bailiffs of the town.[8]

John Morris was instrumental in providing the land for the second site. He came from an established Cambridge family, and a previous John Morris had been twice mayor in Edward II's reign, while, under Edward III, six other members of the family had also held this office; also, several had represented the borough in parliament. As early as 1279, a member of the family held property in the parish of St Botolph, while the Hundred Rolls (a census taken in the 13th century) show a 'Nicholas Morice' as the owner of four houses in the parish. In 1392, a Sir John Morice founded a chantry in St Botolph's Church and, fifty years later, when Doket was the vicar, a Thomas Morice, who may have been a relative of Doket's parishioner John Morris, willed £40 for beautifying the Lady Chapel in the north aisle.[8]

In July 1447, Doket acquired the new site, as a gift from John Morris. This consisted of an area between the present Queens' Lane and the river, on which the Old Court and Cloister Court now stand. Most of this was the site of the outbuildings and garden of a house belonging to John Morris and his wife, Elizabeth, and let to a Benet Lyster; this was on the river bank, and was the end house of a row of houses along the present Silver Street. To the east of this property were six tenements, the first four of which were owned by John Morris and John Battisford of Chesterton; these, together with the land associated with Morris's riverside house, were made over to the King on 1st August 1447 by the President and fellows of St Bernard's College. In this deed, the land associated with Morris's house, with its large garden, is stated to have been received:

'ex dono et concessione predicti Johannis Morys et Elizabeth uxoris sue'.[8] This made possible the King's charter of 21st August 1447, which refounded the College on the riverside site. (The riverside house and additional tenements on Silver Street would be acquired by Queens' by about 1460). The charter of the 21st of August 1447 has survived, and is held in the Cambridge University Library. The name of the College, 'Sancti Bernardi', the President, 'Andream Doket', and the four fellows, are identical with those in the original charter of 3rd December 1446.

However, it was not long before the Queen, seventeen-year-old Margaret of Anjou, made a request to her husband that she become the first Queen to found a Cambridge college. Searle speculates that Margaret's involvement may have been prompted by Doket, when he found that she was more approachable than the King, who was busy with affairs of state and his own foundation.[2] King Henry had founded King's College in 1441 and, as indicated by her petition, Margaret may have been inspired by his: 'mooste noble and glorieus collage roial',[2] as well as by the Countesses of Clare and Pembroke, who had each founded colleges in the 14th century. However, in contrast to her husband's foundation, she was to refound an existing college in her name. Margaret's petition is held in the Cambridge University Library: [2]

'Margaret

RH (the King countersigned the petition)

To the King my souverain lord.

Besecheth meekly Margarete queen of Englond youre humble wif, Forasmuche as youre moost noble grace hath newely ordained and stablisshed a collage of seint Bernard in the Universite of Cambrigge with multitude of grete and faire privilages perpetually appartenyng unto the same as in youre lres patentes therupon made more plainly hit appareth In the whiche universite is no collage founded by eny queen of Englond hidertoward, Plese hit therefore unto youre highnesse to yeve and graunte unto youre seide humble wif the foundacon and determinacon of the seid collage to be called and named the Quenes collage of sainte Margerete and saint Bernard, or ellis of sainte Margarete vergine and martir and saint Bernard confessour, and thereupon for ful evidence thereof to have licence and pouoir to ley the furst stone in her owne persone or ellis by other depute of her assignement, so that beside the mooste noble and glorieus collage roial of our Lady and saint Nicholas founded by your highnesse may be founded and stablisshed the seid so called Quenes collage....to laud and honneure of sexe femenine, like as two noble and devoute contesses of Pembroke and of Clare founded two collages in the same universite called Pembroke halle and Clare halle the wiche are of grete reputacon for good and worshipful clerkis...And she shal ever preye God for you'. But it has been suggested that her motives may not all have been included in this petition:

'this Queen beholding her husband's bounty in building King's College was restless in herself with holy emulation until she had produced something of the like nature, a strife wherein wives without breach of duty may contend with their husbands which should exceed in pious performances'.[4]

Margaret was born in March 1430, the daughter of René, Duke of Anjou. As noted by the late Brendan Bradshaw, historian and fellow of Queens', in the College 'Record' of 1994:

'...it was Margaret's misfortune to become the bride of the English king in 1445 at a moment of particularly intense Francophobia in England. It was just as the tide in the Hundred Years' War had begun to turn against the English...the marriage made her, in fact, a diplomatic pawn in the quest for a peaceful resolution to a war which the English crown was no longer capable of sustaining...Margaret became identified with, and a scapegoat for, a highly unpopular peace policy'. She was aged 15 when she married the naive and inept Henry VI in April 1445, at Tichfield Abbey, and her life as Queen would be marked by civil war, tragedy and her husband's serious mental illness. (The contemporary accounts of Henry's behaviour indicate a present-day diagnosis of a type of schizophrenia). However, Edward Hall, 1497-1547, in 'The Union of the Two Noble and Illustre Families of Lancastre and Yorke...', (originally published in 1548, and subsequently known as 'Hall's Chronicle'), writes of Margaret, in the London edition of 1809:

'The Quene his wife, was a woman of a great witte, and yet of no greater witte, than of haute stomache, (ie high courage), desirous of glory, and couetous (courteous) of honor, and of reason, pollicye counsaill, and other talentes of nature, belonging to a man, full and flowing: of witte and willinesse she lacked nothing, nor of diligence, studie, and businesse, she was not unexperte: but yet she had one point of a very woman: for often tyme, when she was vehemet (vehement) and fully bente in a matter, she was sodainly like a wether-cocke, mutable, and turning. This woman perceiving that her husbande did not frankely rule as he would... determined with her self, to take upon her the rule and regiment, bothe of the kyng and his kyngdom...This manly woman, this coragious quene... practised daily the futheraunce of the same'.

The College of St Bernard then returned their charter into Chancery for the second time and resigned their lands to the King, with a petition that he grant them to Queen Margaret together with a licence to found:

'another college in honour of the glorious virgin St Margaret and of St Bernard, on the ground late of John Morys of Trumpington esquire'.[2]

The King agreed, so St Bernard's college was again dissolved and:

'Reginale Collegium Sancte Margarete et Santi Bernadi in universitate Cantebr.', ('The Queen's College of St Margaret and St Bernard in the University of Cambridge'), was established in a charter dated the 30th March 1448, which granted to Margaret of Anjou the lands of St Bernard's College and licence to found a College.[2] This document was very similar to that granted for St Bernard's College in 1447 and the reasons given for the foundation were (after translation):

'the extirpation of heresies and errors, the augmentation of the faith, the advantage of the clergy and the stability of the church', as well as for: 'study and prayer'.[1]

Shortly following this permission, on the 15th April 1448, Margaret issued a further (and final!) charter founding the College, which repeated most of the King's charter of 30th March.[2]

Margaret was to take a leading role in ruling the kingdom, and Bradshaw summarises her subsequent misfortunes:

'the long, vicious and debilitating "Wars of the Roses", ending in victory for the Yorkists; the coronation of Edward of York as king in 1461, and the final installation of the Yorkist dynasty (after a brief re-adeption of Henry VI in 1470-71); the death of the Lancastrian heir in a desperate bid to turn the tables (Tewkesbury 1471); the murder of the hapless Henry VI, imprisoned in the Tower (1471); the long imprisonment of Margaret herself; the forfeiture of her estates in France, effectively to compensate Louis XI (her cousin) for securing her ransom in 1475; her impoverished last years wandering listlessly in Northern France; and finally death, a broken and prematurely aged woman in 1482'.

We know little about the four fellows appointed by the charters of 1446, 1447 and 1448. However, Peter Hirforde (Hirford, Hyrford, Hyrforde), a D.D. and a benefactor to Queens', who was nominated as one of the framers of the Statutes in the three foundation charters, had become a fellow by March 1449.[2] Searle reports that:

'On 22 Feb. 1412-3,[10] Peter Hirforde, B.A., in the new chapel of the university before Eudo la Zouch, LL.D the chancellor, and the venerable congregation of the masters, regent and non-regent, renounced the conclusions and opinions of Wycliffe, and took an oath that he would never teach, approve or defend those conclusions, opinions, books or treatises, but resist the same and all favouring them in the schools or elsewhere, to the utmost of his power'.[2] (John Wycliffe, 1320-84, was an influential dissident within the Catholic priesthood, who attacked the luxury of the church and advocated the translation of the Bible into the vernacular).

Work began on the buildings for the new college in 1448,[1] and Searle assumes that a papal bull was obtained for the foundation of the College, as was usual for most colleges and universities.[2] However, if so, it is now lost. Henry VI granted 200L to his wife's foundation, which is shown in a document dated 4th March 1449:

'It is shewed unto us by our welbeloved the President and Felowes of the College of saint Margarete and saint Bernard in our university of Cambrigge which is of the foundation of our moost dere and best beloved wyfe the Quene, how that, for as much as the seid president and felows have not wherwith to edifie the seid College in housing and other necessaries but only of almesse of Cristes devoute people thereto putting theire hands and dedes meritorye nor that the seid edification is not to be perfourmed at any wise withoute that the supportation of our moste noble and benygne grace be shedded unto them in this partie- we have yeven them CCli'.[11]

It is claimed that the foundation stone was laid on behalf of the Queen in the south-east part of the chapel by Sir John Wenlock, her chamberlain, on the same date as given for the signing of her foundation charter, the 15th April 1448. An early manuscript, quoted by Searle, recorded the inscription as:

'Erit Domine nostre regine Margarete Dominium in refugium et lapis iste in signum', and suggested that it meant: 'The power of our

Lady queen Margaret shall be our refuge and this stone (laid in her name) the sign of her protection'.[2] However, as noted on the College website, it would be surprising if these two events had occurred on the same day, and the writer of this account may have falsely stated that the stone-laying ceremony was on the same day as the charter date. Fuller (Thomas Fuller, 1608-61, priest and historian), quoting another source, tells us that the stone was inscribed:

'Erit dominae nostrae Reginae Margaretae dominus in refugium & lapis iste in signum', which Fuller translates as: 'The Lord shall be for a refuge to the Lady Margaret and this stone for a signe').[4] However, its present location is not known. (John Wenlock, later 1st Baron Wenlock KG, was a soldier, diplomat, courtier and politician. He fought on both sides in the Wars of the Roses and was killed in the battle of Tewkesbury in 1471). Just over six years later, the chapel was consecrated by William Gray, Bishop of Ely.[6]

The first buildings:

There is convincing evidence that the architect of the first buildings at Queens' was Reginald Ely, who was another of Doket's parishioners. Ely was chief mason at King's College, probably from about 1441, and is mentioned on a 'patent roll' (issued by the Crown) as master mason in 1444.[8] He continued as master mason at King's until all work on the chapel was halted just before Edward IV's accession in March 1461. On the 10th February 1461, King Henry, then a prisoner of the Duke of York, (later Edward IV), granted a special pardon to:

'Reynold Ely of Cambridge, mason, alias maister mason of the college of St Marys and St Nicholas, Cambridge',[8] showing that Ely must have found it expedient to try to insure his position under the imminent new regime. Although the construction of King's College was a slow process initially, the early buildings of Queens' made rapid progress under the control of Doket, working in tandem with Ely. No accounts for the stonework and brickwork of the Old Court at Queens' survive, but there are two extant agreements for the structural timber work.

The first is dated 14th April 1448, and is made with John Veyse, or Weyse, draper of Elsenham, Essex, and Thomas Sturgeon, carpenter. The latter was the master carpenter at King's and a colleague of Ely during the first phase of building at King's. This contract was for the construction of the woodwork for a part of the first court for £100, and involved the north and east sides, as well as the eastern half of the south side:

'This indenture made the xiiij^{the} day of Aprile the yer of the reign of our sovreign lord the king Herry the sixt six and twenty betwen master Andrew Dokett p^{r}sident of the Quene college of seynt Margret and seynt Barnard and the fellows of ye seid college of the one party, and John Veyse of Elesnam in the shire of Essex draper and Thomas Sturgeon of the seides town and shire carpenter on the other party bereth witteness that...the seides John Veyse and Thomas Sturgeon...make or do for to be made well and sufficiantely an howse w^{t} in the said college as in werk of carpentre...'.[2,3]

This was completed within a year and, on the 6th March 1449, a second contract was signed for work on the remaining part of the Old Court, which included the hall roof and the roofs, floors, middle walls and stairs of the buttery, pantry and kitchen:

'This indenture made the sixt day of March...between maister Andrewe Dokett p^{r}sidente of the Quenes colage of sente Margret and sente Barnard of Cambrigge maistere Pers Hirford and maistere Thomas Heywood, of the seide colage felowes on the one party, and John Weyse of Elesnam in the shire of Essex draper and Thomas Sturgeon of the seides town and shire carpenter on the other party...the wich hall shall be and contayn in lenketh L fete of the standard and in brede xxiij fete (ie the Hall is to be 50 feet long and 23 feet wide)'.[2,11]

By the time the second contract was signed, the north range of the Old Court, facing the Carmelite Friary to the north, must have been already built, as it was specified that the timbers for the next stage of building should: 'accord with the other side wich is now redy framed next the Freres'.[8] There is reference to the brick and stone structures, and the work was to be done:

'in as hasty wise as thei may goodly after the walles of the seid howses be redy'.[2]

The design of the Old Court had an important influence on later college buildings in Cambridge and, two generations later, the plan probably influenced the future President of Queens', John Fisher, and his architect, at the construction of St John's College.[8] When Queens' College was planned by Doket and Ely, there was no Cambridge college whose original plan had included the comprehensive facilities of gate-tower, chapel, hall, kitchen and living rooms. The date of the subsequent riverside building at Queens' is not known, but it is earlier than that of the adjacent cloister walks, which were built around 1494-95, and it has been considered probable that it was built in Doket's lifetime, perhaps around 1460.[8]

The early buildings were supported by two important gifts: £200 from the King in 1449, as noted above, and £220 from the Bishop of Lincoln in about 1450. By 1450, the Old Court was probably complete, except for the gate-tower and the north-west corner; the latter would eventually provide the fellows' parlour, underneath a room for the President.

President in troubled times:

The early history of Queens' was set against the power struggles of the Wars of the Roses, with the overthrow of the Lancastrian Henry VI in 1461 by Edward IV, and Doket may have approached Elizabeth Woodville, Edward's Queen, (previously a lady of the bedchamber to Queen Margaret), for patronage, as she became the second royal foundress of the College. (In the present day, Queens' College is referred to with the apostrophe after the 's').

Bradshaw provides an succinct account of the new Queen:

'She was a mature dame of 27, already widowed, who had the good sense to withstand Edward's importunate advances in the calculating manner of Anne Boleyn later, until the King, at his wit's end, finally agreed to marriage- at first by means of a clandestine service on May Day 1464...the seeds of later tragedy were already sown in Edward's love-match with Elizabeth. Firstly there was the Queen's lowly birth (although she had royal ancestry through her mother, Jacquetta of Luxembourg). This elicited almost as much resentment as Margaret's French identity...She came to her royal groom lumbered with a horde of needy and greedy relatives whose "great expectations" she was, in honour bound, to fulfil...the list included two sons by her first marriage, five brothers and seven unmarried sisters. The inevitable outcome was political tension as the Woodville "cormorants" gobbled up the royal patronage...The Woodville clan, for instance, practically cornered the aristocratic marriage market, to the bizarre extreme of Elizabeth's 20 year old brother snapping up the 67 year old and twice widowed Duchess of Norfolk- who, as it happened, contrived to outlive her third husband by 17 years...in this situation a fatal personality flaw revealed itself in the Queen consort. It took the form of over-weaning ambition for her Woodville kindred and a well-neigh infinite capacity to resent those who thwarted her efforts, most especially her Yorkist relatives. Nemesis struck...on the premature and unanticipated death of Edward IV in 1483, leaving a thirteen year old boy next in line of succession- Edward V...what ensued is so familiar...the interception of the young king and his Woodville escort on their way to London by the supporters of Richard of Gloucester; his confinement in the Tower for "safe-keeping" and his subsequent "disappearance" together with his younger brother...the assertion of the claims of Richard III and the outbeak of bloody internecine warfare; Henry Tudor's daring opportunistic bid for power... finally the consequent invalidation of the marriage of Edward and Elizabeth. True, Henry VII took to wife Elizabeth's eldest daughter and namesake...But the outcome for the Queen dowager was penury and obscurity until her death in 1492 when, as her will reproachfully explained, "having no worldly goods to bequeath to the Queen her daughter, or her other children, she left them merely her blessing"'. (Elizabeth Woodville is buried in St George's Chapel, at Windsor Castle). Jonathan Holmes, fellow of Queens' and former Dean of Chapel, adds an interesting postscript in the College 'Record' of 2001:

'...the elder of Elizabeth's two sons by her first marriage, Thomas Grey, was created Marquis Dorset in 1475. His grandson Henry Grey became Duke of Suffolk and married the neice of

Henry VIII (himself of course, a grandson of Elizabeth Woodville)- their eldest daughter was the ill-fated nine day queen Lady Jane Grey. A much later descendent of Thomas Grey, George Grey, Earl of Stamford, matriculated at Queens' in 1755. He presented the College with the portrait of his ancestor Queen Elizabeth Woodville that is the centrepiece of the 18th century panelling in old Hall…'.

The following description of Queen Elizabeth Woodville is given in 'Hall's Chronicle':

'She was a woman more of formal counternaunce than of excellent beautie, but yet of such beautie & favor, that with her sober demeanure, lovely looking, and femynyne smylyng (neither to wanton nor to humble), besyde her toungue so eloquent, and her wit so pregnant, she was able to ravishe the mynde of a meane person, when she allured and made subject to her, ye hart of so great a King'.

In a licence for the College to hold property to the annual value of £200, granted by King Edward in 1465, the College was described as: 'de patronata (patronage) Elizabeth regine Anglie',[1] and there is a record of a visit by the Queen to the College in 1468.[2] But although Elizabeth was still referred to as patroness in 1473 , she was also named: 'vera fundatrix' (foundress), in the first set of College Statutes issued in 1475, thus disregarding Margaret's previous role.[1,12] These Statutes, which will have been prompted by Doket, specified a President and twelve fellows, (normally all priests), and three scholars; this reflected a substantial increase since Margaret's first foundation, and demonstrated that the College had the interests of the church and clergy as its priority. The study of theology rather than law was encouraged, as fellows were not permitted to study law until three years after taking the M.A. degree, and then only with the consent of the President and a majority of the fellows.[1] The President was required to reside one month a quarter, which the fellows could reduce to one month in the year.[13] He was to be paid £3 6s 8d a year, with an additional 2s a week during residence. Fellowships were intended for the poor, and fellows were required to resign if they should obtain an annual income of £5 or more.

Every member was required to be in College by 8pm in winter or 9pm in summer. There were to be daily lectures on the Bible for much of the year and, at table in hall, fellows were to converse in Latin, unless the President relaxed this rule at festivals.[13] (The latter was only abolished-officially- in 1838).

Doket must have fostered good relations with another previous lady of the bedchamber to Queen Margaret, Lady Mary Roos, who, in 1469, enabled the College to buy: 'serteyn lands' sufficient to support five fellows with a stipend of £6 3s 4d each. As Searle records:

'So liberal a benefactor to the college as Lady Margery Roos deserves more than a passing mention. She...married while still young John lord Roos of Hamlake, who was killed 22 March, 1421, in the 23rd year of his age, while serving the king in France... Lady Margery married her second husband, sir Roger Wentworth,, whom also she survived...She died 20 Apr. 1478, and was buried under her window of St Margaret and St Bernard on the north side of the college chapel, which she seems to have given...From her the earls of Cleveland were descended'.[2]

In her will of 1477 she gave the College many books and vestments, and some plate for the use of the chapel. She also left £10 and an engraved vessel as a personal legacy to Doket.[2,3]

In 1475, the College obtained another important asset, namely land on the west side of the river, which was then an island. Doket seems to have initiated this by requesting that letters patent, (ie a written order issued with the authority of the Crown), be sent on behalf of the College to the mayor, bailiffs and commonality of Cambridge, by King Edward, Queen Elizabeth and their son, Prince Edward. This led the borough, on October 6th 1475, to grant this land to the College.[11]

One of Doket's means of attracting endowments was to offer to place the names of benefactors on the 'bede-roll' of the College, for whom prayers were to be said by the fellows on the anniversaries of their deaths.[12] An example of this is shown in a document dated 3rd March 1474:

'This endenture made between maister Andrewe Doket president of the Quenes college in the university of Cambrigge and the ffeliship of the same college on that oon partie, and Robert Rocheford grocer and Robert Carvell mercer, citezenis of London on that other partie witnesseth: that the seid president and ffeliship have received the day of the date of these presentes of the seid Robert and Robert for the soule of Edmund Carvell late citizen and grocer of London now dede xx li. sterling to thentent that the seid Edmond shall be taken and receyved as benefactour of the forseid college...And also that the soule of the same Edmond shall be remembered among other benefactours of the same college...'.[2,3] In the same year, Doket received the last part of a payment of £320 from Dame Alice Wyche, a widow of an alderman, to buy lands in Lincolnshire. Also, on the 13th February 1478, Doket received from Dame Elizabeth Yorke, widow of William Yorke of London, £40 to endow masses for the souls of the Yorkes, their children and friends.[3]

During the unsettled state of England in the 1470s, Doket sought protection by obtaining two general pardons from Edward IV, in 1470 and 1473.[2] The first was dated 1st September 1470, just before Henry VI's brief restoration, and related to all offences before 25th December 1469. The second was dated 29th May 1473 and extended to all offences before 30th September 1471. Further, Edward issued an order, on 4th October 1474, to the treasurer and barons, not to molest the College.[2] As the second pardon was lost, the college sent John Ripplingham to the Court of Chancery to obtain a copy and the pardon was confirmed on 21st October, 1480.[2]

Edward died in 1483, having been briefly deposed in 1470-71, and was soon succeeded by his brother Richard III, following the (almost-certain) murder of Edward's sons, the 'Princes in the Tower'. (This heralded a further two years of civil war, ending with Richard's defeat at Bosworth in 1485 and the accession of Henry VII).

Doket was probably on good terms with Richard, who, as Duke of Gloucester, had founded four fellowships in the College in 1477. The establishment of these is shown in a document issued by Edward IV dated 10th April 1477, which permitted his brother to give the: 'manor and advowson of Foulmire' (Fowlmere) to the

College. This grant is made in a document dated the 17th July 1477, signed by the Duke of Gloucester:

'Wittnesseth that the sayde duke...have given...to the sayde president and feleus and theire successours for evermore the lordship of Fulmere ...and also the advowsyn of the parish chirche of Fulmr to be appropred to the sayde college for ever for continuall prayers and remembraunce of the sayde duke...'. This allowed four fellowships to be founded, with stipends of £8 per annum, for priests who were to:

'pray satisfactorie for the prosperuse astates of Richard the sayde duke of Gloucetr and dame Anne his wife...Also the sayde president and felaus of the sayde college shalle make the forsayde Richarde duke of Gloucetr to be assorted and nombred amonge the benefactours of the sayde college'.[2]

As King, Richard made a grant to the College of land which belonged to his wife Queen Anne and, in a licence of the 25th March 1484, he permitted the College to own property to the annual value of 700 marks. In the grant made on the 5th of July, 1484,[2] the College is described as:

'quod de fundatione et patronatu prefate consortis nostre existit', (existing as the foundation and patronage of our aforesaid consort).[2,13] Therefore, Queen Anne can- arguably- be considered as a third royal foundress of Queens'. (Anne Neville's first marriage had been to Edward of Westminster, the only son of Henry VI and Margaret of Anjou, who was killed at the battle of Tewkesbury. Anne then married Richard, when Duke of Gloucester, in 1472. Her only child, Edward, Prince of Wales, died in April 1484, and she predeceased her husband by five months, dying in March 1485 aged twenty-nine).

Sadly (for Queens'), Richard's benefactions were lost to the College after the accession of HenryVII:

'As for King Richard the third, his benefaction made more noise than brought profit therewith...which soon after was justly resumed by King Henry the seventh and restored to the right owner thereof'.[4] However, Doket died soon after the College had received the further endowments from Richard, and before there was any suspicion that the income would soon be lost.

The change of regime led to a reduction in the number of fellows to 13.[11]

Richard had proved to a be a greater supporter of the College compared with his brother and, in 1484, he and his Queen had been thanked by the University for (in translation):

'very many benefits upon this his University of Cambridge, and especially has lately liberally and devoutly founded exhibition for four Priests in the Queens' college. And now also the most serene Queen Anne, Consort of the same Lord the King (that most pious King consenting and greatly favouring) has augmented and endowed the same college with great rents...'.[2]

Richard's badge of a boar's head is still used by Queens':

'...a crosier, and pastoral staff saltire, piercing through a boar's head in the midst of the shield...bestowed upon them by Richard the Third (when undertaking the patronage of this foundation) in allusion to the boar which was his crest...'.[4]

Fuller, writing in 1655, describes 'Andrew Ducket' as:

'a good and discreet man, who, with no sordid but prudential compliance, so poised himself in those dangerous times betwixt the successive kings of Lancaster and York, that he procured the favour of both, and so prevailed with Queen Elizabeth, wife to King Edward IV, that she perfected what her professed enemy had begun'.[4]

Church appointments:

By the 1470s, Doket was spending less of his time in Cambridge,[1] but the 1475 Statutes provided for the continuous oversight of the twelve fellows by the appointment of a 'Superior', elected for life and responsible for governance, discipline and religious observance. This enabled a President to be elsewhere for much of the time, and the early Presidents were often absent, holding various church appointments.[1] However, Doket was not an absentee President for the early part of his career.

He remained the rector of St Botolph's until 1470, when he was succeeded by a John Chapman B.D., after a commission set up by the Bishop of Ely had confirmed that Queens' College had the right of patronage:

'the Church of St Botolph is now vacant by the resignation of Andrew Doket, who resign'd it on St Mary Magdalen last, & that Queens college is the true Patron of it, & that before they were so, Benet College was in possession of it, who presented Andrew Doket to it; & before that, the Prior and Canons of Bernwell were in possession of it: wch Right of Presentation wch Bernwell Priory and Benet college formally had, now belonged to Queens college, as manifestly appeared...'.[2] The commission was headed by: 'Wm Malstar, Licenciate in Decrees', whose monumental brass (c1492) can still be seen in the chancel of Girton Church, Cambridge.[2]

Although Doket had no need for additional income, as he was a man of some means,[1] he was clearly energetic and ambitious and, from 1467, he took up four church appointments in other parts of the country: prebendary of Ryton at Lichfield Cathedral, during 1467-70; Chancellor of Lichfield Cathedral during 1470-76, in exchange for the previous appointment at Lichfield; canon of the royal chapel of St Stephen's, Westminster; and the Provostship of the collegiate church of Cotterstock, near Oundle. (A collegiate church provided daily worship and was maintained collectively by a college of canons. Cotterstock had, at one stage, a Provost, twelve chaplains and two clerks).

Doket was still rector at St Botolph's when he was appointed at Lichfield in 1467; at Lichfield, as elsewhere, the holding of several offices was very common, particularly among the non-resident clergy.[14] But his appointment at Westminster was exchanged for the Cotterstock appointment, with a Dr Walter Oudeby in 1479. Unlike some of his contemporaries, Doket seems to have taken his church appointments seriously, as he resigned two of these post before taking up their successors.[3]

Memorials, will, burial and an epitaph:

Doket did not leave an intellectual legacy; there is no record of his degrees, but to the end of his life he was styled 'magister', so he was probably not a doctor in any faculty.[8] Also, it has been noted:

'that there are no signs that he was in any way a promoter of that new learning which, before his death, was beginning to be heard of in Cambridge'.[15]

In 1472, Doket drew up an inventory of all the College's goods for which he was responsible. This included a catalogue of the Library entitled:

'Inventorium omnium et singulorum honorum Collegii Reginalis Cantebrigie, factum et renovatum ibidem per Andream Dokett, presidentem ejusdem, primo die mensis Septembris, Anno Domini millesimo cccclxxij'. However, none of the 199 volumes listed remains in the Old Library.[16]

Apart from references in various documents, there are few extant objects which are associated with Doket. However, Jesus College, Cambridge, has a twelfth-century volume, which was owned by Doket while he was rector of St Botolph's.[2,3] This includes sermons of St Ambrose and is inscribed: 'lib magri Andree Doket rectoris sci Botulfi Cantabr.'.[2] Also, there is a monumental brass in Balsham Church, Cambridgeshire, on the grave of a clergyman, John Blodwell, who was an acquaintance, and possibly a friend, of Doket, as there is a document which includes an acknowledgement by Blodwell's executor that 'Andrea Dokett' had returned certain books he had borrowed from Blodwell. The first work mentioned contained commentaries on the five books of the Decretals, (letters of a Pope containing decisions relating to canon law), by John Andreae, a celebrated professor of canon law at Bologna who died in 1349.[2] (Blodwell was born in Shropshire in about 1380 and, after having studied law at Bologna, he practised in Rome before returning to several church offices in England, including rector of Balsham in 1439. After going blind, he died in 1462 and is buried in the chancel of Balsham church, where his monumental brass shows him standing under an arch).[2]

The outer arch of the main Queens' College gateway has a carved keystone representing the half-length figure of a cleric, with tonsured head, a cape (a sleeveless outer garment which covers the wearer's upper back, shoulders and upper chest) and the upper part of what is probably an ankle-length cassock. He holds a scroll in his right hand. The gate was completed before the spring of 1450 and it has been assumed that this is a contemporary portrait representing Andrew Doket holding the foundation charter.[8,17]

Doket made his will on the 2nd November 1484 and died on (or around) the 4th November, having been President for thirty-six years and overseen a foundation of four fellows grow to a society of seventeen. His will, in Latin, is reproduced by Searle.[2] Bequests included 40s per annum to the College from St Bernard's Hostel, for bread, wine, wax and lamp oil to maintain the chapel services; the remainder of the income from the Hostel was to be held by his executors for life and, on their death, the Hostel was to become the property of the College.[11] Another provision in Doket's will was for almshouses, which he had established nearby for three poor women, who were required to pray for his soul and those of the benefactors of the College.[3] The properties were to be managed by his executors and, afterwards, by the College.[11] His almshouses were on the north side of Silver Street, to the east of Queens' Lane, but they were demolished in 1836, after being sold to St Catharine's College. Sadly, we do not have any images of them.[2] Other bequests included money for the President and fellows of Queens', and for the local poor, especially in St Botolph's parish. Also, he bequeathed to the College a house near St Botolph's Church; this was to be sold and the proceeds invested in land or tenements, with the resulting income to be applied at the discretion of the executors. On the death of the executors, this property was to be passed to the College. The residue of his goods were left to his executors: 'John Rypplyngham' and 'William Thurkylle'. His will also directed that his death should be commemorated each year in the College chapel with prayers for his soul's eternal rest. However, this was discontinued at the Reformation.[11]

Doket's will also makes particular mention of Reginald Ely; they had been the owners of adjacent houses on what is now Silver Street, and it has been suggested that:

'the relations between Doket and Ely...were those of mutual regard and even intimacy'.[8] One of Doket's bequests to the College (quoted with modern spelling) was:

'so that they may observe the exequies for my soul and the soul of Reginald Ely and the souls of all benefactors of the said college in the church of St Botolph, Cambridge, on the anniversary day of Reginald Ely'.[8] Ely died in 1471; in his will he describes himself as: 'mason of Cambridge' and wishes to be buried in St Botolph's church:

'where I am a parishioner, on the north side of the said church before the image of St Christopher'.[8] (The exact position of his grave is not known, but may be marked by a slab with the indents of brasses beside a pillar about halfway along the north aisle). Among his bequests, Queens' is mentioned twice, firstly, in relation to Masses to be celebrated in the College chapel and, secondly:

'I will that a chaplain fellow of the Queen's college in Cambridge have eight marks of legal money of England to celebrate for my soul and the souls of my parents and benefactors and all faithful departed for one whole year within the same college. I will that every chaplain being at my exequies and mass have, and each one shall have, 4d. of money aforesaid...I will that the college of St Margaret (in its early years Queens' appears often to be called by this name) have for ever the tenement in which James Belly dwells'.[8] It is surprising that, among his many bequests, none was made to King's College.

As the named executors of Doket's will declined the task, the University's Vice-Chancellor granted letters of administration to the President and fellows of the College on 23rd April 1485. It was Doket, rather than the fellowship, who determined his successor as, in his will, he named Thomas Wilkynson; it has been suggested that the College's subsequent acquiescence demonstrated Doket's: 'overpowering domination' over the fellows.[1,3]. Doket's age at death has been estimated as 74;[12] he was buried in a crypt of the College chapel, (now the Memorial Library), and what was assumed to be his gravestone, with a monumental brass effigy, was described in the 18th century by the antiquary William Cole,[7] although the latter's account in 1768 indicates some uncertainty as to the brass's attribution:

'Directly in the middle of the antechapel, and close by this last, lies an old grey marble with a small brass figure on it of a priest in a praying posture, but the inscription at his feet is torn away: this I have heard belong'd to Andrew Dockett the 1st president here, and who died in 1484.'.[6,7] Browne and Seltman, in their 'Pictorial History' of the College,[17] reproduce a rough sketch by Cole of an effigy on a monumental brass, showing a full-length figure; this was made on the page in the 'Cole manuscripts' which is opposite and adjacent to the above quotation, and the drawing (inspected by the author) is titled: 'Dr Andrew Dockett's Monum.t.' This shares characteristics of the presumed carving of Doket on the arch of the main gate, namely, tonsured head, cape, cassock and a scroll, although in Cole's sketch, the latter is held half open with both hands. (Cole's full-length sketch also indicates a cope, ie a long cloak, open at the front, worn exterior to the ankle-length cassock). (William Cole, 1714-82, was a Cambridgeshire clergyman whose extensive manuscript collections on the history of Cambridgeshire and Buckinghamshire are in the British Library). Cole, discussing whether 'Andrew Duckett' was a 'Franciscan Fryar' (see above) states:

'...we have no authority to support that opinion, especially if that be his Tomb Stone, which tradition assigns him, in ye Antechapel of this College; where his Portrait in brass in a Doctors Habit, without Mitre or Crosier expressly informs us he never was of ye Episcopal order. And I think also it may be doubted whether he was of ye order of St Francis; when we find he was both Rector of a Parish & Dignitary in a Cathedral Church...being a Minorite or Franciscan Friar could neither be Rector of a Parish Church nor Master of a College according to the Rule of his order...After he had prudently governed his College 36 years he died Nov 6 1484 (Note: Searle gives his date of death as the 4th of November) and was buried in the Chapel of his own College under a gravestone of grey Marble; exactly in the middle of the antechapel, under the steps as you ascend into the Choir. In Vol:2. p17 of these Collections is an awkward Sketch of it. He is in a Doctors Habit, But being continually trod on twice a day as People go into the Chapel it is no wonder that the strokes are worn away and that it is now almost a plain smooth piece of Brass'.[7] (However, despite Cole's comment, there is no evidence that Doket was a Doctor of theology). Browne and Seltman report that College records show that the brass was added in 1563-64, about eighty years after Doket's death. Sadly, Doket's monumental brass, if indeed it was the one sketched by Cole, has disappeared, although there are three stone slabs with substantial remnants of other monumental brasses from the original chapel, now attached to the wall of the present College chapel. The original chapel was subject to extensive alterations in 1773-75, which included removal of the tombstones and monuments,[7,13,18] but Cole is recorded to have seen the chapel several times before these changes, including a visit on July 2nd 1768.[6,18] A crypt exists below part of the present Memorial Library, containing several identified coffins, but the location of any remnants of Doket's tomb is not known.

Gray provides Doket with a fitting epitaph:[11]

'Dokett had been spared to govern his foundation during the most critical period of its existence. Its prosperity was largely, perhaps almost wholly, due to his personal exertions and to the wisdom wherewith he had shaped its course through the stormy years of war and revolution. He had commenced with four Fellows: the number of Fellows was now seventeen; the buildings were practically completed, and the College was not inadequately endowed'.

References

1. Twigg, J. A History of Queens' College, Cambridge 1448-1986.
   The Boydell Press. 1987. pp 3-6,9,10,65,66.
2. Searle, W.G. The History of the Queens' College of St Margaret and St Bernard in the University of Cambridge. 1446-1560.
   Deighton, Bell & Co; Macmillan & Co. London. 1867. pp 3,4,15-31,38,39,47,52-59,72,73,76-78,80,88,89,97,100.
3. Underwood, M.G. Dokett (Doket), Andrew. In: Oxford Dictionary of National Biography. Online. 2004.
4. Fuller, T. The History of the University of Cambridge from the Conquest to the year 1634. Deighton, J. & J.J., Stevenson,

T. London. Reprinted 1840. (Original edition 1655). pp 161-64.

5. Dyer, G. History of the University and Colleges of Cambridge. Longman, Hurst, Rees, Orme, and Brown. London. 1814. p 150.
6. Wright, T., Longueville Jones, H. Le Keux's Memorials of Cambridge Vol. 1. Tilt and Bogue. London.1841. 'Queen's College' pp 3,22,23.
7. The Cole Manuscripts, in the British Library. (Add MS 5803, folios 10v-19; Add MS 5808, folios 120v-123v).
8. Oswald, A. Andrew Doket and his Architect. In: Proceedings of the Cambridge Antiquaries Society. Vol.XLII. 1948. pp 14-19,25,26.
9. Willis, R. The Architectural History of the University of Cambridge.
   Vol.1. University Press. Cambridge. 1886. pp 248,259.
10. From 1155 to 1752, the civil and legal year in England began on the 25th March (Lady Day); ie 22nd February 1449 was written as 22nd February 1448 or 1448-9.
11. Gray, J.H. The Queens' College of St Margaret and St Bernard. F.E.Robinson. London. 1898. pp 16,19,35-38.
12. Venables, E. Doket, Andrew. In: Dictionary of National Biography. Vol.15. 1885-1900.
13. Roach, J.P.C. (ed). The colleges and halls: Queens'. In: A History of the County of Cambridge and the Isle of Ely: Volume 3, the City and University of Cambridge. British History Online. 2018.
14. Southwark, C.M. The Canons of Lichfield Cathedral in the last Quarter of the Fifteenth Century. University of Birmingham Research Archive, e-theses repository. Online. 2012.
15. Mullinger, J.B. A history of the University of Cambridge. Longmans, Green & Co. Lonsdon. 1888. p 57.
16. Searle, W.G. Catalogue of the Library of Queens' college in 1472.
    Cambridge Antiquarian Society Communications. Vol.2, 1864. pp 165-93.

17. Browne, A.D., Seltman. C.T. A Pictorial History of the Queen's College of Saint Margaret and Saint Bernard. Printed for the College. 1951.
18. Willis, R. The Architectural History of the University of Cambridge. Vol. II. University Press. Cambridge. 1886. pp 8,10,40.

CHAPTER 2

Thomas Wilkynson (Wilkinson). President 1484-1505.

Summary.

In his will, Andrew Doket recommended that Thomas Wilkynson should be his successor as President, and he was duly elected by the fellows in 1484. Wilkynson was the rector of both Harrow-on-the-Hill and Orpington, and not obviously influential, although he would have known many church dignitaries. Doket's reasons for his choice are unknown.

Wilkynson was not resident in Cambridge and, as President, would be an infrequent visitor to Queens'.[1] But, at the time, absentee Presidents were not thought to disadvantage the College, particularly if they achieved prominent positions elsewhere.[2] He was appointed at a time of apparent prosperity for the College, following the endowments of Richard III, but these were soon to be restored to previous owners after Richard's death in 1485. Nevertheless, after the initial reduction in the College's finances, Wilkynson's time as President seems to have been characterised by stability and gradual development. The cloisters, between the Old Court and the riverside building, were built in the 1490s.

Wilkynson resigned as President in 1505 and, although his reasons are unknown, this may have been the result of pressure from the King's mother, Lady Margaret Beaufort, who wished to provide a Cambridge base for Bishop John Fisher, her collaborator in several projects for the University, who was elected in Wilkynson's place.[1,2] Although Fisher does not appear to have taken an active interest in Queens', and resigned as President in 1508, there is no doubt that the interests of the College would have been protected by such a powerful figure.

Wilkynson's Presidency coincided with the early development of 'Renaissance Humanism', which, in Cambridge, would be dominated by Fisher and Erasmus.[2] This was an intellectual movement which reached England from Europe in the mid-15th century and would be an important feature of English university life in the 16th century, involving the expansion of scholarship beyond the traditional teaching of theology. 'Humanism' relates to disciplines that study various aspects of human society and culture; its initial focus was on the literature and languages of antiquity, but it would also encompass grammar, rhetoric, (ie the use of language), poetry, history and moral philosophy, (ie the concepts of right and wrong). The movement was also associated with a recognition of a need to improve the quality of the education of the clergy.

In Cambridge, humanism developed in the early 16th Century mainly through the foundations of Lady Margaret Beaufort and the work of Fisher, who helped to establish her benefactions. Lady Margaret was deeply religious, and Fisher had been her chaplain and confessor in the 1490s.[2]

Fisher's Chancellorship of the University has been considered to have:

'marked the spring of Renaissance Cambridge, no less surely than it witnessed the Indian summer of the medieval university'.[2,3]

Timeline.

1479. Rector of Harrow-on-the-Hill.

1483. Accession of Richard III.

1484. Death of Andrew Doket, (c4th of November). Thomas Wilkynson elected President, (c11th of November).

1485. Death of Queen Anne.

1485. King Richard killed at Bosworth, (22nd of August). Accession of Henry VII.

1485. In November, the first parliament of Henry VII leads to the loss of Richard III's endowments to Queens'

1486. Henry VII marries Elizabeth of York, daughter of Elizabeth Woodville.

c1495. The College's north and south cloisters built.
1503. Death of Queen Elizabeth of York.
1505. Thomas Wilkynson's resignation as President; he is succeeded by John Fisher, Bishop of Rochester and Chancellor of the University since 1504.
1509. Death of Henry VII. Accession of Henry VIII.
1511. Appointed prebendary of Ripon Minster, (January). Dies, (December). Buried in All Saints' church, Orpington.

An absentee clergyman, who resigned as President after twenty-one years to provide a Cambridge base for Bishop John Fisher.

Andrew Doket, in his will, had written (as translated):

'I desire and so far as lieth in me, I enjoin all the Fellows of the said College as my successor Mr Thomas Wilkynson'.[1,4]

Doket died on or around the 4th November 1484, and the fellows duly elected Wilkynson, probably around the 11th November, as the Statutes of 1475 required the election of a new President on the eighth day of a vacancy. However, he was not in Cambridge at the time. He held two church appointments, rector of St Mary's Church, Harrow–on-the-Hill and rector of All Saints' Church, Orpington, Kent.[1,4] (He had received the appointment at Harrow in 1479 from Cardinal Bourchier, Cardinal Archbishop of Canterbury, on the death of Thomas Winterbourne, Dean of St Paul's, and, after his own death, he would be succeeded as rector of Harrow by Cuthbert Tunstall, who would become Bishop of London, then of Durham).

As President, he resided sometimes in Harrow and sometimes at Orpington, as shown by entries in the College accounts giving the expenses incurred in visiting the President at 'Harwe' or 'Horpington'. It seems that the President was only an occasional visitor to Cambridge; for example, when he was required for elections to fellowships, for the audit and for the Stourbridge Fair.[4]

Wilkynson's previous history is obscure; he may have been a fellow of the College, as there is a document of 1480 in which he is associated with John Ripplingham and Ralph Songar, who were fellows of Queens'.[1] Although he is described on his monumental brass as 'M.A.', Searle, in his history of the College of 1867, notes that his name appears in the records of Cambridge University in 1479 as being (in translation): 'able to start in theology', which suggests that he had taken the degree of B.D.[1]

After the Presidential election, the executors of Doket's will, John Ripplingham and William Thurkylle, renounced their roles and, in April 1485, the University's Vice-Chancellor, Thomas Tuppyn, D.D., granted letters of administration to 'Mr Wilkynson, President', and the fellows of the College, Ralph Songer, Dionysius Spycer and Hugh Trotter.[1]

Wilkynson assumed office soon after Richard III had seized the throne, when the King's past and more recent endowments to the College promised a prosperous future. However, after Richard's death at Bosworth in 1485, these endowments would soon be lost, when they were restored to previous owners.

Possible reasons behind Richard III's generosity are given by Thomas Fuller, (1608-61, churchman and historian), in his 'Church History of Britain', 1655, as quoted by Searle:[1]

'After this bloody act (the seizure of the throne) King Richard endeavoured to render himself popular. First, by making good laws in that sole Parliament kept in his Reign...yet this would not ingratiate this Usurper with (the people), the dullest nostrils resenting it done, not for love of vertue, but his own security...Next he endeavoured to work himself into their good will, by erecting and endowing of Religious Houses; so to plausiblelize himself, especialy among the Clergy...He is said also to have given to Queens College in Cambridge five hundred marks of yearly rent; though at this time, I believe, the College receives as little benefit by the Grant, as Richard had right to grant it. For, it was not issued out of his own purse, but given out of the lands of his enemy, the unjustly proscribed Earl of Oxford; who being restored by Henry the Seventh, made a resumption thereof'.

Although at least some part of the estates granted in 1484 had belonged to Queen Anne's mother, the Countess of Warwick, this was also lost to the College and reverted to King Henry VII in 1487.[1,4]

The time during which the College held the lands of Richard's gift was little more than a year, as the King was killed on the 22nd August 1485, about five months after the death of Anne Neville, his Queen. The first Parliament of Henry VII, which met in November 1585, heralded the loss of all the estates with which Richard had endowed the College as Duke and King, and Fuller makes the charitable claim that:

'the college no whit grieving thereat, as sensible no endowment can be comfortable, which consists not with equity and honour'.[5]

The only memorial of Richard III in the College's possession is a letter recommending a William Ustwayte for a fellowship, dated the 29th December, which Searle considers must be in either 1483 or 1484; if it was the latter, it would have been received during Wilkynson's tenure:

'By the King R.R. To our trusty and welbeloved the Master and felowes of o^{r} college called the Quenes College in o^{r} unive^{r}site of Cambrigge.

Trusty and welbeloved we grete you wele. The good and vertueux disposicion, whiche oure welbeloved Sr William Ustwayte bacheler of arts by credible report unto Us...move Us to write unto you at this time, Desiring and hertily praieng you, that...ye will doo the said Sr William to be elect among you as oon of the felowes of our college...Yeven under our signet at our palois of Westm^{r} the xxix^{tl} day of December'.[1]

The consequences of the new regime are reflected in the bursars' account books; in Easter 1485, there are seventeen fellowships, while the four endowed by Richard, when Duke of Gloucester, are soon lost.[1]

But there were to be new endowments, and a fellowship was founded in 1491 by Lady Joan Ingaldesthorpe, a cousin of the previous benefactor Lady Margaret Roos. She gave the manor of Great Eversden for the endowment of a priest, to sing and pray for her soul and those of her friends, with a salary of ten marks. Also, the President and fellows undertook to provide a priest as a fellow, following the bequest of twelve tenements in Bermondsey Street,

Southwark, made to the College by a John Barby.[1] Another, (of several), benefactors during Wilkynson's tenure, was Dr John Drewell, canon of St Paul's, who died in 1494 and bequeathed land to maintain two fellows and a Bible-clerk. Drewell's executor, William Wilde, was also a benefactor. A further endowment involved the right to present a fellow of the College to the rectory of St Andrew's, Canterbury, but this was lost at the Dissolution of the Monasteries.[4] In 1502, the College received from Hugh Trotter, D.D., Treasurer of York Minster and formally a fellow, £253 6s 8d., which was used to buy an estate at Fulbourn. Trotter had been a fellow of Queens' until 1490, when he became Provost of the collegiate church of Beverley.[1]

King Henry and Queen Elizabeth made many visits to Cambridge[4] and, on September 1st 1498, when they were travelling from Lynn (known as King's Lynn after 1537) to Huntingdon, it appears that they visited Queens', as the bursar's accounts for this year includes:

'In expensis adventus Regis et regine ....', (expenses on the arrival of the King and Queen).[1]

Queen Elizabeth of York, (the daughter of Elizabeth Woodville), died in February 1503, aged 38. She was the first Queen since the foundation of the College not to claim the positions of Patroness and Foundress, but she may have taken some limited interest in the College, as there is a fragment of a document, with her signature in the margin, concerning the election of a 'scoler' named Billington.[1]

Wilkynson resigned as President in April 1505, and it is likely that Lady Margaret Beaufort, the King's mother, had persuaded Wilkynson to stand down and to recommend, as his successor, Bishop John Fisher, who had recently, (in 1504), been appointed Chancellor of the University, and who required a Cambridge base.[1,2]

Wilkynson's recommendation of Fisher as his successor is referred to in a letter from those associated with the College to the President, dated April 12th 1505:

'Ryght reverent and worschypfull and to us att all tymes most syngular and specyall good mastr, Wee yor scolars and dayly beedmen humblie recomend us unto yor mast^{r}schyp And for as mysch as wee underston be y^{r} lett^{rs} of the moste excellent p^{r}nces, my lady the kyngs mother and allso by y^{r} lett^{r}s that ye be at this tyme myndyt to resigne the p^{r}sidentship of this our colage called the qwenys colage, so that ye myght knowe our mynds in this thing, wherefor we write unto yower maist^{r}ship at this tyme signifyyng unto you y^{t} we ar fully det^{r}minate and doth promyse you to elect such a man as is thoght unto you necessary and profitable unto this our colage the lorde bisshop of Rochest^{r} (ie John Fisher)...Frome Cambrige in haste the xijth daye of Ap^{r}ll.'[1]

Several years later, in January 1511, Wilkynson was appointed to the prebend, (ie a form of canonry with a role in the administration of a cathedral or collegiate church), 'of Studley Magna'[1], in the collegiate church of St Peter and St Wilfred, known then as Ripon Minster.[1] (After his death, he was succeeded in this post by Christopher Joyce, a relation of Cardinal Bainbridge, Archbishop of York, 1508-14). However, Wilkynson died later that year, on the 13th December 1511, and is buried in his benefice, All Saints' Church, Orpington. (The church was mentioned in the Domesday Book, while some Saxon work is still visible). The stone slab over his grave has a monumental brass attached, depicting a priest, above the following inscription:

'Orate pro aia Thome Wilkynson Arcium magistri quondam p^{r}bendarii in ecclia sancti Wulffranni de Rippon et rectoris de Harowe sup^{er} montem et Orpyngton qui obiit xiij^{o} die Decembris a^{o} dni m b^{c} xj^{0} cui^{9} aie p^{ro}picietur Deus.'[1]

References

1. Searle, W.G. The History of the Queens' College of St Margaret and St Bernard in the University of Cambridge. 1446-1560. Deighton, Bell & Co; Macmillan & Co. London. 1867. pp 104-06, 118-26.
2. Twigg, J. A History of Queens' College, Cambridge 1448-1986. The Boydell Press. 1987. pp 14, 18, 66.

3. Lamb, J. (ed), A Collection of Letters, Statutes, and other Documents...illustrative of the History of the University of Cambridge during the period of the Reformation. London. 1838.
4. Gray, J.H. The Queens' College of St Margaret and St Bernard. F.E.Robinson. London. 1898. pp 37-38.
5. Fuller, T. Church History of Britain. 1655.

CHAPTER 3

John, Cardinal Fisher. President 1505-08.

Summary.

When John Fisher became President of Queens' in 1505, he was Chancellor of Cambridge University, Bishop of Rochester and closely associated with Lady Margaret Beaufort, King Henry VII's mother, who was a major benefactor of the University. He would develop a reputation as England's foremost theologian and, as such, would cross swords with Henry VIII. He was Chancellor of the University for just over thirty years and instrumental in implementing Lady Margaret's foundations and benefactions, in particular Christ's and St John's Colleges. However, despite Fisher's importance in the history of the University, his three years as President of Queens', while providing him with a Cambridge base at a critical time for the foundation of Christ's College, was not associated with an active interest in the College. He resigned as President in 1508.

It has been previously noted (see Chapter 2) that the intellectual movement of 'Renaissance Humanism', which involved a widening of the scope of University scholarship, was, in Cambridge, dominated by Fisher and his friend Erasmus, who was considered the greatest Humanist scholar of the time. But although Fisher was influential in this movement, and in enticing Erasmus to Cambridge, his embrace of Humanism did not extend to many of the ideas of the 'Reformation', which involved a schism in Western Christianity initiated by Martin Luther. Fisher's adherence to traditional Catholic theology and authority led to his prolonged opposition to King Henry VIII's attempts to divorce Queen Catherine of Aragon. Subsequently, Fisher's refusal to accept both Henry's remarriage and the King's assumption of the title 'Supreme

Head of the Church of England', culminated in his trial for high treason and his beheading on Tower Hill. He was recognised as a Catholic martyr and canonised in 1936. He is buried without his head at the Chapel Royal of St Peter ad Vincula, at the Tower of London.

Timeline.

c1469.	Born in Beverley, Yorkshire.
1483.	Undergraduate at Michaelhouse, (a College founded in 1323, which merged with King's Hall to form Trinity College in 1546).
1488.	B.A. .
1491.	Fellow of Michaelhouse. M.A. . Ordained priest.
1494-95.	Senior Proctor of Cambridge University. Meets Lady Margaret Beaufort, the King's mother, at Greenwich.
1490s.	Chaplain and confessor to Lady Margaret Beaufort.
1491-94.	Vicar of Northallerton.
1494-98.	Master of Michaelhouse.
1501.	D.D. .
1501-04.	Vice-Chancellor, Cambridge University.
1502.	Lady Margaret's Professor of Divinity.
1504-35.	Bishop of Rochester. Chancellor, Cambridge University.
1505-08.	President of Queens', following the resignation of Thomas Wilkynson. (Fisher needed a Cambridge base, while overseeing the foundation of Christ's College).
1505-06.	Three royal visits to Queens'.
1508.	Resignation as President, citing non-residence. Robert Bekynsaw elected in his stead.
1509.	Death of Henry VII. Accession of Henry VIII.
1511-14.	Erasmus resident in Cambridge, based at Queens'. (This was due to Fisher's influence).
1527.	Appointed confessor to Queen Catherine.
1529.	Tribunal at Blackfriars; Fisher defends the validity of King Henry VIII's marriage to Catherine of Aragon, thus opposing the King's wishes for a divorce.

1534.	Fisher refuses to take the 'oath to the succession', which recognises Henry's divorce and remarriage.
1535.	Fisher refuses to confirm Henry as 'Supreme Head of the Church of England'. Created a Cardinal, (21st of May). Charged with 'High Treason' at Westminster Hall, (17th of June). Beheaded on Tower Hill, (22nd of June).
1886.	Beatification.
1936.	Canonisation.

Theologian. Bishop. Long-serving Chancellor of Cambridge University, who was instrumental in founding Christ's and St John's Colleges. Promoter of Humanist learning. Catholic martyr and Saint. A short-term President.

John Fisher was born in Beverley, Yorkshire around 1469. Robert Fisher, his father, was a merchant who died young, leaving two children, John and his brother, Robert. His mother remarried; she had three more sons, and a daughter who became a nun. Both John and Robert were educated at a collegiate church of priests in Beverley, where John's progress led to him being sent to the University of Cambridge, 'distant from his native soil about eight days' journey southward'.[1] He entered Michaelhouse in 1483, under the supervision of William Melton, Doctor of Divinity and Master of that College, graduating B.A. in 1488 and M.A. in 1491. (Michaelhouse was a College of Cambridge University, founded in 1323, which would merge with King's Hall to form Trinity College in 1546). His ascent in the University was rapid; he became a fellow of Michaelhouse in 1491, the year he was ordained, and he became Senior Proctor for the year 1494-95. (The Proctors had considerable powers to regulate the activities, discipline and finances of the University, and acted for the University on all kinds of business). It was while on official business at the court in Greenwich that he met, and must have impressed, Lady Margaret Beaufort, mother of King Henry VII. Subsequently, he became her protégé, chaplain and, in 1497, her confessor. Fisher writes:

'She chose me as her director...to guide her life, yet I gladly confess that I learnt more from her virtue than ever I could teach her'.[1] In 1494 he was elected Master of Michaelhouse, after William Melton had received an appointment at York. In 1501 he became Vice-Chancellor of the University and, in 1502, having recently obtained a doctorate in theology, he was appointed to the University's first professorship, the 'Lady Margaret's Professor of Divinity'. (Lady Margaret would also endow a University Preacher in 1504). In 1504, Henry VII appointed Fisher as Bishop of Rochester and, in the same year, in recognition of his increasing eminence and influence, he was elected Chancellor of Cambridge University. He was to remain Chancellor for just over thirty years, despite his resignation in 1514 to allow the University to elect Thomas Wolsey, who had become a controlling figure in most matters of state, and powerful in the Church as Archbishop of York. However, Wolsey declined the office, and Fisher was re-elected as Chancellor for life, having previously required annual endorsement.[2]

The King's appointment of his mother's chaplain as Bishop of Rochester was unexpected and, at first, Fisher refused the offer. But he was persuaded to accept, in part by his old friend the Bishop of Winchester, Richard Fox, who had been in the service of Henry VII during his exile and had obtained important state appointments after the battle of Bosworth in 1485. Fisher's reaction to his appointment was given in a speech of welcome to Henry VII on his visit to Cambridge in 1506, (translated from the original Latin):

'I whose sudden elevation to the episcopate was the subject of general surprise, since I was young in years, had never held any office at court, nor as yet been enriched with benefices'.[1]

Fisher was consecrated by William Warham, Archbishop of Canterbury, in the chapel at Lambeth Palace. 'I have in my days promoted many a man unadvisably', Henry VII wrote to his mother about her confessor, 'and I would now make some recompense to promote some good and virtuous man'.[1] Unlike Fisher, many of the bishops at that time were lawyers by education and career, including Warham, who was Lord Chancellor, and

Richard Foxe, who was Lord Privy Seal and the King's chief minister. But there were three bishops at the time who had made their names as university officials and college presidents.[1] The diocese of Rochester had a low income and, usually, the bishop would hope to obtain further promotion. (At the time of Fisher's death the revenue from Rochester was about £300 annually, that from Ely was £2,134, while Lincoln yielded £3,300).[1] However, Fisher would refuse offers of further promotion and wrote (as translated and first published in 'The Life and Death of that renowned John Fisher, Bishop of Rochester', in 1655):

'Although some others have greater rents and fatter benefices than I, yet I have in stead thereof less charge and cure of souls; so that when account shall be made of both (which undoubtedly will be very shortly) I would not wish myself in better state of living the value of one hair'.[1] Soon after his appointment, he summoned the priors and monks under his authority, reminding them of their vows, and visited all his parish churches, dismissing some priests whom he judged as unworthy. Also, he regularly carried out the routine pastoral tasks of preaching, confirming children and caring for the needy.[1]

'Wheresoever he lay, either at Rochester or elsewhere, his order was to enquire where any poor sick folk lay near him, which after he once knew, he would diligently visit them...Besides he gave at his gate to divers poor people (which were commonly no small number) a daily alms of money...That being done every one of them was rewarded likewise with meat; which was daily brought to the gate...If any strangers came to him, he would entertain them according to their vocations with such mirth as stood with the gravity of his person...and when he had no strangers, his order was now and then to sit with his chaplains, which were commonly grave and learned men...And the most of his sustenance was thin potage sodden with flesh, eating of the flesh itself very sparingly...He wore most commonly a shirt of hair and many times he would whip himself in most secret wise...he laid him down upon a poor hard couch of straw and mats (for other bed he used none) provided at Rochester in his closet, near the cathedral church, where he might look into the choir and hear

Devine Service; and being laid, he never rested above four hours at a time...'.[1]

Because of Fisher's involvement with Lady Margaret, her patronage became more focussed on Cambridge, where, at the instigation of Fisher, she founded two colleges, Christ's and St John's. Christ's College had been originally founded as 'God's House' in 1437, to provide more grammar-school masters in England, and was refounded as Christ's College in 1505, with a substantial endowment from Lady Margaret. But before this project was completed, Fisher was planning another, involving the development of a religious institution in Cambridge, the Hospital of St John the Evangelist. This had an ancient foundation, dating from around 1200, but was in a run-down state and, in March 1509, Lady Margaret obtained the agreement of the Bishop of Ely for the suppression of the hospital and arranged to endow a new foundation in its place. However, these plans were upset by her death in June 1509 and it was not until 1511 that St John's College received its foundation charter. In addition, there were problems in obtaining money from Lady Margaret's estate, as there were attempts by the King and Lady Margaret's former household servants to obtain part of the endowments, and it was not until 1512 that the Court of Chancery allowed her executors to contribute to the foundation. But, to raise sufficient revenue, Fisher still had to dissolve three small monasteries and to contribute personally, before the College was opened in 1516.[2] Also, it has been suggested that an oration by Fisher in the unfinished King's College Chapel, in the presence of Henry VII and Lady Margaret in 1507, had persuaded the King to provide £5000 for its completion.[3]

Thomas Wilkynson resigned as President of Queens' in 1505, probably as a result of pressure from Lady Margaret on behalf of Fisher, and he recommended that the fellows elect Fisher in his stead. It has been claimed that this was because Fisher, as Bishop of Rochester, needed a Cambridge base to oversee Lady Margaret's foundation of Christ's College, to which she had given a major endowment in 1505. He does not seem to have been much more that a benign figurehead at Queens', and he resigned in 1508, citing his non-residence. However, in 1505, Lady Margaret was involved in obtaining a gift of thirty-one acres to Queens', from the Duke of Buckingham.[2]

There were three royal visits to Queens' while Fisher was President.[2] In 1505 there was a visit from Lady Margaret Beaufort, and then one from the King accompanied by the future Henry VIII. In 1506 the King came again, this time with his mother, when they were on their way to the shrine of St Mary at Walsingham. Cooper,[4] (Charles Henry Cooper, 1808-66, antiquarian and historian, coroner and town clerk of Cambridge), has recorded an account of the latter visit:

'First, The Maior with hys Brederen rode to meet the Kyng, two or three mylle owt of the Towne; Also Mr. Molory then Shereff of the Shire bore his rodd, and gave hys attendance, and as he approached here the Unyversyte, within a quarter of a mylle, ther stode, first all the four Ordres of Freres, and aftir odir Religious, and the King on Horsbacke kissed the Crosse of everyche of the Religious, and then ther stode all along, all the Graduatts, aftir their Degrees, in all their Habbitts, and at the end of them was the Unyversyte Cross, wher was a Forme and a Cushin &c as accustomed, where the Kyng dyd alight, and there the Byshopp of Rochestre, Doctor Fisher then beyng Chaunceller of the Unyversyte, accompanied with odir Doctors, sensyd &c the Kyng, and aftir made a little Proposition, and welcomed hym; and then the Kyng took hys Horse ageyn & rood by the Blackfriers, throughe the Towne, to the Queens Colledge, wher hys Grace was at that tyme lodgged, and ther rested the space of a Houre, & then did on his Gowne and Mantell of the Gartier, and all odir Knyghts of the Ordre there being present, gave their attendance in the Habit of the Ordre, as apperteyneth, and roode from the Kyngs Logginge to the Chappell of the Kyngs Colledge… The Byshopp of Rochestre, being there Chaunceller, did the Divine Service, both the Even, the Day, both at Mattens &c. and sang the Mass of Requiem on the Morrow'. To accommodate the King at the riverside building at Queens', Fisher temporarily moved out to Michaelhouse, where he had been the Master.

There were two further royal visits to Queens' when Fisher was Chancellor; Catherine of Aragon came in 1521 and Henry

VIII visited for two days in 1522.[2] (There is a room named the 'queen's chamber' in the building next to the river). Also, Cardinal Wolsey stayed at Queens' in 1520.[2]

Fisher notified the fellows of his intention to resign the Presidency in 1508, citing non-residence, and they replied asking for a nomination for his successor. He then recommended Dr Robert Bekensaw, fellow of Michaelhouse, who was duly elected. Lady Margaret was notified in the following letter from the fellows, and she would have been interested in the appointment, as Bekensaw was her almoner, around this time:[5]

'Noble and excellent p^{r}nces, ow^{r} g^{r}cius lady, after most humble submission w^{t} dew rev^{r}cy, plesyth yor goodness y^{t} where as of late hit lykyd ye rev^{r}ent father in Godde o^{r} specyall good lord bysshop of Rochester to surches and leve ye p^{r}sidentshipp of o^{r} college to ye right gret hevynes of us all, we...gave hym full power to assyne and chose for his successaur...he hath for the sayd rome assynged ye right worschypfull M. Bekensaw, we have be or full consent electe and chosyn ye same o^{r} president, gladly content so to do the rather y^{t} we might answer and accomplish in this behalf yor g^{r}cius ples^{r}, which to regard and tender we specially and syngulerly be bownd...'.[5]

In 1509 Fisher preached at the funeral of Henry VII and, just a few months later, at a service held thirty days after the funeral of Lady Margaret, who died two months after her son:[1]

'In his sermon, he compareth her in four points to the blessed and noble woman Martha, the sister of Mary; that is to say in nobility of person, in discipline of her body, in ordering her soul to God, and lastly in hospitality and charitable dealing to her neighbours...And yet when she was in health, she never failed on certain days in the week to wear sometimes a shirt and sometimes a girdle of hair, that full often her skin was pierced therewith'.[1] These duties demonstrate Fisher's position at the heart of the establishment and it is unlikely that he could have foreseen the trouble ahead in his relationship with the new regime.

Fisher's enthusiasm for 'Renaissance Humanism' has been noted, (see Chapter 2), and he was responsible for arranging that the pre-eminent Dutch Humanist scholar, Erasmus, came to reside at Queens' between 1511-14. Erasmus, who was renowned throughout Europe, originated in the Netherlands and lived in France, England and Italy, before his final destination of Basel. He visited England several times between 1499-1516, and had a personal connection with Queens' as early as 1497, when he was in Paris at the English Hall of Residence together with a Robert Fisher, who may have been John's brother but it has also been claimed that he was his cousin.[2] Also, in 1498, Erasmus was tutor to William Blount, Lord Mountjoy, whose companion was Richard Whitford, a fellow of Queens'.[2] On Erasmus' second visit to England, in 1506, Fisher invited him to Cambridge for the visit of the King and Lady Margaret.[2]

Twigg, (John Twigg, author of the history of the College of 1987), has described Erasmus' hopes for self-advancement and royal patronage following his next return to England in 1509 and, when this was not forthcoming, his increasing disappointment, leading to his leaving Cambridge in 1514.[2] In 1511, soon after the beginning of his two and a half years at Queens', he was appointed to lecture on Greek at Cambridge, the first to do so, although he notes: 'the audience is small'.[2] Later, he lectured on theology, having being appointed as 'Lady Margaret's Professor of Divinity' in 1511, a post which he held until 1515; also during his stay, he worked on his Greek edition of the New Testament and his edition of the works of St Jerome.[3] (His 'Novum Instrumentum omne' was the first New Testament in Greek to be published, in 1516, and contained parallel Greek and Latin texts). However, the first of the thirty-one letters he wrote from Cambridge to Andrea Ammonio, who was in the papal service in London, complained about his journey from London, and did not indicate any enthusiasm for Queens', as he writes (as translated- as are the subsequent quotations): 'I expect I shall stay at this college for a few days, anyway';[6] also, soon after arrival he was taken ill, perhaps from his recurrent problem of gallstones. As he did not like the College ale, he asked Ammonio to send him a cask of Greek wine but, of the four that he eventually received, two arrived unsealed and undrinkable. His generally negative feelings for the weather, his finances and Cambridge continued:

'What a University! No one can be found who will write (ie copy) even moderately well at any price...Cambridge townsmen go beyond the inhospitable Britons, who have malice joined to their clownishness'.[2,6]

Unsurprisingly, Erasmus liked to escape to London to see his friends John Colet, (the founder of St Paul's School), and Sir Thomas More, (Lord Chancellor during 1528-32), while, in 1513, he wrote: 'We are shut in by the plague and beset with highway robberies'.[2] But, in addition to Fisher, four of the fellows of Queens' were close friends[2] and, in later years, he wrote in more positive terms about Cambridge colleges:

'...there's so much religion and so marked a sobriety in living that you'd despise every form of religious regime in comparison if you saw it'.[2] But he did not return to Cambridge on his three further visits to England after 1514. A letter from Erasmus to Fisher after his time at Queens' warned him not to spend too much time in his library at Rochester by the unhealthy Medway:

'Nor do I forget howe Passionately you love that library which is to you a very paradise'.[1]

Erasmus, while critical of the abuses in the Catholic Church, continued, until his death in 1536, to recognise the authority of the Pope and, before Henry VIII's break with Rome, he was in correspondence with Henry and Queen Catherine. This is described in an account of various 'Letters and Papers. Foreign and Domestic...1524-30';[7] in 1528, Erasmus, writing to Henry:

'Thanks him for his letter inviting him to England, at a time when he is troubled by various afflictions, labours, and ill health. Was afraid of the length of the journey, perils by robbers, and the annoyance of the sea, but yet sent his servant to England as a preliminary step. Since his departure at Easter time, was so sorely attacked by disease that he thought he should have died. Hears from the servant, who is returned, that bands of soldiers are prowling everywhere, and that the duke of Gueldres threatens war. If he can do anything by his pen to please the King, he will not fail'. His letter to Queen Catherine, in the same year, is also described:

'The nobility of her birth, her exalted rank, and her marriage with a most prosperous sovereign, are as nothing in contributing to her happiness, compared with her Majesty's gifts. It is most rare to find a lady, born and brought up at Court, placing all her hopes and solace in devotion and the reading of Scripture. Would that others, widows at all events, would take an example from her, and not widows only, but unmarried ladies, by devoting themselves to the service of Christ. He is a solid rock, the spouse of all pious souls, and nearer to each than the nearest tie. The soul that is devoted to this husband is not less grateful in adversity than in prosperity. He knows what is expedient for all, and is often more propitious when He changes the sweet for bitter. Every one must take up their cross, there is no entrance into heavenly glory without it. These are blessings which none can take away. Hopes the book which he has dedicated to her Majesty will receive her favourable attention'.

As noted above, the decade 1510-20 saw Fisher's efforts in establishing St John's College, whose Statutes promoted Humanist interests, including the use of Hebrew, Greek and Latin.[3] Fisher wished to learn Greek and it is claimed that Erasmus was his tutor at Rochester during the latter's last visit to England in 1516. It seems that Fisher had a working knowledge of the language, as it was sufficient for him to use Erasmus' edition of the Greek New Testament.[3] Fisher was unusually conscientious as a bishop, with an impressive record of residence, which was, no doubt, facilitated by his having few other major responsibilities. Although he was twice nominated by Henry VIII as an English delegate to the Fifth Lateran Council during 1512-17, tensions between England and France prevented these missions, and the only time he left England was to attend the meeting of the Kings of England and France on the 'Field of the Cloth of Gold' in 1420.[3] His concerns and efforts for pastoral care and preaching are well documented; he was an esteemed preacher, and his sermons comprised his first published work.[3]

Despite the long-established saying about the 'Reformation': 'Erasmus laid the egg and Luther hatched it',[2] Erasmus, as well as Fisher and Sir Thomas More, opposed Luther's more radical ideas and, in the 1520s, Erasmus was active in opposing Protestant heresy, which was contrary to official Catholic doctrine. Fisher's orthodox stance was reflected on the 12th May 1521, when Cardinal Wolsey presided over a ceremony outside St Paul's Cathedral to promote a public decree (bull) by the Pope against the views of Martin Luther, at which Fisher had been chosen to preach the sermon. During the 1520s, Fisher published several detailed and scholarly works defending traditional Catholic theology; in particular, his 'Confutatio' (Refutation, 1523), and 'De veritate' (The truth, 1527). These were frequently reprinted, widely quoted, and had a significant influence on the deliberations at the Catholic Church's 'Council of Trent' (1545-63), which considered the Church's response to the Reformation.[3] Fisher was very concerned about heresy at Cambridge and, in 1521, visited several times to preach in relation to a student who had defaced a Catholic poster, which had displayed an indulgence (pardon) issued by Pope Clement VII; his reaction to this incident is reported in an account published in 1655:

'He (Fisher) was greatly moved at the detestable and wicked deed, and thereupon fell in hand immediately to find out the doer, first by trying the handwriting, and after by other means, but all in vain...At last, in a public convocation...he declared what great displeasure might justly inserve at the hands of Almighty God and the King, in case this horrible fact would be left unpunished. After that, what a great discredit it would be to their whole University... if now such a malefactor should escape and not be enquired of... he moved the author to repentance, and by confession of his fault to ask forgiveness at God's hands. Which if he would do by a certain day...he promised on God's behalf remission; but if on the contrary part he would obstinately persist and continue in his secret naughtiness, that then such remedy should proceed against him, as Christ ordained and his Church hath always observed against those kind of malefactors who like rotten members are by the censure of excommunication cut off from the body of the church...So every man departed till the appointed day that the excommunication should be pronounced...the Chancellor there moved the malefactor the second time to repentance and confession of his offence; but the spirit that before suggested this wicked attempt into his heart, would by no means suffer him to hearken to any amendment. Wherefore, the Chancellor...causing a bill of excommunication to be written, took the same in his hands and began to read it; but...even before them all he could not refrain from weeping...and so left off without further proceeding in the excommunication for that time. Nevertheless appointing a third day for their purpose...this third day being at last come it was declared by the Chancellor...that no tiding could be learned of this ungodly person, and so ordering himself after a grave and severe manner as well in his countenance as other gesture of his body, he pronounced this terrible sentence from the beginning to the ending, against this desperate wicked person, but not without weeping and lamentation, which struck such a fear into the hearts of his hearers...such was the bitterness of his words and the gravity of his sentence'.[1]

A further illustration of Fisher's religious zeal occurred after a fellow of St John's had expressed heretical views, when, at the next revision of the College's Statutes, Fisher ensured that any member who was even suspected of heresy could be removed from the College. However, this potential over-reaction was never used.[3] As the decade drew to a close, Fisher had a considerable reputation as a theologian, which was to lead, eventually, to unfortunate consequences. In 1527 he was consulted by the King as to whether his marriage to Catherine was invalid, as she had been previously married to his brother. Although Henry wanted Fisher to support these doubts, Fisher considered that papal authority, which had been given for the marriage, could resolve any scriptural uncertainty, and he was to continue to oppose the King's efforts to obtain a divorce. At a tribunal held at Blackfriars in 1529 to consider the validity of the King's marriage, Fisher, once again, opposed the King in an emotional contribution.[1] The subsequent six years saw Fisher as the King's main opponent in this matter and, in 1531, it is claimed that there was an anonymous attempt to silence him by poisoning his soup. But Fisher refused the meal, which was then given to his servants and the local poor, leaving two persons dead.[1] Despite Fisher's opposition, the King's divorce was declared by the Archbishop of Canterbury, Thomas Cranmer, in 1533 and, soon after, Fisher was arrested and placed into the custody of Stephen Gardiner, Bishop of Winchester, until Anne Boleyn had been crowned Queen in June of that year.

Richard Rex,[3] (Professor of Reformation History and fellow of Queens'), has described how Fisher's resistance to the King's wishes included close communication with Eustace Chapuys, who was Charles V's ambassador to England, and who relayed advice to Fisher from Charles V in relation to possible imperial and papal action against Henry VIII. (Charles V, an uncle of Catherine of Aragon, was Holy Roman Emperor and King of Spain). Also, Fisher met with the 'Holy Maid of Kent', (Elizabeth Barton), whose preaching and predictions of disaster for Henry, if he were to divorce Catherine, had a wide following.[3] She had:

'declared unto sundry persons that many times she had certain visions revealed unto her, touching the King's doings in his matter of divorce, by what means she could not tell, but (as she thought) they came from God. But true it is that divers times being in her trance...she uttered such words touching the reproving of heresies... she would say that it was showed unto her in her vision that the King had an ill intent and purpose in him...minded for his voluptuous and carnal appetite to marry another...'.[1] Subsequently, she became a nun in Canterbury and was: 'famous almost over all the realm'.[1] She met with Fisher and also with the King, who decided to bring charges of high treason against her and against the various clerics who had supported or met with her, as such meetings had given her credence. Elizabeth Barton, and those clerics who had initially supported her, were duly convicted and executed, while Fisher and several others, including his chaplain, were considered guilty of the lesser offence of 'misprision', involving the deliberate concealment of knowledge of treason or felony, despite the fact that her pronouncements were public knowledge. But Fisher was merely sentenced to loss of goods and imprisonment during the King's pleasure; although he probably paid a fine, he did not lose his liberty.[1]

Fisher's opposition continued and, in 1534, he refused to take the 'oath to the succession', required of all adult males.

Fisher was summoned by the Archbishop of Canterbury and other commissioners, and appeared before them on the 13th April

1534. He is reported to have asked to be allowed to consider the oath further and, after his return to his lodgings in Lambeth Marsh, he was visited by many of his friends who thought they would not see him again. These included the Master and fellows of St John's College. When he returned to the commission he is reported to have replied:

'... if you will needs have me answer directly, my answer is: that foreasmuch as mine own conscience cannot be satisfied, I do absolutely refuse the oath'.[1] This resulted in his imprisonment in the Tower of London on the 21st April, with just one servant and, on January 2nd 1535, he was deprived of the bishopric of Rochester. Sir Thomas More also appeared before the commission and was committed to the Tower four days later. They were to exchange letters while in the Tower, one of which was intercepted and read by the King and his council, leading to their being kept in increased security. Although the King sent various bishops and laymen to try and persuade Fisher to take the oath, he continued to refuse. Subsequently, it was claimed that he had denied that Henry was 'Supreme Head of the Church of England', as had been declared in the 'Act of Supremacy' in 1534. It is reported that when several members of the privy council came to him asking if he would acknowledge Henry as Supreme Head, Fisher replied:

'My lords, you have here demanded of me a question so doubtful to answer that I wot not almost what to say to it with mine own safety. And therefore this new Act seemeth to me much like a two-edged sword: for if I answer you directly with denial of the King's supremacy, then am I sure of death; and if on the contrary part I acknowledge the same contrary to mine own conscience, then am I sure of the loss of my own soul. Wherefore, as near as I can to avoid both dangers, I shall desire your lordships to bear with my silence; for I am not minded to make any direct answer to it at all.'[1]

In May 1535, after Fisher had been in prison for more than a year, the King sent Richard Rich, a lawyer, to see him, and it is claimed that the King used Rich's report of their conversation to establish charges of high treason. Also, the King's commission of enquiry searched Fisher's house at Rochester, removing his books and money belonging to the diocese of Rochester. A description of this search confirms previously-noted claims as to an aspect of Fisher's religious devotions:

'I cannot omit to tell you of a coffer standing in his oratory, where commonly no man came but himself alone; for it was his secret place of prayer...But when it was open, they found within it, instead of gold and silver, which they looked for, a shirt of hair, and two or three whips, wherewith he used full often to punish himself, as some of his chaplains and servants would report'.[1]

Pope Paul III created Fisher a Cardinal in May 1535, hoping that this would induce the King to show clemency, but this had the opposite effect. After the King heard about the promotion, it is reported that he sent his secretary, Thomas Cromwell, to ask Fisher if he intended to accept the Cardinal's hat. (A Cardinal's hat, a badge of office, had been sent to Fisher, but the delivery had been prevented). Fisher is reported to have replied:

'I know myself far unworthy of any such dignity, that I think of nothing less than such matters; but if he do send it to me, assure yourself I will work with it by all the means I can to benefit the Church of Christ; and in that respect I will receive it upon my knees'.[1] It is also reported that, on hearing of Fisher's answer, Henry stated:

'Yea, is he so lusty? Well let the Pope send him a hat when he will. But I will so provide that, whensoever it cometh, he shall wear it on his shoulders; for head shall he not have to set it on'.[1,2]

Fisher was brought to trial in Westminster Hall on the 17th June. He was ill and frail and:

'rode part of the way on horseback, in a black cloth gown, and the rest he was carried by water, for that he was not able to ride through for weakness'.[1] His indictment read:

'that he maliciously, traitorously and falsely had said these words: "The King, our sovereign Lord, is not supreme head in earth of the Church of England"... he pleaded "Not guilty" '.[1] Richard Rich testified against Fisher, who is reported to have claimed that Rich had told him that the King:

'had sent him (ie Rich) unto me in this secret manner to know my full opinion...he told me that the King willed him to assure me on his honour and in the word of a King, that, whatsoever I should say unto him by his secret messenger, I should abide no danger nor peril for it'.[1] However, he was convicted by the jury of twelve men and sentenced to death by the Lord Chancellor. Before his return to the Tower he addressed the commissioners again, clearly stating that:

'His Grace cannot justly claim any such supremacy over the Church of God...Wherefore I pray God, His Grace may remember himself in time and hearken to good counsel for the preservation of himself and his realm, and the quietness of all Christendom'.[1]

At about five o'clock on 22nd June , Sir Edmund Walsingham, Lieutenant of the Tower, came to Fisher, who was asleep in his room in the Bell Tower, and told him he would be executed later that morning. Subsequent events are reported as follows:[1]

' "Well", then said he ..."let me by your patience sleep an hour or two; for I have slept very little this night; and yet, to tell you the truth, not for any fear of death, I thank God by reason of my great infirmity and weakness." And after he was waked, he called to his man to help him up. But first of all he commanded him to take away the shirt of hair...and to convey it privily out of the house; and...to lay him forth a clean white shirt and all the best apparel he had as cleanly brushed as might be..."this is our marriage day and it behoveth us therefore to use more cleanliness for solemnity of that marriage"...being so weak, he was scant able to go down the stairs. Wherefore at the stair's foot he was taken up in a chair...and carried to the Tower gate...to be delivered to the sheriffs of London for execution...and carried to the scaffold on the Tower Hill ... Then was his gown and tippet taken from him; and he stood in his doublet and hose...a long, lean and slender body, having on it little other substance, besides the skin and bones..."Christian people, I am come hither to die for the faith of Christ's holy Catholic Church and I thank God hitherto, my stomach hath served me very well thereunto, so that yet I have not feared death. Wherefore I do desire you all to help and assist me with your prayers, that at the very point and instant of death's stroke, I may in that very moment stay steadfast without fainting in any one point of the Catholic Faith, free from any fear. And I beseech Almighty God of His infinite goodness to save the King and this realm, and that it may please Him to hold His holy hand over it and send the King good counsel". These or like words he spoke with such a cheerful countenance, such a stout and constant courage and such a reverend gravity...the people were astonished thereat...Then came the executioner and bound a handkerchief about his eyes...he laid his holy head down over the middest of a little block, where the executioner, being ready, with a sharp and heavy axe cut asunder his slender neck at one blow...And about eight of the clock in the evening, commandment came from the King's council to such as watched about the dead body...that they should cause it to be buried. Whereupon two of the watchers took it...and so carried it to a churchyard there hard by, called All Hallowes, Barking...they digged a grave and...tumbled the body... without either sheet or other accustomed thing belonging to a Christian man's burial. The next day after his burial, the head, being somewhat parboiled in hot water, was pricked upon a pole and set on high upon London Bridge...I cannot omit to declare unto you the miraculous sight of the head, which, after it had stood up the space of fourteen days upon the bridge, could not be perceived to waste nor consume...but grew daily fresher and fresher, so that in his lifetime he never looked so well...wherefore the people coming daily to see this strange sight, the passage over the bridge was so stopped with their going and coming that almost neither cart nor horse could pass. And therefore...the executioner was commanded to throw down the head in the night time into the river of Thames'.[1]

However, his body was soon to be reburied next to the body of Sir Thomas More in the Chapel Royal of St Peter ad Vincula in the Tower of London,[5] while the tomb that Fisher had prepared for himself in St John's College chapel was removed. But his reputation was kept alive by Catholic Humanists associated with St John's, and a biography of Fisher was eventually printed in 1655.[1]

He was beatified by Pope Leo XIII in 1886 and canonised by Pope Pius XI in 1935. He is commemorated by Catholics on the 22nd June, the anniversary of his execution. In 1985, the 450th anniversary of his execution, there was a commemoration service in St John's College chapel, at which Cardinal Basil Hume delivered the address.

In addition to Fisher's material contributions to Cambridge University, his wider influence is noted by the late Brenden Bradshaw, (historian and fellow of Queens'):

'...when Fisher came up to Michaelhouse...as an undergraduate in 1483 Oxford was *the* English university and Cambridge was nowhere in the league. When he died in 1535 Cambridge had already entered upon one of its most glorious epochs as a centre of the new humanist learning. The achievement was in no small measure that of John Fisher. Personally he lent the weight of his influence as Chancellor to the promotion of the New Learning...His two new foundations were designed as humanist colleges and he brought Erasmus, the prince of humanists, to Cambridge for a stay which lasted three years (1511-14)...for Fisher the most important aspect of humanism was not the promotion of language and literature studies in Latin and Greek but the new conceptions of education which it provided, namely the formation of the whole human being. It was in leading the university away from the medieval view of its function...that Fisher made his most notable contribution as Chancellor'.[8]

References

1. Various authors. Saint John Fisher, The Earliest English Life: Introduced by Philip Hughes. Burns Oates and Washbourne Ltd. London 1935. (First printed in 1655 as 'The Life and Death of that renowned John Fisher, Bishop of Rochester').
2. Twigg, J. A History of Queens' College, Cambridge 1448-1986. The Boydell Press. Bury St Edmunds.1987. pp 18-28, 135-36.
3. Rex, R. Fisher, John (St John Fisher) In: Oxford Dictionary of National Biography. Online. 2004.
4. Cooper, C.H. Annals of Cambridge. Warwick and Co. Cambridge. 1842. p 281. (Quoting Ashmole, Institution Laws & Ceremonies of the Order of the Garter, 558, 487).

5. Searle, W.G. The History of the Queens' College of St Margaret and St Bernard in the University of Cambridge. 1446-1560. Deighton, Bell & Co; Macmillan & Co. London. 1867. p 140.
6. Chainey, G. A Literary History of Cambridge. The Pevensey Press, Cambridge. 1985.
7. Letters and Papers, Foreign and Domestic. Henry VIII. Vol.4. 1524-1530. Published by HM Stationery Office. 1875. British History Online.
8. Bradshaw, B.I. Bishop John Fisher (1469-1535). In: The Record, 1986. Queens' College, Cambridge. Online. 2020.

CHAPTER 4

Robert Bekensaw (Bekynshaw, Bekynsaw, Birkenshaw, Bekensall, Beconsall, Bekenshall, Bekonsawe). President 1508-19.

Summary.

Robert Bekensaw was recommended by Bishop John Fisher to be his successor as President of Queens', and was a protégé of Lady Margaret Beaufort, whose patronage the fellows hoped to secure.[1] He has been succinctly described as: 'an assiduous collector of church offices', (in particular, a canon of Windsor), 'active at Court' and 'firmly non-resident'.[2] Although he visited the College for elections and the regular audits, he was not a benefactor, and left no significant mark on Queens'. However, he presided over the College during Erasmus' residence at Queens'.

He resigned for unknown reasons in 1519, but lived for a further seven years.

Timeline.

c1476. Born in Croston, Lancashire.

1493. B.A., Cambridge University.

1496. M.A. .

1500. University Proctor.

1502. B.D. .

1505-26. Vicar of Croston.

1506-07. Dispensation from residence at the University because of his service with Lady Margaret Beaufort.

1507. D.D. .

1508-19. President of Queens'.

1509-10. Chaplain and almoner to Catherine of Aragon. (Chaplain by 1509; almoner before July 2010).

1509. Death of Henry VII and Lady Margaret Beaufort. Accession of Henry VIII.

1511-14. Erasmus resident mainly in Cambridge, based at Queens'.

1512. Rector of Bradwell-super-Mare, Essex, (in the gift of Catherine of Aragon).

1512-25. Canon of St George's Chapel, Windsor Castle.

1513-16. Treasurer of Lincoln Cathedral.

1517. Dean of the collegiate church of St John Baptist, Stoke-by-Clare, Suffolk.

1519. Resigns as President.

1523. Prebendary of All Saints', Hungate, at Lincoln Cathedral.

1526. Dies, (21st of January), aged about 50.

A churchman and courtier, who presided (at a distance) over Erasmus' residence at Queens'.

Robert Bekensaw, (this spelling of his name is in the letter of the fellows of Queens' to Lady Margaret Beaufort, informing her of his election as President),[1] was born in Croston, Lancashire, in about 1476, the son of George Beconsall (or Bekonsawe).[1] He graduated B.A. from Cambridge in 1493 and progressed in his University career with further degrees and offices: M.A., Proctor, B.D., D.D., and a fellowship at Michaelhouse, (a College founded in 1323). As previously noted, (see Chapter 3), Bishop John Fisher, who had also been at Michaelhouse, recommended Bekensaw to be his successor at Queens'. Around this time, or soon after, Bekensaw was chaplain and almoner to Lady Margaret Beaufort, King Henry VII's mother, and he was in attendance at the court when elected as President on or about the 6th of July 1508.[1] However, Henry VII died in April 1509, as did Lady Margaret Beaufort two months later. (The inscription on her tomb in Westminster Abbey was composed by Erasmus who was paid 20s.).[1] Subsequently, a general pardon was issued to the College for all offences committed before 23rd April, the second day of the new reign.

We know little about this President apart from the list of his church offices and a few references to him in contemporary University and College records; for example, in 1506-07, he obtained a dispensation from residence at the University because he was in the service of Lady Margaret Beaufort. (In the University's Grace–book, his name appears as 'Bekynshaw').[1] Another reference, in March 1519, records that:

'Dr Bekensaw and the fellows of the college by indenture granted permission to John Craforth, M.A. one of the fellows to go to the court or any other place for his learning or profit for three years with the full stipend of a resident fellow, £6. 13s. 4d., John Craforth agreeing to resign his fellowship on the Lady-day then next ensuing...'.[1] During Bekensaw's time, poor scholars often paid for lodging and tuition by service, and it is recorded that four poor scholars were paid 16d. for two days work in cleaning the outer and inner courts, while another poor scholar received 6d.: 'for cleaning the Court and cloister of the College'.[3] Bekensaw will, no doubt, have been consulted in 1511 about a debate recorded in the College archives over the statute limiting the number of fellows who could come from a diocese or a county, as there was a move to change this rule for a fellowship established with an endowment from Hugh Trotter, a former fellow.[1,2] Eventually it was decided that this fellowship was to be held by someone from the diocese of York, an arrangement which lasted until 1838, when all restrictions as to the birthplace of a fellow were removed.[1] Cooper,[4] (Charles Henry Cooper, 1808-66, antiquarian and historian, coroner and town clerk of Cambridge), provides another glimpse into University life in these times:

'The Plague prevailed here again this year, (1514), on which account, the University assemblies were discontinued for one term'.[4]

While the time spent in Cambridge by the famous scholar Erasmus was the result of his friendship with John Fisher, his extended stay at the University was during the Presidency of Bekensaw, who is likely to have met Erasmus during his visits. Unfortunately, although it is generally accepted that Erasmus was resident at Queens' at times during 1511-14,[2] there are no references to this in the College archives,[2] and what we know of his association with the College is based only on his letters. Indeed, he may also have stayed in other venues while at Cambridge, and Searle, in his history of he College of 1867, claims that Erasmus may have lived for a time with a bookseller named Garret.[1] If this was so, the latter would have been well acquainted with his habits, and there is evidence that this was the case, as Roger Ascham, (1515-68, alumnus of St John's College, scholar and tutor in Greek and Latin to Elizabeth I), writes in 1544:

'Pastimes for the minde only, be nothing fit for studentes, because the body, which is most hurt by study, should take no profite at all thereat. This knewe Erasmus very well, when hee was here in Cambridge: which, when he had been sore at his book (as Garret, our bookbynder, hath very oft told me) for lack of better exercise, would take his horse, and ryde about the market hill and home againe'.[1] Although there are discrepancies in the various accounts of Erasmus in Cambridge, Fuller, (Thomas Fuller, 1608-61, priest and historian), writes in 1655:

'Queens' College accounteth it no small credit, thereunto, that Erasmus (who no doubt might have picked and chose what house he pleased) preferred this for the place of his study, for some years, in Cambridge...where a study on the top of the south-west tower in the old court still retaineth his name...He often complained of the college ale... as raw, small and windy...Erasmus had his lagena or flagon of wine (recruited weekly from his friends at London) which he drank sometimes singly by itself, and sometimes encouraged his faint ale with the mixture thereof. He was public Greek professor, and first read the grammar of Chrysoloras to a thin auditory, whose number increased when he began the grammar of Theodorus...Some years after he took upon him the divinity professor's place (understand it the Lady Margaret's), invited thereunto, not with the salary so small in itself, but with desire and hope to do good in the employment'.[5] However, the location of his rooms remains uncertain, and Twigg, in his history of the College of 1987, states:

'He did not live at the top of the turret known as "Erasmus' Tower", although this story was in circulation as early as the 17th century; his rooms were apparently below that, on the same staircase...'.[2] He made repeated visits to London from Cambridge and, in 1511, went on a pilgrimage to the shrine of our Lady of Walsingham, Norfolk, when he donated a copy of Greek iambic verses as an offering.[1]

Bekensaw's many church appointments included vicar of Croston, his family's parish, from 1505 until his death,[1] and, by 1509, he was chaplain to Catherine of Aragon as well as her almoner before July 1510.[1] While President he became rector of Bradwell-super-mare, Essex, in 1512, (in the gift of Catherine of Aragon) and, in the same year, canon of St George's Chapel at Windsor Castle.[1] Also, in 1513 he was appointed treasurer of Lincoln Cathedral, but resigned in 1516. He was inducted as Dean of the collegiate church of St John the Baptist at Stoke-by-Clare, Suffolk, (under the patronage of the Queens of England), in 1517. Also, he was rector of Chagford, Devon, and succentor, (assisting in the preparation and conduct of the liturgy), of Wells Cathedral.[1]

After 1512, Bekensaw lived mainly at Windsor and, later, at Stoke, and the fellows were obliged to travel to consult him when necessary, as shown in the College records:

'1513...Item pro expensis m^ri^ Staynbank quum equitavit ad magistrum collegii tunc Wynsorie manentem...'[1] (Also for expenses M^ri^ Staynbank when riding to the master of the college then staying at Windsor...).[1] However, he is recorded as coming to Cambridge for elections of fellows and bible-clerks, and for the audits.[1]

Bekensaw resigned as President in 1519, but there is no record of his reasons. He died in 1526, aged about fifty, after having collected yet another church appointment in 1523, as prebendary of All Saints' Church in Hungate, at Lincoln Cathedral. He left a somewhat unimpressive bequest of 40s to the University and was not a benefactor of Queens'.[1]

References

1. Searle, W.G. The History of the Queens' College of St Margaret and St Bernard in the University of Cambridge. 1446-1560. Deighton, Bell & Co; Macmillan & Co. London. 1867. pp 144-49, 152-59.
2. Twigg, J. A History of Queens' College, Cambridge 1448-1986. The Boydell Press. 1987. pp 20, 21, 84.
3. Gray, J.H. The Queens' College of St Margaret and St Bernard. F.E.Robinson. London. 1898. p 63.
4. Cooper, C.H. Annals of Cambridge. Volume I. Warwick and Co. Cambridge. 1842. p 297.
5. Fuller, T. The History of the University of Cambridge from the Conquest to the year 1634. In: Church History of Britain. 1655. (1840 Edition, edited by Prickett and Wright. Cambridge University Press. Cambridge). pp 165, 175.

CHAPTER 5

John Jenyn (Jenynges, Jennings, Jenynn). President 1519-26.

Summary.

John Jenyn was educated at Queens' and served as a fellow, bursar, principal of St Bernard's Hostel, Dean and Vice-President. In 1509 he was presented as vicar of Harrow-on-the-Hill by Thomas Wilkynson, the rector of this living and former President. Jenyn was elected President in 1519, probably because of his: 'considerable experience of college business'.[1] He presided over the College during visits from Cardinal Wolsey, Catherine of Aragon and Henry VIII.

Unfortunately, in 1525, he became involved in a bitter dispute with the fellows about his expenses as a non-resident President, which led to his forced resignation. However, he is recorded as visiting the College subsequently, so perhaps all was forgiven?

Timeline.

1495.	At this time he was M.A. and a fellow of Queens'.
1496-98.	Bursar of Queens'.
1499.	Principal of St Bernard's Hostel.
1501-02.	Dean of Chapel.
1503.	University Proctor.
1505.	Vice-President.
1509.	Death of Henry VII. Accession of Henry VIII. Vicar of Harrow-on-the-Hill, (presented by Thomas Wilkynson, ex-President and rector of Harrow).
1519.	Resignation of Robert Bekensaw. Elected President of Queens'.

1520.	D.D. .
1520.	Visit of Cardinal Wolsey to Queens'.
1521.	Visit of Catherine of Aragon to Queens'.
1522.	Visit of Henry VIII to Queens'.
1525.	Dispute begins between Jenyn and the fellows of Queens' with regard to the President's expenses.
1526.	Forced to resign as President.
1538.	Dies.

A former fellow and Vice-President of Queens', who was elected President in 1519. Hosted Cardinal Wolsey and two royal visits, but was forced to resign after a dispute about his expenses.

John Jenyn was the first President to have been educated at Queens'. He was a fellow before Easter 1495 and held several College offices: bursar, Dean of Chapel, Principal of St Bernard's Hostel, ('principalis exterior hospitii sancti Bernardi'), and Vice-President in 1505.[2] Also, in 1503, he served as a University Proctor, (see Chapter 3).

On the 19th of November 1509, he was presented as vicar of Harrow-on-the Hill by Thomas Wilkynson, who was the rector of Harrow and the former President of Queens'. Jenyn remained in this living until his death. Although he does not seem to have been a fellow after 1510, he was employed by the College in 1516-17 to look after College property in Bermondsey Street, Southwark, as shown by the following record:

'Item paid to mr Jenyn vycar of Harrow of the hill for such somes as he hadd paid to Thomas Hall, carpentar for the frame at Barmyssay street...'.[2]

Jenyn was elected President in 1519, 'probably chosen on account of his considerable experience of college business acquired under previous absentees',[1] even though he would remain non-resident.

The University was preparing for a visit from Cardinal Wolsey, (Lord High Chancellor of England and Cardinal Archbishop of

York), the following year, who would be staying at Queens', presumably due to the influence of Bishop Fisher, the University's Chancellor and a previous President of the College. The chapel and cloisters were whitewashed, and Wolsey was treated to a feast of swans. One of the two orations from the University to Wolsey was made by Henry Bullock D.D., a fellow of Queens' and a friend of Erasmus:[3] 'being delivered before the imperial ambassadors and several bishops'.[4] The Proctors' accounts include:

'Gifts to the Cardinal: for wine, £3. 6s. 3d; for carrying the same to Queens coll. 12d…for 6 swans, 28s. 8d…'.[4]

Queen Catherine of Aragon was the next important visitor and stayed at Queens' for three days in 1521. She had intended an earlier visit as, in 1519, her servant had enquired;

'whether Cambrigge stood cler from eny contagious sykkenesse or no, forasmoche as hir Grace entended to take hir Georney to o^{r} lady of Walsyngham'.[2] Soon after her visit, the Queen recommended that a John Lambert should be elected to a fellowship, but the College resisted this request, writing in reply that there were doubts as to Lambert's learning and that:

'…whan they resayvyd yor g^{r}cios letters, they did not knowe hys v^{r}tu nor lernyg, wherfor icontynetly after that they had red yor seid g^{r}cyus lette^{r}s they iq'red of hys frendes & acq^{a}yntan I the univ^{r}syte and specially of hys masters and tutars whiche had knowledge botht of hys v^{r}tu & of hys lernyg, and demaunded of theym whed^{r} they wold depose for hy, and they asweryd and seid they wold not depose (ie give information) for hym'.[2] (In the first sentence of the College's reply, the Queen was referred to- flatteringly but inaccurately- as yet another foundress:

'Moost excellent and gracyos p^{r}nces yowre orators and scolers the mast^{r} and felowes of youre college callyd the quenes college in Camb. humblie beseches yowre grace to be good and gracios fownderes (ie foundress) (unto) theym';[2] also, the College writes as 'the mast^{r} and felowes of yor (ie your) coledge'). But despite the lack of local endorsement for Lambert, the College then suggested that he should be examined by them: 'but he wold not'; nevertheless, they made a further attempt to comply with Catherine's request, offering Lambert:

'an honest chamber and x markes for won year and hys lernyg, and yf they myght perceyve i the meane tyme that he wer virtuus & like to be lernyd that thane they wil elect & chose him felaw, as yor g^{r}ce wold have theym to do...'. But this was also refused.[2]

However, despite the misgivings, John Lambert was subsequently elected as a fellow, although only for a short time during 1521-22.[2] But his luck ran out in 1538 when he was executed by burning at Smithfield, London, for his persistent denial of the 'real presence' in the Holy Eucharist.[2,3] He had been tried before the King, at a time when Henry wanted the good opinion of the Catholic powers in Europe. Lambert's Protestant views were in ironic contrast to those of his previous patron, Queen Catherine.

The second Royal visit to Queens' during Jenyn's time was that of Henry VIII himself in 1522. He, like Wolsey, feasted on swans,[2,3] while: 'The Kyngs Present' from the University included:

'Twelve grete Pyks, (Pikes) 55s. 8d.
12 grete Elys, (Eels) 13s.
8 grete Tenchis, 15s.
8 Bremys, 26s. 8d.
Foure Swanys, 20s.
Two Cranys wylde, 6s. 8d.
Two Cranys tame, 10s.'.[4]

Other College events during Jenyn's Presidency included visits, in 1518 and 1522, by Dr Matthew Makarell, the Abbot of Barlings Abbey, who was to be executed after the 'Lincolnshire Risings' in 1536.[2] (This rebellion, followed by further uprisings known as the 'Pilgrimage of Grace', was a protest against the suppression of Catholic religious houses. Barlings Abbey, founded in 1154, was subsequently closed and destroyed). Also in 1522, on a lighter note, there are references to one of the comedies of Plautus, performed by members of the College in the hall.[2]

But, by 1525, Jenyn's relationship with the College was approaching: 'a most inglorious end'.[3] The fellows were very unhappy with their President's expenses, such as the allowances he claimed for his scholar, his horses and the wages of his servants.

A particular complaint was that Jenyn would receive expenses for regular travel to London, falsely claiming to be occupied with College business.[2] Simon Heynes, fellow, and a later President, was sent to London several times to relay these complaints to Cardinal Wolsey and the other counsellors of the Queen.[2] The affair dragged on for about eighteen months, but Jenyn was eventually forced out in 1526. However, he visited Queens' several times afterwards, so he must have made his peace with the fellows.[3] He continued as vicar of Harrow until his death in 1538.

When Heynes became President in 1529, the rules for the President's allowances were reviewed. Henceforth, the President would have his commons (food) during residence, the commons of one servant at all times, but the commons of a second servant only during residence. The College would not provide his servants' wages. Further, the President would be:

'content to have three horses founde when he lith at this college, otherwise he shall provide for his horses himself'; like the fellows, he would pay for firewood, candles and rushes, while expenses on College business would be allowed only after the advice and consent of the fellows. Thus, future Presidents were enjoined not to do what John Jenyn had done![3]

References

1. Twigg, J. A History of Queens' College, Cambridge 1448-1986. The Boydell Press. Bury St Edmunds.1987. pp 27, 67.
2. Searle, W.G. The History of the Queens' College of St Margaret and St Bernard in the University of Cambridge. 1446-1560. Deighton, Bell & Co; Macmillan & Co. London. 1867. pp 161-67.
3. Gray, J.H. The Queens' College of St Margaret and St Bernard. F.E.Robinson. London. 1898. pp 64-66.
4. Cooper, C.H. Annals of Cambridge. Voilume I. Warwick and Co. Cambridge. 1842. pp 303-11.

CHAPTER 6

Thomas Forman (Farman, Foreman). President 1526-28.

Summary.

Thomas Forman was elected President in 1526, when he was rector of All Hallows, Honey Lane, in the City of London. He was known to Queens' as a previous fellow, bursar and Dean, but he was a controversial figure, due to his pronounced views in support of the Reformation. The motives of the fellows for his election are uncertain.[1]

Forman was one of several prominent supporters of the Protestant Reformation in Cambridge, who included Thomas Bilney, John Lambert, (see Chapter 5)), Robert Barnes, (Prior of the Augustine friars), Simon Heynes, (a fellow of Queens' and a future President) and William Tyndale, who translated the New Testament into English.[1,2] Bilney, Lambert, Barnes and Tyndale were among the many to be executed for their religious beliefs under King Henry VIII's regime, although Tyndale met his end near Brussels. Meetings of those in Cambridge who supported the ideas of the Reformation took place at the 'White Horse' Inn, near Trumpington Street, which was nicknamed 'Germany'.[1,2,3]

In 1528, Forman was suspended from saying Mass or preaching, because he possessed works by the leading reformer Martin Luther. He was also accused of being implicated in the distribution of the banned English version of the New Testament, which had been translated by Tyndale. After interrogation, Forman died, perhaps in custody, in September 1528.

Timeline.

1509.	Accession of Henry VIII.
1514.	Fellow and bursar of Queens'.
1516.	Ordained in London.
1517-18.	Dean of Queens', (also in 1519-20).
1522.	B.D. .
1524.	D.D. .
1525.	Rector of All Hallows, City of London.
1526.	John Jenyn resigns as President of Queens'; Forman is elected to succeed him.
1528.	Suspended from his duties by the Bishop of London for possessing works by Martin Luther. Dies in September.

London clergyman. Suspended for his support of the Reformation. Died after arrest and interrogation, perhaps in custody, after less than two years as President.

Thomas Forman was educated at Cambridge, graduating B.A. in 1512 and M.A. in 1515. He was elected a fellow of Queens' in 1514 and ordained in London in 1516. (Surnames at this time often had various spellings, in his case including 'Farman' and 'Foreman'; also, he has been named as 'Robert'. He appears as 'Thomas Forman' in the Cambridge Alumni Database, online). He was bursar of Queens' in 1514, as well as Dean in 1517-18 and 1519-20. He graduated B.D. in 1522 and D.D. in 1524. On the 7th of February 1525, he became the rector of one of the wealthiest parishes in London, All Hallows, Honey Lane, on the presentation of the Grocers' Company.[1] (This was a parish church in the City of London, but was not rebuilt after being destroyed in the Great Fire of London in 1666).

In 1526 he was elected President of Queens' after the forced resignation of the previous incumbent, John Jenyn. While the date of his election is not recorded, he is named as President in a document dated the 12th of January, 1527.[1,3] It is likely that the fellows of Queens' were aware that he held controversial views, as he had been one of the members of the University who supported the ideas of the Reformation in its early stages.[1] (The English Reformation, in which the Church of England broke away from the Pope and the Catholic Church, was the result of a complex interaction between the followers of reformers such as Martin Luther and supporters of King Henry, who was determined to divorce Catherine of Aragon, even at the cost of defying the Pope).

Forman was part of a group of reformers which met at the 'White Horse' Inn, situated on Trumpington Street, opposite the west end of Benet Street, and:

'which was therefore called "Germany" by their enemies. This house was chose, because they of King's college, Queens' college, and St John's were wont to come with more privacy at the back door'.[1] Their stated aim was: 'to confer and discourse for edification in Christian knowledge'.[4] The back entrance was from Milne Street, (the present Queens' Lane), which provided a relatively unobserved approach, in particular for those from King's College and Queens'.[4] A leading member of this group was Thomas Bilney, a member of Trinity Hall, who studied law before his ordination in 1519. He is described as:

'an indefatigable student, whose high attainments and winning disposition averted the ridicule which some harmless eccentricities and a remarkably diminutive stature might otherwise have invoked...'.[2] Another prominent member was Robert Barnes, a Norfolk man, who had studied at Louvain and was Prior of the Cambridge house of Augustinian friars; Cooper, (Charles Henry Cooper, 1808-66, antiquarian and historian, coroner and town clerk of Cambridge), records:

'On Christmas eve, (1525) Robert Barnes, D.D. Prior of the Augustine friars, preached in St. Edward's church...He declaimed against the superstitious observance of holidays; the pride, pomp, and avarice of the prelates and clergy; the rigour and abuses of the ecclesiastical courts; the corruptions and errors of the church; and the persecution of the advocates of religious truth. For this sermon he was accused of heresy before the Vicechancellor, and afterwards convened before Cardinal Wolsey and other bishops in London...'.[3] William Tyndale, famous for his translation of the

New Testament into English, was also associated with this movement, when resident at the University from 1514 to 1521.[2] The Queens' contingent consisted of Forman, Simon Heynes- a future President of Queens', and John Lambert.[4] As noted previously, (see Chapter 5), Lambert's recommendation to be a fellow of Queens' by Queen Catherine of Aragon had been initially resisted, although, eventually, he became a fellow for a short time during 1521-22. In the 1530s he was making a living teaching Greek and Latin, but was accused of heresy by the Duke of Norfolk in 1536.[5] However, it was not until 1538 that he was put on trial for denying the real presence of Christ in the bread and wine of the Eucharist, and burnt at the stake. Lambert was close to Thomas Cromwell, (the King's first minister, who was eventually beheaded), and it is reported that Cromwell cried throughout his friend's execution.[5] Bilney was also martyred, in 1531, as was Barnes in 1540, after a very eventful career, which included a return to the establishment's favour. William Tyndale is the subject of a whole chapter in 'Fox's Book of Martyrs', which was published in 1563, and it is claimed that:

'After the Bible itself, no book so profoundly influenced early Protestant sentiment as the Book of Martyrs...';[6] it describes Tyndale's death, near Brussels:

'At last, after much reasoning, when no reason would serve, although he deserved no death, he was condemned by virtue of the emperor's decree. Made in the assembly at Augsburg. Brought forth to the place of execution, he was tied to the stake, strangled by the hangman, and afterwards consumed with fire, at the town of Vilvorde, A.D. 1536; crying at the stake with a frevent zeal, and a loud voice, 'Lord! Open the king of England's eyes'.[6]

J. Bass Mullinger, (Lecturer in History at St John's College, Cambridge, writing in 1888), notes that, in the time of Forman's Presidency:

'The whole university was divided into two bitterly hostile parties, and signs were not wanting that before long the fires of persecution might be lighted to decide the struggle'.[2] In February 1526, before his Presidency, it is claimed that Forman had prior knowledge of a planned search of the University, by a

Sergeant-at-Arms from London, for forbidden books in the rooms of those suspected of supporting heretical ideas,[7] and that Forman was able to warn his colleagues, so that many of the books were hidden in time. However, it was because of his possession of banned books, which he admitted during an interrogation by the Bishop of London, Cuthbert Tunstall, in March 1528, that Forman was suspended from saying Mass or preaching.[1] This is also referred to by Fuller, (Thomas Fuller, 1608-61, priest and historian), who mentions:

'Doctor Foreman, of Queens' College, who therein concealed and kept Luther's books when sought for to be burnt'.[9] Also in 1528, Robert Necton, a bookseller, was arrested and implicated Forman in the distribution of Tyndale's banned New Testament in English.[5] Forman was then arrested and it is known that Sir Thomas More was present at his interrogation. Forman's curate at All Hallows, Thomas Gerrard, (Garret, Garrett, Garrard), was also arrested, because of his involvement in the distribution of banned books. Gerrard had graduated M.A. at Oxford University in 1524 and had been awarded a D.D. at Cambridge. He had become Forman's curate at All Hallows in 1526 and, subsequently, was active in distributing banned books to scholars of both Universities. After his arrest in 1528, he was examined before the Bishop of Lincoln, who thought that he was:

'a very subtyll, crafty, soleyn, and untrue man'. However he was eventually pardoned by Cardinal Wolsey, before returning to favour and obtaining various appointments. (But, in 1537, his beliefs would lead to his arrest once again and, after a public recantation which was thought to be ambiguous, he was sent to the Tower of London. Eventually, he was burnt at Smithfield, London, in July 1540, together with Robert Barnes and William Jerome, at one stake).[1] Necton also implicated another associate of Forman, his servant Geoffrey Usher, in the purchase of various banned books.[1,9]

Some of these events are chronicled in the 'Letters and Papers, Foreign and Domestic. HenryVIII...', published in 1875, which contain descriptions of the original documents.[10] A letter of the Bishop of Lincoln writing to Cardinal Wolsey in March 1528 is described thus:

'Since he (ie the Bishop) wrote last about Oxford, has had fresh information about the corruption of youth by Mr. Garrett, and the erroneous books he brought thither, which it is thought came from a bookseller in London...Many books were found hid under the earth. The chief companions of Garrett in this business were Mr. Clarke, Mr. Freer, Sir Fryth, Sir Dyott, and Ant. Delabere; and it appears by Garrett's writing that Dr. Farman of Honey Lane, has had books from him, and his servant John Goodale, has often brought books from London to Garrett...Prays God to extinguish those abominable errors...' .

Forman, as rector of All Hallows, Honey lane, is mentioned on three further occasions in the above source:

'Proceedings for heresy. Thursday 19 March, Cuthbert bishop of London, in an inner chamber in his palace, forbade Robert Forman, S.T.P., rector of All Hallows, Honey Lane, to perform mass or preach, for retaining Luther's books after their condemnation...'...

'Robert Necton's confession...Since Easter he (ie Necton) has bought of Geoffrey Usher, of St. Antonyes, with whom he became acquainted a year ago (because he was servant to Mr. Forman, the parson of Honey Lane, to whom sermons this respondent much resorted), eighteen New Testaments of the small size, and twenty-six books, all of one sort... and two others...'...

'Anne Boleyn to Wolsey'....after dealing with other matters, the following is added as a PS: 'Begs that for her sake he will remember the parson of Honey Lane'.[11] Therefore, it seems that Anne Boleyn, writing in August 1528 before her coronation, had taken an interest in Reformation ideas, and appears to be asking for clemency for Forman.[7] However, although he did not become yet another martyr, he died in September of the same year, perhaps in custody.[12] His benefice of All Hallows was filled on 31st October 1528.

References

1. Searle, W.G. The History of the Queens' College of St Margaret and St Bernard in the University of Cambridge. 1446-1560. Deighton, Bell & Co; Macmillan & Co. London. 1867. pp 171-74.

2. Mullinger, J B. A History of the University of Cambridge. Longmans, Green, and Co. London. 1888. pp 80-83.
3. Cooper, C.H. Annals of Cambridge. Warwick and Co. Cambridge. 1842. p 311.
4. Gray, J.H. The Queens' College of St Margaret and St Bernard. F.E. Robinson. London. 1898. pp 67-68.
5. Wikipedia. John Lambert (martyr). Online. 2019.
6. Foxe's Book of Martyrs. Oxford University Press. Oxford. 2009.
7. Wikipedia. Thomas Forman (reformer). Online. 2019.
8. Fuller, T. The History of the University of Cambridge. In Church History of Britain. 1655. 1840 Edition, edited by Prickett and Wright, Cambridge University Press. Cambridge. p 202.
9. Thomas Gerrard. Wikipedia. Online. 2020.
10. Letters and Papers, Foreign and Domestic. Henry VIII. Vol.4. 1524-1530. Published by HM Stationery Office. 1875. British History Online.
11. Letters and Papers, Foreign and Domestic. Henry VIII. Vol.4. 1524-1530. Appendix. Published by HM Stationery Office. 1875. British History Online.
12. Rev. Dr Jonathan Holmes. Dean of Chapel Emeritus. Queens' College, Cambridge. Personal communication following consultation.

CHAPTER 7

William Franklyn (Frankleyn, Franklin, Franklen, Frankelyn, Frankelayn, Frankeleyn). President c.September 1528-c. January 1529.

Summary.

Although William Franklyn had been educated at Cambridge, (he is recorded by this name in the Cambridge Alumni Database, online), he had no documented association with Queens' and we know nothing of the circumstances surrounding his election as President. But Franklyn had important connections as, at the time of his election, he was Chancellor of Durham Cathedral and, therefore, associated with Cardinal Wolsey, who, in addition to his other appointments, had become Bishop of Durham in 1523. It appears likely that it was Wolsey who recommended Franklyn to the fellows of Queens', at a time when the previous incumbent had fallen foul of the establishment. Franklyn would have been seen as a safe pair of hands during a period of ongoing religious turmoil.

However, Franklyn seems to have been too busy to undertake even the minimally-required duties as President. In any event he resigned as President, probably after a mere four months. Initially, he may have looked upon the appointment as yet another source of unearned income, which required little of his time, and he had significant responsibilities in the north of England. In 1525 he had been appointed as a counsellor to the King's illegitimate son, the Duke of Richmond, who became the President of the North and, around the time of his election, Franklyn was involved in negotiations with the Scots. (He had a record of several years of service in the north, which included being instrumental in the recovery of Norham Castle in 1513, for which he had received a grant of arms).

In 1536 he became Dean of Windsor and, in 1537, he assisted at the baptism of the future Edward VI and at the funeral of Queen Jane Seymour. However, his final years were overshadowed by illness and, in 1553, he resigned as Dean of Windsor. He retired to Chalfont St Giles, where he died in 1556.

His Presidency of Queens' appears to have had little or no significance within his extensive curriculum vitae or within the annals of the College.

Timeline.

c.1480.	Born at Bledlow, Buckinghamshire. Educated at Eton College.
1496.	Admitted to King's College, Cambridge.
1504.	Bachelor of Canon Law.
1509.	Accession of Henry VIII.
1510.	Vicar of Thurleigh, Bedfordshire.
1513.	Active in recovering Norham Castle following the Battle of Flodden Field. (Subsequently, he received a grant of Arms).
1514.	Chancellor of Durham Cathedral.
1515.	Archdeacon of Durham. Rector of Easington. Master of the Hospital of St Giles, Kepier, County Durham. (For the next several years he was active in directing border warfare).
1518.	Prebendary of Heydour-cum-Walton, at Lincoln Cathedral.
1518-28.	Prebendary of Howden Minster, Yorkshire.
1520s.	Prebendary of Eveston in the collegiate church of Lanchester, County Durham. (On its dissolution he received £1 3s. 8d.).
1522.	Rector of Houghton-le-Spring, County Durham.
1523.	Cardinal Wolsey becomes Bishop of Durham; Franklyn offers to yield the Chancellorship to Wolsey's steward.
1525.	Counsellor to the Duke of Richmond (aged 6), the President of the North.
1526.	Prebendary of Stillington at York Minster.
1527.	Henry VIII informs Queen Catherine that they must separate. (Anne Boleyn would be crowned Queen in 1533).

1528. Death of Thomas Forman, President of Queens', perhaps in custody. Elected President. Involved in negotiations with James V of Scotland.

1529. Resigns as President, probably after about four months in office. (The duration of his time as President has been disputed).

1531. Serving in Scotland.

1534. Act of Supremacy, by which Henry VIII is declared Supreme Head of the Church of England. Present at Holyrood, Edinburgh, when James V of Scotland swears to observe a negotiated peace.

1535. A member of the Council of the North and is commissioned to tax the clergy. Prebendary of the College of Auckland St Andrew, County Durham. (He received £3 on its dissolution).

1536. Dean of Windsor, with the associated posts of Registrar of the Order of the Garter and Dean of Wolverhampton, then part of Staffordshire.

1536-41. Dissolution of the Monasteries. (Monasteries and other religious institutions were disbanded and their incomes were appropriated by the Crown).

1536-37. Lincolnshire uprisings followed by the 'Pilgrimage of Grace'. (This latter uprising was the direct result of confusion and anger at the Dissolution of the Monasteries).

1537. Rector of Stanmore, (he retreated there when plague struck Windsor). Assists at the baptism of the future Edward VI and at the funeral of Queen Jane Seymour.

1540. One of the signatories, as Dean of Windsor and Archdeacon of Durham, of the decree declaring the marriage of Henry VIII and Anne of Cleves to be invalid. Rector of Chalfont St Giles in exchange for his resignation from his Lincoln prebend.

1540s. Often absent from Windsor through illness.

1553. Accession of Queen Mary I. Resigns as Dean of Windsor. Retires to Chalfont St Giles.

1556. Dies at Chalfont St Giles and is buried in the parish church.

A prominent clergyman, statesman and administrator, who resigned the Presidency after about four months in office. Dean of Windsor.

William Franklyn, who became Dean of Windsor in 1536, was born around 1480 at Bledlow, Buckinghamshire.[1] He was a scholar at Eton College and came to King's College, Cambridge, in 1496. He graduated in Canon Law in 1504. After ordination, he was vicar of Thurleigh, Bedfordshire in 1510 and, in 1514, he was appointed Chancellor of the diocese of Durham, with power to appoint justices of the peace, coroners, stewards, bailiffs and other officers. He would collect many other clerical appointments, most of which must have been just a source of revenue; in 1515, he became Archdeacon of Durham, rector of Easington and Master of the Hospital of St Giles, Kepier, County Durham.

He was also involved in directing border warfare with the Scots and received a grant of arms for his part in recovering Norham Castle, in Northumberland, by his: 'prowes and pollice' (prowess and policy).[1] In 1513, James IV of Scotland had invaded England and taken Norham Castle, but it was soon retaken in the same year after James was slain at the battle of Flodden Field. Subsequently, the castle was inspected by Franklyn on the 29th August 1515, as recorded in a letter from Franklyn to Thomas Wolsey, described in the 'Letters and Papers, Foreign and Domestic, of Henry VIII';[2]

'Came to Norham on Tuesday the 28th; found it well fortified with "contremures and murderers". The long wall from the S.W. of the dungeon to N.W. of the kitchen, in length 44 yards, in height 30 feet, is 28 feet thick with the contremure, the chapel walls 8 feet thick, 30 feet long, 18 wide, with a closet over the same; "and so from the S.W. of the dungeon unto the N.E. part of the dungeon" '. Scotland's Regent, John Stewart, c1481-1536, the Duke of Albany, had recently brought an army against the Hume family on the Scottish borders and captured Hume Castle but, as Franklyn goes on to report, in the same letter, Lord Hume, (the Lord Chamberlain), retook the castle on the 26th of August, 1515:

'The Lord Chamberlain has retaken from Albany on the 26th Aug. the castle of Hume; keeps prisoner its captain the Lord Lemyng's uncle. Next day he pulled it down, razed the walls, "and dammed the well for ever more". This day Will. Hume his brother has taken the Castle of Blackater. Albany is in Edinburgh, his army, to the number of 40,000, at Burgh Muir. He and his council have resolved that on Friday next the Duke's commissioners, Sir Will. Scot, Sir Rob. Lawdor, and Master Hals, shall meet Dacre and Magnus at Coldstream. The King and his brother are under Borthwick's keeping at Stirling. The Duke has in Dunfermaline the Abbot of Kelsay, Davy Hume, the Laird of Wetherborne, Sandy Hume, the Laird Blayneherne, and Adam Tinmo, the constable of Hume. The kinsmen of the Humes, who are fully resolved to destroy the Duke before Sunday next, will know what the Duke intends with his army and great ordnance. Dacre sends letters on Saturday. Norham, Wednesday, 29 Aug. By your chaplain, William Frankelayn'.

In September 1523 there was a further threat of invasion by Albany, and Franklyn, the Earl of Surrey (Thomas Howard, 1473-1554, the 2nd Earl of Surrey from 1514 and the 3rd Duke of Norfolk from 1524), and Sir William Bulmer, Sheriff of Durham, viewed the Norham defences. This is recorded in a letter from the Earl of Surrey to Cardinal Wolsey, on the 27th of September 1523, which is also described in the 'Letters and Papers, Foreign and Domestic, of Henry VIII':[3]

'Albany has arrived, it is said with 8,000 men and 600 horses, of which 200 are barded (ie with body armour)...Came out of Scotland last Friday, and arrived at "this town" (Berwick) at 10 at night as weary as ever man was. Went next morning and saw Wolsey's castle of Norham, where he found the Chancellor of Durham (Frankeleyn) and Sir Wm. Bulmer. Viewed the house thoroughly, and devised certain platforms and ramparts which can be made in six days, so that Albany could not take the place in eight. The outer ward could not be held for one day; but there is no help for that. Went also to Wark, where he caused Caundishe to make new bulwarks, by which it will be able to sustain a ten day's siege. The outer ward might be lost in two days, and the enemy nothing nearer the donjon, "which is the strongest thing that I have seen. I would the keep at Guisnes were like it". Wishes Albany would come to try its strength, he has so trimmed it with ordnance...'.

During 1518-22 Franklyn acquired a further four clerical appointments, (prebendary of Heydour-cum-Walton at Lincoln Cathedral; prebendary of Howden Minster, Yorkshire; prebendary of Eveston, Lanchester, County Durham; and rector of Houghton-le-Spring, County Durham), and became a close associate of Cardinal Wolsey after the latter had been appointed Bishop of Durham in 1523, 'in commendam'; (ie in absentia but receiving the revenues). In various letters to Wolsey, he gave advice about increasing the profitability of the diocesan collieries and lead mines, and getting parliamentary confirmation of certain rights of the diocese.[1] He was anxious to obtain Wolsey's good opinion and he offers to resign the Chancellorship to Wolsey's steward:

'I am yonge now and maye take payne and labour being of full myend to applie my self to do your grace the most honour plesure and service that may lie in my power'.[1] However, this offer was not accepted.

Franklyn's reputation as an administrator led, in 1525, to his appointment as a counsellor to the Duke of Richmond, King Henry's illegitimate son, when Richmond, aged just 6, was made President of the North. Richmond is described by Franklyn as:

'a chylde of excellent wisdome and towardnes, (with) good and quyk capacitie, retentyve memorie, vertuous inclinasion to all honor, humanitie and goodness'. He considers that it would be hard to find: 'any creature lyving of twise his age hable or worthy to be compared to hym'.[1]

After yet another clerical appointment, as prebendary of Stillington at York Minster, he was elected President of Queens', probably around September 1528. He is mentioned as President in a deed of the Goldsmith's Company dated October 1528, but the exact dates of his Presidency are uncertain.[1] The previous incumbent, Thomas Forman, had recently died, perhaps in custody, after interrogation for his possession of the writings of Martin Luther, (see Chapter 6), and the fellows may have wished for a safe pair of hands, at a time of religious conflict, being prepared to accept a recommendation from Wolsey. However, we have no information about his election and he had no known previous contact with Queens'. But although Franklyn was accustomed to having the income from appointments that involved few or no duties, he soon resigned the Presidency, probably after about four months.[4,5] He may have been too busy with his responsibilities in the north to fulfil even the minimally-required duties as President as, in October 1528, probably soon after his election at Queens', he was appointed a commissioner to negotiate with the Scots. Further service in Scotland is recorded in 1531, and, in 1534, he was involved in a meeting at Holyrood, Edinburgh, when the King of Scots, James V, swore to observe a negotiated peace.[5] In 1535, as a member of the Council of the North, he was commissioned to tax the clergy and, somewhat ironically, in the same year he received yet another source of income as a prebendary of the College of Auckland St Andrew, County Durham.[1]

Franklyn was installed as Dean of St George's Chapel at Windsor Castle in 1536, together with the associated offices of Registrar of the Order of the Garter and Dean of the chapter of canons at St Peter's Collegiate Church at Wolverhampton, Staffordshire. Over the next four years he accumulated two further benefices, as rector of Stanmore, where he went in 1537 when there was plague at Windsor,[1] and rector of Chalfont St Giles in 1540. In 1537, he assisted at the baptism of the future Edward VI and then at the funeral of his mother Queen Jane Seymour. At the baptism, on the 15th October, Edward's half–sister Mary was godmother, while his other half-sister Elizabeth carried the chrisom, (a piece of cloth laid over a child's head to keep the consecrated oil from being rubbed off). However the baby's mother, the Queen, became ill on the 23rd October and died the following night.

Franklyn's signature, as both Dean of Windsor and Archdeacon of Durham, is attached to the decree of the 9th of July 1540, declaring the marriage of Henry VIII and Anne of Cleves to be invalid.[5]

From about 1540, Franklyn was often subject to illness, during a time when he was involved in the prosecutions of several Windsor men for heresy. Among these: 'Persons persecuted at Windsor A.D. 1543' was a future President of Queens': 'Dr. Haynes, dean of Exeter' while, among the 'Persecutors', was: 'Master Franklin, dean of Windsor'.[6] These events are described in 'The Actes and Monuments of these Latter and Perilous Days, Touching Matters of the Church', by John Foxe, 1516-87, first published in 1563. The following extract is transcribed from the original spelling:

'The trouble and persecution of four Windsor men, Robert Testwood, Henry Filmer, Anthony Peerson, and John Marbeck: persecuted for righteousness' sake, and for the gospel...In the days of Master Franklin, who succeeded Dr. Sampson in the deanery of Windsor, there was, on a time, set up at the choir door, a certain foolish printed paper in metre, all to the praise and commendation of our Lady, ascribing unto her our justification, our salvation, our redemption, the forgiveness of sins, &c, to the great derogation of Christ. Which paper, one of the canons, called Master Magnus, (as it was reported) caused to be set up in despite of Testwood and his sect. When Testwood saw this paper, he plucked it down secretly. The next day after was another set up in the same place. Then Testwood, coming into the church, and seeing another paper set up, and also the Dean coming a little way off, made haste to be in at the choir door, while the Dean stayed to take holy water, and reaching up his hand as he went, plucked away the paper with him. The Dean, being come to his stall, called Testwood unto him, and said that he marvelled greatly how he durst be so bold to take down the paper in his presence. Testwood answered again, that he marvelled much more, that his Mastership would suffer such a blasphemous paper to be set up; beseeching him not to be offended with what he had done, for he would stand unto it. So Master Dean being a timorous man, made no more ado with him...the Lords of the Garter (as their custom is yearly to do) came to Windsor to keep St. George's feast, at which feast the Duke of Norfolk was President; unto whom the Dean and Canons made a grievous complaint on Testwood; who, being called before the

Duke, he shook him up, and all to reviled him, as though he would have sent him to hanging by and by. Yet, nevertheless, Testwood so behaved himself to the Duke, that, in the end he let him go without any further molesting of him, to the great discomfort of the Dean and Canons'.[6]

Testwood was a musician and chorister, who became involved in several disputes with the Windsor clergy. Also, he is reported to have abused the pilgrims in St George's Chapel and smashed the nose off a statue of the Virgin Mary.[7] He was eventually condemned to death in 1543 and executed by burning, together with his Windsor associates, Anthony Peerson and Henry Filmer.

Foxe's description of Franklin as: 'a timorous man' could accord with his record as a persecutor of reformers under Henry VIII, followed by a switch of allegiance to a Protestant agenda under Edward VI.[8]

He was involved in the transfer of some of the revenues of St George's Chapel to the crown and:

'in consequence of the complaints against him on that account was obliged to resign the deanery about the close of 1553'.[1,4,5] This occurred soon after the accession of Queen Mary in July 1553, and his successor was named in February 1554. He retired to Chalfont St Giles and, in 1545, he resigned his appointment at the Hospital of Kepier and many of his benefices. He died in 1556 and is buried in the parish church at Chalfont St Giles. In his will he:

'bequeathed goods and money for uses then deemed pious, but soon afterwards adjudged superstitious'.[4,5]

References

1. Knighton, C.S. Franklyn, William. Oxford Dictionary of National Biography. Online. 2004.
2. Letters and Papers, Foreign and Domestic. Henry VIII. Vol.2. 1515-1518. Published by HM Stationery Office. 1875. British History Online.
3. Letters and Papers, Foreign and Domestic. Henry VIII. Vol.3. 1519-1523. Published by HM Stationery Office. 1875. British History Online.

4. Searle, W.G. The History of the Queens' College of St Margaret and St Bernard in the University of Cambridge. 1446-1560. Deighton, Bell & Co; Macmillan & Co. London. 1867. pp 175-76 .
5. Cooper. C.H. Athenae Cantabrigienses. Volume 1. Cambridge. Deighton, Bell & Co.; and Macmillan & Co. London: Bell & Daldy, Fleet Street. 1858. pp 141, 547.
6. Foxe, J. The Acts and Monuments of the Church. Vol. II George Virtue, Ivy Lane, Paternoster Row. London. 1844. p 602. See also: John Foxe's The Acts and Monuments. 1576 Edition. Book 8. Online.
7. Ford, D.N. Berkshire in the Reign of Henry VIII. Nash Ford Publishing. Wokingham. 2009.
8. William Franklyn (priest). Wikipedia. Online. 2019.

CHAPTER 8

Simon Heynes (Haynes, Heyns, Heynys). President 1529-37.

Summary.

Simon Heynes was educated at Cambridge University and became a fellow of Queens' in 1519. He served in various College offices before his election as President in 1529. Previously, he had been one of an influential group of supporters of the Reformation in Cambridge and had been active in complaining about one of his predecessors as President, John Jenyn.

Soon after his election, he started to resolve the problems of Jenyn's Presidency, by agreeing, with the fellows, new rules for limiting Presidential expenses and authority. But, in view of the College's financial problems, he was granted extensive powers to manage the College estates.

He became an influential member of the establishment, served as a diplomat, and often preached before the King.

In 1537, he resigned as President due to his appointment as Dean of Exeter. However, as a reformer, he was not popular with the Cathedral's chapter, and their complaints led to his brief imprisonment in 1543.

He remained active in national affairs after the accession of Edward VI and was one of the compilers of the 1549 Book of Common Prayer, the first English-language version of the Church of England's liturgy.

Timeline.

1509. Accession of Henry VIII.

1516. B.A. .

1519. M.A. . Fellow of Queens', (until 1528).

1519-20. Bursar of Queens'.

1520s. One of the group of reformers, at the beginning of the English Reformation, who met at the White Horse Inn, in Trumpington Street, Cambridge.

1520-21. Dean of Queens'.

1525-26. Active in complaints against the President, John Jenyn.

1528. B.D. . Rector of Barrow, Suffolk.

1529. Elected President, (around January). Agrees, with the fellows, a set of rules which define more clearly the President's authority, duties and expenses. These are then included in a revision of the Statutes, confirmed by papal authority. In February, there is an agreement with the fellows conferring on the President 'now being', substantial powers over the estates of the College. He is one of the delegates of the University Senate, tasked with determining the opinion of the University concerning the King's proposed divorce.

1529-35. Heynes improves the parlous state of the finances of the College, by retrenchment and selling off some estates.

1530. Thomas Smith elected a fellow of Queens'.

1531. D.D. .

1532-24. Vice-Chancellor.

1533. Delivers letters to the King requesting confirmation of the privileges of the University. Witnesses Archbishop Cranmer's declaration that the King's marriage is null and void.

1534. After winter at court, often preaching before the King, Heynes is sent by the court, together with John Skip, to preach at Cambridge against papal supremacy. Vicar of Stepney, Middlesex, (he resigned in 1537). A Proctor of the University, involved in disputes with the town.

1535. Thomas Cromwell, the Chancellor of Cambridge University, is also appointed Visitor of the University. The King requires the University to renounce all obedience to the Pope, and to promote various reforming ideas. Sent to France, during May-December, with Christopher Mount, to entice the Protestant reformer Philip Melancthon to England. In October, the King is acknowledged by the University as

Supreme Head of the Church of England. Appointed a canon of Windsor in December.

1536. Act of Parliament: 'extinguishing the authority of the bishop of Rome' and requiring an oath to be taken of everyone: 'promoted or preferred to any degree of learning in any university within this realm'.

1536. Rector of Fulham, Middlesex.

1537. Resigns as President, (before 20th June). In July is appointed Dean of Exeter, a post which is vacant by the removal of Reginald Pole. Attends the baptism of Prince Edward.

1538. Sent on a mission to Charles V in Spain, accompanied by Edmund Bonner, where they meet Sir Thomas Wyatt, the ambassador. Rector of Newton Ferrers, Devon.

1540. One of the signatories of a document invalidating the marriage of Anne of Cleves to Henry VIII.

1540. A prebendary of Westminster.

1543. Brought before the Privy Council; briefly imprisoned.

1547. Accession of Edward VI.

1549. A commissioner for visiting and reforming the University of Oxford. One of the five who preside over a public disputation in the Oxford Divinity School. Publication of the 1549 Book of Common Prayer, (Heynes had been involved in its preparation). Marries Joan.

1552. Dies. (His wife Joan will marry the next President, William Mey).

Priest, University administrator, courtier, statesman and ambassador. Active in the English Reformation and involved in the preparation of the 1549 Book of Common Prayer. His Protestant views were, at times, controversial.

Simon Heynes was born around 1495 and, after his education at Cambridge University, he graduated B.A. in 1516 and M.A. in 1519.[1] He became a fellow of Queens' in 1519, and Searle, in his history of the College of 1867, states that he was bursar in

'1519-20' and Dean in '1520-21', although he was then only in: 'minor orders' as an: 'acolyte' of the Norwich diocese.[2] (This was a rank of the Catholic Church ministry which was lower than the so-called: 'major orders' of priest, deacon and subdeacon). He was ordained, presumably in the rank of 'priest', in 1522 and, in November 1528, after graduating B.D., he became rector of Barrow, near Bury St Edmunds. Soon afterwards, in around January 1529, he was elected President. It is likely that he was non-resident.

Heynes has already appeared in previous Chapters, firstly, in Chapter 6, as one of the reformers who used to meet at the White Horse Inn, on Trumpington Street,[2] which was the prelude to his career as a leading figure in the English Reformation. Secondly, he was active in the fellows' campaign against the then President of Queens', John Jenyn, in 1525, travelling to London on several occasions to seek Cardinal Wolsey's support for Jenyn's removal. When he became President in January 1529, he was involved in the provision of a new set of College Statutes which defined more clearly the President's authority, duties and expenses. While the President would be able to allocate rooms, examine and approve accounts, and delegate College business outside Cambridge, certain procedures, such as signing leases, would need the agreement of the fellows.[3] Thirdly, he was one of those: 'persecuted' at Windsor for heresy when William Franklyn was Dean of Windsor.

Heynes has a further mention in accounts of Jenyn's Presidency, when a dispute between Heynes and another fellow had to be settled by arbitration:[2,3]

'On 10 Apr...1524, a bond for £40 was given by Dr Jenin, president, and the fellows of the college, to Dr Robert Shorten, master of Pembroke hall...and Dr William Capon, master of Jesus college...commissioners of Cardinal Wolsey, that they would "suffer the ward, arbitrement, ordinance and judgement" of the said commissioners to be made between Anthony Maxwell and Symon Heynys, clerks, "to take effect according to the same in every point; withowt ony maner let or disturbance of the seyd president and felaws" '. While the nature of the disagreement is unknown, this, and a number of subsequently- documented events, suggest that Heynes had a somewhat quarrelsome nature!

Very soon after Heynes' election, a document dated the 20th January 1529 was drawn up as a consequence of Jenyn's disputed behaviour; as noted above, this specified limits to the President's authority:

'Matiers of variaunce before this tyme depending betwixt the master or president of this college M. doctor Jenyn and the felowes of the same, now clerly determined and ended for a perpetuall qwietnes within this college by thassent and consente of Mr Haynes now president of this college and all the felowes thereof, as hereafter articularly folowith. ...Whereas Doctor Jenyn had of the college haye, litter, provender for his horses within the college and his horss shoing and also xiii[d] every day whan he ridd in causis collegii (ie college business) for the hier of his horses, It is now concluded and by the said maister and felowes fully determynd that the president now being and his successors shalbe only content to have iii horses fownde whan he lith at this college, that is to say hay litter provender for thre horses and he shall not aske ony other allowance of the college for his 3 horsses, which he shall bye at his owne coste and charge with sadellis, bridollis and all other things to them apperteyning...It is therfore by the said maister and felowes determynd, that the maister of this college shall never ride to London nor to nou other farr place in causis collegii except he first cownsaile with the felowes and have ther advise and consent before: so that if the materes that he wold ride or may be cumpasid well and conveniently otherwise, that than the maister to remayne at home and not to put the college to ony charge'.[2]

Soon after Heynes' election, the Easter term was dissolved:

'...till the morrow of the Visitation of the Virgin, (the 3rd of July), for fear of the plague';[2] in the same year, the Statutes given by Queen Elizabeth Woodville were altered and the new ones confirmed by papal authority.[2]

When Heynes assumed the Presidency, the College's finances were in a parlous state and the fellows acted to give him the necessary authority to remedy the situation; on the 12th February 1529, he was given sweeping powers over the budget and estates:[2]

'M[d]. That the xiith day of February in the chapel of this college it was determynd and agreed by the Maister of this college and felowes of the same that theis things following shall perteyne to the maister or president aforesaid to do by vertue of his office... First it is agreid by the seid president and felowes that the president of this college now being, (ie the agreement does not extend to future holders of the office), by vertue of his office or rowme, shall by his discretion leate or sett forth all londes of this college to ferme...Also, auctorite is given to the president now being to sell all woods perteyning to this college which are convenient to be fellid...In witness wherof as well the maister or president as well also all the felowes hath setto their hands the day and yer above written: Per me Simonem Heynes, presidentem collegii'. (This is followed by the signatures of eight fellows).[2]

Over the next several years there were various sales of College property and estates, including St Paul's Hostel and the adjoining White Hostel, on the site of the present Rose Crescent, which had been a source of loss due to necessary repairs. Fellowships were amalgamated, and estates were sold at Prettiwell; these had been given in 1479 to found a fellowship, but rent had been owing. Other estates was sold at Gilden Morden (given in 1474), Holbeach, Whaplode and Multon, (given by Lady Alice Wyche). Also, St Bernard's Hostel, which can be considered as Doket's inspiration for the foundation of Queens', was sold to Corpus Christi College in 1535.[2]

In 1534, an Act of Parliament gave to the Crown the 'firstfruits', (payments made by the new holder of certain offices), and a tenth of the annual income from all ecclesiastical property. Valuations were carried out by commissioners and, while King's and St John's were the two richest colleges, with incomes of £731 and £507 respectively, Queens' was in a creditable third place with £230. The firstfruits were paid by each incoming fellow and these changes required Queens' to reduce the number of fellows from twelve to ten:

'Whereas by the kyng our soveraigne lord and his parliament it is enacted at the last session that every monasterie and colledge amomg other things shall pay the xth part of the clere yerly valor of all ther rentes to the kyng ower soveraigne lord and his heires, so that this hows cannot susteyne the old accustomed number of prestes fellows and scholars with other charges and also pay the seid xth part, It is therefore agreed and determined bi the seid president and fellows the day and yere abovesaid, that when and as sone as the romes of prestes within the said colledge may be void, no mo prestes shalbe in wagis according to the statutes of this cledg but only ten…' .[2] However, the Universities were released from this burden in 1536.

In February 1530, Henry VIII was actively pursuing his quest to obtain the Church's sanction to divorce Queen Catherine, by canvassing support for his professed doubt on the legality of the marriage, and he ordered Cambridge University to give an opinion on this matter. This was referred by the Senate to a committee of 29 'syndics', (ie members of a Senate committee), which included Heynes, and the majority opinion was to be considered to be that of the University. A list of the committee's names was sent to the King by both Stephen Gardner, (the King's secretary), and Edward Fox, (Provost of King's College and the King's almoner), which indicated those, including Heynes, who supported the King's views and, on the 23rd May 1533, Heynes duly witnessed Archbishop Cranmer's declaration, at the priory of Dunstable, that the King's marriage to Catherine of Aragon had been null and void from the beginning.[2]

In 1533, when Heynes was Vice-Chancellor of Cambridge University during 1532-34, there were disturbances related to the election of the University's senior officials, the Proctors:

'Apon St Denys Eve was there a greate Cumpany of Lawyars a Jettyng (rioting), wch came to the Quenes College, & to dyvers other Howses yn the nyght, abowte ten of the clocke, making a Proclamatyon at every Gate, after thys fasshyon, How yes, How yes, Take hede whome ye make youre Proctor, for fere of that that shall cum after yf ye do Standysshe wrong; Loke ye, make ye Stronge, &c. The next nyght after, they came agayne to every House with a greater Cumpany, by erstymatyon there were 3 or 4 score knocking lykewyse at the Vycchancelors Gat, byddyng them cum owte, Knavys, Cowards, & Heretyks, whereupon the

Cumpany drove them away with Stones, and they cryed fyre, to fyer the Gate...That nyght also, between 7 and 8, they got Mr. Palley, of Christ's College, owt of the Howse by a trayne, and so bette hym sore, and also polde of hys here, and the morrow after, at 8 of the Clocke, Doctors, Masters, Pryncypalls, or Presydents, assemblyd at the Vycechauncelors commawndment, & they determined every Presydent shuld be redy with a certayne Men apoynted, yf they wer sent for yn the tyme of the Electon of the Proctors...'.[4] As Vice-Chancellor, in October 1533, he went to London with letters to appeal for the confirmation of the privileges of the University. He remained there for the winter, often preaching before the King and, in January 1534, he became vicar of Stepney, Middlesex. Later in the year, he was sent from the court to Cambridge, with a Dr John Skip, (or Skyp, afterwards Bishop of Hereford), to preach in support of the King's Supremacy and against the authority of the Pope. However, support for the Pope was:

'stoutly maintained by a considerable number in the University...A public disputation was held on the question of whether the Pope had granted to him by God and shown in the scriptures, any greater authority or power in the kingdom than any other foreign Bishop. This was determined in the negative, and an instrument...passed the seal of the University on the 2nd of May, and was sent up to the King'.[2,4] A week later, on the 9th May 1534, the Vice-Chancellor was in London, presumably having increased his stock of the King's good graces.

We know that Heynes was in London on the 9th of May as this was the date that he wrote to the deputy Vice-Chancellor, Dr Buckmaster, to convene the Masters, doctors and Presidents to consult upon the defence of the University privileges in relation to a number of disputes with the townsmen:

'...every man by the townes men ones indited must be compelled to answer before the Kyngs Justices, to their extreme trobill, gret cast, and perpetual infringing of our privileges...Also, I pray yow remember that ye send letters to Mr Crumwell, thankyng hym for his goodness and to desire him to contynew'.[4] In other letters, the townsmen are described as: 'wonderfull malicioucse' and as pursuing: 'ther seyde sute with uncharitable lyes'.[2] In view of the ongoing disputes, the University appointed several of its doctors, including Heynes, to be its representatives before the Privy Council:

'On the 24th July, (1534), Sir Thomas Audley lord Chancellor of England, Dr Cranmer Archbishop of Canterbury, the Duke of Norfolk, and the Marquis of Exeter, met at Lambeth Palace, when there appeared...Dr Haynes on the part of the university...where it was decreed by the said Lordes that Styrbridge Faire was in the subarbes of Cambridge, and that the Vicechancellor or his commysary might kepe courte cyvyll ther for plees wheare a scolar was the one party. Item, that in the same faire the university had the oversight, correction, and punyshemente of all weightes and measures, of all maner of victayall, of all Regraters and Forestallers. Item, It was determined that spyces be vytaill. The expenses of the university this year for journies to London, &c. in consequence of the disputes with the townsmen, amounted to nearly £80'.[4]

Also in 1534, there was a visit to Cambridge by Alexander Alane, (or Ales), a Scottish reformer, who had been invited by Cranmer and Thomas Cromwell and designated a: 'King's Scholar', with a brief to lecture on the theology of the German reformers. He came to Queens' and was pleased with his surroundings, writing to Martin Bucer, (a German Protestant Reformer), in 1550:

'...habui jucundissimum sodalitium in collegio Reginae', (I had a delightful companionship in Queens' College). But as he could not get money from Cromwell, and as his views were not popular with his audience or the Vice-Chancellor, (by then Dr John Crayford), he soon departed for London.[2,5]

In October 1535, Thomas Cromwell, (then Principal Secretary, Master of the Rolls and Chancellor of the Exchequer), who, recently that year, been appointed Chancellor of the University, was also appointed as 'Visitor' with additional powers for:

'promoting piety, and extirpating error, heresy, superstition, hypocrisy, and idolatry; and requiring the university to renounce all obedience to the pope of Rome, and that his authority (ie the

King's) be received as supreme under God'.[2] Queens' was required to provide two daily lectures, one in Latin and one in Greek, the contents of which were prescribed. Further, the University and colleges were instructed to deliver their records and accounts:

'...into the hands of master Thomas Cromwell, the king's visitor-general, to await his good pleasure'.[2] Accordingly, on or about the 25th of October 1535, the University and the several colleges acknowledged the King's Supremacy and renounced the authority of the Pope.[2] The following year, in June 1536, Parliament passed an act: 'extinguishing the authority of the bishop of Rome', and requiring an oath of acceptance to be taken by every person:

'promoted or preferred to any degree of learning in any university within this realm'.[2]

In a letter written in 1535 or 1536, Heynes is noted as a regular preacher before the King:

'Doctour Heyns prechithe before the kyng, as he is appoynntid every Wedynsday this Lent, and on Wedynsday in the Ymbre he saide in his sermone, that God hathe brought the truthe of his worde to light, and princis be the ministeris of it to give comaundement that it shold goo forward, and yet is no thynge regarded, and make of hym but a Cristmas king'.[2]

Heynes was increasingly employed on royal business and, in May 1535, he was sent to France, with Christopher Mont, described as:

'an honest German, who was long employed by the Crown of England'.[2] (Mont was born in Koblenz and had become an agent of Thomas Cromwell in 1531. He supported Luther's ideas and had been sent on missions to Germany in 1533-34, latterly to obtain the support of the German princes for the King's divorce). Heynes writes to Cromwell on the 22nd July 1535:

'Received your command yesterday, by Mr.Gostwike, to prepare to go on the King's affairs beyond sea. How many horses and servants shall I take? For I am farr unlike furnished for suche a jorney. I beseech you because I never went of on such business before that my instructions may be plainly and fully set forth. London, 22 July'.[6] Their main task was to invite the noted

German reformer Philip Melancthon to England. Melancthon was still in Germany and Mont went to meet him, but he could not be persuaded to come to England, although he and Mont did become friends. (Philip Melancthon was a collaborator with Martin Luther and an influential theologian of the Protestant Reformation). Subsequently, in August 1535, Heynes was:

'ordered to go to Paris there to understand the opinions of the Learned and their affection, how they stood inclined both to the King's proceedings and to the Bishop of Rome's usurped power and authority'.[2]

Further preferment came Heynes' way in December 1535, when he was installed as a canon of Windsor and, in 1536, rector of Fulham, while his most influential clerical appointment followed in 1537, when the King nominated him as Dean of Exeter, following Reginald Pole's removal from this office. This led to Heynes' resignation as President of Queens', in the same year. As Dean of Exeter he attended the baptism of Prince Edward, (later Edward VI), in October 1537.[2] (Reginald Pole was the grandson of the first Duke of Clarence, a brother of Edward IV, who had been- allegedly- executed by drowning in a butt of Malmsey wine. Pole had been appointed Dean of Exeter in 1527, but he broke with the King in 1536, the year that he was created a cardinal, as he did not support the divorce or the Supremacy. But he returned from exile in 1553 on the accession of the staunchly Catholic Mary I and, two years before his death in 1558, he was appointed Archbishop of Canterbury).

The appointment of a reformer as their Dean was not popular with the conservative chapter of Exeter Cathedral, which led to various quarrels over Heynes' authority, expenses and the various liturgical practices which he wanted to abolish,[1] Heynes viewed the south west of England warily, as shown by letters to Cromwell in 1537, (edited with modern spelling):

'On my arrival here I enquired of my brethren in the chapter house for the injunctions left by the King's visitors, in order to see them put in execution. No one present knew who had them, and "if I had them (it was said) they imported nothing else but that we should do as we have done in times past, and live after the old fashion". Some supposed that Dr. Brerwood hath a copy, but as yet I can get no knowledge of them, I beg your lordship therefore to send me such injunctions, signed with your own hand, as you would have kept by this cathedral church and other like, and I will see them executed within this "closs". I like the people of this town very well, but, as far as I have yet seen, the priests of this county are a strange kind, very few of them well persuaded or anything learned. I thank your lordship for the King's gracious letters to the chapter in my favour for the fruits of the residence of my prebend here, because I have compounded with the King's officers both for the corps of the prebend and for the residence. The canons have deferred their answer till St. Matthew's day, but, without your continued favour to me, I have small hope that they will do as the King desires: hitherto their answer is that I shall have the fruits of the vacation at 4l. a year and no more but I beg you will not take this for their resolute answer...

Exeter, 21 August.

You commanded the provincial of the Grey friars to take one John Arthur, friar, and bring him up to you. He is this day taken by one called Cardemaker and delivered to the mayor till the pleasure be known of Sir Thos. Denyse, recorder of the city. This is a perilous county, for God's love let the King's grace look to it in time'.[7] He preached reform, destroyed images throughout the diocese and, in the words of John Hooker, (English historian, writer, antiquary and Chamberlain of Exeter 1555-1601), was: 'marvellous hated and maligned at'.[1] Exeter Cathedral contained the tomb of Bishop Edmund Lacy, (c1370-1455), who had been a friend of Henry V and had been present at the battle of Agincourt, and after his death:

'many miracles were said and devised to be done at his tomb, whereupon great pilgrimages were made by the common people to the same'.[2] But Heynes caused particular offence by discouraging pilgrims, and by removing Lacy's monumental brass from the stone slab. (The latter can still be seen on the north side of the choir).[2]

In 1538, Heynes was sent, with Edmund Bonner, (a future Bishop of London who would later join with Pole in persecuting Protestants in the reign of Mary I), on a near impossible mission to Charles V in Spain, with the aim of assisting the ambassador there, Sir Thomas Wyatt, to dissuade the Holy Roman Emperor from taking part in a general council which might unite Catholic nations against England.[1] (Charles was Catherine of Aragon's nephew and not sympathetic to the King). But they were offended by their off-hand treatment by Wyatt, and Bonner, in a letter from Blois to Cromwell, on the 2nd September 1538, charged the ambassador with traitorous correspondence with Reginald Pole and of speaking disrespectfully of the King.[2,8] However, Cromwell was a friend of Wyatt and ignored these complaints but, after Cromwell's downfall in 1540, Bonner and Heynes would renew their accusations. (Bonner would then be Bishop of London, while Heynes' favour with the King would be evident by his signature on the decree annulling the marriage of Henry to Anne of Cleves in 1540). But although Wyatt was arrested in 1541 and sent to the Tower, he successfully defended himself before the Privy Council and was acquitted, as there was no direct evidence against him. While he admitted that he had sent an envoy to Pole, he claimed that this was only to find out Pole's intentions, and that Heynes and Bonner, who both failed to testify, had agreed to this.

Sir Thomas Wyatt (1503-42) was prominent at court and in the establishment. He served as an ambassador for several important missions and is recognised as a poet, (see below), having introduced the sonnet to English literature. His father had been a Privy Councillor to Henry VII and an adviser to Henry VIII. Wyatt attended St John's College, Cambridge, graduating B.A. in 1518 and M.A. in 1520. He was married in 1520, but separated from his wife soon after 1524. There were contemporary rumours that Wyatt had some kind of romantic relationship with Anne Boleyn in the early 1520s, and although Nicholas Harpsfield, (appointed Archdeacon of Canterbury in 1554), wrote an account claiming that Wyatt went to the King in an attempt to dissuade him from marrying her, claiming that his views were: 'by my own experience as one that have had my carnal pleasure with her',[9,10] this has been considered to be fake news! In 1525, Wyatt accompanied Thomas Cheney, (later, Sir Thomas Cheney, K.G. , diplomat and Lord Warden of the Cinque Ports), on a diplomatic mission to France and, in 1527, he was selected for a mission to the Papal Court with Sir John Russell to petition for the annulment of the King's marriage to Catherine of Aragon. It has been claimed that, on this mission, he was captured by the armies of Charles V before making an escape. In 1533 he was the 'Royal Ewerer' at the coronation of Anne Boleyn, pouring scented water on her hands. Wyatt had known Anne since childhood, as their families were closely connected, (his sister Margaret attended Anne Boleyn on the scaffold), and Anne's execution in 1536 may have given his rivals an opportunity to act against him, as he was briefly imprisoned for an assault on Henry Brandon, Duke of Suffolk. However he retained the King's favour, was knighted and, in 1536, was made Sheriff of Kent. As noted above, he met with Heynes and Bonner in 1538. He died in 1542, aged 39, while travelling to Falmouth to meet a delegation from Charles V. His son, Sir Thomas Wyatt the younger, was executed for rebelling against Mary I. The first verse of his father's poem 'I am as I am' reads:

'I am as I am and so will I be,
But how that I am none knoweth truly;
Be it evil be it well, be I bond be I free,
I am as I am and so will I be'.[11]

In 1539, the 'Statute of the Six Articles' was passed, which affirmed certain Catholic doctrine and practices; this prompted two bishops to resign and Heynes to write a letter to: 'some certain men of the court':

'...admiring how the king could pretend authority of Scripture for those articles, there being not any express word of God written for them: unless men use Scripture (said he) for proving these... Nothing ought to be decreed nor made by man to be an article of our faith, except the same be manifestly grounded upon Holy Scripture written, or at the least wise manifestly and plainly deduced out of Holy Scripture written...'.[2]

The 1540s brought new cathedral foundations and, in 1540, Heynes was appointed a prebendary, by a new foundation charter at Westminster:

'as a reward for the services he did in Embassies he was employed about by the king'.[2] He was given one of the best houses and was often resident.[1] However, as noted in Chapter 7, he was one of those: 'persecuted' for heresy at Windsor in 1543. This followed accusations by the Treasurer and Chancellor of Exeter:[12]

'...for preaching against the superstitious use of holy bread and holy water, and that he should say in one of his sermons (having occasion to speak of matrimony) that "marriage and hanging were destiny", whence they would have gathered treason against him, because of the king's marriage, as though he had an eye to that'.[2] After appearing before the Privy Council on the 15th March 1543, he was committed to the Fleet prison on the following day, but was released on the 5th July: 'by the mediation of friends',[12] although he was reprimanded for: 'sowing...many erroniows opinions'.[1]

However, after the accession of the staunchly Protestant Edward VI in 1547, Heynes' views chimed with the new regime, and he was increasingly active. He was a justice of the peace for Devon; Visitor of Exeter Cathedral; involved in Lord Northhampton's divorce case; Visitor of Oxford University and of the colleges of Windsor and Winchester; a member of the heresy commissions of 1549 and 1551; and Treasurer of Westminster, where his disposal of church ornaments again demonstrated his reformist credentials.[1] In Oxford, he was one of the five who presided at a public disputation held in the Divinity School for three days between Peter Martyr, Dr William Tresham, canon of Christchurch, and others, concerning the doctrine of Transubstantiation.[2] He was one of the compilers of the 'Order of the Communion' of 1548 and, together with William Mey, (the next President of Queens'), was involved in the preparation of the Book of Common Prayer of 1549, which, for the first time, provided the Church of England's liturgy in English.[2]

Clerical marriage became permitted in 1547 by the Convocation of the Clergy and House of Commons and, in 1549, Heynes married Joan, the daughter of a Nicholas Wallron.[1] Their son Joseph was born in 1550, who, as well as his younger brother Simon, would attend Cambridge University.[1,2] In 1575, the latter

Simon Heynes received a grant of arms when he lived in Mildenhall, Suffolk.[2] In 1578, Joseph Heynes purchased the manor farm at Newbury, Barking, which had been granted to Sir Richard Gresham at the dissolution of Barking Abbey. Also, the manor of Wangay was granted to Joseph Heynes by Queen Elizabeth in 1601; this was sold by his son in 1623. Joseph Heynes died in 1621 and is buried in Barking Church.[2]

Heynes made his will in July 1552 and died in October. His estate contained lands near Mildenhall in Suffolk, and it has been suggested that this was his birthplace.[1] His widow married the next President of Queens', William Mey, (the Dean of St Paul's, who died in 1560), and her third husband was Thomas Yale, Chancellor and Vicar-General to the Archbishop of Canterbury, and Dean of the Arches, (ie the judge in the ecclesiastical court of the Archbishop of Canterbury). Yale also had close connections with Queens', as a fellow during 1544-57 and bursar in 1556. Joan died in 1587.[1]

Several extant books which had belonged to Heynes were donated to the Queens' library by Thomas Yale. One of these, St Cyprian's Works, (Cypriani Opera, studio curaque D.Erasmi Rot. Basil. 1525), contains Heynes' signature and has a horn window, consisting of a rectangular piece of transparent horn fixed to the front of the book to protect the label, which states that the book was given to Queens' on the 6th January 1562 by Thomas Yale.

During Heynes' Presidency, Thomas Smith was elected a fellow of Queens' in 1530 and would become eminent as a classical scholar, Protestant statesman, and Secretary of State under both Edward VI and Elizabeth I. In his University career, he was appointed Professor of Greek soon after taking his M.A. degree and, in 1538, he was made Public Orator. In 1540 he became the first Regius Professor of Civil Law and, in 1543, he was elected Vice-Chancellor.[5] He was a supporter of Heynes and commended:

'the king's reformation of religion, his encouragement of every art, and his judgement shewn in the men that he selected for preferment; among these...Dr Heynes, then dean of Exeter...',[2] whom he described as:

'a man of remarkable integrity, piety and liberality to the studious'.[5]

References

1. Knighton, C. S. Haynes (Heynes), Simon. Oxford Dictionary of National Biography. Online. 2004. (Revised 2008).
2. Searle, W.G. The History of the Queens' College of St Margaret and St Bernard in the University of Cambridge. 1446-1560. Deighton, Bell & Co; Macmillan & Co. London. 1867. pp 167-210.
3. Twigg, J. A History of Queens' College, Cambridge 1448-1986. The Boydell Press. Bury St Edmunds.1987. pp 70, 84.
4. Cooper, C.H. Annals of Cambridge. Vol. 1. Warwick and Co. Cambridge. 1842. pp 361-69.
5. Gray, J.H. The Queens' College of St Margaret and St Bernard. F.E.Robinson. London. 1898. pp 71, 85.
6. Letters and Papers, Foreign and Domestic. Henry VIII. Vol.8, January-July 1535. Published by HM Stationery Office. 1875. British History Online.
7. Letters and Papers, Foreign and Domestic. Henry VIII. Vol.12, June-December 1537. Published by HM Stationery Office. 1891. British History Online.
8. Wikipedia. Simon Haynes (priest). Online. 2019.
9. WordPress.com. Renaissance Humanism comes to English letters: Wyatt. 'I am as I am'. Online 2019.
10. Harpsfield, Nicholas. A treatise on the pretended divorce between Henry VIII and Catherine of Aragon, ed. Nicholas Pocock. London: for the Camden Society.1878.
11. Tillyrand, E.M.W. The poetry of Sir Thomas Wyatt. London. The Aldine edition of the British Poets by C.Whittingham.1831.
12. Foxe, J. The Acts and Monuments of the Church. Vol. II George Virtue, Ivy Lane, Paternoster Row. London. 1844. p 608.

CHAPTER 9

William Mey (May, Meye). President 1537-53 and 1559-60.

Summary.

William Mey graduated as Bachelor of Civil Law at Cambridge in 1526 and, subsequently, became a fellow of Trinity Hall, Cambridge. In 1531 he proceeded Doctor of Civil Law and received his first significant promotion, as Chancellor of the Ely diocese. The year 1534 saw the first of his many subsequent appointments to various commissions and benefices, when Archbishop Thomas Cranmer nominated him to be part of a visitation to the Norwich diocese, although he would not be ordained until 1536.

An active supporter of the Reformation, he was elected as President of Queens' in 1537 after the resignation of Simon Heynes. A major event in the history of the College took place the following year, when the property and land of the adjacent Carmelite monastery were surrendered to the College.

In 1545, an Act of Parliament put the colleges at risk of dissolution and, in 1546, Mey, (who had recently been appointed Dean of St Paul's Cathedral), was a member of a three-man commission to investigate the finances of the Cambridge colleges. Their favourable report, together with the lobbying of Thomas Smith, (fellow of Queens', Regius Professor of Civil Law and Clerk to the Council of Queen Catherine Parr), mollified Henry VIII and saved the University and colleges from significant penalties or dissolution.

Subsequently, Mey served on several important commissions, and was involved in the preparation, and later revisions, of the 1549 Book of Common Prayer. However, after the accession of the staunchly Catholic Mary I, Mey resigned as President in 1553, to be succeeded by William Glynn, who himself resigned in 1557. The next President, Thomas Pecocke, was in office only until 1559, when he also resigned after the accession of Elizabeth I. Mey was then restored as President.

However, Mey's second tenure was not to last for long. The following year he was nominated as Archbishop of York, but he died on the day of his election, the 8th August, 1560. Four days later he was buried in the choir of St Paul's Cathedral.

As previously noted, (see Chapter 8), he had married Joan, the widow of his predecessor as President, Simon Heynes.

Timeline.

c1505. Born in Suffolk.

1526. Bachelor of Civil Law at Cambridge University.

1529. Employed by Queens' to obtain papal confirmation of the revised Statutes.

1530. Thomas Smith elected a fellow of Queens'.

1531. Doctor of Civil Law. Chancellor of the Ely diocese, (later, he would become vicar-general and prebendary at Ely).
Date unknown: Fellow of Trinity Hall, Cambridge.

1534. Appointed by Archbishop Cranmer to a visitation of the Norwich diocese.

1535. Rector of Bishop's Hatfield, Hertfordshire, although not in priest's orders. Thomas Cromwell appointed Chancellor of Cambridge University.

1536. Ordained subdeacon, deacon and priest by Bishop Goodrich of Ely. The start of the Dissolution of the Monasteries.

1537. Resignation of Simon Heynes as President of Queens'; Mey is elected in his stead.

1538. Member of a commission that produces an account of the main articles of faith: 'The godly and pious Institution of a Christian Man'. Land and materials to the north of Queens' are surrendered to the President and fellows by the Carmelite friars. Rector of Littlebury, Essex.

1540. Rector of Balsham, Cambridgeshire. Execution of Thomas Cromwell, who is replaced as Chancellor of Cambridge University by Stephen Gardiner, Bishop of Winchester.

1541. Prebendary of Ely.

1544. John Mey, brother of William Mey and a future Bishop of Carlisle, matriculates as a 'pensioner' at Queens'.

1545. An Act of Parliament puts the colleges at risk of dissolution. Prebendary of Chamberlain's Wood at St Paul's Cathedral, London.

1546. Dean of St Paul's Cathedral. Member of a three-men commission to investigate the Cambridge colleges; the findings, together with the support of Thomas Smith, (fellow of Queens', Regius Professor of Civil Law and Clerk to the Council of Queen Catherine Parr), saves the University and colleges from significant penalties or dissolution.

1546. Sent on a diplomatic mission to France, with Sir William Petre.

1547. Death of Henry VIII. Accession of Edward VI. The Regency Council is led by Edward Seymour, Duke of Somerset. Somerset becomes Chancellor of Cambridge University, replacing Bishop Gardiner.

1548. Member, with Sir Thomas Smith, (appointed a Secretary of State and knighted in 1548), of a commission to visit the University with power to amend college statutes.

1549. Publication of 'The Book of Common Prayer', (Mey had contributed to its compilation).

1552. A revised version of the Book of Common Prayer is published, and will be enforced by the Act of Uniformity. The Duke of Northumberland is appointed Chancellor of Cambridge University, but will be executed in 1553 for his support of Lady Jane Grey. Death of Simon Heynes; Mey will soon marry his widow, Joan.

1553. Death of Edward VI. Accession of Mary I. Mey resigns as President and is succeeded by William Glynn. Deprived as Dean of St Paul's. Bishop Gardiner reappointed as Chancellor of Cambridge University.

1556. Reginald Pole, (the last Catholic Archbishop of Canterbury), appointed Chancellor of Cambridge University after the death of Bishop Gardiner.

1557. Resignation of William Glynn following a visitation to the University and colleges. Thomas Pecocke elected President.

1557. Rector of Pulham, Norfolk, and of Longstanton St Michael, Cambridgeshire.

1558. Death of Mary I. Accession of Elizabeth I. Prebendary of Wenlakesbarn at St Paul's.

1559. Sir William Cecil, (later Lord Burghley), appointed Chancellor of Cambridge University after Pole's death. Mey and Sir Thomas Smith advise Cecil during the resolution of a major dispute at Queens' between the President (Pecocke) and a rival faction. Pecocke then resigns. Mey is restored as President of Queens' and also as Dean of St Paul's. A member of another commission to reform the University, and of a commission to take the oath of ecclesiastics.

1560. Dies on the day of his election as Archbishop of York.

Priest. Supporter of the Reformation. Dean of St Paul's Cathedral. Contributor to the report which saved the Cambridge colleges from dissolution. Resigned as President after the accession of Mary I, but was restored under Elizabeth I.

William Mey was born in Suffolk. He graduated Bachelor of Civil Law in 1526, and Doctor (LL.D) in 1531. He became a fellow of Trinity Hall, but had some connection with Queens', as he was employed by the College in 1529 to obtain papal confirmation of its revised Statutes.[1] He was a friend and executor of another fellow of Trinity Hall, Richard Smith, who was one of the reformers who met at the White Horse Inn (see Chapter 6), and Mey was also a supporter of the Reformation.[1]

In 1531 he became Chancellor to Bishop Nicholas West of the diocese of Ely and, after the latter's death in 1533, became a protégé of his successor, Bishop Thomas Goodrich. His career progressed further in 1534, when Archbishop Thomas Cranmer appointed him to a commission for visiting the Norwich diocese, which was initially opposed by the Bishop, Richard Nykke, (Nix), an ultra-conservative Catholic. Further preferment came his way in 1535, when he became rector of Bishop's Hatfield, even though he was not yet an ordained priest. This was rectified the following year, when he was ordained subdeacon, deacon and priest, in the same ceremony, by Bishop Goodrich.[1]

He was elected President of Queens' in June 1537 following the resignation of Simon Heynes and, in the same year, he was appointed, by Archbishop Cranmer, as a commissioner for producing an account of the main articles of faith:

'to set forth a truth of religion purged of errors and heresies'.[1] This duly appeared, titled: 'The godly and pious Institution of a Christian Man', (also termed: 'The Bishops' Book'), which was an attempt by the bishops to promote unity and define church doctrine. We do not know the circumstances of his election as President, but Simon Heynes may have recommended him as a fellow reformer.[1] Futher clerical preferments followed in 1538, 1540 and 1541, as rector of Littlebury, Essex; rector of Balsham, Cambridgeshire; and prebendary of Ely, respectively.

An important event in the history of the College occurred early in Mey's Presidency, when it gained the adjacent land north of the College. This followed the surrender, to Mey and the fellows of Queens', of the neighbouring monastery of the Carmelite friars on the 8th August 1538. The Carmelites, or White Friars, had come to England at the time of Richard I and had moved their monastery from nearby Newnham to the town of Cambridge in around 1290. Carmelites from various English monasteries came to study in Cambridge, returning after graduating in Divinity. But when it became apparent that the dissolution of religious houses was imminent, and that the Carmelites would be willing to surrender the site, (probably thinking that they would get better terms from the College than from the Crown),[1,2] a letter from Queens' was dispatched to Thomas Cromwell, perhaps composed by Thomas Smith. (As noted in Chapter 8, Thomas Smith had been elected a fellow of the College in 1530 and would became a renowned classical scholar, lawyer, and Protestant statesman). The letter, quoted with modern spelling, explains the position:

'There is a convent of Carmelites adjoining our College. It is small, and has been diminished by the recent sale of part of the ground to King's College. Owing to the decline of false religion and the consequent failure of the revenues got by mendicancy the Friars have nearly all left the house. Only a few are left, who do keep up the name of a convent somehow, but even these, as they can no longer maintain themselves or keep a roof over their heads, would gladly, with the royal permission, retire. We have no doubt therefore that the King's Majesty will soon convert the convent to better uses. If the King would grant the convent to some College, especially our College, although the ground is not very extensive, it will be a great acquisition to us and His Majesty will confer a favour on the University, will grant what is essential to us and will perhaps not be unpleasing to the King and his descendants. For whenever royalty has come to Cambridge, it has almost invariably stayed in our College, because the College lies away from the noise of the town, because it is near the river, or because it is pleasantly situated. Accordingly, if the ground shall become the site of a granary or a tanyard, it may be an annoyance to the College and a nuisance to royalty. But if it is assigned to the College, to which it is most necessary, we shall not only rejoice endlessly in the grant for our own sakes, but shall also be mightily pleased, because we hope that royalty also will reap some benefit from the grant.'[2]

On the 8th August 1538, the Carmelites duly surrended their property to Mey and the fellows:

'Be it known to all men, that we George Legat prior of the howse of friers Carmelites in Cambridge, commonlie called the White Friers, and the covent of the same howse...gladly ffrely and willynglie do give and graunt and surrender in to the hands of the right worshipfull Mr William Mey, doctr. In law civil...all that owr howse and grownd called the White friers in Cambridge, with all and singular the appertinences therof and therunto belonging...'.[1] However, on the 17th August, a royal communication was addressed to Dr Daye, (the Provost of King's College), Dr Mey, and two fellows of Queens', (Richard Wilkes and Thomas Smith), ordering them to take possession of the monastery for the King, and to draw up an inventory of the property:

'Henry the eight by the grace of God king of England and of Fraunce, defender of the feyth, lord of Irelande, and in erth immediately under God supreme hedd of the church of Englande, To our trusty and welbeloved chapelains George Deye doctor of dyvinitie provost of our colleadge of Cambridge, William Maye doctor of the lawe maister of the Quenys Colleadge within the same town, Richard Wilkes and Thomas Smyth M^rs^ of Arts and to two of you, greeting: Forasmuch as we understande, that the house of the White freers within that our towne and uniuersitie of Cambridge remayneth at this present in suche state, as it is neyther used to the hono^r^ of God nor to the benefite of our common wealth, myndyng for the conversion of it to a better purpose to take it into o^r^ own handes...The which surrender so made, We wooll that ye shall take possession of the said howse, and soo to kepe the same to o^r^ use tyll further knowleage of o^r^ pleasor...Given under o^r^ privie seale at the castell of Arundell...Thomas Cromwell'.[1,3]

This was followed by a deed of surrender to the Crown dated the 28th August and, on the 6th September 1538, an inventory of all the moveables belonging to the friars was taken, titled:

'The inventory of all and singular ye movable goodis off the howse of the white ffreers in Cambrydge taken by Doctor Maye master off the Quenes college in Cambrydge & Richarde Wylkys & Thoas Smythe felows off the same colledge...'.[1]

Subsequently, the College set to work to demolish the buildings and, in November 1542, Mey purchased all the stone, slate, tile, timber, iron and glass for £20.[3] Some of the glass from the monastery, with portraits of ten of the friars, is preserved in the windows of the Old Library at Queens', and are some of the earliest English portraits painted on glass.[4] The record of the sale is as follows:

'Memorandum that we...the Kings officers of the revenues of the augmentacons of his crowne...have bargained and sold and by these p^r^sentes do bargayne and sell to William Maye doctor of the lawe and master of the Quenes college wtin the universite of Camebrige for the some of xx^{li} poundis sterlinge...all the stone, slate, tyle tymber yorne and glasse of the late howse of the white ffriers...'.[1] But it was not until 1544 that the site was granted by the King to a John Eyre of Bury, who soon sold it to Mey on the 8th November. The final transaction took place on the 30th November 1544 , when;

'...William Mey of Cambridge, doctor of laws, did (for a certain sum received of the president and fellows of Queens' college) grant to them the site of the Carmelites or White friars in Cambridge, which he lately bought of John Eyre, of Bury, esq., with the intent that the site which he had purchased with the college money of masre Eyre should be made sure unto the said college'.[1]

In 1545, Parliament passed an Act which provided for the dissolution of colleges,[1] by putting all the foundations in the Universities at the King's disposal. An attempt to avoid possible disastrous consequences for the Universities is described in a contemporary account:

'wher certain officers in the court and others then in authorytie under the King, importunstely suyng to hym to have the Londes and possessions of both unyversities surveyed, they meaning afterwards to enjoye the best of ther Londes and possessions... certain frendes of the university perceyving the sequel like to tourne to a myschefe sayd to the kinge for avoyding the gret chargis that shuld be susteyned therein not to send any of his costly officers to that purpose: and thereupon he sent his commyssion to Mthew Parker than Vicechancellor, to John Redman (afterwards) Master of Trynitie colleage, and to William Meye Master of the quenys college, to surveye them and to make report to his highnes what the state of the revenues, and what nombre wer susteyned therewith'.[6] Therefore, the commission would consist of friends of the University, who duly received their instructions:

'To our trusty and well-beloved Doctor Parker Vicechauncelor of the University of Cambridge and to our trusty and well beloved Chapleynes Doctor Redman and Doctor Maye and to every of them.

Bi the King,

Trusty and Well beloved we great you well and let you wete that where as our most lovynge and obedyent Subjectes in this our last cession of parlyament have frely gevyn and graunted unto us full powre and auctorytie to ordre, alter, change and reforme all the Colleadges, hospitalles, Chauntryes, and free chapelles wythin this our realme of Inglande...And consydering that the good establishment of the Colleges of our Universityes of Oxforde and Cambridge...And by these our letters gyve unto you full power and auctorytie not only to call before you the Masters and Hedes of every of the Colleges...to learne the very trouthe howe the same foundations statutes and ordenaunces be observed of what values kindes and naturys the hole possessions be which belonge to every souche Colleage...Ands of all the premisses to mak unto us a certifycate fayer written in parchment subscrybed with your hondes...Geven under our signet at our honour of Hampton Courte the xvith of January in the xxxviith yere of our Reigne'.[5,6]

But the composition of the commission did not lay all anxieties to rest and, before the onset of the enquiry, the University composed a letter to Queen Catherine Parr, urging her intercession with the King on its behalf. This was duly delivered by Thomas Smith, who was then, as noted above, Clerk to the Queen's Council.[2,6] The Queen gave an encouraging reply:

'...Apon the confidence of wyche yowr accomplyssehement to my expectation zele and request I (accordyng to your desyres) have attempted my lorde the Kynges Majesty for the stablysschement of your lyvelyhod and possessions in whyche notwythstandyng hys majesties propertye and interest throghe the consent of the highe courte of parlament hys hyeghness beyng suche a patrone to good lernyng dothe tender you so muche that he well rather advance lernyng and erecte new ossasion thereof than to confound those your ancyent and godly instytutions... Scribeled with the hand of hyr that prayeth to the lord and immortal god to send you all prosperous Successe in godly lernyng and knowledge. From my lord the Kynges Majesties manoere of grenewyche the xxvite of February. Kateryn the Queen K.P.'.[6]

In 1546, the three commissioners duly presented a summary of their findings to the King at Hampton Court, and Dr Parker writes:

'In the ende the said commyssioners resorted up to Hampton courte to present to the king a brief summary wryten in a fayr shete of vellum (which very book is yet reserved in the college of corpus christi) describing the revenews, the repryses, the allowances, and nombre and stipend of every colleage, which boke the King diligently persued...'.[6] Fortunately, the King was persuaded that the colleges should not suffer dissolution or any significant penalty and, moreover, that he should found another college. (This would be Trinity College, founded in 1546 with the merger of two existing colleges and seven hostels). Indeed, the King:

'In a certen admiration saide to certen of his Lords which stode by, that he thought he had not in his realme so many parsons so honestly maynteyned in lyvyng bi so little lond and rent'. But he did not understand why the colleges: 'shulde seame to expend yerly more than ther revenues amounted to', until he had been informed that the colleges received additional income from fines, charges from renewal of leases, and sales of timber.[5,6]

In 1545, Mey became a prebendary of St Paul's Cathedral and, in the following year, he was elected Dean of St Paul's, but only after some delay following his nomination. This hold-up had caused the Privy Council to write to the Chapter, instructing them to proceed with the election of: 'Dr William Mey, the King's chaplain'.[1] This may have been due to the opposition of Edmund Bonner, the Bishop of London, who was an opponent of some aspects of the Reformation.

In 1546, Mey and Sir William Petre, (a Secretary of State), were sent by the King to Calais to negotiate with envoys from the King of France. Mey was described by Sir William as:

'a man of the most honest sort, wise, discrete and well lernyd, and one that shall be very mete to serve His Majesty in many ways'.[7]

After the accession of Edward VI in 1547, the reformers' influence increased, and Mey, as well as Heynes, were among the 'Visitors' appointed to inspect the western dioceses.[1] Also:

'...letters passed the University seal, empowering Sir William Paget High Steward of the University, William Mey Dean of St. Paul's, Sir Thomas Wendy the King's Physician, Sir Thomas Smyth, Sir William Cecil Master of the Requests and John Cheke the King's Tutor, to determine all disputes between the University and Town'.[6]

Henry VIII died in January 1547 and Thomas Smith was to prosper under the regime of the first Duke of Somerset, Protector to the new King, Edward VI. Smith became Provost of Eton, Dean of Carlisle, (despite his lay status), and a Secretary of State. He was knighted in 1548. Although he lost influence under Mary, he was restored to favour under Elizabeth, and reappointed Secretary of State in 1572. He was the author of a pioneering study of the English social, judicial and political systems: 'De Republica Anglorum: The Maner of Gouernment or Policie of the Realme of England', published in 1583, which, in the 1609 edition, was titled: 'The Commonwealth of England and the Maner of Gouernment thereof'.

In 1548 Mey and Smith were among those who were appointed commissioners for visiting Cambridge University with power to amend and alter the statutes of the colleges,[1,2] and they subsequently imposed some additional statutes, or 'injunctions', on the University. The commission also had the power to dissolve some colleges to found a College of Civil Law and:

'to constitute a Medical College in some other fit place in the University by assigning one of the Colleges for the study of Medicine', but these projects were not pursued. The commissioners began their work on May 6th 1549, by attending a sermon at Great St Mary's Church from Bishop Nicholas Ridley, (Bishop of Rochester and Master of Pembroke College, Cambridge, who would be burnt as a Protestant martyr in Oxford in 1555), before assembling in King's College Chapel, where they were given various books and statutes for their inspection. Sir John Cheke produced a book of new Statutes:

'synged with the Kynges hand and subscribed with the cownsell: he red every word therein and delivered it unto the Vyce-chancellor'. The Bishop of Ely then gave a:

'short proposition wherein among other he dyd chefflye exhorte all men to be obedient unto the Kynges proceedings, and to renownce all papystrye and superstytyon, and to bring in bylls every man of all thynges worthy reformacon, as well in the universyte and colleges as of every private person'.[2] College visitations followed, and it was the turn of Queens' on 20th May 1549, which led to revisions of the 1529 Statutes:

'On the Munday which was the xxth day thei sate at the Quenes college and made an ende and supped ther'.[2] Members of Queens' were prominent in the 'disputations' associated with the visitation. One debated subject was:

'Transubstantiation could not be proved by Scripture, nor be confirmed by the consent of ancient fathers for a thousand years past', which was opposed by Dr Glynn, ex-fellow and the next President. Another disputee was Andrew Perne, fellow of Queens' and subsequent Master of Peterhouse, who was on the opposite side to Glynn in discussions of the Lord's Supper.

In 1548, Mey, together with the Archbishop of Canterbury and other: 'notable learned men',[1] (who included two members of Queens', Heynes, ex-President and Dean of Exeter, and Dr John Taylor, previously a fellow of Queens', Master of St John's College, Cambridge, and a future Bishop of Lincoln), were appointed to prepare the 'Order of the Communion', which was published in the same year, and 'The Book of Common Prayer and administration of the Sacraments, and other rites and ceremonies of the church', which was published in 1549. The latter was the first book of the liturgy of the Church of England in English.

In 1549, Mey was appointed to yet another commission, tasked with suppressing heresy and reforming ecclesiastical laws, further demonstrating his reputation as a reliable administrator. He is described as being:

'well skilled in the constitution both of Church and State, and there was scarce any considerable step taken towards the reformation of the prevailing corruptions and abuses without consulting his opinions'.[2] This latest appointment involved the examination of his own bishop, Edmund Bonner, who was Bishop of London 1539-49 and again during 1553-59. Although actively involved in Henry VIII's break from Rome, Bonner reverted to Catholicism under Edward VI and, in 1549, he was deprived of his bishopric and detained in the Marshalsea prison. He remained a prisoner until the accession of Mary I in 1553, when he was then restored and became known as 'Bloody Bonner' for his persecution of heretics:

'This cannibal in three years space three hundred martyrs slew. They were his food, he loved so blood, he spared none he knew'.[8] However, his fortunes would change again under Elizabeth I and he was in prison again at his death in 1569. Although his defenders claimed that he no control over the fates of the accused and that he always tried to reconcile them with the Church, an account by John Foxe (1516-87), supports an opposing view:

'Two willow twigs were then brought to him (Bonner), and causing the unresisting youth to kneel agaist a long bench, in an arbor in his garden, he scourged him until he was compelled to cease for want of breath and fatigue. One of the rods was worn quite away'.[9]

In 1549, as part of a protracted process of hostilities towards Bonner, Edward VI wrote to instruct the commission, which included both Mey and Sir Thomas Smith, (quoted with modern spelling):

'Edward the Sixth, & To the most reverend father in God, Thomas, archbishop of Canterbury, metropolitan and primate of England, the right reverend father in God, Nicholas bishop of Rochester, our trusty and right well-beloved councillors, Sir William Peter (Petre) and Sir Thomas Smith, knights, our two principal secretaries, and William May, doctor of the law civil, and dean of Paul's, greeting: It has come to our knowledge, that where we, by the advice of our most entirely beloved uncle Edward, duke of Somerset, governor of our person, and protector of all our realms, dominions, and subjects, and the rest of our privy council, did give to the right reverend father in God Edmund, bishop of London, upon certain complaints before made unto us, and other great considerations, certain injunctions to be followed, done, and executed; and, in a sermon appointed to him to preach by us with certain articles, and for the more sure knowledge, keeping, and observing, did exhibit the same in writing unto him by the hands of our said uncle, in the fulfilling of our council: all this notwithstanding, the said bishop hath, in contempt of us, (as it may appear) overslipped and not observed certain of the said things so by us enjoined, and others so perversely and negligently done, that the things minded of us to reformation, and for a good quiet of our subjects and our whole realm, be converted, by the wilful negligence or perversity of him, to a great occasion of slander, tumult, and grudge amongst our people, as it hath been denounced to us in writing by certain honest and discreet persons, and otherwise called. The which things if they be so, we...have appointed you...to call before you as well the denouncers of the said faults, as also the said bishop...with full power and authority to suspend, excommunicate, commit to prison, or deprive the said bishop...In witness whereof we have caused these our letters to be made patents. Witness ourself at Westminster, the eighth of September, in the third year of our reign'.[10]

'The Acts and Monuments of the Church' by John Foxe, contain a detailed account of the proceedings, (edited with modern spelling):[10]

'Upon Wednesday, the tenth day of September, in the year of our Lord 1549, and in the third year of the reign of King Edward the Sixth, Thomas Cranmer, archbishop of Canterbury, metropolitan and primate of all England, associated with Nicholas Ridley, then bishop of Rochester, Sir William Peter, knight, one of the King's two principal secretaries, and Master William May, doctor of the civil law, and dean of Paul's, by virtue of the king's commission, sat judicially upon the examination of Edmund Bonner, bishop of London, within the archbishop's chamber of presence, at his house in Lambeth, before whom there then also personally appeared the said bishop'. At a subsequent session, in the chapel of Lambeth, the commission comprised the Archbishop, the Bishop of Rochester, Petre and Mey, but, in addition, Sir Thomas Smith. The presence of the latter drew Bonner's objections:

'My Lord, the last day that I appeared before you, I remember there sat in the king's Majesty's commission, your Grace, you my

Lord of Rochester, you Master Secretary Peter, and you Master Dean of Paul's; but now, I perceive, there sitteth the Master Secretary Smith, who, because he sat not at the beginning, nor took there the commission upon him, ought not so to do: for by the law, they that begin, must continue the commission'.[10] This cat and mouse game was to continue for some time and Bonner was to voice the particular enmity between himself and Smith:

'I therefore, Edmund, bishop of London, having perceived and felt by all the sayings, proceedings, and doings of you Sir Thomas Smith, knight, one of the two principal secretaries to the king's Majesty, in this matter attempted and moved against me, that ye have been, and yet continually are, a notorious and manifest enemy of me the said Edmund, and much offended that I should in any wise allege and say, or use any such things for my most defence, as the law giveth me licence and liberty to do...'.[10] But, as noted above, his protestations were in vain; he was deprived of his bishopric and detained in the Marshalsea, a notorious prison in Southwark, London. Also, Mey was one of the judges of Georg van Parre, a Dutchman tried in 1551 for the heresy of 'Arianism', for which he was burned,[1] and, in 1552, he was appointed to assist the Lord Chancellor in hearing submissions.

It was around this time that he married Joan, the widow of his predecessor, Simon Heynes.[1] They were to have a son William and a daughter Elizabeth, who married John Tedcastel, of Barking, Essex.[1,7] Elizabeth died in 1596, aged 43, and is buried at St Margaret's Church, Barking, where there is a monumental brass of her and her husband, inscribed:

'Here under lieth ye bodies of John Tedcastle Gent and Elizabeth his wife daughter of William Mey Doctor of Laws and had issue betweene them ix sonnes and vii daughters...'.[1] Her half-brother, Joseph Heynes, is buried in the same church.[1]

As a leader of the Reformation in England, Mey made many changes at St Paul's during Edward VI's reign:

'1547. Item after Ester beganne the servis in Ynglyche (English) at Powles at the commandment of the dene at the tyme, William may, and also in dyvers other pariche churches...'.

'1549 The ij^{de} sonday of Lent preched Coverdalle, and whan hye masse was done the dene of Powlles, that was that tyme William May, commandyd the sacrament at the hye autre to be pulled down'.

'1550. Item on Sente Barnabes day was kepte no holiday through alle Londone at the commandment of the mayer, and at nyght was the aulter in Powlles pullyd downe, and as that day the vayelle was hongyd up beneathe the steppes and the tabulle sett up there...'.

'Item at Chrystmas was put downe in Powlles the Rectores Chori (the 'Rulers of the Choir': several priests, wearing copes, presiding over parts of the service) with all their coppys et processione, and no more to be usyd'.

'1551. Item...was the grattes besyde the hye alter in Powlles closed up, that the pepulle shulde not loke in at the tyme of the comunyone tyme and the vayle (an altar cloth) hongyd up...and then was the tabulle remevyd, and sette benethe at the vayele northe and sowthe; and on Esterday the dene, then beynge Wyllyam Maye, dyd mynyster hym-selfe'.

'1552. Item...the qweer (choir) of Powlles had a commandment from the dene from Cambryge at the byshoppe of Cantorberes visitation that he shulde leve the playnge of organs at the devyne servys, and soo lefte it'.[1,11]

Soon after the Catholic Mary I succeeded her Protestant half-brother in 1553, Mey, together with Archbishop Cranmer and Sir Thomas Smith, were brought before the Queen's commissioners, which prompted the newly-restored Bishop Bonner to write:

'This day is looked that Mr Canterbury must be placed where is meet for him; he is become very humble and ready to submit himself in all things, but that will not serve; in the same predicament is Dr Smith my friend and the dean of St Pauls (Mey) with others'.[1]

Mary quickly released Stephen Gardiner, Bishop of Winchester, from detention, who resumed his previous office as Chancellor of Cambridge University and, on the 20th August 1553, the Queen sent a letter to the Chancellor and heads of houses at Cambridge, ordering them to restore the Statutes which pre-dated the Reformation. The Chancellor sent his chaplain, Thomas Watson, to carry out this instruction and, after his visit to Queens', the Vice-President and a Mr Bernard were sent to Mey, who was in London, to inquire about the old College Statutes of 1529.[1,5] Under the new regime, Mey soon lost most of his appointments, including Dean of St Paul's and, in November 1553, President of Queens'. But he retained his canonry in Ely and must have accommodated himself to the new religious requirements to some degree as, in 1557, he became rector of Pulham in Norfolk and rector of Stanton St Michael, Cambridgeshire.[1,7] Also, he seems to have had rooms in College during 1555-58.[1] His successor as President in 1553, William Glynn, who reintroduced Catholic forms of worship to the College, was a loyal Catholic who had been forced to resign as Lady Margaret's Professor of Divinity in 1549.[5] (Glynn would resign as President in 1557 and be succeeded by Thomas Pecocke). In 1555, the University was ordered to subscribe to new articles of religion, and a majority of the fellows of Queens', nine in number, did so, but, during Mary's reign, about 90 Cambridge alumni went into exile, including John Aylmer, a Queens' graduate, who had been tutor to Lady Jane Grey.[5] The religious upheavals had a major impact on Queens'; while there were 22 fellows in 1553, at an inspection during 1557 by visitors appointed by Cardinal Pole, there were just 11 fellows, mostly absent, and only three of them were priests.[5,12]

After Mary's death and Elizabeth I's accession in 1558, Mey's fortunes changed again. The Chancellor of Cambridge University, Sir William Cecil, (appointed in 1559 in succession to Cardinal Pole), asked Mey for help to resolve a major dispute between the then President of Queens', Thomas Pecocke, and a rival faction of the fellows. At issue was Pecocke's attempts to install Catholic fellows after Elizabeth I's accession, as well as alleged illegal absences and unseemly behaviour of his supporters. Cecil took advice from Mey and Sir Thomas Smith, as well as from a committee, and a compromise ensued; fellows supported by Pecocke were admitted, but Pecocke resigned under pressure from the court. Cecil hoped that this would:

'avoid all such inconveniences as was supposed wold have insued, and they all together henceforth lyve in more quiet than hitherto they have don'.[5] Pecocke, was: 'fully minded to give over his interest and title',[1] and Mey resumed his Presidency in 1559. In the same year, Mey's brother John, a fellow of Queens' and a future Bishop of Carlisle, became Master of St Catharine's College, Cambridge.[5] Also, Mey resumed his Deanship of St Paul's in 1559, replacing Dr Henry Cole:

'June the 11th being St Barnabas day the Apostles' mass ceased, and no mass was said any more at St Paul's...and now Dr Mey, sometime dean of St Paul's, took possession of his place in the church as dean: and that afternoon was none of the old evensong then, and so abolished'.[1]

Later in 1559, Mey was appointed to two commissions, for the reorganisation and reform of Cambridge University and for the taking the oaths of ecclesiastics. The visitation to the University began in September 1559 and, at Queens', the Statutes, as revised under Edward VI in 1549, were re-established.[1] Also in 1559, he was one of the seven churchmen, together with Sir Thomas Smith, who were appointed to make further revisions to the Book of Common Prayer, which was re-introduced in that year.[1] In December 1559, Mey, as one of the: 'chiefest civilians in those times',[1] signed the Queen's commission to consecrate Mathew Parker as Archbishop of Canterbury. In 1560 Mey was nominated as Archbishop of York, but there were delays in confirming the appointment and Sir William Cecil wrote, on his way to Scotland in June 1560, to Sir William Petre:

'I perceive grete lack hereaway of a Bishopp of York. I think if yow wold move her Majesty, she wold pass the congee d'Eslyer for Dr Maye; suerly the sooner it be doone the better'.[1] But Mey died on the day of his election, the 8th August 1560, at the estimated age of 55, and was buried in the choir of St Paul's. His funeral sermon was preached by Bishop Grindal of London.[7] An inscription on Mey's monument in St Pauls' has not survived, although it is recorded by Searle in his history of Queens' published in 1867.[1]

Mey's will was made very shortly before his death:

'In the name of God amen. The vijth daye of Auguste in the yere of ower Lorde God 1560 I Willm Mey Doctor of lawes deane of the cathedral churche of Paules in London beinge ffeble and sicke in boddie but of good memory and understandinge thankes be given to God, doe make and ordaine my laste will and testamente in manner and forme followinge, ffirst comyttinge my soule to the infinite merce of God and my boddie yerthe to yerth... Item I do give to Jone my wyef xx^{li} of lawfull money. And I give my saide wyef all the money plate vtencill lynnen and juells which she had when I married her or by Doctor Heynes her late husbande. And further I give her all my landes gardens howses closes and tennents in sainte Edmunds bury or any where elce within the Countie of Suff: untill my Children Willm or Elizabeth doe come to theire severell ages of xxj.tye yeres...Also yf my Wyfe myne Executors and Supervisors will sell my landes and woodes boughte in Bedforde, then I will the Quenes Colledge in Cambridge to have the prefermente of hit payenge after xviij. yeres purchas... Item I do give all manner of righte interest tytle or state that I or myne heire have or myghte have or claime in the cittie or circute as hit is now distincted of the late suppressed house of the Whitefriers besides the queens Colledge in Cambridge to the saide Colledge for ev^{r}...And I nominate to be supervisors of this my will the reverente father Edmonde (Grindal) bishoppe of London Mr John Mullens Archdeacon of London and Thomas Yale doctor of lawes...'.[1]

References

1. Searle, W.G. The History of the Queens' College of St Margaret and St Bernard in the University of Cambridge. 1446-1560. Deighton, Bell & Co; Macmillan & Co. London. 1867. pp 212-40, 287-94.
2. Gray, J.H. The Queens' College of St Margaret and St Bernard. F.E.Robinson. London. 1898. pp 88, 92-93.

3. Willis, R. The Architectural History of the University of Cambridge. Vol II. Cambridge: Cambridge University Press. 1886. p 3.
4. Browne A.D., Seltman, C.T. A Pictorial History of the Queen's College of Saint Margaret and Saint Bernard. 1448-1948. Printed for The College. 1951. p 130.
5. Twigg, J. A History of Queens' College, Cambridge 1448-1986. The Boydell Press. Bury St Edmunds.1987. pp 32-38, 70.
6. Cooper, C.H. Annals of Cambridge. Volume I. Warwick and Co., Cambridge. 1842. pp 430-31.
7. Cooper. C.H. Athenae Cantabrigienses. Volume 1. Cambridge. Deighton, Bell & Co., and Macmillan & Co. London: Bell & Daldy, Fleet Street. 1858. pp 207-08.
8. Foxe, J. The Acts and Monuments of John Foxe: A New and Complete Edition. G. Townsend, S.R.Catley. Vol.VIII. Seely and Burnside. London. 1839.
9. Foxe, J. Fox's Book of Martyrs. Pantianos Classics. Printed in Great Britain by Amazon. (Original published in 1563). p 168.
10. Foxe, J. The Acts and Monuments of the Church. Vol. II George Virtue, Ivy Lane, Paternoster Row. London. 1844. pp 786-89, 807.
11. Chronicle of the Grey Friars of London. Ed. J.G.Nichols for the Camden Society, 1851. See also: The Chronicle of the Grey Friars: Edward VI. British History Online.
12. A History of the County of Cambridge and the Isle of Ely. Vol.3. The City and University of Cambridge. The colleges and halls: Queens'. Victoria County History, London, 1959. British History Online.

CHAPTER 10

William Glynn (Glyn, Glynne). President 1553-57.

Summary.

William Glynn was born in Anglesey in about 1504. After graduating at Cambridge, he was elected a fellow of Queens' in 1530 and subsequently served the College as junior bursar, senior bursar and Dean. In 1544 he was elected as Lady Margaret's Professor of Divinity and, in 1546, he was a foundation fellow and first Vice-Master of Trinity College, Cambridge. Despite his Catholicism, he kept some of his appointments under the Protestant regime of Edward VI, although he resigned his Professorship in 1549.

After the Catholic Mary I's accession, his religious views were again in tune with orthodoxy and in 1553 he was appointed to replace the reformer William Mey as President of Queens'. In 1554, the University appointed him as a delegate to Oxford to debate with the future Protestant martyrs Cranmer, Ridley and Latimer, who had been accused of heresy. During the following year he was part of an embassy to the Pope and, on his return, he was consecrated Bishop of Bangor.

However, a visitation to Cambridge University and the colleges in 1557 exposed a picture of discord and laxity at Queens', and although we do not know Glynn's reasons for his resignation later in the year, it is probable that, as an absentee President, he did not feel able to provide the leadership that the College now required.

He died the following year and is buried in Bangor Cathedral.

Timeline.

c1504.	Born in Heneglwys, Anglesey.
1526.	B.A. .
1530.	Fellow of Queens'. M.A. .
1532.	Junior bursar of Queens'.
1553.	Senior bursar of Queens'.
1537.	Archdeacon of Anglesey.
1538.	B.D. .
1539.	Dean of Queens'.
1544.	D.D. . Lady Margaret's Professor of Divinity. Resigns his fellowship.
1546.	Foundation fellow and Vice-Master of Trinity College, Cambridge.
1547.	Death of Henry VIII. Accession of Edward VI.
1549.	Resigns as Lady Margaret's Professor of Divinity under pressure from the Protestant regime of Edward VI. Participates in a disputation before commissioners visiting Cambridge University.
1550-53.	Rector of St Martin's, Ludgate, London.
1551.	Chaplain to Thomas Thirlby, Bishop of Norwich.
1552.	Rector of Heneglwys, Anglesey. (Date unknown: Rector of Rhoscolyn, near Holyhead).
1553.	Death of Edward VI. Accession of the Catholic Mary I. The reformer William Mey resigns as President. William Glynn is elected in his place.
1554.	Incorporated D.D. at Oxford University. Glynn is one of the divines who disputes with Cranmer, Ridley and Latimer at Oxford.
1554-55.	Vice-Chancellor of Cambridge University.
1555.	One of the ambassadors sent to Rome. Ridley and Latimer burnt at the stake in Oxford. (Cranmer will suffer the same fate the following year). Appointed Bishop of Bangor and Archdeacon of Anglesey.
1557.	Gynn is absent in Wales during a visitation to Cambridge University and the colleges. Queens' is visited in January 1557, when various failings are reported. Glynn resigns as

President; Thomas Pecocke is elected in his place. The corpses of the reformers Bucer and Fagius are burnt at Cambridge.

1558. Dies. Buried in Bangor Cathedral.

Clergyman and academic. Replaced William Mey as President after the accession of Mary I. Bishop of Bangor, who resigned as President after failings at Queens' were exposed in 1557.

William Glynn was born in Heneglwys, Anglesey, in about 1504, the son of the local rector.[1] He graduated B.A. at Cambridge in 1526 and M.A. in 1530, the year in which he was elected as a fellow of Queens'. He played an active role in the College, serving as junior bursar in 1532, senior bursar in 1533 and Dean in 1539-40. After proceeding B.D. in 1538, he became D.D. in 1544, the same year that he was elected the Lady Margaret's Professor of Divinity. When Trinity College was founded in 1546, by the amalgamation of the existing foundations of Michaelhouse and King's Hall, he was one of the foundation fellows and the first Vice-Master. But, as he was not a reformer, the accession of the Protestant Edward VI in 1547 led to his resignation from his professorship in 1549.[1,2]

Edward VI appointed a commission to visit the University, which included William Mey and Thomas Smith (see Chapter 9), and Glynn played a prominent part in the disputations which took place before the visitors in 1549. These debates included Glynn opposing the claim that:

'Transubstantiation (the Catholic doctrine that the bread and wine in the rite of the Eucharist becomes the body and blood of Jesus Christ) could not be proved by Scripture, nor be confirmed by the consent of ancient fathers for a thousand years past'.[2]

However, despite his Catholicism, Glynn must have adapted himself to the Protestant regime, as he became rector of St Martin's, Ludgate, London, in 1550 and of Heneglwys in 1552. Also, in 1551, he was chaplain to Thomas Thirlby, Bishop of Norwich.

His fortunes were to improve after the accession of the Catholic Mary I and, in 1553, he was elected President of Queens' at the expense of William Mey, who lost most of his appointments after the change in regime. Mary wrote to the University insisting on the restoration of old statutes and practices which had been:

'muche altered broken and almost utterly subverted' by the Reformation.[3,4] With only three exceptions- Gonville Hall, Jesus and Magdelene, every Cambridge college received a new head, while the Chancellor of the University, the Duke of Northumberland, lost his for his initial support of Lady Jane Grey as a successor to Edward VI.[2] Glynn re-introduced Catholic practices at Queens', including prayers for the souls of the dead. Also, the chapel desks and organ were repaired and a gilt cross purchased.[4] In 1555, the University was instructed to subscribe to new articles of religion and nine fellows of Queens', a majority, complied.[4]

Glynn was in for a busy schedule during his first years as President, which saw him as a delegate to Oxford in 1554 to debate with the future Protestant martyrs, Cranmer, Ridley and Latimer. Also in 1554, he was elected Vice-Chancellor of the University, but resigned during his year in office because, in early 1555, he was appointed as part of an embassy to the Pope.[1,3] His fellow ambassadors included Bishop Thirlby (then of Ely), Anthony Browne, (Viscount Montague) and Sir Edward Carne. They were instructed:

'to make the queen's obedience to his holiness, and to obtain a confirmation of all those graces, which cardinal Pole had granted in his (ie the Pope's) name'.[1] This journey, over about six months, is described in detail by one of Bishop Thirlby's entourage, in 'Miscellaneous State Papers From 1501 to 1727 in Two Volumes Vol. I. Edited by Philip Yorke, 2nd Earl of Hardwicke, printed by Steahan and Cadell, London, in 1778', (available online). When the party reached Rome:

'...the Lords (ie Montague and the Bishop), went to the Court, accompanied with divers Bishops, Noblemen and Gentlemen, and there had open audience. As they passed by the castle of St Angelo, the Lords were saluted with a great peal of ordnance.

The Pope sat in a conclave, where he was chosen (the Sistine Chapel) in a great high chair, having a very rich cope upon him, a mitre of a wonderful price upon his head. The place where he sat was railed in, that the people might not come and trouble the orator. The Cardinals sat in benches, within the rails, round about the Pope's Holiness...After my Lord my Master, the Lord Bishop of Ely, had ended his oration made to the Pope, then all the Englishmen of the Lords train were called for, and let come within the rails, to kiss the Pope's Holiness's foot, who had a crimson velvet slipper on, that had a cross of silver laid upon it. That done, the Pope blessed them, and so they departed sanctified...The fifteenth day the Lords dined and supped with the Pope at the palace of St Mark...and the same night they took their leave of the Pope, who gave my Lord Montagu a table diamond, with a ring, esteemed at 2000 crowns; and my Lord of Ely my master, a cross of gold. They made great bonfires in Rome because we were reconciled to the church of Rome and the castle shot off much ordnance'. (This Pope was Paul IV, recently elected on the 23rd of May 1555; during his strife-ridden papacy he developed a reputation as a harsh persecuter of the Jews, particularly in Ancona where 24 Jews were hanged for refusing to convert, and ordered the Jews of Rome to be restricted to a ghetto).

After Glynn's return, his career progression was further marked by his consecration as Bishop of Bangor in late 1555.[2] The ceremony was performed by Edmund Bonner, Bishop of London, Thomas Thirlby, Bishop of Ely, and Maurice Griffin, Bishop of Rochester.[1] In the following century, Thomas Fuller (priest and historian, 1608-61), quoted by Gray in his history of the College of 1898,[2] provides a glowing estimate of his character:

'An excellent scholar, and as I have been assured by judicious persons, who have seriously perused the solemn disputations (printed by Master Fox) betwixt the Papists and Protestants, that none of the former press his arguments with more strength and less passion than Dr. Glynn: though constant to his own, he was not cruel to opposite judgments, as appeareth by the appearing of no persecution in his diocese: and his mild nature must be allowed to be at least *causa socia* or the fellow cause thereof'.

In 1554, the Convocation of Canterbury, (the assembly of bishops and clergy of the Canterbury province of the Church of England), had sent letters to the University with propositions on the nature of the 'Real Presence', (ie of the body and blood of Christ), in the Eucharist, and on an intent to hold a disputation at Oxford with Archbishop Cranmer, Bishop Ridley and former-Bishop Latimer, whose religious views were now considered heretical by the Catholic regime. Cambridge University had approved the then currently-acceptable religious doctrines and, as the accused bishops were Cambridge alumni, it was decided to send six delegates to try and persuade the accused heretics to agree to the current orthodox views. Glynn was one of those selected, and on this visit his D.D. degree was 'incorporated' at Oxford University.[1,2] Although he was an old friend of Ridley, Foxe (John Foxe, 1516-87, quoted by Searle[1]) claims that Glynn's behaviour to him at the disputation was, despite the above character reference, 'contumelious', (ie abusive, humiliating, contemptuous, insulting):

'Dr Glynn began to reason, who (notwithstanding master Ridley had always taken him for his old friend) made a very contumelious preface against him. This preface master Ridley therefore took the more to heart, because it proceded from him. Howbeit he thought, that Dr Glyn's mind was to serve the turn; for afterwards he came to the house wherein master Ridley was kept, and, as far as master Ridley could call to remembrance, before Dr Young (the vicechancellor of the university of Cambridge) and Dr Oglethorp, he desired him to pardon his words. The which master Ridley did even from the very heart, and wished earnestly that God would give not only to him but unto all others the true and evident knowledge of God's evangelical sincerity, that, all offences put apart, they being perfectly and fully reconciled might agree and meet together in the house of the heavenly Father. Glynn's words were these: I see that you elude or shift away all scriptures and fathers: I will go to work with you after another sort: Christ hath here his church known in earth, of which you were once a child, though you now speak contumeliously of the sacraments. To this the bishop replied:

This is a grievous contumely, that you call me a shifter-away of the scripture and of the doctors. As touching the sacraments I never yet spake contumeliously of them…'.

(Clearly, friends should avoid the subject of religion, as well as politics).

On the death of Bishop Stephen Gardiner, Cardinal Pole became Chancellor of Cambridge University in 1555 and, at the beginning of 1557, now Archbishop of Canterbury, he ordered a visitation of the University and colleges:[1]

'Cardinal Pole, as the Pope's legate, deputed Cuthbert Scott Bishop of Chester, Nicholas Ormanet, DD and LL.D the Pope's Datary, Thomas Watson Bishop elect of Lincoln, John Christopherson Bishop elect of Chichester and Master of Trinity College, and Henry Cole, DD and LL.D Dean of St. Paul's and Provost of Eton College, to visit the University, with a view to the more complete re-establishment of the Catholic religion'.[5] All graduates were instructed to appear before the visitors at Great St Mary's Church on the 11th January between eight and ten, a mass was celebrated at King's College chapel and a Latin sermon was preached at Great St Mary's:

'inveighing against heresies and heretics as Bilney, Latimer, Cranmer, Ridley, &c'.[1,2] by Thomas Pecocke, who would soon replace Glynn as President of Queens'. During the visitation over the next several weeks, Cambridge witnessed the bizarre spectacle of the posthumous trial and condemnation of the Protestant reformers Martin Bucer and Paul Fagius, prior to the burning of their exhumed corpses in the market place, together with a cartload of heretical books. Before the visitors left, on the 17th February, new University Statutes were issued after a mass at Great St Mary's.[1]

Martin Bucer was a German Protestant reformer who had been exiled to England in 1549 and, with the support of Thomas Cranmer, influenced the second revision of the 'Book of Common Prayer'. He died in Cambridge in 1551 and was buried in Great St Mary's Church before a large crowd. Sir John Cheke, (scholar and statesman, 1514-57), writes of Bucer:

'We are deprived of a leader than whom the whole world would scarcely obtain a greater, whether in knowledge of true religion or in integrity and innocence of life, or in thirst for study of the most holy things, or in exhausting labour in advancing piety, or in authority and fulness of teaching, or in anything that is praiseworthy and renowned'.[6] A brass plaque on the floor of Great St Mary's marks the original location of his grave. Paul Fagius was another German Protestant reformer who sought refuge in England. One of his previous appointments was that of Professor of Old Testament Studies at Strasbourg and, in 1549, he was appointed Hebrew lecturer at Cambridge University. He died from plague in 1549 and was buried in St Michael's Church, Cambridge, where a memorial was set up in 1560.

Glynn was absent in Wales during the visitors' inspection of Queens' on the 18th January 1557, which is described by John Mere, who was both the Registrary, (who compiled and maintained the University's records), and the Esquire bedell, (a ceremonial and administrative role), of the University:[2,5]

'xviii Januar. On Monday as before with some snow. It. The visyters came to the Quenes college di. Houre before vij, and in the gate howse a forme sett with carpet and cusshyns, where first the president (John Dale, the Vice-President, Chaplain and Cross-Bearer of the University) received them with holy water and sensings in a cope, and all the company in surplesses with crosses and candlesticks. After that they went to the chapel processionaliter and had masse of the Holy Gost songe, which don they sitting styll in the stalles the president delivered the certificat of all the comanyes names and I (ie John Mere) called them, and then they wente upp to the awlter and so to the vestrye perusinge all things as they did at the kings college. Then they wente to the master's lodgings and there sate in examination until vx, at what tyme the Vic. Came and fet them to S. Maryes, but Dr Thomas Watson the bishop of Lincoln, and Dr Cole Provost of Eton and dean of St Pauls, two of the visitors, remained styll at the Quenes college and there dyned and continued tyll after iiij of the clocke'.

However, the subsequent dinner, provided by the College for Dr Thomas Watson and Dr Cole, caused the visitors to complain, in a manner reminiscent of some modern attempts to avoid criticism by those in the public eye. The following account from Foxe's 'The Acts and Monuments of the Church' is quoted by Searle:[1]

'The commissioners (for they were marvellous conscionable men in all their doings) had great regard of the expenses of every college where they should make inquisition. Wherefore, to the intent that none of them should stretch their liberality beyond measure, or above their power, they gave charge at the beginning, that there should not in any place be prepared for their repast above three kinds of meat at the most...Thereupon when they came to Queenes college the 18th day to sit upon inquiry, and one capon chanced to be served to the table more than was prescribed by the order taken, they thrust it away in great displeasure. These thriving men, that were so sore moved for the preparing of one capon, within little more than one month, beside their private refections, wasted in their daily diet well nigh a hundred pounds (£82.10s. 4d.) of the common charges of the colleges, so that the university may worthily allege against them this saying of our Saviour, 'Woe unto you that strain out a gnat and swallow up a camel' '.

At a later stage of the visitation there was further friction when, on the 8th February, the visitors, (as recorded in 'Annals of Cambridge' by Charles Henry Cooper, published in 1843):

'sente for the Presidente of the Quenes College and all the felowes, and on the 12th, betwyxte I and ii my Lord of Lynkolne and D Cole went to the queens college and called many together into the Chappell and ther remained an howre. As Ormanet was sittinge at Trinitie Colledge, John Dale, one of ye Queenes colledge came to him, whom he had commaunded before, to bring with him the pixe. (A box or vessel in which the materials for the Eucharist were kept). For Ormanet told them he had a precious Jewel, (the same was a linen clout that the Pope had consecrated with his own handes) which he promised to bestow upon them for a gifte. But Dale misunderstanding Ormanet, in stede of that Pixe, brought a chalice & a singing cake (called the hoste) (ie bread or wafers) the which he had wrapped up & put in his bosome.

When he was come, Ormanet spake him courteouslye, demaundinge if he had brought him the thinge he sente him for to whom he aunswered he had brought it then geve it me (quod he), Dale pulled out the chalice & the singing cake. When Ormanet sawe that, he stepped somewhat back as it had been in a wonder, (and, in a puzzling overreaction) calling blockhead, & litel better then a mad man, demaunding what he ment by those thinges, saying, he willed him to bring none of that gere, & that he was unworthy to enjoy so high a benefite, yet notwithstanding forasmuch as he had promised before to give it theym he would performe his promise. Whereupon with great reverence and Ceremonye, he pulled oute the lynnen clothe and layed it in the chalice, and the bread with it, commaunding theym both for the holiness of the thing, and also for the autour of it, to kepe it among them with suche due reverence as belonged to so holy a rellique'.[1,5]

The visitors' enquiries were wide-ranging, including how the restored Statutes of 1529 had been observed,[1,2] and Gray[2] notes their conclusions that Queens' was an organisation in a state of: 'discord and division'. This may have been the main reason for Glynn's subsequent resignation, as, because of his duties in Wales, he would have been unable to provide the input that was clearly required. (At this time, the College consisted of only eleven fellows, while just three were priests. As well as the President, seven of the fellows were absent).[2] Complaints to the visitors had included that the President was absent without the consent of the fellows and had neglected his duty to urge the junior fellows to take priests' orders.[4] Also, that Latin was not being spoken at mealtimes, women were often in the College, some residents stayed out late and wore their hair long, some did not attend services and no Dean of Chapel had been appointed.[4] A further irregularity was that John Mey, the previous President's brother, owed the College the considerable sum of £40; however, this did not prevent his future eminence as Master of St Catharine's College, Cambridge, and Bishop of Carlisle.

Glynn resigned as President sometime between September and December 1557. Since his consecration as Bishop of Bangor in

1555, he had been active in his diocese, as shown by the following account by his successor Bishop Humphrey Humphreys, (in office 1689-1701), quoted by Searle:[1]

'Upon his first coming to Bangor he held there a Diocesan Synod or Convocation, which began on Munday next after Trinity Sunday 1556 and wherein after a Solemn Procession, and the Masse of the Holy Ghost, he preached, and then ordered the Decrees and Canons of the last Provinciall and Legatine Synod to be read, and admonished the Clergy to obey them... Then was read the Pope's Bull of plenary Indulgence (ie remission of the entire time of punishment after death for sins committed in life), and a Mandate from the Bishop (Bonner) of London to observe the Contents. After this, and Conference with the Clergy about severall matters relating to the public State of the Diocese: It was unanimously decreed, there should be two Diocesan Synods at Bangor every year...at which all the Clergy in the Diocese were to be present, to appear in their Surplices for Procession, and to bring their Boxes, to have consecrated Oyle for the Chrisme. And lastly the Clergy presented the Bishop with a Benevolence of 100 Marks, according to the antient and laudable custome of the said Diocese, upon the coming of a new Bishop. At the next Diocesan Synod...he ordered the aforesaid Decrees of the Legatine Synod to be read again, and strictly admonished the Clergy to observe them, under the Penalties therin contained...at Bangor Nov.4 1557 he monished the Clergy to pay their Arrears of Subsidies, to exhibite Terriers (a glebe terrier was a written survey of lands and property in a parish, which were owned by the Church) and Inventaries of their Church goods by the next Synod, under pain of Deprivation, and injoyned Residence and Hospitality. He was a zealous Papist, but no Persecuter, that I can finde. On the contrary, tho' he deprived many of the married Clergy, he generally gave them some other Living instead of that they were deprived of, and often permitted them to exchange'.

He died the following year, 1558, and was buried in his Cathedral, on the north side of the choir, before the High Altar. He is described on a brass plate as:

'Guielmus Glyn natus in insula Mona, (Anglesey was first recorded as 'Mona' by various Roman sources) Cantebrig. Doctor Theologie, episcopus Bangor...'.[1]

References

1. Searle, W.G. The History of the Queens' College of St Margaret and St Bernard in the University of Cambridge. 1446-1560. Deighton, Bell & Co; Macmillan & Co. London. 1867. pp 245-54, 260-61.
2. Gray, J.H. The Queens' College of St Margaret and St Bernard. F.E.Robinson. London. 1898. pp 94-100.
3. Fuller, T. The History of the University of Cambridge from the Conquest to the year 1634. Deighton, J. & J.J., Stevenson, T. London. Reprinted 1840. (Original edition 1655). p 252.
4. Twigg, J. A History of Queens' College, Cambridge 1448-1986. The Boydell Press. Bury St Edmunds. 1987. pp 30-36.
5. Cooper, C.H. Annals of Cambridge. Volume II. Warwick and Co., Cambridge. 1843. pp 112, 124-25.
6. Hall, B. In: Wright, D.F. ed., Martin Bucer: Reforming church and community. Cambridge University Press. Cambridge, 1994.

CHAPTER 11

Thomas Pecocke (Peacock, Peacocke). President 1557-59.

Summary.

Thomas Pecocke was born in Cambridge and educated at Cambridge University. He was a staunch Catholic and, before his election as President of Queens', a fellow of St John's and Trinity Colleges, with various Church appointments.

William Mey had been elected President of Queens' in 1537, but, as he was an active reformer, he was forced to resign in 1553, after the accession of the Catholic Mary I. An era of religious conflicts formed the background to the subsequent rapid turnover of Presidents; Mey was replaced by William Glynn, who resigned in 1557, after failings at Queens' had been exposed by a visitation to the University. Glynn was succeeded by Pecocke, but the latter's two-year tenure was marked by serious disputes within the fellowship and he resigned as President in 1559, after Elizabeth I's accession in 1558 had brought a return of Protestantism. Mey was restored in his place, but Mey's death the following year precipitated the election of the fourth President in the seven years since Mary's accession. In retirement, Pecocke lived in Cambridge and probably died soon after 1581.

Timeline.

c1511.	Born in Cambridge.
1533.	Fellow of St John's College, Cambridge.
1534.	B.A..
1537.	M.A.. William Mey elected as President, (see Chapter 9).
1547.	Fellow of Trinity College, newly-founded in 1546.

1553.	Death of Edward VI. Accession of the Catholic Mary I. The Protestant William Mey resigns as President and is succeeded by the Catholic William Glynn, (see Chapter 10).
1554.	B.D. . Chaplain to Thomas Thirlby, Bishop of Norwich, (who would become Bishop of Ely later this year). Canon of Norwich.
1555.	Continues his association with Bishop Thirlby, now Bishop of Ely. Present at Ely (9th October) when the 'Ely Martyrs' (Pigot and Wolsey) are condemned; they are burned on Cathedral Green, Ely, on the 16th October. Rector of Little Downham, Cambridgeshire.
1556.	Canon of Ely. Resigns as canon of Norwich.
1557.	A visitation is appointed to investigate Cambridge University and the colleges. Pecocke preaches an anti-Protestant sermon before the visitors. Failings at Queens' are exposed. Resignation of William Glynn, (Bishop of Bangor and absentee President); Pecocke is elected President in his stead.
1557-59.	Serious disputes at Queens' between Pecocke and the fellowship.
1558.	Rector of Barley, Hertfordshire, (January). Death of Mary I, (July). Accession of Elizabeth I.
1559.	Pecocke resigns as President. William Mey is restored in his place, (see Chapter 9). Begins retirement in Cambridge.
c1581.	Dies in Cambridge.

A Catholic cleric. Fellow of St John's and Trinity Colleges and canon of Ely. A short-term President, 1557-59, who was elected under Mary I. He resigned under Elizabeth I, after a tenure marked by disputes at Queens'.

Thomas Pecocke was born in Cambridge around 1511. His probable father was another Thomas Pecocke, 'burgess' of the town, whose will of 1528 containes the following bequest:

'Item. I bequethe to my sone Thomas Pecocke xli. To be payd to hym at xxti. Yeres of age, yf that he be a mane of the world, and yf that he wyl be prieste, yt to be payd to hym when the same day that he schall syng hys fyrste masse'.[1]

He was educated at St John's College and elected a fellow of his College in 1533.[2] He graduated B.A. in 1534 and M.A. in 1537.[1] In 1542 he was among those at St John's who made unsuccessful objections about the Master, John Taylor, who had Protestant leanings.[3] His mother died in 1546 and left him a house and two tenements in Cambridge.[3]

A visitation to the University and colleges under the Protestant regime of Edward VI took place in 1549, during the Presidency of William Mey (see Chapter 9), and Richard Rex, (Professor of Reformation History and fellow of Queens'), informs us that:

'Peacock was identified by the protestant visitors as one of a group of hardline papists at Trinity, where there was "such a nest of them as the like cannot be espied within the realm". Once Redman, (the Master of Trinity), himself had been induced to subscribe to the Book of Common Prayer (apparently with some reservations), resistance collapsed.'[3]

Pecocke's career advanced after the accession of Mary I in 1553. He was subsequently ordained and took his B.D. in 1554, the same year that Thomas Thirlby, Bishop of Norwich, (and a native of Cambridge from Holy Trinity, the same parish as Pecocke), appointed him as his chaplain and a canon of Norwich.[3] Bishop Thirlby moved to the diocese of Ely later in 1554 and, in 1555, appointed him rector of Little Downham, Cambridgeshire. In 1556 he became a canon of Ely, in exchange for the canonry at Norwich. In 1555, as the Bishop's chaplain, he assisted at the trial for heresy of the 'Ely Martyrs', Wolsey and Pygot, who were condemned on the 9th October.[1,2] William Wolsey was a 'Constable' at Upwell, near Wisbech, who objected to the doctrine of transubstantiation, after he had studied an illicitly-obtained New Testament Bible in English. He came to official notice when he avoided Mass and was brought before the Ely Assizes. Another local man, Robert Pygot, a painter and builder, was also summoned to court for not attending church, because he believed that:

'...he that is in the true faith of Jesus Christ is never absent, but present in the Church of God' and, after subsequent detention in prison, both men were tried and convicted of heresy by a church commission. Pecocke was also present in Ely a week later on the 16th October, when both these men of humble origin were taken to Cathedral Green for execution by being burned at the stake, after a sermon preached by Pecocke.[3] They died reciting Psalm 106, on the same day as the more illustrious martyrs, Bishop Ridley and former-Bishop Latimer, were burned at Oxford. On the 1st April 1555, Pecocke signed the articles in which the University subscribed to Catholic doctrine and, in 1558, he was presented by Bishop Thirlby as rector of Barley, Hertfordshire.

William Mey, a reformer, had been President of Queens' since 1537, before being replaced by William Glynn in 1553, after the accession of the Catholic Mary I, (see Chapters 9 and 10). However, Glynn was appointed Bishop of Bangor in 1555 and was an absentee President when there was a visitation to the University and colleges in 1557, during Mary's regime. This was under the authority of Cardinal Pole, Archbishop of Canterbury, the Pope's legate and the University's Chancellor, (see Chapter 10). The visitation began on the 11th January and after a Mass at King's College chapel, it was Pecocke who delivered the Latin sermon at Great St Mary's Church:

'before the whole university and the visitors, inveighing against heresies and heretics, as Bilney, Latimer, Cranmer, Ridley, &c.'.[1]

As noted previously, (see Chapter 10), the visitors found various failings at Queens' and Gray summaries their findings that Queens' was in a state of: 'discord and division'.[4] This situation probably led to Glynn's resignation and Pecocke's election as President, in about October 1557.[1]

Unfortunately, during Pecocke's Presidency the problems at Queens' only increased, as his tenure was marked by serious disputes between the President and some of the fellows. Twigg, in his 1987 history of the College, describes a dispute involving claims that Pecocke had abused his extensive powers to manage the College's estates.[5] The President was accused of undue favour to a friend, Thomas Leete, who had sold land to the College, and some fellows claimed that he had been given £10 more:

'then his lande was worthe by our estimation which was appoyntid to vewe the landes he solde to the colleadge', and that Leete had been given:

'certyn of the colleadge woode under pretence, that it is custome to geve always the colleadge woode to all copiholders to buylde what they would therewith'. But the main cause of friction was a disagreement concerning elections to fellowships.[4] The President and six fellows, a majority, had arranged the election of three new fellows, which was considered to be an attempt to fill vacancies with unsuitable men, but with Catholic views, before any further religious upheavals. Three candidates were opposed by the Vice-President, (who was the future President John Stokes), supported by four fellows, who appealed to Sir William Cecil, who had become Chancellor of the University in 1559 after Cardinal Pole's death.[1] Searle quotes the undated: 'Protest of the minority of the society of Queens' college against the election of sirs Hendmare (or Hyndmer), Welles and Harnesse' as fellows:

'Beynge unjustlye greved by the manyfolde prejudiciall doyings of Mr Peacocke Master of our Colledge, and often gentlye desiring redresse therof at his hande...he...elected three by common fame most unworthy in all the townne, not knowen or sene ever before to us...we appealed for reformacon to have the saide pretensid election disanullid or rather pronounced as yt ys of no force...because the said election was attemptit contrarye to the statute...Objections agaist suche as theie have chosen: Sir Hyndmer one elected by theme a common player at dyse or cardes and therbye the better acquainted with theme and speciallye with Gardyner, with whome he hathe bene in a maner contynuallye at cardes or dyse at the basketmakers and other places where theye use the said exercyse.

Item the reporte of him in Christes college ys, that he ys unlerned, for that he never kept their so muche as his owne probleame nor anye other exercyse, as others do of his place and tyme...

Item one Sir Welles butler of Pembrokhall was by them elected, whiche ys reported bothe in the said housse and otherwhere to be a very stubbornne unquiet quarrellinge and chydinge fellowe...

Item one Sir Harnesse of Sant Johns was also elected lykwyse by theme, of whome as yet we have asked or lerned verye lytle, savinge that he ys reported to be unlerned...

As concerning other brechys of the statutes by our m[r] and his evyll regiment...We will not troble your woorshipes withal at this tyme, reservinge them to place and tyme more convenient'.[1]

Subsequently, Sir William Cecil wrote to Pecocke instructing him not to proceed further in the election or admission to fellowships, and to Dr Pory (the Vice-Chancellor), Dr Parker (the future Archbishop of Canterbury) and Edward Leedes (afterwards Master of Clare Hall), on the 21st March 1559, appointing them arbitrators between the two factions. They concluded that two of the three disputed candidates were satisfactory, and Cecil, on the 28th of April, writes to: 'my loving frende mr Pecocke the mr of Quenes college in Cabrige', informing him of the outcome, although, (in contrast to a subsequent letter), he appears to endorse all three candidates:

'After my hartie commendacions. Understanding by sir Thomas Smyth and Doctor May my frends somewhat more of the estate of your colledge and the statutes therof, who bothe for the good will they beare to the colledge hath ben autors to me for the matter, and for the tyme they have ben there and the rule they have borne there, do best knowe theffecte of your statutes, I have moved the Quenes highness herin that for so muche as the eleccon of the fellows is past and (as I can learne by them whom I take to be best sene in the statutes of the colledge) not against your orders there, hir highness hath declared unto me, that it is not hir pleasur to staye their admission...And therefore...ye shall procede to the admission of them according to your statutes... Having in mynde this that as hir highness is so well mynded to learning as never prynce was more...Fare ye well.From the courte the xxviij[th] of April 1559'.[1] But a compromise had been reached to ensure peace, as Pecocke's had agreed, no doubt under pressure, to step down as President, as noted by Cecil writing on the 5th of May to: 'my assured loving friend M[r] Doctor Parker' as follows:[1,4]

'After my very hartie commendations. Foras muche as I am credibly informed that the two young men lately chosen to be ffellowes in the Quenes Colledge be both forward in learning and also well mynded in the service of God, so as by their admission into the same howse our common cause of religion shall no whitt be impaired or hindred, and for that also I understand by Sir Thomas Smith that Mr Pecocke nowe president of the said colledg is fully mynded to gyve over his interest and title in the same to Doctor Mey, (which thing I like very well), I have therefore sent downe my letters for their admission accordingly. And to th'intent that as in the beginning of this matter I made you partaker of the paynes for the understanding therof, so finally to participate with you the determination of the same, I have sent you a copie of the said letters inclosed herin, whereby you shall perceive what I have done therin. I doubt not but as the younge men by their admission shall thinke themselves benefited, so shall thither parte who moved some dowte therin, by changing of the master, avoide all suche inconveniences as was supposed wold have insued, and they all together henceforth lyve in more quiet than hitherto they have don.

And thus I bid you hartely farewell. From the court the vth day of May 1559. Youre assured loving frend W. Cecill'.

Despite the mention of just two fellows in the above letter, all the three controversial fellows are described in College records as having been admitted at about the time of their disputed elections and none of these elections was overturned. Hendmare appears in the College records in the year to September 1559, while Harnesse continued as a fellow until 1560 and Welles to 1564.[1] Pecocke quietly retired later in May 1559, and a degree of goodwill towards him was indicated by a present of £4 from the restored President and the fellows.

In 1559 Parliament passed two Acts: The Act of Supremacy, which designated the Queen as the Supreme Governor of the Church of England, and The Act of Uniformity, which required the use of the revised Book of Common Prayer, (similar to the 1552 vesion), and attendance at an Anglian Church once a week, or be fined the significant sum of 12 pence. But Pecocke refused to subscribe to the royal supremacy and lost his Church appointments. In retirement, he remained in Cambridge,[1,2] and there is a record of him in 1563, when he gave the churchwardens of Holy Trinity parish in Cambridge an annuity of 20 shillings, payable from income from the Crane Inn.[1] But Rex describes one escape from his apparent obscurity:

'A letter written in 1567 by none other than Nicholas Sander, a leading Catholic refugee on the continent, indicates that Thomas Peacock was one of four English priests who met the grand inquisitor in Rome in 1564 and personally received from him faculties to reconcile schismatics to the Roman Catholic church. Peacock certainly returned to Cambridge thereafter, but it is not known what use, if any, he made of these special powers'.[3] There is a final record of him in 1581, when he gave £20 to the corporation of Cambridge to fund a distribution of 16d. a month to the prisoners in the Tolbooth, (the main municipal building). He left no will and probably died soon afterwards.[2,3]

There was an event of wider historical interest at Queens' during Pecocke's Presidency, namely, the admission, as a fellow-commoner in November 1558, of Edward de Vere, soon to become the 17th Earl of Oxford. He was: 'a considerable figure in Elizabethan England' and, from an early age, brought up in the household of Sir Thomas Smith, (see Chapter 8). When he inherited the Earldom in 1562, he moved to the household of Sir William Cecil, then Secretary of State, marrying Cecil's daughter in 1571. He went on to develop a reputation as a poet, playwright and patron of the arts, but he had a volatile temperament, troubled relationships and an hedonistic lifestyle. He was in and out of favour with Queen Elizabeth, although, in 1586, she gave him a large pension to relieve the financial problems caused by his extravagance. While there is no convincing evidence that any of his plays survive, in the last century de Vere has been proposed as the most promising of the alternative (but unlikely) candidates for the authorship of Shakespeare's works.[6,7]

References

1. Searle, W.G. The History of the Queens' College of St Margaret and St Bernard in the University of Cambridge. 1446-1560. Deighton, Bell & Co; Macmillan & Co. London. 1867. pp 253, 264-67, 271-78, 282-83.

2. Cooper. C.H. Athenae Cantabrigienses. Volume 1. Cambridge. Deighton, Bell & Co.; and Macmillan & Co. London: Bell & Daldy, Fleet Street. 1858. p 460.
3. Rex, R. Peacock, Thomas. In: Oxford Dictionary of National Biography. Oxford University Press. Oxford. 2008. Online.
4. Gray, J.H. The Queens' College of St Margaret and St Bernard. F.E.Robinson. London. 1898. p 101.
5. Twigg, J. A History of Queens' College, Cambridge 1448-1986. The Boydell Press. Bury St Edmunds.1987. p 116.
6. O'Brien, P. The Historical Record. In: The Record 2010. Queens' College, Cambridge. Online. 2020.
7. Edward de Vere, 17th Earl of Oxford. Wikipedia. Online. 2020.

CHAPTER 12

John Stokes (Stokys). President 1560-68.

Summary.

John Stokes was educated at Queens'. In 1544 he was ordained and became a fellow of the College, before serving in several College offices. In 1556 he became Vice-President and, during the presidency of Thomas Pecocke (1557-9), he was active in opposing attempts to fill vacant fellowships at Queens' with Catholic candidates. In January1560, he was appointed Archdeacon of York and, in August, was elected President of Queens' after the death of William Mey, who had been restored to the Presidency after Pecocke's resignation. Stokes was President during Elizabeth I's visit to the University and colleges in 1564, during which he took part in the divinity disputations and hosted the Queen during her short visit to Queens'. He died in 1568, aged about 45 and is buried in the original chapel at Queens'.

Timeline.

1537.	William Mey elected President.
1538.	A Bible-clerk at Queens'.
1541.	B.A. .
1544.	M.A. . Fellow of Queens'. Ordained.
1547.	Accession of Edward VI.
1548.	Junior bursar.
1549.	Senior bursar. B.D. .
1551.	Dean.
1553.	Accession of Mary I. William Mey resigns as President and is succeeded by the Catholic William Glynn, (see Chapter 10).
1556.	Vice-President. Chaplain and librarian to the University.

1557.	Resignation of William Glynn. Thomas Pecocke elected President, (see Chapter 11).
1557-9.	Opposes Pecocke's choices of candidates for fellowships at Queens'.
1558.	Accession of Elizabeth I.
1559.	Pecocke resigns as President. William Mey is restored in his place, (see Chapter 9).
1560.	Archdeacon of York. Death of William Mey. Elected President of Queens'. (Date unknown: rector of Mexborough, Yorkshire).
1564.	Prebendary of Beckingham at Southwell Minster, Nottinghamshire. D.D. . Visit of Queen Elizabeth 1 to the University and colleges.
1565-66.	Vice-Chancellor of the University.
1567.	Appointed to examine a dispute involving the 'Lady Margaret Preacher', William Hughes B.D. .
1568.	Dies, aged about 45. Buried in the original Queens' chapel.

Served in various College offices. Archdeacon of York. President in 1564 during the visit of Elizabeth I to Queens'. Buried in the original College chapel.

John Stokes came to Queens in 1538 as a 'bible-clerk', aged about 15, graduating B.A. in 1541.[1] He proceeded to M.A. in 1544 and, in the same year, he was ordained and elected to a fellowship. He went on to fill several College offices: junior bursar in 1548, senior bursar in 1549 and Dean in 1551.[1,2] He had proceeded B.D. in 1549.

Unlike some of his predecessors as President, Stokes must have conformed to the changes in religious requirements, as he retained his fellowship during the reigns of Edward VI, Mary I and Elizabeth I, becoming chaplain of the University during the regime of Mary I and gaining preferment under Elizabeth I. However, as Vice-President during Pecocke's Presidency, he led the opposition to the President's attemps to fill fellowships with Catholic candidates, (see Chapter 11).

Soon after Elizabeth I's accession in 1558, when the Catholic Pecocke was still President of Queens', Sir William Cecil, the University Chancellor, prepared a list of those deserving of patronage entitled:

'Spiritual Men without Promotion at the present'.[1] This included William Mey, who was soon to be restored as President, as well as: 'Stokes, Col. Regin.'. In January 1560 he was appointed Archdeacon of York[1] and, in August of the same year, he was elected President of Queens', following Mey's death.

In 1563, Stokes was one of the signatories of a letter to the Chancellor, Sir Willian Cecil, soliciting a change in the method of electing the Vice-Chancellor, namely that the heads of colleges should nominate two candidates, one of whom would then be selected by the 'regents' (ie senior members of the University), rather than by the then current system of an election involving the whole University:[1]

'That honorable place wherin God hath set youe, and the greate pleasure which ye have alredy shewed to our universitie dothe bolden us for the quietnes & comoditie of the same, presently to crave your honors helpe. Forasmuch as there hath of late manifestlye appeared not only ambition in seekinge the vicechancelorship and a known and confessed faction about it, but also utter contention & displeasure risinge of importune and untimely laboringe (which things in such a place sore blemishe the gospel & the preachers thereof) we felinge theise & sundrie other incommodities in our severall Colledges, with grief are constrained to seke remedie for the same, and therefore most humbly beseche youre honor to procure by the Quenes Majestses bill assigned, that yearly from henceforthe, thre dayes afore the election, towe auncient & fitt men (two ancient and fit men) being named by the heads of Colledges the Regents shall chose the one of them...experience doth persuade us that this remedie obtained, will worke throughout the whole universitie muche quietnes, love & concord...bridle the untamed affections of younge Regents... and cause that more skilfull and auncient vicechauncelors maye be chosen herafter...and we shall not only (as we have great cause the Lord knoweth) most hartely praye for your honors preservacion, but also be redie to do youe what service we maye to our lyves end From Cambridge this 17th of Januarie, 1563.

Your honors most bounden and humble orators...John Stokes...' .[3]

1564 was an eventful year for Stokes, who became a prebendary of Beckingham at Southwell Minster, Nottinghamshire, obtained the D.D. degree and was appointed to take part in the public religious disputations scheduled for Queen Elizabeth's visit to the University in August.[1] This is described in detail by Cooper's 'Annals of Cambridge' Volume II, published in 1843:

'On the 15th of July, Edmund Grindal, Bishop of London, wrote to the Vicechancellor and Masters of Colleges, signifying that he had understood from Sir William Cecil that the Queen's Majesty intended in her progress to see Cambridge...he therefore advertised them to put themselves in all readiness to pleasure her Majesty, and to welcome her with all manner of scholastical exercises, viz with sermons both in English and Latin, disputations in all kind of faculties, and playing of comedies and tragedies; orations, and verses, both in Latin and Greek, to be made and set up of all students in the way that her Majesty should go or ride... Upon Friday the 4th August, Sir William Cecyl, having a sore leg, came with his lady, in a coach, about three a clocke in the afternoone, and tooke up his lodging at the Master's chambers of St John's College: where he was received with an oration. And when he had reposed himself awhile he sent for the Vicechancelor and all Heads...And there with them (after he had taken every one by the hand, and enquired their names and functions) he at large discoursed of all things, touching his former instructions. And added that order should be diligently kept of all sorts, and that uniformity should be shown in apparel and religion, especially in setting of the communion table. And so, for that time, he dismissed the whole company; willing and commanding the bedells, to wait upon the Vicechancellor homeward, for the bedells would have remained with the same Sir William, being High Chancellor...The 5 August, being Saturday, about eight a clock, the said Sir William Cecyl sent for the Vicechancellor, and all the Heads, and shewed them, that the Lord Robert, High Steward of that University

(Robert Dudley, Earl of Leicester) had sent him word that he would come that morning to the University...And there, (at King's College) after he had saluted Sir William Cecyl, he first did peruse the Queen's lodging, and after the church, and the way that the Queen should come to the same. And so both taking their horses, they ridd unto his lodgings at Trinity College...where the Master at the gate received his Honour with an oration. And so brought him, through the whole company, being in number 201 persons, unto the hall...And the University gave unto his Honor two pair of gloves, a march-pain, (a forerunner of marzipan), and two sugar-loaves...And that done, they did take full order for the receiving and entertaining of the Queen's Majesty; and so departed, requiring the Vicechancellor to dinner...At two a clock all the whole University, at the ringing of the University bell, assembled at King's College...First, at the corner at the Queen's College and Martin Gill's house, was set a great falling-gate, with a lock and staple. From that place, unto the King's College Church west door, stoode, upon both sides, one by one, all the University. From the gate stood the Scholars; then the Batchellors of Arts, then the Batchellors of Law, then the Master Regents; then the Non-regents and Batchellors of Divinity, Then, at last, the Doctors in their degree; and every one in habits and hoods. The last Doctor and the Vicechancellor stood upon the lowest greese of the west doore. And by him the three Bedells. The whole lane, between the King's College and the Queen's College, was strawed with rushes, and flags hanging in divers places, with coverlets, and boughs; and many verses fixed upon the wall...All the Scholars had in commandment, at the Queens Majesties passing by them, to cry out "Vivat Regina", lowly kneeling. And, after that, quietly and orderly to depart home to their colleges...The King's College Church was hanged with fine tapestry, or arras of the Queen's, from the north vestry dore, round by the communion-table, unto the south vestry dore; and all that place strawed with rushes... Also a fair closet glazed towards the quire, was devised and made in the middle of the rood loft; if the Queens' Majestie perhaps there would repose herself; which was not occupied...The bells both of the Colleges and also of the Towne were rung most part of the afternoon And such churches was were negligent herein, were afterwards called upon, and were fined...All these things being in this wise ordered, the Queens Majestie came from Mr. Worthington's house at Haslingfield, where she lay all night, by Granchester. And, by the way, the Dukes Grace of Norfolk, the Earl of Sussex, the Bishop of Ely, and divers other honorable personages, met with her Majestie, and so conveyed her toward the town...The house at Haslingfield in which the Queen lodged, is described by Bishop Robynson as a sufficiently magnificent structure, erected by Dr Thomas Wendt, Physician to the Queen, and as being then occupied by Mr Worlington or Worthington one of the gentlemen pensioners, who possesed it in right of his wife....The Queen arrived in Cambridge about 5 o'clock in the afternoon, having been attended throughout her progress from Haslingfield by a vast concourse of persons, who rent the air with acclamations of "Long live the Queen".

Sir William Cecyl all this while sat upon his horse at the gate beyond the Queen's College, and caused certain of the guard to keep the streete, with strict commandment as was given before... Then came the Trumpetters and by solemn blast, declared her Majestie to approach. Then followed the Lords in their order and degree. Her almoner, the Bishop of Rochester bareheaded, with the Bishop of Ely. Then Garter King at Arms, in his royal cote; with divers Serjeants at Arms. Then the Lord Hunsdon with the sword, in a royal scabbard of goldsmith's work. And after him, the Queens Majestie, (with a great companie of ladies and maids of honor) who, at the entering at Queen's College, was informed, by Mr. Secretary, of the Scholars, of what sort they were. And the like he did of all other companies and degrees...She was dressed in a gown of black velvet pinked, a call upon her head, set with pearls and precious stones; a hat that was spangled with gold, and a bunch of feathers...When the Queens Majestie came to the west door of the church, Sir William Cecyl kneeled downe and welcomed her Grace, shewing unto her the order of the doctors. And the Bedells, kneeling, kissed their staves, and so delivered them to Mr. Secretary; who likewise kissed the same, and so delivered them to the Queens hands, who could not well hold them all And her Grace gently and merrily redelivered them, willing him and other magistrates of the University, to minister justice uprightly, as she trusted they did Or she would take them into her own hands, and see to it. Adding, that, although the Chancellor did hault (for his leg was sore, as is before-mentioned), yet she trusted that Justice did not hault...Then Mr William Master of the Kings College, orator, making his three curtesies, kneeled downe upon the first greese or step of the west door...and made his oration, of length almost half an hour...When he had done, she much commended him...Then she alighted from her horse, and asking of what degree every Doctor was offered her hand to be kissed. And four of the principal Doctors bearing a canopy, she under the same, entred into the church...'. After the ceremonies: 'the Queens Majestie came forthe of her traverse, and went towards the lodging by a privy way...And as she went, she thanked God that had sent her to this University...' .[3] (Cooper's account draws on several sources including a Latin narrative by Nicholas Robynson, Bishop of Bangor and a fellow of Queens' during 1548-63).[2,4]

At the service in King's College chapel the following day, the sermon was preached, in Latin, by Andrew Perne D.D., formerly a fellow of Queens' and now Master of Peterhouse. He took as his text Romans, Chapter 13 verse 1 ('Let every soul be subject unto the higher powers. For there is no power but of God: the powers that be are ordained of God'). Gray, in his history of Queens' published in 1898, comments:

'And who could more fully enforce the duty of obedience to princes than the tolerant divine who had steadily obeyed Henry VIII, Edward VI and Queen Mary, no less than her present Majesty: He attacked the Anabaptists, denounced the arrogance of the Pope, commended Henry VI and Henry VII for their benefactions to the University...His object was to stimulate Elizabeth to do the like,"privily moving and stoutly exhorting her Highness to the lyke, by their example" '.[3,4]

Cooper's description continues:

'....Mr. Andrew Perne, D.D. ready in his Doctors cope, was by the Bedells, brought to the pulpit...The Preacher, after he had done his duty, in craving leave by his three curtseys, and so kneeling, stood up, and began his matter...About the midst of his sermon, her Majesty sent the Lord Hunsdon to will him to put on his cap which he did unto the end. At which time...she sent him word, that it was the first sermon that ever she heard in Latin, and she thought, she should never hear a better...'.[3] In the evening, the Queen attended a performance of Plautus' "Aulularia" in King's College Chapel.[4] (The comedies of Plautus, c254-184 BC, are the earliest Latin literary works to have survived, although the ending of "Aulularia" is missing. The play's themes include the stock figure of a miser, the lust of an old man for a young woman, and servants outwitting their superiors). The account continues:

'.... she departed back, by the same way, to the play "Aulularia Plauti" For the hearing and playing whereof, was made...in the body of the Church, a great stage containing the breadth of the church from the one side to the other...Upon the south-wall was hanged a cloth of state...for her Majesty. In the rood-loft, another stage for ladies and gentlewomen to stand on...At last her Highness came, with certain Lords, Ladies, and Gentlewomen... And so took her seat, and heard the play fully'.[3]

On the following day, disputations in philosophy and medicine took place in Great St Mary's Church, where William Chaderton, a future President of Queens', was a disputant in philosophy.[4] Cooper describes the programme on Monday 7th August:[3]

'Against one a clock was provided in S. Maries Church, for disputations, a great and ample stage, from the wall of the Belfrey-head, unto the Chancell In the east end was made a spacious and high room for the Queens Majestie...When all things were ready, and after the ringing of the University bell, the Queen's Majestie came to the said place, with royal pomp. At whose entering all the Graduates kneeled, and cryed modestly, "Vivat Regina"...When the Respondent had ended his oration, four Masters of Arts (standing near her stage and looking westward) replied. (Cooper notes that these were: 'Thomas Cartwright fellow of Trinity College, William Chaderton fellow of Christ's College, afterwards Bishop of Lincoln, Thomas Preston and Bartholomew Clarke fellows of King's College'). With whome her Majestie was so much pleased, that she by divers gestures declared the same; and sundry times stayed the Proctors from taking them up…'. Both the Monday and Tuesday were taken up with lectures, disputations and plays, while, on the morning of Wednesday the 9th August, the Queen visited the colleges, before the disputations in divinity in the afternoon. However, her visit to Queens' was brief, cut short due to lack of time:

'From thence her majestie came home by the Queens' College, and S. Katherine's Hall, only perusing the houses because it was almost one a clock', so that the oration at Queens', prepared by Robert Some B.A., a fellow, was not delivered.[3,4] Later in the day:

'At three of the Clock the University bell rang to the disputations in divinity, unto which her Majestie came, as before'.[3] These involved Stokes, who had been appointed to oppose the statement:

'Civilis magistratus habet authoritatem in rebus ecclesiasticis' (The civil authorities have the authority in ecclesiastical matters).[1] The Queens' last full day at Cambridge ended with another play, provided by the students of King's College.[3]

The Queen departed on Thursday, the 10th August, after various eminent men were made Masters of Arts. These included Robert Dudley, Earl of Leicester, and Sir William Cecil:[5]

During the Queen's visit, Queens' College was host to several of her entourage: 'the cofferer, the Masters and other officers of the Household',[4] while an inventory of the colleges, which had been presented to the Queen, showed that Queens' consisted of:

'The President or Master, Fifteen Fellows, of whom two were Bachellors in Divinity, Six were Masters of Arts, and seven were Bachellors of Arts, Six Pensioners in fellows commons, of whom one was Bachellor in Divinity, and two were Masters of Arts, Twenty-three Scholars and Bible Clerks, of whom four were Bachellors of Arts, Fourteen Pensioners in scholars commons, Six Sizars or Poor Scholars'.[3]

In 1565-66 Stokes was Vice-Chancellor of the University and, in 1567, he was appointed, together with the then Vice-Chancellor,

(Richard Longworth), Dr Whitgift (Lady Margaret's Professor of Divinity) and others, to examine a dispute involving William Hughes, B.D., the 'Lady Margaret's Preacher' of the University and a former member of Queens'. He had offended the people of Leicester by certain doctrines that he had preached there, in particular his views on the: 'descent into hell'.[4] However, the matter appears to have remained unresolved and Sir William Cecil, (the University's Chancellor), and Archbishop Parker, forbade further discussion of the issues raised.[1,4] (Hughes would become Bishop of St Asaph in 1573).[1]

Stokes died in April 1568, probably aged about 45,[1] and was buried in the original College chapel. After the reconstruction of the chapel in 1773-75, some of the displaced monuments, attached to slabs of stone, were moved into the ante-chapel and, in 1925, the four which remained were moved again to their current location. Stokes' monument is one of these four, and can now be seen attached to the wall of the ante-chapel of the new chapel. A rectangular border, formed by an inscribed brass strip, is attached to the gravestone and, while the original effigy is missing, an inscribed brass plate remains. This reads, (translated from the Latin by Dr David Butterfield, fellow of Queens'):

'Your body is buried under this sad tomb, venerable man,
and it is due to be happy food for hungry worms.
But your soul Christ took up to heaven, and
we have faith that it takes its place on the right hand of the father.
For your deeds were proof of living faith,
And are hereafter to be celebrated every day.
Pour forth prayers, so that Christ may always and for ever
Provoke others to follow this man's outstanding deeds'.

The translation of the inscription on the border reads:

'John Stokes, Professor of Sacred Theology and Master of this College, died on 29 April in the year of the Lord 1568, who founded four studentships in this College and left sixpence every week from his tenements and lands in Oakley, which he gave to the College near his death to the value of £9 13s 4d and bestowed many outstanding acts of kindness upon the College'.[1,6]

References

1. Searle, W.G. The History of the Queens' College of St Margaret and St Bernard in the University of Cambridge. Part II 1560-1662. Sold by Deighton, Bell & Co; Macmillan & Co. London. 1871. pp 297-300.
2. Cooper. C.H. Athenae Cantabrigienses. Volume 1. Cambridge. Deighton, Bell & Co.; and Macmillan & Co. London: Bell & Daldy, Fleet Street. 1858. p 252.
3. Cooper, C.H. Annals of Cambridge. Volume II. Warwick and Co., Cambridge. 1843. pp 179-207.
4. Gray, J.H. The Queens' College of St Margaret and St Bernard. F.E.Robinson. London. 1898. pp 107-09.
5. Fuller, T. The History of the University of Cambridge from the Conquest to the year 1634. Deighton, J. & J.J., Stevenson, T. London. Reprinted 1840. (Original edition 1655). p 263.
6. Monumental Brasses. Queens' College Cambridge. Online. 2020.

CHAPTER 13

William Chaderton (Chadderton, Chaterton, Chatterton). President 1568-79.

Summary.

William Chaderton, an ambitious priest, was born in Manchester. He was educated at Cambridge and became a fellow of Christ's College in 1561. He was a disputant in philosophy during the visit of Elizabeth I to Cambridge in 1564. He was elected Lady Margaret's Professor of Divinity in 1567 and President of Queens' in 1568. After proceeding D.D., he was appointed Regius Professor of Divinity in 1569. His remaining time in Cambridge, as a significant University administrator, was marked by his involvement in various religious and personal disputes, within the University and at Queens'. Chaderton supported the moderate Anglicans against an active Puritan movement in the University.

He was appointed Bishop of Chester in 1579 and, during his tenure, he opposed the: 'dangerous infection of popery' in the north of England.

In 1595, his labours were rewarded by futher promotion to the richer See of Lincoln, but this still required his efforts to confront Catholicism. He preached before James I on the latter's progess to London, following his accession in 1603. In his final years he lived in Holywell, Cambridgeshire, and died in 1608. He is buried in Southoe parish church, Cambridgeshire.

He had married soon after his election as President and his granddaughter, Elizabeth Jocelin, is remembered for writing a book of advice to her unborn child, before dying soon after the birth.

While in his public life he was concerned with preaching and opposing Catholicism, he was devoted to his family and to music. His eight-volume copy of the remarkable 'Polyglot Bible' can be seen in the Queens' Old Library.

Timeline.

c1537.	Born at Nuthurst, near Manchester.
1553.	Accession of Mary I. Entered Magdalene College, Cambridge.
1555.	Matriculated at Pembroke College, Cambridge.
1558.	Death of Mary I. Accession of Elizabeth I. B.A. .
1559.	Ordained.
1560.	Death of William Mey, President of Queens'; John Stokes is elected in his stead.
1561.	M.A. . Fellow of Christ's College.
1564.	Visit of Elizabeth I to the University, when Chaderton is a disputant in philosophy.
1566.	B.D. .
1567.	Lady Margaret's Professor of Divinity.
1568.	D.D. . Elected President of Queens' after the death of Stokes. He soon marries Katherine, daughter of John Revell of London. Chaplain to Robert Dudley, Earl of Leicester. Archdeacon of York.
1569.	Regius Professor of Divinity. Resigns as Lady Margaret's Professor, to be succeeded by a controversial troublemaker, Thomas Cartwright.
1570.	Rector of Holywell, (in Huntingdonshire until 1972, now in Cambridgeshire). Purchases a nearby estate.
1574.	Prebendary of Fenton, at York Minster. Resigns the archdeaconry of York. Canon of Westminster.
1577.	Death of Sir Thomas Smith, (see Chapter 8).
1579.	Appointed Bishop of Chester and resigns as President of Queens' and as Regius Professor of Divinity. Warden of the Collegiate Church of Manchester. Rector of Bangor.
c1581.	Moves residence to Manchester.
1595.	Bishop of Lincoln.

1603. Death of Elizabeth I. Preaches before James I at Burghley House, on the King's progress from Scotland after his accession.

1608. Dies suddenly at Southoe, Cambridgeshire. Buried in Southoe parish church.

Ambitious priest. Lady Margaret's Professor of Divinity and, subsequently, Regius Professor of Divinity. Supported moderate Anglicans against Puritan Protestants. Elected President in 1568, but resigned in 1579 to become Bishop of Chester, where he opposed northern Catholic practices. Bishop of Lincoln from 1595 until his death in 1608. Preached before King James I. A devoted family man.

William Chaderton (generally spelt with one 'd') was born in about 1537 at Nuthurst, a district of Moston, near Manchester, the second of three children of Edmund Chaderton and his wife, Margaret Cliffe of Cheshire.[1,2,] His family could trace their forebears to Geoffrey de Trafford, who had received the manor of Chadderton, (spelt with two 'd's, now a town in Greater Manchester), in about 1200.[1] Chaderton attended Manchester Grammar School, proceeding, initially, to Magdalene College, Cambridge, before transferring to Pembroke College where he matriculated in 1555.[1,2] He proceeded B.A. in 1558 and M.A. in 1561, when he was elected a fellow of Christ's College. He was ordained in 1559.[2]

He achieved local prominence in 1564 during Elizabeth I's visit to the University, when he was appointed to take part in the public disputations in philosophy in Great St Mary's Church on 7th August: 'to her great satisfaction'.[1] These also involved Thomas Byng, fellow of Peterhouse, putting the propositions: 'Monarchia est optimus status reipublicae' (Monarchy is the best form of government) and: 'Frequens legum mutatio est periculosa' (Frequent changes in the law are dangerous),[3] (see Chapter 12). The other disputants included Thomas Cartwright, who would become notorious in the University.[3] It has been suggested that it may have been on this occasion that Chaderton made himself known to Sir William Cecil, the University's Chancellor, as well as to the Earl of Leicester, High Steward of the University, whose chaplain he was to become.[1]

Searle, in his history of the College published in 1871, quotes a politically incorrect anecdote, relating to Chaderton's early years in Cambridge:

'This Dr William Chaterton, (sic) now Bishop of Lincoln, and before of Chester, I may remember in Cambridge a learned and grave Doctor; though for his gravity he could lay it aside when it pleased him, even in the Pulpit. It will not be forgotten in Cambridge while he is remember'd, how preaching one day in his younger yeeres, a wedding Sermon, (which indeed should be festivall)...Mr Chatterton is reported to have made this pretty comparison, and to have given this friendly caveat: That the choice of a wife is full of hazzard, not unlike as if one in a barrell full of Serpents should grope for one Fish; if (saith he) he "scape harm of the snakes, and light on a fish, he may be thought fortunate, yet let him not boast, for perhaps it may be but an Eele, &c." Howbeit he married afterwards himself, and I doubt not sped better that his comparison'.[3]

In 1566 he proceeded B.D. and, in 1567, his career was significantly advanced by his appointment as the Lady Margaret's Professor of Divinity. The following year, 1568, with the support of Cecil, he was elected President of Queens' after the death of John Stokes,[1] and duly wrote thanking Cecil in a letter in Latin, signing off as:

'Tui honoris et valetudinis studiossimus (Devoted to your honor and health) Guielmus Chadertonus'.[1] In addition to succeeding Stokes as President, Chaderton also replaced him as Archdeacon of York. He proceeded D.D. in 1568. Soon after his election as President, when he was chaplain to the Earl of Leicester, he wrote to his patron notifying his intention to marry and asking for consent.[3] This was duly given in a reply from the Earl to:

'my loving chaplain Mr. Chaterton' from: 'your loving friend and master',[2] while Searle quotes an early comment on its contents:

'In which letter I must own the earl's gravity diverts me...He writes like a saint and as for women (if we did not know his true character better) one would think he would hardly touch them'.[3] Chaderton duly married Katherine, daughter of John Revell of London.

A further advancement came in 1569, when the heads of the colleges wrote to Sir William Cecil recommending that Chaderton succeed Dr Whitgift as Regius Professor of Divinity:

'as one most fit in their Judgements to succeed in his Place'.[3] He was duly elected, having resigned from the Lady Margaret's professorship, and held the office until he left Cambridge as Bishop of Chester. (Whitgift became Archbishop of Canterbury in 1583).

During Chaderton's remaining decade in Cambridge, he took a leading part in University affairs. For example, in 1569, he became involved in a dispute involving the town, when he was sent by the Vice-Chancellor and heads of houses to the Chancellor, Cecil, to ask him to persuade the Duke of Norfolk, (the High Steward of Cambridge), to withdraw his patronage from the town's corporation.[1] Also, various religious controversies would require his time and patience during his Presidency, in particular involving Thomas Cartwright.

Cartwright had succeeded Chaderton as Lady Margaret's Professor of Divinity and soon began to use this position to express challenging 'Puritan' views. Those in sympathy with this movement would show their dissatisfaction with current practices by such means as refusing to wear a surplice and cap and walking out of college chapels when the service was begun in Latin. Cartwright, in his lectures on the Acts of the Apostles, bitterly attacked the existing Church government[1] and, in 1570, Chaderton wrote to Cecil with his concerns:

'True it is such seditions, contention, and disquietude, such errors and schismes openlie taught and preached, boldlie and without warant, are latelie growne amongst us, that the good estate, quietnes, and governance of Cambridge, and not of Cambridge alone but of the whole church and realme, are for great hazarde unles severlie by authorities they be punished...

(Cartwright, who) alwaies stubburnlie refused the cappe and such like ornaments, dothe now for his daylie lectors teache such doctrine as is pernitious and not tollerable for a Christian commonwealth'.[4] Cartwright was duly suspended and then deprived of his professorship. Initially, Chaderton delivered the Lady Margaret's lectures in Cartwright's place.[1] One of Cartwright's supporters, Edward Dering, wrote to Cecil in 1570 describing the heads of houses who were opposed to Cartwright's teaching as: 'enemies of God's gospel, or faint professors, or secretly papists,' and saying of Chaderton (and of Dr Mey of St Catharine's College):

'ther is smalle Constancie ether in ther Life or in ther Religion'.[3] (Dering, 1540-76, a priest and academic, was a fellow of Christ's College).

In 1572, Chaderton was one of those heads of houses who, with the Vice-Chancellor, expelled William Clark, a fellow of Peterhouse, from the University, and admonished John Browning, a fellow of Trinity, for preaching against the established Church of England.[3] Also, Chaderton was involved in several other skirmishes in support of the moderate Anglicans against the Puritans.[1] For example, in 1569, Chaderton, with other heads of houses, lobbied Cecil recommending a Dr Kelk as Master of St John's College in preference to a Dr Fulke, who was supported by the Puritans.

In 1570, Chaderton became rector of Holywell, Cambridgeshire, and bought a nearby estate associated with a property known as Moyne's Hall, which, while now modernised, can still be seen.[2] He was rector until 1579, while the estate was subsequently bequeathed to his family.

In 1572, Chaderton wrote to Cecil, (who had been created Lord Burghley in 1571), requesting the Deanery of Winchester, to relieve him from: 'the wearisome duty of lecturing',[2] but without success. (Perhaps surprisingly, in view of this comment, the younger members of the University seem to have had a positive view of Chaderton, as he is described as:

'...beloved among the schollers, and the rather for that he did not affect any soure and austere fashion, either in teaching or government, as some use to doe; but well tempered both with courage and courtesie'.[3] However, there may have been less attractive aspects of his personality, as, in 1572, he expressed views which were considered to be a discreditable attempt to attack the reputation of the Bishop of Ely, in the hope of providing ammunition for his deprivation, so that Chaderton could succeed him. This involved Chaderton preaching a sermon at St Paul's Cross, against a sect that had recently established itself near Cambridge, which he declared was: 'a mighty deformity'.[3] This was a thinly veiled criticism of Richard Cox, Bishop of Ely, for not enforcing religious conformity,[1] and Searle quotes the opinion that the sermon was given to:

'expose the Bishop of Ely, who now lay under a Cloud at Court, in consequence of his steady refusal to give up part of the revenues of the see to certain favourites of the queen. For Chaderton indeed had hoped, as was thought, that the bishop for his firm denial would be deprived and that he himself would succeed him...And yet so did the Archbishop (of Canterbury) write to his Brother of York viz. "that he had searched out this Report...and had found these News to be enviously uttered: and that Chaterton talked his Pleasure of the Bishoprick of Ely, which he looked to enjoy"...'.[3] (St Paul's Cross was an open air pulpit in the grounds of Old St Paul's Cathedral).

In 1577, an important event in the history of Queens' occurred, with the death of Sir Thomas Smith, a former fellow and, subsequently, a leading statesman as Secretary of State and Ambassador to France. One of Sir Thomas' last services to the University was the introduction of the Act of 1576:

'for the Maintenance of the Colleges in the Universities, and of Winchester and Eaton', requiring one third of all college rents to be paid in wheat or malt, which increased the revenues of the colleges.[3,4] His bequest to Queens' included his Greek and Latin books, 65 of which remain in the Old Library. Many contain, in the margins, a mixture of annotations, portraits, sketches and translations in his own hand. He also bequethed his own hand-made celestial globe to Queens', which can be seen in the College's Old Library.[3] There is a record of Smith visiting the College in 1571, when he had:

'a marchpane (an early version of marzipan) and a pottle of Ippocras (spiced wine)'.[4] In 1573 he had given the College a rent charge of £12. 7s. 4d. to found two readerships, in arithmetic and geometry, (each to provide a daily lecture), and two scholarships. Three text books were specified for the use of the readers and it was ordered that:

'The which two lectures are not to be redd of the reader as of a preacher out of a pulpit, but "per radium et eruditum pulverem", as it is said, that is with a penn on paper ot tables, or a sticke or compasse in sand or duste to make demonstracon, that his schollers maie both understand the reader and also do it themselves and so profit'.[3,4] The scholars were ordered not to proceed to B.A.:

'befor that they be well expert in the parts of Arithmatique, addition, subtraction, multiplication, division, and extraction of roots as well of whole numbers as of fractions bie the judgment of the reader of arithmetique upon the said readers oth', nor to M.A.:

'before he hath redd and do understand the first six bokes of Euclide, bie the judgement of the reader of geometrie, upon the saide reader of geometrie his oth'.[3] Also, there was a balance of £1 which was:

'to be emploied at one or two daies in the year to amende the cheare of the fellows and scholars in such one daie or two as it shall please them at the assignation of the president or his viceregent to hear and see the exercise of the said Artes and how the schollers have profited therein, or otherwise at the said Mr. and felloes pleasure'.[3,4] Sir Thomas would have been gratified to know that an annual 'Sir Thomas Smith Feast' would become, and continues to be, a premier social event in the Queens' calendar.

In 1576, Chaderton faced a dilemma when the Queen wrote to the College asking them to elect a Thomas Hughes as a fellow, to fill a recent vacancy. But as Sir Thomas Smith was proposing his nephew Clement Smith, the College hesitated to comply, which resulted, a few months later, in a letter from Lord Burghley urging that the College act on the Queen's wishes. Luckily, three other vacancies soon occurred and both candidates were admitted later that year.[3]

As President, Chaderton required a good deal of patience to keep the peace at Queens', which was disrupted by several unruly fellows. Apart from Robert Some, who preached a violent sermon at Great St Mary's attacking, as did Cartwright, the government of the Church, there were three others: Ralph Jones, William Middleton and Edmund Rockrey, whose behavior led them to be deprived of their fellowships. However, each of the miscreants was subsequently restored to his fellowship by the Chancellor, Lord Burghley, no doubt causing the President a good deal of frustration.

Jones was twice admonished by Chaderton for: 'sowing discord and quarrelling', before being expelled for financial irregularities as bursar.[3,4] But the Chancellor restored him on payment of the disputed money and on condition that he would: 'quietly to behave himself in the College hereafter'.[4]

William Middleton was elected a fellow in 1572 and, according to the College Statutes, was required to proceed to M.A. in 1574. But, for unknown reasons, the President and a majority of the fellows refused him the College 'grace', (a formal proposal to the Regent House), to proceed to the degree. To avoid losing his fellowship he used admirable initiative and went to Oxford to take the degree but, at a meeting in the chapel on the 8th July 1575, the President and most of the fellows, having sent Middleton out, decided that this would not fulfil the Statutes and removed him from his fellowship. However, he was supported by Some, Jones and Rockrey, as well as by Henry Goad and Andrew Arnold, who all wrote to Lord Burghley:

'...Mr. Mideltones grace to proceade master of arte was propounded accordinge to ordre amonge the master and fellows, he havinge done and perfourmed all his actes in the schooles...but that was denied him by the master and moste parte of the fellows, and he finallie staied without anie cause alleadged againste him'.[3] The Chancellor must have agreed with a contemporary source that:

'...the bishop of Chester, then being master of that colledge, stood very peremptorilye upon the like exemption and pretence of breache of oathe',[3] as Middleton was restored to his fellowship, although not to his seniority:

'At the instance of the righte honorable Sr. Wm. Cecill, Lord Burgheley, and Chauncellor of this Unyversytie, the said Wm. Mydleton, upon his humble submyssyon & promes to lyve orderlie and quietlie hereafter, was shortlie after Mychelmas "eodem anno predicto" (1575), chosen agayne fellow and so became a junyor and lost both his allowance and senioritie'.[3,4] (However, Middleton must have been a difficult colleague, as, ten years later, he was brought before the next President:

'Anno Domine 1585. Mr Middleton baccheler of Divinitie fellow of the house was admonished by the master...for cumminge with fowr of the fellows to geve the master ane admonitione for gevinge and bestowing a chamber upon one of the fellows... thereby sowinge and raysinge contentione both between master and fellows and fellow and fellowe and slander to the house...and was charged to surcease frome such disorderly and contentious practises and dealinge, upon the peril furder to ensewe, upon the atatute de seminandis discoriis. Umphry Tyndall Testibus John Jegon Willm Laurence'.[3,4]

Perhaps the most disruptive of the four fellows was Rockrey, who had been elected a fellow in 1561 and was a supporter of Cartwright. In November 1570, Chaderton convened a meeting of the College as had been ordered by the Vice-Chancellor, Dr Whitgift, and warned the fellows not to speak against the new University Statutes of 1570. But Searle tells us that:

'Rockrey boldly denounced them, as impairing the liberty and privilages of the university, asserting that some of them were directly against God's word, and remarked that godly princes might be deceived by hypocrites and flatterers, as David was by Ziba...he was on the same day bound over...that he should "personallye apeare ffrom tyme to tyme wthin this towne before the vicechaunc. or his deputie, untyll such matter be determined and ended, as is and shalbe laied against hym by Mr Dr Chaderton"...the following day, 27 Nov., he appeared before Dr Whitgift the vice-chancellor, Dr Chaderton and other heads, when certain articles were objected to him, to which the vice-chancellor required a faithful answer. Rockrey refused to reply... The following day Robert Some, M.A. fellow of Queens', entered into a surety...that Rockrey "should remayne, contynew and quietly kepe his chamber, as a trew prisoner, onles he were called fourth by the vicech. or his deputie, untyll such matter were ended, which is objected against hym"...'.[3] But Rockrey had his supporters and, in January 1571, Lady Elizabeth Hoby, the widow of Sir Thomas Hoby and a sister-in-law of Lord Burghley, wrote to the Chancellor from her residence, Bisham Abbey, Berkshire:

'...I understand that one Edmond Rockery of Cambridge is in truble for certaine words spoken by him...at my ernest request to be good unto him...And therefore assuring myself that if yow knew him so well as I do (he had lived in her house as tutor to her children)...yow woold altogether alter your opinion of him...'.[3] But when, in February, he was ordered to: 'revoke his rashness' he refused and:

'Mr Edmunde Rockrey was pronounced non-socius, beinge expelled out of the colledge and university for his grete disobedience, disorder and contumacy, as well by the authority of the Quene's Mat^ies^ counsel, as also by the sentence of the Lorde Burgheley chancellor of the universytie and the residue of M^rs^ of Colleges then there present. Hiis testibus W. Chaderton p^r^sidens collegii...'.[3,4] Nevertheless, once again, the Chancellor showed his usual tolerance and, in July 1571, Rockrey was restored to his fellowship, although he was never to be given any important College appointment. But any confidence that the Chancellor had in him was misplaced, as he continued to be a thorn in the flesh of Chaderton, Queens' and the University; he signed a protest against the Statutes, refused to wear clerical and academic dress and did not take Communion. In January 1575, Chaderton wrote to Burghley:

'...There is one Mr Rockrey in our College whom your L moved me to receive again into the College. Since his return I could never by any advice or charge bring him to receive the Communion in the College once amongst us, neither yet to keep any order in apparel and ceremonies, whereby doth rise some inconvenience in our College, for reformation whereof I most humbly beseech your L to let me know your mind how I should deal with him, otherwise our laws and orders will fall into great contempt'.[3] Later in 1575, Chaderton discussed the situation with Lord Burghley at the latter's residence, Theobalds Palace, Herfordshire, (subsequently demolished), but, true to form, Burghley counselled delay for a year.[4]

After another letter from Chaderton at the end of this period, and more delay, it seems that Burghley decided to try to reduce further conflict by the time-honoured strategy of promoting troublemakers, and created Rockrey a prebendary of Rochester Cathedral in 1577. Although this would have relieved the tensions at Queens', Chaderton's problems with Rockrey were not over, as Rockrey refused to resign his fellowship for a further two years, although Chaderton considered that his fellowship was not tenable with his new preferment. Considerable correspondence ensued,[3] and a frustrated Chaderton wrote to Burghley in January 1579:

'only I beseech your L. to consider that if there should be any extraordinary toleration, first it will touch my oath...2dly I shall be in danger for not executing the statute upon the offender, 3dly I shall daily be molested to grant a continual absence, which will prejudice both learning and good manners...And lastly that liberty, which is already granted unto the seniors doth greatly hinder the preferment of young men'.[3] However, Rockrey did resign his fellowship later that year, although Chaderton had, by that time, taken up his appointment as Bishop of Chester.

Rockrey's future career went on to illustrate that any fundamental changes in personality are, generally, no more than minimal. At Rochester, in about 1584, his propensity for conflict must have surfaced again as he was suspended from: 'the ministerial function', for four years.[5] However:

'he is said to have been distinguished for his learning and abilities, and to have been an admired and popular preacher'.[4,5]

In 1575, the College enjoyed an heraldic visitation by Robert Cooke, Clarencieux (now Clarenceux) King-at-Arms, who made a grant of a crest to the College Arms:

'...at the request of William Chaderton now doctor of divinitie and President of the said Colledge and the fellows of the same Colledge, I have assigned, geven, and graunted unto these their saide armes the Creast or Cognoiscance hereafter following...The same to use, beare and shewe in all places honest according to the auncient lawe of armes at theire liberty and pleasure...Rob Cooke, Alias Clarencieulx (sic) Roy Darmes'.[3]

A story which would be of human interest in any age took place in 1576, when the minister of Trinity parish was imprisoned by the Vice-Chancellor and heads of houses for irregularly marrying a Mr Byron, a scholar at Queens', to a Miss Beaumont. This is described in a letter to the Chancellor from the Vice-Chancellor:

'...Ther hath fallen out of late here in Cambridge such an evill example so notoriously known, and so nearly touching the credit of the universitie...also did thinke it my part and duty therof to advertise your Lordship...The matter is touching a seacret contract and marriage betweene the soonn and heyer (heir) of Mr Jhon Byron of Nottinghamsheere and a daughter of Mr Beamounds of Leicestershere sojourninge with his family here in Cambridge... the younge Gentleman a great heyer, a schollar of Queenes Colledge, a pupil about the age of 19 yeres, committed to the charge of a Tutor in the same Colledge, the marriage without either consent or privity of the Gentleman's parents or tutor, the solemnizacion close and seacreat without banns or licence for the minister to marry theim, the younge gentleman sence conveyed into the country wherby I cannot take ordre for the restoringe of him to his Tutor, until his father's pleasure be knowen, beside the greatest inconvenience of all (if it fall out trew) of a precontract pretended sence the said marriage between the said scholler and another yonge gentlewoman of the town. This matter beinge in itself evill, in common report here very famouse, and in example in this place pernitious, beside the note of infamy herof like to redound to the whole university...'.[3,4] It seems that a Miss Beaumont and her relations were trying to secure a good prospect in the face of local competition! No doubt the affair would have come to the notice of the President.

When President, Chaderton was appointed a prebendary of York and a canon of Westminster in 1574, (resigning the archdeaconry of York), but he was out of favour in early 1579, as shown by a description of a letter from Lord Burghley to Chaderton, quoted by Searle:

'showing the queen's dislike of the clergies meddling with state affairs in their sermons; touching also the queens's readiness to hear what they had to say of that kind in private, and the perverse temper of some preachers: seemingly a rebuke for what he himself (ie Chaderton) had preached there'.[3]

Nevertheless, promotion as Bishop of Chester came in 1579, due to the influence of his patron the Earl of Leicester.[3] He resigned as Regius Professor in 1580, and was consecrated in St Gregory's Church, (built against the walls of St Paul's Cathedral, but destroyed in the fire of London in 1666), by the Archbishop of York and the Bishops of London and Rochester. In 1580 he was appointed rector of Bangor, and Warden of the Collegiate Church of Manchester, giving him extra income.[2] His time at Chester was occupied by opposition to Catholicism and, in 1580, he was appointed as an ecclesiastical commissioner in the north for discovering and convicting Catholic recusants, (ie those who were not conforming to the requirement to attend Anglican services).[3] His fellow commissioners included Henry Hastings, Earl of Huntingdon, who was Lord President of the North, the Archbishop of York, and the Earl of Derby.[1] Despite the resilience of Lancashire Catholicism, he was commended for his efforts but, in 1583, he was accused by a tenant, who he called: 'a malicious varlet', of holding back £3000 in fines levied by the ecclesiastical commission and was warned by Lord Burghley that:

'to avoid doubtful reports made of you in this matter, you shall do well to make answer speedily'.[2] However, the allegations were soon disproved, after Chaderton had produced his excellently-prepared accounts. He may (possibly) have been belatedly reassured as to likely support from his superiors, if needed, when he was informed that he had never been doubted![2]

In 1581 he moved his residence to the Collegiate Church in Manchester:

'He was a learned man, liberal and given to hospitality, and a more frequent preacher than other bishops of his time. He resided in Manchester, till the too frequent jarrings between his servants and the inhabitants of the town occasioned him to remove his habitation to Chester'.[1,3]

There were many Catholics in the north, and it was claimed that, of 8512 recusants in England, 2442 were in his diocese, and while:

'...his continual exertions to reduce them to conformity brought him much odium',[3] he was commended by the establishment for the care and pains he had taken to purge his diocese of the: 'dangerous infection of popery'.[1] He was strict in the matter of clerical dress and suspended some clergy for refusing to conform.[1]

Queen Elizabeth had become worried about the general trend, among even conforming Anglicans, of having regular meetings for prayer and examination of the Scriptures, as she believed that these could introduce potentially devisive new rites and practices. Therefore, in 1577, she had written to all bishops demanding their suppression. But it seems that, in 1581, the Archbishop of York, Edwin Sandys, considered that even Chaderton, the scourge of the northern Catholics, needed to be reminded of this:

'My lord, (ie Chaderton) yow are noted to yelde to muche to general fastings, all the daie preachinge and prayinge. Verilie a good exercise in time and upon just occasion, when yt cometh from good auctoritye. But, (when there is none occasion, nether the thing commanded by the prince or a synod) the wisest and best learned cannot like of yt, nether will her majestie permitt it...The devill is craftie; and the younge ministers of these oure times growe madd'.[3] But, in 1584, while the Puritans were in favour at Court, Chaderton was admonished by the Privy Council for the lack of religious exercises in his diocese![1]

In 1590, a visitation to the Chester diocese found that many ministers were reluctant to wear the surplice, and Chaderton gave them two months to conform. However, he wrote to the Archbishop requesting some tolerance of the nonconformists, but without success. Therefore, in 1591, Chaderton ordered each parish to provide two surplices and to certify every three months that they were used.[2] But, like many wearisome bureaucratic exercises in every age, this seems to have been quietly forgotten.

Several vignettes record other aspects of Chaderton's life before his next promotion to Lincoln in 1595: in 1586, Queen Elizabeth required him to provide three men, with £25 each, to buy a horse on the continent, as his quota for the 1000 needed to be sent to assist the United Netherlands against the King of Spain,[3] while, in 1593, he preached the funeral sermon of the Earl of Derby. (Chaderton had been close to the Earl and his son, Lord Strange, having lent money to the family and been a frequent guest of the fourth Earl, preaching to his household seven times during 1587-90).[2] Also, in 1591 we find the fIrst of two references to disruptions to the smooth running of his household:

'One Henry...servant to William Bishop of Chester, was found dead hanging on a tree beyond Blacon-head', and, in 1592:

'William Geaton, servant to the Lord Bishop of Chester, was arraigned at the Assizes, holded at the Castle the 27th of Aprill, for the murdering of Ja:Findlorve a seller of Scottish cloath, for which fact the said Geaton was condemned and hanged in chains upon Grapnell Heath, near the place where the deed was done'.[3]

In 1595, Chaderton was elected Bishop of the richer See of Lincoln and resigned the Wardenship of Manchester College. Later the same year, Archbishop Whitgift wrote to him asking him:

'to admonish the Preachers within his Diocese to exhort the Wealthier sort of their Parishioners to contribute more liberally towards the Relief of the Poor'.[3]

In 1603, Chaderton was a witness to a significant time in British history when, on the 24th April, at Burghley House, Stamford, Lincolnshire, he preached before James I, who was then on his progress to London to assume the throne following the death of Elizabeth I.[3] Chaderton prepared to meet James as he entered his diocese and dressed his servants:

'in tawny liveries, with facings of changeable taffeta yellow and red, being the colours now chiefly esteemed',[2] and asked his archdeacons and officers to accompany him with their servants in the same outfits. Later in 1603, as 'Visitor' of King's College, Cambridge, he was asked to resolve disputes in the College but, writing to Burghley, he reported that the: 'younger fractious sort' had not accepted his judgement, chanting: 'We appeal to the King', forcing him to leave fearing violence.[2] Ageing may have been responsible for his growing reputation for weakness and, in 1605, Sir Thomas Lake describes him as: 'aged and fearful...old and weak', because of his inability to properly discipline his clergy,[2] even though, in 1604, 93 ministers had appeared before Chaderton at his ecclesiastical court at Huntingdon. Chaderton told the King that he was waiting for a direct order from the Archbishop: 'which fearfulness the king much mislikes', and the King wanted firmer action.[2] But Chaderton, writing to Robert Cecil, Viscount Cranbourne, (soon to be Earl of Salisbury), in 1605, says that:

'I will by the grace of God use all the best means I can devise, by conference and brotherly exhortations, with mildness and discretion to win them'.[2] However, pressure from the King led to the eventual deprivation of eight of his incumbents and the suspension of nine curates.[2]

Chaderton continued his efforts against papist recusants and, during 1606-07, there are many records of those who had been accused of not attending their parish church and appearing before him at Buckden, Cambridgeshire, to take the oath of conformity.[1] At this stage of his career he is described as: 'a remote and somewhat inscrutable figure'.[2] He did not examine ordination candidates personally and rarely preached, but he was an active judge in his ecclesiastical court.

The bishops of Lincoln had a property at Buckden, but Chaderton did not live there because his income was not sufficient for its restoration, a situation due, so he claimed, to the terms of his predecessors' leases.[1,2,3] But he had bought an estate at nearby Southoe, Cambridgeshire, and:

'He lived in Holywell, "in good state", in his house called 'The Place', allowing the episcopal palace at Buckden to fall into ruin'.[1] The house may have belonged to him while he was President, as, in the College records for 1576, we find:

'Item to one for cariage of a letter to our master to Holliwell aboute the colledge busines'.[1] He made his will in March 1608: 'full of infirmity...believing assuredly' in his salvation.[2] His property was to pass to to: 'my loving and dear wife' Katherine, and then to his grandaughter, Elizabeth. Elizabeth also inherited a dowry, consisting of various plate, his set of viols, his lute, a bandora (a plucked stringed-instrument), recorders, and music books.[2] He died in 1608 and is buried in the chancel of St Leonard's, the parish church of Southoe. He has no monument and the engraved stone over his grave has been removed.[1]

As previously noted, he had married Katherine soon after his election as President. They had one daughter, Joan, who, in 1582, aged eight, was married to ten-year-old Richard Brooke, son of Thomas Brooke of Norton in Cheshire. (Richard would be subsequently knighted). The couple lived with Chaderton in Manchester and, in 1586, the marriage was formally confirmed after the couple's agreement,[2] although they were to separate after the birth of a daughter, Elizabeth, in 1595.[1] The courtier and author Sir John Harington (1561-1612), in mocking vein, writes:

'The Bishop was removed to Lincoln, where he now remains in very good state, having one onely daughter married to a Knight of good worship, though now they living assunder, he may be thought to have no great comfort of that matrimony, yet to her daughter he means to leave a great patrimony so as one might not unfitly apply that Epigram written of Pope Paulus and his daughter...

Thou hast a daughter, Paulus, I am told,
and for this daughter thou hast store of gold.
The daughter thou didst get, the gold didst gather
Make thee no holy, but a happy father...'.[1]

Chaderton willed that his only grandchild, Elizabeth, should receive a dowry of £2000 and all his lands after his widow's death.[2] After Elizabeth's parents separated, she and her mother returned to Chaderton's house, and the Bishop ensured that she was well educated.[5] In 1616, she married Tourell Jocelin of Cambridgeshire and, anticipating the risk of childbirth, she wrote 'The Mother's Legacy to her Unborn Child', which was first published in 1624 and had several subsequent editions. It includes religious advice as well as instructions to her husband and has been regarded as:

'one of the most significant works of the time because of the intimate view it gives of the mindset, beliefs and ideals of women of the time'.[6] She left advice for both a son and a daughter; but, for the latter, her views would probably disqualify her from being invited to address a modern university audience:

'I desire her bringing up may bee learning the Bible, as my sisters doe, good housewifery, writing, and good works: other learning a woman needs not; though I admire it in those whom God hath blest with discretion, yet I desired not much in my owne, having seene that sometimes women have greater portions of learning than wisdome, which is of no better use to them than a main saile to a flye-boat, which runs it under water...'.[6]

This book of advice was published with an: 'Approbation' by a Dr Thomas Goad, who informs us that Elizabeth was:

'from her tender years carefully nurtured, as in those accomplishments of knowledg in Languages, History, and some Arts, so principally in studies of Piety...In Cambridgeshire she was made a Mother of Daughter, whom shortly after, being Baptized and brought to her, she blessed, and gave God thanks that her self had lived to see it a Christian: and then instantly called for her winding sheet to be brought forth and laied upon her. So...she ended her Praiers, Speech, and Life together, rendring her Soul into the hand of her Redeemer...'.[3] She was buried in Oakington, as was her husband in 1656. Her daughter Theodora married a Samuel Fortrey and the baptism of two of their children is recorded:

'Travers Fortrey daughter of Samuell Fortrey esquire and of Theodory his wife baptized January ye 3^{d} 1650. Samuell Fortrey sonn of Samuell Fortrey esqe. And of Theodory his wife Baptized March ye 2^{d}. 1651'.[1,3] Another son, James, entered the service of James II and, after the Revolution of 1588, spent some time at Queens' as a fellow- commoner;[3] he died in 1719.

In 1589, Chaderton had presented to Queens' his copy, printed in 1569, of the 'Biblia Sacra Herbraice, Chaldaice, Graece, & Latine', also known as the 'Biblia Polyglotta' or 'Plantin

Polyglot Bible', printed in Antwerp by Christopher Plantin between 1568 and 1573. (Plantin wished to prove his loyalty to Philip II of Spain by producing a Bible in five languages- Hebrew, Greek, Latin, Classical Syriac and Aramaic- which Philip promised to finance. Each of 1,200 copies consisted of eight volumes: the first four contain the Old Testament, volume five the New Testament and volume six the complete Bible, while the last two volumes contain dictionaries). The volumes are still held in the Queens' Old Library.

Although Chaderton had no son, his nephew, Roger Parker, (a fellow-commoner of Queens' in 1582, who became Dean of Lincoln), benefited from his patronage.[2,3]

References

1. Chaderton, William. Dictionary of National Biography. Smith, Elder & Co.1885-1900. Edited 2013. Online.
2. Haigh, C. Chaderton, William. Oxford Dictionary of National Biography. 2004. Online.
3. Searle, W.G. The History of the Queens' College of St Margaret and St Bernard in the University of Cambridge. Part II 1560-1662. Sold by Deighton, Bell & Co; Macmillan & Co. London. 1871. pp 304-346.
4. Gray, J.H. The Queens' College of St Margaret and St Bernard. F.E.Robinson. London. 1898. pp 113-19.
5. Cooper. C.H. Cooper, T. Athenae Cantabrigienses. Volume 1I. Cambridge. Deighton, Bell & Co.; and Macmillan & Co. London: Bell & Daldy. Fleet Street. 1861. p 482.
6. Jocelin, Elizabeth. Dictionary of National Biography. Smith, Elder & Co. London. 1885-1900. Online.

CHAPTER 14

Humphrey Tyndall (Tindall, Tyndale, Tyndal). President 1579-1614.

Summary.

Humphrey Tyndall was born in 1549 to a distinguished family. He was a fellow of Pembroke Hall in 1567 and ordained in 1572. In 1578, he was chaplain to Robert Dudley, Earl of Leicester, and officiated at Dudley's secret marriage to Lettice Knollys, Lady Essex.

In 1579, aged only 30, he was appointed President of Queens', due to the support of Lord Burghley, (then Lord High Treasurer and Chancellor of Cambridge University), who wanted a reliable candidate to support Elizabethan religious policy.

Tyndall was Vice-Chancellor of the University in 1585-86 and, for many years, was active in the governance of the University. This involved various religious controversies and ongoing disputes with the Mayor and burgesses of the town.

In 1591 he was installed as Dean of Ely and remained in this office until his death in 1614. He is buried in the south sisle of the choir in Ely Cathedral.

He was married in 1593 but his children did not survive childhood. He bequeathed his books to Queens'; these included volumes that had been the property of Lord Burghley.

The rumour described by the historian Thomas Fuller (1608-61), that Tyndall was offered the crown of Bohemia, is not substantiated. However, he had descent from Margaret, wife of Sir Simon Felbrigg. She was from a Bohemian noble family and maid of honour to Richard II's wife, Anne of Bohemia.

Timeline.

1549.	Born in Hockwold, Norfolk.
1555.	Said to have matriculated at a curiously early age, at Gonville Hall, Cambridge.
1558.	Accession of Elizabeth I.
1559.	Sir William Cecil appointed Chancellor of Cambridge University; (he would be created Lord Burghley in 1571).
1564.	Visit of Elizabeth I to the University.
1566.	Scholar of Christ's College. B.A. .
1567.	Fellow of Pembroke Hall.
1569.	M.A. .
1570.	Issue of new Statutes for Cambridge University. Junior bursar, Pembroke Hall.
1572.	Senior bursar, Pembroke Hall. Ordained by the Bishop of Peterborough.
1576.	Licensed as a preacher of the University.
1577.	Vicar of Soham.
1578.	Chaplain to the Earl of Leicester. Officiates at the private marriage of Leicester to Lettice Knollys, the widow of the 1st Earl of Essex.
1579.	President of Queens', with support from Leicester and Lord Burghley.
1582.	D.D. .
1585-86.	Vice-Chancellor.
1586.	Chancellor of Lichfield Cathedral. Prebendary of Alrewas. Archdeacon of Stafford.
1588.	Prebendary of Southwell, Nottinghamshire.
1591.	Dean of Ely. Rector of Wentworth.
1593.	Marries Jane Russell.
1595.	Assists in drawing up the 'Lambeth Articles'. Visit of the 2nd Earl of Essex to Queens'.
1598.	Death of Lord Burghley, who is succeeded as Chancellor of the University by the 2nd Earl of Essex.
1601.	Execution of the 2nd Earl of Essex, who is succeeded as Chancellor by Sir Robert Cecil, subsequently the 1st Earl of Salisbury, son of Lord Burghley.

1603. Death of Elizabeth I. Visit of James I to Hinchingbrooke, where he meets members of the University, on his progress to London after his accession to the throne.

1614. Dies in Ely. Buried in Ely Cathedral.

Dean of Ely. Active in the governance of the University. The subject of an 'improbable tradition' that he was offered the crown of Bohemia.

Humphrey Tyndall was born in 1549 into a well-established family, a son of Sir Thomas Tyndall of Hockwold, Norfolk, and his second wife, Amye, daughter of Sir Henry Fermor of East Balsham, Norfolk. It is claimed that he matriculated as a 'pensioner' of Gonville Hall, Cambridge, in 1555, when he can only have been about six years old, and although Searle, in his history of Queens' published in 1871, quotes another pensioner of Gonville Hall who matriculated aged eight, Tyndall's example is very unusual.[1] But he is unlikely to have been in residence for several years, as he proceeded B.A. in 1566, aged about 17, and M.A. in 1569. He became a scholar of Christ's College and was elected a fellow of Pembroke Hall in 1567. He went on to hold office at Pembroke Hall, as junior bursar in 1570 and senior bursar in 1572.[1,2] Also in 1572, he was ordained by Edmund Scambler, Bishop of Peterborough, who had been a student at Queens'.

During William Chaderton's Presidency, (see Chapter 13), Thomas Cartwright, as Lady Margaret's Professor of Divinity, had expressed challenging Puritan views, attacking the existing Church government. This led to his suspension from his professorship and from his fellowship at Trinity College, but this firm action, taken to try and keep the University free from religious controversy, was opposed by most of the younger Masters of Arts, who had a vote in the 'Regent House'.[3] Therefore, to ensure that such opposition would not prevent effective action in future disputes, the heads of colleges pressed for changes to the University's Statutes, which received the royal assent in 1570, despite strong protests. The main changes were that the governing body (the Caput) and the Vice-Chancellor were to be elected by the heads of colleges, rather than by the wider franchise of the Regent House. At that time, Humphrey Tyndall was one of the younger members of the Regent House who protested about the changes and, in 1572, he signed a letter authorising letters to be sent to various noblemen:

'for reformation of certain matters amiss in the new statutes of the university'.[1,2] But he did not support the divisive demands of Puritan activists, and his orthodoxy was recognised in 1576, when he was licensed as a preacher of the University. In 1577, he became vicar of Soham, a living in the gift of Pembroke Hall, and proceeded B.D. .[1]

In 1578, as chaplain to Robert Dudley, the 1st Earl of Leicester (third creation), who was the 'favourite' of Elizabeth I from her accession to her death, Tyndall had a small but significant part in Leicester's turbulent life history when he officiated at the Earl's second marriage. Robert Dudley's father, the Duke of Northumberland, had been executed for his attempts to prevent the accession of Mary I, and Robert had been condemned to death for his role in attempting to secure the throne for Lady Jane Grey, before being released in 1554. His first wife, Amy Robsart, had died in 1560 after falling down a flight of stairs, and her death caused a scandal as he was suspected of arranging her murder, despite the finding of a coroner's jury that her death had been an accident. He did not remarry for 18 years, to avoid losing the Queen's favour, but he eventually married Lettice Knollys, widow of Walter Devereux, the 1st Earl of Essex, and a first cousin once removed of the Queen. (Essex's death from dysentery in 1576 had sparked another rumour of Leicester's homicidal activities, this time that he had arranged Essex's poisoning). This marriage was conducted secretly, by Tyndall, in September 1578, at Leicester's country house at Wanstead, in the presence of just a few relatives and friends.[4] Leicester did not tell the Queen, but nine months later, after she had been informed of the situation, there was a furious royal outburst. She never accepted his marriage, and his new wife was banished from the court. The Calendar of State Papers 1581-90 contain, as quoted by Searle:

'Depositions of Ambrose earl of Warwick' (elder brother of Robert Dudley), Roger lord North, sir Francis Knollys and Humphrey Tyndall clerk, relative to the secret marriage of the earl of Leicester with Letitia countess of Essex at Wanstead house 21 Sept. 1578...his said brother (ie Leicester) and the said countesse of Essex were marryed together after the order of the booke of Comon Prayers by one Mr Tindall a servaunt and chaplein to his brother Leicester, in such like manner and forme as other folks are accustomed to be marryed, Att which tyme he wellremembreth Sr Frauncis Knowlles, father unto the Countesse did give her for wife unto the aforenamed erle of Leicester in the sight and presence of this deponent, the erle of Pembrooke, the lord North, Sr Frauncis Knolles, Mr Tindall, and Mr Richard Knowlles all which were present and saw the said marriage solemnized as he hath deposed...'.

Tyndall himself is quoted in the next section:

'As this deponent (ie Tyndall) now remembreth...as his chaplein...He (ie Leicester) signifyed that he hadd a good season forborne marriage in respect of her Ma[tes] (Majesty's) displeasure, And that he was then for sundry respectes and especially for the better quiettinge of his owne conscience determined to marry with the right honorable countesse of Essex; But forsomuch as ytt might not be publicqlie knowne without great daunger of his estate, he moved this deponent to solemnize a marriage in secret between them, and fyndeinge this deponent willinge thereunto, he appointed him to attend for the dispatch therof the next morninge about seven of the clock which he this deponent did accordinglie, And theruppon betwixt seven and eight of the clock in the next morninge beinge Sondaie, this examinat was conveyed up by the lord North into a little gallery of Wanisted howse openinge upon the garden, into which gallery their came within a while after togetheir with the aforesaid erle of Leicester, the right honorable the erle of Pembrooke, the erle of Warwick and Sr Frauncis Knolles, and within a little after them the countesse of Essex herself attired (as he now remembreth) in a loose gowne, And then and their he, this deponent, did with the free consent of them both, marry the said right ho: Robert Dudeley erle of Leicester and the ladie Lettice countesse of Essex togeither, in such manner and forme as is prescribed by the Communyon booke, and did pronounce them lawfull man and wife before God and the world, accordinge to the usuall order at solemnization of marriages...this examynat was att that tyme full minister and had byn ordered by the reverend father in God the lord bishop of Peterborough in anno 1572, for proof wherof he exhibited at the tyme of this examination his letters of orders under the authenticall seales of the said bishop...'.[1]

Tyndall probably had some concerns about his role in the marriage, given Leicester's anxieties and the secrecy of the occasion, but must have decided that he did not want to risk the loss of his patron's support. In 1578 there must have been rumours of William Chaderton's impending promotion as Bishop of Chester and of Tyndall as a candidate for his replacement as President of Queens' as, in July 1578, a fellow of Queens', David Yale, wrote to Lord Burghley, the University's Chancellor, asking that the Earl of Leicester (in translation from the Latin):

'might not be allowed to exert his influence over the fellows in favour of Mr Tyndall, whom he considered to be unfit to be president on account of his youth and inexperience in college affairs'.[1] A footnote (in English) to the letter requests:

'That the free election of ye M^r^ of the Q.Colledg in Cambridg may be permitted to the fellows'.[1] However, Tyndall was recommended by the Chancellor and duly elected President in July 1579. Burghley will have wanted to promote a defender of religious orthodoxy, such as Tyndall, as part of his policy to support the Elizabethan religious settlement.

Soon after becoming President, he commissioned the building of a College brewhouse, which caused some complaints, as this was financed by the sale of several trees. This was unpopular with both the Chancellor and the previous President, Bishop Chaderton, who lamented that the trees had been:

'the ornament, bewty, and defence of the colledge', and hoped that: 'a longe row of very fayre ashes' may be saved.[1,2] Chaderton wrote to Lord Burghley, who then wrote to the Vice-Chancellor, Dr John Hatcher:

'...When I wrote my letters of late to the master and fellows of the Q. college to stay the fall of certain woods, growing within the precinct and view of that college, misliking greatly that any such attempt should be made there...who as I understand by your answer have so far proceeded in their bargain, that they cannot well of themselves revoke the same, and have suffered some fall to be made of part of the same woods...I...pray you to take the pains...to view the said woods or other trees...and to take order to stay the fall therof by your authority...From the court at Westminster...Your assured friend W.Burghly'.[1] The Vice-Chancellor duly replied:

'...I went thither to view the same...we found that some trees were felled in divers places and carried away...most of them that are yet standing, notably putrified, not like long to continue...We also called before us all the fellows of the said college, whom we find to agree in one voice, that the fall of the said wood was made of the master and them all upon great deliberation and not for any respect of private gain, to the master or any of them...we think your Honour will be satisfied and contented with the doings of the said master and fellows, whom we find very careful of the said college in all respects...'.[1] This seems to have allowed the matter to be dropped.

Tyndall was elected Vice-Chancellor of the University in 1585-86 and, in 1586, Chancellor of the Cathedral Church of Lichfield and Archdeacon of Stafford. At Queens', the discord during Chaderton's Presidency, which had involved one of the fellows, William Middleton, has already been described, (see Chapter 13), and, in 1585, Middleton was again in dispute with authority, when he disagreed with Tyndall over the allocation of fellows' rooms.[5] The year brought another headache for Tyndall, when he was faced with conflicting demands from the court and the fellows to fill a vacant fellowship. The fellows wrote to Lord Burghley in support of an Alexander Richardson, while Tyndall wrote in reply to Burghley, explaining his position:

'My dutie in most humble wyse unto your Ld^{p} remembred. I have receaved lately your Honours letters, by wch yt seemeth your Ld^{p} conceaveth hardley of me, that I should not yeald to y^{r}

choise of one Alexander Richardson to be fellowe of our house, having a sufficient number of voyces for his election...the place now voyde was resigned up by one Mr Stoone, chaplain to my Ld. Chancellor, upon the motion of his Lorde, in my hands, in behalf of one Anstill M^r^ of Arte...'. Tyndall goes on to explain that, in addition to the promise to Anstill, a third candidate had been put forward by the Queen:

'...yt hath pleased the Queens Maj. To recommende one Dammeporte unto us to be chosen Fellow of our colledge...I trust therefore that I have just cause to stand for the choise of Anstill...And thus claiming most humbly of your L: for the more quiet and peaceable government of the colledge, which hitherto I have enjoyed, that the younger sorte may not receave anye incouragement by your Honours favour...I humbly take my leave...Your Ld^ps^ most humbly to command. Umphry Tyndall'. The President did receive the Chancellor's support, as Richardson was not elected, while both the court candidates received fellowships.[1,5] During Tyndall's year as Vice-Chancellor, one of the many contentious sermons of those times led to the preacher, John Smith of Christ's College, being questioned before the Vice-Chancellor and heads of colleges. Smith had claimed that the performance of plays in the colleges, on Saturday and Sunday evenings, was in breach of the observance of the Sabbath, but he agreed to explain his views in a further sermon, which was to be submitted to Tyndall for his agreement before delivery. (Tyndall was opposed to extreme Puritan views, and believed that: 'liberty should not run wild to licence').[2]

In 1586, the heroic death after the battle of Zutphen of Sir Philip Sidney, poet, courtier, scholar and soldier, (and the nephew of Robert Dudley, Earl of Leicester), prompted the publication of a collection of verses by different members of the University. Searle quotes Tyndall's Latin contribution:

'In obitum D. Philippi Sidnei clarissimi fortissimique equitis, Carmen, (an ode to the death of the most gallant knight Philip Sidney)....Hum.Tindallus'.[1]

In 1588, Tyndall was a signatory of a letter from the Vice-Chancellor and heads to Lord Burghley, complaining that the stationers and printers of London had reprinted books originally printed at the University Press, in particular, a Latin dictionary compiled by the University printer:

'To the Right Honourable the Lord of Burghlie, Lorde Highe Treasurer of Englande and most loving Chancellor of the Universitie of Cambridge...Wheras ther hath bene an ancyent privilage graunted to this Universitie for the mysterie of printinge and the same by her most excellent Majestie in oure Charter most gratiously confirmed, and of late yeares by your honours favourable approbation put in practyse...we finde yt a verie hard matter, either for our Universitie to maynteine this royall privilage, or for oure Printer to doe anie good by his trade, by reason of the Companie of Stationers and Prynters in London who as they have heretofore taken divers of his Copies and printed them againe to his greate losse and hinderance, so doe they still threaten to attempt the lyke hereafter namely and specially with a Dictionarie of his owne compiling, and lately set oute by him and this they challenge as their owne right and proper copie, by vertue of a generall clawse graunted to them from her Majestie, To prynte all Dictionaries whatsoever...in oure judgment (this) extendeth to suche bookes and dictionaries only, as were then extant...and not to any that should afterward come forthe, for elles might yt... hinder the setting forth of manie good and profitable bookes, if learned men might not make choyse of their printer...but must all come to the Printers in London only...we are bold to become humble suters to your Honoure, that...we may mainteyne a print in our Universitie with credyt, according to her Majesties intent and the tenore of our Charter, and also our Printer may followe his trade with some profyt, and not be molested as heretofore... Thus hoping that...your honour will be readie to procure her Majestie to shewe this and all other gratious favour, needfull for the maintenance of good learning, to her pore Universitie...'.[6]

In 1589, Tyndall will have met John Hall, who matriculated at Queens' in the Michaelmas term. He went on to marry Susanna, daughter of William Shakespeare, in 1607, but also to become a physician, preparing some of his case notes, in Latin, for eventual publication. He died in 1635 and, after translation, these were published in 1657 as: 'Select Observations on English Bodies of Eminent Persons in Desperate Diseases'.

In 1591, Robert Whalley, a fellow of Queens' since 1587, died at the early age of 28 and was buried in the College's old chapel. His memorial brass was one of the few that survived damage at the hands of the Puritans in the next century and, in 1925, was moved, with just three others, from the walls of the old chapel to the walls of the ante-chapel of the new chapel. The College website notes:

'Unusually, for a monument to an academic in a college chapel, the effigy is shown in secular dress of the high fashion of the period'. The inscribed plate at the foot of the effigy, (translated from the Latin by Dr David Butterfield, fellow of Queens'), reads:

'Whalley lies here (that faithful fellow);
here pleasantly lie Robert's ashes, here too his bones.
God in his providence placed him in the celestial garden
during spring, for no later winter ever blasted the old man…'.

In December 1591, Tyndall was installed as Dean of Ely and also as rector of Wentworth, and he remained as Dean until his death, spending much of his time in Ely:

'The Master of the Colledge at that time (c1611) was Doctor Tyndal, who was Dean of Ely, and resided for the most part there…'.[1]

Searle relates that Queens' was peripherally involved in the aftermath of the lingering death, in 1592, of the wife of Sir Henry Cromwell of Hinchingbrooke. This was ascribed to withcraft, and three inhabitants of the village of Warboys, John Samwell, his wife Alice and their daughter Agnes, were charged with having killed her. After torture in prison, Alice Samwell confessed, and was duly convicted of bewitching Lady Cromwell, as well as several others. After all three were hanged, their goods became the property of Sir Henry, who gave them to the corporation of Huntingdon, on condition that Queens' would provide a preacher, every year on Ladyday, for a sermon against the sin of witchcraft in one of the churches of Huntingdon.[1] An account of the events leading up to this is quoted by Searle:

'About 10 Nov. 1589 Jane, one of the five daughters of Robert Throckmorton esq, of Warboys...fell into a strange kind of sickness; she would sneeze for half an hour together, and then lie in a swoon, afterwards she would begin to swell and heave up her belly, so as none was able to keep her down...After some days an old woman Alice Samwell, aged nearly 80 years, who lived next door, came in to see the child, who then, frightened at her appearance, called her a witch...A Cambridge physician, Dr Barrow, having tried the effect of his prescriptions without success, suggested witchcraft as the cause of her illness...about a month after, they (her parents) found that their other four daughters...were attacked in a similar way, and that they all agreed in placing their affliction to the account of old Alice Samwell, a charge also brought by the six women-servants of the house, who were afflicted in the same manner as the daughters... Lady Cromwell came to visit them, and at once, as always happened when strangers came to see them, the children all fell in to their fits, and this so touched lady Cromwell's heart that she sent for mother Samuel and charged her with witchcraft...and she afterwards fell very strangely sicke, with fits like the children, and so continued till she died about a year and a quarter after being at Warboys...The three (Samwells) were then condemned to death...and so they were executed...To conclude this Relation, since the Death of these Persons, the Children have continued well, without any Fits at all, enjoying their perfect Health'.[1] The contract between:

'the Burgesses of ye Boroughe of Huntington in the Count. of Hunt. of thone part And the p^r^sident and fellowes of the Coll. Of Ste Margaret and Ste Barnarde comonly called ye queens coll. In Cambr. On thother parte...', specified that:

'the said p^r^sident and fellowes shall for ev^r^more provide and fynde one Sufficient Doctor of Divinity or Bachelor of Divinitye to preache and make one Sermon yearly at and w^th^in some Churche w^th^in the Towne of Hunt. Uppon the feaste daye of the annuntiacon of the blissid virgine for ev^r^more, In wch sermon the said preacher shall preache and Invaye againste the detestable practise synne and offence of witchcraft Inchauntement Charme and Sorcerye,

And...the said Burgesses...shall the same daye paye or cause to paid to the said preacher and sermon maker ffortye shillings... tenn shillings the said preacher shall bestowe and distribute to the moste needye and poore people dewellinge and abiding w^th^in the said Borough of Huntington (sic)...'.[1] The corporation accounts of Huntingdon show that these sermons were preached in the period 1771-1812, while earlier records are missing.[1]

In 1593, Cambridge was affected by the 'plague', (as it would be again in 1610), which caused an exodus to the country and the banning of public assemblies until February 1594.[1]

In September 1594 there was a flood caused by excessive rain, which caused various expenses to Queens':

'Item allowed to 6 men for remooving the beere out of the cellar at the fludde...'.[1]

In 1595, the President and fellows wrote to Lord Burghley regarding a disputed College lease:

'...We become humble suitors unto your Hon. Ld^p^ to vouchsafe that favour to our colledge...that we may not be pressed to lett this lease before ye due tyme...This in all humbleness we crave of her Maj. By our humble letters...Your Ld^ps^ most humbly to command. The M^r^ and fellowes of the Queens colledge Umphry Tyndall...'.[1]

An episode of religious controversy occurred in 1595, when a William Barret, a fellow of Gonville and Caius College, preached a fiery sermon attacking the doctrines of John Calvin:

'with some sharp and unbecoming speeches of that reverend man, and other foreign learned Protestant writers'.[2] This led to his being summoned before:

'the consistory of the doctors, and there enjoined the following recantation: "Preaching in Latin not long since in the University Church many things slipped from me both falsely, and rashly spoken...I do make this public confession, both repeating, and revoking my errors...Last of all, I uttered these words rashly against Calvin, a man that hath very well deserved of the Church of God; to wit, that he durst presume to lift up himself above the high and Almighty God...and I do most humbly beseech you all to pardon this my rashness...and I do promise you, that by God's help I will never hereafter offend in like sort..." '.[7] However the recantation:

'...was done accordingly: but not with that remorse and humility as was expected...',[7] '...in such a manner as to give great offence, and to induce a very general disbelief in his sincerity'.[8] This led to a further summons and a threat of expulsion, after which he appealed to Archbishop of Canterbury, John Whitgift, (who had been a pensioner at Queens', matriculating in 1549),[2] and revoked his retraction. The Vice-Chancellor and heads asked the Primate to settle the matter and Barret was then summoned to appear before Whitgift at Lambeth, while Tyndall and William Whitaker, Regius Professor of Divinity and Master of St John's, were delegated to represent the Vice-Chancellor and heads.[2] Eventually, in March 1597, after many delays, Barret agreed to sign a further recantation and Whitgift wrote to the Vice-Chancellor: 'stating that Barret intended to depart the realm...'. Subsequently:

'...he got beyond sea and embraced the roman catholic faith, ultimately returning to England, where he lived as a layman until his death'.[8] The visit of Whitaker and Tyndall to the Archbishop also led to the compilation of nine statements to define the doctrines of 'Calvinism', which became known as the 'Lambeth Articles'. These were drawn up by Whitaker, with imput from Tyndall, Richard Fletcher, (Bishop of London), and Richard Vaughan (Bishop-elect of Bangor). After approval by Whitgift and other bishops, they were sent to the University of Cambridge in Novenber 1585, not as new laws but as an explanation of current doctrine:

'...the Archbishop addressed a letter to the Vicechancellor and Heads, to whom it was brought by Dr. Whitaker and Dr. Tyndal, on their return from London. In this letter he said his earnest and hearty desire was to have the peace of the church generally observed in all places, especially in this University, of which he was a member. That for the better observation and nourishing of such peace, he and others had with some care and diligence drawn out and set down certain propositions which they were persuaded to be true, and a copy wherof he then sent them, praying them to take care that nothing should be publicly taught to the contrary...And especially, that no bitterness, contention, or personal reproof or reproaches, should be used by any towards any. And that the propositions nertheless must be so taken... thinking them to be true, and correspondent to the doctrine professed in the Church of England...'.[6] However, it appears that they were not sanctioned by the Queen and they were never added to the Church of England's 'Thirty-Nine Articles', which had been finalised in 1571 to determine the Church's doctrines and practices. On the 5th December 1595, Sir Robert Cecil, Secretary of State, wrote to Whitgift that he was commanded by the Queen:

'to send unto his Grace, to acquaint him, that she misliked much that any allowance had been given by his Grace and the rest, of any such points to be disputed, being a matter tender and dangerous to weak ignorant minds, And thereupon that she required his Grace to suspend them'.[6] On the 13th December, the Vice-Chancellor and seven other heads, including Tyndall, wrote to the Archbishop referring to their great loss by the recent death of Dr Whitaker, and proposed:

'God willing, every one in their places, for preserving of that peace, to employ their special care and endeavour, and to continue the course of doctrine in those points among them, according to the direction and cautions his Grace had thought meetest'.[6] (The Lambeth Articles related to the complex and variable concepts of predestination and justification; the former involves a belief that all events have been willed by God, while the latter refers to God's act of removing guilt and punishment for sin. Predestination was supported, as the fourth Article states that those not predestined to salvation are inevitably condemned for their sins).

Lord Burghley died in 1598 and he was succeeded as Chancellor of Cambridge University by Robert Devereux, 2nd Earl of Essex, who would be executed in 1601, following an abortive rebellion. Lord Essex was the son of Walter Devereux, 1st Earl of Essex, and Lettice Knollys, whose second marriage to Robert Dudley, Earl of Leicester, had been conducted by Tyndall. The new Chancellor did not have any previous connection with Queens', although one of his ancestors was Anne, sister of Elizabeth Woodville, (see Chapter I). Fuller tells us that:

'Upon the death of William Cecil, Lord Burghley, Robert Devereux, Earl of Essex was chosen Chancellor of the University. Coming to Cambridge, he was entertained in Queens' College, where the room he lodged in, is called Essex chamber to this day, and where the pleasant comedy of Lelia (Laelia) was excellently acted before him'.[7] However, Searle notes that:

'The college accounts make no mention of a comedy at this time, nor indeed of the earl's visit',[1] and although the 'Essex Chamber' in the President's Lodge at Queens' has Lord Essex's Arms displayed in stained glass in the bay window, it is not certain that he ever stayed there.[9] But he is documented as having visited the College earlier, on March 1st 1595, when he saw a comedy, which has been claimed to have been 'Laelia':

'...The next Morning 1st March after my lord the Earl of Essex & ye rest were come. The Orator entertayned them in the Regent Howse, with an oration, it being no Congregation. After that oration they herd Dr Whitaker read, & then went to Dyner to Queenes Coll: wher after Dyner they had a Comedy, the day being turned into night'.[9,10]

The College website notes:

'George Meriton and George Mountaine were Fellows of Queens' who had acted in the performance of Laelia seen by the Earl of Essex, and who were subsequently asked by Essex to act with him in a performance of a *Device* at Whitehall in front of the Queen on the anniversary of her accession in November 1595', while John Weever, who was an undergraduate at Queens' at the time, (and a subsequent antiquary and poet, who, in 1599 published 'Epigrammes in the Oldest Cut, and Newest Fashion' and, in 1631, 'Ancient Funerall Momuments'), wrote an epigram referring to the occasion, which mentions 'Laelia'.

Twigg, in his history of Queens' of 1987, notes the improvements in the status, accomodation and lifestyle of college heads during the 16th century and, at Queens', the Long Gallery of the President's Lodge was built in the Elizabethan era, for which Tyndall commissioned a significant amount of panelling. Tyndall married Jane, daughter of Robert Russell of West Rudham, Norfolk, probably in 1593, as the parish register of Hockington (Oakington) in that year has the entry:

'Maste^{r} Maste^{r} was married the xx day of December.', which has been considered to apply to the Master of the College.[1] Fuller criticises Tyndall for paying too much attention to his wife: 'non sine Collegii detrimento' (not without detriment to the College),[1,5] while Jane Tyndall was the first President's wife who is recorded as having visited Queens'.[5]

Charles Henry Cooper's 'Annals of Cambridge' of 1843 includes a number of letters written during the 1590s, co-signed by Tyndall as a college head.[6] On 2nd December 1592, the University was asked to prepare a comedy in English, to be acted by students before the Queen at Christmas. But the Vice-Chancellor and heads wrote to the Chancellor asking for more time:

'...How ready wee are to do anything that may tend to her Majesties pleasure, wee are very desirous by all meanes to testify, but how fitt we shall be for this is moved, having no practise in this Englishe vaine...and do find our principall actors...very unwilling to playe in Englishe...we would gladly desire some further limitation of time for due preparation, and liberty to play in Latyn...From the University of Cambridge, this fourthe of December, 1592. Your Lordships most humble to be commaunded...Umphry Tyndall...'.

In 1593, the Vice-Chancellor and heads wrote to Lord Burghley, wishing to renew their application to ban travelling players, because of the risk of the spread of infection:

'It is now longe since wee presumed to offer unto your good lordshipp a supplication as toucheinge a restrainte from publicke showses and commen plaies...Which hath induced us also at this time to undertake the renewinge of that sute, the rather in regard of Gods greate goodnes towards us, who haveinge hitherto somewhat straungely preserved us, from such infection as hath greatly touched many other partes of this land, are the likelier to finde the continuance therof, y^{f} by your honorable meanes wee may be freed from that badd kinde of people, who are (as wee thincke) the most ordynary cariers and dispersers therof... Cambridge, the xvijth of July, 1593...Umphry Tyndall...'.

In 1594, the Vice-Chancellor and heads wrote to Lord Burghley requesting his help to resolve a legal dispute involving a John Brooke, vicar of Campsall, Yorkshire, a living in the gift of the University:

'...this bearer John Brooke...after peaceable and quiet possession in the mansion house of the said vicaredge by him injoyed by the space of twenty yeres...was aboute three yeres last past, by the procurement of one Mr Lee, a gentleman of that country, pretendinge title unto the said vicaredge house, forceablye and with greate violence and outrage done to his wyfe and chikdren, in unseemely manner expelled and throwen oute of the said house...he was...restored to his former possession...his sone Mr. Henry Lee, hath begon a newe sute in the Kings benche, purposinge (as it may seeme) to weary this man with tedious suites and excessive chardge...very humblye prayeinge your good lordship, that for the avoidinge of further chardge and for the more speedy administration of Justice in this behalfe, the same would be pleased to recaull the cause backe againe into the Courte of Exchequor where it was begone and proceeded in, and is now redy for heareinge and determininge... Cambridge, this syxt of June, 1594...Umphry Tyndall...'. Also in 1594, there was a dispute concerning the appointment of 'taxors', who represented the University's rights to intervene in the town's trade. It was the turn of King's College to nominate one of the taxors, but their nominee attracted opposition:

'When the Taxors elect came to the Regent House to be admitted to their offices, a body of the Regents refused admittance to the King's College Taxor, and a great tumult ensued'.[6] Lord Burghley was duly informed by the Vice-Chancellor and heads:

'...Wee have therefore resumed at this tyme in a case of great extremitye and consequence semblably to resort unto the sanctuarye of your worthie Justice and wisdom for aide and direction. Such a notorious ryotte and disorder latcly happening amongst us, and yet also in some degree continueing as in case it be not forthwith severely mette with, it is very likely to shake the groundworke of all peace and government...For the severe punishment whereof wee most humbly crave some ayde and direction from your honorable Lordship, the rather for that if there be not some especiall example made of it by the removing out of the Universitie some of the principalls of this tumult after such a precedent, we have cause to feare the confusion of our whole estate...From Cambridge, the xvjth of Oxtober, 1594. Your lordships humble and bounden to be commanded...Umphry Tyndall...'.

In 1595, there was an attempt to subject the proceedings of the University Courts to review in a 'Court of Error', which led to a letter of protest to the Chancellor:

'...That whereas all causes and occasions personall, of what state and condition soever...concerninge either scholer or scholers servant in the Universitie, are definitively to be hearde tried and ended before the Chauncellor for the Universitie, or in his absence before the Vicechancellor for the time beinge...one James Ansell, haveinge beene latelie sued before Mr Vicechauncellor...hathe notweithstandinge procured a writt of error owte of the Kinges benche to state further proceedinge in it here, and to remove it wholy owte of this Courte thither, to the manifest breach of our priviledges, and to the utter overthrowe of all, if this course maie be suffered. Wherin our verie humble sute unto your Lordship is...to be a meane (means) to my lord Cheife Justice of England... that we maie have his lordships honorable favoure to contynue our wonted course for the Administration of Justice as in times past wee have done withowte interruption...From Cambridge Your lordships most bounden and readie to be comaunded... Umphry Tyndall...'.

In 1596, Robert Wallis, the Mayor of Cambridge refused to take the oath for the conservation of the University's privileges and this led to a meeting, in December, between the Vice-Chancellor and the Mayor, with many assistants, at Great St Mary's Church, when Wallis again refused to take the oath. This was reported to the Chancellor in a letter signed by various University and civic dignatories, including Tyndall:

'John Jegon...Vicechauncellor of the Universitie of Vicechauncellor reade the order for the oathe set downe by the right Honorable the Lords Keeper and Treasurer, and then demaunded of the Maior whether he would receave the oathe accordinge to the order agreed upon by their honorable Lordshipps The Maior answered That he did thincke himself not bounde by that order to take the oathe, because their lordshipps in their lettres had referrence unto the Maior and Burgesses for the time to come, and not for the time beinge...Ita testamur...Umphry Tyndall...'.

This was in the context of several recent disputes between the University and town and, in November 1596, the town authorities had submitted a list of 16 complaints to the Lord Keeper of the Great Seal and the Lord Treasurer:

'Injuries and Misdemeanors by the Universitie of Cambridge and the Officers and Ministers therof offered and committed to the Maior, Baylyffes and Burgessses of the same Towne, generallie and perticulerlie...these generall misdemeanors, besides manie outeragious particuler offences, are used and committed by the Universitie and pryviledged persons, wherof the Maior, Bayliffes, and Burgesses humblie praie and desire reformation'. A letter from Burghley to the University on the 27th November, which attempted to be even-handed, received a dismissive reply from the Vice-Chancellor and heads, including Tyndall, on the 10th December:

'Right honorable, We receaved of late, together with your honors letters, a schedule contayninge certayne articles of complaint exhibited by the Maior and Burgesses of the towne of Cambridge, against us...our unkinde neighboyrs the Townesmen, who beinge challenged for inftinginge our accustomed priviledge (which all that bare office amonge them have yearely sworne to maintayne), they have in their displeasure nowe againe renewed such ould complaintes, as have bene answered to their shame oftentimes heretofore, and are utterly untrue; the which this our present short and direct answer, we hoope will justifie, if it may please your Honor to vouchsafe the readinge therof...Cambridge this 10th of December, 1596...Umphry Tyndall...'. (Some specific answers to the complaints were attached to this letter).

The town-gown disharmony continued and, in June 1597, the Vice-Chancellor and heads wrote again to Lord Burghley:

'...All matters of variance and grief betwixt both bodies have been referred, at the direction of the lord chief justice of England, to conference among ourselves...Notwithstanding all this, they still injuriously exhibit complaints against us of untruths, foul and odious, as of late to your honour, and to the lord North in court, and here to the lord chief justice...They summon our known privileged persons to their town sessions they award process against them...they take scholars' horses to serve post upon ordinary commission and generally they adventure to do anything against our charters with such unwonted boldness and violence, that we shall be driven of necessity to seek relief extraordinary...we most humbly crave your honour's direction, ready to attend your pleasure in person...At Cambridge, the 23d of June, 1597. Your honour's in all duty most bounden... Humphry Tyndal...'. The situation had not improved by September:

'To the right honorable the lord Burghley...Whereas not longe since in way of answere and defence of ourselves we were bolde to acquaint your Honor in generall with Injuries done to this Universitie...since that tyme we finde their attempts to be more and more audacious and injurious unto us...Wherefore we humblie crave that your honor will be pleased...to... give us your Honors allowance and aide to deale wth them here...Your Honors most bounden ever...Umphry Tyndall...'. Later that year Robert Wallis was re-elected Mayor and, on Michaelmas Day (29th September), took an oath to conserve the University's privileges, but in a very irreverent manner. The Vice-Chancellor, Tyndall and the University Bedell informed Lord Burghley that:

'...on Michaelmas daye laste Anno 1597, the said Maior toke his oathe moste unreverently with his head covered'. A more detailed statement was attached, signed by Jegon (Vice-Chancellor), Tyndall and two notaries:

'...one of the bedles tendied a testament, whereupon the Maior laying his hand, his head being covered, so continued untill the oath was fullie read through...This done, D Tyndall rounded the deputie recorder in his eare, asked him whether he ever sawe an oathe so taken before, Whereunto the recorder made none aunswer...'.[6] The Vice-Chancellor and heads wrote again to Lord Burghley in October:

'...we heare of nothinge, but threatninge termes, unfitting his (ie the Mayor's) person and our estate, the conceipte and censure whereof, we most humbly referre to your Honors wisedome...Your Honors most entirely bounden ever...Umphry Tyndall...'.

November 1597 brought further problems to the University, which were shared by the other English University, when a Mr Davies of the Inner Temple, a member of the House of Commons, alleged:

'...many corruptions in the Masters of Colleges in the Universities of Oxford and Cambridge, in the abusing of the possessions of their Colleges, contrary to the intents of the founders, converting the benefit of the same to their own private commodities'.[6] This provoked an indignant response in the form of a letter to the Chancellors of both Universities, signed by both Vice-Chancellors and selected heads, including Tyndall:

'...Whereas one Mr Davies, of the Inner Temple, hath openly, in the lower House of Parliament, uttered some Speaches, greatly tendinge to the utter discreditt of the Governers and Heads of Colledges generally of both the Universities we are bolde to presente unto your Lordshipps Honourable Consideration our cause of griefe...humblye prayinge...that...Mr Davies may be compelled to make such proofe as he can of all these sclanderous matters...wherein as we seeke not to cover any faulte...that neyther this libertie of speache...may have free passage, if there be noe just cause therof, nor that for the faults of a few (if any such be) a general Sclander and Infamy may be brought upon all the rest...we...greatly feare, that, by colour of these scandalous Informations...some new Statute may passe, to the generall prejudice of both the Universities...'.[6]

In 1603, although King James I did not visit Cambridge during his progression from Scotland to London to assume the Crown, he received the homage of the University at the house of Sir Oliver Cromwell, (an uncle of the future Protector), in Hinchingbrooke.[2] Fuller describes the occasion:

'Until at last his majesty came to Hinchinbrook, nigh Huntingdon, the house of Master Oliver Cromwell...But it was the banquet, which made the feast so complete. Hither came the heads of the University of Cambridge, in their scarlet gowns, and corner caps, where Mr. Robert Naunton the Orator made a learned Latin oration, wherewith his majesty was highly affected. The very variety of Latin was welcome to his ears, formerly almost surfeited with so many long English speeches made to him as he passed every corporation. The heads in general requested a confirmation of their privileges...which his highness most willingly granted'.[7]

In 1605, one of Tyndall's duties was to certify that the College was in conformity with the requirement to wear surplices in chapel and he writes:

'According to Mr. Vice-Chancellor's appointment, I do hereby certify that the Fellows, Scholars and Students of our Colledge as usually before time, so at this present, do continue y[e] conformity in Divinis Officiis, both in Surplisses and Hoods, every one according as the University Statutes do require, and also in due observation of the Communion Book'. This is accompanied by the names of ten:

'ministers, who being now present at home have shewed letters of orders'.[2] Also in 1605, Tyndall received, together with the Vice-Chancellor and certain heads, a letter from the Privy Council requiring their help with the investigation of a case of suspected witchcraft, as Cooper relates:

'The strong interest taken by the King in cases of witchcraft is well known. A person of the name of Knightley was charged about this time with bewitching two young women. He was therefore committed to custody, and the young women were sent to Cambridge. Shortly afterwards the following letter was sent..."To our Loving Frends, Dr Cowell Vicechan. Dr Goade Provost of King's Coll. Dr Tindal Master of Queens Coll. And Dr Nevill Master of Trin. Coll....By his Majesties Speciall dyreccion two yonge Mayds were sent of late to Cambridge that are suspected to be bewitched & also one Knightley...being vehemently suspected to be the doer therof. Because his Majestie is desirous to be satisfied whether theis passions those Mayds do seem to suffer doe proceede of any naturall cause or supernaturall, his Highnes pleasure is you shall call unto yow some skilfull Phisitions & learned Devines to consider very advisedly of the state they are in & that order may be taken to minister unto them such things as shall be thought fitt for remedy of their disease if the cause be naturall...Concerning Knightley you are to use the assistance of some of the Justices of the Peace...both to examine him uppon those Informacions already given against him and ani further evidence or proofe that shall be brought unto you...whereof expecting to be particularly advertised from you...From the Court at Whitehall... ".'.[11] Luckily for Knightley, the physicians' opinion was that:

'very confidentlie & assuredlie they pronounce the disease, though somewhat Straunge & extraordinarie & of much difficultie to be cured, yet to be naturall, the longer staie of them (ie of the two women)...at this tyme to be unexpedient, the tyme of the yeare for Medicines proper for their disease to grow now unreasonable, & the aire of the Countrey where they have lived together with exercise & orderlie government of them to be more convenient'.[11] (This indicates the importance of botany to the physician's art at the time, as well as providing a masterclass in the art of avoiding unwelcome responsibility!)

In 1607, the acting of plays in some colleges caused considerable disturbances. On the 20th February:

'there was foul & great disorder committed at the time of a comedy in King's college by most rude and barbarous throwing of many great stones at and through the hall windows, with loud outcries and shoutings by multitude of scholars and others, for the space of about two hours together, there being then assembled the hall full not only of the inferior sort, but also of divers young noblemen doctors bachelors in divinity and masters of arts, to their great offence annoyance and disturbance, beside the breaking of many other windows about the said college, and a great post of timber pulled out of the ground, and therewith divers running at a strong gate, the same was broke open'.[11] This led the Vice-Chancellor and heads, including Tyndall, to issue:

'A decree for reforming great disorders at publick assemblies in the University', which laid down various punishments depending on the degree of offence and their University status. For less serious offences:

'...if such offenders shall be non-graduates or a privileged person, then (being non-adult) they shall be corrected in the schools by the rod...'.[11] (Windows had also been broken at Queens' on theatrical occasions, as the accounts for 1595 record:

'Item for repairing th'hall windowes after the plaies...').[1,2] A further decree was issued, with the same signatories, including the Pro-Chancellor and 'Umphry Tindal':

'A decree for reforming night jetters, keepers of greyhounds, &c. Where there hath divers times fallen sundry disorders, specially in the night-time...and where also divers scholars...have used to shoot in guns, cross-bows, and stone-bows...and also usually have kept greyhounds and some of them hunting horses...to the destroying of game and misspending of their time...That whatsoever scholar or student or any reteyning to them, shall hereafter be found and convicted...shall incurr respectively (according to the degree of his offence) the several penalties above specified for the disturbers of publick assemblies...'.[11] Also in 1607, George, fourth Earl of Huntingdon, visited the College, where his grandson, later the fifth Earl, was in residence. His entertainment cost £4 5s. 4d. .[2] Subsequently, the fifth Earl, Henry Hastings (1586-1643), gave the College £100, with which 102 books were bought and bound with his arms and motto; he was a Puritan and most of the collection relate to reformation texts and early Church writings. (Tyndall produced the first inventory of the Old Library and commissioned its remodelling in 1612-13).

It may have been that, towards the end of Tyndall's long Presidency, the fellows were wanting a change as, in 1608, when Tyndall became ill, one of the fellows, George Montaigne, (also written as Mountaigne, Mountaine, and Mountain, who had distinguished himself as an actor in 1595- see above- and would become Archbishop of York), wrote to the Chancellor, the Earl of Salisbury, requesting a free election in which he expected victory. Also, three years later, when Tyndall's health was again in question, George Meriton, (a previous fellow, and also previously mentioned for his acting skills- see above- who would become Dean of York), prematurely obtained a royal mandate to be elected President. In 1614, when Tyndall's death did finally leave a vacancy, Montaigne was still hoping for the Presidency, but was defeated by John Davenant, a current fellow.[5]

Tyndall signed his will on the 12th of March 1614, the year of his death:

'The last will and Test. of Humfrye Tindall...I Humfrye Tindall Dr in Divinity and president of the Queens college in Cambridge, Dean of Ely, being of good memory...do make and ordain this my last will and testament in manner and form following: First my soul into the hands of my only Saviour and Redeemer Jesus Christ, and my body to the grave, there to rest until the day of judgement...I give to the president and fellows of Queens college in Cambridge to my successors use all the seeling and wainscoting of my chambers and lodging I have, which (I take) amounteth to two hundred and fifty pounds or thereabouts more than I have received from the college or any other benefactors towards the same. Further I give to the use of the society of Queens college aforesaid all my books in folio which are not in the library already...I do also give unto Jane my wife all the rest of my goods and chattels whatsoever unbequeathed...And I do appoint my brother Mr Francis Tindall supervisor of this my last will and testament, by whose advice I would have my said wife to be ruled and counselled. And I give to him for a remembrance of me my seal ring...'.[1] The abovementioned books were 58 in number and remain in the Old Library. They include books from the library of Lord Burghley, the bindings of which are stamped with the Cecil family arms. In one of these, 'The Sermons of Reverend Father Johann Ferus', there is an inscription which translates as:

'Given by Humphrey Tindall. Humphrey Tindall was a former Prefect of this College and left this legacy on his death on 12th October, anno Domini 1614'. The 'seeling and wainscoting' were part of extensive building work involving the President's Lodge,[2] and tree-ring dating is consistent with the construction of the Long

Gallery of the Lodge during Tyndall's Presidency. He died at Ely in October, 1614, aged 65.

His widow, Jane, went on to marry an alderman of London, Henry Jay, and then a third husband, Sir Henry Duke of Cossington, Kent.[1] There is a report that Tyndall had several sons, but it seems they all died without issue.[1] Among the registered burials at St Botolph's Church, Cambridge, we find:

'Johannes filius (son of) Umfridi Tyndalli Decani Eliens. Sep. 12°. Febr. 1610',[1] and it is significant that no child is mentioned in his will. In addition to his bother Francis, he had an elder brother, Sir John Tyndall, and two sisters, Susan and Ursula. Francis Tyndall was an auditor of Queens' in 1611, who died unmarried and left £40 to the College to buy a basin and ewer or to be spent otherwise at the President's discretion, while Sir John Tyndall matriculated at Queens' in 1553, was a LL.D of Lincoln's Inn, a master in chancery and was knighted in 1603.[5] One of his sons, Deane Tyndall, was at Queens' and died in 1678, aged 92. But Deane's father, Sir John, had not been so fortunate; he was murdered in 1616 by a John Bertram, to whom Sir John had given an adverse judgement.[1] Also, Simon Tyndall, a fellow of Queens' during 1599-1612, may have been Humphrey Tyndall's nephew.[9]

Tyndall is buried in Ely Cathedral on the south aisle of the choir.[12] His tomb has a life-size brass effigy and the following inscription:

'The body of the woorthy and reverend Prelate UMPHRY TYNDALL Doctor of Divinity, the Fourth Dean of this Church, and Master of Queenes Colledge in Cambridge doth here expec't the coming of our Saviour.

In presence, government, good actions, and in birth,
Grave, wise, courageous, Noble, was this earth;
The poor, ye church, ye colledge saye here lyes,
A friende, A Dean, A Maister, true, good, wise'.[1,2] His sister, Ursula, is also buried in the Cathedral, where she has provided a lasting memorial to the marital decisions in her life:

'Ursula Tyndall by birth.
Coxee by choice.
Upcher in age and for comfort.

Anno Aetatis 77.'[2]

There is an intriguing account by Fuller in his 'History of the University of Cambridge', originally printed in 1655:

'...Dr. Humphrey Tyndall, Dean of Ely...of whom passeth an improbable tradition:-That in the reign of Queen Elizabeth he was proffered by a protestant party in Bohemia to be made king thereof. Which he refused, alleging, That he had rather be Queen Elizabeth's subject, than a foreign prince. I know full well that crown is elective. I know also that for some hundreds of years it has been fixed to the German Empire. However, because no smoke without fire, or heat at least; there is something in it, more than appears to every eye. True it is that he was son to Sir Thomas Tyndall of Hockwold in Norfolk, and how Bohemian blood came into his veins I know not...'. A footnote in a later edition, printed in 1840, adds:

'Sir William Tyndale, of Hockwold in Norfolk, made Knight of the Bath by Hen. VII at the creation of Arthur, Prince of Wales, was then declared heir to the kingdom of Bohemia, in right of Margaret, his great-grandmother, neice of the King of Bohemia, and daughter to the duke of Theise. Dr. Humfrey Tyndale was great-grandson of this Sir William Tyndale'.[7] The 'Margaret' referred to was Margaret Felbrigg, the first wife of Sir Simon Felbrigg K.G.. She died in 1416 and is buried in Felbrigg Church, Norfolk. The inscription on the memorial brass to her and her husband, translated from the Latin reads:

'Here lie Simon Felbrigg, knight, former Standard bearer to the most illustrious lord, our lord the King Richard the Second. He died on the ..day of the month of .. in the year of our Lord 14.. and the lady Margaret formerly his wife, of the nation and noble blood of Bohemia and formally maid of honour to the most noble lady Anne, Queen of England; she died on the 27th day of June in the year of our Lord 1416; upon whose souls may God have mercy; Amen'. However, the blanks that were left for Sir Simon's death could never be filled in, because he married again and was buried with his second wife in Norwich.

Another account, by Francis Blomefield, (1705-52, priest and antiquarian), published in 1808, informs us that:

'Sir Simon Felbrigg was standard bearer to King Richard II... He married first, Margaret, daughter and heir (as our historians say) to the Duke of Silesia, and Theise in Germany, (nephew to the King of Bohemia), cousin to Anne, Queen-consort of Richard II, King of England...who came into England with that Queen, on her marriage, in 1381, and was one of her maids of honour... Alana, daughter and heir of Sir Simon Fellbrigg, by his first lady, was...the wife of....Sir William Tyndale of Dean, in Northamptonshire, to be her first (husband), by whom she had issue; and her grandson, Sir William Tyndale of Hockwold in Norfolk, was made Knight of the Bath, at the creation of Arthur Prince of Wales, son of King Henry VII and declared heir (in right of his grandmother, Margaret) to the kingdom of Bohemia'.[13] (Note: Margaret was –according to the first part of the account and other sources, *great*-grandmother of Sir William Tyndall of Hockwold). Yet another source, John Nichols, printer and antiquarian (1745-1826), claims that:

'a delegation of Bohemian boyars were sent to England to offer him (ie Sir William Tyndall) the throne but that he refused....'.[14] (There were two Tyndalls named 'Sir William'- the various accounts of the family involve several different spelling of the surname- firstly, Sir William Tyndall of Deene- also Dene, Dean- K.G., who married Alana, the daughter of Sir Simon Felbrigg and Margaret, and, secondly, their grandson Sir William Tyndall of Hockwold. Nichols appears to be referring to the latter). Information compiled by the 'The Tyndale Society', founded by the late Professor David Daniell of University College, London,[15] claims, (with other sources), that Humphrey Tyndall's descent from Alana- daughter of Sir Simon Felbrigg and Margaret- and her husband Sir William Tyndall, began with their son Sir Thomas Tyndall, followed, in a direct line of descent, by Sir William Tyndall K.B., 1452-97, (although variations of these dates have been claimed), Sir John Tyndall and, finally, Humphrey's father Sir Thomas Tyndall.

Unfortunately, the story is futher complicated by reports that Humphrey and the second Sir William were not the only members of the Tyndall family to be offered the Bohemian throne. Searle quotes another account related to the second Sir William's son, Sir John Tyndall, drawn up by 'Thomas Tyndall of Eastwood', a relative of Humphrey, who was an agent of Lord Burghley and lived in France during 1586-1600. At the time Searle was writing, this account was in the possession of a member of the family, John Warre Tyndall, Perridge House, Somersetshire:

'Margaret daughter and heir of Semovitz duke of Teschen, (in Silesia), by Elizabeth daughter of John (Count) of Luxemburg... and of his wife Elizabeth queen of Bohemia; the said Elizabeth being sister of Charles the 4th, Emperor, and aunt unto Wenceslaus and Sigismund, Emperors, and of Anne Queene of England, married to Richard 2nd: so that Queen Anne and Margaret were right cousins germaine.This Margaret came over with Queen Anne, and married with Sir Simon Bigod of Felbrigg K.G. standard bearer of England in the reign of Henry 5th...they of Austrich clayme Bohemia by a deed of Transaction, whereby it was conditioned and agreed (1515) that whichever house died first without male issue, the other should succeed. But the States of Bohemia sent to present the kingdom to Sir John Tyndall K.B., as his right by his great grand mother (in fact, his *great*, great, grandmother) Margaret of Teschen. He accepted the ornaments of a King, but refused the kingdom, to the ruin of his ancient and honorable house. The Baron of Slavatta in Bohemia told me in Paris, that of right a Tyndall should be their king...'.[1]

Searle also relates a fourth claim, this time relating to Humphrey Tyndall's father, from a book published in 1630 by Robert Johnson in London: 'Relations of the most famous kingdomes and commonwealths thorowout the world':

'Their Kingdom (Bohemia) is meerely elective, although by force and faction now almost made hereditary to the house of Austria, which it seems it was not, when as within these two Ages, that State made choice of one M.Tyndall an English gentleman father to M. Doctor Tyndall Master of Queenes College in Cambridge, sending over their Ambassadors to him, and by them their presents, which story is famously known in Cambridge'.[1]

However, in a detailed analysis,[16] Jonathan Holmes, (fellow and former Dean of Chapel at Queens'), points out that while the claim of Margaret's royal descent in the above report is contradicted by other evidence, Margaret may have been, (among other possibilities), the daughter of Premislav I, Duke of Teschen, the ambassador from Bohemia who was involved in the negotiations for the marriage treaty between Anne and Richard II. Also, Holmes suggests that, while the above claims of Margaret's royal ancestry cannot be substantiated, it remains possible that she had other Bohemian royal lineage. He concludes:

'It is quite clear, however, that the Tyndall family really did believe themselves to be descended from Bohemian royalty and that this was public knowledge…'.

In summary, the various sources are confusing, but we can assume that Humphrey Tyndall was directly descended from Margaret, who is buried in Felbrigg Church, who was related to the nobility of Bohemia, (and possibly to Bohemian royalty), and became the wife of Sir Simon Felbrigg. However, there are reports that no fewer than four generations of Tyndalls were approached as possible claimants for the throne of Bohemia, namely Margaret's great-grandson Sir William Tyndall, his son Sir John Tyndall, his son Sir Thomas Tyndall and his son Humphrey Tyndall.[1] If there was any basis to these reports, a likely time for an approach to the Tyndall family would have been during the interregnum for the Bohemian Crown, 1440-53, when the succession of the son of the previous King, Albert, was not recognized by the Czech nobility. However, Sir William Tyndall, Margaret's great-grandson, and the first recipient of the above claims, would have been a child at about the end of that period, as one report gives his date of birth as 1443 and another as 1452. However, Holmes points out that after the death of the Bohemian King George Podebrady in 1471, there were several claimants to the throne, and it does seem possible that, at some point (or points) in Bohemia's turbulent history, there were communications between members of the Bohemian establishment and the Tyndall family, including in the last years of Elizabeth I, when some of the Bohemian establishment may have been looking for a Protestant candidate for the throne. (In 1619-20, the throne of Bohemia would be briefly occupied by the Protestant Frederick V, the Elector Palatine, who was married to Elizabeth, daughter of James I of England). At a more prosaic level, perhaps a suggestion may have been made to Humphrey Tyndall, after a few drinks, that he might apply for the throne of Bohemia if he became tired of Cambridge politics, in view of previous rumours of Bohemian approaches to his family. This may then have led to his alleged response, embellished in the retelling with an offer of the crown, that he would rather be Queen Elizabeth's subject than a foreign prince.

References

1. Searle, W.G. The History of the Queens' College of St Margaret and St Bernard in the University of Cambridge. Part II 1560-1662. Sold by Deighton, Bell & Co; Macmillan & Co. London. 1871. pp 350-97.
2. Gray, J.H. The Queens' College of St Margaret and St Bernard. F.E.Robinson. London. 1898. pp 113-34.
3. Mullinger, J.B. A History of the University of Cambridge Longmans, Green, and Co. London. 1888. p 123.
4. Jenkins, E. Elizabeth and Leicester. The Phoenix Press. 2002.
5. Twigg, J. A History of Queens' College, Cambridge 1448-1986. The Boydell Press. 1987. pp 42-43, 68-72, 80, 93.
6. Cooper, C.H. Annals of Cambridge. Volume II. Warwick and Co., Cambridge. 1843. pp 457, 519-87.
7. Fuller, T. The History of the University of Cambridge from the Conquest to the year 1634. Deighton, J. & J.J., Stevenson, T. London. Reprinted 1840. (Original edition 1655). pp 164, 284-97.
8. Cooper. C.H. Cooper, T. Athenae Cantabrigienses. Volume 1I. Cambridge. Deighton, Bell & Co.; and Macmillan & Co. London: Bell & Daldy. Fleet Street. 1861. p 237.
9. Queens' College, Cambridge. 2019. Online.
10. Moore Smith, G. C. Laelia. A comedy acted at Queens' College, Cambridge probably on March 1st 1595. University Press. Cambridge.1910.
11. Cooper, C.H. Annals of Cambridge. Volume III. Warwick and Co., Cambridge. 1845. pp 13, 14, 24-26.

12. Bentham, J. et al. The history and antiquities of the conventual and cathedral church of Ely. University Press. Cambridge. 1771. pp 228-29.
13. Blomefield, F. North Erpingham Hundred: Felbrigg. Online. 2019.
14. Tyndall. Wikipedia. Online. 2020.
15. The Tyndale Society. 2020. Online.
16. Holmes, J.M. A Bohemian Mystery. The Record, Queens' College, Cambridge. 2009. Online. 2020.

CHAPTER 15

John Davenant. President 1614-22.

Summary.

John Davenant was born in 1572, the son of a wealthy merchant tailor. He was educated at Queens' and became a fellow of the College in 1597. He served in several College offices, was ordained, and graduated B.D. in 1601. His academic prowess attracted notice and, in 1609, he was elected as Lady Margaret's Professor of Divinity. He became President of Queens' in 1614 and his seven years in office was a time of prosperity for the College, which attracted an increasing number of students.

In 1615, King James and Prince Charles visited the University, when Davenant took part in the theology disputation.

In 1618, Davenant was selected by King James as one of the four representatives of the English Church at the Synod of Dort, which had been called to resolve doctrinal conflicts within european Protestantism. His contributions enhanced his reputation as a leading theologian and, in 1621, he was appointed Bishop of Salisbury. He succeeded his brother-in-law, Robert Townson, the son of the under-cook at Queens', who had died leaving a widow and many children.

Davenant, a bachelor, provided the Townson family with a home in the episcopal palace, and two of his Townson nieces were to marry subsequent Bishops of Salisbury. Davenant was active in promoting the interests of several other family members, including his nephew Thomas Fuller, the Church historian.

Bishop Davenant appears to have been universally respected, and is reported to have been benevolent and cheerful, despite never losing his dignity and gravitas. His twenty years at Salisbury were marked by various religious tensions involving the Puritan movement. In 1627, he published: 'An exposition of the Epistle of St Paul to the Colossians', which attracted theological plaudits and has been reprinted in the present century. Despite his theological expertise, he angered King Charles in 1630, when, in a sermon, he touched upon controversial ideas which the King had declared to be forbidden topics for preaching or discussion. He was called before the Privy Council, but an abject apology led to the matter being dropped and the King allowed his hand to be kissed before the Bishop's departure.

He died in 1641, at a time of uncertainty and division in Church and State, which heralded the Civil War. He is buried in Salisbury Cathedral. 'Few men appear to have been more honoured and venerated by all parties than Bishop Davenant'.[1]

Timeline.

1572.	Born in London, the son of a wealthy merchant tailor, (ie a tailor who also sells the cloth for the clothes he makes).
1587.	Admitted as a 'pensioner' to Queens', (ie he pays fees for board and tuition).
1591.	B.A. .
1594.	M.A. .
c1597.	Ordained.
1597.	Fellow of Queens'.
1599.	Lector Graecus (Greek lecturer) at Queens'.
1600.	Decanus sacelli (Dean) at Queens'.
1601.	B.D. .
1608.	The Earl of Salisbury, (Robert Cecil, University Chancellor), writes to the Vice-Chancellor recommending Davenant as the next Lady Margaret's Professor of Divinity.
1609.	Rector of Fleet, Lincolnshire. Elected Lady Margaret's Professor of Divinity. Proceeds D.D. .
1612.	Vicar of Oakington, Cambridgeshire, but resignes later in the year. Rector of Leake, Nottinghamshire.
1613.	Visit of Prince Charles, (Prince of Wales), and the Elector Palatine to Cambridge. Davenant takes part in the theology disputation.

1614. Death of Humphrey Tyndall; within a few hours, John Preston, fellow of Queens', travels to London to lobby the King's influential favourite, the Earl of Somerset, for a free election for the next President. Davenant is elected President and will support Preston, whose reputation will attract many pupils to Queens' from influential families.

1615. King James and Prince Charles visit the University. Davenant takes part in the theology disputation.

1616. Davenant is among those who visit the King at Newmarket to receive: 'certain directions' for the University.

1618. Becomes a royal chaplain. King James sends Davenant, George Carleton (Bishop of Llandaff), Joseph Hall (Dean of Worcester) and Samuel Ward (Master of Sydney Sussex College), to represent the English Church at the Synod of Dort, during November 1618-April 1619. (This was a council of the european Protestant churches). At Queens', building of the Walnut Tree Court is completed; this is needed because of the College's success in attracting pupils.

1620. Rector of Cottenham, Cambridgeshire.

1621. Davenant becomes Bishop of Salisbury, succeeding his brother-in-law Robert Townson, who was the son of the under-cook at Queens'. Consecrated, (with William Laud, Bishop of St David's, Wales, and Valentine Carey, Bishop of Exeter), by several bishops, including his previous rival for the Presidency, George Montaigne, Bishop of London. There is a conflict between Crown and Parliament, when Parliament produces the 'Great Protestation'. (James will soon dissolve Parliament, in February 1622).

1622. Resigns as President and is succeeded by John Mansell.

1625. Death of James I and the accession of Charles I.

1626. Davenant gives £100 to the Queens' library.

1627. Davenant publishes: 'Exposition of the Epistle of St Paul to the Colossians'.

1628. Preaches a sermon to Parliament.

1630. Davenant preaches before King Charles and the court at Whitehall, when he offends the King by addressing the issue of predestination. (The King had forbidden preaching on certain disputed aspects of theology as defined in the 'Thirty-nine Articles of the Church of England', finalised in 1571). Davenant is called before the Privy Council, but no further action is taken after he promises future obedience.

1633. William Laud is appointed Archbishop of Canterbury; (he supported changes in Church ceremonial, thus alienating those of Puritan persuasion. He would be accused of treason in 1640 and executed in 1645).

1634. Death of Davenant's sister, Margaret Townson, who, with her many children, had lived with her bachelor brother during her widowhood.

1640. King Charles is desperately short of money and is forced to summon another English Parliament, the 'Long Parliament', which shows marked hostility to the King. This heralds the onset of the Civil War in 1642.

1641. The King's unpopular servants, Archbishop Laud and the Earl of Strafford, are arrested and confined in the Tower of London. Strafford is executed. Davenant dies on the 20th April of 'consumption'. (Thus he was spared the traumas and further religious conflicts of the Civil War). His nephew, Thomas Fuller, the eminent historian, is one of the family present at his uncle's death. Davenant is buried in Salisbury Cathedral.

Theologian with impressive academic ability. One of the four royal delegates to the Synod of Dort. His Presidency was marked by a period of prosperity at Queens'. Bishop of Salisbury from 1621 until his death in 1641.

It is claimed that John Davenant was descended from a Sir John Davenant who lived in Headingham, Essex, during the era of Henry III, who reigned during 1216-72.[1] He was born in Watling Street, London, in 1572, and baptized at All Hallows, Bread Street, on the 25th May. He was the second son of John Davenant, a wealthy merchant tailor. After attending Merchant Taylors'

School, he came to Queens' as a fee-paying 'pensioner' in 1587, graduating B.A. in 1591 and M.A. in 1594. He was elected a fellow of Queens' in 1597, but only after the death of his father, who had insisted that he refuse a previous offer of a fellowship, on the basis that acceptance would be:

'a bending of these places from the direct intent of the Founders when they are bestowed on such as have plenty'.[1] Davenant held several offices at Queens': 'examinator' (ie in charge of exams) during 1598-99, lector Graecus (Greek lecturer) during 1599-1600 and Decanus sacelli (Dean) during 1600-01. He was ordained during this period and graduated B.D. in 1601.

His academic prowess became apparent, and William Whitaker, Master of St John's College and Regius Professor of Divinity:

'hearing him dispute said that he would in time prove the Honour of the University'.[1] This was an accurate prediction and, in 1608, Robert Cecil, (Earl of Salisbury and Chancellor of the University), wrote to the Vice-Chancellor:

'When I understand your permission to proceed to the election of the Divinity Reader of the Lady Margaret, though I have no purpose to prevent Mr Playfayer, formally interested in the same, yet I have thought to recommend unto you one Mr Davenant, B.D. and Fellow of Queens' College, well known among you, and do request that if the reputation of his parts and learning be equal with his competitor, you would acknowledge my inclination and suffrage with him, and make choice of him to the Readership'.[2] This referred to an impending election to the Lady Margaret's Professorship of Divinity, when the incumbent, Thomas Playfayer (or Playfere), was seeking re-election. Despite Salisbury's entreaties, Playfayer was re-elected, but he died in 1609 and, the next day, the Vice-Chancellor wrote to Salisbury supporting Davenant as the successor. He was was duly elected and re-elected in 1612, holding the position until he left Cambridge in 1622.[2] In 1609, he became D.D. and was one of the University preachers during 1609-12.[2]

In March 1612, Davenant was appointed vicar of Oakington, a living in the gift of Queens', but, for reasons unknown, he resigned later in the year. However, this short tenure produced an anecdote related by Davenant's nephew, the historian Thomas Fuller (1608-61):

'A reverend doctour in Cambridge, and afterwards bishop of Sarisbury, was troubled at his small living, Hoggington (Oakington), with a peremptory anabaptist, who plainly told him: "It goes against my conscience to pay you tithes, except you can show me a place of Scripture whereby they are due to you". The Doctour returned: "Why should it not go much against my conscience, that you should enjoy your nine parts, for which you can show no place in Scripture?" To whom the other rejoined, "But I have, for my land, deeds and evidences from my fathers, who purchased and were peaceably possessed thereof by the laws of the land". "The same is my title", said the Doctour; "tithes being confirmed unto me by many statutes of the land, time out of mind". Thus he drove that nail, not which was of the strongest metal or sharpest point, but which would go best for the present. It was argumentum ad hominem, fittest for the person he was to meddle with, who afterwards peaceably paid his tithes unto him...'.[2]

The following year, 1613, saw a visit to Cambridge by Prince Charles, Prince of Wales, accompanied by the Elector Palatine. As was usual with royal visits, disputations were arranged and Davenant took a leading role at the proceedings at Great St Mary's Church, moderating the debate in theology:

'It was well for all sides, that the best Divine in my Judgement, that ever was in that place, Dr Davenant held the Rains of the Disputation; he kept within the even Boundals of the Cause; he charmed him with the Caducaean Wand (ie the staff carried by Hermes in Greek mythology) of Dialectical Prudence; he order'd him to give just Weight and no more...Such an Arbiter as he was now, such he was, and no less, year by year, in all Comitial Disputations (ie relating to an assembly); wherein whosoever did well, yet constantly he had the greatest Acclamation.[1]

The death of Humphrey Tyndall in 1614 had been anticipated by the fellows at Queens', in particular by John Preston, who wanted Davenant to be the successor. Indeed, Tyndall's possible demise had been considered before, as described in Chapter 14, when the President's ill-health in 1608 had prompted one of the fellows, George Montaigne, to write to the Chancellor asking for a free election when the vacancy occurred, in which he expected victory. In 1614 Montaigne was now Dean of Westminster, but he still coveted the Presidency and was a strong candidate. Preston acted very quickly following Tyndall's death, by travelling to London to lobby the King's influential favourite, the Earl of Somerset. Thomas Ball's 'Life of Dr John Preston', in Samuel Clarke's 'The Lives of Thirty-Two English Divines', 1677,[3] is quoted by Searle in his history of the College of 1871:

'...Doctor Tyndall died...There were very many that had their eyes upon it, but Doctor Mountain (ie Montaigne) in a special manner, who was often heard for to professe, he would rather be Master of that Colledge than Dean of Westminster. But Master Preston had another in his eye. Doctor Davenant...for his worth and parts was already chosen Margaret Professour, and read in the Schools with much applause those excellent Lectures upon the Colossians which are now printed; Him Master Preston pitched upon, but knew it must be carried very privately; for the mountain (ie Montaigne) was already grown into some bignesse, was one of parts, and first observed in acting Miles gloriosus in the Colledge, and had been Chaplain unto the Earl of Essex, but like the Heliotrope or flower of the Sun, did noe adore Sir Robert Carr, already Viscount Rochester, the only favorite...Master Preston having laid his plot before-hand had taken care that word should be daily brought him how the old Doctor did...and laid horses and all things ready; and upon notice of his being dead, goes presently and was at London, and in White-Hall...His businesse was only to get a free election...But knowing also with whom he had to do, makes some addresses unto Viscount Rochester in the behalf of Doctor Davenant, who being unacquainted with his Chaplains appitite to that particular, was fair and willing to befriend a learned enterprise. (Montaigne was chaplain to Robert Carr, a 'favourite' of the King, who was created Viscount Rochester in 1611 and had been advanced to the Earldom of Somerset in 1613). So Master Preston returns unto the Colledge...

and assembling Doctor Davenants Friends...and so they went immediately to Election, and it was easily and fairly carried for Doctor Davenant, who being called, was admitted presently. But when Doctor Mountain understood that Doctor Tyndal was departed, he sends and goes to Court and Colledge for to make friends: But alas the game was played, and he was shut out. Never did Aetna or Vesuvius more fume but there was no cure...'.[1]

However, the accuracy of this account is uncertain and appears biased against Montaigne, who, rather surprisingly, received the news of Tyndall's death within a day, as he writes a letter of condolence to the College, dated the following day, advocating a free election:

'To the Rightworshipf^ll^ the Senior fellow of Queenes Colledg now at home and the rest of y^r^ worthy socy.

Gentlemen, Having lived long in that Colledg and brought up in the same under Dr Tindall, I could doe no lesse then condole his death wth youe and ye Colledg, from whome, whilst I lived ther, not only my self but the whole Colledg receaved so much good...If I were worthy to advise youe, the first thing I would have done should be an humble supplication to his Matie for a free Election... and then, if that be granted, I nothing doubt but God will bless the rest...A faythful sevant and friend George Montaigne. Westminster this 13th of Octob. 1614'.[1] However, Montaigne may have been making the best of the situation if he knew that permission for a free election had already been given, earlier in the day. (Montaigne, who was elected a fellow of Queens' in 1592, went on to have an outstanding career, as Bishop of Lincoln in 1617, of London in 1621, of Durham in 1627, and finally, as Archbishop of York in 1628, the year of his death).

During Davenant's seven years as President, he was a strong supporter of John Preston as tutor, whose reputation attracted many students, often as 'fellow-commoners' from well-connected families.[4] (A fellow-commoner was a rank of student above pensioner and sizar but below nobleman. He paid more fees than a pensioner and had more privileges, such as being able to 'common', or dine, at the fellows' table). This led to Preston being described as: 'the greatest pupil-monger in England'.[4] This was a time of prosperity for Queens', which led to further accomodation to be built in the 'Walnut Tree Court'; this was completed in 1618, while a shortfall in the funding of £172 1s. 2d., was provided by Davenant, who was subsequently repaid.[4] John Preston had been an exceptionally industrious student, and one contemporary, reporting on his sleep habits, notes that:

'he made it short; and whereas notwithstanding all endeavours, there was one in college that would always be up before him, he would let the bed cloths hang down, so that in the night they might fall off and so the cold awaken him'.[5] Preston was elected a fellow of Queens' in 1611 and, for the next 17 years until his death, he was very influential in Cambridge as a preacher with Puritan sympathies.[6] Under Davenant, Preston was Dean and catechist (ie teacher of religion) as well as tutor, and his sermons were so popular that the College chapel was often full before the fellows arrived. This led the Vice-Chancellor to restrict attendance to members of the College.[4,6] His responsibilities as tutor led to his intervention to break up the relationship between one of his pupils, Sir Capel Bedell, and the daughter of Dr Newcombe, commissary to the Bishop of Ely. But Dr Newcombe was not at all pleased and, using his authority in the diocese, forbade Preston to preach an afternoon sermon at the parish of St Botolph, in which Newcombe lived, although a congregation had already arrived. But, after Newcombe had left, Preston defied the veto and preached: 'a very savoury and holy sermon'.[4] Newcombe then went to Newmarket to complain to the King, who directed the Bishop of Ely to investigate. This resulted in Preston being summoned before the heads of colleges, including Davenant, when he was reqired to apologise to Newcombe and then to preach another sermon at St Botolph's instructing people to attend their own parish churches rather than elsewhere.[4] This sermon, on: 'prayer as a means to growth in grace', must have made an impression, as Gray, in his history of the College of 1898, relates that: 'They came to scoff and they stayed to pray'.[4] However, he was forbidden to preach outside Queens' without permission of the Vice-Chancellor. But he was soon in favour again and, with the support of George Villiers, Earl of Buckingham, (a 'favourite' of James I, and soon to be Duke of Buckingham in 1623), he was appointed a chaplain to the Prince of Wales in 1621.[4] In 1622, after Davenant's departure from Queens', Buckingham's influence facilitated Preston's election as Master of the strongly Puritan Emmanuel College, and it has been suggested that Preston was not keen to remain at Queens' without Davenant's support, as: 'the Fellows for the most part were not his friends'.[4] In 1624, Preston declined the offer of a bishopric (at Gloucester) to take up an appointment as Lecturer at Holy Trinity Church, Cambridge, which was an important position for proclaiming Puritan ideas.[6] In 1625, he was present at the death of King James at Theobalds House, Hertfordshire, and accompanied the new monarch, Charles I, to London for the latter's proclamation. But his influence declined, and his career was cut short by his early death in 1628.

King James, together with Prince Charles, visited the University in 1615, when Davenant took part in the disputation in theology with the other divinity professor at Cambridge, John Richardson, which was moderated by the Vice-Chancellor, Samuel Harsnet. Davenant proposed that: 'the Pope has no temporal power over kings', while Richardson opposed the claim, referring to the excommunication of Theodosius by St Ambrose. This annoyed the King, who said that St Ambrose had acted most arrogantly; Richardson must then have decided that retreat was the best option: 'and so sitting down, he desisted from any farther dispute'.[4] Another of the disputations, in philosophy, involved John Preston and Matthew Wren of Pembroke Hall, later Bishop of Ely. The question was: 'whether dogs could make syllogisms' (ie a reasoned deduction from two propositions). Preston said they could, arguing that:

'The major proposition in the mind of a harrier is this: The hare is gon either this or that way: and with his nose he smells out the minor (ie one of the propositions), namely, She is not gon that way, and follows the conclusion, Ergo, this way, with open mouth'. After Wren's objections, the King intervened and described the case of one of his own dogs that was right, when all the rest had gone wrong. The event ended with the moderator asking his Majesty to:

'consider how his illustrious influence had already ripened and concocted all these Arguments and Understandings, that wheras in the morning the reverend and grave Divines could not make Syllogismes, the Lawyers could not, nor the Physicians, now every Dog could, especially his Majesties...and the king went off well pleased with the businesse'.[4] Also, Preston was involved with a different aspect of the royal visit, when the play 'Ignoramus' was performed before the King at Clare College. One of Preston's students at Queens', Morgan, was chosen to play the part of the heroine, Rosabella, but Preston objected to his pupil appearing in women's clothes. However, he was overruled by the youth's guardians. (Morgan would be killed in 1643 at the first battle of Newbury in the civil war, fighting for King Charles, who was in personal command of his army). Other members of the cast included several future luminaries: Lord Holles; the Earl of Northampton; the Bishop of Peterborough; the Dean of Canterbury; and the Master of Corpus Christi College. The fact that several of the cast were ordained attracted some comment.[4]

In 1618, Davenant was selected by the King to represent the English Church at the Synod of Dort, (also known as Dordt or Dordrecht). This was a meeting initiated by the Dutch Reformed Church to resolve doctrinal disputes which had followed the rise of Arminianism, a brand of Protestantism based on the ideas of the Dutch theologian Jacobus Arminius. His supporters, known as 'Remonstrants', had published 'The Remonstrance' in 1610, which consisted of five controversial doctrinal statements. This was submitted to the States General of the Netherlands, who arranged the Synod of 1618 in an attempt to settle these conflicts. Also, there were political overtones, as the Arminians were suspected to be working for Philip III of Spain. (The Synod took place towards the end of the Twelve Years' Truce, 1609-21, which interrupted the Eighty Years' War, 1568-1648, between the Seventeen Provinces- of what are now The Netherlands, Belgium and Luxembourg- and their Spanish sovereigns). However, the Remonstrants did not cooperate with the procedures of the Synod and, in their absence, the final conclusion was a rejection of Arminianism. In due course, the thirteen Remonstrant ministers at the Synod were ordered to leave the United Provinces, while a prominent supporter of the Remonstrants, Johan van Oldenbarnevelt, was accused of treason and beheaded only four days after the Synod had ended.

Davenant's fellow delegates were George Carleton- Bishop of Llandaff, Joseph Hall- Dean of Worcester, and Davenant's friend Samuel Ward- Master of Sidney Sussex College, Cambridge. Before their departure, they were all summoned to attend the King at Newmarket, to receive his instructions, which included:

'on all occasions, you inure (ie accept) yourselves to the practice of the Latin tongue...'. Two of the delegates, Davenant and Ward, had a further meeting with the King, for two hours, at Royston on October 8th, before travelling to Dort via Middelburgh and The Hague. Davenant was accompanied by his nephew, Edward Davenant, at that time a fellow of Queens', after the latter's leave and allowances had been granted by the College.[4] The oath of admission to the Synod was as follows, (the spelling reflects that the following account was published in 1897):

'I promise before God, whom I believe and adore, the present Searcher of the heart and reins, that in all this Synodal action, wherein shall be appointed the examination, judgement, and decision, was well of the known five Articles and difficulties therein arising, as of all other Doctrinals, that I will not make use of any Humane Writing, but only of God's Word for the certain and undoubted Rule of Faith, and that I shall propound nothing to myself in this whole cause, besides the glory of God, the peace of the church, and especially the preservation of the purity of Doctrine therein...'.[2]

Morris Fuller, who was vicar of St Mark's, Marylebone Road, London, had been educated at Queens', and was a descendant of Davenant's sister Judith, (as was the historianThomas Fuller). In his account of Davenant's life (published in 1897) he describes the proceedings:[2]

'...These four divines had allowed them by the states ten pounds sterling a day: threescore and ten pounds by the week: an entertainment far larger than what was appointed to any other foreign Theologues; and politickly proportioned, in grateful consideration of the greatness of His Majesty who employed them. And these English divines...freely gave what they had freely received, keeping a Table general, where any fashionable foreigner was courteously and plentifully entertained...for a month or more the King received from them no particulars of their proceedings, whereat His Majesty was most highly offended. But afterwards, understanding that this defect was caused by the countermands of an higher King, even of him who gathereth the wind in his fist, stopping all passages by contrary weather...(he was)...highly pleased, when four weekly despatches...came altogether to His Majesty's hands...It was not till after the Synod had been opened for a considerable time that the Arminian divines put in an appearance. They could see at a glance the treatment they might expect...The Calvinists were determined to make the Arminians answer in their way. The Arminians were equally resolved to choose their own way...It was therefore resolved to dismiss the Arminians as incorrigible...Having thus got rid of their troublesome opponents, the Calvinists then proceeded to discuss, and of course to condemn, their opinions...A fierce passage of arms took place...The English Divines were still the most moderate, reasonable and charitable of the assemblage...The four English and the Scotch Deputy (Walter Balcanquall, fellow of Pembroke Hall) formed a College, and agreed upon joint opinions among themselves, which they proposed to the Synod. (Dr Hall had returned to England due to ill-health and had been replaced by Dr Goad, chaplain to the Archbishop of Canterbury)...As a rule their views seem to have been received with marked deference...Upon most points they seem to have been pretty unanimous, Upon the "Extent of Redemption" however they differed. Bishop Carleton and Dr Goad held that Christ died only for the elect; Drs Davenant and Ward, that he died for the whole world...the doctrine of Redemption as a blessing to be universally proposed and offered to all men, was so little relished by the Synod of Dort, that it is clear, nothing but the threatened loss of the English deputies induced its insertion...Dr Davenant declared he would sooner cut off his hand than rescind any word of it: in which he was supported by Ward, and it was ultimately agreed to...(Davenant's position was a compromise: that while Christ died for all men, not just for the elect, not all would receive salvation). On 23rd April 1619, the Canons were signed by all the members of the Synod. Arminians were pronounced heretics, schismatics, teachers of false doctrines...The synod ended on April 27th 1619. The English delegates received £200 to finance their return journey and a commemorative gold medal...they were very graciously welcomed by the King with every mark of high and royal approbation...'.[2]

After an absence of seven months at the Synod, the delegates were received by the King who: 'after courteously entertaining of them, favourably dismissed them'[4] and Davenant returned to his duties at Cambridge, where his lectures were:

'appreciated and attended with an eager crowd of listeners...

I was present (said a gentleman of the period) oftentimes also in the public lectures in the schools, upon points of controversy, especially those of Dr Davenant...in which he most clearly confuted the blasphemies of Arminius, Bestius, and the rest of that rabble of Jesuited Anabaptists; by all which my knowledge was much increased'.[2]

The four English delegates to the Synod would all be rewarded by further preferment and, in 1621, Davenant was appointed as Bishop of Salisbury, having been recommended by John Williams, Dean of Westminster, who states:

'Twelve years he had been Public Reader in Cambridge, and had adorn'd the Place with much Learning, as no Professor in Europe did better deserve to receive the labourer's Peny at the twelfth Hour of the Day'.[1] But this promotion was considered unusual, as he had not previously held significant Church office, and the bishopric of Salisbury had a substantial income. Many leases of the land of the See:

'were but newly expired when Davenant came to this See; so that there tumbled into his coffers vast summes'.[2] But letters written to his friend Samuel Ward before his move to Salisbury, show his reluctance at leaving Cambridge:

'Good Sir…I hope…I shall obtein leav to hould my Mastership some time, wch yf I doe, (& it bee so thought fitt,) I shall not bee unwilling to continew my payns in ye Lecture-reading for a time, My body may bee tossed up and down to other places, but Cambridg will alwaies have my heart…your assured loving friend John Davenant. May 15 1621…'.

'Sir, I have spent heer many dayes in much sorrow; and could wish my selfe at Cambridg…My sister is still but weak in body, & troubled in minde; yet I have persuaded her to goe down into ye country amongest her children…I hope to bee sett at liberty, return to Queens Colledg…I hope to obteine some reasonable time for houlding my Mastership, but what will bee granted as yet I know not…I know not how soon I may resigne ye divinity Lecture, I pray bethink your selfe of a Successor, & yf you would undergoe ye payns, I doubt not but ye whole univrsity would bee gladd of it, & never look after any other…Your very loving friend John Davenant. Westminster May 27th, 1621'.

'Sr…I suppose I shall not hould ye Mastership beyond ye next Audit: and for my Lecture I purpose to give it over at ye end of Michaelmas terme…Your very loving friend John Saru, Elect. Queens Colledg, August 5, 1621'.[2] (Davenant was indeed succeeded as Lady Margaret's Professor of Divinity by Dr Ward). It is reported that when he took his leave of Queens', Davenant asked an elderly College servant, John Rolfe, (or Roise or Rosse) to pray for him. Rolfe replied that he rather needed his lordship's prayers:

'Yea, John, said he, and I need thine too, being now to enter into a calling wherein I shall meet with many great temptations'.[2]

In the year of Davenant's appointment as Bishop, his nephew Thomas Fuller, the future Church historian, was admitted as a student to Queens', on the 19th June 1621, aged thirteen. His tutors were his cousin, Edward Davenant, and John Thorp, a future prebendary of Salisbury. It is reported that he took his degree with unusual credit in 1625, in the same year as his cousin Robert Townson, (son of the late Robert Townson, Bishop of Salisbury), was elected a fellow. Fuller was not so fortunate, possibly because the Statutes did not allow two fellowships to be held by natives of his county.[2] But his uncle continued to promote his interests as shown by a letter to Dr Ward dated July 17th, 1626:

'Good Dr Ward, I hope you will make a jorney this summer into these Western parts and visit us here in Salisbury on your way…I would intreat you to cast about, where I may have yo best likelihood for preferring my nephew Sr ffuller (the academic title of "Sir" was applied to graduates and those in holy orders) to a fellowship, yf hee cannot speed in Queens Colledg. Dr Mansel (now President of Queens') has not yet given mee no answer one way or other, but I think ere long hee will…Your very loving friend, Jo. Saru'.[2] A further letter to Dr Ward, written from Lackham, near Chippenham, the seat of Henry Montagu, First Earl of Manchester, whose family knew the Fullers, is dated 23rd September 1627:

'…I have writt unto the Master of Queens Colledg, to know what likelihood ther is for ye preferment of my nephew Thomas ffuller unto a fellowship…I am resolved (yf ther bee no hope ther) to seek what may bee done els-where, and herein I must crave your favour and assistance. I pray therefore (yf you can prefer him in your own colledg) let mee intreat your best assistance therein: or yf you have no means to do it there, make trial what Dr Preston thinks may bee doune in Immanuel Colledg. In briefe, I should bee glad to have him spedd of a fellowship in any Colledg…'.[2] Dr Ward received another letter the following month; the matter had still not been resolved and further favours for the Bishop's family were solicited:

'…Dr Mansell has not yet given mee a resolute answer: whether S ffuller bee in possibility of being chosen at their next election or no. But I have now writt unto him and expect a full and finall answer yf ther bee no hope of speeding in Queens' Colledg…I once motioned another matter unto you wch I would desire you still to think of. It was this, that when you know any discreet man, competently provided for, who intends marriadg, you would (as from your selfe), wish him to bee a suiter unto some of our maidens (ie the six Townson girls) wherof two are now marriadgable. My sister will give reasonable portions, and I shall bee ready to doe somewhat for any woorthy man that shall match wth any of them, as occasion is offered mee. The sickness continues so at Salisbury, that I doubt, I shall keep my Christmas here at Laycock...Your very loving friend Jo. Saru. Latcham Oct. 25th, 1627'.[2] Another letter soon followed, on the 28th November, 1627:

'Dr Ward, I hartily thank you for your mindefulness of my nephew Sr ffuller: what Queens Colledg. Will doe for him I know not...As for my nieces ye elder is seventeen yeer ould: a maide of a sober and gentle disposition, and every way fitt to make a good wife for a divine...'.[2] A final letter relating to Thomas Fuller was written almost a year later on October 21st 1628:

'Dr Ward, I am informed they have made a late election at Queens' Colledg, and utterly passed by my nephew. I would the Master had but doune mee that kindness, as not to have made mee expect some kindenes from him. I should have taken it much better, then his doing of lesse than nothing, after some promise of his favourable assistance. I am loat Mr ffuller should be snatched away from ye University before hee bee growen somewhat riper...'.[2]

Having graduated M.A. aged twenty in 1628, Thomas Fuller left Queens' and was admitted to Dr Ward's College, Sidney Sussex, but as a fellow-commoner. This arrangement, which will have provided Fuller with many of the privileges of a fellow, required the payment of higher fees, compared with those required from students ranked as pensioners or sizars, and these expenses may have been met by the Bishop. In 1630, Fuller became a curate at St Benet's Church, Cambridge, and, in 1631, his uncle provided him with the preferment of a prebend at Salisbury Cathedral. He graduated B.D. from Sidney Sussex College in 1635, having been appointed rector of Broadwindsor, Dorset, in 1634. In later life he was admitted D.D. at Cambridge in 1660, he was heard preaching by Samuel Pepys, and he became Chaplain Extraordinary to Charles II. He is remembered for his writings, in particular: 'History of the Worthies of England'; 'Church-History of Britain: From the Birth of Jesus Christ Until the Year MDCXLIII'; and 'The History of the University of Cambridge: from the Conquest to the year 1634'.

Davenant was consecrated as Bishop of Salisbury on the 18th November 1621, in a ceremony with two other newly-appointed divines, William Laud, who became Bishop of St David's (and subsequently Archbishop of Canterbury from 1633, until his execution in 1645), and Valentine Carey, who became Bishop of Exeter. The service was conducted by George Montaigne, Bishop of London (and Davenant's erstwhile rival for the Presidency), assisted by five other bishops.[1] On the next day the new bishops took their seats in the House of Lords.[2] His predecessor at Salisbury had been his late brother-in-law Robert Townson, a son of the under-cook at Queens', who had been elected a fellow of Queens' in 1597, on the same day as Davenant. Townson had been baptised at St Botolph's Church, Cambridge, and admitted to Queens' as a 'sizar' in 1587, aged 12, after his father's death. (This class of student received assistance such as free meals and lodging, and lower fees, sometimes in return for doing a defined job). Townson had progressed to be Dean of Westminster in 1617 and chaplain to King Charles I, before his promotion as Bishop of Salisbury in July 1620. However, he died within a year, leaving his widow with the responsibility of (according to Searle) 15 children:

'Neither plentifully provided for, nor...maintenance, which rather hastened than caused the advancement' of his brother-in-law,[1] as it is reported that Davenant's friends:

'in pity and commiseration for Mrs Townson's case, (and as he was) a single man and well-deserving, (requested that) he might succeed his Brother (in-law) in the Bishoprick, and so make some provision for his children'.[1] The children were, indeed, rescued from penury, and a contemporary at the court of King James claims that:

'it was probably on account of the domestic burthen that thus devolved upon him, rather than from his merit, that our Bishop was excused the payment of the introductory fees, and of the annual pension, which was then, it seems, customarily paid to the crown on all similar appointments, proportionate to the wealth or poverty of the individual'.[1] Also, perhaps concerned about the extent of Davenant's new responsibilities, it is reported that the King: 'charged him not to marry'.[1]

Another account of Davenant's promotion is given in 'Brief Lives' by John Aubrey (1626-67), quoted by Searle:

'...His predecessor, Dr Tounson, married his sister, continued in the see but a little while, and left several children unprovided for, so the K. or rather D. of Bucks (Duke of Buckingham) gave Bp. Davenant the bishoprick out of pure charity. Sr Anth Weldon (Sir Anthony Weldon, 1583-1648, courtier) says, "twas the only bishoprick y^{t} he disposed of without simony, all others being made merchandise of for the advancement of his kindred. Bp. Davenant being invested, married all his nieces to clergie-men, so he was at no expence for their preferment" '.[1]

Bishop Townson's widow lived with her brother until her death in 1634 and is buried in Salisbury Cathedral. Davenant's will, written in 1637, mentions three nephews and six nieces. His nephew Robert Townson was a fellow of Queens' during 1625-33, while two of his nieces were to marry Bishops of Salisbury: Ellen, who married Humphrey Henchman, Bishop of Salisbury 1660-63, (and of London 1663-75), and Maria, who married Alexander Hyde, Bishop of Salisbury, 1665-67. (Their daughter married Sir Henry Parker, ancestor of Admiral Sir Hyde Parker, 1739-1807, who gave the signal which was famously ignored by his subordinate Horatio Nelson at the battle of Copenhagen in 1801). In 1622, Davenant dispensed patronage to his brother-in-law Thomas Fuller, rector of St Peter's Chuch, Ardwinckle, (the father of the historian Thomas Fuller), who was appointed prebendary of Highworth and, on the latter's death in 1632, this position was given to Davenant's nephew John Townson, a son of the previous Bishop of Salisbury.

In January 1622 , Davenant, together with Dr Carey, Bishop of Exeter, and Dr Richardson, Master of Trinity, was invited to St John's College by the Master, Dr Gwyn, for supper followed by a game of cards in the hall.[1] As noted above, Davenant was rather reluctant to resign as President and remained in office until April 22nd 1622, while the College accounts for this month include:

'For a Dinner bestowed on my Lord of Sarisburie at his departure.... 5^{l}. 15^{s}. 2^{d}. For a paire of gloves bestowed on him...1^{l}. 18^{s}. 0^{d}.',[1] and we have a glimpse of him soon after his consecration, when he was asked to attend the King at Newmarket. However, he refused to ride on a Sunday, the Lord's day;

'and came (though a day later to the Court) no less welcome to the king, not only accepting his excuse, but also commending his seasonable forbearance'.[7]

Davenant, his sister, and her large family, were fortunate in his new domestic environment at Salisbury, in the picturesque surroundings of the palace and Cathedral Close; however, Morris Fuller tells us that:

'when Bishop Davenant entered upon his long episcopate at Salisbury of twenty years, he found the state of the diocese far from satisfactory, and in a chronic state of lethargy, following upon the reaction which settled down after the ernestness and zeal of the Reformation era'.[2] The Bishop is reported to have been benevolent and cheerful but never losing his dignity and gravitas. He did not make harsh or unkind judgements, being:

'more sensible of his own infirmities than others, being humble in himself and therefore charitable to others'.[2]

The problems encountered by Davenant at Salisbury reflected the religious conflicts involving the Puritans, whose influence had developed in Elizabeth's reign. They wanted futher reform of the Church of England and:

'it became the right thing yo do, a mark of true patriotism, to abjure anything and everything that savoured in the most remote degree of Rome...What were deemed superstitious observances had ceased, but in their place we find either cold indifference, or unseemly disorders and strife'.[2] In 1630, at the Salisbury Guildhall:

'Divers persons were ordered and enjoined to look to disorders in the church in the time of divine service, and to apprehend the offenders, or certify their names to one or more justices, on Sundays and Holydays'.[2] An example of the challenges to the Bishop's authority was the behaviour of the Recorder of Salisbury, Henry Sherfield, an uncompromising Puritan, who objected to the images in a window of St Edmund's Church in the City. He proceeded to: 'breaking the same with his staff' and, despite a message from Davenant to abstain from further action, threatened to destroy all the remaining windows. This led to his appearance before the 'Star Chamber', of privy counsellors and judges in 1633, where he was convicted, committed to the Fleet prison, fined £500 and ordered to acknowledge his offence.[2] An account of a visit by Archbishop Laud to Salisbury Cathedral in 1634 also reflected the: 'Puritan disorders', and:

'the state of neglect and disorder in which the cathedral and its services were at this time...in most parishes in Wiltshyre, Dorsetshire, and the westerne partes, there is still a Puritane and an honest man chosen churchwardens together. The Puritane always crosses the other in repayres and adorning the church, as also in the presentments of unconformities, and in the issue puts some trick or other upon the honest man, to put him to sue for his charges hee hath been at for the Church'.[2]

King James died on the 27th March 1625, and was succeeded by his son Charles, while later in the year:

'On the 28th of September we find the King and Queen at Wilton, where their Majesties were entertained by William, the third Earl of Pembroke. The council was commanded to meet (at Salisbury) and the Episcopal palace was required for the accommodation of Blainville, the French envoy, but the bishop Dr Davenant refused to relinquish his residence'.[1] Perhaps the logistics of moving his sister and the many children defeated him!

In 1627, Davenant published: 'An exposition of the Epistle of St Paul to the Colossians', based on lectures he had given while Lady Margaret's Professor of Divinity, (and which has been reprinted in the 21st century). It is dedicated:

'To his benignant mother the University of Cambridge, at all times held in highest renown for virtue, piety, and the acknowledgment of sound doctrine, these first fruits of his theological professorship, originally composed therein and now again revised, are willingly and deservedly given, dedicated and inscribed, in token of affection and honour, by her most devoted son, John Davenant'.[2] To the present day, this has attracted plaudits fom theologians; the 'Prince of Preachers', Charles Spurgeon, (1834-92, who regularly preached to over 10,000 in London), in his 'Commenting and Commentaries', considered the work in the first rank of commentaries, and Charles Bridges,

(1794-1869, a preacher and theologian who was educated at Queens'), states:

'I know no exposition upon a detached portion of Scripture (with the single exception of Owen on the Hebrews) that will compare with it in all parts...in depth, accuracy, and discursiveness'. (John Owen, 1616-83, was a University of Oxford theologian who wrote a seven-volume commentary on the Epistle to the Hebrews). Further publications followed, including, in 1631: 'A Treatise on Justification, or the Disputatio de Justitia habituali et actuali, of the Right Rev. John Davenant, D.D. Bishop of Salisbury, and Lady Margaret's Professor, Cambridge, delivered to the divinity students in that University'.

His exposition of the Colossians is refered to in a series of letters to his friend Dr Ward:

'Good Dr Ward; Mr Henchman (Dr Humphrey Henchman, who married his neice Ellen and was Bishop of Salisbury, 1660-63) acquainted mee wth your desire that I should publish my Readings upon ye Colossians. I confess I have always been, and am very backward to putt any thing of mine in print...And besides, I cannot revise them as were fitt; mine eyes not serving mee to read mine own hand. Yet that you may see how easy I am to yield unto ye psuasions of my friends though contrary to mine own minde; I have caused my scholler Vincent to transcribe those my readings upon ye Epistle to ye Colloss: wch hee has now finished. Yf you shall iudg them fitt for ye presse, I will comitt them to your disposition...The king is expected very shortly heer at Wilton: and ye Counsell (as it is sayd) will spend ye greater part of ye Winter heer at Saru, that so they may bee nigh at hand to his Maiesty...Wee have been and are all cleer from ye infection; wch is it yt drawes ye Court and Councell upon us at this time. Omnis comoditas, etc. And thus wth remembrance of my best love; I comitt you to God, & always rest Your very loving friend Jo. Saru. Septemb. 25, 1625'.[2]

Only one of Davenant's sermons is extant, in a published version discovered in the British Museum by Morris Fuller.[2] This was preached at Westminster Abbey on occasion of a public fast, on April 5th 1628: 'One of the Sermons Preached at Westminster

The Fifth of Aprill, (being the day of the Publike Fast;) Before the Right Honourable Lords of the High Court of Parliament, and set forth by their appointment. By the Bishop of Sarum. London, Printed for Richard Badger, and are to be sold by John Stempe at his shop at the East end of S. Dunstan's Church-yard in Fleet-street. 1628'.[2] The Bishop took his text from Jeremiah 3v22: 'Behold, we come unto thee, for thou art the Lord, our God'. His congregation had to contemplate about 11,000 words, which must have lasted for up to two hours, all on an empty stomach! He spoke of:

'a general calamity which out of doubt hangs over us',[8] but believed that prayer, word and sacraments would reunite clergy and laity.

Despite his theological expertise, Davenant was to fall foul of King Charles in 1630, when he preached before the court at Whitehall on a text from The Epistle of Paul to the Romans, 6v23: 'The gift of God is eternal life through Jesus Christ our Lord'. He made the mistake of touching upon the thorny topic of predestination, the subject of doctrines concerning the belief that God has ordained events, such as the salvation of souls. But the King had forbidden preaching on this and other contentious matters, in an attempt to maintain an orthodox doctrine based on the 'Thirty Nine Articles of the Church of England', which had been finalised in 1571. In relation to these, King Charles, in 1628, had declared:

'No man hereafter shall either print or preach, to draw the Article aside any way, but shall submit to it in the plain and Full meaning thereof: and shall not put his own sense or comment to be the meaning of the Article, but shall take it in the literal and grammatical sense'.[2] Thomas Fuller, in his 'The Church History of Britain...', informs us of the consequences of his uncle's indiscretion:

'Two days after he was called before the Privie Councell, where he presented himself on his knees...But the Temporall Lords bad him arise and stand to his defence, being as yet only accused, not convicted'. Archbishop Harsnet of York vehemently condemned the boldness of his offence for about half an hour, while Bishop Laud (who had been consecrated with Davenant) said nothing. Davenant then explained that he had not deliberately gone against the King's instructions and promised, now that he understood His Majesty's mind, that he would obey in future. Fortunately, this ended the matter; he was even allowed to kiss the King's hand before leaving[1] and he was still included in the list of court preachers later in the decade. Davenant describes these events in a letter to Dr Ward:

'...Presently after my sermon was ended, it was signifted unto me by my L. of York, and my L. of Winchester, and my L. Chamberlain that his Majesty was much displeased, that I had stirred this question which he had forbidden to be meddled withal, one way or other...coming unto the Sunday Sermon, one of the Clerks of the Councell told me, that I was to attend at the Councell-Table, the next day at two of the clock...When I came thither, my L. of York made a speech welnigh of half an hour long, aggravating the boldnesse of mine offence...My answer then was, that I was sorry I understood not his Majesties intention, which if I had done before, I should have made choice of some other matter to intreat of which might have given none offence...and so I was dismissed...At my departure I entreated their Lordships to let his Majesty understand, that I had not boldly, or wilfully and wittingly, against his Declaration, medled with the forenamed point...I went the next day to my L. Chamberlain, and intreated him to doe me the favor, that I might be brought to kisse the King's hand, before I went out of Town...When I came in, his Majesty declared his resolution, that he would not have this high point medled withal or debated, either the one way or the other, because it was too high for the people's understanding: and other points which concern Reformation and newness of life, were more needful and profitable I promised obedience herein, and so kissing his Majesties hand, departed...And thus having let you know the carriage of this business I commit you to the protection of the Almighty'.[2]

Davenant hosted several royal visits to the episcopal palace at Salisbury; James I came in 1623 and Charles I in 1625, 1629 and 1632. On at least the last occasion, the King attended a daily service in the Cathedral, and Thomas Fuller, at that time prebendary of Netherby, Yorkshire, reports of having the honour to see the King solemnly 'heal' (ie 'touching for the King's evil') in the Choir of Salisbury.[2] (It was believed that a touch from royalty could heal a skin disease known as scrofula or the 'King's evil', which was associated with swelling of the lymph glands in the neck caused by tuberculosis).

The 1630s saw Bishop Davenant in dispute with the corporation of Salisbury over a charter granted by James I, which encroached on the long-standing rights of the Bishop. However, the dispute was eventually settled.[1] In 1637, we find the Bishop exerting his authority over a disputed issue, namely the proper position of the table for Holy Communion:

'John, by Divine Providence Bishop of Sarum, To the Curate and Churchwardens with the Parishioners of Awborne, in the County of Wilts...Whereas his Majestie hath beene lately informed that some men factiously disposed have taken upon themselves to place and remove the Communion Table in the Church of Awborne, and thereupon his highness hath required me to take present order therein...these Tables should ordinarily be sett and stand with the side to the west wall of the Chancell. I therefore require you, the Churchwardens, and all other persons not to meddle with the bringing donne or transposing of the Communion Table, as you will answer it at your own perile...'.[2]

In the 1630s Davenant and Ward opposed the writings of the Arminians and worked on plans for a union of Reformed churches.[8] In 1640, the year before his death, Davenant, together with his nephew Thomas Fuller and the latter's uncle Dr William Fuller, Dean of Ely, were present at a Convocation directed by Archbishop Laud, which passed various measures for the enforcement of clerical discipline.[2] Shortly before his death, Davenant published: 'Animadversions written by the Right Rev. Father in God, John, Lord Bishop of Salisbury, upon a treatise intituled, God's Love to Mankind'. He died on April 1641, at a time of division and uncertainty in Church and State, which heralded the Civil War. Archbishop Laud had been sent to the

Tower in March, (he would be executed in 1645), and, in the same month, the Commons had passed a vote against the bishops sitting in parliament.[1] Davenant's nephew, Thomas Fuller, was present at his death:

'I cannot omit, how some few hours before his death, having lyen for a long time (though not speechlesse yet) not speaking, nor able to speak (as we beholders thought, though indeed he hid that little strength we thought he had lost, and reserved himself for purpose) he fell into most emphaticall prayer for half a quarter of an hour. Amongst many heavenly passages therein, He thanked God for this his fatherly correction, because in all his life time he never had one heavie affliction, which made him often much suspect with himself, whether he was a true Child of God or no, until this his last sicknesse. Then he sweetly fell asleep in Christ, and so we softly draw the Curtains about him'.[1]

Davenant had been a generous benefactor of Queens', giving £100 to the library in 1626, which enabled the purchase of 130 volumes and, in 1637, he gave the living of Cheverel Magna, as well as income from an estate on the Isle of Sheppey, to fund two scholarships.[1,4] His will had been written in 1638:

'...I John Davenant, Bishopp of Sarum, beinge at this tyme in good health and perfect memory (praised bee God) weightinge with myselfe the frailtie of this mortall life and the certainetie of my death have thereupon judged it fitt and expedient to order and settle myne estate without delaies...First, I comitt and commend my soule into the handes of Almightie God...and as for my earthlie Bodie I bequeath it to the Earth to bee buryed in the Cathedrall Church of Sarum...'. Among an extensive list of bequests, one relates to Queens':

'Item, whereas I have given the Rectory and Parsonage of Newton Toney for ever to the Master and Fellowes of Queene's College, in Cambridge, by a deed, bearinge date the six and twentith daie of October in the thirteenth yere of the raigne of our Soveraigne Lord, Kinge Charles, I doe by this my will ratifie the same, and appoint that all deedes, evidences, writings concerninge the said Rectory beinge delivered unto them with all fitt expedicon...'. But in a codicil dated the 6th April, 1641, Davenant decides that:

'...whereas Humphrey Henchman, Doctor of Divinitie, and Thomas Clarke, clerke, stand seized in fee of and in the advowson of Newton Tonie in the Countie of Wiltes...and whereas by my said last will I doe give and deuise unto Queenes College in Cambridge in fee and for ever all my right, title, interest, use or trust in and to the said Advowson; my will nowe is that the said Humfrey Henchman and Thomas Clarke...have the first presentation to the said church of Newton Tonie...and all my right, interest, trust and use in and to the same (the said first avoydamce excepted), I doe as formerly will and divise to Queens' Colledge in Cambridge...'.[2]

Matthew Nicholas, canon of Salisbury and Dean of Bristol, (afterwards Dean of St Paul's Cathedral, London), preached the sermon at Davenant's burial in Salisbury Cathedral, where his memorial tablet is displayed in the south aisle of the Choir.

References

1. Searle, W.G. The History of the Queens' College of St Margaret and St Bernard in the University of Cambridge. Part II 1560-1662. Sold by Deighton, Bell & Co; Macmillan & Co. London. 1871. pp 405-22.
2. Fuller, Morris. The Life Letters & Writings of John Davenant D.D. 1572-1641 Lord Bishop of Salisbury. Methuen & Co. London. 1897. pp 37-38, 75-91, 110-11, 127-36, 140-51, 166-69, 254-302, 306-54, 424-32, 533-39.
3. Ball, Thomas. Life of Dr John Preston in: 'The Lives of Thirty-Two English Divines (appended to the third edition of 'A General Martyrology'). 1677.
4. Gray, J.H. The Queens' College of St Margaret and St Bernard. F.E.Robinson. London. 1898. pp 136-47.
5. Dever, M.E. Preston, Pupil-Mongering and the Walnut Tree Court. The Record 1994. Queens' College, Cambridge. Online. 2020.

6. Twigg, J. A History of Queens' College, Cambridge 1448-1986. The Boydell Press. 1987. p 42.
7. Fuller, Thomas. History of the Worthies of England. 1662. National Biography. 2018. Online.
8. Larminie, V. Davenant, John. Oxford Dictionary of National Biography. 2008. Online. 2020.

CHAPTER 16

John Mansell. President 1622-31.

Summary.

John Mansell was born in about 1580 in Lincolnshire and came to Queens' as a 'sizar' in 1594. He became a fellow in 1600 and held various College offices before his election as President in 1622, after the promotion of John Davenant to be Bishop of Salisbury. Subsequently, he proceeded D.D. .

Mansell was Vice-Chancellor during 1624-25, when King James I paid his fourth and final visit to the University. During his Presidency, significant local events included the contested election, in 1626, of the controversial figure of the Duke of Buckingham as Chancellor of the University. Mansell supported the Duke, who had been a favourite of James I, in opposition to most of the fellows of Queens'. In 1625, or soon after, he received the first of several letters from the Bishop of Salisbury requesting a fellowship at Queens' for his nephew, Thomas Fuller, the future Church historian; however, much to the annoyance of the Bishop, this was not forthcoming. In 1630, Cambridge suffered a major outbreak of the 'plague', which led to the cessation of University activities for several months.

Mansell died in 1631, leaving a widow and a daughter, Maria, who had been baptised at St Botolph's Church, Cambridge, in September 1630. His wife died in 1636 and is buried in St Clement's Church, Cambridge.

Timeline.

c1580.	Born in Lincolnshire.
1594.	Admitted to Queens' as a 'sizar'.
1598.	B.A. . Scholar of Queens'.

1600.	Fellow of Queens'.
1603.	Death of Elizabeth I. Accession of James I.
1601.	M.A. .
1609.	B.D. .
1609-11.	Senior bursar of Queens'.
1613.	Visit of Prince Charles and the Elector Palatine to Cambridge.
1614.	Death of Humphrey Tyndall. John Davenant elected President of Queens'.
1614-16.	Vicar of Oakington.
1615.	The King and Prince Charles visit the University. The King pays a subsequent visit.
1617.	Relinquishes his fellowship.
1618.	Davenant is a royal delegate to the Synod of Dort.
1621.	Davenant becomes Bishop of Salisbury.
1622.	Mansell is elected President of Queens'. D.D. . Election of John Preston as Master of Emmanuel College.
1623.	The King's third visit to Cambridge.
1624.	Vice-Chancellor, during King James' fourth visit to Cambridge.
1625.	King James dies and is succeeded by Charles I.
1626.	Contested election for the Chancellorship of Cambridge University. The Duke of Buckingham is elected by a narrow margin.
1628.	Buckingham is stabbed to death.
1631.	Mansell dies, leaving a widow and a daughter.

A goodnatured and capable College administrator and churchman.

John Mansell was born in Lincolnshire around 1580 and came from a distinguished family.[1] A John Maunsell had founded priories in Kent in 1257 and had been chief justice of England, while John Weever, (1576-1632, antiquary and poet), in his 'Ancient Funerall Monuments' of 1631, writes:

'I have seene a pedigree of the Mansels from Philip de Mansel, who came in with the Conqueror, until our times. Of this name and familie is that orthodoxall sound Divine and worthy Master of Queenes Colledge in Cambridge, John Mansel Doctor of Divinitie, and a generall scholler in all good literature'.[2] He entered Queens' as a 'sizar' in 1594, as a pupil of Clement Smith, nephew of Sir Thomas Smith, (see Chapters 8 and 9), and graduated B.A. in 1598. (A sizar received financial help in return for menial work- see Chapter 15). Also in 1598 he was made a scholar and elected a fellow in 1600.[1] He proceeded M.A. in 1601 and B.D. in 1609; Twigg, in his history of the College in 1987, informs us that, in his M.A. disputation, he: 'bravely defended Copernicus',[3] whose claim that the sun, rather than the earth, is at the centre of the universe was considered by some to be contrary to biblical teaching. He was in residence in College until 1617, when he resigned his fellowship, and held various College offices, including senior bursar during 1609-11. He was vicar of Oakington during 1614-1616 and he proceeded D.D. in 1622 .

During his fellowship, Elizabeth I died in 1603 and was succeeded by James I. In 1613, Mansell will have witnessed the visit to the University of Prince Charles and the Elector Palatine and, in 1615, of the King and Prince Charles. Also in 1615, the King paid his second visit to the University. Humphrey Tyndall died in 1614, to be succeeded as President by John Davenant and, in 1618, it will have been a talking point in the College that the President had been selected by the King as a delegate to the Synod of Dort, (see Chapter 15).

After Davenant's promotion as Bishop of Salisbury in 1621, he delayed his resignation as President until 1622, when Mansell was elected as his successor after a free election. However, Twigg, in his history of the College of 1987, tells us that this was:

'....after widespread rumours that an outsider would be imposed, and indeed the duke of Lennox wrote to the college urging them to elect another of the Fellows, Lewis Wemis. Lennox was a relation of the King's, but James does not appear to have taken any interest in the business. Mansell was an able college administrator, and a "very moderate goodnatured man"....'.[3] (Lewis Wemis, or Wemys, was a fellow from 1618 to 1624; he came from Scotland and had been elected under a Royal Mandate as he had not been born in England. He would become a prebendary of Westminster). Also, Searle, in his history of the College of 1871, quotes a report:

'that Dr Balcanqual was to be the new master of Queens' college, but afterwards it was believed that the king would grant the fellows a free election'.[1] (Walter Balcanquall, c1586-1645, was born in Edinburgh, where he graduated in 1609. He then came to Pembroke College, Cambridge, where he was elected a fellow in 1611. He was appointed one of James I's chaplains and, in 1618, was sent by the King to the Synod of Dort to represent Scotland. He became Dean of Rochester in 1624 and Dean of Durham in 1639).

Soon after Mansell's election, a major event for the College was the departure of its charismatic tutor and preacher, John Preston, who, in 1622, was elected Master of the strongly Puritan Emmanuel College, (see Chapter 15). This may have been triggered by Davenant's new appointment, as it is claimed that this:

'created Master Prestons cares, Doctor Davenant had been his constant and faithfull Friend, and given countenance upon all occasions to him and all his Pupils. But now who should succeed? And where should Master Preston find another shelter? The Fellows for the most part were not his Friends, envied his numbers (ie of students), and great relations, and there was no man like so to befriend him...He had a long time been successefull in the way of Pupils, but Doctor Davenants leaving of the Colledge troubled him. A great Tutor hath much occasion to use the Masters influence, for accommodation and advancement of his pupils, which now he saw he could not promise unto himself'.[1]

The Master of Emmanuel College, Laurence Chaderton, was aged 85 in 1622 and some of the Puritan fellows thought that his replacement by Preston would enhance the College's reputation and provide more opportunities for advancement, because of Preston's position as chaplain to the Prince of Wales and his support from the Duke of Buckingham. Searle reports that Chaderton was induced to resign, but that this was kept a secret for seven days, until the election of Preston had been accomplished; only then:

'two of the fellows were dispatcht to Queens Colledge to acquaint Master Preston with what they had done, and to desire that at two of the Clock he would repair unto the Colledge to be admitted, and undertake the charge...It was strange news at Queens, and all the Colledge were much affected with it, wondering extreamly that such a great transaction should be carried on with so much secrecy...but there was order given presently, that all the Schollars should be ready against two of the Clock that day, to attend Master Preston and the Fellows to Emanuel Colledge, in Habits suitable unto their several qualities, which was done accordingly; and a very goodly Company attended him from Queens unto Emanuel, where they were cheerfully received and entertained according to the Custome, with a generous and costly Banquet, and then returned unto Queens again; but left Master Preston, the prop and glory of it, at Emanuel'.[1] However, he was not destined to rule for long over Emmanuel; his health declined and he died in 1628.

In March 1623, the King paid his third visit to the University:

'King James came to Cambridge, betwixt the hours of nine and ten in the morning. The young Scholars were placed from Jesus College gate next the street unto Trinity College gates in this manner: the Bachelors of Arts in their hoods and capps; next to them the Fellow-commoners in their capps; after them the Regents and Non-regents in their hoods and capps; the Proctors, Presidents, and Deans of the severall Colleges did walk up and down in the streets, to see every one in his degree to keepe his rank and place. In Trinity College court, against his Majesty's lodgings, our honourable Chancellor the Earle of Suffolk, our Vice-chancellor Dr. Beale, with all the Heads and Doctors, did meet his Majesty, and the Master presented his Majesty with a book very curiously bound...Then the King thanked our noble Chancellor...and as he passed along the court, the Non-regents and Regents, and Fellow-commoners, and the rest standing in their ranks on both sides of the courts and street, sayd with a loud voice, "Vivat Rex, Vivat Rex!"...'.[4] When he dined at Trinity College, he was entertained by a comedy by John Hacket, afterwards Bishop of Lichfield; however, Queens' was liable for a share in the expenses:

'Upon the Kings coming to Cambridg....iiij^{li}. xij^{s}. ix^{d}.'.[1]

Mansell was Vice-Chancellor during 1624-25, when the King paid his fourth and final visit to Cambridge, a few months before his death in 1625, and will have played a significant role in the proceedings:

'In December, the King was at Cambridge and kept his Court in Trinity College. Charles Prince of Wales was also here, and here Mons. De Villiaviler and the Marquis d'Effiat Ambassadors extraordinary from the King of France, had audience of his Majesty, who on the 12th of December signed here, the ratification of the Treaty with France respecting the marriage of the Prince of Wales with the Princess Henrietta Maria. The King was confined with the gout in his hands and arms, but the Prince of Wales, the Ambassadors, and the Nobility, were entertained with disputations in Philosophy and other academical performances. During the King's stay "in an extraordinary commencement, many (but ordinary) persons were graduated doctors in divinity, and other faculties" '.[4] One of the expenses of the visit that devolved on Queens' was:

'To the Kinges Trumpeters (by the M^{r} when the Kinge was here)....0. 10. 0.'.[1]

The King died on the 27th March 1625 and, at Cambridge, Charles I was proclaimed King on the 30th March.[1] The Master of Emmanuel rode with the new King and the Duke of Buckingham to London on the day after James I's death:

'applying comfort now to one, now to another, on so sad an occasion...'.[1]

The Earl of Suffolk, Chancellor of Cambridge University, died in 1626 and this led to a disputed and controversial election for his successor. The Duke of Buckingham was the candidate of the King and court, and Dr Montaigne, Bishop of London and former fellow of Queens', sent his chaplain, Dr Wilson, to Cambridge with a message to the heads of colleges that the King wished them to elect the Duke. Also, Dr Neile, Bishop of Durham, wrote to the Vice-Chancellor:

'Good Mr. Vicechancellor, In my love to the universitie, & your self, I cannot but impart unto you ye effect of that letter which I have written to ye M^{r} of St. John's (which had informed him of the King's pleasure that Buckingham should be elected Chancellor). That being yesternight with his Majestie it pleased Him to declare his desire touching our Election of a new Chancellor...signifying how well it would please Him, if my Lord Duke of Buckingham might be chosen by the universitie...that in effecting thereof we shall not only gain an honorable Chancellor of the Duke, but in a sort purchase his Majestie himself our Royall Patron and Chancellor, in that we fixe our Election upon him whom himself desireth...Nos Deo & I rest. Yo^{r} very loving friend, R.Dunelm. Durham House, May 29, 1626'.[4] But many members of the University's Senate resented the court's interference, probably influenced by the Duke's increasing unpopularity, and decided to support the Earl of Berkshire, the son of the late Chancellor.

Cooper's 'Annals of Cambridge' of 1845 provide a detailed description of subsequent events:

'All the influence of the Court was used to secure the Duke of Buckinghams' election, which however was not carried without opposition from a considerable number of the Senate, who resolved to support Thomas Howard Earl of Berkshire, the son of the deceased Chancellor. The election took place on the 1st of June, when there were 108 votes for the Duke of Buckingham, and 102 for the Earl of Berkshire...This election excited great attention, more particularly as the Duke of Buckingham was at this period under impeachment by the House of Commons. The subjoined letter from Mr. Mead of Christ's College to Sir Martin Stuteville, contains many curious particulars:

"Worthie Sir...To tell you plainly we have chosen the Duke of Buckingham our Chancellor...Our Chancellor my Lord of Suffolk died on Sunday...on Monday, but about dinner time arrives Dr. Wilson (my Lord of London's chaplain) without Letters but with a message from his Lord that we should chuse the Duke; such being his Majesty's desire and pleasure. Our Heads meet after Sermon, when by Dr. Wren, Beale, Maw, Pask, this motion was urged with that vehemency and as it were confidence of authority, that the rest were either awed or perswaded...It was in vain to say that Dr. Wilson's bare word from his Lord was no sufficient testimony of his Majesty's pleasure...that instead of Patronage we sought for, we might bring a lasting scandal and draw a general contempt and hatred upon the University as men of most prostitute flattery...that it would be wisdom to wait our full time of fourteen days, and not to precipitate the Election. To this was answered, The sooner the better...every Head sent for his Fellows to perswade them for the Duke...But the same day about dinner time the Bishop of London arrived unexpected, yet found his own Colledge (Queens') most bent and resolved another way, to his no small discontentment. At the same time comes to town Mr. Mason (my Lord Duke's Secretary) and Mr. Cosens, and Letters from my Lord of Durham (see above) expressly signifying in his Majesty's name (as they told and would make us believe) that his Majesty could be well pleased if we chose the Duke...Masters belabour their Fellows...and yet for all this stirre the Duke carried it but by three Votes from my Lord Andover (ie the Earl of Berkshire) whom we voluntarily set up against him, without any motion on his behalf, yea without his knowledge...(Note: There is a slight discrepancy in the accounts of the voting figures, even allowing for two of the votes for the Duke being reported as 'void by statute')...We had but one Doctor in the whole Towne durst (for so I dare speak) give with us against the Duke, and that was Dr. Porter of Queen's. What will the Parliament say to us?...Joseph Mead. Christ Coll. Jun.3."

...The house of Commons were greatly incensed at the Duke of Buckingham's election, in consequence of his being at the time under impeachment. On the 5th June, the House resolved itself into a Grand Committee...Mr. Herberte reporteth from the Committee, that it conceiveth this House, hath just cause of Offence, at the Choice of the Duke...Upon Question, a letter to be written to the University of Cambridge...to signify unto them, that this house hath taken just Offence at their Election of the Duke to be their Chancellor; and to require them to send some, instructed and authorised, to inform and give Account to this House, of the Manner of their Proceedings...These to be here upon Monday next...6 Junii...Mr. Chancellor of the Exchequer delivereth a Message to the House; that the King, having taken Knowledge hereof, hath commanded him to signify his Pleasure, that the House forbear to send this Letter, Resolved, To defer the further Consideration of this Message till To morrow...7 Junii... The grand Committee tender, in writing, the substance of a Message to his Majesty, in Answer of that sent Yesterday...On the afternoon of the same day (ie 7th of June) Sir Richard Weston Chancellor of the Exchequer, reported the King's answer...That the University of Cambridge and all Corporations derive their Right and Priviledge from him...Concerning the Election itself his Majesty is far from conceiving it a Grievance; for he never heard that Crimes objected, were to be taken as proved; or, that a Man should lose his Fame or good Opinion in the World, upon an Accusation only...On the King's answer being read it was "Resolved, to put off the further Consideration and Debate thereof till Friday Morning"...but no further proceedings respecting the business are recorded, and on the 15th of June the Parliament was dissolved...The letter from the King...approving of the election...is in the following terms: Charles R. Trusty and welbeloved, wee greete you well...you are therein made partakers of our Royall approbation. And wee shall ever conceive that an honor done to a Person wee favour, is out of a loyall respect had unto our self...wee shall ever justify Buckingham worthy of this your election...for wee that have found him a faithfull sevant to our deare father of blessed memory...To our Trusty and welbeloved the Vice Chauncellor, Heads, Proctors and the whole Senate of our University of Cambridge'.[4]

As noted above, the majority of the Queens' fellows did not vote for the Duke, including Dr George Porter, the senior fellow.[1] The new Chancellor, George Villiers, had been born in 1592, the son of Sir Charles Villiers. He had obtained various marks of royal favour, because of his position as the King James' closest advisor, principal 'favourite' and possible lover; these included appointment as Lord Admiral in 1619, and he was created Duke of Buckingham in 1623. He had also been close to the Prince of Wales and he maintained his influence after Charles I's accession. However, he had become increasingly unpopular, attracting blame for various naval, military and political disasters, for buying and selling offices and titles, and for financial impropriety.[1] At the time of his election as Chancellor, the House of Commons was attempting to impeach him, but King Charles came to his rescue by dissolving Parliament later in June. However, in 1628, unfortunately for the Duke, one of the many members of the public who regarded him as a public enemy, John Felton, an army officer, stabbed him to death at the Greyhound pub in Portsmouth. This time the vacant Chancellorship was filled without opposition, by Henry Rich, Earl of Holland.

Although Mansell had been on the side of King and court in the election of Chancellor, Searle reports that, later in 1626, in the case of the Mastership of Caius College, he was:

' "eager" for the college candidate Mr Batchcroft and so opposed to the courtiers Dr Maw (of Trinity), Dr Wren (of St Peter's) and Dr Beale (of Jesus), who were "furious against him" '.[1]

As noted in Chapter 15, Mansell would receive, during 1625-26, the first of several letters from the former President, the Bishop of Salisbury, asking for the preferment of a College fellowship for his nephew, Thomas Fuller, the future Church historian. But this was not to be forthcoming and Davenant expressed his annoyance about Mansell's lack of support in a letter to his friend Dr Ward in 1628. In consequence, Fuller migrated to Sidney Sussex College in 1629.

The President will have noted the death, in 1626, of Sir Edward Villiers, half-brother of the Duke of Buckingham, who had been admitted a fellow-commoner at Queens' in 1601. He had been ambassador to Bohemia and President of Munster. Among his descendents would be the Dukes of Grafton and Cleveland.[1]

In March 1627, the Duke of Buckingham visited the University for the first time as Chancellor. As well as dining at Trinity, he: 'had banquets at divers other colleges', while Queens' contributed two pounds two shillings and four pence: 'For the Dukes entertainment at Trinity college'.[1]

In 1628, Thomas Edwards M.A., a previous student at Queens', was brought before the Vice-Chancellor on a charge that he had preached:

'against consulting with earthly superiors as tutors, husbands, masters, in any doubtful case, but that the person in doubt, ought to find out a man in whom the Spirit of God dwells, one that is renewed by grace, and he should direct him. This he urged with very innecessary warmth'.[1] Edwards defended himself by claiming that his advice, which was not conducive to college discipline, should only be followed if the 'superiors' gave advice contrary to the word of God, but he was ordered to repeat his explanation at St Andrew's Church on the 6th April and to send in a certificate that he had done so. Although Edwards did comply with his required church appearance, he:

'presently left the towne and made noe certificate',[1] and it was not until the following year that the required document was provided, with five signatures including those of the curate of St Andrew's and Laurence Chaderton, the first Master of Emmanuel College, (who lived to the age of 104). Edwards would become a well-known Puritan divine; he was the author of 'Gangraena', a notorious and alarmist work describing the details of heresy, published in 1646.[5] He had been admitted a pensioner at Queens' in 1618, where he met Thomas Fuller who gives us a succinct character sketch:

'I knew Mr Edwards very well, my contemporary in Queen's College, who was often transported beyond due bounds with the keenness and eagerness of his spirit; and, therefore, I have just cause in some things to suspect him...'.[1]

In May 1629 the Corporation of Cambridge made the following order:

'Queen's College having often digged up sodds in the Green by Newnham, for the repairing of their butts (ie archery targets), without any leave or licence from this House, North Harrison and Michael Watson to have conference with the Master and fellows, to the intent it might be known, whether they do it in their own right or in presuming the favour of the town'.[4]

In September 1629, the University Chancellor, Lord Holland, visited the University with the French Ambassador. They dined at Trinity College and visited many of the colleges. The records of Queens' note:

'Contribution to the entertainment of a frenche embassadour...5.13.4.'.[1]

Towards the end of Mansell's Presidency, Cambridge suffered a catastrophic outbeak of the 'plague' from April to October, 1630:

'In April, it was discovered that the plague again prevailed in the town, having been introduced by a soldier who died of it on the 28th of February preceeding. Mr Mead of Christ's College... thus speaks of the state of the University..."Our University is in a manner wholy dissolved; all meetings & Exercises ceasing. In many Colledges almost none left...Our Gates strictly kept, none but Fellowes to go forth, or any to be lett in without ye consent of the major part of our Society, of wch we have but 7 at home...Our Butcher, Baker, & Chandler bring ye provisions to the Colledg Gates, where the Steward & Cooke receive them...Yea we have taken 3 Women into our Colledge & appointed them a Chamber to lye in together. Two are Bedmakers, one a Laundresse. I hope the next Parlement will include us in ye generall Pardon. We have turned out our Porter & appointed our Barber both Porter and Barber, allowing him a Chamber next ye Gates. Thus we live as close Prisoners, & I hope without danger"...Dr Butts the Vicechancellor, whose magnanimous and Christian-like behaviour during this season of affliction obtained general applause, wrote a long letter to Lord Coventry, (the steward of the town)..."There are five thousand poor and not above one hundred who can assist in relieving them...we follow your lordships counsel to keep the sound from the sick; to which purpose we have built nere 40 booths in a remote place upon our commons, whether we forthwith remove those that are infected, where we have placed a German physician who visits them day and night and he ministers to them: besides constables we have certain ambulatory officers who walk the streets night and day to keep our people from needless conversing, and to bring us notice of all disorders...To give our neighbours in the country contentment, we hyred certain horsemen this harvest-time to range and scowre the fields of the towns adjoining, to keep our disorderly pore from annoying them... Myself am alone a destitute and forsaken man not a Scholler with me in College, not a Scholler seen by me without...". The contagion had much abated towards the end of September, but...the effect of the plague was to reduce the number of members of the University for many years...It was not until January 1631, that the town was sufficiently free from the distemper to allow of a cessation of the weekly payments to the poor. Altogether 347 died of the plague and...2,858 persons were relieved by charity'.[4] (Dr Butts was Master of Corpus Christi College, and had been admitted to Queens' as a pensioner in 1592. While most of the other heads had left Cambridge, he remained, with a few others, to maintain order and distribute relief. Because of his brave and humane conduct, he was re-elected as Vice-Chancellor in 1630, but would be found hanged in his room in 1632).[1,5]

These events are briefly reflected in the Queens' records:

'17°. Apr.1630. The colledge brake up, so did the university, to avoid the infection of the plague dangerously spred in the towne. It was then agreed that fellows should have their whole allowance, during the time of the dissolution, whether they were absent or present...Octob. 29. This grant for absence &c. was continued till the audit'.[1] In July 1630, two shillings were spent on: 'pitch, tarr &c. to air the Officers and Schollars Chambers'.[5]

After the plague, in early 1631, Cooper records that:

'the comedy of Senile Odium was performed in Queens' College by the students of that house. It was written by Peter Hausted, M.A. of Queens' College, and was printed at Cambridge in 12mo. 1633'.[4] (Hausted gained his M.A. while at Queens' and proceeded D.D. . He was a flamboyant playwright, poet and preacher, who opposed Puritan dissent in the Church of England).

Mansell died on October 7th 1631, leaving a widow and a daughter.[5] The College records refer to:

'Peeces of Plate taken out of the Treasury for the furnishing of the banquet of the funeral of our late Master Dr Mansel Nov.22,1631'.[1] His will had been made on the 5th of October, very shortly before his death, and he left all his goods to his wife and child. The witnesses were his wife Mary, George Bardsey, (a fellow of Queens' elsewhere named Edmund Bardsey), and his servant, Thomas Church. His daughter Maria was born in the year before his death; her baptism, on the 9th September 1630, is recorded in the register of St Botolph's Church:

'Maria Mansell fil. Joannis Mansell pres. Coll. Regin. Ex Maria uxore'. His wife survived him until September 1636 and is buried at St Clement's Church, Cambridge.[1]

The Bodleian Library, Oxford, contains:

'Various pieces transcribed ca.1599-1601 by John Mansell, later President of Queens' College, Cambridge including an otherwise unknown letter from Sir Philip Sidney to Edward Denny, 22 May 1580...The other contents include university exercises, Mansell's own letters to the President of Queens' College, to members of his family and to friends, as well as letters to him...and various poems in Latin and English'. (MS.D.d152). The original of one of the transcribed letters may have been written by Mansell himself, early in his career, to a potential benefactor, and reflects a perennial problem of youth:

'Where necessity comandeth, and the name of brotherhood giveth hope: bouldness may seeme to be excusable: I writ unto you about Shrovetide, wherof having received no answer: Which by my said letters I so earnestly so desired. I am moaved to doubt you never received them...I am to commence this midsummer, and that upon those conditions that if I neglect it all my hopes and beginnings of preferment, are utterly lost...I can not tell where to hope for 10 or 12 shillings but from your selfe; wherein if you faile me I may be bould to say it of a truth I am cleane undone. Therefore if ever the name of God or man might move you, I beseech you first for God's sake, our hevenly father, secondly for his sake that was our earthly father; to deale with me in compassion, as God hath commanded, and our father desired; namely to be helpful one to another, in what we may...Thus desiring the God of heaven and earth to yield it you many fold, whatsoever you shall please to doe for me; I cease your trouble.'

Two lines of one of the transcribed poems also reflect an enduring issue:

'What doth the foule contagious forme, & smoke,
Of this Tobacco, filthy, stinkinge Weede...'.

References

1. Searle, W.G. The History of the Queens' College of St Margaret and St Bernard in the University of Cambridge. Part II 1560-1662. Sold by Deighton, Bell & Co; Macmillan & Co. London. 1871. pp 447-61.
2. Weever, John. (1576-1632) In: Ancient Funerall Monuments, within the United Monarchie of Great Britaine, Ireland and the Islands Adjacent. 1631.
3. Twigg, J. A History of Queens' College, Cambridge 1448-1986. The Boydell Press. 1987. pp 44, 69, 101.
4. Cooper, C.H. Annals of Cambridge. Volume III. Warwick and Co., Cambridge. 1845. pp 156-57, 170-71, 185-93, 214, 222-28, 239.
5. Gray, J.H. The Queens' College of St Margaret and St Bernard. F.E.Robinson. London. 1898. pp 150-51.

CHAPTER 17

Edward Martin. President 1631-44 and 1660-62.

Summary.

Edward Martin, c1581-1662, was born in Cambridgeshire and admitted to Queens' as a 'sizar' in 1605. He was elected a fellow in 1617 and ordained in the same year. He went on to hold various College offices and, from about 1628 to 1631, he was chaplain to Bishop William Laud, (later Archbishop of Canterbury), who gave his name to the 'Laudian', or 'high church', faction of the Church of England. This advocated an emphasis on the formalities of ritual, as well as certain doctrines, and was opposed by the Puritans and other Nonconformist groups, who believed that the Church of England was not sufficiently reformed from Catholicism. Martin was a consistently zealous opponent of the Puritans and a supporter of the monarchy.

He was elected President of Queens' in 1631 and, in his first year in office, spent a large sum of money on refurbishing the College chapel. He was a staunch supporter of Charles I and, in the run-up to the Civil War, he was one of the heads of colleges who sent his College's silver plate to the King in defiance of Parliament. This led to his arrest by Oliver Cromwell, together with two other college heads, followed by their detention in London and sequestation of their property. Martin was formally ejected as President of Queens' on the 13th March 1644. He remained imprisoned but, in 1648, he escaped from house arrest and lived under an assumed name in Suffolk until he was recaptured in 1650. However, he was soon released and, in about 1653, he travelled to Paris, where he spent most of his subsequent exile. After the Restoration of the monarchy in 1660 he returned to England and, on the 2nd August 1660, was reinstated as President of Queens'. He was installed as Dean of Ely in 1662 but died three days later. He is buried in the original College chapel.

Timeline.

c1581.	Born in Cambridgeshire.
1604.	James I convenes the 'Hampton Court Conference', in response to Puritan requests for reform, to hear the views of representatives of the Church of England. These include prominent Puritans. Agreements on some Puritan demands are achieved and major arguments are avoided, due to James' moderate and inclusive approach.
1605.	Martin is admitted to Queens' as a 'sizar'.
1609.	B.A. .
1612.	M.A. .
1614.	Death of Humphrey Tyndall. John Davenant elected President.
1617.	Fellow of Queens'. Ordained at Peterborough.
1621.	B.D. . The 'Protestation of 1621'. (The House of Commons stated its right to freedom of speech, while King James believed they had no right to debate foreign policy).
1622.	Resignation of Davenant. John Mansell elected President.
1623-26.	Senior bursar.
1625.	Licensed as a preacher by the University.
1625-30.	Vicar of Oakington.
1626.	Votes against the Duke of Buckingham in the election for Chancellor of the University.
1628-31.	Chaplain to William Laud, (Bishop of Bath and Wells, who was advanced to become Bishop of London in 1628 and Archbishop of Canterbury in 1633).
1629.	Start of the 'Personal rule' of Charles I, also known as the 'Eleven-Year Tyranny'. Charles makes peace with France and Spain and causes resentment at home with his religious policies. These include 'High' Anglicanism, with careful attention to ceremonial; he is supported in this by his main political adviser, Bishop William Laud, who is accused of

bringing back Catholicism, and who is strongly opposed by the Puritans.

1630. Rector of Conington, Cambridgeshire. Martin, as chaplain to the Bishop of London, licenses a book: 'An Historicall Narration…', which enrages the Puritans.

1631-38. Rector of Uppingham.

1631. Death of Mansell. Martin is elected President of Queens', with Bishop Laud's support.

1632. Visit of King Charles and the Queen to Cambridge. They attend a comedy by Peter Hausted of Queens', which is poorly received. Martin receives the degree of D.D.: 'by virtue of the King's recommendatory letters', after a payment to the Chancellor's secretary; this proves very controversial and the aftermath is probably one factor that provokes the suicide of the Vice-Chancellor, Henry Butts.

1633. Laud is appointed Archbishop of Canterbury.

1634. In the context of religious conflict in the University between Puritans and 'Laudians' (such as Martin), Peter Hausted (also a Laudian) preaches before the University and gives great offence.

1637. Anthony Sparrow (a future President) preaches a controversial Laudian sermon.

1638. Rector of Houghton Conquest.

1640. The 'Short' Parliament of Charles I, (April-May). The 'Long Parliament' is summoned in November and will be increasingly hostile to the King. (There were concerns that Protestantism was under threat and that Charles was being influenced in the direction of Catholicism by his Catholic wife, Henrietta Maria. Also, it was feared that Charles wished to be an absolute ruler).

1641. In October, the Vice-Chancellor orders bonfires to be lit to celebrate the King's return from Scotland. In December, a list of complaints, the 'Grand Remonstrance', is presented to the King by Parliament. The 'Protestation', an oath to defend against: 'Popist innovations', is required by members of the University.

1642. In January, Charles I attempts to arrest members of Parliament and leaves London soon afterwards.

In March, Charles I visits Cambridge University and receives a show of loyalty.

In June, the King writes from York requesting money for his defence against Parliament. Martin subscribes £100.

In July, the King writes again to the Vice-Chancellor, from Leicester, requesting the silver plate of several colleges. The Queens' plate is handed over in August and reaches the King at Nottingham.

The English Civil War starts on the 22nd of August, when the King raises the royal standard at Nottingham; the Puritans dominate the Parliamentary faction. (These were English Protestants in the 16th and 17th centuries, who wished to purify the Church of England of remaining Roman Catholic practices). On the 30th of August, Martin, together with the Masters of St John's and Jesus Colleges, are arrested by Colonel Oliver Cromwell.

In September, a Parliamentary committee orders that the heads of colleges who had sent the plate of their colleges to the King are to be brought to the Tower of London. (Archbishop Laud was already imprisoned there).

In October, the Battle of Edgehill, the first major confrontation of the war, is inconclusive.

1643. In January, Martin is transferred as a prisoner to the keeper of Lord Petre's house in Aldersgate Street, London.

In March, the House of Lords forbids violence to University property and members.

In April, Parliament orders the confiscation of the private estates of all the clergymen who had assisted the King. Colleges that had assisted the King have their estates sequestered, but this will be reversed in January 1644.

On the 11th of August, Martin, with his fellow heads, are moved to a prison ship, a coal-ship called 'The Prosperous Sarah', at Wapping. Later in the same month they are moved to the Bishop of Ely's house in Holborn. Also this month, Parliament orders various changes in churches and chapels, eg. removing signs of: 'popish superstition' such as stone altars, crosses, images and inscriptions. (Demolition work at the Queens' chapel will take place on 26th December).

The 'Westminster Assembly of Divines', consisting of theologians and parliamentarians, is appointed to review the worship, doctrine and government of the Church of England and will continue until 1653. (Their conclusions in relation to reformed doctrine will lead to the 'Westminster Confession of Faith' in 1646).

1643. Leave of absence is given to all fellows of Queens' from February 1643 to midsummer and is renewed until Michaelmas (September) 1644. A large number of Parliamentary troops are stationed in Cambridge. The University is subjected to: 'plunder and robbery'. The state of the University becomes: 'very deplorable'. Martin is deprived of his Church preferments.

1644. In January, the (2nd) Earl of Manchester is given authority by Parliament to eject members of colleges. A new oath, the 'Covenant', is introduced.

Martin is ejected from the Presidency on the 13th March.

On the 11th of April, Herbert Palmer is installed as President of Queens' in the College chapel by the Earl of Manchester, who will eject many royalist fellows and make new appointments to fellowships.

1644. Trial of Archbishop Laud.

1645. Execution of Archbishop Laud. The battles of Naseby and Langport are decisive Parliamentary victories.

1646. The authority and role of bishops in the Church of England is abolished.

1647. Martin draws up a mock petition to the House of Lords. Death of Herbert Palmer. Election of Thomas Horton as President of Queens' on 19th September.

1648. Martin escapes from house arrest. He lives in disguise in Suffolk until 1650.

1649. Trial and execution of Charles I. Start of the Commonwealth of England.

1650. Martin is taken prisoner but is soon released. He returns to Suffolk for about three years.

1651. The battle of Worcester, in which the forces of the future Charles II are defeated; Charles escapes to France. The end of the English Civil War. The Earl of Manchester is replaced as Chancellor of the University by Oliver St John, a Parliamentary republican and a previous fellow-commoner of Queens'.

c1653. Martin travels to Paris and lives with Lord Hatton.

1653. Start of the Protectorate under the rule of Oliver Cromwell.

1654. Disastrous failure of Cromwell's expedition to annex Hispaniola, (ie the Dominican Republic and Haiti).

1658. Death of Oliver Cromwell. His son Richard succeeds as Lord Protector.

1660. Charles II restored to the throne. On the 26th May, the Earl of Manchester is reinstated as Chancellor. On the 2nd August, the new regime removes Horton as President and restores Martin.

1661. The 'Savoy Conference' meets to revise the Book of Common Prayer and attempts to resolve the conflicts involving Puritan and Nonconformist factions within the Church of England. However, agreement is not reached.

1662. Martin is installed by proxy as Dean of Ely on the 25th April. He dies three days later. In June, a collection of letters by Martin is published. An 'Act of Uniformity' decrees that any minister or University member who refuses to conform to the Book of Common Prayer by the 24th August 1662 will be ejected from the Church of England. This leads to around two to three thousand Puritan and other Nonconformist ministers being forced out of the Church of England in what has been called the 'Great Ejection'.

A partisan President, zealously supporting the monarchy and the 'Laudian' religious faction against the Puritans. Imprisoned during 1642-1648. Ejected from the Presidency in 1644. In exile c1653-60. Reinstated as President in 1660.

Edward Martin's origins are obscure. But in a letter of 1660 he notes: 'the infirmities which accompany seventy-nine years' and, in the College records, he is entered as a fellow of the: 'county of Cambridge'. Thus, he was born around 1581 in Cambridgeshire. He was admitted to Queens' as a 'sizar' in 1605, (ie with financial help in return for some menial duties), proceeded B.A. in 1609 and held a scholarship until he graduated M.A. in 1612.[1,2] He was ordained priest at Peterborough in 1617; in the same year he was elected a fellow of Queens' and proceeded to hold various College offices: praelector geometricus (geometry lecturer) 1617-21, examinator 1623-24, senior bursar 1623-26, censor theologicus and examinator 1624-25, decanus capellae 1625-26 and censor philosophicus 1627-28. In 1628-29 he was 'scrutator' of the University, responsible for examining votes in University elections. In 1621 he proceeded B.D. and was nominated by Queens' as vicar of Oakington in 1625, a living which he held for five years. In the same year he was licensed as a preacher by the University.

The controversy over the election of the Duke of Buckingham as Chancellor of the University has been described in the previous Chapter. While the President and just one fellow voted for the Duke of Buckingham, this widely unpopular court candidate was opposed by the majority of the Queens' fellows, including Martin.[1]

Martin's career would owe much to the support of William Laud, who, as Bishop of Bath and Wells, was promoted to become Bishop of London in 1628. In this year Martin was Laud's chaplain and continued as such until 1631. Searle, in his history of the College of 1871, quotes a letter from Martin during his time with Laud, with an interesting medical reference, which has defied online searches:

'For my very worthy and lovinge friend Mr Merrick Casaubon one of the Prebends of Canterbury, at his lodgings there, these dd.

Worthy frende, All I have to say is my Lo: is come home, and is very well. He came to London last weddensday, and went this day to doe his duty to His Matie. My Lo: of Winchester came here on tuesday was seuenight and was never sicke hee thankes God and you at Canterbury; only he had the episgirtupsy (as the phisitians call it), some two days...your assured frende and Servant Edward Martin London House, Octob. 26. 1629'.[2]

At this time, only the Archbishop of Canterbury and the Bishop of London had the right to license books to be printed and it was their chaplains' duty to examine, and if necessary to censor, all such works. Martin ran into trouble in 1630 when he:

'licensed a Booke for the Presse intituled An Historicall Narration of the judgment of some most learned and Godly English Bishops, holy Martyrs and others, concerning God's Election and the Merits of Christ's death'.[2] This was duly printed in 1631 and contained doctrines which were anathema to the Puritans. William Prynne, who was a prominent opponent of Laud, called this book:

'the greatest affront and imposture ever offered to, or put upon the church of England in any age deserving the highest censure'.[2] He then asked Sir Humfrey Lynde to inform Laud of:

'this desparate Imposture he had obtruded on our Church to his eternall Infamie'[2] and to advise him to call in and burn this: 'dangerous seducing booke'. As Laud took no action, Prynne appealed to Archbishop Abbot of Canterbury, who then acted to suppress the book and Laud does not seem to have given Martin any support, telling the Archbishop that his chaplain had done: 'very ill', but:

'he had given him such a ratling for his paines, that he would warrant His Grace, hee should never meddle with Arminian Bookes or Opinions more'.[2] But this did not mollify Prynne who states:

'that indeed he had ratled him to very great purpose, for no longer then yesterday in the afternoone his Chaplaine Martin Preaching the Passion Sermon at Paules Crosse, publicly broached maintained Universall grace and Redemption, with all the Arminian Errors contained in this Book and condemned in the

Synod of Dort, to the great offence of the Auditors'.[2] But despite his demand that Martin be censured, no futher action was taken, although Martin soon left the Bishop's service. Prynne bitterly notes:

'Doctor Martin for this good service was presently after by this Bishop advanced to a great living, and likewise to the headship of Queenes college'.[1] This 'living' was the rectory of Uppingham, to which Martin was appointed in 1631,[2] the same year that he was elected President of Queens', after the death of John Mansell.

Twigg, in his history of the College of 1987, notes a decisive change in the religious nature of the University in the 1630s, with the development of a 'high' church movement associated with new heads of Colleges, including Martin, who formed a 'Laudian' faction, in support of William Laud, appointed Archbishop of Canterbury in 1633. (Opposed by the Puritans, these high church supporters shared certain theological beliefs, such as the rejection of aspects of predestination, and an emphasis on formality in their religious ritual). In his first year as President, Martin spent a large sum on renovating the chapel and, in 1632, a tax which had been used for the payment of the underbutler was appropriated for this purpose.[1] In 1633, all those at Queens' who were to take a degree were required to attend a service in the chapel according to the liturgy of the Church of England, which would have excluded some Puritan conscientious objectors.[1] The College cook reported that Martin said that: 'he would rather see his son in a whore house' than let him go to the Puritan lecturers in Holy Trinity Church,[3] (despite there being no record of a Presidential wife or family!).

The visit of King Charles and the Queen to Cambridge in March 1632 was associated with two controversial events which involved Queens'. Firstly, the award of several degrees by royal mandate, including that of D.D. to Martin, which attracted disapproval and, secondly, a play acted before the royal couple, 'The Rival Friends', by Peter Hausted of Queens', which was very badly received. Cooper's 'Annals of Cambridge' of 1845 records a contemporary account:

'King Charles & his Queen came from New-Market to Cambridge March 22, 1631 (ie 1632, by the 'New Style' dating introduced in 1752)...The Schollers Bachellors Fellow Commoners Regents & Non Regents were placed in the Streets in like manner as they were when K.James came thither March 1622. They made a great Acclamation as the K. & Q. passed by them, saying, Vivat Rex, Vivat Regina, &c...they came into Trin. Coll. Court...then their Majesties went up into the Lodging next the dining Roome where two Chayres of State were placed for them to sitt in...when their Majesties had dined they went presently into the Hall to the Comedy...The King said that he would show the Queen King's Coll. Chappell...the King led the Queen into the Quire, where they viewed the Windows & stately Structure &c. and then took Coach for Roystone'.[4] (Martin is reported to have received his D.D. on the 20th of March, but there are conflicting accounts of the dates of the various events of the visit).[2] 'The Annals of Cambridge' continues:

'It would seem that two comedies were acted here before the King and Queen, viz.: The Rival Friends, by Peter Hausted M.A. of Queens' College, and the Jealous Lovers by Thomas Randolph Fellow of Trinity College by the students of which House it was performed'.[4]

Searle's account gives further details:

'Before the arrival of the King and Queen there seems to have been a controversy among the heads, as to which should have the precedency. Chiefly, it would appear, through the influence of the Vicechancellor, Dr Butts, Hausted's play was acted first...Hausted undertaking two parts; but the subject was a satire against simony and other scandals of ecclesiastical patronage, and the play was...an unmistakeable failure...Dr Butts...desired to be Vice-Chancellor the third time, because of the King's coming. He hath been observed somewhat to droop upon occasion of missing a prebend of Westminster, which he would have had (as he said) and the Mastership of Trinity. But his vexation began when the King's coming approached, and Dr Comber and he fell foul of each other about the precedency of Queens' and Trinity comedy- he engaging himself for the former. But the killing blow was a dislike of that comedy and a check of the Chancellor (Lord Holland), who is said to have told him that the King and himself had more confidence in his discretion than they found cause, in that he thought such a comedy fitting &c...this came on the protestations of some of both Houses against his admission of the Doctors...The excitement was too much for the vicechancellor's mind, and it gave way, and he hanged himself in his bedroom'.[2,5] (Note: according to the University's records, Thomas Comber had succeeded Butts to become Vice-Chancellor for the academic year 1631-32; but it appears that the handover had been delayed). There was a report of riotous behaviour after Hausted's play, despite the University giving a warning to the students not to engage in:

'any humming, hawking, whistling, hissing, or laughing, be used, or any stamping or knocking, nor any other such uncivill or unschollarlike or boyish demeanor upon any occasion...'.[4,6]

Some of the underlying tensions of the visit are also described in the autobiography of Sir Simonds d'Ewes, 1602-50, an antiquary and politician, who was a member of the Long Parliament. However, as Searle points out, his Puritan views made him far from impartial in his opinions on high church divines such as Martin. Sir Simonds writes:

'The day following (the award of Martin's D.D.) after dinner I left the University...and came safe back to Islington...There passed divers degrees at this time at Cambridge, by virtue of the King's recommendatory letters, of which divers new and unworthy Doctors of Divinity partaking, the whole body of the University took great offence; and in the open Regent's house told Doctor Buts, master of Bennet College, then Vice Chancellor, to his face, that they did *istam graduum nundinationem improbare* (for all these Doctors had paid Mr Sanderson, the Earl of Holland's secretary, large rates for their doctorships, which Earl was now Chancellor of that University,) and so would not give their votes and assents to pass and confirm that dignity to Doctor Martin, Master of Queen's College, in Cambridge, and to the other new doctors; yet Doctor Buts carried business through with much disorder and violence, and pronounced them to have passed and attained that degree. This heaped so much distaste upon him in the said University (Mr Sanderson also being about this time turned out of his place by the said Earl of Holland) that the first day of April, being Easter-day, he hung himself in the morning, in his lodgings in Bennet College aforesaid'.[2] (ie in Corpus Christi College, of which he was Master).

Hausted ran into further trouble in 1634 for his high church views, when he gave great offence to Puritans and the Dutch in a sermon, causing him to be attacked by a mob at the University Church. These events are described by Martin in a letter to Archbishop Laud's chaplain on November 4th 1634:

'Most worthy Sr...next day here preached by chaunce at St Maryes my Curate at Uppingham, Mr Hausted. His sermon I have sent you up as he preached it...I suppose you may find some indiscretions of expression such as may deserve reprehension, advice, councell, but none that can deserve punishment. Yet because hee preached for reverence, alacrity, purity and order in God's service, for adoration in Churches, and bowing at the Bd name, for the surplis and other Ceremonyes, and for that hee preached that himselfe had seene very grave men in that place neglect their duties...Because in one place he told them that the Dutch, who are noted to be naturally slovenly, doe scoffe and gibe at all other nations for two much nicety: Upon this hee was taken immediately from the pulpit, arrested and committed in the Church, drawne through the street from the pulpit to the Consistory wth the greatest uproare and concourse of people that ever I was at any arraignment...Hausted, arraign'd and sentenced...only upon these two points, for taxing the University and abusing nations, namely, the Dutch...I was soe bold to tell him thus much: Now that you have slept upon the business I pray consider what you have done through ignorance, pride and factious zeale, that wh. Was never heard of...for a preist to be hal'd from the pulpit through the street to the consistory...wthout any cause of heresy, treyson or haynous crime pretended...Hee is my Curate in a regular market towne, and nether his poverty nor merits will suffer mee to put him out...'.[2] Hausted was: 'arraign'd and sentenced' by five heads of houses at the University's consistory court but, at later meeting under a new Vice-Chancellor, he was acquitted, exacerbating the religious divide in the University.[1] This was further widened in 1637 by another Laudian fellow of Queens', Anthony Sparrow, (a future President), who gave a controversial sermon and further infuriated his opponents by having it published.[1]

In 1630, Martin is reported to be rector of Conington, Cambridgeshire,[2] (although another source claims him as rector of another Conington in Huntingdonshire)[3] and, in 1638, when two parishes were amalgamated to form Houghton Conquest, Bedfordshire, he was presented to this living, vacating the living of Uppingham.[2,3]

In 1635, because of his high church views, Martin was asked to host a secret visit to Cambridge of a papal agent, Gregorio Panzani, and when viewing an Italian picture, Martin wondered: 'when will such splendour be restored to our church'.[3]

In 1637, Martin was the subject of a critical report to Parliament because of the performance at Queens' of a play, 'Valetudinarium':

'He (Martin) likewise permitted a most prophane Comedy to be acted in his Colledge ffebruary 5 1637 (ie 1638, using current dating). (The compiler of it being a divine and two other of ye Actors men in orders) and this to ye abuse of Religion & Religious men vnder ye name of puritanisme & Puritans. Three of ye principall actors in this play were Ipwichus, Linna, Magneticus, in derision (as was generally supposed) of ye Townes of Ipswich & Lynn & of mr Samuel Ward preacher in Ipswich who had a little before printed a booke de Magnete'.[7] The Queens' website notes:

'The towns of Ipswich and Lynn would have been recognised by the audience as strongholds of puritanism, and so this play appears to have had three comic puritans. It is scarcely surprising that eventually, as the puritans gained influence in government, the theatres were ordered to be closed and the performance of plays banned'.[7] (In the previous century, taking part in drama was a compulsory part of the College curriculum, which was backed up by the possibility of expulsion for refusal to take part, while the 1558 College Statutes specified that two comedies or tragedies should be put on every year. But the above production was the last at Queens' before all plays was banned in 1642).

Martin's turbulent future career was determined by the upheavals within Church and State, which encompassed the Civil War, the execution of Charles I, the English Commonwealth and the restoration of the monarchy in 1660. Charles I was involved in conflicts with Parliament from the beginning of his reign in 1625. He believed in the divine right of kings and there were many objections to certain of his regime's taxes which did not have Parliamentary approval. Also, his religious policies, together with his marriage to a Catholic, were opposed by Reformed groups such as the English Puritans and Scottish Presbyterians.

The Parliamentary session of 1629 ended with disagreements with the King, who would rule alone for the next eleven years, during a period known as the 'Personal Rule' and the 'Eleven-Year Tyranny'. During this time, the King's particular advisors were William Laud and Thomas Wentworth, who would become Baron, then Viscount Wentworth in 1628, and 1st Earl of Strafford in January 1640. (As noted above, the King had appointed Bishop Laud as Archbishop of Canterbury in 1633).

The 'Bishops Wars' of 1639 and 1640, between England and Scotland, can be considered as heralding the civil war to come. These conflicts followed long-standing tensions over the control of the Church of Scotland and, in 1637, Charles had tried to impose uniform practices in both the Scottish Church and the Church of England. But there was a major disagreement about the role of bishops, as most Scots wanted a Presbyterian system, involving government by representative assemblies. In 1638, a 'National Covenant' opposed Charles' instructions and, in 1639, Wentworth was recalled from Ireland, (where he had been Lord Deputy since 1632), to become the King's principal advisor in the crisis of war with the 'Covenanters', in the context of royal bankruptcy. But the Covenanters opposed Charles' attempt to impose his will by force and, in 1639, there was a truce after Charles had joined his forces at Berwick. Charles was then advised by the newly-enobled Strafford to summon a Parliament to grant funds to continue the war; this was the 'Short Parliament', beginning on the 13th April

1640, which brought Charles' eleven years of personal rule to an end. However, many in Parliament resented the King's previous actions, in particular his religious reforms and the royal claim to levy ship money, and Parliament demanded that these matters be considered before any funds be granted. After a futile appeal by the King to the Lords for support against the Commons, the resulting deadlock led the King to dissolve Parliament on the 5th May. At this point we can glimpse Martin in the midst of these events: when the Short Parliament met, a Convocation of the Church of England was also formed, with royal authority to make new 'canon' laws to implement Laud's religious reforms and Martin was one of the two delegates or 'proctors':

'...for the clergie of this diocese (ie Ely) to meet in convocation in the chapter house of St Paul's Cathedral in London 14 April'.[2,8] Although it was a tradition that a Convocation only sat while Parliament was in session, it was allowed to continue after the dissolution of the Short Parliament and produced seventeen new 'canons', including an endorsement of the Divine Right of Kings and the establishment of an oath to support established Church doctrine (the 'Etcetera Oath'), to be taken by members of the learned professions. Not surprisingly, despite approval by the King and ratification on the 30th June 1640, this produced widespread opposition.[2,8]

The Scottish war continued with the advance of Scottish forces, the retreat of Charles' army and a Scottish occupation of Northumberland and County Durham. Charles was forced to sign the Treaty of Ripon in October 1640, which pledged the payment of the Scottish expenses and forced the King to summon another Parliament to grant him further funds. This led to the 'Long Parliament', which met on the 3rd November 1640, (and would continue until 1660), and began to impeach Strafford, who was sent to the Tower of London on the 25th November. Charles, under great pressure from Parliament, which was even more hostile to him than its predecessor, eventually, and reluctantly, agreed to Strafford's execution, which took place on the 12th May 1641 on Tower Hill, before a large crowd. Also in 1641, Parliament passed the 'Triennial Act', which received the Royal

Assent but significantly reduced the King's authority, as the measures included forbidding the levy of ship money, (a tax on coastal cities and counties), without Parliament's consent, and a requirement for Parliament to be summoned at least once in three years. But, in May 1641, Parliament tried to reduce the risk of civil unrest, by asking all males over the age of 18 to take and sign the 'Protestation', an oath of allegiance to the King and a pledge to defend the Church of England against: 'Popish innovations'. Further, in January 1642, the Speaker of the House of Commons, Lenthill, signed a letter ordering compliance. Martin, for unknown reasons, was absent when the oath was taken by the senior fellow of Queens', on behalf of the College.[1] Charles and Parliament hoped that Strafford's execution and the Protestation would reduce the dangerous instability in the country, but hostilities continued between the supporters of Charles and those of Parliament.

In August 1641, Charles visited Scotland to try and enlist support and made various concessions, including the establishment of Presbyterianism. In November 1641, Parliament passed, but only by a narrow majority, the 'Grand Remonstrance', a list of grievances against Charles' government since the beginning of his reign and, around this time, news of rebellion in Ireland led to fears that any army raised to suppress the violence might be used by the King against his opponents. In consequence, Charles was asked to surrender his command of the army and his response was predictable: 'By God, not for an hour'. It has been suggested that his fears that his Catholic Queen would be impeached led to his drastic action of accusing one member of the House of Lords and five of the Commons of treason. On the 4th January 1642, in a famous incident, when backed up by about 400 men, he entered the House of Commons himself, only to find that the five had escaped and, after an oft-quoted response by the Speaker, he declared: 'All my birds have flown'. This incident was politically disastrous for the King, leading to Parliament seizing control of London and the departure of the King to Hampden Court Palace on the 10th January. Two days later he moved to Windsor Castle and, after sending his wife and eldest daughter abroad in February, he travelled north. But in March, the King, accompanied by the Prince of Wales, visited Cambridge University, as described in a letter of Joseph Beaumont, later Master of Peterhouse, to his father:

'... ye Moonday after, he came hither himself, &...graciously turned in & staid a while. At his coming out of ye Coach, which was before Trinity College, ye University being placed ready, saluted him with such vehement acclamacions of Vivat Rex, as I never heard ye like noise heer before upon any occasion...At his parting one tells me that he thus spake to ye Vicechan. "Mr. Vicechane. Whatsoever becomes of me I will charge my Sonn, upon my blessing, to respect ye University"...'.[4] After futile negotiations with Parliament by letter, while various cities and towns declared their support for one side or another, Charles then attempted to obtain weapons from a major depository at Hull, but he was refused admission by the governor, who had been recently appointed by Parliament. Both sides began to raise troops and Charles raised his royal standard at Nottingham on the 22nd August 1642. After the first significant engagement of the Civil War, in which a Parliamentary cavalry detachment was defeated, the first major battle took place at Edgehill in October 1642. But this was inconclusive, as was a subsequent engagement at Turnham Green; Charles then withdrew to Oxford, which would be his headquarters for the rest of the war.

Martin was active in promoting the King's cause in the University.[2] On the 29th June 1642, the King wrote to the Vice-Chancellor from York asking for money, to be repaid at eight percent interest: 'as soon as it should please God to settle the distraction of the kingdome',[2] and Queens' provided a conspicuous demonstration of loyalty; Martin personally subscribed £100 and ten of the fellows a total of £85, receipt of which was duly noted:

'July 2°. 1642. Received the day and yeare above written of Edward Martin, Dr in Divinity, Master of Queen's Colledge in the University of Cambr. The summe of one hundred eighty five pounds, viz. one hundred for himself and foure score and five pounds for the fellows of the said Colledge, wch money is lent unto the King according to the intendment and direction of his

M[ties] letters of the 29 of June last to the Vicechancellr of the said University. I say, Rd by mee, John Poley'.[2] On the 24th July, the King wrote again, from Leicester, requesting that the silver plate of the various colleges be sent to him to avoid its confiscation by the Parliamentary party:

'To our Trusty and well beloved, the Vice-Chancellor of our University of Cambridge.

Charles R. ...being informed of the further readiness of all or most of our Colleges in Cambridge, to make offer of depositing their Plate into our Hands, for the better security and safety thereof...we would have some of every Society to take a just account...that the same proportion, in the same manner may be returned again to them, when it shall please God, to end these troubles...'.[4] Once again, Martin gave his support and, on the 3rd August: '923 ¾ oz. of gilt and white plate' was delivered to John Poley of Pembroke Hall, who had been commissioned by the King to organise the transfer. The list of the plate begins:

'Queenes Colledge, Cambr. Aug, 3, 1642. The Colledge plate in these dreadfull times of Imminent Danger for the Security thereof deposited wth the Kings most excellent Mate (and delivered by his Maties Speciall direction unto John Poley Esquire and Servaunt in ordinary attendaunce to our gracious Prince Charles) upon his Maties letters to that purpose and Royall promise of Restitution either in kind or full value according to the quality of the plate. By the unanimous Act and consent of Master and Fellowes...'.[2] One of the items was a flagon presented by past members of Oliver Cromwell's family, Thomas, John and William Cromwell.[5] Searle reports that Oliver Cromwell had been ordered by Parliament to seize the colleges' plate and was waiting between Cambridge and Huntingson, but that, nevertheless, most of the consignment was delivered to the King at Nottingham.[2] (Twigg states that while Oliver Cromwell and his brother-in-law Valentine Watson prevented most of the colleges' plate from leaving, the Queens' plate, and that of Jesus, St John's and Peterhouse, had been sent early).[1] But the Parliamentary party had strong support in the Eastern Counties and, on the 17th August, Parliament empowered Cromwell and four Cambridge aldermen to take charge of the town.[1] The three heads of houses who had given particular support to the King, namely Martin, Beale of St John's and Sterne of Jesus, were arrested on the 30th August 1642 by Cromwell with a group of soldiers. They were treated:

'with all possible scorn and contempt, especially Cromwell behaving himselfe most insolently towards them, and when one of the Doctors made it a request to Cromwell, that he might stay a little to put up some linen, Cromwell denyed him the favour; and whether in a jeere, or simple malice told him, that it was not in his Commission. Having now prepared a shew to entertain the people, in triumph they lead the captives toward London, where the people were beforehand informed what captives Colonell Cromwell was bringing. In the Villages as they passed from Cambridge to London, the People were called by some of their Agents to come and abuse, and revile them'.[1] However, Twigg considers that this and other accounts of significant ill-treatment after their arrest and imprisonment are unlikely.[1]

On the 1st September 1642, the House of Lords was informed that some heads of colleges in Cambridge who had sent their plate to the King had been arrested, which led to the issue of the following orders:

'To Captaine Oliver Cromwell Sept.1. 1642. It is ordered by the Committee of the Lords and Comons appointed for the safety of the kingdome, That the Bishop of Ely, Dr Martin, Dr Beal, and Dr Sterne bee safely conveyed by you to Blackwall and from thence by water to the Tower of London, where they are to bee kept, till further direction bee given. Essex...'.

'To the Gentleman-Usher or his Deputy to be delivered to the Leiutenant of the Tower of London Die Jovis, 1me Sept. 1642. Ordered by the Lords in Parliament, that the Leiuetenent of the Tower of London shall take the Bodyes of the Lod Bishop of Ely, Mr Dr Beal, Mr Dr Martin, and Mr Dr Sterne into his safe custody, intill the pleasure of this House bee further signified unto him, and this shall bee his sufficient warrant. Jon Brown Cler. Parliam'.[2] It is claimed that Cromwell led his captives:

'through Bartholomew Faire, and so as farre as Temple-Bar, when the Concourse was as thick as the negotiation of buyers and sellers...could make it; they lead these captives leisurely through the midst of the Faire: as they passe along, they are entertained with exclamations, reproaches, scornes, and curses, and considering the prejudice raised in the City of them, it was Gods great mercy that they found no worse usage from them...the people there (ie in the Tower) use them with no lesse incivility within the walls, then the people did without, calling them Papists, Arminians, and I know not what'.[2] Archbishop Laud had already been confined to the Tower and, on the 3rd September, the Lords made an order that he should not meet the Cambridge doctors.[2]

After a few days the three heads drew up a petition, which was presented to the House of Lords by the Chancellor of Cambridge University, the Earl of Holland:

'...May it please your Lo:ps in tender consideration of the premises to graunt your Pet:rs their Libertyes upon their bonds to appeare, whensoever your Lo: shall please to appoint...'.[2] But liberty was not forthcoming and the following order was made on the 24th October 1642:

'It is this day ordered, amd appointed by the Lords and Comons in Parliament assembled, that all the Prisoners in the Tower bee forthw'h kept under such restraint, as that not any Prisoner bee suffer'd to have above two servants, or permitted to have speech, or converse with any other prisoner, or person, but in the presence or hearing of his keeper'.[2] Also, in December, the Commons ordered that:

'all Malignants and Delinquents that were sent for should bear their own charges'.[2] The three heads made a further petition to the Lords in December and petitions were also delivered from the three colleges affected, asking for the release of their Masters in view of approaching audits, the choice of scholars and college officers, the renewing of leases and other business.[2] As these did not produce any movement towards their trial or release, in January 1643, Sir Philip Stapleton, (a member of Parliament, a supporter of the Parliamentary cause, commander of a brigade of cavalry at the battle of Edgehill and a previous fellow- commoner of Queens'), prevailed upon his fellow members of the Committee of the Lords and Commons for the safety of the kingdom, to order that the three Masters be transferred to Lord Petre's house in Aldersgate Street:

'To the keeper of the Ld Peters House in Aldersgate Street. These are to will and require you forthwith and upon sight hereof to take into your safe custody the bodies of William Beale, Edward Martin, and Richard Sterne, Drs in Divinity, who are transmitted unto you from the Tower where they have been prisoners And them you shall safely keep, until you shall receive father order theirin from this Committee. Given at the Committee of the LL[ds] and Commons for the safety of the kingdome this 11 of January 1642 (ie 1643 new style)...'.[2] It was also ordered that the three should:

'upon their removal pay their fees to the Lieutenant of the Tower of London, and the other officers there...'.[2] Further, on the 1st April, Parliament ordered the confiscation of the property of all clergymen who had assisted the King. (William Petre, the 4th Baron, 1626-84, succeeded to the barony aged eleven and, at the beginning of the Civil War, his estates were sequestered by Parliament as he was a Catholic).

In August 1643, Martin wrote to Sir Philip Stapleton:

'Noble Sr, I have beene now these twelve-monthes a Prisoner (never ha- once the liberty to stirre out of dores) in w[c]h time (after the sequestration of all my living and maintenaunce to a farthing: and the taking away of all my cattell and goodes to a Bedstaffe) I am at length (as I heare) design'd to bee sent a ship board: w[c]h to mee can bee no other then Death by another name...Let us therefore, I beseech you...bee preserved in the same Condition to w[ch] your goodness solely preferr'd us...'.[2]

However, this plea was in vain as the following order was issued:

'To the keeper of the prison of Peterhouse in Aldersgate Streete. By vertue of an order this day made by the House of Comons, these are to will and require you to deliver to those appointed by an Ordinance of Parliament for the Militia of London the bodies of Capitaine John Cooper, Dr Beale, Dr Martin, Dr Sterne...to be by them delivered to Georg Hawes master of the ship called the Prosperous Sarah now riding in the river of Thames to be kept in safe custody as Prisoners in the sayd ship by the sayd Hawes, until the pleasure of the House be signified to the contrary: And for this doing this shall be your warrant. Dat. 10 August 1643. Wm Lenthall. Speaker'.[2] An account of subsequent events, 'Mercurius rusticus', was published in 1685:

'They went by Coach from Alders-gate-street to Billinsgate... there to take water one was overheard to say these looke like honest men, and he was not a jot mistaken...but another looking the grave learned Divines in the face, reviled them, saying, that they did not looke like Christians and prayed that they might breake their necks as they went downe the Stairs to take water... but yet they found farre worse by water: being come on ship-board, they were instantly put under Hatches, where the Decks were so low, that they could not stand upright, and yet were denyed stooles to sit on, or as much as a burden of straw to lye on. Into this Little Ease in a small ship, they crowd no lesse than fourscore persons of quality, and that they might stifle one another, having no more breath then what they sucked from one anothers mouths, most maliciously, and (certainly) to a murtherous intent, they stop up all the small Auger holes, and all other in-lets, which might relieve them with fresh aire: an act of such horrid barbarisme, that nor Age, nor Story, nor Rebellion can parallel'.[9] A contemporary account, 'Querela Cantabrigiensis', published in 1646, adds:

'for ten days together they...were kept under deck without liberty to come to breath in the common aire, or to ease nature, except at the courtesie of the rude Saylors, which oftentimes was denyed them'.[10] Further, Sir William Dougdale, (1605-86), in 1681, claims that:

'And did not Mr Rigby (a member of the Commons)...move twice, that those Lords and Gentlemen which were Prisoners... should be sold as Slaves to Argiere, or sent to the new Plantations in the West-Indies, because he had Contracted with two merchants for that purpose'.[10] Although Twigg describes aspects of these accounts as: 'hysterically exaggerated',[1] some royalists detained on prison ships on the Thames are reported to have lost their lives[2] and Martin will have been very relieved that he did not have to remain for long in his miserable situation as, on the 19th August, the following order was made:

'To the Keeper of the Ely House or his deputy. By vertue of an order of the house of Comons...These are to require you to take into your safe Custody, and soe to keepe till further order, the Bodyes of Dr Beale, Dr Martin, Dr Stearne...'.[2] Martin was then transferred from the ship to the Bishop of Ely's house in Holborn.

Around 1643, Martin was deprived of his Church preferments for reasons described by John White, 1590-1645, a member of the Long Parliament and chairman of its Grand Committee of Religion in 1640, in: 'The first Century of Scandalous Malignant Priests':[12]

'The benefices of Edward Marten, Doctor in Divinity, Parson of the Parish Churches of Houghton-Conquest in the county of Bedford and of Dunnington (Conington) in the county of Cambridge, are sequestred, for that he usually prayed openly for the Saints and people departed this life, and that they might be eased and freed of their paines in Purgatory, and hath said, that preaching is prophaned when it is in a dining-roome, or other place not allowed by the Bishop...and hath not preached since he was Parson of Houghton-Conquest in five yeares, not above five Sermons there, and hath substituted there in his absence very scandalous and malignant Curates...and is most unreasonable in adoring of the Altar, making five low cursies in his going to it, and two at it, and then falling downe upon his knees before it...And hath openly preached that the Parliament goeth about in a factious way, to erect a new Religion, and...that hee had lent and given money to the King to maintain this unnaturall warre against the Parliament and Kingdom'.[2,12]

In December 1643, after Trinity College petitioned the House of Lords complaining about falling rents and sequestrations, the Earl of Manchester hoped that the peers would:

'think it better to endeavour the reforming of the University rather than to hazard the dissolving of it'[1] and, in January 1664, Manchester was empowered by an:

'Ordinance for regulating the university of Cambridge and for removing of scandalous ministers in the seven associated counties...', to eject all members of the colleges that were:

'scandalous in their lives or ill affected to the parliament or formentors of unnaturall warre...or wilfully refuse obedience to the ordinances of Parliament...and to place other fitting persons in their room...'.[2] Martin was among the first of several heads to be ejected, by a warrant of the 13th March 1644:

'To the President (ie the acting head of the College) and fellows of Queenes Colledge in Cambridge. By vertue of an ordinance of Parlyament...giving mee likewise power to eject such Masters of Colledges as are scandalous in their lives and Doctrines, or that oppose the proceedings of Parlyament, I doe eject Dr Martin Master of Queenes Colledge in Cambridge for opposeing the proceedings of Parlyament and other scandalous acts in the University of Cambridge. And I require you to sequester the profits of his Mastership for one that I shall appoint in his place, and to cut his name out of the Butteries, and to certifie mee of this your act within one day...E. Manchester'.[2] Also, four Queens' fellows were ejected on the 8th April, for non-residence and not appearing when summoned, and four more on the next day, for refusing to take the 'Covenant' required by Parliament, which supported a Presbyterian system of Church organisation.[1] Martin later wrote that he would:

'embrace any extremity of torture or death', rather than support something: 'so opposite to his Religion, Faith, and all his duties to God and man'.[1]

Queens' had been without an active head since Martin's arrest on the 30th August 1642, a situation that endured until 11th April 1644 when Herbert Palmer was appointed President. During this interregnum, in 1643, Parliament had directed that:

'in all churches and chapels all altars and tables of stone should be taken away and demolished. The communion tables were to be removed from the west end of the chancel, the rails taken away, all tapers, candlesticks and basins to be removed from the communion table and disused, all crucifixes, crosses, all images and pictures of any one or more Persons of the Trinity or of the Virgin Mary, all other images and pictures of saints or superstitious inscriptions in churches and chapels were ordered to be taken away and defaced'.[1] Manchester commissioned William Dowsing to carry out this ordinance in the East of England and the latter's diary records his visit to Queens' on the 26th December 1643:

'We beat down 110 superstitious pictures besides Cherubims and Ingravings, where none of the fellows would put on their Hatts in all the time they were in the Chapell, and we digged up the Steps for three hours and brake down 10 or 12 Apostles and Saints within the hall'.[2]

Archbishop Laud was eventually brought to trial in 1644 and one of the charges against him was that he had accepted superstitious practices and observances in the University of Cambridge. This was supported by three witnesses, including John Wallis (Wallys), a fellow of Queens' during 1644-45 and subsequently Professor of Geometry at Oxford, who testified that:

'Altars, Pictures, Crucifixes, were there of late set up in most Colledge Chappells...in Peter house Chappel there was a glorious new Altar set up, & mounted on steps, to which the Master, Fellowes, Schollers bowed, & were enjoyned to bow by Doctor Cosens the Master, who set it up...Alyers Crucifixes, Candlestickes, Tapers, and bowing to Alters...were brought in since the Archbishops time by means of Byshop Wren, Doctor Cosens, Dr. Martin and others, all Canterburies great favourites...'.[4] After Laud had received a sentence of execution, he requested that Martin, together with Dr Hayward and Dr Sterne, be allowed to visit but:

'the Commons were so cruel and envenomed that a negative was absolutely put on the two former, and when they allowed Dr Sterne to go, it was under condition, that two of his bitter enemies and their tools Stephen Marshall and Herbert Palmer or one of them, was to be always with him, when in conference with the ABishop, which in effect was equal to a refusal'.[2] In his will Laud left Martin his: 'ring with a hyacinth in it' and similar legacies to others that had been his: 'chaplains in house'.[2] He was beheaded on the 10th January 1665.

Martin's house arrest continued, and Searle quotes a letter from Martin, believed to be to Sir Philip Stapleton, written around 1647:

'I found myselfe soe thoughly bereft of all comforts in relation to wch men may any way desire to live in this world, as bereft of all goods, sequestr'd from all livelihood, destitute of frend and inthrald to most strict imprisonment, having not any leave through my life should depend thereon at any time to stire out of doores, for now almost these five yeeres shifted from prison to prison; by land and by water, exhausted of all meanes to buy bread, yet finding a subsistence (though a very poore one) by divine Providence...But, noble Sr, soe it is that being not conscious to myselfe of any injury or damage by mee done to any man living...I am doom'd (by mr Knightly his committee) to bee singled out from all men in my case and to be committed a prisoner to the Marshalsey in Southwarke, where I can nether have convenient lodging, aire, wayes or opportunityes to send to frendes to accommodate mee w^t^h such necessary as may preserve mee from famine, and utter extremity. My humble suite to you is only this that, in case I may not possibly obtain my berty (ie liberty)...yet that I may bee carried to any prison where others of my owne ranke and condition are (as the Fleete or Peterhouse) ...or if this may not bee obtain'd, yet I humbly beseech you (if it bee possible) that by you I may understand from whence and how this arrow is shot at mee, that I may attempt...from thence to procure any remedy...'.[2] However, Martin was not transferred to the Marshalsea prison and was in Lord Petre's house in June 1647, when he drew up what has been described as a 'mock' petition to the House of Lords, written to express his frustrations rather than in the expectation of release:

'written in a manly spirit of boldness, and displaying the detestable hypocrisy and villany of those times and his own sufferings'.[2] It was printed in the same year, titled:

'E.M. A long imprisoned Malignant His Humble Submission to the Covenant and Directory: With some Reasons and Grounds of use to settle and satisfie tender Consciences. Presented in A Petition to the Right Honourable the Lords assembled in

Parliament, in Whitsun-week, in the year 1647…'.[2] Martin asked the Earl of Manchester to present this to the House of Lords in a letter in which he signs off as:

'Your Hon:[rs] poor Annihilated Nothing Edw. Martin'.[2]

Searle informs us that Martin remained in custody until he escaped around August 1648, with the help of a Mr Weldon, who had been ejected as rector of Stony Stanton in Leicestershire. He then stayed with Henry Coke, at Thorington, Suffolk, who was a son of a previous Chief Justice Sir Edward Coke. (Henry Coke, who had been admitted a fellow- commoner at Queens' in 1607, was a member of the Long Parliament until September 1642, when he was excluded for his royalist sympathies). We are told that Martin lived with Coke under the name of Matthews, until he was arrested by some soldiers from Yarmouth in 1650 and taken to London. But he was soon released and returned to Suffolk, living under his own name, before going abroad for most of the 1650s. He then lived mainly with Lord Hatton in the Fauxbourg St Germain district of Paris, but was living in Utrecht in 1656.[3] (Lord Hatton, 1605-70, who was educated at Jesus College, Cambridge, was a prominent royalist and had been a member of the Long Parliament). During his exile Martin was consistently hostile to both foreign Protestants and the Catholic Church. He:

'neither joined with the Calvinists, nor kept any Communion with the Papists: but confined himself to a Congregation of old English and Primitive Protestants…he was offered honorable accommodations by some in the Church of Rome, but he accepted them not, because he said, He had rather be a poor Son of the afflicted, but Primitive church of England, than a Rich Member of the flourishing, but corrupt Church of Rome'.[2]

In the month before the monarchy was restored in May 1660, Martin writes to a Mr Richard Watson, summarising his past misfortunes:

'I…who having been habituated these eighteen years, to nothing but Prisons, Ships, wandrings, and solitude, hath always been very well satisfied with one Meal a day, and at night a Crust of Bread, and a Cup of any Drink. That I most desire everywhere is Cider, or, in defect of that, Water (if it bee anything neer so good as here at Paris) for I drunk no Wine for thirteen years together, before I came out of England'.[2]

Charles II arrived in England at the invitation of Parliament on the 25th May 1660, and Martin returned in the same month. He was restored as President on the 2nd August 1660, at the then advanced age of 79, by a warrant from the Earl of Manchester, who had previously ejected him:

'Whereas I am informed yt Edward Martin, Doctor in divinity and Master of Queenes Colledge in Cambridge hath been wrongfully putt out of his Mastershipp, These are to signifie to all whome it may concerne yt I doe by virtue of an authority given unto me by ye Lords assembled in Parliament, restore him to his sayd Mastershipp, together with all lodgings keyes leigerbookes and scales appertaining to his place, From henceforth to have and injoy all profits rights priviledges and advantages thereunto belonging, unless cause be shewen me to ye contrary within tenn dayes next after ye date hereof…E. Manchester'.[2] On the death of Herbert Palmer in 1647, Thomas Horton had been elected President and, on receipt of the above, accepted the inevitable and withdrew from the College. Martin reflected that the College had been rescued from its: 'Babylonian captivity'.[1]

The Earl of Manchester had himself fallen foul of Parliament, when he had refused to sign the 'Engagement' of 1649, which pledged allegience to the 'Commonwealth of England'. He had been removed from the Chancellorship of the University, but was re-appointed after the Restoration.[5] Both the Chancellor and Martin wanted to avoid a wholesale purge of those appointed at Queens' since 1642, as shown by a letter from Manchester to Martin dated the 13th August 1660:

'Reverend Sr…These are to require you to take care not to remove any from being fellows or schollers in Queens Colledge that are in places vacant by death or other incapacities and likewise yt none be removed from being fellows or schollers till those places be filled which are already void or may immediately made void by voluntary resignations and if such vacant places shall not be enough for the reception of all who are to be restored, then to make roome for ye rest by ye removal only of so many of ye juniors as shall be necessary. Thus with my kind respects to you I rest your friend to serve you, E. Manchester'.[2] Those fellows elected since Martin's ejection were re-elected, while those who had been ejected were duly restored.

On his return, Martin initiated the restoration of the chapel which had suffered under William Dowsing. His friend Henry Coke gave cedar for panelling at the east end, and an organ was re-introduced; also, Martin diverted Herbert Palmer's bequest of £53 for the benefit of poor scholars, to pay for repairs to the chapel.[1] Hoods and surplices were obtained and altar rails were restored. On the 12th January 1661 Martin turned his attention to another (very) important issue, that of College feasts:

'It is agreed upon and decreed by the M^{r} and Fellowes, that the Questionists and Inceptors shall not be allowed to make any feasting or any manner of exceedings, but as followeth; that is to say: For that Fryday when they have their graces first propounded in the university to every messe of Fellowes (6 to a messe) 6^{s}. For every messe of Bachelours, Questionists and generall Sophisters (6 to a messe) 3^{s}. To every messe of Fellowes a quart of sack and 2 quarts of claret, and to every messe of Bachelours Questionists and Sophisters 2 quarts of claret. That they doe not exceed 12^{s}. upon any pretence of provision for the Father and the Bedle at the Questionists Priorum. Edward Martin'.[2]

A draft of a petition, in Martin's handwriting, shows his residual bitterness:

'...the whole College stock is entirely consum'd and lost: the woods and timber upon the grounds fell'd and sold without any account: the Covenants of Leases alter'd: rents extinguished: Royaltyes alienated (which should have belong'd to the maintenance of the Chappell, and God's service and work amongst us)...and the College itselfe so ruinated in edifices and otherwise, that we are in no wayes able to maintaine it...'.[5]

National attempts at reconciliation included the 'Savoy Conference' of 1661, held at the Savoy Hospital in London, which attempted to achieve harmony within the Church of England. The delegates included 12 Anglican bishops and 12 representatives of the Puritan and Presbyterian factions; Searle claims that Martin was: 'one of the managers'.[1] But this did not achieve success, and the Church of England was destined to split, with the exodus of most of the Nonconformists. This followed the passage of several Acts of Parliament, including the 1662 'Act of Uniformity', which made the use of the Anglican Book of Common Prayer compulsory. Also, Martin was a delegate from the Ely diocese to the Anglican Convocation in 1661, which approved the text of the revised Book of Common Prayer before it was submitted to Parliament. In 1662 he was elected Dean of Ely and installed by proxy on the 25th April, but after a tenure of just three days, he died on the 28th April. He is buried in the College's original chapel.

The College library contains an early fifteenth-century English volume, 'Soliloquia', by Augustine of Hippo (354-430), handwritten and lavishly illustrated, containing annotations on its final leaf suggesting that it was the property of Queen Mary Tudor, while a later inscription by Martin shows that he bequeathed it to the College in 1662. However, the College records show that the Library had owned the book before the Civil War, so Martin may have removed the book to safety before his arrest, fearing wartime vandalism.

Soon after his death, a collection of five letters of Martin was published. These had been written while he was exiled in Paris to Richard Watson, who was a fellow of Caius College, Cambridge, and Master of the Perse Grammar School, Cambridge, until being removed from his positions for his religious views. Watson then went into exile in France and, after his return in 1661, he became chaplain to the Duke of York and prebendary of Salisbury. The publication was titled:

'Doctor Martin Late Dean of Ely His Opinion 1. The difference between the Church of England and Geneva. 2. The Pope's Primacy as pretended successive to St Peter's. 3. The Authority of the Apostolical Constitutions and Canons. 4. The discovery of the Genuine Works of the Primitive Fathers. 5. The false brotherhood of the French and English Presbyterians. Together With his Character of divers English Travelers in the time of our Late Troubles, Communicated by five pious and learned Letters in the time of his Exile. London Printed Anno 1662'.[2]

Another English divine in exile in France during the Civil War for his 'supertstitious and Popish practices', was John Cosin, 1594-1672, previously a fellow of Caius College and, after the Restoration, Bishop of Durham, whose relationships with French Protestants were criticised by Martin in the above letters. A subsequent commentator, White Kennet, 1660-1728, Bishop of Peterborough, in his: 'Register and Chronicle, Ecclesiastical and Civil...from the Restauration of King Charles II', states:

'There is also another Pamphlet called Dr. Martin's Letters, fraught with gross Untruths, and railing against the Bishop (ie Dr Cosin) and others whilst he lived amoung the Protestants in France, set out by the Spite and Peevishness of a Pedant Minister RW. And scarce one Line true in all that he writes...his Principles were very rigid, and his Temper sour'd by Sufferings and a tedious exile'.[2] But Martin shows a thoughtful self- reflection in the following letter:

'For I do confesse to you, that the Zeal of Gods Church (though I am now not farr from my grave) constrains mee sometime (I fear in conscience) beyond the bounds of Brotherly Charity, and Christian duty, which God forgive mee...'.[2]

However, his Presidency of Queens' receives an approving judgement from one of his successors, Robert Plumptre:

'...The college books furnish sufficient proofs of his abilities, of his knowledge and taste in classical learning, of his attention to the duties of his office, and of his faithful discharge of them'.[2]

References

1. Twigg, J. A History of Queens' College, Cambridge 1448-1986. The Boydell Press. 1987. pp 44-53, 119, 142-43.
2. Searle, W.G. The History of the Queens' College of St Margaret and St Bernard in the University of Cambridge. Part II 1560-1662. Sold by Deighton, Bell & Co; Macmillan & Co. London. 1871. pp 464-526, 572-83.
3. Milton, A. Martin, Edward. Oxford Dictionary of National Biography. 2011. Online. 2019.

4. Cooper, C.H. Annals of Cambridge. Volume III. Warwick and Co., Cambridge. 1845. pp 249-51, 288-89, 322-28.
5. Gray, J.H. The Queens' College of St Margaret and St Bernard. F.E.Robinson. London. 1898. pp 155-95.
6. Gurr, Andrew. Playgoing in Shakespeare's London. Cambridge University Press. Cambridge. 1996.
7. Academic Drama. Queens' College Cambridge. Online. 2020.
8. Plant, David. The Short Parliament, 1640. BCW Project. Online. 2019.
9. Ryves, Bruno. (1596-1677). Mercurius rusticus. 1685.
10. Barwick, John. (1612-64). Querela Cantabrigiensis, or, A remonstrance by way of apologie for the banished members of the late flourishing University of Cambridge by some of the said sufferers. 1646.
11. Dougdale, Sir William. (1605-86). A Short View of the Late Troubles in England. 1681.
12. White, John. (1590-1645). The first Century of Scandalous Malignant Priests. 1643.

CHAPTER 18

Herbert Palmer. President 1644-47.

Summary.

Herbert Palmer was born in 1601 to a well-established family in Kent, the son of Sir Thomas Palmer of Wingham. He became a fellow-commoner at St John's College, Cambridge, in 1616, where he graduated B.A. and M.A. . But there is a puzzling report that he was: 'denied his degee at St John's on account of personal deformity' and, although there are several references to his small and crooked stature and child-like appearance, it is not clear why he transferred to Queens' as a fellow-commoner in 1622. He was elected to a fellowship at Queens' the following year and was ordained in 1624. He was to show religious zeal throughout his life and held strong Puritan views. However, he is described as a moderate man, who took great care and interest in his pupils' welfare and religious instruction. He became a renowned preacher and, while visiting his brother in Kent, his sermons at Canterbury led to an offer of a Puritan lectureship at a local chuch.

In 1632, he was appointed vicar of Ashwell, Herfordshire, by William Laud, then Bishop of London, and he vacated his fellowship at Queens' the following year.

Despite his Puritan leanings he was a member of the 'Convocation' of the Church of England in 1640, which met with the authority of the King to implement Archbishop Laud's reforms.

The Civil War began in 1642 and, in 1643, Parliament appointed the 'Westminster Assembly of Divines', to restructure and reform the Church of England. Palmer was a leading member of this Assembly, preaching to Parliament and contributing to the 'Shorter Catechism'; this would be published in 1647, the year of his death.

Edward Martin, President of Queens', was arrested in 1642 because of his support for the King, and imprisoned in London, so that the College was without an active Head until 1644, when Martin was officially ejected. Palmer was then installed in his stead by the Earl of Manchester.

Palmer inherited only a few resident fellows and students but, in June 1644, nine new fellows were appointed by Manchester. Later that month, eleven new students were admitted, and Palmer: 'set himself industriously to the promotion of religion and learning'. He was also active in the support of the University, leading a delegation to petition Parliament on its behalf in 1645.

He died in November 1647 after a short illness: 'so great was that unanimity and reciprocal affection between him and the Society that scarce any Head of a Society was taken from them with more general sorrow'.

Timeline.

1601. Born at Wingham, Kent, the younger son of Sir Thomas Palmer, (d.1625).

1616. Fellow-commoner, St John's College, Cambridge.

1619. B.A. .

1622. M.A. . Fellow-commoner, Queens'.

1623. Fellow of Queens'.

1624. Ordained.

1626. Visits his brother at Canterbury and preaches at the Cathedral. Appointed as a 'Lecturer' at St Alphege's Church, Canterbury.

1631. B.D. . Edward Martin is elected President of Queens'.

1632. Appointed vicar of Ashwell, Herfordshire by William Laud, Bishop of London.

1633. Appointed a Cambridge University preacher. Resigns as a fellow of Queens'.

1630s. Develops a system of catechism (ie religious teaching by question and answer). Takes in sons of noblemen and gentlemen as pupils.

1640.	Publication of his catechism: 'An Endeavour of Making the Principles of Christian Religion...Plain and Easie'.
1642.	Appointed a Lecturer at Hitchen by Parliament. Martin arrested and conveyed to London.
1643.	Appointed as an original member of the 'Westminster Assembly of Divines', which is set up to restructure and reform the Church of England. He moves to London, leaving Ashwell in the charge of his half-brother, John Crow, (who will become his successor in 1647).
1643-46.	Preaches to the House of Lords and House of Commons on several occasions, advocating spirituality and Church reforms. He is appointed to preach in several London venues, including Westminster Abbey.
1644.	Publication of his brief spiritual guide to fasting. Martin is ejected as President. On the 11th April, Palmer is installed as President of Queens' by the Earl of Manchester, (see Chapter 17). Nine new fellows of Queens' are appointed and eleven students are admitted.
1645.	In April, Palmer leads a delegation from Cambridge University to petition Parliament and is a signatory of another University petition in August.
1646.	An assessor at the Westminster Assembly.
1647.	Dies after a short illness and is buried at Westminster.

A Puritan clergyman with physical infirmities. Member of the Westminster Assemby of Divines. Appointed President in 1644 after the ejection of Edward Martin. A respected disciplinarian. Died in 1647, aged 46.

Herbert Palmer was born in 1601 at Wingham, Kent, the son of Sir Thomas Palmer, (who died in 1625), and grandson of Sir Thomas Palmer (1540-1626), who, in addition to his knighthood, was created a Baronet in 1621. His maternal grandfather, Herbert Pelham, had been a fellow-commoner at Queens' in 1562.[1] Two of his uncles were knighted: Sir Roger, who was master of the household to Charles I, and Sir James, Chancellor of the Order of the Garter. (Another brother, Sir Thomas, was the 2nd Baronet, who succeeded in 1625 and died in 1656).

His parents provided him with an excellent education from an early age and it is claimed that he could speak French: 'almost as soon as he could speak'. Also, he: 'early shewed the fruits of a religious mother's care'.[1] Aged fourteen, he was admitted as a fellow-commoner at St John's College, Cambridge, graduating B.A. in 1619 and M.A. in 1622. However, Searle, in his history of the College of 1871, quotes a claim that he was: 'denied his degree at St John's on account of personal deformity'.[1] (As will be noted, he was reported to have been of very small stature with a weak and bent appearance). St John's loss was Queens' gain, as he became a fellow-commoner at Queens' in 1622 and, in 1623, he was admitted a fellow, as a result of a royal mandate from James I. Searle notes that such mandates were considered to require compliance,[1] although Edward Martin, a fellow and the future anti-Puritan President, refused to obey the mandate for Palmer and voted for another candidate.[1]

Searle quotes from a contemporary account of Palmer by Samuel Clarke, (a Puritan clergyman and biographer, 1599-1683):[2]

'Although he were a Gentleman, that beside his Fellowship, had an estate of his own and so had the lesse need in point of maintenance, to take the trouble of Pupils upon him, yet (not satisfying himself, to take a place upon him, without performing the Office thereunto belonging) he took many Pupils, of whom he was more than ordinarily carefull, being very diligent both in praying with them in his Chamber, and instructing them in the grounds of Religion; as also keeping them to their studies, and the performance of disputations, and other exercises of learning, privately in his Chamber, beside the more publique exercises required of them by the Colledge, to the great benefit of those that were his pupils'. It is also claimed that he assisted many foreign Protestants who had been forced to leave their Universities.[1]

He was ordained in 1624 and held the College office of Greek praelector in 1626-27, although for most of the year his duties were probably performed by a deputy, as he had leave of absence for a year from November 1626.[1] In April 1626 he wrote: 'an exceedingly sweet and charming letter..."To his most Deare and Honoured Lady mother the Lady Margaret Palmer, from my study at Queenes colledge in Cambridge, April 21, 1626" '.[1] Later in 1626 he visited his brother Sir Thomas at Wingham; he preached at Canterbury Cathedral and also at St George's Church, Canterbury, presumably to great effect, as he was subsequently invited to return and: 'undertake to preach a Lecture among them', with the support of Philip Delme, the minister of the French church at Canterbury.[1] As noted above, he was given a year's absence from Queens' from November 1626, and he accepted this invitation, receiving a licence to preach from the Archbishop of Canterbury, Dr Abbot, before delivering a weekly Sunday afternoon sermon at St Alphege's Church. (A local Puritan radical, diarist and advocate of Parliamentary reform, Thomas Scott, 1567-1635, helped to install Palmer as Lecturer at St Alphege's by giving £10 annually towards his maintenance). He had another year's leave of absence from Queens' from November 1628. However, in 1629, the King instructed that afternoon sermons were to be discontinued and, in due course, Palmer's Puritan leanings were identified as being in conflict with the views of the King and Bishop Laud. As a result, in 1630, the Dean and Archdeacon of Canterbury:

'sent for Mr Palmer a lecturer in Saint Alphage Canterbury on Sunday in the afternoone...Mr Palmer preached a factious Sermon in the Cathedrall Service there...Hereupon the Commissioners willed Master Palmer to desist, and to give Master Platt, the Minister of the said Church roome to do his duty himselfe, until they might heare farther from my Lords Grace of Canterbury, and to him they remitted him...'.[1] However, the Archbishop received a petition in support of Palmer from: 'the gentry and citizens' and authorised him to continue as before. His abilities as a preacher were also evident when he assisted the minister in the French Church at Canterbury, preaching in French: 'to the great astonishment and edification of the whole Congregation'.[1] When he first preached to the French congregation an elderly Frenchwoman exclaimed (as translated): 'What will this child say to us?'. But she is reported to have been overjoyed by his praying and preaching: 'with so much spiritual strength and vigour'.[3]

In 1631 he obtained the B.D. degree and, from June, he had yet another year's leave of absence from Queens'. During the following year, 1632, Bishop Laud appointed him as vicar of Ashwell, Hertfordshire, an appointment which Laud was to cite in his defence when he would be charged as having given:

'all Preferments, only to such men as were for Ceremonies, Popery and Arminianism', (ie not to Puritans such as Palmer).[1] Laud's own account states:

'...Mr Palmer had indeed his Benefice of my giving...but it was at the Entreaty of a great Noble-Man....Mr Palmer was then a stranger to me: Somebody must speak, and assure me of his Wants and Worth, or I cannot give. But if upon this I give it freely, is it worth no thanks from him, because a Noble-Man spake to me? Let Mr Palmer rank this Gratitude among his other Vertues'.[4]

His batchelor existence at Ashwell was an active one; he admitted many sons of noblemen and gentlemen to his house as pupils, taking great pains with their education. He preached twice every Sunday and regularly instructed the children of the parish.[1] He showed pronounced religious zeal, striving to make all his actions:

'according to his constant rule, of being subservient to the glory of God, and the good of souls'.[2] In 1633 he became one of the Cambridge University preachers, whereby he had authority to preach: 'as he should have ocasion in any part of England'.[1] Also in 1633, he resigned his fellowship at Queens'.

The 'Short Parliament', during April-May 1640, was called by Charles I during the crisis of the war between England and Scotland, in the context of opposition to the King's religious reforms and his methods of raising taxes. At the same time that Parliament sat, a Convocation of the Church of England met in London, with authority from the King to revise canon law and to establish Archbishop Laud's reforms; Palmer was chosen as one of the two representatives of the Lincoln diocese.[1] (The Convocation produced seventeen new canon laws including an affirmation of the Divine Right of Kings).

The English Civil War began in August 1642, when the King raised the royal standard at Nottingham and, later that month, the President of Queens', Edward Martin, was arrested and taken to London. In 1643, Parliament appointed the 'Westminster Assembly of Divines' with the task of restructuring and reforming the Church of England. It sat until 1653 and duly produced a new form of Church government, a statement of belief, (the 'Confession of Faith'), two manuals for religious instruction (the 'Shorter and Larger Catecisms'), and the 'Directory for Public Worship'.

At Ashwell, Palmer had worked on a sytem of catechism which taught the faith in a question and answer format. This was first published in 1640 by Roger Daniel, printer to the University of Cambridge, titled: 'An Endeavour of Making the Principles of Christian Religion, namely the Creed, the Ten Commandments, the Lords Prayer, and the Sacraments, plain and easie: tending to the more speedy instruction of the meanest capacities, and weakest memories; and for the making triall also of their understandings, who though they have attained some measure of saving knowledge, yet through the weaknesse of their abilities cannot expresse even that which they do conceive'.[3] The Assembly of Divines appointed a committee to respond to Parliament's request for a directory of catechising and, as Palmer was one of the most respected of around twelve members of the Assembly who had produced catechisms, he had a leading role. But the first draft was a disappointment to the Scottish delegates and, around 1647, the committee decided that two catechisms were needed for the different needs of ministers and children. The 'Larger Catechism,' to assist ministers in teaching to their congregations, was completed in October 1647, and another committee was set up for a 'Shorter Catechism', for teaching the faith to children, with Palmer as chairman.[5] Although Palmer died in September 1647, he is considered to have been an important contributor to the Shorter Catechism, which was completed in November 1647. Both Catechisisms were adopted by the Church of Scotland in 1648 and have remained influential in Presbyterianism, but the work of the Westminster Assembly of Divines was overturned in the Church of England after the Restoration in 1660.

In 1643, he published: 'Scripture and reason pleaded for defensive armes, or The whole controversie about subjects taking up armes: wherein besides other pamphlets, an answer is punctually directed to Dr. Fernes booke, entituled, Resolving of Conscience, &c.: the Scriptures alleadged are fully satisfied. The rationall discourses are weighed in the balance of right reason. Matters of fact concerning the present differences, are examined. Published by divers reverend and learned divines. London: Printed for John Bellamy and Ralph Smith at the signe of the Three Golden Lions neare the Royall-Exchange, MDCXLIII'. Another work appeared in 1645: 'A full answer to a printed paper, entituled, Foure serious questions concerning excommunication, and suspension from the Sacrament, &c.: wherein the said questions, with the particulars under them, and severall arguments and texts of Scripture produced in them, concerning the matter of excommunication and suspension from the Sacrament, are particularly and distinctly discussed. Printed by Richard Bishop, London'.

Another of Palmer's appointments by Parliament was that of one of the fifteen 'Tuesday lecturers' at Hitchin in 1642[3] and, in 1643, he urged the House of Commons to:

'Secure youth in the Universities, and Schools, with the utmost care; and even in Parents houses, what you can, specially the poorer sort. The young ones are the hopes or the bane of the Church and State in the next 20, 10, or 7 years'.[6]

Searle reports that Palmer was a leading member of the Assembly of Divines; he was chosen as an 'Assessor' and was very rarely absent. He appointed a curate (his half-brother, John Crow), to officiate at Ashwell, and preached in various London churches.[1] He was appointed a Lecturer at St James's, Duke Place, and to the charge of a new church in the parish of St Margaret's, Westminster, where he:

'was unwearied in his official duties, continuing ofttimes to speak in publique for the space of six or eight hours on a Sabbath day'.[1,3]

This was the 'Broadway (or New) Chapel', built between 1638-42, on the burial ground for the Church of St. Margaret's, Westminster. (This was replaced by an imposing building, Christ Church, built between 1841-44, but this was destroyed in the

Second World War. The site is now a public garden, the Christ Church Gardens, adjacent to Victoria Street, Westminster). Also, he was one of seven divines:

'that, by appointment of Parliament, did carry on the daily morning lecture at the Abby-Church' (Westminster Abbey), and regularly preached to the House of Commons and the Assembly of Divines.[1] An account of the religious ambience in London at this time is given by Robert Baillie (1599-1662), a Scottish Presbyterian minister, in his 'Letters and Journals' (published by David Laing in 1841):

'This day (17th May 1644) was the sweetest that I have seen in England, Generall Essex...sent to the Assemblie, to entreat, that a day of Fasting might be kept for him...so we spent from nine to five very graciously...Mr. Marshall prayed large two houres, most divinelie, confessing the sins of the members of the Assemblie, in a wonderfullie pathetick, and prudent way. After, Mr. Arrowsmith preached one houre, then a psalme; thereafter, Mr. Vines prayed near two houres, and Mr. Palmer preached one houre, and Mr. Seaman prayed near two houres, then a psalme... God was so evidentlie in all this exercise, that we expect certainlie a blessing both in our matter of the Assemblie and whole Kingdome'.

'On Tuesday last (13th August 1644), there was a solemne Fast for Generall Essex's armie. Mr Palmer and Mr. Hill did preach that day to the Assemblie, two of the most Scottish and free sermons, that ever I heard any where...these two good men laid well about them, and charged publicke and parliamentarie sins strictlie upon the backs of the guilty; among the rest, their neglect to settle religion according to the Covenant...'.[1]

Clarke comments that in Palmer's sermons to Parliament:

'he spared not to declare fully and plainly what God expected from them and freely to reprove what was amisse. For (as he was wont to say) he did not in that place preach BEFORE them ...but TO them (authoritative) as by Commission from God, and how much soever they might be superior to him in other regards, yet he was in that place superior to them, as acting in God's name... notwithstanding any displeasure or danger...'.[2]

In 1645, Palmer was, with Stephen Marshall (a member of the Westminster Assembly of Divines and another powerful preacher), appointed by Parliament to visit Archbishop Laud before his execution and they attended him on the scaffold, although Laud refused their religious ministrations.

As described in the previous Chapter, Queens' was without an active head between Martin's arrest on the 30th August 1642 and Palmer's installation as President on the 11th April 1644. The latter event took place in the College chapel, as recorded in College documents:

'Aprill the Eleventh. 1644. On which day the Right Honoble

Edward Earle of Manchester in pursuite of an ordinance of Parlyament for regulateing and reforming of the University of Cambridge, came in person into the chappell of Queenes Colledge, and by the authority to him committed as aforesaide, did in presence of all the fellows now resident, declare and publish Mr Herbert Palmer to be constituted Master of the said Colledge in roome of Doctor Martin late Master there, but now justly and lawfully ejected...and did put him into the Masters seate or stall within the said chappell, and delivered unto him the statutes of the said Colledge in testimony of his actual investiture and possession of the said charge...notwithstanding hee be not elected nor admitted according to the ordinary course prescribed by the said statutes in this time of distraction and warre...'.[1] The new President then made the following declaration:

'I Herbert Palmer being called and constituted by the Right Honoble Edward Earle of Manchester (who is authorized thereto by an ordinance of Parlyament) to be Master of Queenes colledge in the University of Cambridge, with the approbation of the Assembly of Divines now sitting at Westminster, doe solemnly and seriously promise in the presence of Almighty God the searcher of all hearts, that...I shall faithfully labour to promote piety and learning in myselfe, the fellows, schollers, and students...agreeable to the late solemn Nationall league and covenant by mee sworne and subscribed...and by all meanes to procure the good, welfare, and perfect reformation both of that Colledge and University, so farre as to me appertaineth. Herbert Palmer'.[1]

The new President inherited only a few resident fellows and students. Eight fellows had been ejected on the 8th and 9th April 1644 but, on the 11th June, nine new fellows were appointed by the Earl of Manchester after they had all been approved by the Westminster Assembly of Divines.[6] (One of the new fellows, John Wallis- or Wallys- left after a year to marry. He became Savilian professor of Geometry at Oxford for over fifty years and a leading member of the Royal Society).[6] On the 20th June, eleven new students were admitted and, later in the year, four more new fellows were admitted, including a John Pypard. But the latter would, in 1645, be:

'found disorderlie at a taverne in disorderlie companie at eleven of the clocke of the night and admonished by the expresse consent of the master and major part of the fellows', and there was some criticism as to the quality of the new appointees. However, Pypard seems to have been the exception.[1] One of the new sizars was Simon Patrick, later Bishop of Ely, who describes Queens' at that time:

'Here I found myself in a solitary place at first; for, tho' Mr Fuller in his Church History was mistaken in saying this College was like a Land-wrack (as I think his words are) in which there was one left to keep possession, yet there were about a dozen scholars, and almost half of the old Fellows, the Visitors at first doing no more than putting in a majority of new to govern the College. The other rarely appearing were all turned out for refusing the Covenant, which was then so zealously pressed, that all scholars were summon'd to take it at Trin: Coll: Thither I went and gad it tender'd to me, but God so directed me, that I telling them my age (18 years) was dismiss'd and never heard more of it- blessed be God. I had not been long in the college before the master, Mr Herbert Palmer took some notice of me, and sent for me to transcribe some things he intended for the press; and soon after (on the 7th February 1646) made me the College Scribe...But before I was Batchellor of Arts (in January 1648) this good man dy'd, who was of an excellent Spirit and was unwearied in doing good. Though he was a little crooked Man, yet he had such an authority, that the fellows reverenc'd him as much as we did them, going bare, when he passed thro' the Court, which after his death was disus'd...I remember very well that being a member of the Assembly of Divines, he went oft to London: and sometime stay'd there a quarter of a year. But before he went, he was wont to cause the Bell to be toll'd to summon us all to meet in the Hall. There he made a Pathetical Speech to us, stirring us up to pious Diligence in our studies, and told us with such seriousness as made us believe, that he shou'd have as true an account from those he cou'd trust, of the behaviour of every one of us in his absence, as if he were here present with us to observe us himself...'.[1,7] He is reported to have maintained several poor scholars at his own expense and bequeathed money to the College for this purpose:

'though of a weakly constitution, he was indefatigable in business and was constantly employed in works of devotion and charity. He was a short man and is called by Baillie gracious and learned little Palmer'.[1]

Clarke provides a glowing account of Palmer's performance as President:

'...it cannot easily be believed how exceeding Circumspect he was, how Cautious and wary in the Choice of those, who (as fellows) were to joyn with him in the Government, that they might be learned, pious, and unanimous. The happy effect of which care, in so quiet and peaceable establishment of that Society, as could not easily be expected in so troublesome a time, was, to the great astonishment and Amazement of all, even of those that hated them; and hath had a very great influence upon that happy, and flourishing condition thereof ever since...(He was) extraordinary solicitious, for the constant presence of the whole Society at the publique Worship of God...He took care also for the constant instruction, not only of the young Scholars, but likewise of all the Colledge Servants, in the principles of Religion...he did...make a Decree, that in all future Elections, none should be admitted ...till they did first approve themselves for learning by a publique triall or examination, for two or three days successively in the audience of the whole Colledge, which hath already produced very good effects for the improvement of learning in that Colledge...In his converse with the Fellows, it was his great care to preserve unanimity, that as well Elections as all other affairs of the Colledge, should be carried on by an universal consent; so if...there were any dissent, his usual manner was to defer the determination of it, till every one should see reason sufficient to concur with the rest; and was himself as ready to hearken to any argument produced, though contrarty to his present sense, which he would either fully answer or yield to it: so that scarce anything was overruled merely by plurality of suffrages, but all with universal consent...so great was that unanimity and reciprocal affection, between him and the Society, that scarce ever any Head of a Society was taken from them with more general sorrow'.[2]

In 1645, he led a delegation from the University to the House of Commons to obtain exemption for the colleges from various taxes, which had a successful outcome:[1]

'On the 11th of April, the House of Commons being informed that certain Divines, Heads, and Masters of divers Colleges in the University of Cambridge were at the door desirous to prefer a petition, they were called in, and Mr. Palmer preferred a petition for exempting the societies from public contributions, taxes, and impositions. This petition having been read, the House immediately passed an ordinance for so exempting the Colleges in the University. This was forthwith sent to the Lords for their concurrence, which was obtained the same day'.[8] 1645 was a year when there were serious disputes between the University and Town in respect of their respective privileges, and several petitions, from both sides, were presented to Parliament. On the 5th August, seven heads, including Palmer, signed:

'The humble Petition of the Heads of Colleges in the University of Cambridge, whose Names are Underwritten, in the Behalf of themselves and the whole University...Your Petitioners...do humbly make their Addresses to this High and Honourable Court; humbly praying, that, for avoiding of the Disturbances and Inconveniences that may suddenly arise without some speedy Prevention, you would be pleased to order, That the said Mayor and Bailiffs may forthwith take their Oath, as their Predecessors have done for well near Three Hundred Years and that your Petitioners may be continued in the Possession of their Liberties, as formerly they enjoyed them'.[8] This also met with success, as:

'Upon reading of the Petition of the Heads of Colleges in the University of Cambridge: It is ordered, by the Lords in Parliament assembled, That the said University of Cambridge shall continue in the Possession of their Liberties and Privileges they formerly used and enjoyed, by former Grants and Charters, before these Troubles...'.[8]

Clarke describes Palmer's behaviour during his last, short, illness;

'his deportment therein holy and heavenly; his humility, faith, patience, and submission to God's Will, eminently appearing from time to time, and his discourse full of heavenly expressions till the time of his death', praying that God: 'would provide a faithfull man for Queens Colledge'.[1,2] He died in September 1647, probably on the 11th, and his successor was elected on the 19th of September. He was buried in the New Church, Westminster, the site of the present Christ Church Gardens.

Clarke's 'The Lives of Thirty-Two English Divines' includes a portrait of Palmer showing him as: 'puny and crooked' with a childlike face.[1,2]

In early 1647, he presented about thirty volumes to the College library and he also left a bequest to Queens' of £53 for the support of poor students, although in 1661 this would be diverted to the restoration of the chapel.[1]

References

1. Searle, W.G. The History of the Queens' College of St Margaret and St Bernard in the University of Cambridge. Part II 1560-1662. Sold by Deighton, Bell & Co; Macmillan & Co. London. 1871. pp 464-526, 536, 568, 572-83.
2. Clarke, Samuel (1599-1683). The Lives of Thirty-Two English Divines. 3rd Edition. 1670.
3. Eales, Jacqueline. Palmer, Herbert. In: Oxford Dictionary of National Biography. 2004. Online. 2019.

4. Laud, William (1573-1645). The History of the Troubles and tryal of the Most Reverend Father in God and blessed martyr wrote by himself during his imprisonment in the Tower.
5. Kelly, D.F. The Westminster Shorter Catechism. In: Carlson, J.L.; Hall, D.W. (eds). To Glorify and Enjoy God: A Commemoration of the 350th Anniversary of the Westminster Assembly. Edinburgh: Banner of Truth Trust. 1994.
6. Twigg, J. A History of Queens' College, Cambridge. 1448-1986. The Boydell Press. 1987. pp 54-57.
7. Patrick, Symon. The Works of Symon Patrick, D.D. Ed. A. Taylor. Volume IX. University Press. Oxford. 1858.
8. Cooper, C.H. Annals of Cambridge. Volume III. Warwick and Co., Cambridge. 1845. pp 385-86, 391-92.

CHAPTER 19

Thomas Horton. President 1647-60.

Summary.

Thomas Horton was born in about 1606, the son of a London merchant. He was admitted to Emmanuel College, Cambridge, in 1623, graduated B.A. and M.A., and became a fellow of his College in 1631. While the date of his ordination is unknown, in 1638 he became a Cambridge University preacher and a perpetual curate at St Mary Colechurch, in the City of London.

In 1641, Horton was elected professor of Divinity at Gresham College, London; this was a prestigious appointment at a College founded by Sir Thomas Gresham in 1597. He must have been in favour with the Parliamentary establishment before the Restoration, as he held various appointments and received invitations to preach at influential London gatherings.

After the death of Herbert Palmer in 1647, Horton became President of Queens' after a free election. Although he was resident in London and had not been formally associated with Queens', he would have been considered to be well-placed to provide the College with protection and influence. In 1649 he became D.D. and was Vice-Chancellor in 1649-50.

His marriage in 1651 caused the governors of Gresham College to declare his post vacant, as, by the will of the founder, the incumbant was required to remain single. But Horton obtained a dispensation and would remain in post until 1661.

Soon after the Restoration in 1660, Horton was ejected as President of Queens' by the Earl of Manchester, and Edward Martin was reinstated. In the following year, Horton finally lost his professorship at Gresham College and, in 1662, was ejected from the Church of England for not taking the oath required by the 'Act of Uniformity'. However, he soon conformed and must have built up sufficient favour with the new regime to be appointed vicar of St Helen's Church, Bishopsgate, London, in 1666. There he remained until his death in 1673 and he lies buried in the chancel. His published output contains many sermons but also Latin verses, which commemorate various significant events. He was survived by his wife and daughter.

Timeline.

c1606.	Born.
1623.	Admitted a 'pensioner' at Emmanuel College, Cambridge.
1627.	B.A. .
1630.	M.A. .
1631.	Fellow of Emmanuel. Edward Martin is elected President of Queens'.
1637.	B.D. .
1638.	One of twelve University preachers. Appointed to a curacy at St Mary's, Colechurch, London, by the Mercers' Company.
1641.	Professor of Divinity at Gresham College, London.
1642.	Edward Martin arrested and conveyed to London. Onset of the Civil War.
1644.	Herbert Palmer appointed President of Queens', following Martin's ejection. Appointed by Parliament as a 'trier' for the approbation of candidates for ordination.
1645.	Supports a petition to implement Presbyterianism in the Church of England.
1646.	Preaches before Parliament.
1647.	Preaches before Parliament. Appointed as a preacher at Gray's Inn. Death of Herbert Palmer. Elected President of Queens' on the 19th September.
1649.	D.D. . Execution of Charles I.
1649-50.	Vice-Chancellor.
1651.	Marries. Resigns preachership at Gray's Inn. Obtains a dispensation from Parliament to remain at Gresham College, despite the founder's will stipulating that the professor must remain single.

1653. Preaches before the Mayor and aldermen of London.

1654. Appointed a 'Visitor' of Cambridge University. In November preaches before the Mayor and aldermen of London at St Paul's Cathedral. Petitions Oliver Cromwell for payment of the 'Augmentation' to his College stipend as President.

1656. The governors of Gresham College elect George Gifford to replace Horton, but he obtains another dispensation to remain in post. Horton preaches to: 'the native citizens of London…at Paule's'.

1658. Horton is, again, appointed a 'trier'. Death of Cromwell. Richard Cromwell succeeds as Lord Protector but resigns in 1659.

1660. After the Restoration of the monarchy in May, he obtains a dispensation from Charles II, on the 1st August, to retain the professorship at Gresham College. Ejected from the Presidency of Queens' by the Earl of Manchester on the 2nd August. Edward Martin is restored as President.

1661. Nominated as a delegate to the 'Savoy Conference' but does not attend. In May, the dispensation for Horton to continue as a professor at Gresham College is revoked.

1662. Ejected as a Church of England minister after the 'Act of Uniformity,' but soon conforms to its requirements.

1666. Appointed vicar of St Helen's, Bishopgate, London.

1673. Dies. Survived by his wife and daughter, Judith. Buried at St Helen's Church, Bishopsgate.

A Nonconformist clergyman. Professor of Divinity at Gresham College, London. Installed as President after the death of Herbert Palmer in 1647, but was ejected when Edward Martin was restored as President in 1660 after the Restoration.

Thomas Horton was born in London, around 1606, the son of Lawrence Horton, who was a merchant and a member of the Mercers' Company.[1,2] (The Company received a Royal Charter in 1394 as a trade association for general merchants, and ranks first in the order of precedence of the City Livery Companies). He was admitted to Emmanuel College, Cambridge, in 1623, and graduated B.A. in 1627, M.A. in 1630 and B.D. in 1637. He was a fellow of Emmanuel College in 1631, where John Wallis, subsequently a fellow of Queens', (see Chapter 18), was one of his pupils. (Wallis was a clergyman and mathematician who became Savilian professor of Geometry at Oxford. His contributions included introducing the present symbol for infinity, and he has been described as one of the greatest intellectuals of the early renaissance of mathematics). Wallis writes:

'The first time I had the opportunity of knowing him, was about the year 1632, when he was fellow of Emmanuel Colledge in Cambridge, in which college I had the Honour (and Happiness) of receiving the first of my Academical education and for some part of it under his Tuition'.[1]

After ordination, in 1638 Horton was appointed a Cambridge University preacher and a perpetual curate of St Mary Colechurch, a parish church in the City of London, (sadly, destroyed by the Great Fire of London in 1666), which was in the gift of the Mercers' Company. Although he resigned the living in 1640, he later returned, and an augmentation to his stipend there is recorded in 1649; also, he is recorded as preaching there in 1651, while Searle, in his history of the College of 1871, states that Bishop Brownrigg:

'was a very frequent, if not his Constant Auditor, even though he did not lodg in those parts of town'.[1] (Ralph Brownrigg was Bishop of Exeter from 1642-59, although he was in exile for most of this time and may never have visited his See. He was Master of St Catharine's College, Cambridge, from 1635, but was ejected in 1646 by Parliament).

In 1641 Horton was elected professor of Divinity at Gresham College, London, which had been founded in 1597 with a bequest from Sir Thomas Gresham, the founder of the Royal Exchange, the centre of commerce for the City of London. (There were six other professorships: Astronomy, Geometry, Law, Music, Physic and Rhetoric; an early professor of Astronomy was Christopher Wren). His rival in the election was Benjamin

Whichcote, 1609-83, a Puritan and, from 1645-60, Provost (ie head) of King's College, Cambridge.

Horton must have been well thought of by the establishment before the Restoration in view of his several appointments and invitations to preach; for example, in 1644 he was appointed one of 28 'triers' of candidates for the ministry, named: 'Commissioners appointed for approbation of publique preachers'.[1] The following year he showed his Reformist credentials by supporting a petition asking Parliament to provide Presbyterian government for the Church of England, while, in 1646, he preached a sermon titled:

'Sinnes discovery and revenge, as it was delivered in a sermon preached (on Numb.32. 23) to the right hon. The house of Peers at the Abbey Church at Westminster on Wednesday 30 Dec. 1646, being the day of the monthly publick fast'.[1] In 1647, he and Thomas Valentine, (1586-1665, a member of the Westminster Assembly of Divines), preached before Parliament, this time at St Margaret's Church, Westminster, when they: 'received the thanks of the house'.[1] Also in 1647, he was appointed a preacher of Gray's Inn.[2] (Gray's Inn is one of the four 'Inns of Court' that train barristers in England and Wales). In 1653 and 1654 he preached to the Mayor and aldermen of London, on the latter occasion at St Paul's. Another sermon, in 1656, was, as Horton himself recorded, given to: 'the native citizens of London, in their solemn assembly at Paule's'.[2]

After Herbert Palmer's death in 1647, Horton became President of Queens' after a free election on the 19th September and was admitted on the 2nd October.[1] At the time he was resident in London and it was recognised that he would continue to spend much of his time away from Cambridge.[3] But he would have been considered as able to provide the College with some protection and influence, in view of his favour with Parliament. It seems that the peace and order at Queens', which had been established by Palmer, was maintained by Horton, who was, according to John Wallis:

'very well skilled in the oriental languages, very well accomplished for the work of the ministry, and very conscientious in the discharge of it'.[4] In 1649 he was awarded the D.D., (which was incorporated D.D. in Oxford in 1652), and, in 1649-50, he served as Vice-Chancellor.

The autobiography of Simon Patrick, later Bishop of Ely during 1691-1707, provides glimpses of Queens' just before and during Horton's Presidency, as Patrick arrived at Queens' in 1644 and was a fellow of the College from 1649 to 1658:

'...He (ie Herbert Palmer) was succeeded by a good man (Dr. Horton), but not such a governor: under whom I was chosen fellow of the college, when I was one year bachelor of arts; before which time I had been so studious as to fill whole books with observations out of various ancient authors, with some of my own which I made upon them...It is a great comfort now in my old age to find that I was so diligent in my youth; for in those books I have noted how I spent my time...I desire to take special notice of... God's placing me, when I came thither, in Queen's college, when we were resolved to go to another, and there providing me such a loving kind tutor, of extraordinary affection to me, which he expressed sundry ways exceeding my account...I bent my studies chiefly to theology, and the manner of those times was for young men to preach before they were in holy orders, and the first sermon I preached was at Okeington, (a college living near Cambridge,) April 6th 1651, upon Acts iii.19, Repent and be converted, &c. ...being bound by the statutes of the college to enter into holy orders when I was two years master of arts, I knew no better than to go to a classis of presbyters who then sat; and was examined by them, and afterwards received the imposition of their hands. This afterwards troubled me very much...whereby I was fully convinced of the necessity of episcopal ordination. This made me inquire after a bishop to whom I might resort; and hearing that bishop Hall lived not far from Norwich, of which he was bishop, thither I went with two other fellows of our college...There we were received with great kindness by that rev. old bishop, who examined us and gave us many good exhortations, and then ordained us in his own parlour at Higham...April 5th 1654'.[5]

In 1651, aged about 45, Horton married- his wife was named Dorothy- and he was subsequently reported to be: 'a most jealous husband'.[2] However, this opinion may not have had the modern meaning, perhaps just implying a protective husband. It seems his marriage caused some problems and there may have been pressure on him to resign as a preacher of Gray's Inn, which he did later that year, although in 1655 the Inn admitted the: 'late preacher of this society' as a member.[2] There were certainly problems at Gresham College, because Sir Thomas Gresham's will required the professor of Divinity to be single, so the post was duly declared vacant. But, later in the same year, Horton obtained a 'dispensation' from Parliament, (ie an order to ignore the requirement). Nevertheless, in 1656, the College governors elected George Gifford as a replacement; but although Gifford would be the next professor of Divinity, his succession would not be until after the Restoration.

Following the execution of the King in 1649, Parliament required all heads, fellows, graduates and University officers to take the following oath of 'Engagement':

'I do declare and promise that I will be true and faithful to the commonwealth of England, as the same is now established without a king or house of Lords', which led to two Queens' fellows being ejected for non-compliance in 1650.[1] They were in good company, as the Chancellor himself, the Earl of Manchester, was also ejected in November 1651, to be succeeded by Oliver St John, who, since 1648, had been Chief Justice of the Common Pleas. He had been admitted to Queens' around 1616, where he had been a fellow-commoner,[3] and thus became the second Chancellor of the University to have been associated with Queens', after John Fisher, (see Chapter 3). His career may have been helped by his marriage to his second wife, who was a relative of Oliver Cromwell.[1]

In 1657, tension between the College and the authorities is shown in the following record, made in Horton's handwriting:

'Resolved by the determination of the major part of the Fellowes, that Mr Lauson be not admitted fellow upon the mandate of my Lord Protector, till further addresses be made to his Highness in that behalf, for as much as they are not satisfyed in the condition mentioned in the sayd mandate'.[1] (John Lawson, who had been a pensioner at Queens' in 1648, was not subsequently admitted a fellow. This may have been a loss to the College, as he went on to have an interesting career, graduating M.D. in Padua and becoming President of the Royal College of Physicians in 1694).[1]

In 1650, Parliament provided much-needed additional funding to college heads, in an Act: 'for further provision for ministers and other pious uses', with the following clause:

'And to that end that Two thousand pounds a year given for the increase of the Maintenance of the Masters and Heads of Houses in the respective Universities within this Nation...Provided it do not exceed One Hundred pounds per annum to any one of them'.[6] A list of the annual income of the masterships at Cambridge, and each 'Augmentation' from this scheme, shows that Queens' provided £68 3s 3d. for its President, while the Augmentation was set at £50.[6] However, in 1654, Horton had to petition Cromwell, as he had not received the previous year's Augmentation. While it is not clear whether that year's deficit was ever rectified, Horton was paid the £50 for the year to September 1656.[2]

In 1654, the Lord Protector and Council issued the following ordinance:

'Visitors appointed for both Universities...Whereas the carrying on and perfecting of the Reformation and Regulation of the Universities of this Land, is a work very much conducing to the Glory of God, and the Publique Good, for want of which many inconveniences and evils do and cannot but ensue, Be It Therefore Ordained by His Highness the Lord Protector, by and with the Consent of his Council, That...the Vice-Chancellor of the University of Cambridge for the time being, the Lord Henry Cromwel, Henry Lawrence, Lord President of his Highness Council...Oliver St John, Lord Chief Justice of the Common-Pleas... Doctor Horton, President of Queens Colledge...or any seven or more of them, be and they are hereby Constituted and Ordained Commissioners fot the visiting the said University, and all Colledges and Halls within the said Universities...and...shall consider of the best ways and means for the well Ordering, Regulation, and good Government of the said Universities...'.[6]

In 1659, Horton was involved in another petition, this time on behalf of the University:

'On the 18th of April, the senate constituted Thomas Horton, Benjamin Whichcot and Lazarus Seaman Doctors in Divinity... delegates to exhibit to the Lord Protector (ie Richard Cromwell) the subjoined petition against the erection of a new University at Durham...'.[6] (Clearly the competition was unwelcome! But the two English Universities would be safe until 1832, when Durham University was eventually founded, the first to be established in England for over 600 years):

'To his highness Richard lord protector of the common wealth of England, Scotland, and Ireland, &c.

The Humble Petition of the university of Cambridge, sheweth,

That your petitioners have notice of a grant ready for the seal from your highness to a college at Duresme in bishopric importing to the said college to become an university and bestow degrees of all sorts. Now the said grant being not only prejudicial to but also destructive of the charters and fundamental privileges of this university, which your petitioners are jointly and severally obliged by oath to maintain and assert as being established by act of parliament, and likewise from time to time confirmed to us and our successors...May it please your highness to inhibit the sealing of the said grant untill such time as your petitioners are heard...'.[6]

After the Restoration in May 1660, Horton's fortunes changed; his ejection from the Presidency of Queens' was soon to come and, on the 2nd August 1660, Edward Martin was restored as President of Queens' by the Earl of Manchester, now restored as Chancellor of the University, (See Chapter 17). Horton quietly withdrew. Also, although on the 1st August 1660, Charles II granted him yet another dispensation to continue as professor at Gresham College, this would soon be revoked and, in June 1661, Horton was finally replaced as professor by George Gifford.

However, Horton was still a professor at Gresham College during the Savoy Conference of April 1661, which was convened at the Savoy Hospital in London and attempted to reconcile the factions within the Church of England. This involved twelve

Anglican bishops and twelve Nonconformist (Puritan and Presbyterian) representatives. Each side had nine deputies and Horton was nominated a deputy for the Nonconformists, but it is reported that he did not attend.[2] (Anthony Sparrow, a future President of Queens', was a deputy on the episcopal side). The proceedings were not successful and soon afterwards there was a mass exodus of Nonconformists from the Church of England, after the Church's episcopal traditions were implemented by the 'Act of Uniformity 1662', titled: 'An Act for the Uniformity of Publique Prayers and Administration of Sacramentes & other Rites & Ceremonies and for establishing the Form of making ordaining and consecrating Bishops Preists and Deacons in the Church of England'. This ordered the form of public prayers and other rites as laid down in the Book of Common Prayer, which had been revised in the same year. Acceptance of the Act was required for the holder of any office in government or the Church, and over 2000 clergymen who refused to take the oath were ejected from the Church of England in the 'Great Ejection' of 1662.

Horton was one of those ejected but he soon reversed his position and conformed,[2] although: 'his conformity was of no very strict character'.[1] Nevertheless, in 1666, Horton was appointed vicar of St Helen's Church, Bishopsgate, London, by the Dean and Chapter of St Paul's, with the support of Sir John Langham.[2] (Langham was a merchant, who had been in the House of Commons in 1654 and 1660. He had been committed to the Tower on two occasions for his Royalist views, which, after the Restoration, were rewarded by a knighthood and a baronetcy). Also, in 1671 he was in sufficient favour to be asked to preach at St Saviour's Southwark, (designated as Southwark Cathedral in 1905), before Sir Thomas Twisden and Sir William Morton.[2] (Sir Thomas, an alumnus of Emmanuel College, was in the House of Commons for two periods between 1646-60, became a High Court Judge and presided at the trial of the regicides. Sir William, an alumnus of Sidney Sussex College, also sat in the House of Commons, in 1640 and during1663-65. He fought for the King in the Civil War, and is described as:

'active and violent...of a high spirit and bold...most obnoxious to the justice of Parliament'.[7] After the Restoration his various appointments included Justice of the King's Bench).

Horton was still at St Helen's Church, Bishopsgate, at his death in 1673 and is buried in the chancel. (This is the largest surviving parish church in the City of London and is known for the number of its monuments). He was survived by his wife and a daughter, Judith.[2] Searle provides a list of his publications, including the following sermons: 'The unrighteous Mammon exchanged for the true riches, or a sermon on Luke 16.9, peached at the funeral of William Adams, esq. in the parish church of St Lawrence Jewry, on Tuesday Sept. 3, 1661, by Th. Horton D.D., dedicated to the Haberdashers' Company',[1] and 'Rich treasure in earthen vessels, a sermon on 2 Cor. 4.7. preached Jan.1, 1662-3 at the funeral of Mr James Nalton late minister of God's word at St Leonard's Fosterlane, by Th. Horton, D.D. ...'.[1] His output also included several contributions to collections of Latin verses issued by the University, each written to commemorate a significant occasion, such as peace with Holland, the death of Oliver Cromwell, the accession of Richard Cromwell and the restoration of Charles II[1]:

'The conclusion of peace with Holland (in 1654) was celebrated in a collection of poems published by the University, under the following title, "Oliva Pacis ad illustrissimum celsissimumq. Oliverum Reipub. Angliae Scotiae & Hiberniae Dominum Protectorem de Pace cum Foederatis Belgis feliciter sancita Carmen Cantabrigiense". Amongst the writers were Lazarus Seaman Vicechancellor, John Arrowsmith Master of Trinity College, Anthony Tuckney Master of St. John's College, Thomas Horton President of Queens' College...'.[6]

References

1. Searle, W.G. The History of the Queens' College of St Margaret and St Bernard in the University of Cambridge. Part II 1560-1662. Sold by Deighton, Bell & Co; Macmillan & Co. London. 1871. pp 557-69.

2. Wright, S. Horton, Thomas. In: Oxford Dictionary of National Biography. 2008. Online. 2019.
3. Twigg, J. A History of Queens' College, Cambridge. 1448-1986. The Boydell Press. 1987. pp 57-60.
4. Wallis, J. In: Preface to 'One hundred select sermons upon several texts fifty upon the Old Testament, and fifty on the New'. By Horton, Thomas. Printed for Thomas Parkhurst. 1679.
5. Patrick, Symon. The Works of Symon Patrick, D.D. Ed. A. Taylor. Volume ix. University Press. Oxford. 1858. pp. 417-24.
6. Cooper, C.H. Annals of Cambridge. Volume III. Warwick and Co., Cambridge. 1845. pp 431, 456-57, 460-62, 473-74.
7. Magnotta, M.S.R. Morton, Sir William. In: Oxford Dictionary of National Biography. 2004. Online. 2019.

CHAPTER 20

Anthony Sparrow. President 1662-67.

Summary.

Anthony Sparrow was born at Depden, Suffolk, in 1612 and entered Queens' in 1625. After graduation, he became a fellow of the College in 1633, was ordained in 1635 and held various College offices before the Civil War.

Edward Martin, who was elected President of Queens' in 1631, was a zealous supporter of the monarchy and of the 'high church' faction, which was opposed by the Puritans and other Nonconformists. Sparrow shared his views and, in 1637, preached and published a controversial sermon, which caused great offence to the Puritans. In 1640, he and Martin were identified as religious trouble-makers by a Parliamentary committee.

In 1644, Martin was ejected from the Presidency and Sparrow was one of those ejected from their Cambridge fellowships. Despite his straightened circumstances, he married in 1645, and although he was appointed rector at Hawkedon, Suffolk, in 1647, he suffered a further ejection after just a few weeks, for his use of the prohibited Book of Common Prayer. In 1655 he published (anonymously) his highly influential: 'Rationale upon the Book of Common Prayer', which has had over 100 English editions.

His fortunes were transformed after the Restoration in 1660. He was reinstated as rector at Hawkedon and became Archdeacon of Sudbury. Edward Martin was restored to the Presidency in 1660 and, on his death in 1662, Sparrow was installed in his stead by royal mandate. But this was after a disputed election, when the majority of the fellows had supported Simon Patrick, a future Bishop of Ely.

Sparrow's high church views were rewarded by his appointment as Bishop of Exeter in 1667, when he resigned as President. He obtained further promotion as Bishop of Norwich in 1676 and died at the Bishop's Palace, Norwich, in 1685. He was survived by his wife and several children.

Timeline.

1612.	Born at Depden, Suffolk.
1625.	Admitted to Queens'.
1629.	B.A..
1631.	Edward Martin elected President of Queens'.
1632.	M.A..
1633.	Fellow of Queens'.
1635.	Ordained at Ely.
1637.	Preaches and publishes a controversial sermon, objected to by Puritans: 'A Sermon Concerning Confession of Sins and the Power of Absolution'.
1638-43.	Holds various College offices.
1639.	B.D..
1640.	Identified in Parliament for his views: 'against true religion'.
1642.	Contributes to the £185 sent by the President and fellows of Queens' to the King, shortly before the onset of the Civil War.
1644.	Parliament requires members of the University to take an oath - the 'Covenant'. Ejected from his fellowship on the 8th April by the Earl of Manchester. Edward Martin is ejected as President of Queens' and is replaced by Herbert Palmer.
1645.	Marries Susanna Orrell at Withersfield, Suffolk.
1647.	Death of Herbert Palmer. Thomas Horton elected President of Queens'. Appointed rector of Hawkedon, near Depden, but is ejected within five weeks for using the Book of Common Prayer.
1655.	Publishes the highly influential: 'Rationale upon the Book of Common Prayer'.
1660.	Restoration of Charles II. Reinstated as rector of Hawkedon. Archdeacon of Sudbury. Chaplain to the King. Elected to a

	preachership at Bury St Edmunds. Thomas Horton ejected from the Presidency of Queens' by the Earl of Manchester. Edward Martin restored as President.
1661.	Nominated to attend the Savoy Conference. Prebendary of Ely. Publishes: 'A Collection of Articles, Injunctions, Canons, Orders, Ordinances, and Constitutions Ecclesiastical…'.
1662.	The 'Act of Uniformity'. Death of Edward Martin. Sparrow is elected as President of Queens' by the authority of a disputed royal mandate, although the majority of the fellows had supported Simon Patrick.
1662-24.	Patrick unsuccessfully pursues his claim to the Presidency.
1663.	The Vice-Chancellor and heads decree a more solemn observation of the 30th January, (the anniversary of the execution of Charles I).
1664-65.	Serves as Vice-Chancellor.
1665.	'Plague' in Cambridge.
1666.	Re-emergence of plague in Cambridge. The Great Fire of London.
1667.	Appointed Bishop of Exeter. (Also, during 1668-76, he was Archdeacon of Exeter and Dean of St Buryan).
1676.	Advanced to be Bishop of Norwich.
1685.	Dies at the Bishop's Palace, Norwich; is buried in the nearby chapel. Survived by his wife and several children.

Zealous royalist and 'high' churchman. Ejected from his fellowship at Queens' in 1644. After the Restoration, becomes President in 1662 by royal mandate, following a disputed election. Bishop of Exeter 1667-76. Bishop of Norwich 1676-85.

Anthony Sparrow was born in 1612 at Depden, near Bury St Edmunds, Suffolk, the son of Samuel Sparrow, and baptised at Wickhambrook.[1] He was admitted to Queens' in 1625, graduated B.A. in 1629 and M.A. in 1632. In 1631, Edward Martin had been elected President; Sparrow shared Martin's religious views and became a fellow of Queens' in 1633. He was ordained at Ely in 1635.

The 'high' church movement in Cambridge in the 1630s was characterised by certain aspects of doctine and an emphasis on formality in religious ritual, and was supported by some new heads of colleges, including Martin. But this was opposed by the Puritans and other Nonconformists, (See Chapter 17). Sparrow featured in this conflict in 1637, when he delivered and published a controversial sermon, claiming that priests could hear confession and provide absolution, which outraged the Nonconformist faction. An extract follows:

'A Sermon Concerning Confession of Sins and the Power of Absolution. Preached by Mr. Anthony Sparrow of Queen's College in Cambridge. London: Printed by R. Bishop for John Clark, 1637.

In Dei Nomine, Amen. 1 John 1.9: If we confess our sins, he is faithful and just to forgive us our sins, and to cleanse us from all unrighteousness. If we say that we have no sin, we sin in saying so: for we give God the lie, who by his Prophet hath said, There is none that doth good, and sinneth not, and by his Apostle, that in many things we offend all...The poor Publican's humble confession, with a God be merciful to me a sinner, is the only way to pardon and forgiveness. For if we confess our sins, he is faithful and just to forgive us our sins, and to cleanse us from all unrighteousness...(over 4,000 words omitted)...If we with the prodigal confess...the Father of mercies will behold us with the eye of pity, will melt us with his grace, embrace us with the arms of mercy, will own for us his sons, and clothe us with the robes of righteousness...'. However, Sparrow escaped official censure, probably benefitting from Archbishop Laud's approval.[1]

Sparrow held several College offices between 1638 and 1643: Hebrew praelector 1638-39, (ie with responsibility for students in this discipline), Greek praelector 1640-41, Hebrew praelector again in 1642-43, bursar 1640-42, censor theologicus and examinator 1641-42, and censor philosophicus, 1642-43. He proceeded B.D. in 1639.

But after 1640, Sparrow's high church and royalist views would seriously disrupt his career. In 1640, the King had been obliged to call a Parliament after eleven years of his personal rule and, after the 'short' Parliament of just a few weeks, the 'long' Parliament, was convened in November. This set up a committee to examine the state of religion in the Universities, because of concern over the influence of Catholic doctrine and practices, and Sparrow was one of the Cambridge churchmen, who included Edward Martin, whose: 'audacious and libelling pamphlets against true religion' were noted.[2] In June 1642, Sparrow's royalist sympathies were in evidence when Martin and ten of the fellows, including Sparrow, gave £185 to the King, in response to a royal request for funds, (see Chapter 17). Martin's fate in the Civil War has also been described in Chapter 17, involving his arrest on the 30th August 1642, his subsequent imprisonment, and his ejection from the Presidency on the 13th March 1644. He was replaced by Herbert Palmer, who was installed in his stead on the 11th April 1644. This took place soon after eight of the Queens' fellows, including Sparrow, had also been ejected on the 8th and 9th of April, (see Chapter 18).

Despite his being: 'reduced to great straits',[3] Sparrow was married, in 1645, to Susanna Orrell (or Querall) at Withersfield, Suffolk, and, in 1647, he secured appointment as rector of Hawkedon, near Depden. But this source of income did not last for long, as he was ejected after only five weeks for using the Book of Common Prayer, which had been prohibited by Parliament. His devotion to the established Anglican ritual also led, in 1655, to the anonymous publication of his work: 'A Rationale upon the Book of Common-Prayer of the Church of England'.[1] This would become highly influential and it has had 106 editions in English between 1655 and 2010. It describes and defends the doctrines and forms of worship in the Book of Common Prayer in great detail, and Sparrow's views were an important influence on the revisions to the Book of Common Prayer in 1662. The preface to his 'Rationale' is as follows:

'The Common-Prayer-Book contains in it many holy Offices of the Church: As Prayers, Confession of Faith, holy Hymns,

Divine Lessons, Priestly Absolutions and Benedictions: all of which are Set and Prescribed, not left to private mens fancies to make or alter; so was it of old ordained CON.CARTHAG. Can.106. It is ordained that the Prayers, Prefaces, Impositions of hands which are confirmed by the Synod, be observed and used by all men. These and no other. So is our English Can.13. The COUNCIL OF MILEVIS gives the reason of this Constitution, Can.12, (Lest through ignorance or carelessness, any thing contrary to the Faith should be vented or uttered before God, or offered up to him in the Church)'. (The Councils of Carthage were Church synods held at Carthage during the 3rd, 4th and 5th centuries, while the Council of Milevis was held in AD402, in what is now Tunisia. This was chaired by Aurelius, the Bishop of Carthage, and confirmed the canons of synods held at Hippo and Carthage; also, it produced five disciplinary canons). Sparrow continues to quote the deliberations of the early Church fathers:

'And as these Offices are set and prescribed, so are they moreover appointed to be one and the same throughout the whole National Church. So was it of old ordained. CON. TOLETAN.11.C.3. (That all Governours of Churches and their people should observe one and the same rite and order of service, which they knew to be appointed in the Metropolitan See.) The same is ordered CON.BRACCAR.1.Can.19. and Tolet.4.c.2. It is appointed that one and the same order of praying and singing, be observed by us all, and that there should not be variety of usages by them that are bound to the same Faith, and live in the same Dominion. This for Conformities sake, that according to divine Canon Rom. 15.6 We may with one mind and one mouth glorify God'. The next extract gives a flavour of his detailed consideration of the liturgy:

'Christ is present at the Sacrament now, that first instituted it. He consecrates this also: It is not man that makes the body and blood of Christ by consecrating the holy Elements, but Christ that was crucified for us. The words are pronounced by the mouth of the Priest, but the Elements are consecrated by the power and grace of God, THIS IS, saith he, MY BODY: By this word the bread and wine are consecrated. Before these words (THIS IS MY

BODY) the bread and wine are common food fit only to nourish the body: but since our Lord hath said, Do this, as oft as you do it in remembrance of me, This is my body, this is my blood: as often as by these words and in this faith they are consecrated, the holy bread and blessed cup are profitable to the salvation of the whole man'.

After the Restoration in 1660, Sparrow's fortunes were rapidly transformed; he was soon reinstated as rector of Hawkedon and elected to a preachership at Bury St Edmunds.[1] Robert Plumptre, a future President, writes:

'After the Restoration he resumed possession of his living, but was soon afterwards called up to London to consult with other divines upon the alterations to be made in the Service-Book (the Book of Common Prayer). He was likewise prevailed with by the earnest request and importunity of his friends to become one of the Ministers and Preachers at Bury St Edmund's'.[3] Also, on the 7th August 1660, he was appointed Archdeacon of Sudbury and, on the 31st, received the degree of D.D. from Cambridge by royal mandate, together with other loyal royalists, including the historian Thomas Fuller, (see Chapter 15).[1] The new King seems to have been very liberal with University degrees, as:

'During this reign, mandates for degrees were very common and the total number of degees for which royal mandates issued from the 25th of June, 1660, to the 2nd of March, 1660-1; seems to have been: Doctors of Divinity, 121; Doctors of Civil Law, 12; Doctors of Physic, 12; Bachelors of Divinity, 12; Masters of Arts, 2; Bachelor of Civil Law, 1'.[4]

Further preferment came in 1661, when he was appointed a prebendary at Ely by Bishop Wren.[1] (Matthew Wren had accompanied Charles I to Holyrood Palace in 1633 for his Scottish coronation. He had been a strong anti-Puritan supporter of Archbishop Laud and had been imprisoned in the Tower of London). In the same year, Sparrow published another influential work: 'A Collection of Articles, Injunctions, Canons, Orders, Ordinances, and Constitutions Ecclesiastical: with other publick records of the Church of England, chiefly in the times of K.Edward VI, Q. Elizabeth, K. James, & K. Charles I, published to vindicate the Church of England, and to promote uniformity and peace in the same. 1661; London, Printed by R. Norton for Timothy Garthwait at the Little North-doore of St. Paul's Church 1661'. Also in 1661, Sparrow was chosen as one of the nine deputies (assistants) to the twelve Anglican bishops nominated to attend the Savoy Conference, which unsuccessfully tried to reconcile the orthodox and Nonconformist factions within the Church.

Edward Martin died on the 28th April 1662, just three days after he had been installed, by proxy, as Dean of Ely, (see Chapter 17). This was followed by what Twigg, in his history of the College of 1987, describes as: 'The most blatant example of royal interference' in college elections in the 1660s.[2] There were two candidates for the vacancy, Simon Patrick, a previous fellow, and Sparrow, (then Archdeacon of Sudbury and chaplain to the King), who was the King's choice to be a loyal head who would advance religious peace and orthodoxy in the University. Patrick- see Chapters 18 and 19- had arrived at Queens' as a sizar in 1644 and was a fellow during 1649-58. Before eventual episcopal office, he was chaplain to Sir Walter St. John, (who was a member of Parliament); vicar of Battersea, London; rector of St Paul's, Covent Garden, London; and Dean of Peterborough. Patrick would be appointed Bishop of Chichester in 1689 and advanced to be Bishop of Ely in 1691. He died in 1707 and is buried in Ely Cathedral.

Patrick had relatively liberal religious views, which were not in favour with the new establishment, but he was popular with the younger fellows, while Sparrow was the choice of the restored senior fellows.[2] The election was held on the 5th May 1662, in the College chapel, administered by the Vice-President, Richard Bryan, who, like Sparrow, had been ejected as a fellow in 1644. In one account, the five senior fellows voted for Sparrow and before five votes for Patrick were written, Bryan halted the proceedings and read a letter from the King, in support of Sparrow. A subsequent statement by Sparrow's supporters provides further details:

'After these (letters) were read, we went to a second scrutiny, (ie vote; three were allowed by Statute), and the seniors writt as before for Dr. Sparrow, some others for Mr. Patrick: but before they had written so many suffrages for Mr. Patrick, as had been given for Dr. Sparrow, the senior Fellow broke off that scrutiny and read His Majesties Mandate for the electing Dr. Sparrow. After that, the seniors againe according to their duty writt their suffrages for Dr. Sparrow, and the Senior Fellow, seeing that others were disobedient to his Majesties command, broke off that scrutiny, Dr. Sparrow having then two suffrages more than Mr Patrick. After this the senior Fellow pronounced Dr. Sparrow Master or President...The truth of this we do attest by the subscription of our hands, ready to confirm it by oath, when required. Ambrose Appleby, Edward Kemp, Richard Bryan, Sen. Fellows'.[3] Patrick provides a similar account in his autobiography, although it differs in some details:

'On the 29th of April, 1662, I had news from Cambridge of the death of Dr. Martin, Master of Queen's College; and that the major part of the fellows expressed their desires to have me to be their President...on the fifth of May word was brought me to Trompeton (Trumpington), within a mile of Cambridge, that I was legally chosen by the majority of the fellows, but another admitted, contrary to the statutes. For thus the election was managed. The senior fellow went up to the Communion table, and read the statute, and invoked the Holy Ghost to direct their choice, and they were sworn to choose him whom they knew most worthy. Then he read a letter from the King recommending Dr. Sparrow to their choice, and standing in scrutiny, the fellows came up one by one, and in a paper wrote their suffrages (which I have still to shew); and when he saw that eleven of nineteen had wrote for me, he snatched up the paper, and read a mandamus from the King to choose Dr. Sparrow. They told him he should have produced it sooner, for now it was too late, another being chose by the major part of the fellows, before they knew the King's mind. But the old man, one Mr. Brian, pronounced Dr. Sparrow to be chosen by the King's authority and admitted him. I came to the college when this was done, and staying one night with my friends, returned to London, to advise what was to be done in this case'.[3,5]

Patrick's supporters maintained that if the election was to be by mandate, then Bryan: 'ought to have produced it sooner',[3] and in view of the disquiet, the King ordered the Vice-Chancellor, the two Divinity professors and the Provost of King's College to summon the new President, and the fellows, to the College hall, to confirm the election of Sparrow and to suspend the fellows who had voted for Patrick from all their privileges, except their accomodation and their right to attend chapel, until they accepted the situation.[3]

Patrick began legal action in London on the 8th of May, applying to the King's Bench for a mandamus for his admission as President and, although this was initially refused, a further application on the 12th of May was successful. But this decision did not alter the situation; Patrick provides a detailed account of subsequent events:

'On the 22nd of October I was summoned to appear before some commissioners, whom the King appointed to hear our business. I was advised by some hot persons not to go. But both I and the fellows who chose me appeared on the 30th at Worcester house, before the Lord Chancellor, the Bishops of London, Winchester, Ely and others...where I was thought to speak very pertinently in my own behalf. And the Lord Chancellor...bade us bring what friends we pleased with us the next time they met to examine the business...But...when we appeared again, they were all shut out: and I having then thought fit to entertain counsel, when I came to call Serjeant Keeling to go along with me, he told me he was ordered at that hour to wait upon the King at the council table. So I was forced to desire leave I might plead my own cause as well as I could...some of the fellows had permission to speak, who made it so evidently appear that I was duly chosen, that the counsel on the other side had nothing to reply, but that they were fellows only by the King's grace and favour...At which the Chancellor said, "Well then, he is legally chosen; but will he yield nothing to the King?" I humbly told him I had nothing to yield, but if they pleased to put me in possession of that to which they acknowledged I had a right, they should see what I would do. Upon which he was angry, and bade all our names to be taken and set down in writing, that we might be noted as a company of factious fellows and then bid us withdraw; and we heard no more of this commission, by which we were heard and nothing determined...my business...was moved again...in Westminster Hall. But after a long attendance there, for two years or more, I found it was to no purpose...Therefore, I let it fall, being settled in a better place...(ie the living of St Paul's, Covent Garden)'.[3,5]

Sparrow's zealous high church views reflected the dominant faction in Cambridge in the post-Restoration 1660s and a visitor in 1663 writes that Sparrow and some other heads:

'carried things so high that I saw latitude and moderation were odious to the greater part even there'.[2] In Queens', Sparrow is reported to have been concerned about Nonconformist views, such as Socinianism.[2] (This involved various unorthodox beliefs, such as rejection of the pre-existance of Christ before his being conceived, developed by the Italians Lelio and Fausto Sozzini).

On the 27th of January 1663, Sparrow was one of the eleven heads, who, together with the Vice-Chancellor, signed the following decree for the: 'more solemn observation of the 30th day of January in this University', which was the anniversary of the execution of Charles I:

'...IT IS AGREED by the vice-chancellor and the heads of colleges that every doctor in divinity being head of a college shall according to seniority preach in Saint Marys church at nine of the clock in the forenoon on the said thirtieth of January: and if any shall fail so to preach or to procure one of the heads of colleges or a doctor in divinity to preach for him he shall forfeit six pounds thirteen shillings and eight pence to the use of the common chest... IT IS FURTHER AGREED that on the same day there shall yearly be a speech at two of the clock in Saint Marys church (or such place as the vice-chancellor shall assign) to be made by such as the vice-chancellor shall appoint'.[4] In March 1663, Sparrow will have been involved in the visit to the University of: 'the King's natural son James Duke of Monmouth', at this time about fourteen years of age':[4]

'The University entertained the Duke with a banquet and a comedy at Trinity College, and the King is said to have been highly gratified with the attention paid to the Duke on this occasion'.[4]

In 1664, the Vice-Chancellor and heads:

'ordered that all in pupillari statu that shall go to coffee houses without their tutors leave shall be punished according to the statute for haunters of taverns and alehouses'.[4] The rationale for this action is explained by an account of the life of the Rev. Dr. John North, who was admitted to Jesus College in 1661:

'...And the scholars are so greedy after news (ie newspapers from London) (which is none of their business,) that they neglect all for it; and it is become very rare for any of them to go directly to his chamber, after prayers, without doing his suit at the coffee-house; which is a vast loss of time grown out of a pure novelty, for who can apply close to a subject with his head full of the din of a coffee house!'.[4]

Sparrow served as Vice-Chancellor during 1664-65, and is mentioned in a contemporary account of events in Cambridge during the year, but only for an invitation that he did not accept:

'Mr. Mayor, Mr. Recorder, ye Alderman as many as pleased... went on fishing according to custome. They had 3 boates with netts, they drew Newnham pitt, Cambridge Mill pitt & soe fisht downe to Bullen, (Bullen Grove was the eastern extremity of Stourbridge Common) where we had our fish drest ye charge of this for wine bread & cheese in ye boate & after at Bullen together with boathire came to £5. Od. Money. ye mace did not goe with ye Mayor. None were in Gownes. The Mayor & Aldermen invited with them ye Vice Chancellor then Do^r^. Sparrowe but he went not, also Do^r^. Fleetewood, Do^r^. Dillingham & Do^r^. Steyt who went & dyned with them at Bullen'.[4]

In August 1665 there was an outbreak of 'plague' in Cambridge and, on the 1st of September, Stourbridge Fair was prohibited. (This event dated from 1211 and was, at its peak, the largest fair in Europe). On the 12th September, the Corporation made an order:

'in regard the infection of the plague is in divers parts of this kingdome & in some measure in this Towne & in respect all publique meetings within this Towne are prohibited both by the University & Towne'.[4] On the 10th of October, the University discontinued sermons at St Mary's Church as well as academic exercises and, although Cambridge appeared free of infection in March 1666, there was a serious recurrence of the plague in the following summer. But there was at least one positive outcome from this outbreak: Isaac Newton retreated from Trinity College to his family home at Woolsthorpe Manor, Lincolnshire, for two extended periods during 1665-67. These were when he made major advances in his ideas, in particular involving light and gravity, the latter allegedly stimulated by his observing the fall of an apple from a tree in the Manor garden. In 1666 there was another major disaster- the Great Fire of London.

The Queens' records provide snapshots of the everyday functioning of the College during Sparrow's Presidency. In 1664, £6 0s. 2d. was paid: 'for heightening ye walls' of the fellows' garden, which was stocked with:

'jasmins, gilliflowers and strawberies', 'Peach and Apricote-trees', and '5 apple-trees'. Twelve elms were planted in the area west of the river and various other expenditures are noted: a 'lime-house' was built; 'Curtains for the lodging' cost 16 shillings; '12 Russia-leather chairs in ye lodgings' cost £5 1s; and the hall was paved with stone. In 1665, £2 10s. was paid for the: 'organ-mender'; £2 8s for: 'sixe turky chaires for ye lodging'; and 2s.: 'for dressing ye bore', (ie a boar's head at Christmas). In 1666, the: 'subcoquus' (under-cook) received £1 14s. 8d. for scouring the pewter and, in 1667, £31 was paid for building the orchard wall.[3]

The Queens' chapel contains a notable triptych over the altar, which is attributed to a late fifteenth-century workshop in Brussels in the charge of the 'Master of the View of Saint Gudula', so-named because of a painting from this workshop, of the Collegiate Church of St Michael and St Gudula, (now Brussels Cathedral), which is in the Louvre, Paris. The three panels are from what was originally a much larger altarpiece and, while the earliest reference to them in the College records is in 1717, it is not known how and when they came to Queens'. But the late Peter Spufford, (Professor of European History and fellow of Queens' during 1979-2017), believed that it is most likely that Sparrow acquired them for the College during his Presidency. Spufford further argued that, in the sixteenth century, the panels had probably been given to the church at Long Melford, Suffolk, which contains an inscription appearing to refer to the paintings. Subsequently, they would probably have been removed and stored during the Civil War and Parliamentary era, possibly at nearby Kentwell Hall, before coming to the notice of Sparrow, who was Archdeacon of Sudbury and knew the area well.[6]

In 1667, when he was aged 55, Sparrow's fortunes improved further, when he was appointed Bishop of Exeter. As previously noted, he had married in 1645, and he and Susanna are reported to have had six daughters.[3] In his later years he is described as:

'...a man of a very ready apprehension and good judgment, but complained of the weakness of his memory. He was very strict in his devotions, public and private. Besides those in his retirements, he never failed to have the Litany read in his family every evening about six or seven o'clock'.[3] During 1668-76 he was also Archdeacon of Exeter and Dean of St Buryan. (The parish and church of St Buryan are about five miles west of Penzance, Cornwall).

Sparrow was very concerned about any dissent from Anglican orthodoxy, as demonstrated by a sermon given in Truro: 'The Bishop of Exons Caution to his Diocese Against False Doctrines', which was published in 1669. (This had eight English editions up to 1984). Also, he objected to the 'Royal Declaration of Indulgence' of 1672, (in which Charles II aimed to extend religious liberty to Protestant Nonconformists and Catholics, by suspending punishment for those not attending Anglican services), writing to Gilbert Sheldon, Archbishop of Canterbury:

'I see daily to my heart's grief the poor sheep committed to my trust snatched out of the fold by cunning wolves and I know not how to bring them back'.[1]

In 1676, Sparrow was transferred to the more valuable See of Norwich, where he would encounter serious factional conflict between the Church and:

'the sizeable nonconformist minority fearful of the rising tide of aggressive Anglicanism'.[1] This led to his complains of:

'some clamouring loud against me for prosecuting schismatics, and some who profess great loyalty and zeal for the church, as loud complaining because we do not proceed violently beyond the rule of law'.[7] He died at the Bishop's Palace in Norwich in 1685 and is buried in the nearby chapel.[1] His bequests included £100 for the rebuilding of St Paul's Cathedral and £100 to Queens'. His widow was still alive in 1693. One of his daughters, Joan, (d.1703), was the wife of Edward Drew (d.1714), of The Grange, Broadhembury, Devon, a canon of Exeter Cathedral.[8] Two other daughters are also reported to have married clergy of Exeter Cathedral.[1]

References

1. Ginn, R.J., Kelsey, S. Sparrow, Anthony. In: Oxford Dictionary of National Biography. 2008. Online. 2019.
2. Twigg, J. A History of Queens' College, Cambridge. 1448-1986. The Boydell Press. 1987. pp 47, 144-45.
5. Gray, J.H. The Queens' College of St Margaret and St Bernard. F.E.Robinson. London. 1898. pp 201-11.
4. Cooper, C.H. Annals of Cambridge. Volume III. Warwick and Co., Cambridge. 1845. pp 481, 508-17.
5. Patrick, Symon. The Works of Symon Patrick, D.D. Ed. A. Taylor. Volume ix. University Press. Oxford. 1858. pp 417-24.
6. Spufford, P. The Altarpieces in the College Chapel. The Record. 2008. Queens' College, Cambridge. Online. 2020.
7. Spurr, J. The Restoration Church of England, 1646-1689. Yale University Press. New Haven-London. 1991. p 82.
8. Vivian, J.L. (ed). The Visitations of the County of Devon: Comprising the Heralds' Visitations of 1531, 1564 & 1620, Exeter, 1895. p 307.

CHAPTER 21

William Wells. President 1667-75.

Summary.

William Wells was a royalist clergyman about whom little is known. He was a fellow of Queens' in 1638, but was ejected in 1644 by the Earl of Manchester, acting on behalf of the Civil War Parliament, for refusing to take the oath supporting the 'Solemn League and Covenant' of 1643.

After the Restoration, he was appointed, in about 1665, as rector of Little Shelford, Cambridgeshire, and, at dates unknown, he married, was appointed rector of Sandon, Essex, and obtained a doctorate of Divinity at Cambridge. In 1667, he was appointed Archdeacon of Colchester.

When Anthony Sparrow, President of Queens', was appointed Bishop of Exeter in 1667, Wells, who may have been nominated by Sparrow, was elected as his successor by royal mandate. He served as Vice-Chancellor during 1672-73 and during his Presidency he will have been present at several visits of notables to the University and at the installation of the Duke of Monmouth as Chancellor in 1674.

He died in office in 1675 and was survived by two daughters. He was not actively associated with any significant events in the College or the University, but perhaps he can be considered to have provided a safe pair of hands at Queens', during a time of national recovery.

Timeline.

1631. Edward Martin is elected President of Queens'.

1638. William Wells is a fellow of Queens'.

1642. Start of the English Civil War.

1644.	Edward Martin is ejected as President and replaced by Herbert Palmer. On the 26th September, Wells is ejected from his fellowship.
1647.	Death of Herbert Palmer. Thomas Horton succeeds as President.
1660.	Restoration of Charles II. Edward Martin is reinstated as President.
1662.	Death of Edward Martin. Anthony Sparrow succeeds as President.
c1665.	Appointed rector of Little Shelford, Cambridgeshire.
1665.	Rector of Sandon, Essex, (date of appointment unknown).
1667.	Appointed Archdeacon of Colchester, (2nd February). Sparrow becomes Bishop of Exeter and resigns as President. Wells is appointed President by royal mandate.
1669.	Visit of Cosimo de' Medici, Prince of Tuscany, to the University.
1670.	Visits of the Duke and Duchess of York (October) and the Prince of Orange, later William III (November), to the University.
1671.	Visit of the King to the University.
1672-73.	Vice-Chancellor.
1674.	Duke of Monmouth installed as Chancellor of the University, in London.
1675.	Dies in office. Survived by two daughters.

A royalist clergyman ejected from his Queens' fellowship in 1644. Appointed President in 1667 by royal mandate. Left no significant mark on the College or University.

We know nothing about the early life of William Wells, until Gray, in his history of the College in 1898, reports that he was elected a fellow of Queens' in 1638.[1] He features again in accounts of the ejections of Queens' fellows during the Civil War, after Edward Martin's removal as President, (see Chapter 18).

In 1644, Parliament passed:

'An ORDINANCE for Regulation the University of Cambridge, and for the removing of Scandalous Ministers in the seven Associated Counties',[2] which gave the Earl of Manchester sweeping powers over the University, including:

'he shall have power to eject such as he shall judge unfit for their Places...and to place other fitting persons in their Roome, such as shall be approved of by the Assembly of Divines sitting at Westminster'.[2] Also, the Earl of Manchester was given the power: 'to administer the late Covenant',[2] that is to require an oath of support for the 'Solemn League and Covenant', which was an agreement, in 1643, between the Scottish 'Covenanters', (who supported the Scottish system of Presbyterian church government), and the leaders of the English Parliament.

The President, Edward Martin, was removed on March 13th 1644 and, on the 8th April, four Queens' fellows, including the future President Anthony Sparrow, were ejected for non-residence and not returning to Cambridge. The following day, four more were removed for refusing to take the oath of the Solemn League and Covenant. Ejections continued and, on September 26th, it was Wells's turn, when he and Arthur Walpole were removed, also for refusing to take the required oath.[1] (Walpole had been a fellow since 1635 and, unusually, was a Doctor of Medicine).

There follows a long absence of Wells from known records, although Gray tells us that he was married.[1] The 'History of Little Shelford', Cambridgeshire (online), lists many of the rectors of All Saints Church, and Wells is recorded as rector from c.1665 to his death in 1675. At unknown dates he was awarded the D.D. degree from Cambridge and became rector of Sandon, Essex.

The next sighting in records is on the 2nd February 1667, when he became Archdeacon of Colchester.[3] This was within the diocese of London, whose Bishop, from 1663 to 1675, was Humphrey Henchman, a previous fellow of Clare College, who had helped the future Charles II escape the country after the battle of Worcester in 1651. Also in 1667, Anthony Sparrow became Bishop of Exeter and resigned his Presidency. There is a claim that the King allowed Sparrow to recommend his successor,[4] before Wells' election by royal mandate. Although it is reported that there was no opposition to his election,[1] the King may not have wanted to take any chances that his wishes would be ignored, after the dispute over Sparrow's election, (see Chapter 20).[4] The date of Wells' election, September 26th, was the anniversary of his ejection in 1644![1]

Several visits of notables to Cambridge occurred during Wells' Presidency, and no doubt he will have been involved in the celebrations, although not with a significant role. In 1669:

'On the first of May, Cosmo de Medicis, Prince of Tuscany afterwards Grand Duke by the title of Cosmo III., visited Cambridge...came from Newmarket up ye Peticury to ye Rose Taverne in Cambridge...in his Coach & 6 horses with a postilion, there came alsoe along with him 2 other Coaches. He then was about ye age of 28 yeares, a proper man, very thick in person & very swarthy in his favour...Mr. Mayor & ye Aldermen in their scarlett, & ye Bailliffs Treasurers, & 24ty in their Gownes, went... to visitt him. Which was in the Chamber at ye Rose next St Michael's Churchyard...by his interpreter (he) thankt Mr. Mayor for ye Civility & said it was a fine Town, he liked it well...The University alsoe, soone after ...did visit him...the Vicechancellor & Doctors in their Scarlet met ye Prince in ye middle of ye Regent Walke & soe conducted him to ye Regent House...Thence ye Prince went to his Inne & dyned & then again to ye schooles, where there was a Philosophy Act, & from thence went to Kings Col. Chappel where they had a music divertisement...from thence...to St Johns Col...& from thence came to Trinity Col... & then they went to ye Comedy house where they had a Comedy... composed for ye Italian meridian...he seemed to like ye Comedy very well...he went from hence on Sunday morning ye 2nd May, 1669...'.[2] Another account describes the scene when the Prince met the University representatives:

'...As soon as the magistrates were gone, there immediately appeared, in grand procession, preceded by the mace-bearers, the college of the doctors, consisting of fourteen heads of the university (probably including Wells), drest in doctors' robes of scarlet cloth, edged with ermines' skin, which was spread round the neck like that of the large cap of the cardinals' robes...His highness received them graciously...'.[2] (Cosimo III, 1642-1723, Grand Duke of Tuscany from 1670 to his death in 1723, was descended from the Italian de' Medici family that first rose to prominence in the Republic of Florence in the 15th century and, in the late 16th century, one branch were created the Grand Dukes of Tuscany. Cosimo succeeded his father Ferdinando as Grand Duke in 1670, the year after his visit to Cambridge, but would rule over a realm in decline, eventually to near bankruptcy. He married Marguerite d'Orleans, granddaughter of Henri IV of France, and although he was succeeded by his son Gian Gastone in 1723, the latter would be the last Grand Duke. On his death in 1737, there was an absence of male heirs and control of Tuscany passed to the Austrians).

In 1670, Cambridge received two royal visits. In October the Duke and Duchess of York who, with the Duchess of Cleveland:

'arrived in cambridge in one coach...During their stay here the University presented the Duke and Duchess of York with two fair quarto bibles...'.[2] (The Duke of York would become James II, while his Duchess, Anne Hyde, daughter of Edward Hyde, Lord Chancellor between 1660 and 1667, and mother of the future monarchs Mary and Anne, would die the following year). In the following month:

'...the Prince of Orange (afterwards King William the Third) visited the University...The Prince and his retinue arrived in Cambridge from Newmarket...about 10 in the morning. There were three coaches, in the middle one of which were the Prince and Lord Ossory. Mr. Herring the Deputy Mayor, with the Aldermen in scarlet, and the Common Council and others in their habits, met the Prince at the hither end of Jesus Lane...Thence he proceeded to the Schools, where many degrees were conferred. The Prince dined at King's College with the Provost, and after dinner went to Trinity College. The same night he left Cambridge for Audley End...The Prince is described as..."between 19 & 20 years of age a well countenanced man, a smooth & meeger face, and a hansome head of hayre of his owne" '.[2] We can reasonably assume that Wells was at the degree ceremonies and possibly at the subsequent dinner.

In 1671 there was a visit to Cambridge from King Charles, on the 4th of October. He arrived in the morning from Newmarket and returned the same evening; but despite this brevity, the cost of his entertainment was a substantial £1,039 5s. 1d.[2], (estimated to be equivalent to about £120,000 in 2020):

'His Majesty this day honored the University and Town of Cambridge with his royal presence, attended by many of the nobility from Newmarket; the Mayor & Aldermen with the trayn Soldiers waited his coming without the Town; the whole body of Students according to their several Orders and Degrees in their Habits, attended in the streets from the first entrance unto the Schools; as he passed by the Market place, the Conduit ran with Claret wine; at the Schools he was received by his Grace George Duke of Buckingham, Chancellor of the University, with the Vice-Chancellor and Doctors, presented with a fair Bible, and a short speech made by the Orator...Through his Majesties great favor, and his Grace the Chancellor's care of the University, no Degrees were conferred upon any, by his Majesties Command, though much desired by many'.[2] After a visit to King's College chapel, including a climb to the roof for the view, and to St. John's College, he was given an early dinner at Trinity College, before leaving at about five o'clock to return to Newmarket.[2]

Wells was Vice-Chancellor in 1672-73, although he gets only the briefest of mentions in Cooper's 'Annals of Cambridge' of 1845:

'Dr Wells the Vicechancellor for the year ending November, 1673, put down the singing of psalms in St Mary's'.[2] Also in 1673, the University published: 'The Foundation of the University of Cambridge, with a Catalogue of the Principal Founders and Special Benefactours of all the Colledges, and total number of Students, Magistrates and Officers therein being', and the entry for Queens' notes:

'A President, 19 Fellows, 27 Scholars, 12 Bible-clerks, and three Lecturers of Hebrew, Arithmetic, and Geometry, besides other Officers and Servants of the Foundation, and Students, The whole number being about 120'.[2] This was similar to the size of the College just before the ravages of the Civil War, although in around 1621 there had been a total of about 230.[1]

In 1673, Wells was involved in a strange incident involving a brush with officialdom in the Ely diocese:

'Dr. Board Surrogate of the Official of the Archdeaconry of Ely, suspended Dr. Spencer the Vicechancellor, and Dr. Wells President of Queens' College, for not appearing at the Archdeacon's Visitations, they being incumbents of benefices in the archdeaconry. This was complained of as a breach of the University privileges and also of the privileges of the Convocation (of the Church of England, in London) then sitting, and of which Dr Spencer and Dr. Wells were members in right of their respective archdeaconries of Sudbury and Colchester...'.[2] But this decision seems to have been reversed!

George Villiers, the Second Duke of Buckingham (second creation), had been installed as Chancellor of Cambridge University in 1671, after the death of the Earl of Manchester. Buckingham had a remarkably complicated and volatile relationship with Charles II and the political establishment, and was associated with various plots and scandals. In 1674, he fell out of royal favour and was replaced as Chancellor by the King's eldest illegitimate son, the Duke of Monmouth, after the King had informed the University:

'Charles R. Trusty and well-beloved we greet you well. WHEREAS we have thought fit to remove from our service and personal attendance George Duke of Buckingham, whereby he is rendered incapable of discharging any longer the office he bore amongst you of chancellor of that our university either to our satisfaction or your benefit... WE DO HEREBY DECLARE the chancellor's office of that our university in the person of the said George Duke of Buckingham to be void...we further hereby recommend to your choice that of our dearly beloved son James Duke of Monmouth as a mark of our indulgent care of your prosperity and welfare. And so we bid you farewell. Given at our castle at Windsor this 11th day of July, in the 26th year of our reign'.[2] Monmouth was duly installed as Chancellor in a lavish ceremony at Worcester House, London, (which was on the present site of the Savoy Hotel and Theatre, and was the venue of the secret marriage of the Duke of York to Anne Hyde in 1660), on the 3rd September, 1674, at which it is likely that Wells was present:

'The day appointed for the Solemnity drawing nigh, the Vicechancellor by the advice of the Heads went to London about a week before to expect the Chancellor's Commands & to give the Heads Intelligence of any new occurrence if occasion should be offer'd...The place made choice of for the generall meeting was Darby (sic) House, where the University stay'd together till they had notice that his Grace was in readiness to receive them. Upon notice whereof they set forward from thence about 4 of the Clock in the afternoon, all in their Habits according to their respective Degrees, to ye number of above 480 persons, in order following:- Four or five of the King's Life Guard well mounted going before to make way through the Croud (which was very great) the Junior Bedle Mr. William Woorts went first in his Bedle's Gown Velvet Cap Gold Hatband & Regent's Hood, holding his Bedle's Staff the round End upward. After him followed the Regents...after them went the Non-Regents Masters, then the Batchelors in Divinity, Next the Taxors, last of all the Proctors with their Chained Books...After the Vicechancellor went the Bishops...Next to the Bishops went the Doctors in Divinity...In this Order...did the Procession advance from Derby House to Worcester House, in the view of a very numerous Company of Spectators in ye Streets & Windows from ye beginning to ye end thereof. The Company, which was very great, being a little composed, the vicechancellor made a speech in English, declaring the singular content & satisfaction of the University in their Relation to a Personage whose virtues were as eminent as his place & Fortune...the Orator, Henry Paman, D.M. Fellow of St. John's College, (who graduated M.D. at Cambridge in 1658, and later became Professor of Physic at Gresham College), addrest himself to his Grace in an Eloquent Speech in Latin...the Orator having concluded, his Grace was pleased in a few but very full & affectionate words to declare himself very sensible of the kindness of the University in this election of him...His Graces Speech being ended...he invited the University up to a long & Spacious Gallery, where was prepared for them an Entertainment whose Variety Neatness delicacy Order & all other Circumstances of Magnificence was beyond Expression...The Chancellor & most of the Doctors supt at a very large Ovall Table plac'd at the upper end of the Roome, & most of the Company besides at 2 long tables plac'd on each side of the Gallery, each Table containing (as was thought) above 150. Besides which there were 2 large Tables spread below Staires...The Company having sat about an hour...his Grace (after some expressions of kindness to the University) took his leave, & was attended...by the Vicechancellor to his Barge which waited his coming at the back Staires belonging to the House...'.[2] It is to be hoped that the new Chancellor's enjoyment of the occasion was not marred by any premonitions of his future execution in 1685, which had been the fate of six of his predecessors!

The last of the few facts we have about Wells is that he died in office in 1675. Twigg, in his history of the College of 1987, notes that he did not leave much of a mark upon the College,[4] and the same can be said about his duties in the University and the Convocation of the Church of England. But, remembering Sir Arthur Conan Doyle's dog that did not bark in the night, ('the dog did nothing in the night-time...That was the curious incident'), the absence of records of significant conflict, difficulties and scandal in the College during his Presidency, suggests a safe pair of hands at Queens' during a period of national recovery. He was survived by two daughters.[1]

References

1. Gray, J.H. The Queens' College of St Margaret and St Bernard. F.E.Robinson. London. 1898. pp 106, 171-72, 211-16.
2. Cooper, C.H. Annals of Cambridge. Volume III. Warwick and Co., Cambridge. 1845. pp 369, 533-34, 544-45, 549, 553-63.
3. Wikipedia. Archdeacons of Colchester. Online. 2020.
4. Twigg, J. A History of Queens' College, Cambridge. 1448-1986. The Boydell Press. 1987. p 148.

CHAPTER 22

Henry James. President 1675-1717.

Summary.

Henry James was born in Somerset, in about 1642, the son of a clergyman. He was elected a fellow of Queens' in 1664 and came to royal notice, becoming one of the honorary 'Chaplains in Ordinary' to Charles II. His one printed work, his sermon to the King at Newmarket in 1674, was published at the King's request and, in the following year, he became President of Queens' after nomination by the King in a royal mandate. In 1681, James received King Charles and Queen Catherine at Queens' and he was appointed Vice-Chancellor in the years 1683-84 and 1696-98.

In 1700, he became Regius Professor of Divinity at Cambridge. In this capacity, he developed a reputation for impressive public performances as an examiner, when summing up and adjudicating disputations. In 1705 he hosted another royal visit to Queens', by Queen Anne.

He died, unmarried, in 1717, after nearly 42 years as President, making him the longest-serving President to date. He is considered to have been an:

'excellent Master, very attentive to the business and interests of the College during his life, and...a considerable Benefactor to it at his death'. However, in 1681, he had described his role at Queens' as: 'drudgery and slavery', in frustration at his lack of further promotion.

Timeline.

c1642. Born in Somerset.

1661. Admitted to Magdalene College, Cambridge, from Eton College.

1662.	Moves to Queens'. (Subsequently graduated M.A. and B.D.).
1664.	Elected fellow of Queens'.
1674.	Publication of: 'A Sermon Preached before the King at Newmarket October 11. 1674 by Henry James'. (Date unknown: Chaplain to Charles II).
1675.	Death of William Wells. James is elected President by royal mandate.
1681.	Visit of Charles II and Queen Catherine to Queens'.
1682.	Duke of Monmouth deprived as Chancellor of Cambridge University.
1683-84.	Vice-Chancellor. (Also in 1696-98).
1685.	Death of Charles II. Accession of James II. Execution of the Duke of Monmouth.
1687.	Prebendary at York. (Dates unknown: proceeded D.D.; prebendary of Canterbury; rector of St. Botolph's Church, Cambridge).
1688.	James II deposed in the 'Glorious Revolution'.
1689.	William III and Mary II accede as co-monarchs. William III visits Cambridge University in October.
1694.	Death of Mary II.
1700.	Appointed Regius Professor of Divinity. Rector of Somersham, Cambridgeshire.
1702.	Death of William III. Accession of Queen Anne.
1705.	Visit of Queen Anne to Queens'.
1706-07.	Acts of Union, uniting England and Scotland as the single state of Great Britain.
1708.	Attempted invasion in Scotland by James Stuart, the 'Old Pretender', son of James II. Death of Prince George of Denmark, (consort of Queen Anne).
1714.	Death of Queen Anne. Accession of George I, Elector of Hanover.
1715.	Failed Jacobite rebellion led by the Old Pretender.
1717.	Dies in office, unmarried. The longest-serving President to date.

Chaplain to Charles II. Elected President by royal mandate. Regius Professor of Divinity. Hosted two royal visits to Queens'. The longest-serving President to date, who was frustrated by his lack of further promotion.

Henry James was born in about 1642, the son of Henry James, rector of Kingston, Somerset and of Crowcombe, Somerset. (The upper storey of the present Church House, Crowcombe, was used by the Carew Charity School during c1660-1872, for about 40 children from poor families in Crowcombe and Clatworthy, and its records show that one of its supporting legacies was from: 'Rev. Dr. Henry James, son of a past rector').[1] James was sent to Eton College and, in 1661, entered Magdalene College, Cambridge, although he moved to Queens' the following year. He was elected a fellow of Queens' in 1664 and was aged only 33 when elected President in 1675. He would become the longest-serving President to date.

He became an honorary 'Chaplain in Ordinary' to Charles II and, in 1664, produced his only published work: 'A Sermon Preached before the King at Newmarket October 11. 1674. By Henry James Chaplain in Ordinary to His Majesty, and Fellow of Queen's College in Cambridge. Printed by His Majesties special Command. London, Printed by William Godbid, 1674'. This begins:

'St. Luke 1. 74,75. –Might serve Him without fear, in holiness and righteousness before Him all the days of our life.

Whoever he be that considers himself, and that seriously reflects upon his own frame and constitution, or those excellent purposes he seems by God and Nature fitted for, can neither conclude himself the Author of his own Being, or design'd to live only to himself, without any regard at all to a Superior.

The perpetual obligations he lies under for being made Man, and that common protection of Life whereby he is supported, the Mercies of Health and Liberty, and the reasonable expectation of Happiness hereafter, must needs mind him of a duty owing to the Benign Parent of all things, to the Comfort and Stay of our Lives, our God and Saviour…'. The sermon concludes with a positive message for his royal patron:

'For why may we not reasonably presume, that when good Kings come to dye, as dye they must, and fall like other Men, Millions of the Spirits of their own just Subjects made perfect, and the Angels of God shall wait their departure hence, and wing their Great Souls with triumph into the Celestial Habitation, there presenting them to the Holy and Undivided Trinity, that they may be incorporated into the Number of Saints, be Crown'd with Diadems of Immortality, and receive an Inheritance incorruptible, and undefiled, and that fadeth not away, reserv'd in Heaven for those who are kept by the power of God through faith unto salvation.

Oh, that this may be the Portion of all Christian Kings, Princes, and Governours, and specially of Him, for whom our Souls desire to bless God, that this may be the Portion of all that study to enlarge the Empire of the Holy Jesus in Truth and Goodness, that Protect His Church, that Defend His Faith, and that this may be the Portion of all the World that live in obedience to that Faith, and make Conscience of Serving God in Holiness and Righteousness before Him all the days of their Life. Amen'. From the Crown's viewpoint, James is described as: 'a vigorous defender of religious orthodoxy'.[2]

In the following year, 1675, following the death of William Wells, James was elected President of Queens', on the 29th of July, by royal mandate, nominated: 'as a particular mark of Our grace and favour towards our said Chaplaines'.[2] This was the third time in succession that the President of Queens' was supplied by a royal mandate. (Gray, in his history of the College of 1898, claims that there was some support from the fellows for Simon Patrick, as had been the case in the election of 1662, and that James was deputed to ask the King that no mandate be sent; but no sources are cited).[1] Twigg, in his history of the College of 1987, quotes a contemporary account of James' election in the diary of Samuel Newton, a local alderman, two days after the death of William Wells:

'This day it is reported that Doctor Belke of that Colledge is to succeed in that Mastership. But on the next morning…came downe from London to that Colledge Mr James one of the Fellowes of that Colledge with a Mandamus from the King for him the said Mr James to be Master, and he was that morning accordingly admitted Master of the said Colledge, and sworne by Dr Boldero, Vice-Chancellor, all done before 11 of the Clock that morning, the King alsoe as it is said then gave the said Mr James who was one of his Chaplins, a Prependayryes place at Windsor'.[3] (Thomas Belke was a fellow of Queens' during 1655-76 and, later, rector of Wickhambreux, Kent, and prebendary of Canterbury).

In 1676, James is one of the signatories of an attempt by the University to curb how some students have behaved since time immemorial:

'WHEREAS there hath lately been much complaint of loose scholars resorting to divers houses in this town of Cambridge infamous for harbouring lewd women, for the preventing of such scandalous wickedness it is ordered and decreed by the vice-chancellor and heads whose names are underwritten That hereafter no scholar whatsoever (excepting officers of the university performing their duty in searching houses) upon whatsoever pretence shall enter into the house of Abraham Achersely at the green dragon in Trinity parish, or of William Shepheard at the three feathers in saint Edward's parish, or of the Widow Gilson at the saracen's head upon the causeway to Queen's College...or into any other house of bad report in Cambridge: and that if any scholar shall presume to disobey this order he shall for his misdemeanour and for his contumacy immediately be expelled from the university...'.[4] Hopefully, this did not give the students any new information! (Yes- I have also heard it before!).

In 1681, Charles II and Queen Catherine visited the University:

'...As they came to the schools, they found the Regent-Walk crouded on both sides with Regents and Non-Regents, through whose joyful Applauses they walk'd till they came near two Chairs of State; the Vice-Chancellor, Heads of Colleges, and all the Doctors standing in their Scarlet Robes...the Royal Pair went to King's College Chapel...From whence they went to Trinity College; and...to St. John's College, where...the Master and Vice-Chancellor...entertain'd their Majesties in his long Gallery, with so much Grandeur and Satisfaction at Dinner...that....he declared at large, how highly he was satisfy'd with his Reception, and the Regard he would always have for the University of Cambridge... In Sum, the whole was so great and magnificent, and withal so zealous and hearty...that the Court was never better satisfy'd with any Entertainment...'.[4] However this account omits another part of their visit, recorded in the Queens' archives, when Charles II and his Queen:

'did us the Honour to visit this College where they staid about an houre'.[2] But the honour was tempered by the cost to the College of £26, (calculated as equivalent to £3,000 today), for presents and a looking-glass for the Queen.[2] William Sedgwick, a later President, writes that the Queen had wanted to use a chamber pot when she was in the Lodge, but the President:

'not being provided of one Handsome enough made her wait till he sent to King's Coll: to borrow a Silver one for her use. She retired into ye Room, now my Study, formerly call'd ye Essex from Q.Eliz's Earl, and Dr James afterwards Christened it (I suppose with some of Her Majesty's Water) "In perpetuam rei memoriam ye Queens' Chamber", which name it still retains'.[2] Also in 1681, the Vice-Chancellor and heads, including: 'Dr James', made the following decree:

'WHEREAS several under-graduates and batchelors of arts have of late neglected to wear such gowns as by order and custom are proper for those of their rank and standing in the university, whereby the common distinction of degrees is taken away...it was this day in consistory RESOLVED ORDERED AND DECREED... that none residing in the university under the degree of master of arts shall hereafter upon any pretence whatsoever be allowed to appear publickly...in mourning gowns...but what by order and custom of the university belongs to their degree and standing...'.[4]

After the Duke of Monmouth's magnificent installation as Chancellor of Cambridge University in 1674, his relationship with his father, the King, had seriously deteriorated. This was in the context of increasing anti-Catholic sentiment, with rumours that Catholics were plotting to seize power, and a concern about the planned succession of the Catholic Duke of York to the throne;

this was associated with Monmouth's increasing popularity, which could make him a rival heir to the throne. Charles II considered Monmouth to be a threat and banished him from the Kingdom in 1679, and although he soon returned, he was banished from court in 1681, after crowds in London had showed him their support. On the 4th April 1682, the King wrote to the University depriving Monmouth of the Chancellorship and recommending Christopher Monk, Duke of Albemarle, as his successor:

'Charles R. TRUSTY & WELLBELOVED we greet you well. WHEREAS the undutifull behaviour of our Naturall Sonn James Duke of Monmouth, hath given us just cause to remove him from our Service, & any further attendance on our Person, whereby he is rendered uncapable of discharging any longer the Office he bore amongst you of Chancellor of that our University...we doe hereby declare the Chancellor's Office...to be void...AND WHEREAS as well the Integrity & constant Loyalty of our Right trusty & Right entirely Beloved Cosin & Counsellor Christopher Duke of Albemarle...renders him every way qualifyd for the discharge of so high a Trust...WE FURTHER hereby recommend him to your choice...GIVEN at our Court at New-Market...'.[4] Albemarle was duly elected and James will probably have been part of the University contingent for his installation ceremony in London:

'For the more solemn Installment of their new Chancellor, the Heads of the University, with other Members to the Number of two Hundred and fifty, repair'd to London, and made a pompous Procession in all their Robes and Habits, from Northumberland-House to Albemarle-House. Here the Ceremony was perform'd with great Decency and Grandeur...The whole was concluded by a noble and splendid Entertainment...'.[4]

In the relatively uneventful year beginning November 1683, James served as Vice-Chancellor, when the issues considered by the University included the regulations for the University Library.[4]

In 1685, James would have been one of the heads in the procession of the University to the Market Place, when James II was proclaimed as King on the 9th February.[4] In his short reign, James II caused some resentment at Cambridge, by his attempts to appoint Catholic or Catholic sympathisers, to University positions, and the Vice-Chancellor, Dr Peachell, was deprived of his office: 'for an act of great disobedience' in resisting a royal mandate. However, he was reinstated in 1688, shortly before the change of regime in the 'Glorious Revolution'.

Twigg, in his history of the College of 1987, notes that most of the University opposed James II's Catholic policies and celebrated his overthrow and the accession of William and Mary, although about 40 University members, (over half of them from St John's College, but only one from Queens'), had to leave for refusing the required oath of allegiance to the new sovereigns.[2] In 1688, after the arrival in London of the Prince of Orange, soon to be William III:

'the mob here (in Cambridge) made dilligent search for those members of the University who were, or were suspected to be, inclined to Popery, many of whom narrowly escaped by getting out of town by private ways'.[4] But the 'Revolution' also provided an opportunity for those who liked an excuse to make trouble:

'13th December 1688. This night & several nights before there were upp in armes a great many in this Towne some nights 2, or 300, (many scholars among them) of ye rabble called the Mobile, who at first under a pretence to seek for papists & such who had favoured them & to ransack their houses for armes, at last came to be very insulting & wherever they pleased to enter men's houses & doe them much mischief...'.[4]

On the 14th February 1689, King William and Queen Mary were proclaimed as co-monarchs in Cambridge,[4] and James must have been concerned when, on the 20th June, the House of Commons received a report that copies of a Declaration by the deposed monarch had been sent to him and the Master of St John's. The Journals of the House of Commons note:

'Sir John Guise acquaints the House, That several of the Declarations of King James the Second have been taken to Cambridge; and that there was one Thomas Fowler at the Door... (who) gave an Account, that they came down by Carriers in Boxes, directed to the Master of Queens' College, and Master of St. John's College...But Sir Robert Sawyer, One of the Burgesses for the University, acquainted the House, That he had received

Information, that the Boxes were both carried to, and now remain with the Vice-Chancellor'.[5]

In October 1689, William III visited Cambridge, when James would have been one of the welcoming heads of colleges:

'On Sunday last, the Vice-Chancellor, the Heads of the Colledges, and Doctors in all Faculties, with several Regents and Non-Regents, in their proper habits, waited upon His Majesty at Newmarket, being introduced into his Royal presence by his Grace the Duke of Somerset, Chancellor of the University...They then waited upon His Majesty to Church, and at their return from thence were conducted to the King's House, where by Directions from His Majesty, they were received and splendidly entertained at Dinner by Sir James Forbes, Clerk of the Green Cloth (who organised royal journeys and the royal household). The next day His Majesty was pleas'd to make a Visit to the University...'.[5]

In February 1695, James may have been one of the heads of Colleges present when the King, at Kensington, was presented with:

'a most dutiful and loyal address from the Chancellor and Senate of the University, condoling the death of the Queen, whom they term "that incomparable Patroness of Religion and Learning"...and praying Almighty God to bless his Majesty with a long life and prosperous reign for the defence of His Church, the Honour and Welfare of this Kingdom and the publick benefit of the Christian World...'.[5]

During 1696-98, James again filled the office of Vice-Chancellor, (for each year in office the incumbant was usually appointed in early November, so that most of each year in office was during the following calendar year), and, in November 1697, as Vice-Chancellor, together with several heads, the University's Proctors and the two members of Parliament for the University, he accompanied the Chancellor, the Duke of Somerset, who presented a loyal address to King William at Kensington. The occasion was the conclusion of the peace of Ryswick and the King's return to England. The delegation also included the Archbishop of Canterbury and the Bishops of Ely, Norwich, Peterborough, Lincoln and Chester,[5] who tell the King:

'We your Majesties most Dutiful and Loyal Subjects, the Chancellor, Masters, and Scholars of your University of Cambridge, do with all humility congratulate your Majesties return to your Kingdoms in safety, as that great and comprehensive blessing, which completes and confirms to us the happiness we owe to your Majesty, in the conclusion of a most honourable Peace...'.[5] Also, the University published a volume of poems to commemorate this event, and James, again as Vice-Chancellor, presented a copy to the King at Kensington in December.[4] (The Peace of Ryswick was a series of treaties ending the 'Nine Years' War' between France and the 'Grand Alliance', which included England, the Dutch Republic, Spain and the Holy Roman Empire).

James remained Vice-Chancellor during most of 1698 and, in April, the University and Town of Cambridge were charged a tax of over £2000, (estimated at over £200,000 today), mainly for disbanding forces and paying seamen. In the same week, James, as Vice-Chancellor, together with other heads, went to Newmarket: 'to congratulate the King on his arrival at that place', also present was the Chancellor, the Duke of Somerset.[5] (James may have been among the heads that accompanied the then Vice-Chancellor, Sir William Dawes, on a similar mission in 1699, when:

'...His Majesty received them very graciously; and they were afterwards entertained at Dinner by His Majesty's particular Command').[5]

As President, James' fortunes increased further, although he was not to receive a bishopric. But he proceeded D.D., received prebends at York (in 1687) and Canterbury and, in 1700, was appointed Regius Professor of Divinity at Cambridge.[1] He then became rector of Somersham, Cambridgeshire, as this benefice had been added to the stipend of his professorship. Also, at an unknown date, he was appointed rector of St Botolph's, Cambridge. But Twigg speculates that his further promotions and preferments did not satisfy someone who was hoping for high ecclesiastical office and, in 1681, he had written to the Archbishop of Canterbury's secretary:

'I was betraied into drudgery and slavery (ie into the Presidency) by some who are gone when I accepted of this place, which I owne to have been the great error of my life and would most willingly expiate by leaving it when ever my superiors shall think fit'.[3] (Let us hope that this was just an off-day!).

Although James only published one work, (his sermon to the King at Newmarket), Twigg notes that he was famed for his performances as a chief examiner or 'moderator'. This was an important role, requiring the delivery of a summing up and adjudication at the end of a disputation, and his efforts were unusually long, learned and detailed. A contempory reports that he had seen:

'the late Professor James so ready and fluent at the work on publick occasions, that strangers have been greatly surprised at it, and could hardly be convinced that there had not been some management and private correspondence beforehand between Professor and respondent'.[2]

William III died in 1702 and, in the absence of a direct heir, he was succeeded by Anne, his late wife's sister. She was proclaimed by the University on the 10th March, and the death of William III was commemorated by the University by the publication of a book of poems. James may have been among the heads at the subsequent presentation of an address to the new Queen, by the Duke of Somerset:

'We your Majesty's most dutiful & Loyal Subjects, the Chancellor, Masters, and Scholars, of your University of Cambridge, who were deeply afflicted at the death of our late Sovereign King William, of most glorious Memory, humbly beg leave to express our hearty sorrow on that sad occasion; and at the same time with unfeigned duty and affection to congratulate your Majesty's happy Accession to the Throne of your Royal Ancestors…'.[5]

Queen Anne came to Cambridge in April 1705, when she visited Queens' to be entertained by the President, after attending prayers at King's College Chapel:[2]

'Her Majesty having been graciously pleased to declare her intentions of Visiting the University of Cambridge…was received a mile out of Town by the Mayor, Aldermen, Common Council, & the rest of the Corporation…Her Majesty proceeded towards this place amidst the acclamations of an infinite number of people, who made a Lane to the end of the Town...The ways were all along strowed with flowers; the bells rung; & the conduits run with wine. In the Regent walk which leads to the Schools, Her Majesty was received by his Grace the Duke of Somerset, Chancellor of the University, in his Habit, at the head of the Doctors...Her Majesty went up into the Regent House, where, as is usual upon so great & extraordinary a solemnity, Degrees in the several Faculties were...conferred upon persons of high Nobility and distinguished Merit. Dr. James, the Queen's professor in Divinity, opened that Ceremony with a very learned & eloquent Speech...From the Schools Her Majesty went to Trinity College... and...was pleased to confer the Honour of Knighthood upon John Ellis Esq. Doctor in Physick, & Vice Chancellor of the University...& Isaac Newton, Esq., formally Mathematick Professor, & fellow of that College: Then about 300 Ladies & Gentlewomen were admitted to kiss Her Majesty's hand. Her Majesty was afterwards entertained at Dinner in Trinity College Hall...Her Majesty went from thence to Prayers in King's College Chapel...After Prayers Her Majesty went to Queen's College, where she was received by Dr. James, in the same manner, & with the same expression of Duty & Loyalty, as she had been in the other Houses...From thence Her Majesty took Coach, and returned the same evening to Newmarket, very well satisfied...'.[5]

In 1708, there was an attempted invasion of Scotland by James Stuart, the son of James II and known as the 'Old Pretender', which prompted the Chancellor to present another address to the Queen, attended by various dignatories including College heads:

'We your Majesty's most loyal and dutiful subjects the Chancellor, Masters & Scholars of the University of Cambridge, BEING highly sensible of the manifest injury design'd to your Majesty's undoubted right & title to these your Dominions, which a pretender from France has threaten'd to invade, humbly crave leave to express our utmost abhorrence of this and all other attempts which may be made to disturb the inestimable happiness We enjoy under your Majesty's most gracious administration...'.[5]

The Queen's consort, Prince George of Denmark, died in 1708, deeply mourned by his wife. The University published a commemorative collection of Latin and Greek verses and amongst the authors was: 'Henry James D.D. President of Queens' College'.[5]

In 1710, James became involved in a controversy over the religious views of William Whiston, a theologian, historian and mathematician, who was Isaac Newton's successor as Lucasian Professor of Mathematics:

'On the 23rd of October, William Whiston M.A. Lucasian Professor, appeared (in pursuance of a citation served upon him the preceding day) at King's College Lodge before Dr. Roderick the Vicechancellor and nine other Heads of Colleges (including: "Dr. James Master of Queens' College and Regius Professor of Divinity")'.[5] But after further meetings, Whiston withdrew from the proceedings and was duly banished from the University:

'October, 30th, 1710. AT A MEETING of Mr. Vicechancellor, and the Heads of Colleges in the University of Cambridge, in the Vicechancellor's Chamber, in King's College, In the said University. WHEREAS it hath been proved before Us, That William Whiston, Master of Arts, Mathematick Professor of this University, hath asserted and spread about in Cambridge, since the 19th day of April, 1709, divers Tenets against Religion, receiv'd and establis'd by Publick Authority in this Realm, contrary to the Forty Fifth Statute of this University ...(and)...did refuse to make any such Confession and Retraction...the said William Whiston...be banished from this University ...C. RODERICK Vicechancellor... HEN. JAMES...'.[5]

In April 1713, at St James's Palace, London: 'several heads of Houses' were again accompanying the Vice-Chancellor, when he presented an address to the Queen on the conclusion of the Peace of Utrecht. (This was a series of treaties between various states, including France, Great Britain and Spain, to end the 'War of the Spanish Succession', which had followed the death of the childless Charles II of Spain in 1700 and involved the battles of Blenheim, Ramillies, Oudenarde and Malplaquet. It was finally agreed that Philip, grandson of Louis XIV of France, would be allowed to take the Spanish throne, while losing his and his descendants' claim to the French throne):

'Most Gracious Sovereign, We humbly beg leave to congratulate your Majesty with the greatest joy, upon the happy conclusion of a peace, and the securing of the Protestant succession, whereof we have the fullest assurances from that perfect friendship which there is between your Majesty and the Illustrious House of Hanover, which we hope no Artifices will ever be able to impair...'.[5]

Queen Anne died on the 1st August 1714 and was succeeded by George I, the ruler of the Duchy and Electorate of Hanover, and the University lost no time in proclaiming the new King:

'On the 3rd of August, Dr Lany...summoned the Heads of Houses, and the Doctors of all Faculties, to meet him at the Schools, where being assembled and attended by the Masters of Arts and Students, they proceeded in their formalities to the Market-Cross, and Proclaimed His Majesty with the usual Solemnity...'.[5] Also, on the 22nd September at St James's Palace, the Duke of Somerset, accompanied by many dignatories including: 'more than twenty Heads of Houses', presented an address to the King from the University:

'May it please your most Sacred Majesty, We your Majesty's most Dutiful and Loyal Subjects, the Chancellor, Masters & Scholars of your University of Cambridge, do most humbly beg leave to approach your Sacred person, to condole with your Majesty, for the death of our late most Gracious Sovereign Queen Anne...At the same time, we cannot but adore the Divine goodness, which has ally'd our Griefs & dispell'd our fears by your Majesty's peaceable accession to the Imperial Crown of these Kingdoms, & your safe arrival to your people...It would be unpardonable folly, & downright infatuation, if any of your Majesty's Protestant Subjects should turn their eyes to a Popish Pretender, who can never reign over us...May your life be long, & your reign happy!...'.[5]

However, there were riots in England after George's coronation in October 1714 and, the following year, the Jacobites, (who wanted to restore the House of Stuart to the throne), started uprisings in Scotland and Cornwall. After Jacobite forces had been defeated at Preston, Lancashire, and had fought an inconclusive engagement at Sheriffmuir, Scotland, James Stuart, the Old Pretender, landed at Peterhead in December 1715. However, he soon abandoned his allies, returning to France in February 1716. During these events, on the 16th August 1715, with the expectation of an invasion, the Chancellor of Cambridge University: 'attended by the Vicechancellor and several Masters of Colleges' presented another address to the King at St James' Palace:

'We presume to appear in your Royal presence to testify our Zeal & Affection to your person & Government, called to it by the just concern we are under from the danger which threatens your Majesty & your people, a danger in which not only the present Age, but even the latest posterity is deeply concerned; for the Liberty & establish'd religion of Britain...we do assure your Majesty that we have & will so instruct the youth committed to our care, that in the dutiful behaviour towards your Majesty they may shew forth an example of those Principles of Loyalty & obedience, which this University, pursuing the Doctrines of our Church, has ever steadily maintained'.[5] In October 1716, after the suppression of the rebellion, an address of congratulation to the King was delivered by representatives of the University in the presence of several heads, but this was delivered to the Prince of Wales at Hampton Court, as the King was in Europe:

'...we had been among the earliest messengers of the common joy and congratulation for your victory over Rebels, had not our intention been frustrated by an unforseen & unexampled impediment, which now being removed, we take the first opportunity to Shew to your Majesty & the world, that it was not our want of duty or affection but our misfortune and calamity...'.[5] (This referred to the delay before presentation of an address which had been drawn up several months previously, in April 1716. But this had run into some opposition in the University, before being eventually approved by the Non-Regent House, 36 for and 15 against, and by the Regent House, 34 for and 14 against).[5] There was a further address from the University to the King on the

12th March 1717, congratuating him on: 'your safe return to your Kingdom of Great Britain',[5] but although this was accompanied, as usual, by: 'several Heads of Houses', James was probably not present on this occasion, as he died 3 days later, on the 15th of March, 1717.

A later President, Robert Plumptre, describes James, despite the latter's views on his Presidential duties, as having been: 'very attentive to the business and interest of the College',[2] and we have many examples of his domestic concerns.

In his second year as President, James decided, with the unanimous consent of the fellows, that only Latin should be spoken in hall at: 'dinner and supper', although some days were excepted. But this must have proved too onerous as, in 1680, there was a further relaxation of the rule, so that English could also be spoken on Sundays and holidays.[1]

James kept a handwritten account of many events and, in several entries, describes recurrent difficulties involving Francis Master, who was a Queens' fellow during 1677-85:

'...Upon Mr Master's confession that he was guilty of that ungratefull and inhuman act, (destroying fruit trees in the President's orchard), and upon owning himself very sorry for it and upon his earnest entreating of my pardon, I was willing to pass it by, after he had subscribed wth his owne hand those words. Viz., "I am asham'd of ye Act"...'.

'Mr. Master, privately admonished for Pernoctation (staying out of College at night) Mar.3, 1678, again privately admonish'd for his loose living...'.

'...in Jan. 1679 came to officiate at Chappell on a Sunday in ye Evening much disorder'd wth drink. In ye same yeare from Shrove Monday until ye Friday in Whitsun-week never at ye Chappell foure times, lieing for ye most part out of ye Coll dureing all that time, and that at houses of noe good note...'.

'Mr. Master return'd to ye Coll about Shrove-tide in ye yeare 1679 and having lain in ye Town for ye most part at ye 3 Tuns for 5 weeks together and never been at Chappell nor in ye Hall dureing all that time, was on 14 Apr: 1680...sent into ye country and not to return without leave, return'd again iin Oct:

since wch time he has liv'd very disorderly lieing for ye most part out of ye Coll...but now, viz Nov. 29, 1680, appearing before myselfe and ye Society at a publick meeting he was then... Admonish'd according to Statute for his scandalous manner of Living & ye reproach he brought upon ye Coll. Hen James'.[1] One can only wonder at the forebearance of James and the fellowship, but there is no record of further problems, and Master must have mended his ways to some extent, as he was appointed to two livings near Canterbury after vacating his fellowship in 1685.[1]

Twigg notes that James' memorandum book shows a detailed interest in financial matters and that he was: 'precise and fair, but fussy, a stickler for the rules'.[2] In the 1680s he recorded his concerns about the College finances and the risk of debt:

'were it not for the absences of men from the College, or for that the number of 15 Priests is not compleat, or the schollarships not full, and we have noe way to be reliev'd but by the Focalia-Bill (sales of timber) which is a mere contingent thing'.[2] He considers that the bursars should be:

'very carefull to retrench all unnecessary expences, especially that of the Audit; which of late yeares amounts to a scandalous sum, and exceeds the ability of our small Revenue as much as it does the measures of a laudable and honest hospitality for our Tenants'.[2] In 1682, he describes the: 'great repaires' which had depleted the reserves:

'This yeare all ye first Court was stripp'd, ye Sparrs wch in many places were very bad new lin'd, all ye upper Windows made new & regular, the great Gate alter'd. ye Gate-House & Regent-Walk (across the Court) new laid with Freestone, ye bow-window in ye Hall repair'd with Freestone & new glass there, ye Dialls new painted...a Cupola new made &c. all w^h make ye moneth acct (monthly account) swell to soe great a sum'.[1] In 1708, James stressed the need to obtain the best possible deal from the charges to College tenants for entry and renewal of leases, (in 1678, the College had tried to eject its tenant at Haslingfield),[2] and he complained that Queens' tenants were obtaining tax exemptions from the College, but passing the tax on to their subtenants.[2]

In 1708, James records a glimpse of everyday College life, when a clergyman:

'came hither to enquire whether Archbishop Mountain did not found two Scholarships and whether his son who is now a boy of ten years old might not have one of them when he came to the University. I told him I did not doubt but that he might, but that in probability I should not live soe long'.[2]

There were tensions with the fellowship in 1715, when seven fellows appealed to the Chancellor to reverse James' refusal to admit William Ayerst to a fellowship after the latter had, allegedly, been elected in 1714. A later speculation was that James had acted:

'on account of his Godson, whom he could no otherwise hope to make fellow.[2] However, he got his way, and Ayerst was not admitted until after James' death. (Ayerst, an Oxford graduate, was a fellow during 1717-18 and would hold several Church appointments, including a canon of Canterbury Cathedral).

James was unmarried and made various bequests; those to Queens' included an estate at Haddenham, Cambridgeshire, and he financed the foundation of four: 'poor scholarships'. Also, an allowance of 2s. 6d. per week provided meat for four poor people, one of whom was to be the College scullion (ie an unskilled kitchen worker), and he gave over £600 for the purchase of a Church benefice for one of the eight senior fellows in holy orders, to be chosen by the President rather than the fellows.[1,2] This allowed the purchase of the living of Grimston, Norfolk. Also, he left his books to the College library and £50 for new purchases. Previously, in 1701, he had given the College £20, specifying that £1 should be paid on Christmas eve to eight almswomen: 'for the purchase of a Christmas dinner...',[1] and such a demonstration of concern for others is consistent with the following very positive appraisal of his Presidency:

'He had proved himself an excellent Master, very attentive to the business and interests of the College during his life, and was a considerable Benefactor to it at his death'.[1]

A monumental tablet to James can be found in the ante-chapel of the present Queens' chapel, and is one of five that were moved from their original positions in the ante-chapel of the old chapel.

References

1. Gray, J.H. The Queens' College of St Margaret and St Bernard. F.E.Robinson. London. 1898. pp 216-31.
2. Twigg, J. A History of Queens' College, Cambridge. 1448-1986. The Boydell Press. 1987. pp 136, 148-52, 179, 190, 203-04, 300-04.
3. Twigg, J. The Appointment of Henry James as President in 1675. The Record 1990. Queens' College, Cambridge. Online. 2020.
4. Cooper, C.H. Annals of Cambridge. Volume III. Warwick and Co., Cambridge. 1845. pp 571-72, 588-97, 600-06, 643-44.
5. Cooper, C.H. Annals of Cambridge. Volume IV. Warwick and Co., Cambridge. 1845. pp 2-10, 29,36-42, 50-51, 71-72, 81-85, 102-03, 111, 121-23, 138-46, 168.

CHAPTER 23

John Davies. President 1717-32.

Summary.

John Davies was born in 1679 in London. After attending Charterhouse School he came to Queens' in 1695 and was elected a fellow in 1701. He soon developed a reputation for classical scholarship, publishing an edition of the writings of Maximus of Tyre in 1703. In 1709, he published the first volume of his most important work, editions of Cicero's philosophical writings.

He was ordained at Ely in 1711, acquiring the Bishop, John Moore, as his patron, who presented him with two benefices in the same year.

On the death of Henry James in 1717, Davies, who was a 'Whig' and supporter of the Hanoverian succession, became President of Queens' in a free election, with the support of the Lord Chief Justice. His political stance was rewarded later in the year, when George I visited the University and Davies received an honorary D.D..

Richard Bentley, Master of Trinity College since 1700, was the foremost classical scholar of his day and a friend of Davies. Bentley influenced Davies' work and provided an appendix for one of the latter's publications. But Bentley's years in Cambridge were marked by conflict due to his temper and challenging behaviour, and Davies was the only head to support his friend, when the University deprived him of his degrees in 1718.

Davies was elected Vice-Chancellor in 1725-26 and served during an uneventful year. We know nothing about his family life, although he was married. He died in 1732 and is buried in the original Queens' chapel.

Timeline.

1675. Henry James elected President of Queens' by royal mandate.

1679. Born in London.

1685. Death of Charles II. Accession of James II.

1688. James II deposed in the 'Glorious Revolution'.

1689. Accession of William III and Mary II as co-monarchs.

1695. Admitted to Queens' after attending Charterhouse School.

1699. B.A. .

1701. Fellow of Queens'.

1702. M.A. . Death of William III. Accession of Queen Anne.

1703. Publishes the first edition of his commentary: 'Maximi Tyrii Dissertationes'.

1709. Junior Proctor of the University. Publishes the first part of a series of new editions of Cicero's philosophical writings: 'M. Tullii Ciceronis Tusculanarum Disputationum'.

1711. Ordained at Ely. His patron, John Moore, Bishop of Ely, appoints him rector of Fen Ditton, Cambridgeshire, and a prebendary of Ely. Proceeds LL.D. . Around this time he becomes one of the Bishop's chaplains.

1712. Appointed rector of Glemsford, Suffolk, (this will be vacated in 1718). Vacates Queens' fellowship.

1714. Death of Queen Anne. Accession of George I, Elector of Hanover.

1715. Failed Jacobite rebellion.

1717. Death of Henry James. Davies succeeds as President of Queens' in a free election, with the support of Thomas Parker, Lord Chief Justice. Visit of George I to the University. As a committed 'Whig' and supporter of the Hanovarian succession, Davies receives the degree of D.D. during the visit.

1718. The only head to support his friend Richard Bentley, Master of Trinity College, when the latter is deprived of his University degrees. Loses an election for Vice-Chancellor to Thomas Gooch.

1719. Spain supports an unsuccessful Jacobite-led invasion of Scotland. The University delivers a loyal address to George I.

1720.	An economic crisis, (the 'South Sea Bubble'), contributes to George I's unpopularity. The University delivers another loyal address to George I.
1725-26.	Vice-Chancellor.
1727.	George I dies abroad. Accession of George II. The University delivers a loyal address to George II.
1732.	Dies. Buried in the original Queens' chapel. A wife, Sarah, is mentioned in his will.

Clergyman. Eminent classicist. 'Whig' and Hanoverian supporter.

John Davies was born in London on the 22nd April 1679, the son of a London merchant, who died when Davies was young, and Elizabeth, daughter of Sir John Turton, justice of the court of the King's Bench.[1] (The list of King's Bench justices state that Turton was dismissed in 1702, having been appointed in 1696). He came to Queens' in 1695, after attending Charterhouse School and graduated B.A. in 1699. He became a fellow of Queens' in 1701, before proceeding M.A. in 1702. In 1709, he served as Junior Proctor of the University, whose duties included representing the colleges in University proceedings. In 1711, at Ely Cathedral, he was ordained deacon on the 21st of September and priest two days later. Around this time, he acquired the Bishop of Ely, John Moore, as a patron, and, later in 1711, Davies was presented by the Bishop to the rectory of Fen Ditton, Cambridgeshire, as well as to a prebend at Ely.[1] Also in 1711, he obtained the LL.D degree and, in the following year, Moore presented Davies with another living, that of Glemsford, Suffolk, which he held until 1718.

The Universities were caught up in the development of party politics in the early eighteenth century, with bitter divisions between 'Whigs' and 'Tories'. Twigg, in his history of the College of 1987, notes that:

'both the Whigs and the Tories represented a complex, shifting mixture of personal alliance, tradition and ideals',[2] but Tories tended to be 'high' church- with an emphasis on ceremony and doctrine, sympathetic to the Jacobites and unenthusiastic about the Hanoverian succession, while the Whigs were more tolerant of variations in religious views and firm supporters of George I and his successors. While Oxford University was a Tory stronghold in the eighteenth century, Cambridge was associated with Whiggism, although Tories won several politically-partisan elections for Vice-Chancellor during the reign of George I.[2]

Davies was a strong Whig supporter and, on the death of Henry James in 1717, he was elected as his successor as President of Queens' by a free vote. Twigg notes that he was supported by Thomas Parker, a Trinity College alumnus, and the future Earl of Macclesfield.[2] (Parker had been elected a Whig Member of Parliament in 1705. He was appointed Lord Chief Justice in 1710 and Lord Chancellor in 1718, but his influence ended when he was convicted of corruption in 1725).

George I had an enthusiastic reception from the University at his visit on the 6th of October 1717:

'About 11 o'clock the King alighted from his carriage at the Regent-walk, in the middle of which he took his seat in a chair of state in the open air...His Majesty was then conducted with a mixture of royal and academical ceremony, to the Regent-house... Hereupon the creation of some of the new Doctors, the only specimen of academical proceedings, which the shortness of time would allow, took place with full ceremonial. After the grace had passed for the degrees of all persons named in the Royal mandate, Dr Bentley, as Regius Professor, presented to the Chancellor three of the number, who were Heads of Houses, Mr. Grigg, Dr. Davies (previously only Doctor of Laws) and Mr. Waterland...He then created the three Doctors of Divinity. The academical business thus concluded, the august company went in procession to the magnificent chapel of King's College, the glory of the University; in the nave of which the King was addressed in another speech from the Provost; his Majesty probably understanding these Latin orations better than anything else which he heard that day...The procession then left the chapel for Trinity College...A distressing mistake now occurred. The Vice-chancellor wishing that his own beautiful college should have its share of the Royal admiration, chose to conduct the procession the back way to Trinity, in order that it might pass by Clare Hall. Thus his Majesty, after a passing glance at that House, was led to the Queen's gate of Trinity: but ... his arrival being of course expected at the King's-gate, the Master and the whole college were drawn up there for his reception, while all the inhabitants of the town were assembled on the outside: meantime the other entrance had been closed...Thus did the King find the entrance of his Royal college barred against him, and was compelled to stand five minutes in the lane, which is described to have been at that time "a most dirty, filthy place"...At length his Majesty obtained admission, and Dr Bentley at the head of the society, meeting him about the middle of the court, bade him "welcome to a college which he might call his own"...'.[3] Another account by Dr David Wilkins, who had also received a doctorate by royal mandate, ends his glowing account of the proceedings, including the King's: 'great deal of satisfaction' at his reception, with the thought: 'What will the Sister University say to this',[3] referring to the political differences between the two English Universities.

The 'Dr Bentley ' in the above account, was Richard Bentley, 1662-1742, whose eventful life is neatly summarised on a blue plaque at his birthplace, Oulton, Yorkshire:

'RICHARD BENTLEY. FRS, DD. Born in 4/5 Bentley Square; educated at Wakefield Grammar School and Cambridge; Keeper of the King's Library at St James' and Master of Trinity College Cambridge. His brilliant translation and reappraisal of classical texts made him one of England's greatest and most controversial scholars'. After a glittering career as a scholar and librarian in London, he was appointed Master of Trinity College in 1700, where he remained until his death in 1742, despite many disputes, feuds and controversies. He antagonised the fellows at Trinity with his various reforms, contemptuous manner and domineering temper, leading, after a decade, to an appeal by the fellows to the College's 'Visitor', the Bishop of Ely, claiming that he had committed 54 breaches of the Statutes. This eventually led to a sentence of expulsion from the Mastership by the Crown lawyers, but it was not executed, and conflict continued for many years. Bentley's problems were not confined to Trinity as, in 1718, the

University deprived Bentley of his degrees for not attending the Vice-Chancellor's court and escalating what started as a minor issue into a major and extended conflict with the University establishment. In 1733, the fellows of Trinity renewed their complaints to the Bishop of Ely, and Bentley was again sentenced to be removed, but the Vice-Master of Trinity, who was a friend, refused to act and Bentley remained in his post.[4]

Davies was a friend of Bentley, whom he supported in the latter's successful bid to become Regius Professor of Divinity in 1717, after the death of Henry James. Also, Davies was the only head to support Bentley in 1718, when a University 'grace' was passed to remove his degrees:[2]

'This unexampled measure was thus effected by more than a double majority: among the dignitaries of the University, a still greater proportion was found on the side of severity. An eye-witness records that a greater display of scarlet robes appeared in the Senate-house on this day, than ever had been seen in the memory of man: of thirty Doctors present, no less than twenty-three voted for the degradation of their brother; and of ten Heads of Colleges, all but one joined in the same cause'.[3] Bentley must have ruffled a lot of feathers!

While Bentley was the preeminent classicist of his day, Davies was also a respected classical scholar, publishing editions and commentaries on the writings of Caesar, Lactantius, Minucius Felix, Maximus of Tyre, and Cicero.[1,2] His first edition of 'Maximi Tyrii Dissertationes' was in 1703,[1,2] while the title page of a later edition reads:

'MAXIMI TYRII DISSERTATIONES, Ex recensione Ioannis Davisii Coll. Regin. Cantab. Praesidis. Editio Altera...Londini Excudit Gulielmus Bowyer Anno MDCCXL'. But Davies' most important works were his editions and commentaries on Cicero's philosophical writings.[2] The first was published in 1709,[1] with an appendix by Bentley, who had a significant influence on Davies' work, while the title page of a 1730 edition reads:

'M. TULLII CICERONIS TUSCULANARUM DISPUTATIONUM Libri V. Cum Commmentario Joannis Davisii Coll. Regin. Cantab. Praesidis. Editio Tertia. Auctior et Emendatior

Cantabrigiae Typis Academicus. Londinenses MDCCXXX'. (After Davies' death, his unfinished edition of Cicero's 'Offices' was in the possession of Bentley's nephew, who was preparing it for publication, when it was destroyed in a fire at a house in the Strand, London).[1,2]

Another friend of Bentley was Joseph Wasse, a fellow of Queens' during 1698-1713.[5] He was also a respected classical scholar, producing editions of Sallust and Thucydidides, and had been one of Davies' students.[2]

The 'Annals of Cambridge' of 1845 provide a detailed account of events leading to Bentley being deprived of his degrees in 1718:

'Dr Conyers Middleton commenced an action of debt in the Vice-chancellor's Court against Richard Bentley D.D. Master of Trinity College and Regius Professor of Divinity. In order to try the right of the latter to a fee of four guineas, which he claimed for creating Dr Middleton on occasion of the King's visit...he (Bentley) called on Dr. Gooch the Vicechancellor at Caius College Lodge, and expostulated with him in high terms, saying among other things which gave offence "that he would not be judged by him and his friends over a bottle"...On the court-day...The Vice-chancellor took his seat, along with six of the Heads as his assessors...who all agreed as to the fact of contempt, and the propriety of inflicting the heaviest punishment in the power of the court- a suspension of the offender from all his degrees. Immediately the Vice-chancellor, uncovering himself, pronounced, in solemn and awful terms, the judgement of the court...This extraordinary act of power...struck with amazement the audience in the Consistory...when they heard such a punishment pronounced upon a Doctor of twenty-two years standing, who possessed the highest preferments, as well as the greatest literary reputation of the whole University. Dr. Gooch was not able to sustain the dignity which such an occasion demanded...he added, with much warmth, (to Mr Lisle, Bentley's representative) "Go tell your friend from me, that if he does not come and make his submission and acknowledge his fault within three days, I will declare his professorship vacant"...'.[3] The feud continued with numerous meetings and appeals, involving the courts, the

Chancellor of the University, the King and the Privy Council, but Bentley did not lose his professorship and his degees were eventually restored in 1724. Although Davies, as a gesture of support for his friend Bentley, opposed the re-election of Dr Gooch as Vice-Chancellor in 1718, he lost the vote 60 to 122, presumably reflecting Bentley's personal unpopularity within the University.[3] Indeed, Gooch was elected Vice-Chancellor for a third year in 1719.[3]

Later editions of Bentley's major work such as: 'Dr Richard Bentley's Dissertation upon The Epistles of Phalaris, Themistocles, Socrates, Euripides and upon The Fables of Aesop. Edited by Wilhelm Wagner. Berlin, S. Calvary and Co. 1874', contain the text of a letter to Davies from Bentley, which provides a vivid illustration of the latter's combative character:

'Copy of a letter from Dr. Bentley to Dr. Davies; found in the latter's Study, after his death, by his Successor at Fen-ditton in Cambridgeshire: xx years after it was written.

Dear Sir, After you left me this morning, I borrowed of Dr. Sike Mr. Barnes's new edition of Homer; where I was told, that I should find myself abus'd. I read over his dedications and prefaces, and there I found very opprobrious words, against enemies in general, and one Homo inimicus in particular which I cannot apply to myself, not being concerned in the accusation. But if Mr. Barnes has, or does declare in company, that he means Me by those expressions; I assure him, I shall not put up such an affront, and an injury too: since I was one of his first subscribers, and a useful director to him, if he had followed good advice. He struts and swaggers, like a Suffenus (Suffenus was a bad poet, ridiculed by another Latin poet, Catullus, c84-54BC), and challenges that same enemy to come aperte, and shew him any fault. If he mean Me, I have but dipt yet into his Notes; and yet I find everywhere just occasion of answers...'.(There now follows a diatribe against various mistakes in the book, interspersed with:... 'Now for this interpolatation alone, his book deserves to be burnt....but our Professor, besides his botching in the words, has sullied even the sense...a piece of ignorance, for which he deserves to be turned out of the Chair...enough to make a man spew, that sees the vanity and insolence of the writer…'). The letter concludes: 'Sir, I write to you, as a common friend, and desire you to shew Mr. Barnes this letter: but not to let him keep it, nor transcribe it. If it be true, that he gives out, that he means Me by those villainous characters; I shall teach him better manners towards his elector. For though I shall not honour him so much, as to enter the lists against him myself; yet in one week's time I can send a hundred such remarks as these to his good friend Will. Baxter; whom I have known these twenty years: who, before the Parliament sits, shall pay him home for his Anacreon. (Anacreon, c582-485BC, was a Greek lyric poet). But, if it be otherwise, that he does not describe Me under those general reproaches: a small satisfaction shall content me; which I leave you to be judge of. For I would not, without the utmost provocation, hurt the sale of his book; upon which he professes to have laid out his whole fortunes. Pray, let me hear from you, as soon as you can. I am &c. Trin Coll. Saturday Evening'. (Joshua Barnes, F.R.S., 1654-1712, was appointed Regius Professor of Greek at Cambridge in 1695, and produced his edition of Homer in 1711).

In June 1719, when Great Britain was part of the 'Quadruple Alliance' against Spain, there was another failed Jacobite rising in Scotland, which had been supported by about 240 Spanish marines and:

'At St James's on the 21st of November, His Grace the Duke of Somerset, Chancellor of the University of Cambridge, attended by Dr. Gooch Vice-chancellour, and a great number of the heads and other Doctors & Members of the University…had the honour to present the following most dutiful and most loyal Address, which passed unanimously in full Senate…MAY IT PLEASE your most Excellent Majesty, To permit us to express before you the joy and satisfaction we feel upon your safe and happy return to this Kingdom; a satisfaction common to us and all your subjects. But as we can never forget your Majesty's Royal Munificence to this University, nor think of it without a sense of the particular Obligation we are under to be zealous in whatever concerns the prosperity of your Majesty & your family; tis our Ambition to appear among the forwardest upon all the happy Occasions of

Congratulations...'.[3] (The 'Royal Munificence' will have referred to the library of Davies' patron, John Moore, Bishop of Ely, which had been purchased by the King for £6,000 and presented to the University in 1715. It had over 30,000 volumes and was considered the greatest benefaction that the University had yet received. Today, this forms the 'Royal Library', within the University Library).

The Chancellor, Vice-Chancellor: 'and a great number of the Heads', presented another loyal address on the 19th November 1720, during the economic crisis caused by the 'South Sea Bubble'; this was a speculation frenzy, when investors lost fortunes by investing in the South Sea Company, founded in 1711 to trade, mainly in slaves, with Spanish America. The King's popularity had declined and he probably appreciated the usual extravagant sentiments in the address.[3]

Davies was elected Vice-Chancellor in 1725 and served for a relatively uneventful year.[3] Many of the heads were present at another address to the King, on 14th of March 1727, the last before the King's death, while abroad, on the 11th of June 1727, when he was succeeded by his son, George II.

The University lost little time in proclaming the new King on the 15th June, and published a volume of celebratory poems. On the 29nd June, at St James's Palace, the Duke of Somerset: 'with a great number of Heads of Houses', presented the University's first address to the new sovereign:

'We come with hearts full of Affection to your Majesty, to congratulate your happy accession to the throne of your Ancestors, & to condole with you for the loss of your royal father, our most honoured & much loved King & Patron, whose memory will be sacred & precious in your University of Cambridge as long as Gratitude continues to be the virtue of generous minds. Under this loss, our greatest comfort is in the prospect now before us, of happy days from your Majesty's known love of the religion, laws, and liberties of this kingdom...'.[3] After a:

'most gracious Answer...His Majesty was pleased to receive them very graciously and they had all the honour to kiss his Majesty's hand'.[3]

In the following year, 1728, George II visited the University:

'His Majesty having signified his pleasure of favouring our University with his Royal presence; on Wednesday the 24th of April, his Majesty being at Newmarket, the Heads of our University waited upon him, to thank him for his intended favour, and to invite him; which his Majesty received very graciously. On the next day he came, attended by about 12 Peers, other Noblemen and Gentlemen; and was met at some distance from the Town by the Mayor and Aldermen on horseback, dressed in their proper habits...'.[3] The King was then subjected to the usual events; a procession, speeches, a degree ceremony at the Regent House, a visit to King's College chapel and then on to Trinity College, where there was:

'a most splendid entertainment consisting of about eight hundred dishes...Whilst he was at dinner, Dr. Bentley stood on his right hand, and discoursed with him very freely...'.[3] Among the 27 doctors that received their honorary degrees, was the preeminent politician of the day, Sir Robert Walpole, whose influence had survived the change of monarch. Apart from the noble and eminent, 286 others also received degrees, paying fees to the University for the privilege. It is to be hoped that this was sufficient compensation for the cost of the visit! The King must have been satisfied, as be donated £2000 towards the cost of the present Senate House, which was begun in 1722 and opened in 1730.[3]

In 1729, Davies was a signatory of a decree from the Vice-Chancellor and heads, concerning the perennial problem of students and alcohol:

'Whereas many and grievous complaints have been made unto us the vice-chancellor and heads of colleges in this university of scholars and students frequenting taverns and other publick houses and there continuing till either by unseasonable hours or great intemperance many disorders and tumults have arisen to the manifest scandal of the university the destruction of all good order and discipline...for the prevention of any such disorders for the future we the vice-chancellor and heads whose names are hereunder written as by statute empowered do order and decree That if any scholar shall at any time resort to any tavern or other publick house otherwise than the statutes do allow, he shall forfeit one shilling amd eight pence...if at a more unseasonable hour or disordered in liquor he shall beside the other penalties be admonished by the vice-chancellor...Any number of scholars under pretence of being of the same year school or county or otherwise assembling together at any publick house shall upon conviction thereof...be suspended from taking any degree till one whole year after the usual time of taking the same...'.[3]

Davies died at Fen Ditton, (where he was rector), on March the 7th 1732, at the age of 52, and is buried in the original Queens' chapel.[1,2,5] The 18th century antiquary, William Cole, describes his monument, which has not survived:

'In ye very middle of ye Chapel & as ye Head of this last lies a very noble Black Marble slab for ye late learned President of the College who in 1709 was Junior Proctor of ye University & succeeded Dr James in ye Office in 1716 at ye time Prebendary of Ely to wch he had been installed 24 Sept. 1711. He was also Rector of Fen Ditton in this County...'.[6]

His will mentions a wife, Sarah, but we know nothing about her, while he entrusted his unfinished manuscript on Cicero's works to a Dr Mead, who gave it to Bentley's nephew, Dr Thomas Bentley, to prepare for publication. Sadly, as noted above, fate intervened in this plan. However, Davies had already left his mark as a classicist.

References

1. Cooper, T. (Revised by Skedd, S.J.) Davies, John. In: Oxford Dictionary of National Biography. 2008. Online. 2019.
2. Twigg, J. A History of Queens' College, Cambridge. 1448-1986. The Boydell Press. 1987. pp 155-57, 180, 216-17.
3. Cooper, C.H. Annals of Cambridge. Volume IV. Warwick and Co., Cambridge. 1845. pp 140, 148-69, 188-89, 192-97, 204.
4. Wikipedia. Richard Bentley. Online. 2020.

5. Gray, J.H. The Queens' College of St Margaret and St Bernard. F.E.Robinson. London. 1898. p 238.
6. Cole, William. The Cole Manuscripts, in the British Library. Add MS 5803, folios 19v-19; Add MS 5808, folios 120v-123v.

CHAPTER 24

William Sedgwick. President 1732-60.

Summary.

William Sedgwick was the son of a rector in Buckinghamshire and was admitted to Queens' in 1716. He became a fellow in 1723 and held several College offices before being elected President in 1732, following the death of John Davies. He held the College living of Oakington, Cambridgeshire and, subsequently, that of St Clement's, Eastcheap, London.

He remained an undistinguished clergyman and served an uneventful year as Vice-Chancellor during 1741-42. During his Presidency he oversaw several building projects at Queens', in particular the construction of the 'Mathematical Bridge' and of the riverside 'Essex Building'. The latter was completed just before his death but only realised part of the original plan. This had been for a much larger building, which proved to be beyond the College's financial resources.

He is described by his successor as: 'a man of weak nerves and an infirm constitution', who, for the last 15 years of his life: 'very rarely went out of the Lodge'. He died in 1760, unmarried, and left generous bequests to the College.

Timeline.

c1700. Born in Buckinghamshire.
1716. Admitted to Queens'.
1717. John Davies elected President of Queens'.
1723. Elected fellow of Queens'. (Dates unknown: M.A., B.D.).
1727. Death of George I. Accession of George II.

1732.	Death of Davies. Sedgwick elected President. Holds the living of Oakington, Cambridgeshire.
1732-24.	Renovations to the hall at Queens'.
c1737.	Rector of St Clement's Church, Eastcheap, London. Vacates living of Oakington.
1740-48.	War of the Austrian Succession.
1741-42.	Vice-Chancellor.
1743.	Battle of Dettingen.
1744.	The University delivers a loyal address to the King
1745.	Jacobite rebellion. The University delivers a loyal addess to the King.
1746.	Battle of Culloden. The University delivers a loyal address to the King.
1748.	Duke of Newcastle elected Chancellor of Cambridge University. Treaty of Aix-la-Chapelle ends the War of the Austrian Succession. The University delivers a loyal address to the King.
1749.	Construction of the 'Mathematical Bridge' at Queens'. Duke of Newcastle installed as Chancellor of Cambridge University.
1756-60.	Construction of the 'Essex Building' at Queens'.
1756-63.	The 'Seven Years' War'.
1757.	Riots in Cambridge over the price of corn.
1760.	Death of George II, (25th October). Death of Sedgwick, (4th November). Leaves generous bequests to the College.

An undistinguished clergyman. Presided over several building projects at Queens'. A significant benefactor of the College.

William Sedgwick was born around 1700, the son of Leonard Sedgwick, rector of Thornton and perpetual curate of Stony Stratford, both in Buckinghamshire.[1] He was educated at Eton College and was admitted to Queens' in 1716. He was elected fellow in 1723 and held several College offices: censor philosophicus, catechist and Dean of Chapel. At unknown dates he graduated M.A. and B.D. .

John Davies, the President since 1717, died on the 7th of March, 1732, and Sedgwick, who was still a fellow, was elected in his stead on the 15th of March. His successor as President (Robert Plumptre) writes:

'Not being of standing for the degree of B.D., he obtained the signatures of a majority of the Heads to a Petition to the King for a Mandate for that degree…'.[1] At the time of his election he was the incumbent of the College living of Oakington, Cambridgeshire, but Gray, in his history of the College of 1898, informs us that he vacated this after he had been appointed by: 'Lord Chancellor Hardwicke' to be rector of St Clement's, Eastcheap, London. The latter preferment presumably occurred in or after 1737, when Baron (later Earl) Hardwicke was appointed Lord Chancellor. St Clement's Church, close to London Bridge, had been rebuilt in the 1680s after the Great Fire of London, to a design by Sir Christopher Wren. During Sedgwick's time, the organist was Edward Henry Purcell, the grandson of Henry Purcell, 1659-95, one of the greatest English composers. Edward Henry Purcell had been appointed organist in 1740; he died in 1765 and is buried in the church.

Soon after his election, during 1732-34, Sedgwick presided over major structural alterations to the College hall, the first of several significant building projects during his tenure. The 16th century panelling in the hall was replaced and, under the direction of Sir James Burrough, a flat ceiling was constructed under the open-timbered roof. (Thankfully, this was removed in 1846!).[1,2] In 1742, the changes to the hall were considered with approval:

'(The hall) very lately was elegantly fitted up according to the present taste and is now by much ye neatest Hall of any in ye University being completely wainscoted and painted with handsom fluted Pillars behind ye Fellows Table at ye upper end of it over wch are neatly carved ye Armes of ye Foundress: at ye lower end of it over ye two neat Iron Doors of ye Screens wch front ye Butteries and Kitchin is a small Gallery for Musick occasionally'.[1,2] (Sir James Burrough was Master of Gonville and Caius College and an amateur architect, whose classical taste influenced several Cambridge buildings).

The Queens' Old Court contains a complex and ornate sundial, and a dial at this site had been constructed in 1642. But, in the 1730s, it received some further attention, as the College accounts note: 'May 1733: Paid Mr Jo: Sharp for drawing ye Dial Plan et'.[3]

Twigg, in his history of the College of 1987, notes that Sedgwick enjoyed the patronage of Lord Chancellor Hardwicke and that, like his predecessor as President, he was a 'Whig', (see Chapter 23).[4] Most of the few glimpses we have of Sedgwick when President are related to College business and, although he served for a year as Vice-Chancellor in 1741-42, this was relatively uneventful.[5] One of his concerns was the composition of the Queens' fellowship; he believed that there were too many non-resident fellows, who did not have much experience of College administration and who may show:

'a want of that affection for the common good of the college which arises from living together in the Society'.[4] This led, in 1735, to the requirement that five junior non-resident fellows should attend the annual audit, while, in 1736, non-residence in excess of six months in a year was not allowed until at least one year after graduating M.A., although there were certain exceptions. (These included employment as a tutor to a nobleman's son or as the chaplain to a peer).[4] Sedgwick did not want fellows to be chosen from those who had just graduated B.A.,[4] and he also complained that Walter Post, a fellow between 1721 and 1733, had received one of the best College livings without the B.D. degree. On a more positive clerical note, we know that Sedgwick officiated in person at the weddings of three College servants in the Queens' chapel between 1742 and 1752. The frequent weddings there at this time were mostly of local people and were conducted by the fellows.[4]

Sedgwick was unmarried, but seems to have had active interests apart from College and University business as, in 1735, Dr Samuel Dale (1659-1739, physician and geologist), saw: 'Hawksby's Pneumatick Engin' in the President's Lodge, while, in 1752, the Lodge contained musical and mathematical instruments and, in a ground room:

'he hath a Printing Press with the Apparatus belonging thereto, wherein he is Printing his Astronomical Works'.[4]

There is a reference to Sedgwick as a tutor, receiving a letter from the Earl of Bristol, who writes to complain that his son Charles, who is under Sedgwick's care, had fallen into bad habits and is:

'to my great surprise rather less improved of late...than he was before...

I wish you could help me to disculpate you entirely on this occasion being otherwise tempted by the great concern this disappointment has thrown me into to suspect your part in this misfortune may not appear quite so blameless as it ought'.[4]

(Charles' father, John Hervey, 1st Earl of Bristol, was a politician who had been ennobled for his support of the Hanoverian succession. He had a total of twenty children, and Charles was one of the seventeen by his second wife; he was born in 1703 and, hopefully, discarded most of his bad habits as, although he never reached the highest offices of the church as his father had intended, he was appointed to a family living and became a prebendary of Ely. The behaviour of two more of Bristol's sons, Tom and Henry, at Christ Church, Oxford, had already given his father serious cause for concern).

Another major project at Queens' in Sedgwick's time was the design and construction of the 'Mathematical Bridge', the subject of countless tourists' photos. This was designed in 1748 by William Etheridge and built in 1749 by James Essex the Younger, (1722-84). But although the present bridge is of the same design as the original, it was repaired in 1866 and completely replaced in 1905. Etheridge was a civil engineer who worked on several wooden bridges, including the supporting wooden structues during the construction of a previous Westminster Bridge; his design for Queens' was unusually sophisticated for the time, while the earliest known reference to the Queens' bridge as the 'Mathematical Bridge' was in 1803.[6] James Essex was the son of a local builder and had studied under Sir James Burrough, before working on many Cambridge colleges, as well as on restorations of Ely and Lincoln Cathedrals. Entries in the College records include:

'1748 Oct 6 Mr Etheridge for the Design & Model of the Bridge £21 00s. 00d.

1749 Sep 30 Mr Essex's Bill for the new Bridge £160 00s. 0d.

1750 Sep 30 Cook...a Supper on finishing the Bridge to Mr Essex's Men £0 17s. 9d.'.[6]

The most ambitious of the works carried out under Sedgwick is known as the 'Essex Building', after its designer and builder, the above-mentioned James Essex, and constructed during 1756-60. It was planned that this should replace all the buildings along the riverfront, but only one wing was completed, adjacent to Silver Street. It is indeed fortunate that the money ran out before most of the 15th century riverside range could be demolished, although about 25 feet of this was lost.[4] The surviving part of the 15th century range is now the oldest building on the river in Cambridge. The funding for the building was a problem as, in 1758, the College had to arrange a loan and Sedgwick provided £1000 in return for an annuity. But the College's debt accumulated, preventing the completion of Essex's design, and financial stability was not achieved for several years.[4] Plumptre provides the following account:

'...And in the year 1756 the Clunch building extending from the Lodge Stair-case by the Town Bridge to the College Kitchen on the outside, and forming nearly two sides of the Court called Erasmus's Court within, being very much decayed, was taken down, and the present useful and ornamental building begun in its place. It was planned and executed by Mr. Essex, an eminent Architect and man of good understanding and character in Cambridge; and was finished (except the fitting up of the rooms) before the death of Mr. Sedgwick in 1760. Towards defraying the expense of it he had advanced £1000, on condition of receiving an Annuity for life from the College, about a year and a half before his death...'.[1] The work was completed in September 1760, when Essex was paid twenty guineas: 'for surveying the new building'.[1] Also, Plumptre gives us a few personal details about his predecessor:

'a man of weak nerves, and an infirm constitution, which he probably render'd still more so by too much indulgence, instead of using proper methods and exertions to strengthen it. For the last 15 years of his life he very rarely went out of the Lodge'.[4] However, we have seen- in Chapter 22- that Sedgwick's account of Henry James' efforts to obtain a suitable chamber pot for the use of Queen Catherine, on her visit to Queens' in 1681, shows that he had a sense of humour!

In 1749, Sedgwick will have congratulated a newly-elected member of the fellowship at Queens', John Mitchell, who would be described in the 1760s, by William Cole, (1714-82, clergyman and antiquary), as:

'a little short man, of black complexion and fat...Fellow of Queen's College, where he was esteemed a very ingenious Man, and an excellent Philosopher. He has published some Things in that way, on the Magnet and Electricity'.[7,8] But, in a more recent- and generous- assessment, he is described as:

'one of the greatest unsung scientists of all time...he... proposed the existence of black holes; suggested that earthquakes travelled in waves; explained how to manufacture an artificial magnet; and, recognizing that double stars were a product of mutual gravitation, he was the first to apply statistics to the study of the cosmos. He invented an apparatus to measure the mass of the Earth. He has been called the father both of seismology and of magnetometry'. Mitchell had been educated at Queens', was ordained deacon in 1749 and served in various College offices during his 15 years as a fellow. In 1760, the year in which he became rector of the College living of St Botolph's, Cambridge, he published a landmark paper in geology: 'Conjectures concerning the Cause and Observations upon the Phaenomena of Earthquakes', for which he was elected a fellow of the Royal Society. (He suggested that earthquakes spread in waves, influenced by the structure of the geological strata of the Earth's crust and he estimated the epicentre of the 1755 Lisbon earthquake). In 1762, he became Woodwardian Professor of Geology but, in 1764, when he married, he resigned as a fellow of Queens' and from his professorship, as celibacy was a condition of both appointments. After clerical posts in Hampshire, in 1767 he became rector of St Michael's Church, Thornhill, Yorkshire, where he would remain for 26 years and continue his scientific work. (The patron of this living was Sir George Savile, his contemporary and friend at Queens'). His visitors in Yorkshire included Benjamin Franklin, (British American polymath, scientist and politician), Joseph Priestley, (another polymath, one of the first to discover oxygen), and Henry Cavendish, (who discoved hydrogen). Mitchell's first wife had died after a year of marriage, leaving a daughter, and he married again in 1773. In 2007, he was the subject of a commemorative blue plaque, which was unveiled on the outside wall of Thornhill parish church, while his memorial tablet is in its Chancel.

His studies of magnetism led to the 'inverse-square law', namely, that the magnetic force exerted by each pole of a magnet decreases in proportion to the square of the distance between them. His work on gravity led to his design of a 'torsion balance', which would be constructed by his friend Henry Cavendish after Mitchell's death and would allow an accurate estimation of the mass of the Earth. (A modern assessment of its significance, in 1987, describes the instrument as:

'the basis of all the most significant experiments on gravitation ever since').[7,8] But it was his work on astronomy which now appears to be the most ground-breaking; this produced evidence for binary stars and star clusters and, in 1783, he suggested that light could be affected by gravity and that there were such objects as: 'dark stars', later to be known as 'black holes'. Mitchell writes:

'If there should really exist in nature any bodies, whose density is not less than that of the sun, and whose diameters are more that 500 times the diameter of the sun...their light could not arrive at us...yet, if any other luminous bodies should happen to revolve about them we might still perhaps from the motions of these revolving bodies infer the existence of the central ones with some degree of probability, as this might afford a clue to some of the apparent irregularities of the revolving bodies...'.[7,8] (In 1767, Mitchell was a member of the astronomical committee of the Royal Society).

As a college head, Sedgwick may have been present at many significant University ceremonies, some of which reflected the various threats and conflicts facing George II's government. The 'War of the Austrian Succession', from 1740 to 1748, involved most of the European powers, including Great Britain, and determined the eventual succession of Maria Theresa as Archduchess of Austria and Queen of Hungary. This included the 'Battle of Dettingen' in 1743, which, while having little effect on later events, is remembered as the last time a reigning British monarch led troops in combat. In December 1743, the Corporation of Cambridge referred to this in their address to the King at St James's Palace, in which they gave congratulations for:

'your Majesty's safe return to your people, from the Dangers of War, to which your Majesty has so freely exposed your most valuable Life...'.[5] Two months later, also at St James's, on the 25th of February 1744, the King was addressed by:

'Dr. George Vice-Chancellor of the University of Cambridge, and his Grace the Duke of Newcastle, High Steward of the Universiity, attended by several Heads of Houses...(who) waited on his Majesty in their Formalities...'.[5] But, on this occasion, the King was reminded of what must have seemed the ever-present threat of a Jacobite invasion:

'We your Majesty's most dutiful and loyal Subjects, the Chancellor, Masters and Scholars of your University of Cambridge, beg leave to express our hearty Detestation and Abhorrence of the insolent and perfidious Design to invade your Majestys Dominions, and impose on us a Popish and abjur'd Pretender...'.[5]

A significant date in British history is 1745, the year of the start of the final Jacobite rebellion and:

'At Kensington on the 20th of September (1745) the Rev. Mr. Prescot, Master of Catharine Hall, and his Grace the Duke of Newcastle, High Steward of the University, attended by several Heads of Houses...waited on his Majesty in their Formalities, with the following Address:- ...We your Majesty's most dutiful amd loyal Subjects, the Chancellor, Masters, and Scholars of your University of Cambridge, humbly beg Leave to express our unfeigned Joy upon your Majesty's safe return to your British Dominions. The unnatural Rebellion lately broke out in Favour of a Popish Abjur'd Pretender, encouraged and Supported (as there is the greatest Reason to apprehend) by a Foreign Power, is an attempt, which we cannot but look upon with the utmost Abhorrence...we will constantly endeavour, by all the Means in our Power, to defeat the wicked and traiterous Designs of those, who aim at the Subversion of your Majesty's Government, and consequently of our Laws, our Liberties and our Religion...'.[5] The situation at this time must have been very worrying as, in the previous month, (August 1745), Charles Edward Stuart, (grandson of James II - known as the 'Young Pretender' and 'Bonnie Prince Charlie'), had begun a Jacobite rebellion in Scotland, raising sufficient support to march on Edinburgh, which had surrendered. On the 21st of September, the day following the University's address, government forces were defeated at the battle of Prestonpans, and it was not until the 16th April in the following year that the King received news of a decisive victory over the rebels and the end of the Jacobite threat. This occurred at the Battle of Culloden, when government forces were under the command of the Duke of Cumberland, who would become known as 'Butcher Cumberland', because of the brutal aftermath of this, the last battle on British soil.

In the month after Culloden, there was a further address to the King at Kensington, on the 14th May 1746, from the University's dignitaries, including: 'several Heads of Houses':

'We your Majestys most dutiful and loyal Subjects, the Chancellor, Masters, and Scholars of your University of Cambridge deeply sensible of the great Importance of the signal Victory lately obtained by your Majesty's Arms under the Command of his Royal Highness the Duke of Cumberland, over the Rebels, beg Leave to offer our most hearty and unfeigned Congratulations to your Majesty on this happy event...'.[5]

On the 5th of December 1748, the University presented another address to the King at St James's Palace, after the final version of the treaty of Aix-la-Chapelle had been signed on the 18th of October, ending the War of the Austrian Succession. The company included the Duke of Newcastle, High Steward of the University, (and soon to become its next Chancellor), as well as several college heads:

'We your Majesty's most dutiful and loyal Subjects...beg leave to approach your Majesty's Throne, with our most sincere and unfeigned Congratulations...Your Majesty's constant and unwearied Endeavours to promote the happiness and Prosperity of your People...and effectual Means you employed in their Vindication and Defence in the Course of the just and necessary War in which your Majesty was lately engaged always afforded us the most rational and well grounded Assurances that they would at length be crowned with the desired success...setling the Ballance of Europe upon a firm and lasting foundation and of restoring to these Nations in particular the great and invaluable Blessings of a safe and honorable Peace...'.[5] (But, unfortunately, there were unresolved issues, which would result in the start of the 'Seven Years' War' in 1756).

The Duke of Somerset, Chancellor of the University for nearly sixty years, died on the 2nd of December 1748, and although the Prince of Wales had been considered as his probable successor, he was out of favour with the King, who recommended Thomas Pelham-Holles, the 1st Duke of Newcastle. He was duly elected and installed in the Senate House, on the 1st of July 1749:

'The University being assembled in the Senate House, a deputation was sent to his Grace, who was at Clare Hall, whence, preceded by the Bedels and several Doctors he came to the Senate House, at the steps of which he was met by Dr. Chapman the Vicechancellor...A band of music having performed a short overture, the Vicechancellor made a congratulatory speech in English. Then he presented the Duke with the patent of office...He was then seated by the Vicechancellor in the chair of state. Mr. Yonge the Public Orator having made a latin oration...Then was performed the Installation Ode... (which ended, after nine lengthy stanzas, with): Full Chorus...

The Muse shall snatch the trump of Fame,
And lift her swelling accents high,
To tell the world that PELHAM'S name
Is dear to Learning as to Liberty'.[5]

Although Newcastle's election was, in the end, undisputed, there had been significant support for the Prince of Wales, who had previously expessed interest in the appointment, and Lord Dupplin, one of Newcastle's strongest supporters, had visited Cambridge in August 1748, when Somerset was ailing, to urge obedience to the King's wishes for the successor. His account of the visit provides further evidence of Sedgwick's chronic infirmity:

'I paid my compliments to the Heads and some particular Fellows...I saw all the Heads except the Vice-Chancellor, who happened to be out when I called, and the Master of Queens' who is in a bad state of health...'.[9]

The 'Annals of Cambridge' of 1845 describe some local difficulties towards the end of Sedgwick's Presidency:

'On the 15th of June, (1757), A mob (chiefly of women) assembled at Cambridge, broke open a storehouse in which were lodged about 15 quarters of wheat, the property of a farmer, who had that day refused 9s. 6d. a bushel for it, and carry'd it all off...On the 16th, the mob assembled again, having intelligence of 27 sacks of flour being lodged at Small-bridges, and notwithstanding the constables attended, about ten they began to assault the place; and after a vigorous resistance in which seven or eight were dreadfully wounded, they carried it, forced the mayor to release one of their number that had been made prisoner, and then went off in triumph. Similar disturbances, occasioned by the high price of corn, took place in various other parts of the Kingdom at this period'.[5]

Sedgwick died on the 4th of November, 1760, just a few days after the accession of George III on the 25th of October. He left considerable bequests to the College, including two freehold estates and a leasehold in Northamptonshire, whose revenues founded two scholarships. Also, he left his library of about thirteen hundred books for the President's Lodge.[1] But as we are told that he rarely left the Lodge in his final years, he may not have been greatly missed. At Queens', his memorial tablet can be found in the ante-chapel of the new chapel, one of five that were removed from the ante-chapel of the old chapel.

References

1. Gray, J.H. The Queens' College of St Margaret and St Bernard. F.E.Robinson. London. 1898. pp 238-44.
2. Willis, R., Clark, J.W. The Architectural History of the University of Cambridge. Vol. II Cambridge University Press. Cambridge. 1886. p 46.
3. History of the Dial. Queens' College Cambridge. Online. 2020.
4. Twigg, J. A History of Queens' College, Cambridge. 1448-1986. The Boydell Press. 1987. pp 165, 180, 186, 212, 312-13.
5. Cooper, C.H. Annals of Cambridge. Volume IV. Warwick and Co. Cambridge. 1845. pp 245-46, 250-55, 262, 268-71, 297.
6. Mathematical Bridge. Queens' College Cambridge. Online. 2020.
7. John Mitchell. Wikipedia. Online. 2020.
8. John Mitchell. Queens' College, Cambridge. Online. 2020.
9. Winstanley, D. A. The University of Cambridge, in the Eighteenth Century. Cambridge University Press. Cambridge. 1922. pp 38, 45.

CHAPTER 25

Robert Plumptre. President 1760-88.

Summary.

Robert Plumptre was born into a distinguished family in 1723; one of his sons would become the sixth of the family to be a fellow of Queens'. He was admitted to Queens' in 1741 and elected a fellow in 1745. The 1st Earl of Hardwicke was a patron to the family and presented Plumptre, (who had been ordained in 1748), to two Cambridgeshire livings in 1752. He married in 1756 and was appointed a prebendary of Norwich Cathedral. He was elected President of Queens' in 1760, after the death of William Sedgwick.

He served as Vice-Chancellor during 1761-62 and 1777-78. He was an advocate of political, religious and University reforms and an influential figure in the University. He died in 1788 and is buried in Norwich Cathedral. He had ten children, nine of whom were living in 1784. He produced a manuscript history of the College, copies of which are in the Old Library at Queens' and in the British Library.

Timeline.

1723.	Born in Middlesex.
1732.	William Sedgwick elected President of Queens'.
1741.	Admitted to Queens'.
1744.	B.A..
1745-55.	Fellow of Queens'.
1748.	Ordained. Duke of Newcastle elected Chancellor of Cambridge University.
1752.	Presented to the livings of Wimpole and Whaddon, Cambridgeshire, by his family's patron the 1st Earl of Hardwicke.

.1756. Marries Anne Newcombe. Appointed a prebendary at Norwich Cathedral.

1756-63. The 'Seven Years War'.

1760. D.D. . Death of George II; accession of George III, (25th October). Death of Sedgwick. Elected President of Queens' on the 12th of November.

1761. On the 14th of September, the University presents an address to George III, after his recent marriage. Plumptre contributes to a celebratory book of verse.

1761-62. Vice-Chancellor. The University presents an address to George III, on the 3rd of September 1762, after the birth of a Prince on the 12th of August. Plumptre contributes to a celebratory book of verse.

1763. The Treaty of Paris is signed on the 10th of February, formally ending the 'Seven Years' War'. The University presents an address to George III on the 14th of April. Plumptre contributes to a celebratory book of verse.

1764. Death of the 1st Earl of Hardwicke. Plumptre successfully promotes the election of the 2nd Earl of Hardwicke as High Steward of Cambridge University.

1768. Death of the Duke of Newcastle, Chancellor of the University. Plumptre enquires about support for the 2nd Earl of Hardwicke as the successor, but this proves insuffıcent to recommend a challenge to the Duke of Grafton, who is duly elected.

1769. Elected as Professor of Moral Theology or Casuistical Divinity.

1773. The start of major renovations to the Queens' chapel.

1774. Member of a University committee to review examinations.

1775-83. The American War of Independence.

1775. Supports the University's controversial address to George III, condemning the American rebels.

1776. The 'United States Declaration of Independence', on July 4th.

1777. His brother Charles, Archdeacon of Ely, provides him with a further stipend by appointing him as his assistant. (Unknown date: appointed a justice of the peace for Cambridgeshire).

1777-78.	Serves a second term as Vice-Chancellor.
1778.	In October, as Vice-Chancellor, presides over a University court which tries Dr. Ewin, who is accused of usury.
1778-82.	At Queens', a building in 'Walnut Tree Court' is partially rebuilt after a fire.
1783.	William Pitt the Younger, Tory statesman, becomes Prime Minister.
1788.	Dies at Norwich on the 29th of October. (Since his appointment as a prebendary at Norwich, he had maintained residences in both Cambridge and Norwich). He is buried in the Cathedral.

Clergyman from a remarkable family, who held several benefices. An advocate of political, religious and University reform. Buried in Norwich cathedral.

Robert Plumpre was born in 1723, in Middlesex, the son of John Plumptre (1679-1751) and Annabella, daughter of Sir Francis Molyneux, fourth baronet.[1] He attended Henry Newcombe's school in Hackney and was admitted to Queens' as a 'pensioner', (paying for tuition and living expenses), in July 1741.[2] After graduating B.A. in 1744, he was elected a fellow of Queens' the following year and would remain a fellow until 1755. He was ordained in 1748 and, in 1752, he was appointed to the livings of Wimpole and Whaddon, Cambridgeshire, by Philip Yorke, 1st Earl of Hardwicke, who was a patron of the Plumptre family.[2] He married in 1756 and, probably as a wedding present, Lord Hardwicke arranged for his appointment as a prebendary of the Cathedral at Norwich, where he would maintain a residence for the rest of his life. In October 1760 he obtained the D.D. degree and was elected President of Queens' on the 12th of November. Plumptre left a manuscript history of Queens',[1,3] in which he gives further details of his early life, describing himself in the third person:

'Robert Plumptre was the youngest of ten children of John Plumptre, Esq. a gentleman of moderate estate in Nottinghamshire, and a Member of Parliament above forty years, most of which time he was representative of the town of Nottingham. He received his school education under Dr. Henry Newcome at Hackney, from whence he was removed to Queens' College in April 1741...He was chosen Fellow March 21st 1745 and his Fellowship had been vacated in 1755 by his being preferred, (in 1752), in succession to his elder brother Charles, (Fellow of Queens' and Archdeacon of Ely), to the rectory of Wimpole and vicarage of Whaddon, both in Cambridgeshire, by the favour of the then Lord Chancellor Hardwicke (High Steward of the University). In Sept. 1756 he married the second daughter of' Dr. Newcome, his former schoolmaster (by whom he has had ten children, nine of whom are living in 1784), and in about a fortnight after, and about two months only before resigning the Seals, his kind and most excellent patron gave him a Prebend in the Church of Norwich. He took the degree of D.D. Oct. 18th, preceeding his election, per saltum, not having till then taken that of B.D.'.[4]

Despite Plumptre having an influential patron, there is no evidence that his election as President was not due to a free vote of the fellowship.[3] Twigg, in his history of the College of 1987, tells us that the Duke of Newcastle, ('Whig' statesman, University of Cambridge Chancellor and Prime Minister in 1760), was informed that: 'a major part of the society...are determined in favour of Dr Plumptre'; also, Twigg notes that the Chancellor would have approved the choice, as Plumptre had a reputation for Whig sympathies,[3] which were associated with support of a constitutional monarchy and of relative religious tolerance. In 1761, Newcastle writes to his friend and political ally the 1st Earl of Hardwicke:

'Everything has passed here, since my coming down, extreamly well...the performances of the young men yesterday were extreamly good and gave great satisfaction...We had last night a very fine entertainment at the new Master's of Queens'. We have constantly drunk your Lordship's health twice a day, as I told you we would'.[5]

The Plumptre family were represented in several generations at Cambridge University, and one of Plumptre's sons (another Robert) was the sixth family member to become a fellow of

Queens', in his case during 1786-96.[3] Plumptre's great-grandfather, Huntingdon Plumptre, had attended Trinity Hall, Cambridge, and graduated M.D. in 1631, and Plumptre's father and two uncles had been students at Queens'. His uncle Henry had been a fellow during 1703-07 and would become President of the Royal College of Physicians;[6] Henry's son, Russell, was Regius Professor of Physic at Cambridge during 1741-93; and Plumptre's brother, Charles, Archdeacon of Ely, was a fellow during 1737-48. During Plumptre's Presidency, two of his sons (Joseph and Robert) and a nephew (Charles), were Queens' fellows. Another of his sons, James, was a fellow of Clare College and a noted dramatist. Plumptre had ten children, and his reformist inclinations for civil and religious liberty had led him to give his daughters:

'an education very different from what generally falls to the lot of even well instructed females'.[1] Indeed, his daughters, Anne, (who became a strong supporter of Napoleon) and Annabella, developed a literary reputation, while his wife and eldest daughters would show their independent spirit by leaving the Church of England.[4] In 1752, Plumptre was presented with the livings of Wimpole and Whaddon, which had been held since 1745 by his brother Charles, before the latter's promotion as Archdeacon of Ely,[1] and Hardwicke's generous patronage of the family led the poet Thomas Gray, (widely known for his 'Elegy Written in a Country Churchyard'), to suggest that Plumptre's rather curious motto: 'Non magna loquimur, sed vivimus', should be (mis) translated as: 'We don't say much, but we hold good livings'.[3] Also, Plumptre's brother, when Archdeacon of Ely, provided him with another source of income in 1777, by appointing him as an assistant.

On the 14th of September 1761, a:

'humble Address of the University of Cambridge, was presented to his Majesty (George III, at Leicester House, London) by his Grace the Duke of Newcastle, the Chancellor, accompanied by...eleven Heads of Houses...',[7] who probably included Plumptre, as a newly- elected head. The occasion was the King's recent marriage, on the 8th of September, to the 17-year old Princess Charlotte of Mecklenburg-Strelitz, who had become

Queen within six hours of her first arrival in London, in a marriage ceremony in the Chapel Royal, St James's Palace:

'We your Majesty's most dutiful & loyal Subjects....feel the warmest sentiments of joy & affection, in offering our Congratulations to your Majesty, on this most happy & auspicious Occasion...Your choice of a Princess for your Consort, endowed with such Virtues, and distinguished for such personal accomplishments, as will add lustre to a Throne, while they alleviate the cares of it, gives the surest prospect of Domestick happiness to your Majesty...'.[7] Plumptre was one of the contributors to a book of celebratory verses for this occasion.

In November 1761, Plumptre was elected Vice-Chancellor and, during his year in office, on the 3rd of September 1762:

'the following Address of the University of Cambridge was presented to His Majesty by his Grace the Duke of Newcastle, Chancellor of the University; accompanied by the Reverend Dr. Plumptre, Master of Queen's College, Vice-Chancellor; his Grace the Duke of Grafton; the Marquiss of Tavistock; the Earl of Halifax...& upward of ninety Masters of Arts, & Batchelors of Law & Physick...'.[7] This was on the occasion of the recent birth of a Prince, on the 12th of August, who would become George IV:

'We your Majesty's most dutiful and Loyal Subjects, the Chancellor, Masters & Scholars of the University of Cambridge, humbly beg leave to present to your Majesty our sincerest congratulations on the safe delivery of the Queen, & birth of His Royal Highness the Prince, and on the prosperous state of Her Majesty's health since the happy event...We have the most firm and just confidence that Princes, educated under the inspection & example of your Majesty & your Royal Consort, will inherit, together with your Crown, all the Virtues necessary to its support & lustre, & to the making a people happy...'.[7] (Sadly, this confidence would not be justified by future events!). Plumptre was again a contributor to the University's celebratory book of verse, which was presented to the King and Queen by the next Vice-Chancellor on the 20th of December, 1762.[7]

The 'Seven Years' War', which had started in 1756, involved many belligerents and extended over five continents, including the

Americas. The end came in 1763, after the victory of a Great Britain-Prussian coalition over a coalition led by France and Spain, which led to the signing of the Treaty of Paris on the 10th of February. This was marked by another address from the University to the King, at St James's Palace on the 14th of April, when the company was noted to be: 'amounting in the whole to near two hundred':

'...We your Majesty's most dutiful & loyal Subjects, the Chancellor, Masters & Scholars of your University of Cambridge, beg leave to...express the warmest sentiments of our Duty & Gratitude to your Majesty for your tender regard to the true happiness of your people, in concluding an expensive, though successful war, by a safe & honourable peace...'.[7] Once more, Plumptre was a contributor to the University's celebratory verses, a copy of which: 'magnificently bound in crimson velvet', was presented to the King on the 1st of June.[7]

The High Steward of Cambridge University was, originally, the deputy to the Chancellor, while in the 18th century it had become an office that honoured prominent individuals. In 1764, the incumbent, Philip Yorke, the 1st Earl of Hardwicke, died, and there was a hotly-contested election for his successor. The two candidates were associated with different Whig factions, and Plumptre was active in supporting his deceased patron's son, the 2nd Earl of Hardwicke, also named Philip Yorke, who was allied to the Duke of Newcastle and the Whigs who opposed the government, while the other candidate, the Earl of Sandwich, was a member of the government headed by Prime Minister George Grenville.[3] (The Duke of Newcastle had been the University's Chancellor since 1748).The contest was close and chaotic:

'The grace for the Earl of Hardwicke passed the Caput, and was carried in the Non-Regent House, the votes being placets, 103; non-placets, 101. In the Regent House the votes were equal, viz. placets, 108; non-placets, 108. The Proctors (who were in different interests) at first disagreed as to the numbers in the Regent House, in consequence of each omitting to mark the other's vote; but when, on rectifying the error, it was found the suffrages were equal, the Senior Proctor insisted on a second scrutiny, which the Junior refused; and the Vicechancellor dissolved the Congregation without the Proctors making any report...'.[7] However, the matter was eventually resolved in the Court of the King's Bench, which issued:

'a mandamus...to the Seal-keepers to put the University seal to the earl of Hardwicke's appointment'.[7] The results reflected the Chancellor's declining influence in the University, and Newcastle:

'in the closing years of his life...was commonly regarded as an impotent old dotard'.[5] He died on the 17th of November 1768, and the Vice-Chancellor called a meeting of college heads for the following morning.

The Chancellor's death had been anticipated, and a letter was read from the Prime Minister, the 3rd Duke of Grafton, (who had supported Hardwicke in the election for High Steward),[5] stating that he would be honoured to be elected Chancellor. But as Hardwicke, as High Steward of the University, was also interested in the succession:

'the President of Queens' communicated to the meeting Lord Hardwicke's sentiments on the same subject'.[5] These, according to a contemporary letter, were that:

'Lord Hardwicke had thought proper to declare his readiness to accept of the Chancellorship'.[5] Consequently, Plumptre and Professor Rutherforth, (Regius Professor of Divinity), agreed to carry out a discreet enquiry and found that:

'about two hundred and forty persons would vote, and that of these Hardwicke could not possibly count upon more than eighty. In these circumstances it would be both useless and ridiculous for him to come forward as a candidate'.[5] Consequently, when the President of Queens', the Masters of Corpus, Jesus, and Emmanuel, and Professor Rutherforth met in conference:

'...they had little difficulty in deciding the...communication they should address to Hardwicke: "Upon consideration of the state of the university, after the best inquiry that can be made in the several colleges and reflecting on the disadvantages of entering so late into an opposition, we are of the opinion that there is no reasonable expectation of making a respectable minority in favour of Lord Hardwicke, and therefore...we think it best that your

Lordship's name should not be made any farther use of on this occasion" '.[5] Accordingly, the Duke of Grafton was elected, unopposed, on the 29th of November.

Plumptre and his family maintained close ties with the Yorke family, receiving further patronage and giving political support.[8] In 1774, the 2nd Earl, who often stayed at Queens', sent his nephew (another Philip Yorke, who was his heir) to Queens', when Plumptre writes:

'The honour which your Lordship and Family does me in thinking of admitting Mr Yorke of this college, and the proof thereby given of confidence in me call for my best and most grateful acknowledgements... My best endeavours shall be used to shew that it has not been misplaced'.[8] Also, in 1781, James Yorke, the 2nd Earl's brother, who was Bishop of Gloucester, sent his son Charles to Queens' and Plumptre informs the Earl:

'I am preparing Rooms here for the B'p's son, whom the B'p informs me he will bring as soon as I can have them ready'.[8] In 1783, James Yorke, now Bishop of Ely, presented Plumptre's eldest son Joseph to the rectory of Newton, Cambridgeshire, while, in 1784, Plumptre supported Hardwicke's successful efforts to achieve the election of William Pitt the Younger as one of the MPs for the University of Cambridge.[8]

Plumptre acquired another University appointment in 1769, when he was elected Professor of Moral Theology or Casuistical Divinity, (founded in 1683, now called the Knightbridge Professorship of Philosophy), but many professors in the 18th century did not lecture, and Plumptre noted that, despite a theoretical requirement to provide specified lectures, the post:

'though small in value...has the recommendations of having nothing to do for it, of interfering with no other preferment, and bringing with it no new residence or old house'.[3] Plumptre supported a rare (and unsuccessful) attempt in the 18th century to introduce University reforms, in this case the provision of annual examinations, and was a member of a committee which proposed their introduction for the sons of the nobility and for fellow-commoners, who had previously been exempt. He also supported additional examinations for pensioners and sizars and was a critic of the standards required for law degees, complaining about the ease by which these could be obtained.[3] He believed this had:

'got to such a height that it most undoubtedly requires some stop to be put to it. It is the refuge of idleness and ignorance, and yet gives advantage over those who employ their time and pains in taking a degree in arts'.[3]

The 'American War of Independence' began with the military defeat of a British attempt to disarm the militia in Concord, Massachusetts, on the 19th of April, 1775. This led to the exposure of political divisions in the University, when the liberal reformers nearly defeated a proposal in the Senate to present a loyal address to the King condemning the American rebels.[3] Although usually on the side of reform and liberty, Plumptre is reported to have been influenced by his patron, Hardwicke, in his support of the address, while the fellows of Queens' were divided.[3] Plumptre writes that he was:

'thought of late to incline towards Toryism, because he abhors the American Rebellion'.[1] The degree of opposition to the loyal address is evident in the account in the 'Annals of Cambridge' for 1775:

'The following address from the University was carried on the 24th of November, by 46 placets to 21 non-placets in the Non-Regent House, and 38 placets to 25 non-placets in the Regent-House. It was soon afterwards presented at St. James's...We your Majesty's most loyal & faithful Subjects, the Chancellor, Masters, & Scholars of the University of Cambridge, in full Senate Assembled, think it our duty at this alarming crisis to approch your Throne... animated with the warmest Loyalty & Affection for your Royal Person & Government, we cannot remain silent Spectators of the unnatural Rebellion, into which many of our brethren in your Majesty's American Colonies have been unhappily seduced: We see their delusion with equal indignation and concern...we fervently implore Heaven to bless your Majesty's Counsels with Success; so that the Crown & Dominions of this Realm may be transmitted with undiminished lustre to your Majesty's remotest posterity'.[7]

Plumptre served a second term as Vice-Chancellor during 1777-78, after a rather unusual situation, when Dr. Thomas,

Master of Christ's College, who had been elected Vice-Chancellor on the 4th of November 1777, claimed that his health would not allow him to take office. (His ailments included: 'gout slightly in one hand').[4] This left the University without a Vice-Chancellor as, after a proposal to excuse him on payment of a fine was rejected, Thomas still refused to be sworn in. This caused a major problem for University business, and Plumptre was asked to stand again by the Master of Trinity College and the Provost of King's College. They will have been relieved to hear that, although:

'he would be as much ashamed to pass the office over to a junior as he was unwilling to take it before a senior', he told them that if Dr. Thomas was formally removed as Vice-Chancellor, he would serve if elected. They agreed that the Senate should, again, be asked to consider Thomas' request to stand down, which was finally approved. The situation was resolved on the 3rd of December, when Plumptre was elected with a large majority and sworn in as Vice-Chancellor on the same day.[4] The 'Annals of Cambridge' provide further details:

'The persons nominated for Vicechancellor were Hugh Thomas D.D. Dean of Ely and Master of Christ's College, and Robert Plumptre D.D. President of Queen's College. The votes were, Dr. Thomas 40; Dr. Plumptre 16. Immediately an Esquire Bedel went to Christ's College, to inform Dr. Thomas of his election. He shortly returned to the Senate House, and reported that Dr. Thomas had stated That he (Dr T.) had laid the state of his health before the University, and that he could not (or should not) send any answer to the information brought him...On the 2d of December, a congregation being assembled, the Senior Proctor communicated the contents of a paper he had received from Dr. Thomas, in which he stated that his age, and infirmities, had rendered him wholly unfit for the high office, to which he had been elected; and quite incapable of discharging its important duties, either with advantage to the University, or with satisfaction to himself...(After further negotiations)...The Senior Proctor then requested the members of the Senate to express their approbation or disapprobation of this excuse...there appeared, placets 62; non-placets 13. The Heads and Presidents immediately proceeded to nominate two persons for the office, when Dr. Plumptre and Dr. Goddard were returned to the Senate, and on the 3rd of December Dr. Plumptre was elected'.[7]

During Plumptre's year in office, he presided over the trial of William Ewin LL.D of St John's College, who had been accused of lending money at exorbitant interest rates to Mr. Bird, a fellow-commoner of Trinity College. This would turn into a protracted legal nightmare. Although Dr. Ewin had written to the Master of Trinity with an apology and a promise not to offend again:

'On the 14th of October, William Howell Ewin LL.D. of St. John's College, appeared in the Vicechancellor's Court in the Law Schools, to answer a charge of having lent money at usurious interest to William Bird a scholar of Trinity College, during his minority, without the consent of his tutor...it appeared that he had in 1775 and 1776 advanced to Mr. Bird, then a minor in stutu pupillari, partly through the agency of a Portugese Jew named Silva, but who also went by the name of A.Grove, the sum of £750. For which he took notes to the amount of £1090. Dr. Ewin made but a sorry defence. The Court was adjourned to the 21st of October, when he again appeared, made some objections, and then slunk out of Court. After being thrice solemnly called and not appearing, the Vicechancellor and nine Heads sentenced him to be suspended from all degrees taken or to be taken, and expelled the University...'.[7] But Ewin appealed to the 'Delegates', a statutary University committee,[4] which, in a spirit of compromise, withdrew the sentence of expulsion, while confirming the suspension of the degrees. As a further setback to Plumptre's authority, Ewin went on to obtain the reversal of the remaining part of the original sentence:

'Dr. Ewin having applied to the Court of King's Bench for a mandamus to restore him to his degrees, that Court after full argument awarded the writ, on the ground that there being no express statute of the University forbidding usury or the lending money to minors, the Vicechancellor's Court had no jurisdiction in the case. Lord Mansfield however censured Dr. Ewin's conduct in the strongest terms, and suggested that a statute to meet such cases in future should be passed, and that the Great Seal should be petitioned that he might be struck out of the Commission of the Peace...Dr. Ewin was restored to his degree of LL.D on the 20th of October (1779). He came to the Senate House in his Gown. The Vice Chancellor objected to it, and he pulled it off before he was reinstated...'.[7] However, a subsequent 'grace' was passed to stop: 'this most pernicious evil' of usury.[4]

Plumptre is reported to have made several errors in a Latin speech as Vice-Chancellor in 1777, but the importance of Latin had been diminishing; while in the late 17th century students were expected to speak Latin at dinner in hall, a century later this practice was discouraged by fines.[3]

Plumptre was a 'Latitudinarian', that is, sympathetic to the views of a 17th century group of theologians, originally from Cambridge, who were 'moderate' Anglicans, believing that very specific doctrines and practices were not necessary and, in the 19th century, it was considered that, under Plumptre, Queens' had been: 'distinguished for its attachment to Civil and Religious liberty'.[9] This was exemplified by Plumptre's opposition to the requirement to subscribe to the 39 Articles of the Church of England by those matriculating or graduating from the Universities of Oxford and Cambridge and by those accepting any ecclesiastical office.[3] He suggests that:

'some other Expedient, than such Subscription to Articles...be substituted in its Place...as effectual to the Preservation of the Church of England, and not so burdensome to its *real* (perhaps *best*) Friends, who wish its Amendment and consequent Prosperity, not (as they have been reproached) its Destruction'.[8] He, and seven of the College fellowship, were among those who signed a petition to Parliament for the abolition of the subscription and its substitution by a simple declaration of belief in the Bible. This has been called the 'Feathers Tavern' petition, signed at the Strand, London, in 1772; the University of Cambridge provided a substantial number of the petitioners, (in contrast to just a few from the University of Oxford), but their efforts were unsuccessful, as they represented a minority view in the Church of England at the time. This issue had also generated a petition signed by undergraduates at Cambridge, which was presented to the

Vice-Chancellor on the 31st of December 1771, by Charles Crawford, a fellow-commoner at Queens':

'...The Humble petition of certain undergraduates...sheweth, That your petitioners apprehend themselves...to be under an obligation of devoting their attention to that course of studies, which is recommended to them by their superiors...that, in consequence of this multiplicity of academical engagements, they have neither the leisure nor the opportunity of inquiring into the abstruser points of theology; that they nevertheless find themselves under a necessity of declaring their unfeigned assent to a set of theological propositions, usually called "the thirty-nine articles of religion," apparently of high argument and great importance... Your petitioners, therefore, intreat...that they may be released from the necessity of testifying their assent to the aforementioned propositions...'.[7] However, this was ignored, and Crawford, who, as we shall see, had an appetite for confrontation, addressed the Vice-Chancellor again:

'Mr. Vice-Chancellor, I wait upon you again concerning the petition of undergraduates, and would beg to be indulged with a few moments hearing. We have received as yet no direct answer to our petition...all mankind with one voice cry out against the imposition we speak of as absurd and illegal, which an arbitary Stuart, in the wantonness of his power, had pleased to establish in the University. What answer, Sir, shall I carry back to the rest of the subscribers?'.[4] Although this plea was followed by the formal rejection of the petition, in 1773 the University did reduce the obligation to a declaration that:

'I...do declare that I am a bona fide member of the Church of England as by law established'.[3,4]

While Crawford was an irritant to the University establishment, he was a considerable nuisance to Plumptre and Queens', due to a pattern of drunken violence.[3] This included an unprovoked attack on a coach's mounted postillion and a threat to throw the senior fellow of Pembroke College through a window. Eventually, he was expelled in August 1773:

'for having been drunk, and for assaulting and beating a waterman in the town, and for making a riot'.[3] But he refused to leave and hired a blacksmith to break into his rooms. Although he left in November, having locked his rooms, thus requiring the College to organise a further break-in, he returned in the summer of 1774, deliberately provoking the College to eject him on two occasions. He then sued the porters for assault. Perhaps wishing to provoke once again, within a week he returned with a pistol and was bound over for breach of the peace. These matters were duly considered by the Court of the King's Bench in 1775 and, no doubt to Plumptre's relief, the judgement was in favour of the porters and the expulsion, and the College was not seriously inconvenienced again:[3]

'Grundon, the porter of Queens' College and others were indicted at the Town Sessions, for an assault on Charles Crawford Esq. late a fellow-commoner of Queens' College. The indictment was...tried at the Lent Assizes before Mr. Justice Willes, when the defendants were convicted, subject to the opinion of the Court of King's Bench...which was argued on the 21st of June...It appeared that Mr. Crawford was expelled the College...by the Master and two fellows...He afterwards came into the college garden with an intent to take possession of his rooms, whereupon the defendants took hold of him and conducted him out of college. This was the assault complained of, for Mr. Crawford contended that his expulsion was illegal...The Court...gave judgement in favour of the defendants (ie the porters), intimating that...the order of expulsion must be taken to be a right sentence till avoided or set aside by the Visitor, and that the defendants acting under it were thereby justified in the assault'.[7]

Crawford may have reminded Plumptre and Queens' of the protracted behavioral problems of another particularly difficult student, John Lloyd, who, in 1767, had disappeared without leave:

'and his friends search'd some days in London for him before they could find him to send him back'.[3] Subsequently, Lloyd:

'did in order to obstruct the discipline of the College enter into an association to miss Chapel a greater number of times than was commonly allow'd them in a week, and then if any exercise was set them to refuse one and all to comply with it'.[3] Although these efforts to incite rebellion were unsuccessful, Lloyd's career as trouble-maker continued and, in 1769:

'a chair bottom was thrown from a college window late one night at a post-chaise in Silver Street, terrifying the horses. A servant sent back by the occupants of the chaise to make a note of the room from which the object had been thrown was met by the students gathered there, including Lloyd, who climbed down from the window to the street, assaulting the servant, and threw him over the rails into a muddy place adjoining to the river...The driver of the chaise, who followed in search of the servant, was also beaten up, and the chaise's occupants...were subjected to indecent and abusive language. One of the townspeople knew Lloyd, and the affair was settled between them afterwards...When Plumptre found out, about a month later...another Queens' scholar who had taken part in the affray...was rusticated...But Lloyd... was spared: he was ordered to make a public apology, and to learn and recite by heart in hall one of Cicero's orations...'.[3] But this was not the end of Lloyd's wayward behaviour as, in December 1768, after learning that he was unlikely to be elected to a fellowship the next January, he:

'violently intoxicated himself with liquor, and in that state did come out into one of the Courts of the College, did there make a great riot and disturbance, and did grossly abuse and violently threaten some of the Fellows of the College whom he supposed not favourably dispos'd towards him, and did strike his Tutor who came to quiet him several blows'.[3] Plumptre describes Lloyd's:

'unmeasurable Self-conceit, pride, Arrogance, caprice, imperiousness, and assuming airs...which it was feared would operate very fatally on the peace and good order of the Society if he was elected into it'.[3] Despite these accounts, Lloyd's brother, William Lloyd, a fellow of Queens' during 1760-c70, accused Plumptre of having: 'exerted some undue influence' to prevent the election of his brother, and although the decision was supported by the fellowship, William Lloyd pursued the case in the Court of Chancery.[3]

In 1780, another student, Reginald Bligh, failed to be elected to a fellowship, which was, he thought: 'the only Chance I stood of obtaining a genteel Livelihood'. It was, perhaps, unfortunate that Plumptre's son Joseph was successful at the same election, as Bligh considered himself to be the more qualified candidate. Bligh then wrote:

'several frantic blustering letters...as testimony to his highly emotional and confused state of mind' and, in December 1780, he was expelled for: 'most false, Scurrilous, defamatory, and malicious Libel'.[3]

While the behaviour of these students is particularly memorable, widespread student drunkenness was a significant problem at this time; for example, in the 1770s, Younge Gilson was rusticated for:

'coming to chapel intoxicated...He kept in a room above me one whole term, in which term, I rarely, tho' I saw him often, saw him sober. And in what company did he get drunk? In no company at all, except bottles of rum and brandy'.[3] In the 1780s, a remarkably modern approach to the problem was instituted; the President awarded an annual prize of five guineas for: 'morals', to the student distinguished:

'by regularity in attendance on Chapel, Hall, and Lectures, frugality in his Expences, and general Propriety of Conduct'.[3]

Plumptre presided over various building projects at Queens', which he describes in his manuscript history of the College:

'...in the summer after his (ie Plumptre's) election, the offices on the North side of the Lodge Gallery were built for him...The inside of the Chapel was likewise entirely refitted as it now appears, in the years 1774 and 1775, and the Library enlarged at the same time by taking into it the principal part of a set of rooms that were between that and the Chapel, making the remaining part into a Gallery to the Chapel for the use of the Master's family'.[4] The antiquary William Cole (1714-82), visiting in March 1773, writes:

'The Chapel in the Spring of 1773 was entirely taken to Pieces and new modelled, tho' it seemed to want it very little; every old and modern Tomb Stone being taken up from the Floor, the Altar Piece taken away, with the stalls and the blew coved Ceiling taking down in order to refit it entirely...The West End was enlarged...

and a curious painted Room above the Entrance into it converted into a Gallery for the Master's family'.[4] All this work required the closure of the chapel for two years and it was reopened on the 5th of May, 1775. Various other works at Queens' included the partial rebuilding, after a fire, of 'Walnut Tree Court', (situated north of the original court), during 1778-82 and, in 1782, Isaac Milner (the next President) was given permission:

'to build a Chemical Laboratory in the Stable Yard adjoining to the Coal-house'.[4]

There are other miscellaneous glimpses of Plumptre in the College context. Despite his reforming attitude and large family, he considered the idea that fellows should marry was:

'so very absurd that I have been, and still am, much in doubt whether it was ever seriously intended...the ruin of the University as a place of education would infallibly and speedily ensue: if restrained to non-resident Fellows, the ruin would perhaps be not quite so expeditious but no less certain'.[3] (Twigg points out that many believed that fellows should be encouraged to move on, in contrast to the modern concept of an academic profession).[3] Plumptre's views are also recorded on another controversial issue, namely the students' use of private tutors, particularly in their final year. At this time, much of the teaching was carried out by private tutors, who were, usually, fellows with few paid teaching duties, who wished to earn extra income. Plumptre reflects that the system:

'on the one hand encouraged idleness in the forgoing years, and on the other occasioned expense to parents and been heavily complained of by them'.[3]

Plumptre died at Norwich on the 29th of October 1788 and is buried in Norwich Cathedral, where a tablet to his memory can be found on the south side of the chancel. Twigg concludes that Plumptre was:

'an active proponent of political, religious and university reform, an important figure within the university. Queens' was inspired by his ideals, although there are hints that he was not the firmest of governors with regard to college discipline and financial arrangements'.[3] His main legacy is his manuscript: 'Historical account of the foundation, benefactors, presidents & fellows, &c.'. This can be found in the Queens' College Archives in the Old Library, while William Cole's copy, with Cole's annotations, is in the British Library.[1,3]

References

1. Chandler, D. Plumptre, Robert. In: Oxford Dictionary of National Biography. Online. 2008.
2. Wikipedia. Robert Plumptre. Online. 2020.
3. Twigg, J. A History of Queens' College, Cambridge. 1448-1986. The Boydell Press. 1987. pp 158-64, 180-99, 208, 301, 481.
4. Gray, J.H. The Queens' College of St Margaret and St Bernard. F.E.Robinson. London. 1898. pp 245-56.
5. Winstanley, D.A. The University of Cambridge in the Eighteenth Century. Cambridge University Press. Cambridge. 1922. pp 139, 142-44, 150.
6. Dictionary of National Biography, Wikisource's edition. Plumptre, Henry. Online. 2020.
7. Cooper, C.H. Annals of Cambridge. Volume IV. Warwick and Co. . Cambridge. 1845. pp 308-35, 363, 378-92.
8. Payne, Reider. Robert Plumptre- 18th-Century President of Queens' and Servant of the House of Yorke. The Record 2009. Queens' College, Cambridge. Online. 2020.
9. Gunning, H. Reminiscences of the University, Town, and County of Cambridge from the Year 1780. George Bell. Fleet St, London.1894.

CHAPTER 26

Isaac Milner. President 1788-1820.

Summary.

Isaac Milner was born in Leeds, in 1750, the son of an unsuccessful businessman who died when Isaac was aged ten. He was then obliged to leave the Grammar School to be apprenticed to a woollen manufacturer but, after seven years, in which he kept up with the study of the classics, he was rescued from the factory by his elder brother Joseph, who had been educated at Cambridge with the help of his previous headmaster and family friends. When Joseph became headmaster of Hull Grammar School in 1767, he employed Isaac as his assistant for two years, before organising his admission to Queens' in 1770.

Milner's exceptional talents became apparent in 1774, when he graduated as 'Senior Wrangler', (ie in first place), in the Mathematics Tripos examination. He was elected a fellow of Queens' in 1776 and, after ordination in 1777, he was appointed rector of the College living of St. Botolph's Church, Cambridge, in 1778.

He was elected a fellow of the Royal Society in 1780 and, in 1783, he became the inaugural Jacksonian Professor of Natural Philosophy.

In 1784, he began an extended continental tour with William Wilberforce, whose campaigning would be instrumental in the passing of the 'Slave Trade Act, 1807'. This was the start of a lifelong friendship.

After the death of Robert Plumptre in 1788, he was elected President of Queens' and, as a leader of the 'evangelical' movement in Cambridge, he would change the religious nature of the College.

In 1792, he was appointed Dean of Carlisle and, in 1792-93, (and also in 1809-10), he served as Vice-Chancellor.

In 1798, he was elected to the prestigious Lucasian professorship of Mathematics, once held by Isaac Newton.

In 1810, he published a revised and re-edited version of the 'Ecclesiastical History of the Church of Christ', which he had co-authored with his brother Joseph. This would become very popular in the 19th century.

He died in 1820, afer a lifetime of recurrent ill-health, with Wilberforce at his side. He is buried in the original Queens' chapel. He was unmarried. His brother Joseph, to whom he had been very close, had died in 1797.

His abilities, which he had demonstrated in theology, chemistry, mechanics and mathematics:

'were of the very highest order; his acquirements most extraordinary; and the versatility of his talents quite wonderful...'.
But perhaps his principal legacy is his memorable reputation:

'He had looked into innumerable books, had dipped into most subjects, and talked with shrewdness, animation, and intrepidity on them all. Whatever the company or whatever the theme, his sonorous voice predominated over other voices, even as his lofty stature, vast girth, and superincumbent wig, defied all competitors...'.[1]

Timeline.

1750.	Born in Leeds.
1756.	Attends Leeds Grammar School.
1760.	Death of father. Apprenticed as a weaver. Death of George II. Accession of George III. Robert Plumptre elected President of Queens'.
1767.	Isaac's brother Joseph becomes headmaster of Hull Grammar School. He appoints Isaac as his 'usher'.
1770.	Admitted to Queens' as a 'sizar' (ie required to carry out some servant's tasks).
1774.	B.A. . Senior Wrangler (ie first place in the Mathematics Tripos exam).

1776. Elected a fellow of Queens'.

1777. Ordained priest. Tutor at Queens'. M.A. .

1778-92. Rector of St Botolph's Church, Cambridge.

1780. 'Moderator' (ie examiner; also in 1783, 1785). Elected F.R.S. .

1783. Elected as the inaugural Jacksonian Professor of Natural Philosophy. William Pitt becomes Prime Minister.

1784-85. Extended continental tour with William Wilberforce.

1786. B.D. , (associated with an impressively memorable 'Act').

1788. Death of Plumptre. Elected President of Queens'. (He will become a leader of the 'evangelical' movement in Cambridge).

1789. Publishes a paper on nitrous acid, a key ingredient of gunpowder. Start of the French Revolution.

1790. William Pitt elected High Steward of the University.

1792. Dean of Carlisle. D.D. .

1792-93. Vice-Chancellor. Presides over the trial of William Frend.

1797. Death of Joseph Milner.

1798. Lucasian Professor of Mathematics.

1801. Act of Union, (forming the United Kingdom of Great Britain and Ireland). William Pitt leaves the office of Prime Minister.

1803. National concern about possible invasion by the French.

1805. Address to the King from the University after the naval victories of Viscount Nelson.

1804. Pitt returns as Prime Minister, (until his death in 1806).

1806. The 3rd Earl of Hardwicke elected High Steward of the University after Pitt's death.

1807. The 'Slave Trade Act 1807'; (this prohibits the slave trade in the British Empire, although the practice of slavery will not be abolished until 1833).

1809-10. Vice-Chancellor.

1810. Publication of a revised and re-edited version of the 'Ecclesiastical History of the Church of Christ', co-authored with his now-deceased brother Joseph.

1811. Supports the formation of a Cambridge branch of the 'British and Foreign Bible Society'. The Prince of Wales becomes the Prince Regent. Death of the Duke of Grafton

	and the election of the Duke of Gloucester as University Chancellor.
1814-16.	Spends nearly two years in Carlisle.
1815.	The University presents an address to the Prince Regent after the Battle of Waterloo. The end of the Congress of Vienna.
1820.	Dies. Buried in the original Queens' chapel. Death of George III. Accession of George IV.

A formidably-talented 'Evangelical' clergyman, with a memorable character. Lucasian Professor of Mathematics. Dean of Carlisle.

Childhood.

Isaac Milner was born on the 11th of January, 1750, in Mabgate, now an inner city area of Leeds, West Yorkshire.[1] He was the third son of an unsuccessful businessman, who died in 1760, and a religiously-inclined mother, who, according to Milner's biographer, his niece Mary Milner:

'was not, indeed, a woman of good temper, but she was remarkable for her sound and vigorous understanding, for the active turn of her mind, and for a vein of shrewd humour which rendered her conversation, uneducated as she was, acceptable to persons of the highest attainments…(In later life): One evening, a party of friends assembled at the house of the Rev. Joseph Milner, (Isaac's elder brother), were discussing, among other religious topics, the character of St. Paul, (when) Joseph Milner expressed very strongly his idea of the privilege and happiness of those persons who enjoyed opportunities of personal intercourse with the apostle; and said, that he could scarcely conceive a higher gratification than to have sat in his company and heard him converse, "Ay, bairn" interposed his mother, in her broad Yorkshire dialect, " but thou would'st not have let him have all the talk to himself,- thou would'st have put in thy word, I'll warrant thee". Joseph Milner, who was, in fact, when he liked his company, a great talker, joined very heartily in the laugh thus raised at his expense'.[2]

Isaac describes his early childhood, in the third person:

'Isaac, when a little boy of six years old, began to accompany his brother Joseph every day to the Grammar School; and at ten years of age could construe Ovid and Sallust into tolerable English, and was then beginning to learn the rudiments of the Greek language. The premature death of their father (when Isaac was aged ten) ruined all the prospects of Isaac's advancement in learning. His mother was obliged to abandon the prosecution of her husband's plan; and, that her son might acquire a livelihood by honest industry, she wisely employed him in learning several branches of the woollen manufactory at Leeds'.[2]

However, the headmaster of Leeds Grammar School, the Rev. Moore, had recognised his brother Joseph's abilities and, with the help of other friends of the family, arranged his education at St. Catharine's College, Cambridge, after which he was ordained deacon and became curate at Thorp Arch, West Yorkshire. In 1767, Joseph was appointed headmaster of Hull Grammar School and a lecturer at Holy Trinity Church, Hull, and was thus able to finance Isaac's education.[3] Initially, he asked the Rev. Miles Atkinson to visit Isaac:

'Upon proceeding to the work-room in which Isaac Milner then laboured, Mr Atkinson found him seated at his loom, with Tacitus and some Greek author lying by his side. Upon futher examination, it appeared, that...his love of classical learning remained unimpaired. After a private interview with Mr Atkinson...the master of the establishment entered the work-room, and addressing young Milner, said to him "Isaac, lad, thou art off". The delight exhibited by the youth, on hearing these words, was declared by Mr. Atkinson to be quite indescribable'.[2] Joseph then invited Isaac to become his 'usher', (ie assistant teacher), and over the next two years, in the words of Mary Milner, Isaac became:

'a tolerably good classic, and acquainted with the first six books of Euclid'.[2] (Joseph became a committed supporter of the 'evangelical' movement and remained in Hull, where he died in 1797).

At Queens': Student 1770; fellow 1776; President 1788.

In 1770, Joseph engineered his brother's admission to Queens', both of them travelling on foot to Cambridge, with occasional lifts in a wagon.[2,4] Isaac became a 'sizar', (ie an undergraduate who received some assistance with expenses in return for some unskilled work for the College), but he resented his menial duties such as ringing the chapel bell and bringing the first dish to the fellows' table, and was teased for his northern accent.[1,5] The story goes that when he was admonished for spilling a tureen of soup he responded:

' "When I get into power I will abolish this nuisance!" This expression...occasioned, as it is said, much merriment among the fellows; who, of course, did not detect, under the rough exterior of the Sizar, the future president of their College'.[2,4] (However, sizars were excuded from waiting at table in 1773, when this duty was undertaken by the President's gardener and the porter).[2,6]

We have another glimpse of his undergraduate days in 1772, when he became unpopular with his peers by being the only student at Queens' to refuse to sign a petition against the compulsory subscription to the Thirty-Nine Articles of the Church of England, which was required when appointed to a Church office, and on enrolment in, or graduation from, the English Universities.[6]

His exceptional talent became apparent in 1774, when he graduated as 'Senior Wrangler' (ie in first place) in the Mathematics Tripos examination. His performance was sufficiently outstanding for the 'moderators' (examiners) to write: 'Incomparabilis' after his name, although he had been despondent about his performance.[2,4] Also, he was awarded the first place of the two annual 'Smith's Prizes' for mathematics and theoretical physics, which had been established in 1769. He is reported to have ordered an expensive seal to mark the occasion, bearing the head of Sir Isaac Newton.

He was elected a fellow of Queens' in 1776. In 1777, his paper, 'Observations on the Limits of Algebraical Equations...', was read at a meeting of the Royal Society on the 26th of February and, in the same year, he proceeded to the M.A. degree, was appointed a College tutor, and ordained priest in the chapel of Trinity College.[2] In 1778, he received the College living of St. Botolph's, Cambridge. However, it is claimed that it was:

'generally understood by the Fellows that the said I. Milner for several years held the living of St. Botolph's in Cambridge, for the express purpose of possessing the income necessary to make him eligible to the...Office of President'.[6]

Academic interests.

In his early years at Queens', he developed a reputation as a notably successful mathematics tutor, and practice papers that he prepared for his students were in such demand that a student from another college bribed a bedmaker to purloin them.[2,6] His academic interests expanded to include chemistry and, in 1782, he delivered chemistry lectures as a deputy for the Professor of Chemistry,[4] while, in the same year, he was granted leave by Queens':

'to build a Chemical Laboratory in the Stable Yard adjoining to the Coal-house';[5] but, unfortunately, he is reported to have developed persistent lung symptoms: 'by incautiously inhaling some noxious gas'.[6] His interests also included mechanics and, when President, he had a workshop in the Lodge with lathes, a furnace, work-benches, grind-stones, bellows and a variety of apparatus.[6] He is reported to have designed and made a lamp:

'as perfect as such an implement could well be. The light was shaded from the reader's eyes; it was thrown strongly upon the paper before him; there was neither shadow nor smoke; and finally the trimming and adjusting gave no trouble worth mentioning. In fact this lamp was a decided "hobby horse" '.[5] In 1794, the College financed the provision of an air pump and: 'pneumatical apparatus', which would be available to the fellows: 'for the purpose of instructing their Pupils in their public Lectures'.[6] He was elected to a fellowship of the Royal Society in 1780 and, in 1783, his interest in chemistry will have marked him out as a candidate for the inaugural Jacksonian Professor of Natural Philosophy, (ie related to the physical sciences), which required the holder to lecture and provide demonstrations.[6] Milner was duly elected, and would remain in the post for nine years, until his promotion to be Dean of Carlisle, during which he developed a reputation as an entertaining public lecturer, alternating each year between mechanics and chemistry. He was considered a: 'first–rate showman', who engendered:

'a high state of interest and excitement...a very capital lecturer...what with him and his German assistant, Hoffman, the audience was always in a high state of interest and entertainment... He did not treat the subjects under discussion very profoundly, but he continued to amuse us, and we generally returned laughing heartily at something that had occurred during the lecture'.[1,2,6] But Milner appears to have viewed the discipline with respect:

'the Subject is intricate & mysterious &...whenever we meddle in it without the utmost care and circumspection, we are likely to involve ourselves in Error & Absurdity'.[1]

In 1787, Milner describes his life as a lecturer:

'In college I lecture from eight to ten in the morning- from that time till four in the afternoon, I am absolutely so engaged that I can scarcely steal half an hour from preparing my lectures, to dine. At half- past five, I get my coffee, go to chapel, and then lie down for an hour.- I then rise, take my milk- look out various articles, and make notes of natural history &c., for the succeeding day. This coming every day, keeps me on such a continued stretch, that I am often very much done up with fatigue...'.[2]

Milner also attracted notice as a moderator in 1780, 1783 and 1785 and, in future years, was:

'frequently called upon to settle the places of men in the higher brackets'.[6] In 1788, when he was asked to decide who was Senior Wrangler between two candidates:

'The examination was conducted with great seriousness and decorum on this occasion; but it not unfrequently happened that, when examining the brackets, Milner was in the habit of indulging in jokes at the expense of those unfortunate men who, when dissatisfied with their situations, had caused him to be called in. Milner had a very loud voice, combined with a peculiar shrillness, by which he could make himself heard a considerable distance.

He was in the habit of calling dull and stupid men sooty fellows; and when he had a class of that description to examine, he would call out to the Moderators, who were at the other end of the Senate House, "In rebus fuliginosis versatus sum", ("I am engaged in sooty matters!")'.[7]

Milner's range of talents was demonstrated again in 1786, when he proceeded to the B.D. degree, no doubt reflecting on his belief that:

'A judicious prosecution of the science of mathematics and natural philosophy is among the very best preparatives to the study of theology'.[3] His opponent in the 'Act' (ie the debate involving the candidate), was William Coulthurst, a fellow of Sidney Sussex College and minister at the Holy Sepulchre Church, Cambridge. (He had been born in Barbados to a slave-owning family and became a joint owner of a plantation in Demerara. But he supported the abolitionist cause and became a friend of William Wilberforce). The Regius Professor of Divinity, Dr. Richard Watson, presided, and was moved to conclude:

'non necesse est descendere in arenam, arcades enim ambo estis', ('there is no need to descend into the arena, for you are both Arcadians', ie inhabitatants of the mythical Arcadia, with its non-attainable perfection). The subject, St. Paul's teaching on faith and works, is said to have been:

'handled by the disputants with a wonderful combination of knowledge, eloquence, and ingenuity, long remembered in the university, and referred to as a type of what a divinity "act" ought to be'.[4] Watson, who became Bishop of Llandaff, would meet Milner again many years later at Lowther Castle, when they were both guests of Lord Lonsdale, and Milner was Dean of Carlisle:

'...Dr Watson...had, many years before, presided in the Schools at Cambridge, when Dr. Milner and Dr. Coulthurst kept the Act which the Bishop had distinguished by his signal approbation...It so chanced, that one day after dinner, at Lord Lonsdale's table...this Act became the subject of conversation, and a discussion arose between the Bishop and the Dean...Dr. Milner...in perfect good humour, had the best of the argument... Dr. Watson, on the other hand, who was in the habit of talking for effect, and who treated the matter with the utmost gravity, became annoyed at his own failure, and at length showed symptoms of being on the very point of losing his temper. At this juncture, the Dean who had a strong sense of the ludicrous, and very little compassion for vexations occasioned by want of temper... exclaimed jocosely, in his usual sonorous tones, "Now, Bishop, will you take the other side, and we'll argue it over again?" The whole scene was felt by all...who ...perceived the imposing character and manners of the stately Bishop of Llandaff, to be exquisitely comic...'.[2] (Milner would proceed to the D.D. degree in 1792).

From 1787, Milner was a member of the Board of Longitude, a government body formed in 1714 to award prizes to encourage the solution of the problem of finding longitude at sea, which would involve the development of accurate chronometers.[1] This would require many visits to London over the years.

In 1798, he was elected to the prestigious Lucasian professorship of Mathematics, once occupied by Isaac Newton, and, although he delivered no lectures, as holder of this office he sat on the committee that monitored a proposal by Thomas Telford, (1757-1834, the renowned civil engineer), to build an iron bridge over the Thames to replace the old London Bridge.[1] However, although the plan was published in 1801, it was eventually dismissed as being too bold an experiment.

Milner was not known for his original work in mathematics or science, but he did contribute to the knowledge of a process to make nitrous acid, which was important in the manufacture of gunpowder. His paper: 'On the production of nitrous acid and nitrous air', was published in the Royal Society's 'Philosophical Transactions' in January 1789, which also included articles by Joseph Priestley, one of the discoverers of oxygen. This would lead to correspondence between them.[1]

Friendship with William Wilberforce.

An important event before Milner's election as President of Queens', was the development of a very close, lifelong friendship with the reformer William Wilberforce, the son of a wealthy merchant. In 1767, Wilberforce had attended Hull Grammar School, where he befriended Isaac's brother, the School's headmaster, Joseph Milner.[8] However, in the following year, after the death of his father, Wilberforce left Hull, as his family had arranged for him to live with relatives in London. In October 1776, he was admitted to St. John's College, Cambridge, and graduated B.A., despite his subsequently-regretted hedonistic lifestyle. He became an M.P. in 1780 and was a strong supporter of William Pitt, who had been a close friend at Cambridge, when the latter became Prime Minister in 1783.

The relationship began in Scarborough in 1784,[4] when Wilberforce asked Milner to accompany him, together with his wife, mother, sister and two or three other ladies, to the south of France. They left in October, in two carriages, to enjoy the usual pastimes of the Riviera, including dinners, cards and gambling, before progessing to Genoa, Italy, and Switzerland.[2,8] Mary Milner reports:

'At Nice, the party entered freely into the English society which the place afforded, and which was composed, for the most part, of persons of high rank. Among other distinguished individuals the Duke of Gloucester was there, with his children, Prince William, and the Princess Sophia; who, like all other young persons who knew him were attracted by Mr. Milner's child-loving disposition...During this journey, the travellers were once in danger of instant destruction; the weight of their carriage having overpowered the horses, when on the very brink of a precipice. The danger was, however, averted by the timely exertions of Mr. Milner, who being possessed of great personal strength, arrested the descent of the carriage in the moment of peril'.[2] But in the latter part of the tour, Wilberforce and Milner read and debated the New Testament in the original Greek, as well as the 'The Rise and Progress of Religion in the Soul' by Philip Doddridge, a leading early 18th century Nonconformist.[4,9] During the tour, Milner is described as:

'sedulously explaining to his friend, his views of the doctrines therein laid down; "until" says Mr. Wilberforce, "by degrees

I imbibed his sentiments" '.[2] While Wilberforce had shown an earlier interest in evangelical Christianity, these travels provoked a major revival of his religious beliefs and he began to get up early to read the Bible and pray, regretting his past life and committing himself to God's work:

'Inwardly, he underwent an agonising struggle and became relentlessly self-critical, harshly judging his spitituality, use of time, vanity, self-control and relationships with others'.[8,9]

(The evangelical movement began in the 18th century, within various denominations of non-Catholic Christians, with an emphasis on religious enthusiasm, on the primacy of faith in Jesus Christ for an individual to be 'saved' from death and separation from God, on regular study of the Bible, on the importance of preaching rather than ritual or doctrinal details, on the experience of conversion- being 'born again', and on the sharing and spreading of the Christian message. In England at this time, it was also associated with anti-Catholic sentiments and with intolerance of other beliefs, and Milner resisted any attempt to allow Nonconformists, as well as Catholics, to study at the Universities).[6]

The tour lasted for most of a year, (although both men briefly returned in the spring of 1785), and Milner is credited with responsibility for Wilberforce's conversion,[6] which contributed to the latter's lifelong concern for reform and, in particular, his parliamentary campaign against the slave trade. This led to the 'Slave Trade Act 1807', which prohibited the slave trade in the British Empire, although the practice of slavery would not be abolished until 1833. Prime Minister Grenville called this:

'a measure which will diffuse happiness among millions now in existence, and for which his (ie Wilberforce's) memory will be blessed by millions yet unborn'.[9] Milner is reported to have provided: 'solid and well-directed advice' for Wilberforce's campaign,[2,6] but it does not sound as if Milner displayed overt religious enthusiasm, as Wilberforce tells us that Milner's:

'religious principles were in theory much the same as in his later life, yet they had at this time little practical effect on his conduct. He was free from any taint of vice, but not more attentive than others to religion; he appeared in all respects like an ordinary man of the world, mixing like myself in all companies, and joining in as readily as others in the prevalent Sunday parties'.[4] Another contemporary view of Milner's faith states:

'I ever esteemed this gentleman to be endowed with one of the most vigorous and penetrating minds I know, but his theological conceptions were always, I confess, one of the inscrutabilities of mystery; a heterogeneous composition of deistical levity and methodistical superstition: disparaging the ceremonies of religion, and performing them with slovenly precipitation'.[1] However, there are many references to his regular attendances at Church services and, in 1793, Milner complains about the current level of religious enthusiasm:

'Then (ie at the Reformation) persons of rank and eminence, some of them at least, attended to the Gospel; now, in general, the lower orders only regard such things, and the great and the high have, all over Europe, forgotten that they have souls'.[6] Also, in 1800, he speaks of the:

'lamentable truth, that the bishops of our country do not understand the real state of religion'.[2]

President of Queens'.

Milner was elected President of Queens' in November 1788, following the death of Robert Plumptre, and he soon began to promote evangelical ideas and practice in the College, as well as to encourage its educational reputation.[4] Gunning, (Henry Gunning, 1768-1854, Senior Esquire Bedell of the University), an unsympathetic commentater on Milner, writes;

'It is very true that the College entirely changed its character, and that the Society, which, under the Presidentship of Dr. Plumptre, had been distinguished for its attachment to Civil and Religious Liberty, became afterwards as remarkable for its opposition to liberal opinions...the number of students increased; but the majority of them were men who in those days were termed Methodists, afterwards Calvinists, and then Serious Christians. Previously to his being President these Low-Church doctrines had been entirely confined to Magdalene College...Dr. Milner soon acquired that entire ascendency over the Fellows, that after a few years no one thought of offering the slightest opposition to his will…'.[5,7]

There is no doubt that Milner could be ruthless in the selection and discipline of the fellows; in 1794, he expelled a non-resident fellow of Queens', Thomas Fyshe Palmer, M.A., B.D. ,[6] as recorded in his own hand, dated January 1794:

'Agreed and ordered, that the Revd Thomas Fyshe Palmer, Fellow of the College, be expelled the College on account of this seditious Conduct. Everyone of the underwritten viz the Master and twelve Fellows, concur in this sentence of Expulsion, and grounded their Judgement upon the Statutes of the College and the Evidence received by them on the subject'. Palmer had become a fellow of Queens' in 1781. He was ordained, but soon left the Church of England and spent the next decade in Scotland, (although retaining his fellowship), founding a 'Unitarian' church in Dundee. In his sermons and pamphlets he advocated various political and religious reforms, including a reduction of war taxation, annual parliaments and universal suffrage and, in 1793, this produced a forceful over-reaction by the government in the aftermath of the French Revolution. He was tried in Perth for sedition and, despite parliamentary support, including from the Whig statesman Charles James Fox and the Whig politician and playwright Richard Brinsley Sheridan, he was sentenced to be transported for seven years to New South Wales. After being taken to London and put in irons for three months of forced labour, he was embarked on the 'Surprize', (a three-deck merchant vessel, which had been launched in 1780), in which, in addition to a variety of convicts and some free colonists, his travelling companions included three of the other four so-called 'Political Martyrs' or 'Scottish Martyrs'. (Thomas Fyshe Palmer, together with Thomas Muir, William Skirving, Maurice Margarot and Joseph Gerrald are named on, and commemorated by, a 90ft tall obelisk on Calton Hill, Edinburgh, which is inscribed: 'Erected by the Friends of Parliamentary Reform In England and Scotland. 1844'). He was fortunate to survive the outward journey, as, after a month, he and one of the other 'martyrs' were close confined, because the Captain had suspected they were planning a mutiny. As he relates:

'I was thrust into a cabin in the midst of that infernal brothel of which I had so often expressed my abhorrence. The language of Newgate was virtue and decency compared with what I was always doomed to hear. My neighbours were divided from me by only a wooden partition, the women were almost perpetually drunk, and as perpetually engaged in clamours, brawls, and fighting. The cabin was not six feet square: it was besides so close and hot under the torrid zone, that we could not bear the weight of our clothes, and were obliged to take it by turns to enjoy the privilege of sitting by the door. With perpetual thirst we only had to drink putrid water. The bed in the cabin was only two feet wide, in which it was meant that we two bulky men should sleep together. We were denied the common privilege of the worst of the felons, to breathe an hour in the fresh air upon the deck. I was refused clean linen. The heat and the confinement was not all that we had to suffer. The ship was so old and crazy, that every wave of the sea dashed the water through its side, and it ran onto my bed...Had I not been under the protection of a gracious Providence, this treatment must have killed me'. But he survived; indeed, when he and the other Political Martyrs arrived at Port Jackson, Sydney, his fortunes improved, as he had been sentenced to transportation but not to servitude. They had letters of intoduction to the governor and, during his exile, Palmer was not subjected to the usual convict regime and able to become involved in various projects, including farming, beer-brewing and trading, writing to a friend:

'The soil is capital; the climate delicious. I will take upon me to say that it will soon be a region of plenty, and wants only virtue and liberty to be another America'. However, he wanted to return to his native shores and, in 1799, together with two colonist friends, he bought an old Spanish boat with the plan to return home, trading on the way. But this was not to be; on an eventful return journey, they were forced to land on one of the Mariana Islands, in the north Pacific, where he died of dysentery in 1802.[6,10]

The strong evangelical movement in Cambridge, which developed at the end of the 18th century, was led by Charles Simeon, a fellow of King's College, but it was Milner: 'who created an enduring evangelical party within the university'.[6]

Milner sought out those who shared his evangelical views and, perhaps surprisingly, in view of his own record as a theologian, he was wary of too much biblical study, concerned that students would become:

'less solicitous to understand and remember the well-tried established arguments for the authority of the Sacred Writings... (and) give too great a weight to minute and trivial objections and difficulties'.[5] A student who left Queens' in 1818 thought that religious views were paramount when being elected to a fellowship there:

'For the profession of certain theoretical opinions, attendance at a certain place of worship, a thorough conceit of their own goodness, and a due contempt and pity for the rest of mankind... is a surer recommendation than talents and learning...'.[6] But Gray, in his history of the College of 1898, marshalls the evidence that Milner's Presidency, although somewhat despotic, was marked by prosperity in terms of student numbers and academic success, including the education of three Senior Wranglers.[5]

Milner changed the nature of the fellowship and quelled resistance by applying pressure to resign, moving some into College livings and, when appointing tutors, recruiting from other colleges when there was not a suitable candidate at Queens'.[6] Milner describes an example of the latter:

'At Queens' we happened unfortunately to have several clever fellows, some time ago, who should have filled our offices of trust as tutors etc. but were disqualified on account of their principles... Our own being very unfit, we went out of college sorely against the wish of several; however, by determining to make no jobs of such things, but to take the very best men I could find, I carried the matter through, in no less than three instances...'.[2] Also, on another occasion:

'Some time ago Queens' College...was in want of a tutor; and there not being a person of my own College whom I judged proper for this truly important situation, I fixed upon Mr. Thomason, (who took his degree from Magdalene as 5th Wrangler in 1796), after looking very diligently through the whole University; and I was certainly induced to appoint him Tutor of Queens' College, entirely on account of his high reputation for learning, good principles and exemplary conduct'.[5] Milner's interest and commitment to educational standards in the College can also be seen in this letter to a tutor:

'The Greek books in which I used to lecture were these: Prose.- Xenophon's Memorab, as an easy book for pupils who know any Greek at all; then Demosthen. Orations, as a harder; Longinus, as still harder and affording to the lecturer a deal to say. Verse.- I used Euripides and Sophocles: In Latin, select parts of Livy, particularly in Second Punic War. In Morals, Locke's Essay is indispensible'.[2,5]

In 1810, he gives his views on student discipline, showing that 'zero tolerance' is not a modern concept:

'...both in our domestic and our public discipline, a more strict attention to the infliction of the lesser censures for the lesser faults, and these censures gradually increasing in severity according to circumstances, would lead to the improvement of our Academical regulations'.[6] However, he advocated the removal of persistent troublemakers and describes the main student offences, as:

'Breaking of lamps and windows, shouting and roaring, blowing of horns, galloping up and down the streets on horseback or in carriages, fighting and mobbing in the town and neighbouring villages; in the day-time breaking down fences and riding over cornfields, then eating, drinking, and becoming intoxicated at taverns or ale-houses; and, lastly, in the night frequenting houses of ill-fame, resisting the lawful authorities, and often putting the peaceable inhabitants of the town into great alarm'.[2,6] (No change there then!). These problems were largely due to students from wealthy backgrounds, who could afford to misbehave.[6]

In the last years of Milner's Presidency, Queens' faced financial pressures and:

'It having appeared that on account of various deficiencies in payments of debts due to the College, and other unforseen circumstances, the Bursar had been obliged to borrow considerable sums of Money at legal Interest...Stocks had to be sold, there was an agricultural depression, and rents were often not paid'.[6]

Milner was, in general, a diligent President, although in later years, ill-health affected his duties. His view of the Presidency is given in a letter to a friend:

'A head of a college is supposed to have little or nothing to do; so I once thought: but he has all the property of the college to manage; and, what is far worse, he has the tempers of parents and guardians to humour about their children and wards. He has abundance of letters to write, and is exposed to many temptations'.[2]

Vice-Chancellor. 1792-93 and 1809-10.

In 1792, Milner was elected Vice-Chancellor, despite his having previously obtained medical opinions about his ill-health and his likely inability to carry out all the duties. Around this time he writes:

'At pesent I am absolutely supported by large doses of the most powerful medicines, repeated several times every day; and although I am thereby enabled to make considerable exertions at home, I can rarely stir out, for any length of time, with safety, and seldom do stir out, without suffering very considerable inconvenience'.[2]

The French Revolution had begun in 1789 and his first tenure as Vice-Chancellor was a time of:

'such great tension and extreme feeling (that) those of liberal or reformist sympathies were in danger of being labelled republicans by reactionary and conservative elements. Feelings grew stronger as the Revolution degenerated into a series of bloody purges'.[6] In this context, in early 1793, William Frend, a fellow of Jesus College, (a reformer who had left the Church of England in 1789 because of his 'Unitarian' beliefs), published 'Peace and Union recommended to the Associated bodies of Republicans and Anti-Republicans', which attacked the Church's establishment and conservative political views, and led to charges in the Vice-Chancellor's court. The 'Annals of Cambridge' report:

'The Rev. William Frend M.A. fellow of Jesus College, this year published..."Peace and Union recommended to the Associated Bodies of Republicans and Anti-Republicans"...On the 4th of March, certain members of the Senate met on the Vicechancellor's invitation at his lodge in Queen's College. They resolved that Mr. Frend should be prosecuted in the Vicechancellor's Court...On the 23rd of April, Isaac Milner D.D. the Vicechancellor issued a summons requiring Mr. Frend's appearance in the Law Schools...to answer a charge...of having violated the laws and statutes of the University by publishing the pamphlet above mentioned, in which religion as established by public authority within this realm and also all ecclesiastical ranks and dignities were impugned...it was alleged that in the pamphlet in question he had...asserted that "ecclesiastical courts, ecclesiastical ranks and titles, are all repugnant to the spirit of Christianity" and profanely reviled and ridiculed the most sacred office of religion'.[10] The subsequent decision of the Vice-Chancellor and heads was that Frend had offended against the University's Statutes and must publically retract his error, which he declined to do, saying that he would: 'sooner cut off this hand than sign the paper'.[5,11] Milner then refused to receive a further plea and issued the following decree:

'I Isaac Milner, D.D., and Vice-chancellor of the University of Cambridge do decree, declare, and pronounce, that William Frend, M.A. ...having refused to retract his error...theVice-chancellor, with the assent of the major part of the Heads of Colleges, has incurred the penalty of the statute, and that he is therefore banished from the university'.[11] Despite subsequent appeals, involving the King's Bench and the Bishop of Ely, the sentence was upheld, although Frend had considerable support among the undergraduates.[6] However, Gunning, who was sympathetic to Frend, is critical of Milner's conduct:

'to an attentive observer of the proceedings in the Vice-chancellor's Court, it was apparent from the first that the Vice-chancellor was determined to convict...In the examination of witnesses, the forms established in courts of justice were constantly violated, and every objection brought forward by Frend, whether founded on the statutes of the University or on the maxims of civil law, were overruled by Dr. Milner'.[5,6,7] It has been suggested that Milner was hoping that his firm action would advance his career.[6]

In 1809-10, when he served again as Vice-Chancellor, he was involved in an unusual case involving:

'An action for slander having been brought in the King's Bench by Thomas Browne D.D. Master of Christ's College, against George Cecil Renouard M.A. fellow of Sidney College, Dr. Milner the Vicechancellor, claimed conusance of the case, (ie Milner considered that the matter should be under his jurisdiction), and his claim was allowed on the 25th of January...The Vicechancellor appointed the 14th of February for proceeding with the cause, when Dr. Browne the plaintiff not appearing, the case was dismissed'.[11] If proceedings had taken place, Renouard, (a classical and oriental scholar and subsequent Professor of Arabic), may have had a strong defence, as Browne would be the first and only Master of Christ's College to be removed from office. (He had acted contrary to the College Statutes and his project to enclose a College estate at Bourn led to a loss of rent and a complaint from the fellows to the 'University Visitor', who ejected him in 1814. He was then found to owe the College £1,300).

Death of Joseph Milner, 1797.

Milner's most important relationship in his lifetime was with his brother Joseph, who, as noted above, had been instrumental in providing his education. Over the years they remained close and the brothers would often visit and stay together in Cambridge or Hull or Carlisle, the latter after Milner's appointment as Dean. In the 1790s, Joseph was engaged in writing what would be a well-known work in the 19th century, his: 'History of the Church of Christ', and Isaac was also involved. Mary Milner writes:

'In the long vacation of this year (1794) Dr. Milner enjoyed, as usual, the company of his brother; being his guest at Hull, and his host at Carlisle. Joseph Milner...was now about to publish the first volume of his History of the Church of Christ...In the preparation of the subsequent volumes of this history for publication, Joseph Milner was assisted by his brother the Dean...'.[2] A subsequent visit by Isaac in 1796 is also described:

'while on his way to Carlisle for the purpose of keeping his residence there, he visited his brother at Hull, and took him with him to spend his school vacation at the Deanery. Mr. Wilberforce, who was at the same time in Hull, on a visit to his aged mother, thus writes in his Diary: "June 9, 1796. Milner preached- very practical and good. Joseph Milner dined with us- simple and pleasant" '.[2] Later in the same year, Joseph writes to a friend:

'I was glad to hear from you on my arrival here with my brother from Carlisle, last Saturday night...The Dean and myself have preached at the cathedral. He has preached several times with great faithfulness and downright plainness on the first and most fundamental truths...My health is pretty good at present, and I am going on with the History; but as I come nearer the Reformation...Indeed the work is very laborious; I did not think it to be so great as it is, before I undertook it...'.[2]

However, in the following year, Joseph's health became a matter of concern and, in October 1797, only a few months after Joseph had been appointed to the important vicarage of Holy Trinity Church in Hull, Milner writes to Wiberforce:

'My Dear Sir, My brother's asthma is but bad. I had thought I should have a very bad account indeed to give of him. He keeps the house, and is, I hope, something better. I cannot persuade him to take sufficient care of himself...'.[2] His condition deteriorated and Milner soon writes again:

'...I must be very short; I am not able to write. A considerable fever, with an increase of asthma, has come upon my poor brother, and brought him to the very gates of death. He still remains in a most critical situation; I very much doubt whether he will recover. This is not fear, but reality...'.[2] This prediction was soon realised and Joseph died on the 15th of November 1797, prompting another letter to Wilberforce on the same day:

'Wednesday Morning, Hull. Oh! My dearest friend, my beloved brother's last words, or nearly so, were, that "Jesus was now doubly, doubly precious to him". Christ called him to himself this morning about seven. I keep to myself as much as possible, and pray- but, indeed, my dear friend, I fear this may be the last letter you will ever receive from me. If the event, which, however, is not worse than the suspense, should prove too much for my weak frame, and already half-broken heart, remember, there was a corner in that heart preserved for you and your half. Oh! That I had followed his steps; or had now strength, as I have some heart, in the dregs of life, to follow them, in warning a thoughtless world! I wish tears would come; I should be easier. Farewell- I had almost forgotten the principal motive that made me struggle to write at this sad moment; viz., that you may lose no time, if you think you can do anything, towards getting a godly vicar. It will be a sad thing if God should punish a careless town by taking away the Gospel from its principal church...Yet- I have a good hope. God does not forsake me. With love to B., Yours, I.M.'.[2]

Dean of Carlisle, 1792-1820.

In 1792, Milner became the first evangelical to achieve high office in the Church, when he was appointed Dean of Carlisle:

'For this preferment he was chiefly indebted to the active kindness of his friend, Dr.Pretyman, Bishop of Lincoln, (Sir George Pretyman Tomline, Bishop of Lincoln since 1787)[5], who, before his elevation to the Episcopal bench, had been tutor to Mr. Pitt... "the Bishop," writes Mr. Milner to Mr. Wilberforce... "espoused my cause with such a glow of friendship as is never to be forgotten". In short, he said, "he should never rest till he saw me settled in a confortable income"...in consequence of the Bishop of Lincoln's representations to Mr. Pitt, he had himself received, from the Prime Minister, "a most handsome and substantial letter", informing him, that he had been recommended to his Majesty for the vacant deanery of Carlisle'.[2] (Twigg, in his history of the College of 1987, reports that the support of Wilberforce had also been influential). Tomline and Milner were of the same age, and the former had been Senior Wrangler at Cambridge in 1772; Milner writes in 1800:

'You must know that the present Bishop of Lincoln and myself were very intimate at Cambridge'.[2] But William Pitt was not generally sympathetic to evangelicals and Milner would never obtain sufficent patronage for a bishopric.[6] Milner remained in the office of Dean for the rest of his life, usually visiting each year, when he presided over Chapter meetings.[5] The years 1814-15 proved an exception, as he stayed for nearly two years, claiming ill-health.[6] This must have caused serious problems for College business, and some undergraduates are reported to have removed the brass knocker on the Lodge door and sent it to Carlisle:

'with the message that perhaps it might be of some use to the Dean of Carlisle, for it was of no use in Cambridge'.[5,6] But Milner made a favourable impression in Carlisle, and his preaching produced such large congregations that: 'you could walk over the heads of the people'.[2] On one of his journeys north he called on a friend in York and found a servant girl washing the doorsteps and, coming across the same scene at his next visit, he said: 'What lass, hast not thou finished that step yet?'.[5]

The 'Bible Society' in Cambridge.

The 'Annals of Cambridge' report that on the 12th of December 1811:

'The Cambridge Auxillary Bible Society was established at a crowded and unanimous public meeting, held at the Town Hall... The Earl of Hardwicke was in the chair. Amongst the speakers were...Rev. Charles Simeon M.A. fellow of King's College, (the leading evangelical clergyman in Cambridge and the founder of the Church Missionary Society in 1799), Dr Isaac Milner Dean of Carlisle and President of Queen's College...The proceedings appear to have excited the most intense interest'.[10] Twigg explains the issues involved: the evangelical movement was resisted by the orthodox churchmen of the Church of England, who also opposed the establishment of a Cambridge branch of the 'British and Foreign Bible Society' (or Bible Society). (This interdenominational movement had been formed in 1804, by an evangelically-minded group which included William Wilberforce, to encourage the wider circulation and use of affordable Bibles). Also, a Cambridge branch was opposed by many senior members of the University:

'who considered that if the young men assumed the character of a deliberating body, it would be productive of great mischief to the university',[7] while Dr Herbert Marsh, Lady Margaret's Professor of Divinity, (and, subsequently, Bishop of Peterborough), believed that it was not right to circulate the Bible without the Prayer Book.[5] The situation posed a dilemma for Milner, who shared the worries of his senior University colleagues, but did not want to offend Wilberforce and like-minded evangelicals, whose influence might have led to further Church preferment. But when Milner spoke, he was in support of a Cambridge branch:

'nobly and manfully, and took shame to himself for being so long in making up his mind'.[6]

In 1813, residual controversy regarding the Bible Society in Cambridge drew Milner into public conflict with Marsh, and Milner informed the Archbishop of Canterbury, in a letter from: 'Queen's College Lodge' dated the 6th of Febuary 1813, that Marsh:

'was pleased, in December 1811, to represent, in a printed address to our Senate, the Church members of the modern society (ie the Bible Society) as neglecting the Prayer Book, and as encouraging a society that might contribute to the downfall of the Established Church. This very uncandid attack (as I thought it) on a number of churchmen who are as sound members of the establishment as Dr. Marsh can wish them to be, induced me, at the public meeting for the formation of an Auxillary Society at Cambridge, to say a few words, in reply to this misrepresentation; and soon after that meeting, appeared, in print, Dr. Marsh's Inquiry, &c., &c., in which I consider myself, among others, grievously misrepresented'.[2] Milner went on to publish: 'Strictures on some of the Publications of the Rev. Herbert Marsh':

'Dr. Marsh appears to me to lay abundantly too much stress on the niceties of Biblical criticism...I do not think, that a minute and accurate investigation of the various readings of manuscripts, or a scientific knowledge of the grounds of preference in settling the very best reading on all cases, ought to be considered as the most important part of divinity...He everywhere takes it for granted, that the poor and unlearned cannot understand the Bible.

Now, whatever doubts may be raised on other points, this is, notoriously, a Popish sentiment, and is, doubtless, the foundation of a large portion of mischievous Popish practice. I differ essentially from Dr Marsh in this point, that the poor and unlearned have not judgement, have not ability, have not leisure, have not inclination, for understanding the Holy Scriptures, and the great fundamental truths contained in them...'.[2] The ill-tempered exchange continued with Dr. Marsh's pamphlet: 'A Reply to the Strictures of the Rev. Isaac Milner', but Milner: 'refrained from publishing any rejoinder', because, according to Mary Milner, his object: 'the permanent advantage of the Bible Society', had been obtained.[2]

A memorable personality.

Many further accounts and anecdotes demonstate that Milner made a memorable impression in a variety of personal and public settings. He was tall, with a large frame which, in his later years, became considerably obese, and elicited the comment: 'the most enormous man it was ever my fate to see in a drawing room'.[6] Gray describes:

'the piece of furniture known as "Milner's chair" in the Gallery of the Lodge, in which two men of ordinary girth can sit, and in which three ladies of slender proportions have contrived to bestow themselves'.[5]

The various descriptives he has attracted include:

'big; boisterous; overpowering; despotic; awkward; arrogant; contemptuous; self-indulgent; an eccentric steeped in corruption and opium addiction; a time-serving reptile; a drug-addled fanatic; a rough loud and rather coarse man; a glutton; the life of the party; sincerely religious; scrupulously conscientious; efficient; thorough; and deeply affectionate'.[2,5,6,12] As well as his close and lifelong friendship with Wilberforce and deep love for his brother Joseph, he had a noticeable fondness for the young. When the future historian Lord Macaulay came to stay in the Lodge aged 12:

'Dean Milner was one of the many valuable friends to whom my dear father was introduced by Mr. Wilberforce...In 1813...I was at school, in the neighbourhood of Cambridge. We had holidays at Easter, but so short...I remember with what delight I learned, on Easter Monday, 1813, that the Dean of Carlisle had sent for me, and that I was to pass the week at the Lodge of Queen's College. My delight was not indeed unmingled with apprehension. I was only twelve years old; Dean Milner must have been upwards of sixty. His figure, which, to a child, seemed gigantic, inspired me with awe. I had also heard some young men...speak with dislike of his rigid opinions, and the sternness with which he exercised his authority...The Dean laid himself out to please and amuse me, as if he had been an affectionate grandfather and I a favourite grandchild. In the first place, he insisted on knowing what I should like for dinner. Then he ransacked his library to find entertainment for me. In the long gallery...I first became acquainted with Moliere and with Richardson. I still remember with what gaiety and interest he talked to me about them...I well remember with what delight I sat by him one morning over a huge volume of the plates of the Encyclopedia, while he explained to me the principle of one machine after another. Then he turned the conversation to Count Rumford's plans in Bavaria, and gave a history of them, so lively, that I have never forgotten it. (Count Rumford had been born Benjamin Thomson in the U.S.A., before being ennobled by the Elector of Bavaria, after a remarkable career)...It was he who discovered the nature of the machinery by which the Invisible Girl diverted and amazed London...This turn of mind, it may be easily supposed, made him a delightful companion for a boy. He had an inexaustible fund of anecdotes about ventriloquism, legerdemain, the performances of automatons, optical delusions, &c...'.[2,5] Also, when two schoolboys visited the Lodge:

'On the second or third day of our visit, he placed us in a bedchamber, and said that he had a curiosity to know how we should translate certain passages from some classic authors, and do a problem or two in mathematics; that we should oblige him. We got into a state of extravagent laughter while closeted together and had not the slightest suspicion that we were undergoing an examination...each of us was admitted to his College on the ground of what we then did'.[6]

As noted above, he is reported to have suffered from chronic ill-health for most of his life, and it has been suggested that he often used this as an excuse to avoid duties that did not interest him. Gunning was of this opinion when he recorded that Milner asked to be excused some duties as Vice-Chancellor on medical grounds and persuaded other heads to take them on.[6] Nevertheless, there are many references to his poor health: for example, it is stated that he was seriously ill soon after his election as President and, in 1802, there is a reference to: 'the Master's indifferent state of health'. Mary Milner's biography contains numerous references to various disabling symptoms, while, in 1799, Milner writes to Wilberforce informing him that he has to take: 'almost twenty grains of opium daily'.[6] But his often-reported indispositions did not stop him maintaining a reputation for being good company; for example, as Vice-Chancellor, he would give dinners on Sundays before the afternoon service at Great St. Mary's Church, which were: 'very merry', while his private parties could be: 'uproarious'.[4,7]

However, in 1803, he faced complaints from some Queens' fellows about his: 'self-indulgence and indolence',[2,6] and Gunning reports that his tour in Europe in 1775 had been at the expense of his duties as one of the two University moderators, leaving his colleague to do all the work, without prior consultation.[6,7] Also, evidence to support a charge of self-indulgence is given by the University Registrary's diary of 1835, 15 years after Milner's death, which reports:

'Today received from the President of Queens' 2 magnificent MS volumes...these had been stolen by Milner and kept in his study'.[6] But he gave significant charitable donations, for example, to the distressed poor of Leeds, his home town.

Final illness, death and legacy.

Towards the end of his life he seldom left the Lodge,[4] and his end came in 1820 when he was visiting Wilberforce in London:

'During the first two or three weeks of Dean Milner's visit to Kensington Gore, his indisposition was not such as to prevent him from using the moderate exercise to which, for years, he had been accustomed. At length, however, a slight affection of the ankle rendered it expedient that he should confine himself to his sofa. Still, nothing like danger was apprehended either by Dr. Baillie, or by himself...Alas! Before... Monday...Dean Milner had been attacked by a difficulty of breathing, and other alarming symptoms, which, though they did not lead Dr. Baillie to forbode a speedily fatal issue, caused him to desire an immediate consultation with some other physician "of experience and high reputation"...as his end drew very near, he became incapable of continued conversation; and being now told, that he was in danger, he grew more composed and calm than he had been before...On the day before his death, he made an attempt to engage in prayer with the servant who attended him; and subsequently desired the same servant to read to him the 14th chapter of St. John's Gospel, a chapter upon which he had, for years, loved to meditate...The night before his death, speaking with much weakness and difficulty, he uttered a few words, conveying to Mr. Wilberforce, who was by the side of his bed, the idea, that he was looking to a better world. On Saturday morning, April 1st, he became decidedly worse; and Mr. W. being called to his room, he said,: "My dear friend, I am leaving you; I am dying". On the same day, about eleven o'clock, he suddenly extended his limbs, uttered three sighs, and ceased to breathe; being in the seventy-first year of his age...A large concourse of friends followed the remains of Dean Milner to their resting-place in the chapel of Queen's College Cambridge...'.[2]

He bequeathed over 3000 books to the College library and £500 for the upkeep of almswomen,[5] while his portrait, by John Opie, 1761-1807, (who painted many emminent men and women, including members of the royal family), remains in the College. A literacy legacy was the five-volume 'History of the Church of Christ', which, as previously described, he co-authored with his brother Joseph. This was to became the most popular English-language history of the Christian Church for several decades, while, in a review in 1959, it is considered that it:

'must thus be reckoned as a book of first importance in the religious history of early nineteenth-century England. Yet, save for a few pages in Abbey and Overton (still the most reliable survey of Evangelicalism after eighty years) Milner's book is now unknown'.[13] In this work, Joseph Milner had tried to emphasise the positive side of Church history, writing:

'The terms church and Christian, in their natural sense respect only good men. Such a succession of pious men in all ages existed, and it will be no contemptible use of such a history as this if it prove that in every age there have been real followers of Christ'.[14] The first three volumes, written by Joseph but amended in manuscript by Isaac, were published in 1794, 1795, and 1797, and republished by Isaac in a revised version in 1800. Volumes four and five, written and edited by Isaac, but with some of Joseph's work, came out in 1803 and 1809. Another edition, re-edited by Isaac was published in 1810 and there would be futher editions after his death.[13]

In conclusion, he was a sincerely religious man, and:

'The abilities of the Dean were of the very highest order; his acquirements most extraordinary; and the versatility of his talents quite wonderful...'.[5,7] Sir James Stephen (1789-1859, a civil servant who made an important contribution to the Slavery Abolition Act of 1833), provides a succinct portrait of a remarkable man:

'He had looked into innumerable books, had dipped into most subjects, whether of vulgar or of learned inquiry, and talked with shrewdness, animation, and intrepidity on them all. Whatever the company or whatever the theme, his sonorous voice predominated over all other voices, even as his lofty stature, vast girth, and superincumbent wig, defied all competitors'.[4]

References

1. Knox, K.C. Milner, Isaac In: Oxford Dictionary of National Biography. Online. 2004.
2. Wikipedia. Joseph Milner. Online. 2020.

3. Milner, M. The life of Isaac Milner, D.D. F.R.S. Seely, Burnside, and Seeley. Fleet Street, London. Second Edition. 1844, and Biblio Bazaar Reproduction Series.
4. Clark, J.W. Milner, Isaac In: Dictionary of National Biography. 1885-1900. Volume 36. Online. 2020.
5. Gray, J.H. The Queens' College of St Margaret and St Bernard. F.E.Robinson. London. 1898. pp 256-69.
6. Twigg, J. A History of Queens' College, Cambridge. 1448-1986. The Boydell Press. 1987. pp 160-97, 201-13, 304.
7. Gunning, H. Reminiscences of the University, Town, and County of Cambridge from the Year 1780. George Bell. Fleet Street, London. 1854.
8. Wikipedia. William Wilberforce. Online. 2020.
9. Hague, W. William Wilberforce: The Life of the Great Anti-Slave Trade Campaigner. Harper Press. London. 2007.
10. Smith, R.A. Thomas Fyshe Palmer, 1747-1802. The Record 1995. Queens' College, Cambridge. Online. 2020.
11. Cooper, C.H. Annals of Cambridge. Volume IV. Warwick and Co.. Cambridge. 1845. pp 448-50, 492-93, 501.
12. Knox, K. Isaac Milner: a time serving reptile? The Record 1993. Queens' College, Cambridge. Online. 2020.
13. Walsh, J.D. Joseph Milner's Evangelical Church History. In: The Journal of Ecclesiastical History, Vol 10. Issue 2. October 1959, pp 174-87.
14. Overton, J.H. Milner, Joseph. In: Dictionary of National Biography, 1885-1900.

CHAPTER 27

Henry Godfrey. President 1820-32.

Summary.

Henry Godfrey was born in 1781, the son of a London grocer. He was admitted to Queens' as a 'sizar' in 1798, and graduated with first class honours in the Mathematics Tripos examination in 1802. He was elected a fellow of Queens' the following year and proceeded to the B.D. degree in 1813.

After the death of the illustrious Isaac Milner in 1820, Godfrey was elected President in a contested and bizarre election, in which he only attracted four votes in the first ballot, in contrast to eight for the Vice-President, William Mandell, and the election was not determined until the fourth ballot, which involved the restricted franchise of the five senior fellows. Much later in the year, the result was contested by a majority of the Society, who submitted two petitions to the Court of Chancery. But, despite sustained opposition to the new President, the Lord Chancellor confirmed the legality of Godfrey's appointment in March 1821.

However, this may have seemed a Pyrrhic victory, as the records of his Presidency contain a litany of disputes within the Society, including a subsequent legal challenge to Godfrey's authority by Joshua King, who would succeed him as President. In 1822, Godfrey proceeded to the D.D. degree by royal mandate, and must have have welcomed some distraction from the Combination Room at Queens', when he was elected Vice-Chancellor for the academic year 1822-23.

He died in 1832, aged 51, and although he may have developed mixed feelings for the College, he was destined to remain within its confines, interred in a crypt under the original

College chapel, where he lies near the select company of Milner and an 18th century Vice-President, David Hughes.

Timeline.

1781.	Born in London. Son of Henry Godfrey, grocer, of Newgate Street.
1798.	Admitted to Queens' as a 'sizar'.
1802.	B.A. , (13th Wrangler).
1803.	Fellow of Queens'.
1805.	M.A. .
1813.	B.D. .
1820.	Death of George III. Accession of George IV, (29th of January). Death of Isaac Milner, (1st of April). Elected PresIdent of Queens'. The election is contested in the Court of Chancery.
1821.	The legality of Godfey's election as President is confirmed by the Lord Chancellor, (27th of March).
1822.	D.D. by royal mandate.
1822-23.	Vice-Chancellor.
1827.	Opposition to the President's candidate for a College appointment leads to a legal challenge to his authority.
1829.	The 'Catholic Relief Act' receives Royal Assent, (13th of August).
1830.	Death of George IV. Accession of William IV.
1832.	Dies on the 16th of October. Buried in the original Queens' chapel.

An undistinguished Queens' fellow, whose Presidency was riven by legal proceedings and dissention within the Society.

Henry Godfrey was born in 1781, the son of Henry Godfrey, a grocer, of Newgate Street, London. He attended St Paul's School, where he was an exhibitioner and, in 1798, was admitted to Queens' as a 'sizar', (ie an undergraduate who received some assistance with expenses in return for some unskilled work for the College). He graduated B.A. in 1802 and was the 13th 'Wrangler'. (A Wrangler denotes the award of a first class honours degree in the final year of the Mathematics Tripos examination). He was elected a fellow of Queens' in 1803, before proceeding M.A. in 1805 and B.D. in 1813. (In 1797, his elder brother Frederick had been admitted to Queens' as a fee-paying 'pensioner', after attending Harrow School).[1]

Isaac Milner died on the 1st of April 1820, and the subsequent election of Godfrey as his successor heralded a time of:

'deep divisions within the society, for a series of bitter disputes broke out after his death, perhaps all the more bitter for having been suppressed for so long'.[2] As Twigg points out, in his history of the College of 1987, it was usual at this time for mastership elections to be contested and Godfrey was opposed by three other candidates: William Mandell M.A., B.D., a fellow since 1803, tutor, Vice-President, an evangelical with notable experience of College business and- as claimed by another fellow, Joseph Jee- Milner's favourite to succeed;[2] George Barnes M.A., B.D., a fellow during 1798-1817 and subsequently rector of Grimston, Norfolk; and the Reverend William Farish of Magdalene College, Cambridge, the brother of Charles Farish, a fellow of Queens' since 1792. (The latter candidate would not receive any support other than from his brother and it is unclear why he was nominated). The conduct of the election is described in detail in an account of the subsequent legal proceedings: 'The Case of The President of Queen's College, Cambridge, Determined in the High Court of Chancery by The Right Honorable Lord Eldon, &c &c. Acting on behalf of His Majesty as Visitor...Edited by Charles Bowdler Esq. ...1821'.[3] This informs us that 16 fellows assembled on the 9th of April 1820 and, after the four candidates were nominated, the votes cast in the first ballot were: Mandell eight; Godfrey four; Barnes three; and Farish one. This was not considered conclusive, as the eight votes for Mandell were balanced by the other eight votes, and did not deliver a required majority. But a second ballot did not resolve the situation, as Mandell received the same eight votes, although Farish switched his support from his brother to Barnes. For the third ballot, Farish, seemingly a loose canon, nominated and voted for another candidate, namely, Edward Anderson, M.A., B.D., a fellow since 1808. However, this new candidate continued to vote for Mandell, while one of Mandell's previous supporters switched his vote to Barnes. At this point, it was considered that the College Statutes devolved the right of election to the five senior fellows, who included both Mandell and Godfrey, together with John Lodge Hubbersty, M.A., M.D., (a fellow since 1781, described as: 'a cotton spinner and a bankrupt'),[4] George Hewitt, M.A., B.D., (a fellow since 1783 and reported to be: 'a scandalous old reprobate'),[4] and Charles Farish, M.A., B.D., (as noted above, a fellow since 1792). Hubbersty and Hewitt had previously voted for Godfrey and, for the final ballot, there were only two candidates, Godfrey and Anderson; we can presume that Mandell saw no point in prolonging the process and he also voted for Godfrey, leaving just Farish's vote for Anderson. Hubbersty, as senior fellow, then pronounced Godfrey as having been duly elected. According to Godfrey's subsequent deposition to the Court of Chancery, there followed some discussion about whether he should immediately proceed to the Vice-Chancellor to subscribe to the declaration of conformity, (ie to the 'Act of Uniformity 1662', which was required before his admission to office), or proceed to take the oath entitled 'Juramentum Praesidentis' as required by the Statutes. Godfrey's subsequent disposition states:

'That the oath entitled 'Juramentum Praesidentis' was then administered to dept, (ie to Godfrey, who continues to refer to himself in this way), by the Senior Fellow, who also, and of his own accord, and without the same being insisted on or asked by dept., then put into the hands of dept. a book containing a Copy of the Statutes of the said College, and delivered to dept. certain Keys belonging to the College Tresury...it was then clearly understood that the dept. would proceed on the following morning to the Vice-Chancellor...early in the forenoon of Monday, the 10th April aforesaid, being the very next day after the Election, and no further or other ceremony having been performed, dept. was accompanied to the Vice-Chancellor of the University by the said Senior Fellow, and the Rev J Jee, M.A, one of the other Fellows of the said College, and in their presence, and in the presence of the Vice-Chancellor, dept. subscribed his name in the Vice-Chancellor's Book to the declaration of conformity to the Liturgy of the Church of England, required by the said Acts of Parliament...And...on the 20th day of April aforesaid, all of the Fellows of the said College who then continued resident therein viz the said J.L.Hubbersty the Senior Fellow, and Messrs Hewitt, Mandell, Anderson, Toplis, Gorham, Jee, and the said J King the Petitioner, being a majority of the whole body of Fellows, did assemble themselves in the Chapel of the said College that the dept. was in their presence introduced by the said Senior Fellow to the Seat of the Master of the said College, and by him Installed therein, as the President of the said College...the said Senior Fellow...recorded in the Register of the said College, the Election of dept as President...as it took place on the 9th day of April aforesaid, and his Admission as President as it took place on the 20th day of the same month...that no objection was made thereto...'.[3]

But several objections were subsequently raised, in particular, whether Godfrey's fellowship was legally held, and whether a delay in subscribing to the Act of Uniformity until the day following the election, invalidated the process. These were the basis of two petitions, delivered in December 1820, which were addressed:

'To the King's Most Excellent Majesty, in his High Court of Chancery, Visitor of Queen's College, in the University of Cambridge'.

The first petition was from Joshua King, (a recently- appointed fellow and the next President), and accused Godfrey of ignoring discussion about the requirement to sign the Act of Uniformity, before asking the Senior Fellow to admit him to the office on the 9th of April. Also, King claimed that Godfrey did not meet the property qualifications required by the President in the College Statutes:

'...and the said H Godfrey was not in fact possessed of such qualification'. (Subsequently, Lord Eldon examined Godfrey's finances and was satisfied that he was, in fact, qualified). This petition concludes:

'Your petitioner therefore humbly prays your Majesty... would be graciously pleased to cause it to be declared, that the said office of President is vacant, and that the said H Godfrey ought to be moved therefrom, and that a new Election ought to take place to fill the same...'.[3]

Mandell was responsible for the second petition, but this was also signed by seven other fellows: Anderson, Toplis (Dean and assistant tutor), Beevor, Jee (bursar and Junior Proctor of the University), Graham, Barham and Dewe. These petitioners claimed that Godfrey's vote had been invalid, as he was a fellow from Middlesex, at the same time as there was another fellow from that County, despite a stipulation in the Statutes that there should not be more than one fellow from Middlesex. (If Godfrey's vote had been discounted, Mandell would have been elected on the first ballot).

In reply, Godfrey claimed that his admission was not completed before the ceremonies in the chapel on the 20th of April, and that, therefore, he had, as required by the Statutes, signed the declaration of faith before his admission was completed. In relation to the second petition, he stated that, from time immemorial, the College had maintained two fellows for Middlesex. The proceedings were protracted and the College was kept in suspense until March 1821, when the Lord Chancellor gave his opinion. This was remarkably lucid, in contrast to the preceeding depositions and arguments. At the start of his judgement he notes:

'This matter comes before me upon two Petitions against the Election and Admission of Mr. Godfrey as President of Queen's College Cambridge, one of these Petitions is offered by the Rev William Mandell, and seven other of the Fellows who have presented it jointly with him, the other Petition is from Mr. King also a Fellow of this Society. There is this difference between these two Petitions namely,- Mr Mandell represents that Mr Godfrey was not duly elected to the office of President, but, on the contrary, that the Petitioner, William Mandell, was duly elected, and ought to have been Admuitted thereto- Mr King, on the other hand, insists, in his Petition, that Mr Godfrey was not duly elected and if duly elected that the office has been since vacated...'. The final part of his judgement was delivered on the 27th of March:

'I ...state the opinion which I have formed with respect to the claim of Mr Mandell to be Master, founded upon his allegation, that Mr Godfrey ought not to have been considered as a Fellow and that (by lessening the number of the Society) Mr Mandell ought to be considered as having been elected by a majority on the first scrutiny. Mr Mandell's Petition assumed the fact that there could not be more than one Middlesex Fellow. According to the Statutes, when they were originally made, that appears to me to have been the intention of the Foundress. But, on looking at the affidavits which have been filed, I find that the practice of electing two Middlesex Fellows has obtained for more than two centuries and a half, and that a form of application to the Crown for a third, is known in the College. Since, therefore, during that long series of years, every Fellow must have forgotten his oath, on the supposition that the Statutes have been violated, and since I apprehend that the Crown could, by a general dispensation, sanction the practice of two Fellows for Middlesex, it did appear to me preferable to refer this usage to a lawful origin, and I conclude, therefore, that Mr Godfrey was a lawful Fellow...It remains to ask,-

I If Mr Godfrey was duly elected and if so,-

II Whether he continues to be Master...this brings us to the point of his Admission, and of his Declaration of Conformity required by the Act 12 and 14 Charles II...I am... disposed... to hold, that the Admission of Mr. Godfrey was not complete when he subscribed before the Vice-Chancellor on Monday morning the 10th April, and that his real Admission was that which was made by the ceremonies of the 20th April...The next question is, Whether the Admission was too long delayed, from the 9th to the 20th April? Now I cannot bring myself to say that it was...I do hereby, after due consideration...Declare that the said Henry Godfrey is now in my Judgement entitled to hold and enjoy the Office of President of the said College and all the emoluments and rights thereunto appertaining, and I therefore do not think it proper to comply with the prayer of either of the said Petitions but it appears to me, nevertheless, to be fit that the Costs of the Petitioners, and of the said Henry Godfrey, and of His Majesty's Attorney-General, relating to the said Petitions, be respectively paid out of the funds of the said College. ELDON.C.'.[3]

Therefore, after almost a year since his election, at which he had received the support of only three of his fellows on the first ballot, Godfrey's position was secure. However, a majority of nine fellows had attempted to dislodge him, including the Dean and the bursar, and the Society continued to face a crisis of morale. Gray, in his history of the College of 1898, suggests that Mandell would have been elected but for: 'the unhappy mental aberration of which he was afterwards the victim',[6] but we have no futher details of this claim and Twigg, in his history of the College in 1987, points out that he remained active for many years and retained his fellowship until his death in 1843, having been University Proctor, University Preacher, Vice-President, Dean and tutor.[2] (A record of him in the year of the disputed election is the publication: 'The Blessedness of dying in the Lord. A Sermon preached in the Chapel of Queen's College, Cambridge. On occasion of The Death of His Late Majesty King George the Third By William Mandell, B.D. Vice-President and Tutor of Queen's College. "The Memory of the Just is Blessed". Cambridge:...Printed by J. Smith, Printer to the University...1820'). However, perhaps Gray's comment was related to Mandell's capacity for very intemperate behaviour, several examples of which are described in Twigg's detailed account of further disputes in the College over the next few years. Relationships must have been particularly difficult in the months after Lord Eldon's judgement, (no doubt exacerbated by contemplation of the costs to be paid) as, in October 1821, Godfrey convened the fellowship:

'for the purpose of taking into consideration frequent interruptions of Harmony and open Violations of Decency which had been stated by a Majority of the Fellows as having prevailed for some time past, in one instance unhappily productive of

Personal Violence'.[2] This led to meetings over six days, four of them consecutive, and:

'several Fellows were censured. William Mandell expressed the "deepest contrition" but was nonetheless "very severely reprimanded" by the president for "repeated Insults in the Hall and Combination Room...open Acts of Provocation...Attacks on Private Character...a want of Delicate Regard to the feelings if several Members of the Society". He promised to "be more circumspect in the whole of my conduct and behaviour". George Hewitt was found guity of "violating order and Decorum in the Combination Room...by striking Mr. Mandell the first Blow and using terms of Reproach to him under the Irritation of great provocation"; Hewitt also tendered his profound apologies'.[2] Perhaps the apologies suggest that Godfrey had displayed some interpersonal skills in managing such difficult colleagues and achieving a degree of resolution. There were futher outcomes from these meetings; Hewitt was censured: 'for accusing the President of Partiality', and it was found that Hubbersty was guilty of: 'Violating Order and Decorum in the Combination Room', but excused censure as: 'he acted under the influence of Passion having been irritated by Gross Provocation'. Also, Anderson was censured at one of the meetings:

' "for tending to asperse most grossly" the characters of three other Fellows present; he quickly apologised, claiming that his remarks were uttered in the "heat of debate" '.[2]

In 1822 there was another serious instance of conflict, when the senior bursar, Jee, was in dispute with the senior fellow, Hubbersty; once again this led to very protracted meetings, over six days:

'Jee admitted to having cast unfair aspersions upon Hubbersty's character, and offered a full apology. The fellows considered that no further action was necessary: Jee's words, they felt, had been uttered "under the influence of peculiar circumstances which might lead him to entertain a mistaken notion of his duty but which by no means afford any justification of his Conduct". But they also rejected Hubbersty's counter-accusation that Jee had brought a "conspiracy" against him; and whilst Jee had "manifested some neglect and betrayed confusion in managing the pecuniary concerns of the College", it was felt that "his integrity and zeal for the best interests of the College have been altogether unimpeached and...his incapacity to conduct its affairs has not been established" '.[2] This dispute may have been related to a previous build-up of hostility between them, as Jee would later claim that, in 1819, Milner had asked him to enquire into Hubbersty's character, and that Hubbersty was rumoured to keep a woman in the town. Also, in September 1821, they had been in a dispute over Mandell's handling of the tutorial account, which required the President's arbitration.[2]

In 1824, Jee made a further contribution to the College's disharmony, when he was fined for being absent from College, refusing to explain his reasons, and for having:

'denied and resisted the Authority of the President in manner and language most contemptuous and insulting'.[2]

In 1827, yet another dispute had to be resolved by the Lord Chancellor in the Court of Chancery, when Godfrey's nominee for senior bursar was opposed by a majority of the fellows. Godfrey did not allow any other nominations, and claimed that the President's agreement was necessary for the office, which provoked Joshua King to present his second petition to the King, as Visitor to the College. The outcome, in the following year, is reported in the 'Annals of Cambridge':

'On the 22nd of June, Lord Lyndhurst Lord Chancellor gave judgement on a petition from certain fellows of Queen's College to the King as Visitor. The judgement was, that by the statutes of the college the concurrent voice of the President is necessary in all college elections. The petitioners' case was argued by Mr. King...'.[7]

In 1822, Godfrey proceeded to the D.D. degree by royal mandate and must have welcomed some distraction from the Combination Room at Queens', when, later in the year, he was elected to serve as Vice-Chancellor for 1822-23.[1] On the 19th of February 1823, as an evangelical, he will probably have supported the considerable majority of the Senate, which voted in support of a petition to the House of Commons which opposed the admission of Roman Catholics to political power.[7] (However, in 1829,

George IV, under intense political pressure, would reluctantly agree to the 'Catholic Relief Act', which permitted Catholics to sit in the Westminster Parliament). On a more positive note, Godfrey, as Vice-Chancellor, was present at two ceremonies to celebrate new college buildings. On the 2nd of July, 1823:

'the first stone of the new buildings of Corpus Christi College was laid by Philip Earl of Hardwicke High Steward of the University, attended by the Vicechancellor, Heads of Houses, Noblemen...who walked in procession from the Senate House... The new buildings were designed by William Wilkins Esq. M.A. of Caius College. They consisted of a Hall, Chapel, Library, Master's Lodge, and numerous apartments for the fellows and scholars...'.[7] In the following month, Godfrey was also present at the start of another building project, involving the same architect:

'On the 12th of August, being the King's birthday, the first stone of a new court at Trinity College was laid by the Right Honourable Charles Manners Sutton Speaker of the House of Commons (deputed by his Majesty to represent him on the occasion), attended by the Vicechancellor, High Steward, Noblemen, Heads of Houses...who came in procession from the Senate House...This new court, (was) called the King's Court...'.[7] Also in 1823: 'This year the Town was lit by gas'.[7]

Godfrey's involvement with University affairs is again recorded in 1829, after a major disturbance:

'On the 9th of April, a great number of Undergraduates, who had taken offence at the Senior Proctor, assembled in front of the Senate House, and on his coming out assailed him with groans, hisses, and offensive missiles. They followed him to the gates of his college, and continued assembled for several hours...'.[7] This prompted a letter from the Proctors to the Vice-Chancellor:

'Sir, We beg leave respectively to state that yesterday the Proctors in the execution of their duty were resisted and most grossly insulted by a large body of the Undergraduates of this University...We therefore feel that the Proctors have not sufficiently the confidence or support of the Heads of Houses to enable them to maintain that discipline which they have engaged to uphold. Under these circumstances we beg leave respectfully to resign the several offices which have been entrusted to us...'.[7] This provoked a rapid response from the establishment and, on the 13th of April, the Vice-Chancellor together with nine heads, including Godfrey, published the following notice:

'Whereas on Thursday last...a great number of Undergraduates assembled together in a tremultuous manner, and, as it has been represented to us, with a premeditated design of insulting certain of the University Officers: We the Vice-Chancellor and Heads of Colleges hereby give notice, that if any persons in statu pupillari shall hereafter meet together in such manner and with such design, and, being so met, shall offer any insult to any University Officer, or, being warned to disperse, shall not immediately comply, they shall, on being duly convicted, be expelled from the University'.[7] But the demonstrators had got their way, as the resignations were not rescinded and new Proctors were elected on the 22nd of April. (Also in 1829:

'On the 19th of May, Mr. C. Green, accompanied by two members of the University, ascended in a balloon from Warwicker's Yard, Barnwell. The balloon descended in the parish of Grendon, near Wellingborough').[7]

While the available records of Godfrey's Presidency mainly focus on the quarrels and divisions in the College, more positive aspects of his tenure include major renovations to the College's Old Library, (which dates from 1448 and is still situated in its original room, with bookcases incorporating medieval lecterns),[4] repairs to the Lodge and the 'Walnut Tree Court' and, in 1822, the Lodge was: 'furnished at the Master's discretion'.[6] In another positive event, in 1823, it was:

'Agreed that in consequence of the depreciation of the value of money it is equitable that the foundation and other scholarships of small amount should be increased...'.[6]

Gray describes an important social change in 1831, when the beginning of the dinner-hour was changed from 3pm to 4pm, while Evening Service was altered to 5.30pm, followed by supper at 8pm. This was the start of a trend to later meals, which allowed time for activities such as boating, cricket, athletics and football.[5]

(Boat races were introduced at Cambridge in 1827 and the Oxford and Cambridge boat race was initiated in 1829).

Godfey will have been aware of a particularly colourful fellow-commoner at Queens' in 1822, namely Charles Philippe Hippolytus de Thierry, the son of an attendant at the Court in Versailles, who had fled to England after the Revolution and claimed the title of 'Baron'. During his time at Cambridge, he met two visiting Maori chiefs and a missionary, Thomas Kendall, who inspired him to arrange the purchase of 40,000 acres in New Zealand, with the aim of establishing his own sovereign state on the North Island. This transaction was documented in 1823, when he received a somewhat dubious: 'Deed of Grant', relating to about 40,000 acres as the property of:

'the Baron Charles Philippe Hippolytus de Thierry, of Bathampton, in the County of Somerset, and of Queen's College Cambridge'. (The Maori chiefs were well-known in Cambridge at the time and were under the protection of Samuel Lee, the Professor of Arabic since 1819. Lee was a remarkable and brilliant linguist who had been a carpenter's apprentice before the accidental loss of his tools had led him to become a school teacher, and who had then entered Queens' as a student in 1813, when aged 30). Many years later, in 1837, Thierry eventually arrived in Hokianga, New Zealand, with about 90 Australians recruited in Sydney, but his dream of a kingdom did not appeal to the local Maori chiefs and, after being deserted by his followers, he was only allowed to occupy a modest plot. But he exaggerated his success to France, requesting that a French colony be established, with himself in charge. While this enterprise appears to have been unlikely to succeed, it has been suggested that his activities may, nevertheless, have been a factor in prompting the annexation of New Zealand by the British Crown, with the Treaty of Waitangi in 1840. Sadly, his reduced acreage did not provide much of a living and he ended his days in poverty, as a music teacher in Auckland, dying in 1864.[8]

Godfrey died on the 16th of October 1832 and, although he may have developed very mixed feelings about the College, he was destined to remain within its confines, interred in a crypt, (which had been rebuilt in 1773), situated in part of the space below the original chapel. He shares this with his illustrious predecessor, Isaac Milner, and with David Hughes, M.A., B.D., whose coffin had been placed there in 1777. (David Hughes had been elected a fellow in 1727, had served in several College offices, including bursar, Dean and Vice-President, and had been vicar of Little Eversden, Cambridgeshire). The College archives and website contain photographs of their coffins, taken in 1986.[4]

References

1. Venn, J.A. Alumni Cantabrigienses. Cambridge University Press. London. 1922-1954.
2. Twigg, J. A History of Queens' College, Cambridge. 1448-1986. The Boydell Press. 1987. pp 220-22.
3. Bowdler, C. (ed) The Case of the President of Queen's College, Cambridge, Determined in the High Court of Chancery. Printed for Joseph Butterworth and Son 43, Fleet-Street and John Deighton and Sons, Cambridge. 1821.
4. Queens' College, Cambridge. Online. 2020.
5. Milgate, M. The Case of President Godfrey. The Record 1998. Queens' College, Cambridge. Online. 2021.
6. Gray, J.H. The Queens' College of St Margaret and St Bernard. F.E.Robinson. London. 1898. pp 271-74.
7. Cooper, C.H. Annals of Cambridge. Volume IV. Warwick and Co.. Cambridge. 1845. pp 541-43, 558-62.
8. Wright, I. A Queens' King, and Maoris in Cloister Court. The Record 1990. Queens' College, Cambridge. Online. 2021.

CHAPTER 28

Joshua King. President. 1832-57.

Summary.

Joshua King was born in 1798 in Lancashire and attended Hawkshead Grammar School, which had educated the poet William Wordsworth. He came to Queens' in 1816, after a brief period at Trinity College, Cambridge, and, in 1819, graduated as the Senior Wrangler, (ie in first place), in the Mathematics Tripos. He was elected a fellow of Queens' in 1820, the year in which Isaac Milner died, and Henry Godfrey became President of Queens'. However, Godfrey's election was contested, and his tenure would be a period of division and conflict within the Queens' Society. King was active in his opposition to Godfrey, presenting two petitions to the Court of Chancery, but College business continued nonetheless, and King served as a successful tutor and senior tutor. He must have gained the trust and confidence of the fellowship, as he was their unanimous choice to be the next President, after Godfrey's death in 1832.

However, King's health soon began to fail; later in 1832 he suffered a stroke and although he made a recovery, this may have left him with some impairment. He suffered a more severe stroke in 1843, after which all his activities were affected by chronic ill-health.

Any residual effects of his first stroke did not prevent his election as Vice-Chancellor for the academic year 1833-34, during which he showed his true colours as a: 'vigorous Tory', by vetoing proposals to allow Nonconformists to proceed to University degrees; also, when 62 members of the Senate petitioned the House of Lords to support the proposal, King organised a counter-petition, defending the status quo.

In 1839, King was elected to the prestigious Lucasian professorship of mathematics, despite having published only one short paper in 1823, although he had developed a reputation as an examiner in the subject. But, after his second stroke, even his examining was curtailed.

During King's Presidency, the University was in dire need of reform, as its main purpose had become restricted to the provision of ordinands for the established Church. The main subjects studied were limited to classics and mathematics, while the rapidly-expanding body of knowledge in the natural sciences was ignored. When the Chancellor of the University died in 1847, the resulting hotly-contested election for his successor reflected the divide between traditionalists and reformers. Prince Albert had been persuaded to stand for election by some of those who wanted change, while the conservatives fielded the Earl of Powis, a Tory politician with a record of defending the interests of the Church of England. Once again, King showed his aversion to reform, by joining Powis' election committee. But, fortunately for the University, Prince Albert was victorious, albeit by a narrow majority.

One of King's contemporaries provides a depressing summary of unfulfilled potential:

'...his reputation in Cambridge was immense. It was really believed that nothing less than a Second Newton had appeared. They really expected his work as a Mathematician to make an epoch in the science. At an early age he became President of Queens'; later, he was Lusasian Professor. He published nothing; in fact, he did no mathematical work. But as long as he kept his health, he was an active and prominent figure in Cambridge, and he maintained his enormous reputation...'.[1]

He died in 1857 and is buried in the original Queens' chapel. He left a widow and three children.

Timeline.

1798.	Born in Lancashire.
1815.	Admitted to Trinity College, Cambridge, in October.
1816.	Admitted to Queens' as a 'sizar' in February.

1819. B.A. . Senior Wrangler.

1820. Fellow of Queens'. Tutor. Petitions the Crown opposing the recent election of Henry Godfrey as President.

1827. Senior tutor. Petitions the Crown opposing the President's authority related to a College appointment.

1830. Death of George IV. Acession of William IV.

1832. Elected President of Queens'. Suffers a stroke but makes a recovery.

1833. Marries Mary Brocklebank.

1833-34. Vice-Chancellor. Vetoes proposals to admit Nonconformists to the University.

1837. Death of William IV. Accession of Queen Victoria.

1839. Elected Lucasian Professor of Mathematics.

1843. Suffers another stroke.

1845-49. Potato blight in Ireland, followed by the 'Great Famine'.

1845. The start of major renovations to the College's chapel and hall.

1847. February 12th: Death of the University's Chancellor, the Duke of Northumberland. The Earl of Powis is proposed as his successor by a group of fellows from St John's College.

February 13th: the Master of Trinity College, on behalf of many who regard this with dismay, writes to Prince Albert's secretary asking if the Prince would agree to a request from a number of heads of Colleges to be a candidate for election as Chancellor.

February 15th: Prince Albert agrees.

February 28th: Prince Albert elected Chancellor.

March 25th: Prince Albert inaugurated as Chancellor at Buckingham Palace.

July: Queen Victoria and Prince Albert visit Cambridge.

1848. October 31st: The Senate approves reforms to the University of Cambridge, after significant opposition.

1849. Resigns as Lucasian Professor.

1850. The Prime Minister, without consulting Prince Albert, institutes a Royal Commission to report on the Universities. Commissioners are appointed.

1851. A Queens' committee is formed to address the College's debts. Another Queens' committee is formed to respond to questions from the Commissioners.

1852. The Commissioners report to the Queen. Death of the Duke of Wellington.

1853. A Queens' committee is formed to examine the report of the Commissioners.

1853-56. Crimean War.

1856. The Cambridge University Act of 1856. A Queens' committee is established to consider the implications of the Act.

1857. Indian Rebellion begins on the 10th of May. Dies at the President's Lodge, on the 1st of September. Is buried in the original chapel of the College. He leaves a widow, Mary, and three children.

A gifted mathematician who only published one paper. A highly-regarded tutor and examiner. An active and prominent traditionalist figure in Cambridge, whose later career was blighted by ill-health.

Joshua King was born on the 16th of January, 1798, the son of David King of Lowick Bridge, near Ulverston, Lancashire, while his mother descended from Michael le Fleming, who, in about 1107, had been granted land in Furness, Cumbria.[1] He attended Hawkshead Grammar School, whose scholars had included the poet William Wordsworth, and afterwards received some instruction in mathematics from John Gough of Kendal (1757-1825), a blind scientific polymath, who acted as a private tutor of mathematics to select pupils, (including William Whewell, who would become Master of Trinity College, Cambridge, in 1841), to prepare them for University.

King was admitted to Trinity College, Cambridge, as a 'sizar' in 1815, (ie an undergraduate who received some assistance with expenses in return for some unskilled work for the College), but transferred to Queens', also as a sizar, in February 1816; it is thought that he was attracted to the evangelical reputation of his new College.[2] He was awarded College prizes in Latin and mathematics and, in 1819, became Senior Wrangler, (ie in first place in the Mathematics Tripos examination), also receiving the first-ranking of the two annual Smith's Prizes for mathematics and theoretical physics, which had been established in 1769. One contempory opinion was that he graduated: 'with higher distinction than perhaps any other man ever did',[2] and this led, the following year, to his election as a fellow of Queens'. He proceeded M.A. in 1822 and, in 1823, he produced his one and only publication, a short paper:

'A new demonstration of the Parallelogram of Forces', which was read before the Cambridge Philosophical Society on the 14th of April and published in the Society's Transactions.[1] In 1838 he proceeded to the LL.D degree by royal mandate, and was admitted to Lincoln's Inn, (one of the four London 'Inns of Court' to which barristers of England and Wales belong), in 1828.[3]

After the death of Isaac Milner in 1820, Henry Godfrey succeeded as President of Queens', after a bitterly contested election, as described in the previous Chapter. Later in the year, two petitions challenging the result of the election were considered by the Court of Chancery, but failed to dislodge the new President. One of these was prepared and presented by King, despite his very recent appointment to the fellowship, and he would present another petition in 1827, this time challenging Godfrey's authority in relation to College appointments. Although the latter petition also failed, Lord Lyndhurst's judgement spoke of Dr King as having:

'argued on behalf of the Fellows of the College with much industry and talent'.[1] But despite the volatile instability of the fellowship during Godfrey's tenure, King was a successful tutor and senior tutor,[1] who must have gained the confidence of his colleagues, as he was their unanimous choice to be their next President. However, he was not in holy orders, as required by the College Statutes, and Gray, in his history of the College of 1898, notes that as King was a 'Tory', and as the 'Whigs' were in power, there was concern that the necessary dispensation from the Crown for his election would not be forthcoming. (The Tories championed Crown and Church, while the Whigs were more sympathetic to religious toleration and political reform). But the dispensation was duly provided.[4]

However, the new President's health soon began to fail:

'...in the year in which he was elected President, Dr. King was seized with a stroke of paralysis; from this he, to a considerable extent, recovered, but a severe attack in 1843 reduced him to an invalid condition, which gained upon him more and more till the time of his decease'.[1]

Nevertheless, in the following year, 1833, he was married to Mary, daughter of the Reverend J. Brocklebank of White Beck, Cumberland,[4] and was elected Vice-Chancellor for the academic year 1833-34. In his first month in this office, on the 2nd of December 1833:

'... a very violent attack was made by an excited mob on the Anatomical Theatre. The riot act was read, and by the exertions of the magistracy and constables peace was restored, though not until considerable damage had been done to the building and its contents. The outbreak was occasioned by the body of an aged pauper, of Trinity parish, named Porter, having been irregularly given up for dissection under a mistaken construction of the Anatomy Act. The body was on the following day restored to the parish officers for interment.'.[5] King was involved, when:

'The Vice-Chancellor headed a party of Master of Arts, and Under-graduates for the protection of the (Anatomical School and) Museum, and succeeded in doing so, though at considerable personal risk and at the expense of some rough handling'.[1]

Reformers, who supported the admission of Nonconformists to degrees and offices in the University, presented proposals for reform during King's year of office as Vice-Chancellor, but he vetoed these in the 'caput senatus'. (This was a committee led by the Vice-Chancellor, in which any member could veto any proposal, before it could be considered by the Senate). But this did not end the matter and, on the 21st of March 1834, 62 resident members of the Senate presented a petition to the House of Lords, asking for the abolition of:

'every religious test extracted from members of the University before they proceed to degrees, whether of Bachelor, Master, or Doctor in Arts, Law, or Physic... Your Petitioners therefore humbly beg leave to suggest that as the legislative bodies of the United Kingdom have repealed the Test Act and admitted Christians of all denominations to seats in Parliament...they think it both impolitic and unjust that any religious test should be exacted in the University previously to conferring the civil advantages implied in the degrees above enumerated'.[5] Predictably, this was soon opposed by King, in a published protest, which had many signatories, including ten other heads of Colleges. This was followed by a petition to the House of Lords, which was organised in the hall at Queens',[6] where it was signed by 258 members of the Senate:

'Your Petitioners...most earnestly pray that your honourable House will not lend its countenance to the changes suggested in the Petition above referred to, and thus in effect formally recognise and sanction dissent from the Established Church within the University itself...'.[5] This was presented on the 21st of April by the Chancellor of the University, the Duke of Gloucester. (Also, in 1835, King was one of seven Tory heads of colleges who secured the election of a Tory Vice-Chancellor, instead of Whig, as the latter supported the admission of Nonconformists).[6]

In 1839, the prestigious Lucasian professorship of mathematics was vacated by Charles Babbage, (1791-1871, who is credited with inventing the first mechanical computer), and eight heads of colleges met on the 17th of January 1839 to determine his successor:[2]

'As president of Queens', King was one of the eight present. Two candidates were nominated- King and...Hopkins- but King won the vote by a majority of seven to one. Even the Master of Hopkins's college voted for King, as, evidently, did King himself '.[2] (William Hopkins, F.R.S. 1793-1866, a mathematician and geologist, was famous as a private tutor of promising undergraduate mathematicians. One of his pupils was George Stokes- later Sir George, 1st Baronet- who would succeed King as Lucasian professor, make seminal contributions to science and mathematics, and serve as President of the Royal Society). King saw the main role of the professorship as having responsibility for the examinations for the Mathematical Tripos and for the two annual Smith's Prizes, which also involved a series of examinations. Although King had been a member of committees in 1827 and 1832 to revise the Mathematical Tripos, and had often examined in the Tripos between 1824 to 1831, when he was Lucasian professor, he examined for the Smith's Prizes on only four occasions, no doubt due to his poor health, which were early in his tenure.[2] (In 1841, it was King's successor, Stokes, who was Senior Wrangler and the first Smith's prizeman).

Academic life was beginning to include a focus on professorial lectures and an interest in new scientific subjects,[2] and, as a non-lecturing professor in poor health, who was not a fellow of the Royal Society, King's reputation and influence was on the wane. This contrasted with the career of William Whewell, (Master of Trinity College, 1841-66), who played a significant role in the development of Cambridge science. In 1848, after the election of Prince Albert as Chancellor, there was an important committee headed by Whewell that proposed a Board of Mathematical Studies, a Natural Sciences Tripos and a Moral Sciences Tripos, but King was not involved. He must have recognised his limitations as, in 1849, he informed the Vice-Chancellor that he would resign as Lucasian professor: 'because of the continued infirm state of my health'.[2] The heads of colleges, but not including King, met on the 23rd of October 1849, when Stokes was elected as his successor, unopposed.

King's opposition to reform was also apparent in the momentous election, in 1847, of a successor to the Duke of Northumberland as Chancellor of Cambridge University. On the 12th of February, the same day as Northumberland's death, several fellows of St John's College publicly proposed the second Earl of Powis as a candidate. Powis was a Tory politician, a defender of the Church of England's interests in Wales, Lord Lieutenant of Montgomeryshire and an alumnus of St John's College, where he had graduated M.A. in 1806. But, as a committed churchman and Tory, he was not an attractive candidate to those such as Whewell, who saw the need for reforms. Therefore, the latter, on the 13th of February, wrote to Prince Albert's Private Secretary, asking if the Prince would be willing to stand for election at the request of several heads of colleges.[7] Events continued to move rapidly and, on the 15th of February, Albert agreed to the proposal if this was: 'the unanimous desire of the University'. Wisely, the Vice-Chancellor, Henry Philpott, (Master of St Catharine's College and a future Bishop of Worcester), was economical with the truth, when he reported that this was, indeed, the unanimous wish of the college heads and, on the 17th of February a delegation to the Prince received his acceptance of the invitation.[7]

The Prince's supporters hoped that Powis would withdraw, but, instead, a lively and acrimonious hustings had begun. At this point, King has a brief mention in the records; an election committee to support Powis was formed in London, after a dinner at the British Hotel, Cockspur Street, at which King was present, together with the President of St John's College. Although the Prince now wanted to withdraw, angry at being misled, he consulted Sir Robert Peel, the previous Prime Minister, asking if he should:

'take a further step in order to stop the possibility of my name appearing in the Contest, and what ought that step to be? If I remain quiet, and my election is carried by a majority, am I to accept or refuse the honour proposed to me? '.[7] Fortunately for the future of the University, he was to accept Peel's advice to permit the election and accept if elected, although he had considerable misgivings.

The contest attracted much argument, emotion and interest. Only senior members of the University had a vote, and many of those in politics and government were urged by Prince Albert's supporters to travel to Cambridge for the election. There were three consecutive polling days and, at the end of the first, held on the 25th of February, Prince Albert had received 582 votes, which only gave him a marginal lead over Powis, whose tally was 572. While the undergraduates could not vote they:

'had also captured the election fever, and vociferously crammed the Senate House throughout the voting'.[7] 'The Times' reports:

'At 12 o'clock an immense number of voters arrived by the London train, and the lower part of the building presented an enormously dense appearance. The general wish seemed to be to get towards the front, to vote and have done with it, and to get back to Town in time. Some not very feeble barriers placed in front of the Vice-Chancellor's little hustings to keep back the flow of the tide, and the wands and staves of the attendants in office, shared the fate of all things fragile'.[7]

On the second day, which merited a further report from 'The Times', Prince Albert increased his lead:

'The row was of a terrific character; missiles of all sorts were employed in assailing the voters, all of whom gladly retreated as soon as they had given in their voting cards, and some refrained from voting at all, after having travelled many miles for the purpose, rather than subject themselves to the fury of the storm raging within the Senate-house'.[7]

At the conclusion of the final day, Prince Albert had received 953 votes, against 837 for Powis, and he was in some doubt as to whether he should accept the result, after such a close contest. But Peel advised:

'the acceptance of the office without reluctance or delay has about it a character of firmness and decision, of supporting friends instead of giving a Triumph to Opponents'.[7] Prince Albert was reassured that he had received the support of a majority of heads and 16 out of the 24 professors, while the resident senior members had voted three to one for him, and he accepted the Chancellorship on the 27th of February.[7] (Powis ungraciously refused the Prince's invitation to the Inauguration, and had further ill-fortune the following January, when he was shot and killed by one of his sons, while shooting pheasants on his estate).

Prince Albert was inaugurated as Chancellor at Buckingham Palace on the 26th of March, 1847, in the presence of many dignatories, including thirteen heads of college; but it is unlikely that King had travelled to London. Later in the year, the Queen visited the University, accompanied by her husband:

'Her Majesty and the Prince left Buckingham Palace on Monday the 5th of July, and travelled by road, to Tottenham, at which place a special train was in readiness to convey them to Cambridge. At the Station...Her Majesty was received by the Mayor and Council...the streets were filled with a countless multitude, who greeted their Sovereign with loud and long-continued acclamations...At the entrance of Trinity College, Dr. Whewell the Master presented the keys to her Majesty...Shortly after two o'clock, Her Majesty being seated on her throne at the upper end of the hall of Trinity College, the doors were thrown open, and his Royal Highness the Prince Chancellor, attended by the Vicechancellor... entered, and his Royal Highness, standing at the foot of the throne, read the following address:- To the Queen's Most Excellent Majesty, the Humble Address of the Chancellor, Masters, and Scholars of the University of Cambridge...'.[5] It is reported that the Queen enjoyed her visit, which included walking with Prince Albert along the 'Backs' of the river Cam, despite thinking that her husband's address was: 'almost absurd',[7] while a subsequent comment on the visit notes that:

'the Poet Laureate, Wordsworth, had composed an Ode of such dismal banality that it gave clear evidence of failing powers or possibly- being a St. John's man and a Tory- lack of personal commitment to his task'.[7]

The new Chancellor's interests and influence would play a significant role in supporting a pivotal period of University reform, which, at least in relation to religious reforms, will have been an uncongenial time for the ailing President of Queens'. The main purpose of the University was still to provide clergymen for the Church of England, while the main studies were limited to classics and mathematics. Over half the students were at Trinity and St John's, where the majority of the fellows were clergymen,[7] and standards of teaching were so low that University teaching had been largely replaced by private tutors. Soon after his election, Prince Albert received a letter from Whewell on the 8th of March, advocating that the University should incorporate: 'some of the most valuable portions of modern science and literature'.[7] But Whewell's vision for change was timid and limited, and Prince Albert moved to enlist additional allies to support his recognition of the need for urgent reform. He asked Adam Sedgwick, to be his official secretary in Cambridge and requested the Vice-Chancellor, Henry Philpott, to provide a list of: 'studies & scientific enquiries pursued at Cambridge at this time', which showed that there were no, or minimal, studies in history, political economy, law, psychology, modern languages, geography, chemistry, art, astronomy, natural history, or science.[7] (Adam Sedgwick, 1785-1873, Professor of Geology, would be an unusual reformer today, as he opposed Darwin's theory of natural selection and was strongly opposed to the admission of women to the University, describing aspiring women students as: 'nasty forward minxes'). Prince Albert also requested the views of the Whig Prime Minister, Lord John Russell, as well as those of his predecessor, Sir Robert Peel, who wrote on the 2nd of November, 1847, complaining about the inadequacy of Whewell's plans for reform:

'The Doctor's (ie Whewell's) assumption that a century should pass before our discoveries in Science are admitted to the course of Academical Instruction exceeds in absurdity anything which the bitterest enemy of University Education could have imputed to its advocates'.[7]

In December 1847 Philpott wrote to his successor as Vice-Chancellor, with his proposals for reform, including an emphasis on the natural sciences and history, noting:

'The exclusive character of our Studies which gives the University the appearance of a place of Education for candidates for Holy Orders only…',[7] and proposing:

'a new Moral Sciences Tripos involving moral philosophy, political economy, modern history, general jurisprudence, and the laws of England', and a new Natural Sciences Tripos. Prince Albert was active in his support of these proposals, which attracted considerable opposition. But the influential Whewell was persuaded to give his acceptance, and the reforms were approved by the Senate on the 31st of October 1848. Although the Chancellor got much of the credit for this in the press, Philpott must be remembered as the main author of the reforms, which would be mirrored at Oxford.

However, despite Prince Albert's credentials as a reformer, he was ignored and deeply offended in 1850, when the Prime

Minister, Lord John Russell, appointed a Royal Commission on the Universities without consulting him. Only after the event, Russell writes to the Chancellor on the 8th of May 1850:

'Sir, Having announced in my place in Parliament the intention of Her Majesty's Ministers to advise that a Royal Commission should be appointed to enquire into the state and revenues of the Universities of Oxford and Cambridge...I am anxious to explain to your Royal Highness, the views of Her Majesty's confidential servants, in recommending this measure for Her Majesty's approbation...'.[5] The proposed threat to the University's autonomy naturally caused consternation at Cambridge and, on the 14th of May, 1850, the Vice-Chancellor writes to Prince Albert:

'...If the proposed plan be preserved in, the Vice-Chancellor can only regard with the deepest anxiety and sorrow the future prospect of the University. The issuing of a Royal Commission, especially after having been earnestly deprecated by so large a number of resident Members of the Senate, will be talken to imply that, in the opinion of Her Majesty's Ministers, the governing body of the University are unfit for their position...'.[5] But despite his feelings, Prince Albert demonstates his political skills when he replies on the 27th of May:

'My Dear Vice-Chancellor...You are already aware that I did not know of the intention of her Majesty's Government to advise the issue of a Royal Commission, in time, before Lord John Russell's speech in the House of Commons, to be able to communicate with the University...I have since felt that it was not unnatural on the part of the University to look with apprenension at the proposed measure, as affording a means to those who may be ill disposed towards these venerable institutions to vent their hostility against them...I am glad, however, to find upon further communication with the Government...that they were anxious... not to expose the University to needless hostility, by the selection of the persons who are to compose the Royal Commission...I would recommend the authorities of the University not to meet it with opposition, but rather to take it as the expression on the part of the Crown and Parliament, of a natural desire to be accurately informed upon the present state of Institutions so closely connected with, and of such vital importance to, the best interests of the nation...Believe me always, Yours truly, ALBERT, C.'.[5]

The Commission was duly appointed on the 31st of August, and consisted of John Graham, Bishop of Chester, (previously Master of Christ's College), George Peacock, Dean of Ely, (a mathematician and fellow of Trinity College), Sir John Herschell, (Senior Wrangler in 1813 and past President of the Royal Astronomical Society), Sir John Romilly, (the Attorney General and a future Master of the Rolls), and Adam Sedgwick (as noted above, Professor of Geology and the Chancellor's official secretary in Cambridge).[5]

Two years later, the 'Annals of Cambridge' report that:

'On the 30th of August the Commissioners for enquiring into the State, Discipline, Studies, and Revenues of the University and Colleges made their report to the Queen...'.[5] The recommendations included the establishment of many new professorships, but the thorny question of admitting Nonconformists to the University was not resolved, although the report considers that:

'The University will be placed, more or less, in a false position, if it estranges itself from this great movement of liberal progress (ie "the equal enjoyment of civil rights on account of differences in religious opinion"). There is a manifest and intelligible challenge to it to throw open the advantages of its system of education, under proper securities, as widely as the State has thrown open the avenues to civil rights and honours...What securities should accompany such a concession to public opinion; what guarantees for internal peace can be provided... are questions on which we do not presume to express an opinion...'.[5] This issue would be partially addressed in the Cambridge University Act 1856, which decreed that:

'No Person shall be required, upon matriculating, or upon taking, or to enable him to take, any Degree in Arts, Law, Medicine or Music, in the said University, to take any Oath or to make any Declaration or Subscription whatever...'. But a declaration of membership of the Church of England was still necessary to hold certain offices, and for membership of the Senate. (It would not be until the University Tests Act 1871, that all religious 'Tests' would be abolished for any degree- other than a degree in Divinity- and for appointment to professorships, fellowships, studentships and other lay University offices).

Before his Presidency, King had made his mark in the College by his reputation as a tutor, by his experience of College business as senior tutor, and by his popularity within the fellowship. But, as noted above, he suffered his first stroke in the year of his election, and a major recurrence in 1843 significantly reduced his involvement in College, as well as University, affairs; however, he presided over a period of relative harmony at Queens', compared with Godfrey's regime. But the College's financial stability was imperilled by the system for the renewal of leases on College property, as the income was divided among the President and fellows, rather than contributing to expenses and savings. This led the College to make an important resolution in 1845 to change the practice, recognising that:

'... the present system of letting the College property by beneficial leases is highly injurious to the permanent interests of the College...'.[4] Thereafter, the number of beneficial leases was gradually reduced, but the debt in 1849 was £10,200, and it was not until 1851 that a committee produced a plan to eliminate this by repayments over 21 years.

Despite these concerns, major renovation works to the chapel and hall were begun in 1845. In the hall, a plaster ceiling was removed to expose the original oak beams, which needed to be replaced, and an oriel window was restored and filled with stained glass, subscribed by members of the College.[4]

In 1851, a College committee was formed to answer questions from the members of the Royal Commission on the Universities and, in January 1853, another committee had the task of examining the Commissioners' report and suggesting appropriate changes to the Statutes. (This would lead to a relaxation of the requirements for some fellows to be ordained and, when the Statutes were amended in 1860, to the freedom of the fellows to marry).[4] In 1856, yet another committee considered the implications of the Cambridge University Act 1856.[6]

In 1849, Alexander Crummell, who is still remembered as a leading African-American figure in the movement for black rights, was admitted as a student to Queens', aged 30.[8,9] He would graduate with a degree in Classics in 1853. He was born free in New York City, although his father was a former slave, and, after a stuggle to gain an education, he overcame prejudice and resistance to be ordained in the New York Episcopal diocese in 1844. In 1848, he came to England to raise funds to build a church for his New York congregation, financed by evangelical and anti-slavery friends who had close ties with British anti-slavery campaigners. He met many influential people, preached and lectured, before enrolling at Queens'; two of his sponsors were William Wilberforce, the anti-slavery campaigner, and Thomas Babington Macaulay, the historian and politician. The choice of Queens' was probably influenced by its evangelical and missionary reputation, as established under Isaac Milner. Crummell writes in 1848:

'An English degree (was) of great value in America', (which could benefit his) 'own family comfort and my children's welfare', (while it was) 'a matter of importance that the standard of learning among the African race, in America, should be raised'...(the) 'very fact of English Philanthropists interesting themselves so much in a black man...cannot but have a lively and startling influence among the prejudiced and the proslavery at home, especially in our (Church)'. After matriculation at Queens' he lived with his wife and (eventually) five childen in nearby Botolph Lane and worshipped at St Botolph's Church. He continued to preach while at Queens', and his sermons and lectures against slavery were often reported in local newspapers; a sermon in Norwich is described as: 'evangelical, intellectual, and eloquent'. Many newspapers reported the death of his eldest son, Alexander, who died from choking on a boot button. Little is known about his undergraduate days; life was not easy, as he records:

'I was often in the hands of doctors. Not seldom I fell into a state of discouragement and despair, on account of my health. Now and then my studies were interrupted'. An incident at his graduation ceremony in 1853 is recorded in the biography of E.W.Benson, Archbishop of Canterbury:

'A boisterous individual in the gallery called out, "Three groans for the Queen's n----- "...a pale slim undergraduate (the future Archbishop)...shouted in a voice which re-echoed through the building, "Shame, shame! Three groans for you, Sir!" and immediately afterwards, "Three cheers for Crummell!" This was taken up in all directions...and the original offender had to stoop down to hide himself from the storm of groans and hiusses that broke out all around him'. (Students in the gallery of the Senate House often proposed three cheers, or groans, for notable figures). In the same year he told friends that he felt unable to do useful work in the Britain or America, and he and his family emigrated to Liberia, which had attracted many African-American former slaves and had declared independence in 1847. He spent nearly 20 years there as a parish priest, teacher and lecturer, but then returned to the USA in 1873 and spent over 20 years as a minister in Washington DC, founding the St Luke's Episcopal Church, the first independent church for a black congregation in the City. He died in 1898, but his reputation endures. Twigg, in his history of the College in 1987, concludes that:

'His considerable influence as a writer, teacher of moral ideals, and opponent of racial persecution is well recognised today in the United States. Over forty publications by him are listed; one of his pamphlets was said to have sold half a million copies. He was a tireless worker for black rights and, despite many reverses, constantly optimistic...He worked for a moral revolution based on philanthropy, honesty, self-restraint and hard work...'.[9]

King's obituary, (quoted in the College's 'Record' and believed to be from 'The Times'),[1] speculates as to what he might have achieved if he had not suffered the strokes, which, after 1843, had reduced a person with:

'his commanding manner, his powers of business, his winning courtesy, his universal popularity'... (to) 'an invalid condition... To a man of his energetic temper and active habits no trial could well have been greater than that which it pleased God to send him; we venture to state, however, upon the best authority, that those who enjoyed his society were not more struck by his vigour and activity when in health, than by his gentleness and patience and

Christian resignation during his lengthened period of infirmity. He was as well as usual till within a week of his death, which took place at the Lodge, on Tuesday, September 1 (1857)'.[1] King's portrait, by William Beechey (1753-1839) remains in the College.

As previously noted, he was married in 1833 and one of his sons, John, after attending Repton School, was admitted as a pensioner to Queens' in 1856, graduating B.A. in 1860 and M.A. in 1863. After King's death in 1857, the family moved to a house in Norfolk, where the 1861 census records Mary King, 62, her daughter Margaret, 26, and her son John, 23: 'B.A. of Queens' College', in Hillington, near King's Lynn, together with an aunt and four servants. In 1862-64, John was a curate at Hampstead, Middlesex and, in 1865-66, a curate of St Botolph's Church, Cambridge. But the family moved back to Cambridge, and the 1871 census finds John, then aged 33, described as a: 'Curate without cure of souls', living with his mother, Mary, then aged 72, and her granddaughter Edith aged 2, at 29, St. Peter's Terrace, Trumpington Street, Cambridge, together with five servants. John died early, aged 40, in 1878.[3]

King's other son, his namesake Joshua, had a more eventful career. After attending Repton School, he was admitted as a pensioner to Trinity Hall, Cambridge, in 1855, and, after graduation, he was appointed to the Indian Civil Service in 1859, initially serving in Bombay as Assistant Collector, Magistrate and Under-Secretary to the Government. His final posting was to Satara, where he served as Senior Collector, Magistrate and Political Agent, before retiring, aged 49, in 1866. He then lived in Bath, where he died in 1927, aged 90, having been a liability to his pension scheme for 41 years.[3]

King's daughter Margaret, noted above in the 1861 census, is one of the main protagonists in the account of the life of Gerard Brown Finch, described in detail by Jonathan Holmes, (fellow and formerly Dean of Chapel at Queens').[10] Finch was admitted to Queens' in 1853, aged 18, to read mathematics, at a time when King was an invalid, living in the Lodge with his wife, sons and 19 year old daughter Margaret. Finch was an exceptional student and, guided by the College lecturer (and future President) William

Campion, and a private tutor, (Stephen Parkinson of St John's College), he graduated as Senior Wrangler in 1857 and became a fellow of Queens'. He was to marry Margaret, although not until 1868, but Holmes speculates that the ailing President may have invited the promising student to the Lodge for encouragement and advice from a former Senior Wrangler, and that this may have been the start of Finch's relationship with the President's daughter. King died just a few weeks after Finch's success; Margaret soon left Cambridge and, on medical advice, Finch also left in the same year on an extended world tour, before deciding to return to Cambridge and become a lawyer. (In due course he would develop a lucrative practice at the Chancery Bar). He maintained his Queens' fellowship, with its modest income, until 1870, making occasional visits to Queens', and he will have renewed or initiated his relationship with Margaret after the latter's move from Norfolk to St Peter's Terrace, Cambridge. Holmes believes that:

'Most likely Gerard and Margaret were waiting until his law practice was firmly established and he could "keep her in the manner to which she had become accustomed", ie with lots of servants'.[10] In any event, they were married in 1868, when Finch was 32 and Margaret was 33. They were to have six children, including Ernest, who was admitted to Queens' in 1889. Margaret died in 1897, aged 62, and Mill Road cemetery, Cambridge, contains a monument to Mary King and her daughter Margaret Elizabeth Finch, whose husbands are buried elsewhere. Finch was married again, to Amelia Janet Kelly, a staff nurse at Addenbrooke's Hospital, Cambridge, and eventually moved to 'Howes Close', a house near Girton, now an hotel. Finch became a Councillor and Alderman of the Borough of Cambridge, a Vice-Chairman of the Cambridgeshire County Council and a Governor of Addenbrooke's Hospital. He died in 1913, aged 77; he was a wealthy man and a considerable benefactor to Queens', contributing to the new chapel and the new residential 'Friars' Building'.

King's funeral in the College chapel was reported in the 'Cambridge Chronicle':

'Last Monday forenoon, the mortal remains of the late Dr. King President of Queens' College, were interred in the antechapel of the College. At an early hour in the morning they were removed from the Lodge to the Hall, whence the funeral procession, under the direction of Messers. Baker and Pain, started at 11 o'clock...The melancholy procession went round the first Court of the College to the Chapel; and the service for the Burial of the Dead having been performed by the Revd W.M.Campion and the Revd W.G.Searle, assisted by the College Choir, the body of Dr. King was deposited in the ground, near that of the late Revd Watson, who died a short time ago during his year of office as Senior Proctor. During the morning, the great bell of St Mary's as is usual upon occasions of this sort, tolled half-minute time, and a dumb-peal (ie muffled) was rung in the evening'.[1]

Fred Finch, a cousin of Margaret's children, reports a conversation he had, in about 1895, with Edward Stone, a fellow of Queens' during 1859-72, who had been an undergraduate during King's last years. It provides a melancholy overview of unfulfilled potential:

'Joshua King, said W. Stone, came up to Cambridge from Hawkshead Grammar School...He became Senior Wrangler, and his reputation in Cambridge was immense. It was really believed that nothing less than a Second Newton had appeared. They really expected his work as a Mathematician to make an epoch in the science. At an early age he became President of Queens': later, he was Lucasian Professor. He published nothing; in fact, he did no mathematical work. But as long as he kept his health, he was an active and prominent figure in Cambridge, and he maintained his enormous reputation. When he died, it was felt that the memory of such an Extraordinary man should not be permitted to die out, and his papers should be published. So his papers were examined, and nothing whatever worth publishing was found'.[1]

References

1. Joshua King 1798-1857. In: The Record. 2004. Queens' College, Cambridge. Online. 2020.

2. Wilson, D.B. Arbiters of Victorian Science: George Gabriel Stokes and Joshua King. In: From Newton to Hawking. Knox, K.C., Noakes, R. (Eds.). Cambridge University Press. Cambridge. 2003.
3. Venn, J.A. Part II. Vol. IV. Alumni Cantabrigienses. Cambridge University Press. London. 1922-1954.
4. Gray, J.H. The Queens' College of St Margaret and St Bernard. F.E.Robinson. London. 1898. pp 277-82.
5. Cooper, C.H. Annals of Cambridge. Volume IV. 'Victoria after 1850': 11-20, 75, 89, 90.
6. Twigg, J. A History of Queens' College, Cambridge. 1448-1986. The Boydell Press. 1987. pp 224, 271.
7. Rhodes James, R. Albert, Prince Consort. Hamish Hamilton. London. 1983. pp 172-79.
8. Meer, S. Capped and Gowned in the University of Cambridge. The Record 2013. Queens' College, Cambridge. Online. 2020.
9. Twigg, J. Alexander Crummell. Queens' College, Cambridge. Online. 2020.
10. Holmes, J. Romance in the President's Lodge? In: The Record. 2010. Queens' College, Cambridge. Online. 2020.

CHAPTER 29

George Phillips. President 1857-92.

Summary.

George Phillips was born in 1804, in Suffolk, the son of a farmer, and managed to acquire sufficient knowledge of mathematics while working on the farm to be appointed as a master at Woodbridge School, when aged about 18. By 1823 he had moved to be a master at the Royal Grammar School, Worcester and, in 1824, he was admitted to Magdalen Hall, Oxford. But he transferred to Queens' after about a year and graduated B.A. in 1829, with a first class degree in mathematics, as 8th Wrangler. He was elected a fellow of Queens' in 1831 and was ordained in 1832.

His academic interests soon changed to oriental languages and, in 1837, he published: 'The Elements of Syriac Grammar'. Nearly a decade later, his life also underwent a major change, when, in 1846, after 15 years of service to the College in various offices, he moved to Sandon, Essex, as rector of St Andrew's Church, which was a College living. This was probably related to his impending marriage to Emily Frances Pilkington, which took place in 1848.

In 1857 Joshua King died, and Phillips must have been singularly popular and respected during his years at Queens', as he was recalled from his country exile to become the next President. He served as Vice-Chancellor during 1861-62 and officiated at the installation of the 7th Duke of Devonshire as Chancellor of the University, following the death of Prince Albert.

During Phillips' presidency, Queens' saw a period of growth, reform and stability, as well as the construction of two new major buildings, the 'Friars' Building' for student accommodation, and a new chapel. The latter was designed by G.F.Bodley, who is considered to have been the leading ecclesiastical architect in England at that time.

Phillips was active in promoting the study of oriental languages in the University and played a leading role in establishing the Indian Languages Tripos and the Semitic Languages Tripos.

He died in 1892, aged 88, having been: 'hale and vigorous to the last'.[3] He was a generous benefactor to Queens', having given £1000 to found a scholarship and a significant donation towards the new chapel. Also, he had been noted for his hospitality. Although his funeral service was held at the College, he was buried in Mullinger, County Westmeath, Ireland, the county of his wife's ancestors. He did not have children, but his wife survived him until 1898.

Timeline.

1804.	Born in Dunwich, Suffolk.
1822.	Master at Woodbridge School.
1823.	Master at Worcester Grammar School. Publishes: 'A Brief Treatise on the Use of a Case of Instruments'.
1824.	Publishes: 'A Compendium of Algebra'. Admitted to Magdalen Hall, Oxford on the 19th of June.
1825.	Admitted to Queens' on the 25th of October.
1827.	Awarded a scholarship.
1829.	B.A. , 8th Wrangler.
1831.	Elected a fellow of Queens'. Ordained deacon.
1832.	Ordained priest. Publishes: 'Summation of Series by Definite Integrals'.
1837.	Publishes: 'The Elements of Syriac Grammar'. (The 2nd edition followed in 1845).
1839.	B.D. . Formation of the Cambridge Camden Society to promote 'Gothic Revival' in church architecture.
1845-47.	Extensive renovations to the College chapel and hall.
1846.	Leaves Cambridge to be rector of the College living of Sandon, Essex. Publishes: 'The Psalms in Hebrew; with a Critical, Exegetical, and Philological Commentary'.

1847. Resigns his College fellowship. Prince Albert is elected Chancellor of the University.

1848. Marries Emily Frances Pilkington, of County Westmeath, Ireland.

1856. The 'Cambridge University Act 1856'.

1857. Death of Joshua King. Phillips is elected President.

1858-61. A College committee is formed to restore the chapel; the subsequent reconstructions are designed by G.F. Bodley.

1859. D.D. .

1860. New Statutes for the College are approved.

1861. The Prince of Wales enrolls at Trinity College, Cambridge, in January. Death of Prince Albert, Chancellor of the University, on the 14th of December.

1861-62. Vice-Chancellor. The 7th Duke of Devonshire is installed as Chancellor of the University.

1861-64. Further renovations to the College hall; the old fireplace is removed and its replacement with an overmantel is designed by G.F.Bodley. (The tiles above the fireplace are designed by the decorative arts firm run by William Morris).

1863. Publishes: 'Short Sermons on Old Testament Messianic Texts'.

1866. Revises his 1837 publication as: 'A Syrian Grammar'.

1869. William Wright, (Professor of Arabic 1870-89), is elected an honorary fellow at Queens', at Phillips' instigation.

1871. The 'University Tests Act 1871'.

1872. The Indian Languages Tripos is established. A Royal Commission is set up to inquire into: 'the Property and Income of the Universities...and of the Colleges...'.

1873. Ford Maddox Brown designs tiles depicting Margaret of Anjou and Elizabeth Woodville, which are added to the existing tiles above the Queens' hall's fireplace.

1875. First examinations for the Semitic Laguages Tripos. Decorations for the walls and roof of the hall are designed by G.F.Bodley.

1876. The 'Royal Titles Act'; Queen Victoria is styled 'Empress of India'.

1877. The 'Universities of Oxford and Cambridge Act 1877'.

1882. New Statutes for the College are approved.
1886. The 'Friars' Building' at Queens' completed.
1887. Donates £1000 to Queens' to found a scholarship. Golden Jubilee of Queen Victoria.
1888. A decision is made to build a new College chapel. Makes a generous donation towards the project.
1891. Consecration of the new College chapel, designed by G.F.Bodley.
1892. Dies at Queens'. Buried at Mullingar, County Westmeath, Ireland.

Grammar school teacher. Mathematician. Churchman. Tutor. Orientalist. College benefactor.

George Phillips was born on the 11th of January 1804, at Dunwich, Suffolk, the third son of Francis Phillips, a farmer. He was baptized at Westleton, Suffolk, on the 5th of February, and the family soon moved to Otley, Suffolk.[1] His academic career had an unusual beginning, as he acquired a knowledge of mathematics in his spare time, while working on the farm.[1] He must have shown early promise as, when he was aged about 18, he was appointed a master at Woodbridge School, Suffolk, and, by 1823, he was a master at the prestigious Royal Grammar School in Worcester. (This is claimed to be the sixth oldest school in the world, with origins in the 7th century, and had received a Royal Charter in 1561).[2] During his time at Worcester, he published 'A Brief Treatise on the Use of a Case of Instruments' in 1823, and 'A Compendium of Algebra' in 1824.[1]

On the 19th of June 1824, Phillips was admitted to Magdalen Hall, Oxford, but, for reasons unknown, he transferred to Queens' on the 25th of October, 1825.[1] (Magdalen Hall would merge with Hart Hall in 1874 to form Hertford College). He was awarded a Queens' scholarship in 1827 and graduated B.A. in 1829, with a first class degree in mathematics, as 8th Wrangler.[1,3] He became a fellow of Queens' in 1831, serving in various College offices over the next 15 years: assistant tutor, Dean, censor theologicus, Hebrew lecturer, praelector and senior tutor.[1,4] He was ordained deacon in 1831 and priest in 1832; subsequently he graduated M.A. and would proceed to the B.D. degree in 1839.

In 1832 he published his last paper on mathematics: 'Summation of Series by Definite Integrals', and his future scholarship would be in oriental languages. In 1837, he published: 'The Elements of Syriac Grammar by the Rev. George Phillips. M.A. Fellow and Tutor of Queens' College, Cambridge. Cambridge: Printed by the University Press, for J. and J.J. Deighton, Cambridge. MDCCCXXXVII'. In the Preface, Phillips writes:

'The following "Elements of Syriac Grammar" are intended for the assistance of those Students in Hebrew, who are desirous of extending their studies to the Syriac Language. This is easily accomplished in consequence of the close affinity, which exists between the two languages both in their structure as well as in the multitude of words which they possess in common. A small portion only of time and labour is quite sufficient for the Hebrew scholar to obtain a moderate knowledge of Syriac...it may be mentioned that the Syriac Language supplies one source of valuable information for the criticism of the Hebrew Bible...But the great claim as it appears to me, which the Syriac has...consists in the Syriac New Testament. The high antiquity of this Version and its use in the early established Syriac Church stamp an importance on it, which can be assigned to no other...the Syriac Language is so nearly the same as that spoken in Palestine in the first age of Christianity, that by many persons it has been termed the vernacular language of our Lord...In Syriac we have the New Testament of which mention has already been made; besides a great quantity of ecclesiastical and historical writings. It must also be especially borne in mind that a very great portion of the history, science and literature of the middle ages is locked up in the Syriac and Arabic languages...'.

(Syriac, together with Latin and Greek, became an important language in the early Christian church and was influential in the development of Arabic).

In the 1830s, Phillips' religious life was influenced by a movement, initially active at Oxford University, which embraced some of the older, Catholic, 'high church', Christian traditions of doctrine and liturgy. This was the 'Oxford Movement', led by John Henry (later Cardinal) Newman and Edward Pusey, which produced a series of publications during 1833-41: the 'Tracts For the Times'. In Cambridge, a parallel and growing attraction to elements of the pre-reformation Church was reflected by a renewed interest in church architecture and a revival of the 'Gothic' style. (See below). This led, in 1839, to the formation of the 'Cambridge Camden Society', which was set up mainly to promote these ideas of church architecture, although many members were sympathetic to the high church movement; Phillips was a member in its early years.[5] The Society's journal, the 'Ecclesiologist', reports in 1845 that:

'Considerable restorations are contemplated in both the hall and the chapel of Queen's College. It was but recently discovered how much mischief the paganizing mania of the last century had inflicted on these two venerable edifices. The roof of the hall proves to be the finest in the University, of beautiful high pitched open timbers, now underdrawn and totally concealed by a flat plaister ceiling. Considerable remains of the internal panelling still exist in the president's lodge. The roof of the chapel was coved and handsomely painted; it is likewise covered with a flat ceiling. This is to be restored forthwith, and we believe a new east window filled with stain glass is also contemplated. In the lodge is still preserved the ancient triptych once belonging to the altar. It is curious, but not very beautiful, German painting, This of course will be restored to the chapel'.[5,6] The work on the chapel was completed by 1847, under the supervision of Phillips, the Dean and the senior bursar.[5] (In 1846, the flat ceiling in the hall would also be removed, prior to a restoration of the roof).

In 1846, Phillips' life underwent a major change, when he accepted a College living and moved to Sandon, Essex, to become rector of the 11th century St Andrew's Church. Also in 1846, he published: 'The Psalms in Hebrew; with a Critical, Exegetical, and Philological Commentary, By The Rev. George Phillips, B.D. ... Fellow and Tutor of Queens' College, Cambridge, and rector of Sandon Essex. In Two Volumes...London: John W. Parker, West

Strand. M.DCCC.XLVI', which would have a second edition in 1872.[1] This was a monumental work, and the first volume runs to 432 pages; Phillips informs us in his preface that:

'In presenting to the public the following Commentary on the Psalms, I beg permission to state briefly the objects which I have had in view. There can be no doubt that, rich as the Church of England unquestionably is in works on theological literature, yet in commentaries on the Old Testament, of a critical and philological character, it is lamentably deficient...it is especially so with respect to the Psalms...a commentary on the whole Book of Psalms...for the edification of the English reader, has not...ever issued from the press of this country...the many other commentaries on the Psalms which the critics of (ie from) Germany have produced...must be regarded not only as unfit for general purposes, but even as injurious when placed in the hands of young students...the fact that no book is so often quoted in the New Testament as the Book of Psalms, must render every attempt at their elucidation most desirable...I...hope that it will prove beneficial to those young persons who are engaged in the acquisition of Hebrew learning, that it will lighten their labours... that thus it may be the means of leading them to...giving to the subject that earnest attention which its immense importance demands...that it may contribute, with God's blessing, to the increase of faith and piety among His people, and so to the glory of His Holy Name...And now that I am about to retire from academic life, to engage in another department of theological labour, I feel much satisfaction that, in submitting these volumes to the public, I am enabled to render to it some account of the manner in which I have employed those opportunities for literary pursuits, which, through the kind providence of God, and the munificence of pious Foundresses of a College, I have long enjoyed'. He resigned his fellowship the following year and appears to have taken his new duties seriously, building a school, restoring the church and renovating his rectory.[1] (In 1894, when Phillips was President, the present Eagle Lectern at St Andrew's, then owned by the College, was given to the Church). This major change in Phillips' life was probably related to his impending marriage to Emily Frances Pilkington, which took place on the 10th of August 1848. She was the younger daughter of Henry Pilkington, 1780-1865, of Tore, near Tyrrellspass, County Westmeath, Ireland. (This branch of the Pilkington family was descended from Richard Pilkington, 1635-1710, Emily Frances' fourth-great-grandfather, who had migrated to Ireland from Lancashire, to establish an estate at Tore).

It may be more than a coincidence that, ten years earlier, Philip Kelland, who had been a colleague of Phillips as a fellow of Queens' during 1835-38, had married another member of this Irish branch of the Pilkington family, Elizabeth Maria Pilkington, (1817-44):

'Elizabeth m. June 1838 to the Rev. Philip Kelland, late fellow of Queen's Coll. Cambridge, and professor of mathematics at the University of Edinburgh'.[7] (She was to die in 1844, as the mother of two children). Perhaps Phillips met his future wife due to Kelland's family contacts?

In the 1851 census, we find George Phillips aged 47, his wife Emily Frances aged 38, and his sister, Charlotte aged 42, at Sandon, together with three servants. Phillips would be a witness at his sister's wedding to Frederick Burr in 1854, when the bride was 46 and the groom 43. Sadly, Frederick Burr died in 1856. Also, Charlotte Burr is found in the company of her brother and sister-in-law in the 1891 census, as a visitor at Queens', aged 83. (She was to die in the December of the following year, her brother having died in the February). Phillips and Emily Frances did not have children; she died in 1898.[1]

Joshua King died on the 1st of September 1857, and Phillips was elected his successor as President on the 9th of September.[3] Gray, in his history of the College of 1898, claims that William Campion, a fellow since 1850, (and Phillips' successor as President), was Phillips' rival in the election, gaining support from the younger fellows, while the senior fellows thought that, at the age of 37, he was too young.[3] Phillips must have been popular and respected in his former life at Queens', to have been recalled from his country exile. Gray also tells us that on the day of his election, Phillips makes the following note:

'Agreed to give Policeman No.4 of the Cambridge Police Force two pounds for his exertions in extinguishing the fire in the College on August 25th, 1867'.[3] (This had been caused by the carelessness of a previous member of the College, who was staying for a few days, when the College was almost deserted, and was extinguished by the two or three people who were still resident, together with the policeman).

Before his departure from Cambridge in 1846, Phillips had been involved with renovations to the College chapel and, in January 1858, very soon after his election, he formed a committee, which included Campion, to consider further structural and decorative changes. These, according to the 'Ecclesiologist' were sorely needed:

'Queen's College Chapel has undergone a few improvements, but is still a miserable place. Some very inferior glass, by Mr. Barnett, of York, has been inserted in the east window...The flesh is a ghastly sort of white; and all the hair is in round curls, in the same colour; an absurd piece of conventionalism. The whole design and colouration is vulgar in the extreme...We have seldom seen money more thrown away...'.[8] The committee chose the young architect George Frederick Bodley, 1827-1907, who favoured the 'Gothic Revival' style, to design and oversee the works.[5] Bodley had been a pupil of his relative Sir George Gilbert Scott, the designer of London's Albert Memorial, and would be responsible for numerous new churches, as well as church repairs, alterations and furnishings, during his long and successful career, becoming recognised as the leading ecclesiastical architect in England.[9] In due course he would design the new Queens' chapel. ('Gothic' architecture developed in Europe during the middle ages, and involved pointed arches, together with such features as vaulted ceilings, buttresses, window tracery, slender pillars, pinnacles and spires, associated with rich colours and decorations). Bodley had connections to the College; his elder brothers had been undergraduates at Queens' during 1840-44 and 1844-48, as had John Fowler, who married his sister in 1858.[8] Extensive work on the chapel took place during 1858-61; some adjacent rooms were transformed into an organ loft and vestry, the bottom four feet of the east window were bricked up to allow a screen to be placed behind the raised altar, and a window was moved. Also, two new stained glass windows were installed. The 'Ecclesiologist' duly notes its approval:

'The work at Queen's college chapel is now finished, and is a most valuable specimen of modern art. We are glad to find that the fellows are not content with this good beginning, but are endeavouring to make the music of their services worthy of their architecture'.[8]

In 1860, on the 30th of June, new Statutes for the College were approved.[10] The background to this has been outlined in the previous chapter; in summary, a Royal Commission had been constituted in 1850 to make wide-ranging enquiries into the University, which was followed by the 'Cambridge University Act 1856'. This authorised the appointment of Statutory Commissioners with powers to revise the Statutes of the University and colleges, and those proposed for Queens' were published in the London Gazette in May 1860. The Commissioners' subsequent summary of the changes affecting the fellowship included, but with some exceptions:

'...limited tenure has been adopted as the rule...There is no obligation to enter into orders... A Fellowship is not vacated by marriage...'.[10] However, as noted in the previous chapter, it would not be until the 'University Tests Act 1871', that all religious 'Tests' would be abolished for degrees and appointments, although, again, there were a few exceptions.

Phillips was elected Vice-Chancellor in 1861, the year in which Edward, the Prince of Wales had enrolled at Trinity College, and, soon afterwards, Prince Albert visited his son at Madingley Hall, (Edward's nearby residence), to confront him with his recent wayward behaviour. But the Prince Consort's health was rapidly deteriorating and he died on the 14th of December, just a few weeks after Phillips had assumed office. It would fall to Phillips to officiate at the installation of his successor as the University's Chancellor, namely, William Cavendish, the 7th Duke of Devonshire. This will have been a reunion, as Devonshire had graduated with Phillips in 1829, when, although the Vice-Chancellor had obtained a creditable first class degree as 8th Wrangler, he had been outclassed by the future Chancellor, who had been 2nd Wrangler and a Smith's prizeman.[3] At the ceremony, those receivimg honorary degrees included the Chancellor's son, (himself a future Chancellor), and the Marquis of Lorne, (later the 9th Duke of Argyll and husband of Princess Louise, fourth daughter of the Queen). This was followed by a dinner given in the Long Gallery of the President's Lodge at Queens'.[3]

The next project in the College which involved Bodley, was work on the hall during 1861-64. This included a new fireplace and overmantel, the latter incorporating a series of decorative tiles produced by Morris, Marshall, Faulkner & Co, founded by William Morris, (probably the 19th century's most celebrated British designer), and others, including Dante Gabriel Rosetti. (The latter was a member of the 'Pre-Raphaelite Brotherhood', a group of painters, poets and critics founded in 1848, who favoured paintings with detail, strong colours and complex compositions; Morris was a later follower of their principles). Another artist who followed the principles of the Brotherhood was Ford Maddox Brown, who designed two further tiles, depicting the two Queens' foundresses- Margaret of Anjou and Elizabeth Woodville- which were added to the overmantel in 1873.

Phillips held strong conservative views in matters of religion and did not support new ideas in biblical criticism.[1] He had proceeded to the D.D. degree in 1859 and, in 1863, published: 'Short Sermons on Old Testament Messianic Texts'. But he was now, primarily, an orientalist and, in 1866, revised his 1837 work, which was now titled: 'A Syrian Grammar'.

An important development in Phillips's promotion of Hebrew and Semitic languages was his success in persuading Dr William Wright, a noted orientalist, to relocate to Cambridge and, in 1869, Phillips arranged his election as an honorary fellow at Queens'. He became a fellow in the following year. From 1861 to 1869, Wright had been an assistant in the Department of Manuscripts at the British Museum, while from 1869 to 1870 he was Assistant Keeper at the museum. (Previously he had been Professor of Arabic at University College, London, during 1855-56 and Professor of Arabic at Trinity College, Dublin, during 1856-61). Also, Phillips was instrumental in getting Wright appointed to the Sir Thomas Adams professorship of Arabic at Cambridge in 1870, which he held until his death in 1889.[3] His catalogues of manuscript collections, in the British Library and the Cambridge University Library, are still consulted today, as is his: 'A Grammar of the Arabic Language'.[11] Also, Phillips played a leading role in the establishment of the Indian Languages Tripos in 1872 and of the Semitic Languages Tripos, for which the first examinations were held in 1875. (These were the predecessors of the Oriental Languages Tripos, established in the 1890s).[5]

In 1875, the existing, very colourful, decorative scheme for the walls and roof of the College hall, much photographed by present-day tourists, was designed and overseen by Bodley.[12] This involved the gilding of 885 lead castings of stars in the roof and the painting of Latin Graces around the walls.

Yet another Royal Commission was set up in 1872:

'to inquire into the Property and Income of the Universities of Oxford and Cambridge and of the Colleges and Halls therein', and this led to the 'Universities of Oxford and Cambridge Act 1877'. This was then followed by another revision of the Statutes for Queens', which was approved in 1882. Among the various changes related to fellowships:

'the requirements of celibacy, Anglicanism and previous membership of the University disappeared...'.[10]

The last half of the 19th century was a period of major educational reform in the Universities. Scientific advances, as well as social and political changes, led to an expanding curriculum, which then led to renewed tensions between the respective roles of University and college teaching. An increased provision and focus on University teaching was needed to support the wider range of specialised subjects, but this was resisted by the colleges, as a threat to their autonomy and finances, as college revenues were taxed to provide University appointments. An opinion in 1877 claims:

'as with a few brilliant exceptions the Professors are notoriously useless as teachers...The great increase, for instance, which is asked for in the number of professorships appears to me to be wholly unnecessary, and the money, which would be required to establish them, would be spent to comparatively little purpose. For some reason or another the professorial system as a whole has failed to supply an efficient teaching power in Cambridge'.[13] Phillips was also a supporter of college teaching, and claims, although without any supporting arguments, that:

'Every college is able to provide ample instruction for its pupils, not only in the old subjects of study, viz. classics and mathematics, but also in the new'.[3,13] But Phillips' Presidency saw various educational reforms at Queens' and, in 1873, a committee was set up to examine:

'the causes which result in the present low state of the College and to suggest measures for removing them and increasing the general usefulness of the College'. This led to a range of measures to make Queens' more attractive to students and to lift educational standards'.[5]

The last decade of Phillips' Presidency saw the construction of two major new buildings. The urgent need for new accommodation for an inceasing number of undergraduates was first discussed in January 1885 and, by June, a plan was approved to build on a site which was then used as a private kitchen garden by the President.[3,5] Twigg, in his history of the College of 1987, tells us that Phillips did not want to lose his seeond private garden, and had to be pacified by the provision of the exclusive use of the fellows' kitchen garden.[5] As he was over 80, perhaps the fellows did not think they would have to wait too long to regain their privilege! By the end of 1885, the design had been approved and the contractors hired. The architect was William Milner Fawcett, 1832-1908, a graduate of Jesus College, who rose to be Vice-President of the Royal Institute of British Architects; he worked on many of the buildings and colleges in Cambridge, as well as on the restoration of churches and houses throughout the country. (In 1875, he had restored the east frontage of Queens').[5] The resulting 'Friars' Building', with thirty-two sets of rooms, was completed in 1886, but it was taller than the other College buildings and the 'Cambridge Review' believed it would: 'ever be an eyesore to lovers of the backs'.[5] (This critic would have something interesting to say about Queens' buildings near the river in the next century!).

It was not long before a second major project was completed. With the increased number of undergraduates, the chapel was found to be too small and, despite the expense and scope of earlier renovations to the original chapel, it was decided to build a replacement. In January 1887, Bodley was approached for designs and a decision to proceed was taken a year later.[5] The cost was raised by subscriptions and the project was finally authorised in June 1888.[3] Construction took place during 1889-91, and the new chapel was consecrated by the Bishop of Ely, (Lord Alwyne Compton, fourth son of the 2nd Marquess of Northampton), on the 13th of October 1891, after which Phillips presided over a dinner in the College hall.[3] Gray notes that:

'The Chapel is in the late English Gothic style...The proportions are lofty...The sides show windows of three lights... These windows are tall, and the tracery, graceful and characteristic of the style, is certainly very effective...'.[3] On two of the wooden panels on the oak screen in the ante-chapel are the letters 'A.D.' and 'G.P.'; these are the initials of the first President and of George Phillips, as the current President.[3] The East Window and all the windows on the north side of the chapel are the work of the Kempe Studio, which was under the personal direction of Charles Eamer Kempe (1837-1907):

'the most influential English stained glass designer and maker of the late nineteenth and early twentieth centuries'.[14]

Phillips died at Queens' on the 5th of February, 1892, having been: 'hale and vigorous almost to the last'.[3] The University paid him a last tribute when he became one of the five distinguished members of the University for whom Handel's Dead March was played at Great St Mary's during the Lent term of 1892. (One of the others was the 7th Duke of Devonshire, the Chancellor, who had died on the 21st of December 1891).[3]

Phillips had presided over a period of growth, reform and stability at Queens', to which he had been a generous benefactor. He had given £1000 to found a scholarship in 1887 and had made a significant donation towards the new chapel.[1] Also, he had been noted for his hospitality.[1] His funeral service took place in the College on the 11th of February, but he was buried at Mullingar, County Westmeath, the county of his wife's ancestors.[1] She would survive him until 1898.

References

1. Clark, J.W. (revised by R.S. Simpson) Phillips, George. In: Oxford Dictionary of National Biography. 2018. Online.
2. Wikipedia. Royal Grammar School, Worcester. 2020. Online.
3. Gray, J.H. The Queens' College of St Margaret and St Bernard. F.E.Robinson. London. 1898. pp 282-93.
4. Queens' College Cambridge. Fellows 1800-1899. 2020. Online.
5. Twigg, J. A History of Queens' College, Cambridge. 1448-1986. The Boydell Press. 1987. pp 272-77, 294, 298, 314-15.
6. Queens' College Cambridge. The Old Chapel. 2020. Online.
7. Pilkington of Tore. In: Burke's Landed Gentry of Ireland. 1899.
8. Queens' College Cambridge. Old Chapel. 2020. Online.
9. Wikipedia. George Frederick Bodley. 2020. Online.
10. Queens' College Cambridge. Statutes. 2020. Online.
11. Wikipedia. William Wright (orientalist). 2020. Online.
12. Queens' College Cambridge. Old Hall. 2020. Online.
13. Winstanley, D.A. Later Victorian Cambridge. Cambridge at the University Press. 1947.
14. Barlow, A. The Kempe Windows. The Record. 2007. Queens' College, Cambridge. Online. 2020.

CHAPTER 30

William Campion. President 1892-96.

Summary.

William Campion was born in 1820, in Ireland. He was admitted to Queens' in 1845 and graduated B.A. in 1849, with a first class degree in mathematics as 4th Wrangler. He was elected a fellow of Queens' in 1850 and very soon became joint tutor, and then sole tutor. He was a: 'vigorous and stimulating' teacher, and several of his pupils achieved the highest Tripos honours. His energy was noted in the wider University and he became the Secretary to the first Council of the Senate. He also served as University Proctor and an examiner for the Moral Sciences Tripos.

He was ordained in 1855 and would be an active churchman, with a tendency towards liberal theological views; he was rector of St Botolph's Church, Cambridge, (1862-92), Rural Dean, (1870-92), and an honorary canon of Ely, (1879-96). In 1866 he co-authored a popular and learned account of Anglican ritual: 'The Prayer Book Interleaved'. He proceeded D.D. in 1870.

He was popular and active in College, Church and University spheres. In 1867 he gave evidence to a Parliamentary Select Committee, which provides insight into some of the main educational issues of the time.

In 1867, he was the favoured candidate of some of the younger fellows to succeed Joshua King as President; however, the majority decided that greater experience was required and Campion would have to wait a further 25 years before being elected President in 1892.

After a brief and uneventful tenure, he died, after a short illness, on the 5th of February, 1896. He was unmarried. He is buried, together with his sister, in the Mill Road Cemetery, Cambridge.

Timeline.

1820.	Born in Maryborough, County Laois. Ireland.
1845.	Admitted to Queens' as a 'pensioner'.
1846.	Elected a scholar of the College.
1849.	B.A. , 4th Wrangler.
1850.	Elected a fellow of Queens'.
1850-53.	College mathematics lecturer. (Date unknown: Sadleirian Lecturer).
1852.	M.A. .
1853-92.	Tutor.
1855.	Ordained priest at Ely.
1856.	Member of the first Council of the Senate and its Secretary. The 'Cambridge University Act, 1856'.
1857.	Death of Joshua King. George Phillips elected President.
1858.	Member of the College committee to restore the chapel; the works are designed by G.F.Bodley.
1860.	B.D. . New Statutes of the College are approved.
1861.	An examiner for the Moral Sciences Tripos, (also in 1862 and 1867). Death of Prince Albert.
1861-64.	Renovations to the College hall.
1862.	Appointed the University's 'Lady Margaret Preacher'. The 7th Duke of Devonshire installed as Chancellor of the University.
1862-64.	Appointed the University's 'Whitehall Preacher'.
1862-92.	Rector of St Botolph's Chuch, Cambridge, (a College living).
1865.	Appointed Proctor of the University.
1866.	Co-author (with W.J.Beamont) of the popular: 'The Prayer Book Interleaved'.
1867.	Gives evidence to a Parliamentary Select Committee on the state of the University and colleges.
1870.	D.D. .
1870-92.	Rural Dean of Ely.
1871.	The Universty Test Act, 1871.

1875.	Decorations for the College hall are designed by G.F.Bodley.
1876.	The Royal Titles Act; Queen Victoria is styled 'Empress of India'.
1877.	The Universities of Oxford and Cambridge Act, 1877.
1878.	Is noted to be spending most of his time on the parochial work of St Botolph's Church.
1879-96.	Honorary canon of Ely.
1882.	New Statutes for the College are approved.
1886.	The 'Friars' Building' at Queens' completed.
1891.	Consecration of the new Queens' chapel.
1892.	Death of George Phillips, (5th of February). Elected President of Queens', (23rd of February). Publishes: 'The Beauty of Holiness. A Sermon preached by the Rev. W.M. Campion... September 27, 1892'.
1896.	Dies at Queens', (20th of October). Buried at Mill Road Cemetery, Cambridge.

Mathematician. Tutor. Churchman. Active in College, Church and University affairs.

William Magan Campion was born in Ireland on the 28th of October, 1820, the second son of William Campion of Maryborough, County Laois.[1,2]

He came to Queens' as a fee-paying 'pensioner' in 1845, but did not spend all his time in the library, as he is recorded as having been involved in the running of the boat club as a student.[3] On the 12th of October, 1846, he was elected a scholar of the College, (on the same day that George Phillips, the next President, accepted the College living of Sandon, Essex),[4] and, in 1849, he graduated B.A. in the Mathematics Tripos, as the 4th Wrangler. He was elected a fellow of Queens' on the 12th of January, 1850 and:

'became almost at once joint tutor and soon sole tutor of the College. He was a vigorous and stimulating teacher'.[4] Gray, in his history of the College of 1898, notes that several of his pupils achieved high honours: as 3rd Wrangler in 1856, Senior Wrangler in 1857 and 1858, and 5th Wrangler in 1859.[4] He was the College's mathematics lecturer during 1850-53 and, at an unknown date, a Sadleirian Lecturer.[5] (Lady Mary Sadleir had founded lectureships at nine colleges, which had originated in 1710: 'for the full and clear explication and teaching that part of mathematical knowledge commonly called algebra'. However in 1860, the bequest was used to establish a professorship).[6] In subsequent decades, he would also serve the College as Dean, steward and praelector. In 1851 he was ordained deacon and, in 1855, a priest, at Ely.[1] Gray tells us that:

'the energy and ability displayed by the Tutor of Queens' speedily marked him out as a leader among the rising young men of the University. This was shown by his election to the first Council of the Senate and his appointment to be the first Secretary of that body'.[4]

Joshua King died in 1857 and although Campion had been a fellow for only seven years, some of the younger members of the society saw him as their favoured candidate for the vacancy; but the senior members wanted more experience and recalled George Phillips for the Presidency.[4] It would be 25 years before Campion would, eventually, be Phillips' successor, but he would make a major contribution to the College in the interim.

In the last chapter we have seen that Phillips' tenure was associated with major renovations and new buildings at Queens', and that Campion was a member of the committee set up in 1858 to renovate the College chapel. He was one of the Queens' fellows who were members of the Cambridge Architectural Society, which promoted chapel restoration and a more elaborate ritual, including the reintroduction of choral services.[3] The committee chose the architect and designer G.F. Bodley for the renovation project; this would be a prescient choice, as he would develop a reputation as the leading English ecclesiastical architect of his time and, subsequently, he would be responsible for the design of a new chapel at Queens'.

In the 1860s, Campion was an active churchman; he proceeded B.D. in 1860 and, in 1862, was appointed as the University's 'Lady Margaret Preacher'. Also, during 1862-64, he was the University's 'Whitehall Preacher'. In 1862 he was appointed to the College living of St Botolph's, Cambridge, which he would hold for 30 years, until becoming President in 1892. In 1866 he published, with W.J.Beamont: 'The Prayer Book Interleaved with Historical Illustrations and Explanatory Notes Arranged Parallel to the Text, by The Rev. W.M.Campion, B.D. Fellow and Tutor of Queens' College, and Rector of S.Botolph's, and The Rev. W.J.Beamont, M.A. Fellow of Trinity College, and Incumbent of S.Michael's, Cambridge. With a Preface by The Lord Bishop of Ely. Second Edition, Revised and Enlarged. Rivingtons, London, Oxford, and Cambridge. 1866'. The authors explain their purpose in the 'Editors' Preface':

'Pobably at no period, since the Reformation, has the national Church occupied the attention of intelligent men in foreign lands and of all classes in our own land, to so large an extent as she does at the present day. Her internal strength has, of late years, been marvellously recruited; and, as a consequence, her energies have rapidly expanded. But her growing activity, encouraging as it is to her faithful members, has stimulated the attacks of opponents, who have exaggerated the peculiarities of her ritual into defects or distorted them into blemishes. On the one hand she has been assailed as inclining too much to the practices and doctrines of the Church of Rome; on the other as having too little sympathy with the primitive usages of Christianity. In each of these cases her Prayer-book is made the chief object of attack. Hence we are of opinion that an intimate acquaintance with the history of the formation of the Prayer-book, as well as with the contents of its Offices, is a most desirable, we had almost said an indispensable, element in the education of all churchmen...Under these circumstances it has appeared to us that a portable edition of the Prayer-book, accompanied by compendious notes, arranged, as far as possible, face to face with the text illustrated, was wanted in our ritualistic literature...we have given a short account of the origin, development, and alterations of the various Services...As a popular explanation of many matters ordinarily apprehended with some vagueness, and also as a sort of syllabus to the student of Church ritual, we ask for an indulgent acceptance of the Interleaved Prayer-book. W.M.Campion W.J.Beamont Cambridge, Christmas, 1865...

Editors' Preface to the Second Edition. In issuing a second edition of the Prayer-book Interleaved, we have availed ourselves of several hints given in reviews...Thus a short account of the origin and use of the vestments prescribed in the First Prayer-Book of Edward VI has been introduced...further historical details respecting the course followed in making the successive revisions of the Prayer-Book have also been given...WM.Campion W.J.Beamont Witsuntide, 1866'. This learned and popular work ran to 395 pages.

In the University of the 1860s, Campion was an examiner for the recently-established Moral Sciences Tripos, (in 1861, 1862 and 1867), while, in 1865, he served as a University Proctor. In 1865, we have a record of his views on one of the current issues which was being considered by a committee of the Senate, namely, how to improve the standards of the ordinary degrees; the committee's report stated that:

'the scanty and imperfect training of a large number of our students, and their want of adequate elementary knowledge on entering the University, constitute one of the principal difficulties with which the University has to contend in any endeavour to inprove the course of education for the ordinary class of students'... (and that there is) 'no way in which this difficulty can be effectively obviated, except by the institution of a general University examination, which all students shall be required to pass before, or shortly after, commencing residence in the University'.[7] But this proposal attracted much opposition, including from Campion, who declared that:

'such an examination as that proposed would be an undue interference with the colleges'.[7] In 1867, he gave evidence to a Parliamentary 'Select Committee on the Oxford and Cambridge Universities Education Bill', (published as a 'Special Report' in 1867), which is fortunate for the historian, as his views are recorded on several aspects of University and college life: namely, the expanding curriculum, changes in the nature of college fellowships, student accommodation, student recruitment, and social changes in the colleges.

The University curriculum had been significantly expanded in 1848, with the establishment of the Natural Sciences Tripos and Moral Sciences Tripos, (the latter encompassing psychology, philosophy and political economy), and their first examinations took place in 1851. However, until 1861 they could only be taken after obtaining a B.A. in another subject and, at Queens', only one student had taken the Natural Sciences Tripos before 1863, while, in relation to the Moral Sciences Tripos, there was only one before 1867. But, as noted above, Campion had been an examiner for the Moral Sciences Tripos and he told the Select Committee that the standards in these new subjects had improved.[3]

The Select Committee also heard Campion's views on the effect of the changes in the new College Statutes of 1860 on College fellowships. As noted in the previous chapter, after 1860, with some exceptions, there was no obligation to enter into holy orders, and a fellowship was no longer incompatible with marriage. Also, fellowships had a limited tenure of ten years. (But fellows in holy orders could remain after 10 years if unmarried, and a major College office could only be held if the fellow was unmarried). Campion saw: 'no reason to be dissatisfied' with the revised arrangements, which, by allowing some married fellows, were a substantial change.[3] (The 'University Test Act 1871', and further revisions to the Statutes in 1882, which followed the 'Universities of Oxford and Cambridge Act 1877', would see the complete disappearance of the requirements of celibacy, Anglicanism and previous membership of the University, in relation to fellowships).[8] But, in 1867, Campion was against the idea of formally opening all fellowships to College outsiders, as, although such were regularly recruited by the smaller colleges, a formal competition would require an examination, and he believed that: 'the multiplication of such examinations is an evil'.[3] (The College did not want to lose any of its autonomy; also, it was thought that such an arrangement would favour richer candidates, who would have more opportunity to prepare for such an examination). At Queens', fellows were usually chosen from the first 15 Wranglers in Mathematics and the first 15 places in the Classical Tripos, and Campion considered that:

'men who take high places in the triposes are provided for by fellowships, and they get their fellowships at their own colleges'.[3] However, this system was not universally popular and, in the next century, it was recalled that:

'so little were the rights of the Fellows to elect respected, that the candidate was told by the Tutor to come up for the day of the meeting to be admitted'.[3]

In the early 19th century, the increasing number of Cambridge students had required the use of licenced lodging houses in the town and, in his evidence to the Select Committee, Campion reported that, recently, he had had: 'the greatest difficulty' in finding such accommodation.[3] The committee were clearly worried about student behaviour outside the discipline provided within college walls, but they were reassured by Campion that the colleges were concerned that each lodging house should have a good reputation; many were kept by college servants and most keepers reported those who came in after 10pm. But the committee eventually raised what was, perhaps, their main concern, when Campion was asked if students were exposed to great temptations by maidservants in lodging houses. Campion's reply, while demonstrating a probably-successful attempt at humour, showed a complete lack of political correctness, and may not have completely reassured the parliamentarians:

'Considering the specimens of servants...that I have seen, I should say that they are not'.[3] He believed that Cambridge was not a particularly immoral town and that the moral dangers of lodging houses had been exaggerated, but regretted that the students out of College: 'cannot so thoroughly realise the collegiate system'.[3] (Twigg, in his history of the College of 1987, informs us that, in the early 1880s, more than half the Queens' students were in lodgings, a similar proportion as in the rest of the University, but, by 1894, only 16% were in lodgings, following the construction of the 'Friars' Building').

The Select Committee was also interested in the 1860s equivalent of the contemporary preoccupation with students' access and diversity. Twigg notes the claim of Sheldon Rothblatt, (in 'The Revolution of the Dons', 1968), that:

'one of the aims of the university reforms was to ensure that Cambridge did not lose its traditional connections, and to exclude the rising non-professional middle classes unless they were prepared to accept Cambridge values and style',[3] and Campion told the committee that it was not possible for the University to take in more students from the new middle classes, because:

'I do not see what is to become of them after their University course'. He claimed that Cambridge already took in some of this group, including:

'all who can make their University course profitable; and I believe that with the present great pressure in the country you will not get persons who are going into commerce, or who are going into trade, or what I might call the lower professions, to come and spend two years at the University...no man, I conceive, however distinguished he was in...examination, and however sure of getting a scholarship, would come to Cambridge if he intended, after coming to Cambridge, to go into a merchant's office in Liverpool; for the merchant would tell him that it would serve his purpose much better to go into the office at once'.[3] This argument is increasingly heard today, particularly in relation to the newer Universities, but Twigg considers that Campion was lacking in candour, in view of the prevailing middle-class interest in University education; this judgement is supported by Campion's claim that:

'the great advantage which the men get in coming to Cambridge is by rubbing against each other, and a man gets to learn what he is properly worth; in fact, as we say, the conceit gets taken out of him', and that a Cambridge degree:

'represents not only a certain amount of general education... but it also represents the social training which may be given during three years' residence'.[3] This reasoning is clearly in conflict with his first-quoted argument citing the need for the professional utility of a degree, and it is interesting to note that all these issues remain relevant to the present identity and culture wars in the United Kingdom.

The social elements of a Cambridge education were also raised by the Committee when Campion was asked about the role of sport in University life, in the context of expections that students would be involved in sport and subscribe to college sports clubs. When asked:

'A person could hardly be attached to a college without subscribing to a cricket and boat club could he?', Campion replied: 'No', and when asked about refusal to subscribe, he stated:

'I have no doubt there are instances, but then they are rare instances of men of iron determination, and you cannot expect that every man would do so.[3] (Twigg reports that in 1887, at a meeting of the 'Amalgamated Clubs' at Queens':

'several members spoke on the urgent necessity of all the men in the college taking an active part in the various branches of sport').[3]

During the 1870s, Campion would retain his significant involvement in Church matters and, in 1878, he was noted to be: 'devoting most of his time to parochial work at St Botolph's'.[3] This was when Arthur Wright, a fellow since 1867, had become assistant tutor to Campion and would take over many of Campion's College duties.[3] Wright had been obliged to go out of College for five years after his election as a fellow, returning as Dean in 1872. This had involved him in an exchange of correspondence with Campion, when trying to negotiate a permanent tenure for his fellowship as a condition for his return. But although, in Wright's subsequent account, Campion told him that:

'I must on no account insist on that, for it would never be granted me', Wright held out for his terms, recalling:

'If I came to Cambridge, it would be to stay, and after five or six letters had passed my terms were granted. So unwilling were the seniors of that day to admit any reform'.[3] In 1870, Campion was awarded the D.D. degree and appointed Rural Dean of the Ely diocese; he would continue in this office until elected to the Presidency in 1892. In 1879, he was appointed to an honorary canonry of Ely Cathedral, which he retained until his death in 1896. At Queens', he would have been involved in the oversight of the decorations for the hall in 1875, designed by Bodley.

As described in the previous chapter, the 1880s saw two major building projects at Queens', the 'Friars' Building' for student accommodation, completed in 1886, (to which Campion contributed), and a new College chapel. Wright subsequently claimed that Campion was instrumental in the initial stages of proposing the latter:

'the idea of building a new chapel came from a walk in the country which he (Wright) took with Campion. Wright suggested enlarging the existing chapel, and although Campion thought this an impractical idea, he offered to subscribe £1000 towards the cost of a new chapel if Wright would take the responsibility for arranging its construction'.[3] Events moved swiftly; Bodley drew up plans in 1887, a decision to proceed was made in 1888, the funding was soon raised by subscription, and the building was consecrated in 1891.

When Phillips died, on the 5th of February 1892, Campion was elected President in his stead on the 23rd of February. Gray, tells us that this was:

'hailed with delight by the past members of the College, most of whom had been his pupils'.[4] His Presidency was to be short and relatively uneventful. The new chapel organ was celebrated in a ceremony on the 27th of September, 1892, and Gray, who will have been present, states that of the old members of the College attending:

'Most of them will remember the sermon preached by the President on the occasion',[4] (which may leave some of us wondering about the minority who managed to put the event out of their minds!). Campion's address, which was duly published, was entitled: 'The Beauty of Holiness'.[9] In his final years, Campion, despite his high church sympathies, was on the side of the more liberal theologians of the time, advocating freedom of choice in many rites and practices, and accepting the relevance of the growing movement of Biblical criticism.[3] In relation to the latter, in 1892 he writes:

'The questions raised, though involving matters which affect Christian doctrine, must be discussed as literary questions. They cannot be decided by mere ecclesiastical authority'.[3] He regretted the disputes between Anglicans, and believed that:

'respecting some of the accessories of public worship... Predilections for such things indifferent and prejudices against them have broken the unity of the Church'.[3] During Campion's Presidency, the academic reputation of the College, to which he had been a major contributor during the early years of his career, was maintained, as Queens' students achieved the highest honours in the Mathematics, Law and Natural Sciences Triposes during 1894-96, and, in the year after his death, in the Classics Tripos.[4] He died, unmarried, aged 76, after: 'a very short illness',[4] on the 20th of October, 1896. He is buried in Mill Road Cemetery, Cambridge. The inscription on his stone monument reads:

'In Memory of ALICIA ANNE CAMPION June 18 1876 aged 51 also of her brother WILLIAM MAGAN CAMPION DD President of Queens College d October 20 1896 aged 76'. (At the time of her death, his sister was living at 7, Trumpington Street, Cambridge). The monument's carved floral decorations are accompanied by the College's coat of arms.

The 'Cambridge Review' considers that:

'Without being exactly a prominent man in the history of his time, he was for several years conspicuous in the annals of the University and the Town...His was one of those lives, of which we have seen many examples, which are closely bound up with the history of the College to which they belonged and to which they gave their life's work'.[3]

Some personal memories of Campion are recorded in an article for the College magazine, 'The Dial', in 1938 by Harold Temperley, the son of Ernest Temperley, the latter a fellow of Queens' during 1871-89:

'I remember my father, Ernest Temperley...talking about its inception, (ie the plan to build what became the 'Friars' Building'). The matter was discussed one night in the Combination Room, and old Dr Campion showed up magnificently...offering a subscription of one thousand pounds. I always understood that the old President (Dr Phillips) did not like the project, because it meant giving up his second garden. Anyhow, it was built...During the excavations, thirteen skeletons, plus a horse's skull, were dug up...Dr Campion was a great character, Rector of St Botolph's, the only Rector in

Cambridge as he was fond of saying, and as picturesque a figure as could be imagined. He was never seen...without a top hat, and looked the perfection of benevolence. His rooms were often thronged with strange characters from Newnham parish, towards whom he was a real father. He once pulled a boy out of Newnham millpond with a boat hook and saved his life by applying artificial respiration. Newnham was a real village in the old days, and Dr Campion a rural rector, attending mothers' meetings, discussing the right way to feed cows, and the way to prevent boys going to the bad. Dr Campion was not only a great scholar and an eloquent preacher, but a most engaging and entertaining companion for old and young...He delighted a mother in the parish one day by telling her that her child of three looked like a cornfield, with cornflower blue eyes, cheeks as red as poppies, and hair as yellow as the grain...I remember the first stained glass window being put up in St Botolph's. It was the gift of Dr Campion...In his last years Dr Campion was President, and my brothers and myself were often in the Lodge. We used to go to tea with him, and he taught us to fish, leaning out of the window over our shoulders, as we dangled our rods in the Cam...The picture of him in the college by Mr Brock is an excellent one, but I don't think anything could represent what he was in life, full of benevolence, wit, eloquence, learning, and alive to the very finger tips even when over eighty (Note: in fact, he died aged 76)...There was something unique in the college, in its picturesque chatacter, in its strange old-world simplicity, in its remarkable remoteness and seclusion and self sufficiency.The impression it made on you was that of tasting some old and rare wine. This wine at least had a bouquet and a body, rich and full as the finest Burgundy'.[10]

References

1. Wikipedia. William Campion (mathematician). 2020. Online.
2. Campion, William. A Cambridge Alumni Database. University of Cambridge. 2020. Online.
3. Twigg, J. A History of Queens' College, Cambridge. 1448-1986. The Boydell Press. 1987. pp 225-42, 257-59, 274-77, 286, 291.

4. Gray, J.H. The Queens' College of St Margaret and St Bernard. F.E.Robinson. London. 1898. pp 283-84, 293.
5. Queens' College Cambridge. Fellows 1800-1899. 2020. Online.
6. Wikipedia. Sadleirian Professor of Pure Mathematics. 2020. Online.
7. Winstanley, D.A. Later Victorian Cambridge. Cambridge at the University Press. 1947. p 156.
8. Queens' College, Cambridge. Statutes. 2020. Online.
9. Campion, W.M., The Beauty of Holiness. A Sermon preached by the Rev. W.M.Campion, D.D. ...September 27, 1892, Cambridge. 1892.
10. Temperley, H. Some Memories of Old Queens'. The Dial. Easter 1938. Queens' College, Cambridge. Online. 2021.

CHAPTER 31

(Sir) Herbert Edward Ryle, K.C.V.0. . President 1896-1901.

(Clergymen do not use the title associated with knighthood).

Summary.

Herbert Edward Ryle was born in 1856, the second son of John Charles Ryle, rector of Helmingham, Suffolk, who would be appointed Bishop of Liverpool in 1880. His mother died in 1860 and Herbert Edward remembered being held up by his nurse at the attic window, to view his mother's funeral.

In 1868 he was admitted to Eton College, where he achieved exceptional academic and sporting success, winning the prestigious 'Newcastle' prize for classics. In 1875, he proceeded to King's College, Cambridge, to study classics, but, after an impressive start to his University career, an injury at football not only restricted his mobility, but led to a period of depression; although he was awarded a degree, he did not sit the examinations. However, in 1879, he resumed his studies, this time in theology, and proceeded to win several prizes. He achieved a first class degree in theology in 1881.

He was elected a fellow of King's in 1881 and was ordained priest in 1883. In the same year he married Nea Adams; they would have three sons, but only one would survive to adulthood. In 1886, he was appointed Principal of St. David's College, Lampeter. But he was very ambivalent about leaving Cambridge and returned, after just two years, as the Hulsean Professor of Divinity.

In 1896, after the death of Edward Campion, he was elected President of Queens', where he was to display his lifelong skills of attracting affection, respect and admiration.

In 1900 he was appointed Bishop of Exeter and, for the second time, reluctantly left Cambridge to do what he considered to be his duty. However, after only two years, he was promoted to be Bishop of Winchester.

He had suffered severe angina in 1904 and, thereafter, it was difficult for him to fulfill the demanding schedule he set himself. As a result of his chronic ill-health, he made another reluctant move, in 1910, to become Dean of Westminster, a prestigious role, but one which would be less physically demanding. During his tenure, Westminster Abbey would witness the Coronation of George V, many special services during the Great War, and the burial of the 'Unknown Warrior'.

He died in 1925 and is buried in the Abbey, near to the grave of the Unknown Warrior. He was survived by his wife, son and grandchildren.

Timeline.

1856.	Born in London. Second son of John Charles Ryle, rector of Helmingham, Suffolk, and, subsequently, Bishop of Liverpool.
1860.	Death of his mother.
1861.	His father remarries and moves to be rector of Stradbroke, Suffolk.
1866.	Attends a private school at Wadhurst, Sussex.
1868.	Admitted to Eton College.
1875.	Admitted to King's College, Cambridge.
1877.	Sustains a seriously disabling injury at football.
1879.	Awarded an 'aegrotat' degree for the Classical Tripos, (ie he is deemed unable to take the exams due to illness).
1879-81.	Studies theology; achieves several prizes and first class honours in the Theology Tripos.
1880.	His father is appointed as the first Bishop of Liverpool.
1881.	Elected a fellow of King's College. (He will be a Professorial fellow 1888-1901 and an honorary fellow from 1901).
1882.	Ordained deacon at Lincoln. M.A. . Engaged to be married.
1883.	Marries Nea Newish Adams. Ordained priest.

1884.	A son dies soon after birth.
1885.	Birth of a son: Edward.
1886-88.	Principal of St. David's College, Lampeter.
1887.	Elected in November as Hulsean Professor of Divinity at Cambridge.
1888.	Returns to Cambridge.
1889.	Birth of a son: Roger. Select Preacher of the University, (and again in 1892, 1895 and 1899). Death of his step-mother.
1892.	B.D. .
1895.	D.D. .
1895.	Appointed honorary canon of Ripon, Yorkshire.
1896.	Death of Edward Campion. Elected President of Queens'. Appointed honorary chaplain to the Queen.
1897.	Death of his son, Roger.
1898.	Warberton Lecturer at Lincoln's Inn, London.
1898-1901.	Chaplain-in-Ordinary to the Queen.
1899.	Start of the Second Boer War.
1900.	Appointed Bishop of Exeter. Death of his father.
1901.	Consecrated as Bishop in January. Resigns as President of Queens'. Elected an honorary fellow of Queens'.
1902.	End of the Second Boer War.
1903.	Translated to be Bishop of Winchester.
1904.	Suffers a severe attack of angina.
1910.	Reluctantly accepts the offer of the Deanery of Westminster, as he has had an extended period of ill-health. Death of Edward VII on the 6th of May.
1911.	Installed as Dean of Westminster on the 29th of April. Officiates at the coronation of George V on the 22nd of June. Created C.V.O. . The Parliament Act 1911 restricts the power of the House of Lords.
1912.	Prolocutor (ie Chairman) of the Lower House of Convocation, Province of Canterbury, of the Church of England.
1914.	Start of the Great War, on the 28th of July.
1918.	End of the Great War, on the 11th of November.
1920.	Issues an appeal, (The Dean Ryle Fund), for the maintenance of Westminster Abbey. The 'Unknown Warrior' is buried at Westminster Abbey on the 11th of November.

1921. Created K.C.V.O. . The gravestone of the Unknown Warrior is unveiled on the 11th of November.

1922. Irish Free State established on the 6th of December.

1923. Officiates at the wedding of the Duke of York, (later George VI), at Westminster Abbey.

1924. His health declines.

1925. Returns to Westminster after five months during which he had been nursed at Bournemouth. Dies on the 20th of August. Is buried in Westminster Abbey, close to the grave of the Unknown Warrior. Is survived by his wife, son and grandchildren.

Theologian. Biblical scholar. College fellow. Principal of St David's College, Lampeter. A short-term President of Queens'. Bishop of Exeter and of Winchester. Dean of Westminster.

Herbert Edward Ryle was born in Onslow Square, London on the 25th of May 1856. He was the second son of John Charles Ryle, rector of Helmingham, Suffolk, and his second wife, Jessie Elizabeth, daughter of John Walker, of Crawfordton, Dumfriesshire.[1]

His father, John Charles Ryle, who would be appointed as the first Bishop of Liverpool in 1880, was born in 1816, the eldest son of John Ryle, a wealthy banker and Member of Parliament.

John Charles had been educated at Eton College and proceeded to have a brilliant career at Christ Church, Oxford, as a scholar and athlete. Although he had experienced a religious conversion at Oxford, he did not plan a career in the Church, and joined his father's bank, became a magistrate, and hoped to get into Parliament. But, in 1841, his father's investments failed and his future prospects were transformed. He recalls:

'We got up one summer's morning with all the world before us as usual, and went to bed that night completely and entirely ruined'.[2,3] This was:

'the blackest chapter of my life...I never had any particular desire to become a clergyman', (but took orders) 'because I felt shut up to do it and saw no other course of life open to me'.[3] In 1841, he was duly ordained deacon by the Bishop of Winchester at Farnham Castle, (his son Herbert Edward's future home), and accepted an offer of a curacy at Exbury in the New Forest. Although he resigned after two years, because his health: 'broke down', he was then appointed rector of St Thomas', Winchester, and would serve nearly 40 years as a parish priest. In 1844 he became rector of Helmingham, Suffolk, and married Matilda, who died from tuberculosis in 1847, leaving an infant daughter, Georgina. In 1849 he married his second wife, Jessy Walker, but she soon began to suffer from chronic ill-health and died of kidney disease in 1860, after giving birth to three sons: Reginald John, Herbert Edward and Arthur Johnston, and a daughter, Jessy Isabella. The rector was left with five children, aged between fourteen and two, and his relationship with the local squire, John Tollemache, the patron of the living, had broken down to the extent that there was: 'a complete suspension of friendly relations between them'.[3] This led to his accepting the offer of the nearby living of Stradbroke, and he moved his family there in 1861. Later in the year he was married for the third time, to Henrietta Amelia Clowes, who would be a loving stepmother to her new family. John Charles Ryle became a well-known 'evangelical' in the Church, (see Chapter 26); he was well over six feet tall with a commanding presence and was noted for his preaching and writings. In 1880, he was appointed as the first Bishop of Liverpool, on the recommendation of the outgoing Prime Minister, Benjamin Disraeli, who, allegedly, wanted an evangelical in the position, to annoy the in-coming Prime Minister, the 'High Church' William Gladstone.[2]

The only memory that his son, Herbert Edward, had of Helmingham, was of being held up by his nurse at the attic window of the rectory to see his mother's funeral. At Stradbroke, he and his siblings grew up in a household focussed on religious devotion. A visitor in the 1860s writes:

'Mr Ryle, with his gigantic figure and stentorian voice, was perhaps rather formidable to a youthful visitor, but he was very kind and hearty, and I soon felt at home. The atmosphere of the house was...devotional: daily Bible readings, somewhat lengthy family prayers, and a good deal of religious talk...'.[3] In 1866, when Herbert Edward was aged ten, he joined his brother at a small private boarding school at Wadhurst, Sussex, when his father writes:

'I left the dear boys at Wadhurst last night...Poor little Herbert cried most bitterly at parting...'.[3] Later in the year, a letter to Herbert Edward from his step-mother, identifies a rather surprising trait in his temperament, which, it is to be hoped, he managed to suppress in his future career:

'My dear Herbert...I am very glad to hear you are quite well again-throwing stones or filliping pebbles you see may be dangerous sometimes, and you will not wonder at my having mercy on the poor sheep when you and R. were slinging stones at them...Best love to you from Arthur and from your very affect. Mother, H.A.Ryle'.[3] After two years, Herbert Edward was taken to Eton College by his father, to compete for an entrance scholarship, and did sufficiently well to be accepted as an 'Oppidan', (ie living in a boarding house in the town); he was subsequently admitted to the College in 1869. Herbert Edward had demanding expectations of himself and was determined to achieve the College's most prestigious prize. This was the 'Newcastle Scholarship', awarded annually, which involved examinations in Greek, Latin, and Divinity. He succeeded on his third attempt, in 1875, when one of the examiners was E.W.Benson, the future Archbishop of Canterbury. Many years later, Herbert Edward was to recall:

'It was one of the severest ordeals of my life. Possibly my work for it was almost intemperate. But the aspiration for the "Newcastle" was one that was deeply implanted in boyish ambition; and as the bare possibility of it arose above the horizon of school life, it became the object of extraordinarily intense effort...'.[3] In addition he gained his colours for the College's football XI.

In 1875, after a distinguished school career, Herbert Edward, (who will now be referred to as 'Ryle'), was elected a scholar of King's College, Cambridge, where, of the 40 undergraduates,

13 were Old Etonions. He continued to excel, winning the Carus Greek Testament prize for undergraduates in his first term and the divinity prize in 1876. He won yet another prize in 1877 and studied hard for the Classical Tripos which he was due to take in 1879. Also, he was expected to represent the University at athletics. But he then experienced a major setback; he sustained a knee injury playing football, which not only halted his sporting activities, but seems to have resulted in a serious lack of mobility and disabling symptoms of depression. His biographer tells us that:

'Lack of exercise and overwork produced so serious a condition of health that it became apparent that a prolonged rest must be the only remedy'.[3] This so affected his studies for the next two years, that he graduated in 1879 only with an 'aegrotat' degree, which signified that he was not examined because of illness. But he was sustained by several trips to Europe with friends; in 1878 he was in Switzerland, as one of his travelling companions recalls:

'We had to share the same room sometimes, and I cannot forget that Ryle had the most extraordinary way of getting into bed, a method of his own invention. When all was ready, he would run across the room, leap into the air, and, with a sudden twist, so arrange matters that he fell flat on his back on the bed. One night...when man and bed met, there was a terrific crash; the boards under the mattress gave way, and the man disappeared... he was very respectful to the Swiss beds after it, and the settling of the consequent little bill'.[3] In 1879, while at Dresden, he had sufficiently recovered physically to take part in some sports and won several events; but this was a mistake, as he injured his knee again and had to be carried back to his hotel: 'in a faint'. The Queen of Saxony, who had been present, subsequently inquired about his progress and, when convalescing, another solicitous lady, a Mrs Adams, took him out for drives, together with his future wife, her daughter Nea.

His academic fortunes were about to inprove; in 1879, he began to read for the Theology Tripos and, in the same year, won the Carus Greek Testament Prize for Bachelors of Arts and, in

1880, the Crosse Scholarship. In 1881, he obtained a first class in the Theological Tripos and won three other University prizes, which led to his election as a fellow at King's College on the 25th of April. Thereafter, for nearly two decades, his life would focus on teaching, scholarship- in particular, critical studies of the Old Testament- preaching and writing, culminating with his election as President of Queens':

'His charm of manner, his infectious zest for all forms of healthy amusement, his ready sympathy with all sorts and conditions of men, made it easy for him to enter into friendly relations with the undergraduates, who, while they could not but feel respect for his intellectual distinction, yet saw in him nothing of that pedantry or stiffness which makes some College "dons" appear to their juniors as beings belonging to another world'.[3]

At Easter 1882, he travelled to Rome to meet Nea Adams and her parents, and he and Nea became engaged. His father, now Bishop of Liverpool, took an optimistic view:

'Herbert is a sensible fellow, and I do not think he would choose a fool- or an unbeliever or a papist- or one who is not a lady'.[3] In December 1882 he was ordained deacon by the 'Visitor' of King's College, Bishop Christopher Wordsworth, (a nephew of the poet, William), at Lincoln Cathedral. On the eve of this occasion Ryle writes:

'May God direct into a better channel my ambition, my love of study, my love of society. May God grant His special blessing upon my own work in Cambridge- theological study, and particularly the study of the Bible... May God bless with every blessing my own darling Nea, that she may have peace in soul and joy in heart...so that when the call comes to summon us hence, we may be found ready to go, with the firm faith that we shall meet again in Heaven'.[3] His father officiated at their marriage, in August 1833, at the Holy Trinity Church, Marylebone, London, and Ryle was ordained priest by the Bishop of Lincoln in the following December.

The couple began married life in a furnished house in Trumpington Street, Cambridge, but then moved to a newly-built house at 12, Hervey Road. In 1884, they had the sorrow of the death of their first child, soon after his birth, but their second son,

Edward, was born the following year and, for several years, their lives became settled. But, in 1896, the first of several upheavals in the Ryles' life occurred, when he applied for the post of Principal of St David's College, Lampeter, Wales, which had become vacant when the incumbent was appointed Bishop of Chester; Ryle had links with the College, having been an examiner for their B.A. degree. (St David's had been founded as a theological college and had recived a royal charter in 1828. It had achieved the right to award the B.D. degree in 1852, and the B.A. degree in 1865, while in 1971 it became 'St David's University College', as part of the University of Wales). However, he was very ambivalent before confirming his candidature, and when it was rumoured that he would withdraw, it needed a letter from a member of the Lampeter staff to help him make up his mind:

'If ever a man had a call to any place, you are that man, and I can conceive of no reasons sufficiently weighty for your declining the call...We were unanimously agreed (an unusual thing in such matters) in our willingness and even wish to work with you as our Head...and we cannot help feeling more than sorry that you have been unable to try our sincerity'.[3] This, and other appeals prompted Ryle to finally decide to apply, as he explains in a letter of the 28th of July:

'I wish to let you know...I have sent up my name for Lampeter...Cambridge owes a great responsibility to Lampeter on the occasion of this vacancy...I only wished to do my duty for the University; and possibly the invitations I had received, coupled with the absence of University candidates, indicated a line of duty...I wish to work for the Church and for Cambridge: whether away from the University or at the University...I do not wish to think of private interests or gratification...I am not racing for a prize. I only announce my readiness, if wanted, to serve elsewhere...I have gone through days of torment as to what was right...'.[3] Ryle was kept waiting for news of the success of his application until September, as the Bishop of St David's, who was responsible for the final decision, had mislaid the papers, giving the Ryles only three weeks to establish themselves in Wales. He writes to a friend on the 22nd of September:

'...it is simply horrid having to go away...We are both so near the point of breaking down whenever we bid adieu to a friend... On Monday next I go to Aberystwyth and look for a lodging where the family may rest until our future home is ready for us; and on Tuesday I go to Lampeter where the Bishop is going to institute me on the 29th. Nea, the infant, nurse and our servants (who bless them! Go with us)...will, I hope, be able to come and settle down by the end of next week, Oct.2'.[3] But although there was some delay in providing the necessary renovations to the Principal's house, the new Principal was given an immediate welcome by his eight colleagues, who were hoping for harmonious relationships, an overhaul of the College's finances, and development of the curriculum.[3] In December, 1886, he received encouragement from Edward Benson, Archbishop of Canterbury:

'My dear Principal- May I offer you my real congratulations on your taking of office, - so sacred and so important to the Church and country- and assure you of my prayers for a great blessing on your labour in raising a holy seed of priests and preachers and teachers...I was at once so sorry for your departure from Cambridge, and so filled with a sense of what you might do for Wales, that I could not forbear to say so...'.[3]

For the short time he would be in post, the promise of his appointment was fulfilled:

'The business of the moment was to consolidate...Here Ryle's tact, good temper, moderation, conciliatory temperament, and constitutional methods were of admirable service to the College... life there, if uneventful, was very happy...Ryle was not only Principal but also Professor of Greek, and one of the Professors of Theology. He at once made his mark as a teacher...His earnestness, sincerity, and deep religious sense, made him a real spiritual and moral force...'.[3]

However, after only just over a year, Ryle sent in his name as a candidate for the Hulsian Professorship of Divinity at Cambridge, which had became vacant when the previous incumbent had been elected as Lady Margaret's Professor of Divinity, the University's oldest professorship. (The Hulsian Professorship of Divinity had been founded in 1860, from bequests made by John Hulse,

1708-90, for a prize, scholarships and lectureships). While this was a surprise to many, Ryle considered that he had made it plain that he would consider himself free to return to Cambridge if he believed his services were required. He felt it was his duty that his name should be considered for the professorship, as the focus of his scholarship- the study and 'Higher Criticism' of the Old Testament- was an increasingly important area of controversy in Anglican theology. Ryle believed that, in the words of his biographer, (the Rev. Maurice Fitzgerald, who was his chaplain when he was Bishop of Winchester):

'This task of commending new truth to inquiring and earnest minds was of vital importance to the future of religion',[3] and he felt bound to offer himself as a candidate, at the risk of disappointing friends in Lampeter. On November the 19th, he received the news that he had been elected and was faced with the task of informing his colleagues, who did not know of his application:

'Ryle came into the Common Room, where some of the members of the staff were sitting, and said that he had been offered the Hulsean Professorship and was going. Though he had every right to go...he was apologetic and genuinely distressed that he had not stayed as long as his colleagues had hoped. He was... wrong in the conception, if he entertained it that the brief tenure of office had hardly been worth while...It had been well worth while...The Principal's house was a centre of hospitality warm and genial. Dinners with happy chats, games of tennis of an afternoon, long talks on the beautiful lawn as the enchanting summer light faded away...'.[3]

The Ryles returned to Cambridge in 1888 and moved into a new house, 'Meadowcroft', on the Trumpington Road, where he would keep pigs. In his letter to the electors for the Hulsean Professorship he had stated:

'As a student of Theology it is my highest desire to give myself up to work upon the Old Testament. The great problems raised by recent criticism seem to make a special claim upon the enthusiasm and courage of the younger generation of students...'.[3] He believed that:

'The theology of no generation exactly resembles that of its predecessors...It too sifts tradition...rearranges ideas, states old truths in new lights, casts aside crudities, and sooner or later drops superstitions'.[4] For example, he argues that the early chapters of Genesis were: 'neither accurate science nor literal history', but contained:

'under the form of a symbolism for which a phase of rudimentary and erroneous science in Palestine was the chosen vehicle, (there are) spiritual truths which belong to the very foundation of our faith'.[4] But the new ideas of the so-called 'Higher Criticism' were regarded in some influential Anglican circles as: 'little less than treasonable'.[3]

For the next thirteen years at Cambridge, Ryle was an active lecturer, preacher and writer; among his published books were: 'The Early Narratives of Genesis' (1892), 'The Canon of the Old Testament' (1892), and 'Philo and Holy Scripture' (1895).[1]

Before his election as President of Queens', his second son Roger was born in 1889 and, in the same year, he was appointed Select Preacher of the University, (and again in 1892, 1895 and 1899). He proceeded to the B.D. degree in 1892 and to the D.D. in 1895, while in the same year he was appointed an honorary canon of Ripon Cathedral, Yorkshire. His lectures were meticulously prepared and a former pupil provides evidence of their reception:

'I read Theology after taking my degree, and for two years enjoyed his lectures...The memory of his friendliness and encouragement to a completely undistinguished disciple is as fresh as if it had all happened yesterday. As a teacher he was so clear and direct, and so easy to follow; never any sort of parade of learning...at the same time stimulating us to dig for ourselves... the satisfaction of the postgraduate time always centres round Dr. Ryle'.[3]

Edward Campion, President of Queens', died on the 20th of October, 1896, and, unusually, the fellows looked for a replacement from outside the College, as they had to take into account that the income of the President had been considerably reduced during the agricultural depression and that there were no internal candidates of a suitable age and sufficient financial means.[3] (The 'Great Depression of British agriculture', during about 1873-96, was caused by a fall in grain prices, resulting from the cultivation of the American temperate grasslands). The fellows issued a unanimous invitation to Ryle, which he accepted, and his diary for the 1st November notes the: 'extraordinary sensation produced by the surprise of unexpected appointment'.[3] The Ryles received over two hundred letters of congratulation, including one from John Willis Clark, (Registrary of the University and co-author of 'The Architectural History of the University of Cambridge...' Cambridge. University Press, 1886):

'Oh! You foolish young people! Why take these irrevocable steps without consultation?...you will simply eat your heart out in trying to effect the impossible...We shall no longer, it is true, be able to say that the province of the Heads is universal ignorance...I hope that I may be alive when you are Vice-Chancellor...It is pleasant to think of the delightful Lodge in the hands of you and Nea. But I am afraid that you will find it almost hopelessly uncomfortable as a home. I have views on nearly every part of it-so do please let me come and have a talk with you about it...I really think that I...know more about it than anybody else does... We shall all, I am sure, be very pleased to think that you will be nearer to us. This love of dwelling in a cabbage-garden in the suburbs is a very real drawback to academic life and influence...'.[3] Luckily, Clark was wrong in his forecast of Ryle's work at Queens'. Although he would only serve for just over four years, he established excellent relationships with the fellows and undergraduates, and the number of the latter increased from 78 to 98 during his tenure.[3] Ryle was installed as President in the chapel on the 21st of November 1896; he then dined in hall, before the senior fellow proposed his health in the Combination Room. He preached in the chapel the following day and, two days later, introduced himself to the undergraduates at a meeting in the hall. One lasting effect of this occasion, is that, in the light of the poor morale and performance of the College's Boat Club, he suggested a change of design of its blazer to its current white with green trimmings. (As a previous member of the Boat Club, the author felt compelled to include this bit of ephemera. This coincided with the start of a marked improvement in the performance of the College boats, and Mrs Ryle embroided a new flag for the Club). He re-opened a staircase leading to his study so that he would be readily accessible to undergraduates, he was a regular attender at College sporting events, and he would often entertain the undergraduates in the Lodge with musical activities and social gatherings. A contemporary recalls, 25 years later:

'In University entertaining the Ryles made it their special delight to break down the last remnants of the old traditional etiquette which built up walls of division between seniors and juniors, while it tended also to keep apart socially those whose interests lay in different directions. Ryle would rejoice in gathering round his board men of science, theologians, and Divinity students, while undergraduates and young M.A.s would find themselves introduced at evening parties to dons, professors, and their wives in a way that was far less usual in those days than it is now. Music was always a prominent feature in the home, and one remembers the keen interest Ryle took in the famous Cambridge performance of Gluck's opera "Orpheus", conducted by Sir Charles Stanford, when many University ladies were performers, Mrs. Ryle and Lady Stanford amongst the number. At Queens' Lodge...their cultivated taste and knowledge found scope in restoring and furnishing appropriately the long gallery, which is one of the glories of Cambridge...'.[3]

From the 1880s, several colleges supported missionary work in London and, shortly after Ryle had been elected President, he was one of the speakers at a large meeting organised to set up 'Cambridge House', the University's mission in South London. The Bishop of Rochester, the principal speaker, was the guest of the Ryles and recalls that he:

'distinctly remembers feeling that Ryle and John Selwyn (Master of Selwyn College) were the two Seniors who really understood and would follow up and throw weight into the attempt',[3,4] while Ryle writes:

'the future historian of the Church will find few more remarkable features of healthy and hopeful life than that series of School and College Missions and University Settlements, in which men of all schools of thought have sought to link the fortunes and the happiness of the students of the land with the barren monotony and heathen hopelessness of thousands in East and South London'.[4]

However, Ryle's remaining time in Cambridge was not all- as Jonathan Swift (1667-1745) would have said- 'sweetness and light'. For example, in 1896, the question whether to award degrees to women was an ill-tempered and divisive issue, as although a University committee had recommended that women at Girton and Newnham Colleges should receive a diploma and the titles of several degrees, 2130 undergraduates, (out of a total of 2856), signed a petition against this in May 1897, while the Cambridge Union Society:

'strongly condemned the recommendation of the Women's Degree Syndicate', by 1063 votes to 138, presciently stating that there was:

'a real danger that as women, attracted to Cambridge in large numbers by the new titles, come in at one door, men may go out by the other'.[3] Ryle had been a supporter of reform, but in view of the hightened emotions, he, together with three other prominent University members, published a statement shortly before the decisive vote in the Senate House, which would not enhance his chances of a memorial statue today:

'Our intention to support the recommendations of the Degrees for Women Syndicate has, we believe, become generally known to members of the Senate. It is our duty therefore to inform them that we now feel compelled, most reluctantly, to abandon that intention. Our opinion that it is desirable to grant to women who are successful in our Tripos Examinations some such distinction as that recommended by the Syndicate has undergone no change; but the opposition which the Report has called forth has compelled us to look at the question from an entirely different point of view. We are forced to ask ourselves whether an extension of privilege to women students ought to be granted at all, unless supported by a majority...such as that by which the Grace for admitting women to University Examinations was passed in 1881. The removal of a grievance which, after all, has pressed upon a comparatively small number of persons, can be bought at too high a price when considerably more than half of the resident members of the Senate are known to be bitterly opposed to the measure, and would view it, if carried, as a grave betrayal of trust...the benefit conferred upon those for whom we are risking so much would be of doubtful value. They would find the University hostile instead of friendly'.[3] The vote, on the 21st of May 1897, defeated the proposal, 1707 to 661. After this, no doubt some considered themselves betrayed and did not see Ryle in the same adulatory light as his biographer, who cites his: 'calm judgement' (and) 'the courage to meet the risk of being misunderstood'.[3] Also, Ryle's relations with his students were less than friendly on several occasions; for example, when he took a noticeably hard line against misbehaviour. Although he had encouraged the Boat Club, he objected to the consequences of its success in 1898 and deprived five students of their scholarships and exhibitions after a celebratory bonfire in the College. This led to a petition signed by: 'almost every member of the College in statu pupillari'. Also, in 1898, when a rugby blue was sent down for a year, there was a demonstration in his support and a student newspaper informed its readers:

'the Tutorial Body of Queens' is attempting a return to the Inquisitorial barbarities of medievalism'.[4] But Ryle still maintained considerable support; some influential students then wrote a letter denying:

'all connection with the article or with the sentiments expressed therein'.[4]

But such difficulties did not affect the Vice-President's assessment of Ryle's character, and in 1925 he recalls:

'When Dr Ryle was elected President in 1896 he was still under forty. He came to us with all the fresh vigour of a man still young. He had many great gifts, none greater perhaps than his wonderful power of sympathy. There cannot often have been a man who possessed as he did the gift of putting himself in touch with the hopes, the fears, the prejudices, the difficulties of anyone with whom he might be thrown into contact by accident or design. He was as winning as he was wise, as sincere as he was sympathetic. These were qualities of infinite value to a Professor and the Head of a House. No wonder that his counsel was widely sought, and his influence very widely felt'.[5]

The Ryles suffered a tragedy in 1897, when their younger son, Roger, died aged eight. He had undergone an operation for the removal of adenoids, which was performed at the Lodge. Roger had come in from the garden asking: 'He will only send me to sleep fot three minutes?', but did not recover consciousness from the anaesthetic. A family friend recalls:

'The parents met this crushing blow with the fortitude and unselfish courage which only the highest faith can give; and those who lived with them through this time of intense sorrow can never forget the lessons learnt in that stern school. The Chapel service for the little lad's funeral was one which will ever stand out in the memory of the friends who came and helped to sing the hymns of praise which the father and mother had chosen…the father's heart was so deeply wounded that never again would he face life with quite the same glad buoyancy…something had gone from him which would never return. Not a week later the elder boy went away for the first time to his private school, and the house which had been so joyous with the children's voices became at once strangely silent and empty, for that chapter also was now ended… he decided in those first days of desolation that the nursery toys should go at once…it is the only way…We could never do it at all, if we leave it now'.[3]

Ryle had developed a wide reputation by preaching and lecturing outside the University; for example, in 1889 he preached at Westminster Abbey on Trinity Sunday. He had became B.D. in 1892 and D.D. in 1895. In 1896 he was appointed honorary chaplain to Queen Victoria and, after the first time he preached before the Queen at St George's Chapel, Windsor, he told his father that he could not bring himself to look towards her but:

'had great relief in the visage of Sir Walter Parratt and his porcupine hair, which confronted him from the organ'.[3] He dined with the Queen at Windsor Castle on the 28th of February, 1897, who informed him:

'I was very much pleased with your sermon; I wished to tell you- yes, it was a good subject. And that is the way we want subjects treated, in a practical sort of way'.[3] This occasion was also memorable as he did not own a court suit and was dressed in an ill-fitting and precariously-pinned outfit borrowed from the Dean of Windsor.[3] His place in the establishment was further consolidated when he received promotion as Chaplain-in-Ordinary to the Queen in 1898.

In 1899, Ryle visited his ailing father at Lowestoft. His step-mother had died in 1889 and the Bishop was: 'so evidently enfeebled in step, hearing, and memory', that Ryle advised his father's resignation. The Bishop remained in Lowestoft, dying there in 1900. In a letter to a friend, Ryle recalls:

'In the country life of Suffolk he was everything to us- taught us games, natural history, astronomy, and insisted on our never being idle, and carefully fostered our love of books...The task of arranging for the funeral and of transferring the body from Lowestoft to Liverpool has meant heavy work...The church was filled with clergy and gentry. The graveyard was crowded with poor people who had come in carts and vans and 'buses to pay the last honours to the old man...'.[3] Later in 1900, the Ryles, together with their son Edward, joined family friends for a holiday in Switzerland. On their return they spent a night in London, as Ryle's diary records:

'All three of us attended Hippodrome performance; 2 to 6!! Extraordinary performances of all sorts- acrobatic- performing dogs- clowns- scenic effects- conjuring- a Siberian story- astonishing athletic performance of trapeze man who from standing position took forty-five back somersaults in the air without slightest pause or apparent fatigue!'.[3]

Ryle's biographer considers that he must have been expecting the offer of a bishopric and this came in 1900, when he received a letter from the Prime Minister, as he records in his diary:

'Nov. 30, S. Andrew's Day.- A letter at 8 A.M. from Lord Salisbury, with her Majesty's Permission to offer me the See of Exeter. A painful and troubled day. It is evidently to all intents and purposes a command: and the duty must be faced. But in these days no man knowing as I do what the work is- ...can wish to undertake it...S. Andrew's Day Festival at (Girton) Church...

Hymns and Anthem- procession- with choir of 5 elderly rustics and schoolmaster. Women voices from Girton College. Preached on John I, 40, and got further away from this haunting offer than before throughout the day. Returned 9.30, and wrote letter 10.0 P.M. to Marquis of S. accepting..Dec. 1.- Very bad night...It has been a greater shock to me than I could have supposed possible'.[3,4] The news was made public on the 4th of December, and he notes:

'Terrible distress in College at the announcement. Letters and telegrams all day long'. On the 20th of January he attended the chapel at Queens', when his diary notes:

'Arthur Wright preached, with very kindly- much too tender- references to myself. Vry hard not to give way. The College makes me feel weak as water'.[3] In a letter to the College debating society, he writes:

'I feel the approaching severance from the College will be to me one of the great sorrows of my life; and the fact of its being so arises from the happiness and the intimacy of the relations in which I have been privileged to live with all members of the College'.[4]

Ryle was consecrated Bishop of Exeter on the 25th of January, 1901, at Westminster Abbey, three days after the death of Queen Victoria, so that the new Bishop took the Oath of Allegiance to King Edward VII. Ryle notes:

'The service was most sustaining, and compelled one to look up from the unworthiness of personal powers to the unseen Personal Presence...I have a shrewd suspician that I could never have work more full of interest and influence than the one I am resigning'.[3] On the 8th of February he handed his resignation to the Vice-President of Queens', received gifts from members of the College, dined in hall and shook hands with the undergraduates in the Combination Room. On the following day, his last in Cambridge before before travelling to Exeter, his diary reads:

'H.C. at 8.0 and was much upset...After lunch went alone to cemetery and visited dear little R's grave...'.[3]

Ryle was enthroned at Exeter Cathedral on the 12th of February:

'Thenceforward he was involved in a ceaseless whirl of duties which scarcely left him a leisure moment', and soon gained the confidence of the clergy and laity.[1,3] The theologically controversial issues of the time included the 'Invocation of Saints' and 'Prayers to the Virgin Mary' and, in 1904, Ryle published a collection of his views on Church doctrine in: 'On the Church of England, Sermons & Addresses'. But his time in Exeter was to be limited by the consequences of the death of Archbishop William Temple, in December 1902. Ryle preached a Memorial Sermon at Canterbury Cathedral on the day after the funeral and, in January 1903, the Bishop of Winchester was appointed as the next Archbishop of Canterbury. The Prime Minister, Arthur Balfour, then offered Ryle the bishopric of Winchester. Once again Ryle suffered distressing ambivalence, but:

'sorely against his will he accepted the burden of fresh office thus thrust upon him',[3] and he preached his farewell sermon at Exeter on the 22nd of January. In March he writes:

'We have passed through horrid times of anxiety and making-up-one's- mind...I had a bad time of it, as you may well imagine... The offer to me was put very strongly, and the Archbp. Told me it had the very cordial approval of the King. The trio of Prime Minister, King, and Archbp. were a formidable combination; against which the private feelings of attachment to our new home and surroundings and friends could not, patriotically, make resistance. The people here are, as we are, genuinely distressed at this early separation...'.[3]

Ryle was enthroned in Winchester Cathedral on the 23rd of April, 1903, and would serve for eight years. His next move would result from various chronic symptoms of ill-health and he had suffered feelings of weakness, exhaustion and chest pain at the end of his time at Exeter. Continuing ill-health may have have affected his judgement in his early days at Winchester, as even his admiring biographer considers that a peremptory letter to his clergy in June 1903, while still a stranger to the diocese, was an uncharacteristic mistake. The new Bishop writes:

'...I learn that some of the Clergy are anxious to be informed of my wishes upon certain disputed matters...By laying down my explicit ruling upon such matters I may come into collision with the predilections of some devout and earnest fellow-workers. Nevertheless it is better that quite plain directives should be given by the Bishop than that there should be any feeling of uncertainty among Clergy or Laity...I feel confident that a Diocese gains more from the loyal adhesion of the Clergy to Episcopal ruling upon "burning questions" than from the absence of plain directions...I therefore desire it to be understood throughout the Diocese...That the use of incense is not permitted...that the Invocation of the Blessed Virgin and Devotions addressed to the Saints are not permitted...that the Celebration of the Holy Communion without the minimum number as prescribed in the Book of Common Prayer is not permitted...that the omission of the Commandments in the Service for the Holy Communion is not permitted...that the Administration of the Consecrated Elements with the recitation of only one clause is not permitted...that the introduction of pictures, figures, ornaments, etc., into churches is not permitted without a faculty duly obtained...I need not assure you, my brethren, that my single aim is to promote unity and peace...that we may give ourselves whole-heartedly to the spiritual duties with which we are each one of us entrusted...Yours sincerely, Herbert E. Winton: Farnham Castle May 27, 1903'.[3] He had not been universally welcomed at Winchester, and the letter, which only affected a few churches, was not well received. However, eventually, he would recover his reputation, and his resignation in 1911 would be widely regretted.[1]

In January 1904, while dictating letters at his official residence at Farnham Castle, he had a severe attack of angina which confined him to bed and, the following week, this was compounded by symptoms diagnosed as appendicitis. But athough he was not fit enough for surgery, he gradually recovered. However, he was unable to undertake public engagements for about nine months and, although he became well enough to maintain a busy schedule of engagements, there continued to be concerns about his health. There is no doubt that his energy would have been taxed by the routine that he set himself; the letters from Farnham Castle numbered about 12,000 each year, he spent much time travelling, and he would visit London for several days each month. His biographer, his chaplain at this time, reports:

'There was always an underlying feeling of anxiety, for we never travelled without taking with us remedies, lest he should have another attack of angina'.[3]

In 1908, the Ryles celebrated their silver wedding at Farnham Castle:

'A company of some 400 guests of all conditions and degrees assembled, and all the couples were photographed at the expense of their hosts. Music was provided by the band of the Gordon Boys' Home, and boys from that Home gave a gymnastic display in the garden. Tea was served in the courtyard of the Castle, and the Keep was illuminated at night...'.[3]

The Bishop of Winchester was always a member of the House of Lords, but Ryle did not often attend and only spoke on three occasions. When attending meetings which required a stay in London, such as the Convocation of the Anglican Province of Canterbury, Ryle was usually to be found in rooms in the Lollard's Tower at Lambeth Palace, which had been assigned for his use by the Archbishop of Canterbury in 1903. One of his duties was as Prelate of the Order of the Garter and he attended the Order's investiture ceremonies held by the King for the King of Norway in 1906 and for the King of Portugal in 1909. Both the Bishop and Mrs. Ryle became friendly with the Duchess of Albany, (the widow of Prince Leopold, the youngest son of Queen Victoria), who paid several visits to Farnham Castle.

In April 1910 he developed a new and disabling symptom: 'the mischief in his foot'.[3] which led to considerable pain and discomfort, and he was confined to bed for a month in the summer. His engagements became an increasing struggle and, at the end of the year, he was again bed-ridden. But there was one positive event in the autumn which would have lifted his mood: the engagement of his son Edward, who had attended Cambridge University, where he had been Secretary and President of the University Athletic Club.

However, his fortunes were about to improve; on the 9th of December he told his chaplain that the pain in his foot had lessened for the first time in several months, and two letters arrived on the 13th, from the Prime Minister and the Archbishop of Canterbury, offering him the Deanery of Westminster. The Prime Minister, Herbert Asquith, writes:

'My Dear Lord Bishop- As you are aware, the Deanery of Westminster will shortly be vacant. It has been suggested to me that you might be disposed, from considerations of health, to exchange the labours of your See for the comparative quiet, and the leisure for scholarly pursuits, which the Deanery offers. If this is the case, it would be a great satisfaction to me to advise the King in that sense. If I have been misinformed, or if (as is more than probable) you prefer, on a balance of reasons, to remain where you are, you will (I trust) not take it amiss that I should, in strict confidence, have put the choice before you'.[3] The Archbishop's letter notes:

'It is one of the great positions of central responsibility in the Church, calling for a man of first-rate thought and scholarship, and (above all) common sense of the deepest Christian kind...'.[3] For the fourth time in his career, Ryle found himself very conflicted whether to accept a new appointment. Although Westmister Abbey is a 'Royal Peculiar', so that the Dean is not responsible to the Bishop of London but to the Monarch, this was not a natural promotion. Also, the Ryles enjoyed the countryside and their home at Farnham Castle. But, after further consultations with friends, he decided that, in view of his uncertain health, he should accept the offer; as he told his son: 'After all, in some ways it's rather a dog's life'.[3] On the 22nd of December he writes to the Prime Minister:

'Dear Mr. Asquith- I fear I have delayed too long in sending my answer to your kind letter. It has, indeed, occasioned me sore perplexity as to what was my duty...On the whole...the impression seems to be that the present work represents too severe a strain to make it wise to decline the offer of a post so unique and, in a sense, so congenial as well as honourable. Although, therefore, the withdrawal from this See will be a most keen distress, yet I should not feel justified in running the risk of possibly not being able a short time hence to do the full measure of work...I decide therefore to inform you that I consent to your kind proposal to mention my name to the King in connection with the approaching vacancy of the Deanery of Westminster; and I respectfully tender you my thanks for the great honour which such a proposal implies...It would be difficult to express what I have gone through, in arriving at the conclusion contained in this letter. I pray God it is right. I am, dear Mr. Asquith, yours sincerely, Herbert E. Winton'.[3]

Before taking up his new appointment, on the 24th of January 1911, he celebrated his son's wedding at St Paul's, Knightsbridge and, on the next morning, accompanied by his biographer, he set off on a visit to Egypt, where he hoped his health would improve. He had: 'electrical treatment' to his foot, but had to rest at his hotel for several weeks before being able to take short walks. They left Egypt for Italy on the 30th of March, and, on the 16th of April, he ceased to be Bishop of Winchester. He returned to London on the 27th of April and, on the 29th , was installed as Dean of Westminster, at a service at Westminster Abbey. However, most of the building was closed to the public, as King George V, (who had succeeded to the throne in May 1910), was awaiting his Coronation, which was scheduled for the 22nd of June. The Abbey was being prepared by the Office of Works and, at his installation, the new Dean processed from the Jerusalem Chamber into the Abbey:

'through passages of new deal planks, lighted by electric light, and guarded by policemen and detectives'.[3] The ceremony was witnessed by only a small congregation of officials, choristers, bedesmen, neighbours, and personal friends. While redecorating and renovating the Deanery, preparation for the Coronation was Ryle's main preoccupation for his first two months in office. The first of five rehearsals of the Coronation processions was on the 6th of June: 'which the Dean in his weak state found so fatiguing...', and his erstwhile chaplain at Winchester was needed by his side on Coronation day:

'He certainly needed someone by him, for the ceremony was long and exhausting, and during its course I was obliged to dose him twice with sal-volatile and once with brandy and water, of which I carried supplies in the pockets of my cassock'.[3] But all went well; the King was pleased and, soon afterwards, Ryle was appointed C.V.O. .

Ryle's physical incapacity limited his outside engagements, but he was an active presence in the Abbey. However, the harmony which he achieved with his colleagues and officials would soon be overshadowed by the Great War, while, in his first two years, there were several demonstrations in the Abbey by the Suffragettes. The Dean describes one of these in a letter to his wife, dated the 10th of August, 1913:

'The Suffragists disturbed our morning service. There was an enormous congregation, people standing in the aisles all the time. And these Maenad criminals in the N. transept had occupied two pews, to the right and left. After the 7th Commandment they set up yowling: at first we thought some one had a fit or a seizure, but the howling became more tuneful and in unison. Needless to say I went on steadily with the Commandments: Alcock worked his organ energetically; the boys shook a bit but steadied themselves down: the vergers, assisted by the congregation, ejected about a dozen...Fortunately my sermon was not interrupted; and peace and order prevailed...but the offence as an outrage leaves an indelible impression'.[3] There was no sign that the demonstrators succeeded in attracting the Dean's attention to the underlying issues, and his reaction is mirrored by his biographer:

'It is difficult to realise today (ie in 1928) that people were to be found so dead to all sense of reverence and decency. But so it was. And none but an optimist as to the range of human folly can feel confident that, in days of public excitement, we are secure from ever witnessing some similarly lamentable scene'.[3]

In 1914, with the outbeak of the Great War, the Abbey and its Dean became:

'as it had never so completely been before, the spiritual home and centre of both nation and Empire. It was the Dean's aim to make it such...'.[3] The Abbey would host many public occasions, such as the Anzac Service in 1916 and the Memorial Service for Lord Kitchener, as well as services for the reception of the colours of regiments about to go to the front. It was the Dean's responsibility to protect the fabric of the Abbey; some window glass and monuments were removed, and air-raid watchmen were required every night. But the Ryles were spared one potential source of anxiety when their son, after attempting to join the Army, was judged physically unfit for service. The Dean's view of the war was, according to his biographer:

'...as a whole-hearted patriot, profoundly convinced of the righteousness of the Allies' cause, and of the necessity of fighting to the death against Prussian militarism'.[3] On Christmas Day 1916, he preached a controversial sermon critical of the U.S. President Wilson:

'...he (ie President Wilson) was of opinion that the nations who were leagued to disarm this evil demoniac of national militarism had the same aim in view as the perpetrators of these crimes...he had entirely misapprehended the European situation. Did anyone suppose that peace would be honourable which regarded the assailants and the defenders of humanity as having the same aim in view?'.[3] This achieved wide publicity in the U.S.A. .

Fortunately, the Abbey did not suffer any significant damage, but in 1917 the Dean writes:

'I saw Sir Edward Henry (Commissioner of Police) yesterday and he advised that in the event of a raid in the middle of the service (which God forbid) we should carry on...If such an interruption occurred in the middle of the sermon, I think the Choir and Organist should be prepared to sing some well-known hymn, like "Oh God, our Help"...It would be impossible for a preacher to continue, or for the congregation to listen, whilst explosions were going on. We may take it for granted that the King would not budge an inch...But...People who wish to leave the Abbey will have to be told to retire quietly.[3]

On the day before the end of the War, the 10th of November, 1918, Ryle notes:

'A wonderful and memorable day- the whole country waiting in expectation for the news of the signing of the Armistice. Last night a wildly enthusiastic reception was given at the Lord Mayor's Banquet in the Guildhall...reaching a whirlwind climax in the welcome accorded to Lloyd George...it had been one of the great days in the history of the country- the suspense, the agitation, the hope, the strength of religion'.[3] On the 11th of November he continues:

'At 11.0...Shouting, bugles, cheering soon filled the air. The streets full of excited people. A great rush to Buckingham Palace, where King and Queen had a splendid and enthusiastic reception. At 12.0 I took Mid-day Intercession...I was in scarlet and took the service from the High Altar. Abbey packed with people...What an overthrow of greatest military autocracy of modern times!'.[3]

During the War, the Dean had often been in the company of the King. In 1913, as ex officio Chaplain of the Order of the Bath, he had suggested to the King that Installation ceremonies should take place in the Abbey, as had been the case up to 1812; this duly occurred in July 1913, and again in 1920 and 1924. Also, there had been many special services which the King had attended. After the War, the first part of the funeral service for Edith Cavell was held at Westminster Abbey, also in the pesence of the King. (The War heroine, a hospital nurse, had been executed by firing squad in 1915 for helping Allied servicemen to escape from German-occupied Belgium). Her coffin, covered with the Union flag, was carried on a gun carriage through streets lined with mourners. After the service, the procession left to the sound of Chopin's Funeral March and the coffin was taken to Liverpool Street Station for transport by train to Norwich, for burial in the Cathedral. Ryle received further royal approval in 1921 with the award of the K.C.V.O., (although clergymen do not use the title of a knighthood). Further royal occasions at the Abbey included the wedding of the Duke of York, later George VI, in 1923.

After the War, the Abbey's finances were in a: 'desperate state of things'.[3] Repairs to the fabric were required, while significant debts were owing and, in 1920, a public appeal was launched in 'The Times', with a letter from the Dean. Donations were received from the King and the Ecclesiastical Commissioners, but the £250,000 target for the 'Dean Ryle's Fund', was only partially successful, raising just £170,000. Nevertheless, he resisted the offer of one donation of £30,000, as he had been asked:

'if I wd. Secure baronetcy for him or his son; quietly told him it must not be thought of. We parted good friends ! –but-'.[3] (As this honour was used by James I in 1611 for the express purpose of raising funds, its history could, perhaps, have justified acceptance of the proposal by someone less scrupulous than a former President of Queens'!). In his post-war years, Ryle would devote considerable time to Church committees; he was active in the preparation of an Enabling Act, which gave the Church more autonomy, and was prolocutor (ie chairman) of the lower house of the Convocation of Canterbury.

The tomb of the Unknown Warrior is, probably, the best-known monument in Westminster Abbey. The idea of a symbolic burial of a soldier to commemorate all those killed in the Great War came from an Army chaplain, the Rev. David Railton, after he saw a grave in a garden at Armentieres with a rough cross, on which were pencilled the words: 'An Unknown British Soldier'.[6] In August 1920 he wrote to Ryle, who then took up the suggestion and obtained the approval of the King, the Prime Minister and the Cabinet. Orders were issued for the exhumation of an unidentified British Empire serviceman from each of the Aisne, Arras, Somme and Ypes battlefields. On the 7th of November 1920, the remains of the four soldiers were brought to the Military Chapel at St Pol sur Ternoise, where the British Army had its Headquarters. They were each covered by a Union Flag, and Brigadier General L.J.Wyatt, having no idea from which area each body had come, chose one, which, on the 9th, was placed in an oak coffin recently arrived from England, made from a tree from the Royal Palace at Hampton Court and bound with iron bands. The other three bodies were reburied. On the morning of the 10th of November 1920, the coffin was taken to Boulogne and a mile-long funeral procession passed through the streets as a military band played Chopin's Funeral March. The coffin reached England on a Royal Naval destroyer and was conveyed by train to Victoria Station. The next morning, the 11th of November 1920, the coffin was placed on a gun carriage and an: 'enormous' crowd watched as it proceeded to the Cenotaph, where it was met by the King. At 11 o'clock, the coffin was carried through the north transept door of

Westminster Abbey. The aisle was lined with 100 holders of the Victoria Cross, while the congregation included 1000 widows and mothers of fallen servicemen and 100 nurses wounded in the course of their duties. Within five days, over a million people had visited to pay their respects.

It was not until the 11th of November the following year, 1921, that the gravestone of black marble from Belgium was unveiled; as the Dean notes in his diary, this was: 'a great day for Westminster Abbey'.[3] He had been responsible for composing the inscription for the grave:

'Beneath this stone rests the body of a British Warrior/ Unknown by name or rank/ Brought from France to lie among the most illustrious of the land/ And buried here on Armistice day 11 Nov: 1920, in the presence of His Majesty/ King George V/ His Ministers of State/ The Chiefs of his Forces/ And a vast concourse of the Nation/ Thus are commemorated the many multitudes who during the Great War of/ 1914-1918 gave the most that man can give life itself/ For God/ For King and Country/ For loved ones Home and Empire/ For the sacred cause of justice and the freedom of the world/ They buried him among the Kings because he had done good toward God/ And toward His House'

Ryle had many engagements in 1924; in May he revisited Lampeter and, in June, he preached the University sermon at Cambridge. But his health was failing and he preached for the last time at the Abbey on the 29th of July; on the 2nd of October he was taken to Bournemouth and remained in a nursing home until the 7th of January 1925, when he was moved to the Highcliffe Hotel. But he seemed not to realise the seriousness of his condition, as in April he writes:

'We are staying on here for another 4 weeks or so, and then return to the Deanery. My strength is, I hope, slowly returning…'.[3] But although he returned to the Deanery in May, his condition continued to deteriorate and, in the summer, he would often be wheeled in his bath-chair in the College garden or sit out above the south cloister. He died on the 20th of August 1925, and his funeral was held on the 25th of August.

Ryle's grave is in the centre of the nave of Westminster Abbey, near the grave of the Unknown Warrior, and is marked by a stone which reads:

'Not by might nor by power but by my spirit. Herbert Edward Ryle K.C.V.O. D.D. Dean of Westminster 1911-1925. Born 25 May 1856. Died 20 August 1925. Bishop of Exeter 1901-1903. Bishop of Winchester 1903-1911. Thou wilt shew me the path of life. In thy presence is fullness of joy'. His stall plate, as Dean of the Order of the Bath, is on the south stalls in the Lady Chapel, and his coat of arms is on this Chapel's west window.

His tenure as Dean is also commemorated, and admirably summarised, by a memorial tablet over the entrance to the Dean's Verger's office, in the south aisle:

'This stone set here by the Dean and Chapter of this Collegiate Church commemorates the life and work of HERBERT EDWARD RYLE, Bishop, Dean of Westminster from 1922-1925. In that period King George V was crowned; the Empire passed through five years of war; the body of the Unknown Warrior was laid here; also the ceremonies of the installation of the Knights of the Most Honorable Order of the Bath were revived; a great sum was gathered for the repair of the Abbey; and the love borne by the citizens of the Empire towards this place was more and more surely evidenced and established. "Thanks be to God for all his mercies" '. It is to be hoped that Ryle would have approved of his memorial, as he had refused many demands for burial or commemoration within the Abbey. In July 1924, a letter in 'The Times' had proposed a memorial to the 6th Lord Byron in the Abbey, signed by a galaxy of distinction, including Lord Balfour, H.H. Asquith, D. Loyd George, G.M. Trevelyan, Thomas Hardy and Rudyard Kipling. However, the Dean's response displays a very modern concern about statues and memorials:

'Sir-...The elequent and influentially signed letter in your columns of the 14th inst...calls for an answer...Two new facts I should like to mention: The available room for monuments in the Abbey is distressingly small...The Abbey is not a mere literary Walhalla. There are many names of great persons in English literature who have no memorial upon our walls...Byron was a great poet, though probably he does not rank as high now as he seemed to do a hundred years ago. Unfortunately Byron, partly by his openly dissolute life and partly by the influence of licentious verse, earned a world-wide reputation for immorality among English-speaking people. Westminster Abbey primarily stands to witness for Jesus Christ. A man who outraged the laws of our Divine Lord, and whose treatment of women violated the Christian principles of purity and honour, should not be commemorated in Westminster Abbey...It may be replied that there are names of various dissolute persons commemorated in the Abbey. It may be so. I regret the low standard of opinion in the 18th century...In conclusion, let me say that in my decision I have the unanimous support of the Chapter...Herbert E. Ryle, Bishop, Dean of Westminster'.[3]

Of the many tributes after his death, his former Dean at Winchester writes:

'I never knew a man quite so sympathetic and tender-hearted, quite so charitable in his judgement of others, even when he did not agree with their views- so loyal in friendship, so ready to give help and counsel- and, withal, so unaffectedly modest that he always appeared to esteem others better than himself'.[3]

In a sermon preached at the Commemoration of Benefactors at Queens' in 1980, Dr D.M. Thompson, University Lecturer in Divinity, considers Ryle's place in the historical context of the College, as:

'one of that important group of young scholars at the end of the nineteenth century who sought to secure the acceptance of the principles of biblical criticism in the Church of England...though not well-known, he illustrates very well the way in which Queens' has a series of figures who played a not unimportant part at crucial stages in the history of the Church in moving thought into a new era. Erasmus and John Fisher are clear examples of this at the turn of the sixteenth century; John Smith, (a fellow from 1644 to 1652, and an influential theologian within the 'Cambridge Platonist' movement, which advocated reason, and freedom of the will), is another from the seventeenth century; and Isaac Milner, to whose influence the conversion of William Wilberforce was largely due, is identified with the evangelical revival in Cambridge at the end of the eighteenth and the beginning of the nineteenth centuries'.[7]

References

1. FitzGerald, M.H., revised by Hawke, J. Ryle, Herbert Edward (1856-1925). Oxford Dictionary of National Biography. Online. 2020.
2. Keith's Histories. The Life of John Charles Ryle (1816-1900). Online. 2020.
3. Fitzgerald, M.H. A Memoir of Herbert Edward Ryle. Macmillan and Co. Ltd. London. 1928.
4. Twigg, J. A History of Queens' College, Cambridge. 1448-1986. The Boydell Press. 1987. pp 230, 264, 281-84.
5. The Dial. No.52. 1925. Queens' College, Cambridge. Online. 2020.
6. The National Association of Funeral Directors. The Story of the Unknown Warrior's coffin. Online. 2020.
7. Thompson, D.M. In: The Record. 1981. Queens' College, Cambridge. Online. 2020.

CHAPTER 32

Frederic Henry Chase. President 1901-06.

Summary.

Frederic Henry Chase was born in 1853, the son of the rector of St Andrew-by-the-Wardrobe, Blackfriars, London. He was admitted to Christ's College, Cambridge, in 1871, and graduated B.A. in 1876, being placed a modest eighth position, (for a scholar of his future eminence), in the first class of the Classics Tripos. But it is reported that he was in poor health at the time. Later in the year he was ordained deacon and served as a curate at Sherborne, Dorset. The following year he was ordained priest and married Charlotte Elizabeth Armitage; they would have a daughter and three sons, one of whom would serve as his chaplain when he was Bishop of Ely.

In 1879 he returned to Cambridge, as curate of St Michael's Church, and proceeded M.A. in 1880. In 1881 he became Lecturer in Theology at Pembroke College and, in 1884, tutor at the newly-established Cambridge Clergy Training School, (now Westcott House). He was appointed Principal of the latter in 1887 and in the same year published: 'Chrysostom: A Study in the History of Biblical Interpretation', one of several works which would develop his reputation as a Biblical scholar, theologian and 'higher critic' of the historical and scientific accuracy of aspects of the New Testament. He was appointed Lecturer in Theology at Christ's College from 1893 to 1901 and proceeded D.D. in 1895. In 1900, he delivered the 'Hulsean Lectures', which were published in 1902 as: 'The Credibility of the Book of the Acts of the Apostles'.

He was elected President of Queens' in 1901 and, later in the year, the Norrisian Professor of Divinity. He became widely-admired for his work as Vice-Chancellor during 1902-04, and for his contribution to College life.

He was appointed Bishop of Ely in 1905, resigning the Presidency early in 1906, and soon made his mark by raising funds to set up an extensive charitable foundation for: 'destitute young women of the diocese'. His theological expertise was harnessed by the Church in a long-drawn-out process of revising the 'Book of Common Prayer', and he made a significant contribution to the revised version which was agreed by the Church in 1927. But he was spared witnessing the rejection of the revisions by Parliament in 1928, as, having resigned his See in 1924 due to ill-health, he died the following year. He is buried in Brookwood Cemetery, Surrey, and is commemorated by a plaque in Ely Cathedral.

Timeline.

1853.	Born on the 21st of February. Son of Charles Frederic Chase, rector of St Andrew-by-the-Wardrobe, Blackfriars, London.
1871.	Admitted to Christ's College, Cambridge, as a 'pensioner'.
1875.	Awarded the Powys Medal for Latin hexameter verse.
1876.	B.A. , (placed 8th in the first class of the Classics Tripos). Ordained deacon at Rochester.
1876-79.	Curate at Sherborne, Dorset.
1877.	Ordained priest at Salisbury. Marries Charlotte Elizabeth Armitage at Sherborne.
1878.	Birth of daughter, Elizabeth Armitage, at Sherborne.
1879.	Birth of son, Frederic Alliston, at Sherborne, (a future chaplain to his father, when Bishop of Ely).
1879-84.	Returns to Cambridge, as curate at St Michael's Church.
1880.	M.A. .
1881-90.	Lecturer in Theology, Pembroke College, Cambridge. Initially resides at 14, Brookside, Cambridge.
1883.	Birth of son, Charles Allen.
1884.	Wins the Kaye Prize for a theological essay.

1884-87. Tutor of the Cambridge Clergy Training School, (now Westcott House).

1886. Birth of son, George Armitage.

1887-1901. Principal, Cambridge Clergy Training School.

1887. Publishes: 'Chrysostom: A Study in the History of Biblical Interpretation'.

1891. B.D. . Publishes: 'The Lord's Prayer in the Early Church', in the Dean of Westminster's 'Texts and Studies' series.

1893-1901. Lecturer in Theology, Christ's College.

1893. Publishes: 'The Old Syriac Element in the Text of Codex Bezae'.

1895. D.D. .

1900. Hulsean Lecturer at Cambridge. Contributes three articles for 'Hastings' Dictionary of the Bible'.

1901. Death of Queen Victoria. Accession of Edward VII. Herbert Ryle resigns as President of Queens'; Chase is elected as his successor. Elected Norrisian Professor of Divinity.

1902. Publishes: 'The Credibility of the Book of the Acts of the Apostles'.

1902-04. Vice-Chancellor.

1905. Honorary fellow, Christ's College.

1905. Appointed Bishop of Ely; consecrated at Westminster Abbey. Resigns as Norrisian Professor. Resides at the Bishop's Palace, Ely.

1906. Resigns as President of Queens'.

1907. Convenes a meeting which leads to the 'Ely Diocesan Association for Rescue, Preventative and Penitentiary Work'.

1910. Death of Edward VII. Accession of George V.

1914. Start of the Great War, on the 28th of July.

1918. End of the Great War, on the 11th of November.

1924. Resigns as Bishop of Ely, due to ill-health.

1925. Dies on the 23rd of September at Bexhill, Sussex. Is buried at Brookwood Cemetery, Surrey.

Prominent theologian and Biblical scholar. Educator. Bishop of Ely.

Frederic Henry Chase was born on the 21st of February, 1853, at the rectory of the church of St Andrew-by-the-Wardrobe, Blackfriars, London, where his father, the Rev. Charles Frederic Chase, held the living; his mother, Susan, was the daughter of John Alliston.[1] He was baptised on the 11th of June. (St Andrew-by-the-Wardrobe was so named because, in 1361, Edward III moved his Royal 'Wardrobe', or storehouse, to just north of the church, but this and the church were destroyed in the Great Fire of 1666. The present church, designed by Sir Christopher Wren, was seriously damaged in the Second World War, but was rebuilt in 1961). Although his sister Mary Evelyn, who was born in 1855, would live until 1918, two other siblings would survive less than a year, while another sister, Ethel Constance, died in 1865, aged four.

Frederic Henry was educated at King's College School, London, before being admitted to Christ's College, Cambridge, in 1871, as a 'pensioner', (ie a fee-paying student). (King's College, London, had been founded by George IV and the Duke of Wellington in 1829, and the school was its junior department, located in the basement of the College's premises in the Strand, London. It moved to its present site at Wimbledon in 1897). He was elected to a scholarship at Christ's College, Cambridge, and, in 1875, won the Powys Medal for Latin hexameter verse. He graduated B.A. in 1876, but while he was placed in the first class of the Classics Tripos, he was only in the eighth position, which would not have predicted his future reputation as a theologian and scholar. But we are told that this was:

'in the face of bad health, which at one time threatened to terminate his University career'.[2]

Later in 1876, Chase was ordained deacon at Rochester and appointed to a curacy at Sherborne, Doset. (The magnificent Sherborne Abbey, which had been a Saxon cathedral from AD705, had, since the Dissolution of the Monasteries, been Sherborne's parish church). In 1877, he was ordained priest at Salisbury and married Charlotte Elizabeth, daughter of the Rev. George Armitage, vicar of St Luke's, Gloucester. Two of their four children were born in Sherborne: their daughter, Elizabeth Armitage in 1878, and their son, Frederic Alliston, in 1879.[1] (Frederic Alliston would be admitted to Pembroke College, Cambridge, in 1898, and would serve as chaplain to his father, when Bishop of Ely).[3] A second son, Charles Allen, would be born in Cambridge in 1883, and a third, George Armitage, (a future Bishop of Ripon and Master of Selwyn College, Cambridge), in 1886.

Chase returned to Cambridge with his family in 1879 and served as curate at St Michael's Church until 1884. He graduated M.A. in 1880, B.D. in 1891 and D.D. in 1895. He was Lecturer in Theology at Pembroke College from 1881 until 1890, and at Christ's College from 1893 until 1901. Also, from 1884, he was tutor at the Cambridge Clergy Training School, (now Westcott House), and became its first Principal in 1887. (This had been set up in 1881, due to the influence of Brooke Foss Westcott, Regius Professor of Divinity at Cambridge since 1870, and a future Bishop of Durham).

Many publications would establish Chase's reputation as a theologian and Biblical scholar. In 1887, he produced: 'Chrysostom: A Study in the History of Biblical Interpretation', which he dedicated: 'To the Memory of my father'. (John Chrysostom, c347-407, was Archbishop of Constantinople and a prolific author in the early Christian Church). Chase was among those who applied 'higher criticism' to the New Testament, which challenged aspects of its historical and scientific accuracy[4] and, in his preface to the above, he writes:

'...the views about the Bible which the great teachers of Antioch held were not the same as those which had approved themselves a century before. There had been progress, but there had been no revolution. Newer methods of interpretation were transforming, not destroying, the older system. The responsibility of accurately investigating the actual words of Scripture was keenly felt, but the spiritual side of God's Revelation through the typical literature of Israel and of the Christian Church was not overlooked. The claims of criticism, so far as they could be understood then, and the claims of devotion were reconciled'.[5] In 1891, Joseph Armitage Robinson, a future Dean of Westminster and of Wells, (who was then vicar of All Saints Church, Cambridge, and would be elected to the Norrisian Professorship of Divinity at Cambridge in 1893), founded and edited a series of publications: 'Texts and Studies. Contributions to Biblical and Patristic Literature', which would produce 29 volumes up to 1922, and Chase was a contributor to the first volume, with: 'The Lord's prayer in the early church'.[1] In 1893, he published: 'The Old Syriac Element in the text of Codex Bezae',[6] based on the 'Codex Bezae Cantabrigensis', held in the Cambridge University Library. (This is a manuscript book of most of the New Testament, written in both Greek and Latin, dating from the 5th century. For several centuries it was in a monastic library at Lyon, before being stolen by French Huguenots in 1562. In 1581 it was in the hands of the Protestant scholar Theodore Beza, who gave it to Cambridge University, as a place of relative security). Chase dedicates this to:

'The Right Reverend Brooke Foss Westcott D.D. Lord Bishop of Durham This essay is dedicated as a slight expression of gratitude for the inspiration of his teaching…'.

In 1901, Herbert Ryle resigned as President of Queens' following his appointment as Bishop of Exeter, and Chase was appointed as his successsor. Twigg, in his history of the College of 1987, notes that Ryle had been active in all aspects of College life and that the election of Chase would have reflected a wish to maintain this pattern.[4] In 1925, the Vice-President of Queens' remembers Chase's Presidency:

'He (Chase) had been building up a growing reputation, and soon showed that he was capable of the responsibilities which, one after the other, were laid upon him. Before he had been in the Lodge six months he was appointed Norrisian Professor of Divinity, in another twelve months he became Vice-Chancellor. His easy mastery of business, his calm temper, and his unfailing courtesy made him, by general consent, an almost ideal chairman. And what a lovable man he was to those who knew him! Always the same sincere, frank, courteous, cordial gentleman, quite unspoilt by prominence and promotion, because he was quite unspoilable...It was a matter of great satisfaction to Dr Chase that, when he took up his residence in the Palace at Ely, (ie after his appointment as Bishop in 1905), he was allowed to retain a set of rooms in the College...Between them Dr Ryle and Dr Chase were with us little more than ten years. But these ten years were vitally significant in our history. Their work is to be appraised, not by length, but by its results. And both of them have carved their names deep in the history of the College...'.[7] Both Presidents served during a period of expansion of the College, and Gray, in his history of the College of 1898, notes that, while in 1887 there were 24 'freshmen', (ie the annual intake of undergraduates), this had increased to 60 in 1909.[8]

In the late nineteenth century there had been a growing awareness of the poverty and deprivation of the inner cities, and many 'settlements' or 'missions' were established by the Universities and independent schools, where student volunteers could visit and try to provide social, financial, spiritual and educational help to the local communities. In May 1899, a Boy's Club had been founded on Peckham High Street, London, by a local clergyman, but this soon ran into financial difficulties, and it was then 'adopted' by Queens' in Chase's first year as President, as noted in the 'Cambridge Review':

'On Thursday, October 10th, (1901), the Queens' College Boys' Club was inaugurated at Peckham, the President and several past and present members of the College attending'. The same publication also reports a fund-raising event for the 'Mission' in 1903:

'A most successful concert was held in the Hall on May 12th, on behalf of the funds for the Queens' College Mission in South London. Quite 200 were present. A feature of the evening was the excellent violin playing of Mr J.D. Morgan. Mr Lascelles' sleight of hand was also highly appreciated'. The Mission moved to a new site at Rotherhithe Street in 1911 and there was a name-change to 'Queens' House' in 1928; but, in 1940, it was:

'Agreed regretfully to close the Queens' House Mission at Rotherhithe owing to the war'. However, although under new management, the premises were re-opened in 1941 and close contacts with Queens' continued for several years, until the building was demolished in 1964.[9]

As noted above, Chase served as Vice-Chancellor during 1902-04 and, when he was due to leave Queens' for Ely, 'The Times', of the 5th of July 1905, notes:

'It was not, however, till Dr Chase became Vice-Chancellor in 1902 that his capabilities as a man of affairs were suddenly revealed to the University. He had had no great experience of the intricacies of University business, but he seemed to grasp difficulties with tact and shrewdness, and this was especially noticeable on the occasion of the King's visit to open the new Science Schools. Christ's College has recently made him an honorary Fellow together with the Dean of Westminster. He has been in recent years a frequent and welcome speaker at the meetings of societies of all parties in Cambridge. As Bishop he will be greatly helped by Mrs Chase…'.[2] Also, a member of the College summarises the achievements of the departing President:

'It was in the middle of the Long Vacation that we heard of our President's nomination to the See of Ely. At first we were "struck all of a heap", even though the news was not quite unexpected…Among his writings, special mention should be made of "The Old Syriac Element in the Codex Bezae". In this book he did perhaps more than anyone else has done, to solve the origins of the "Western" Text of the New Testament…The ripest product of his pen is his article on "The Gospels in the light of Historical Criticism", published in the recent volume of Cambridge "Theological Essays". It summarises the results of many years of careful study and deep thought on some of the greatest questions of our faith, such as the Resurrection and Miracles of Our Lord. When we remember that the most notable triumphs of the modern School of Theology at Cambridge have been achieved in this very region of the historical study of the Gospels, we can understand the importance of such an essay from Dr Chase's pen…For, after all, it is not as theologian, but as President, that we in Queens' know him, and, knowing, are proud of him…He is not to us a figure-head, but *our* Master: not *in loco parentis* (with all that those words suggest!) but something more. All through the busy years of his Vice-Chancellorship, he managed to keep in close touch with the College,- in real contact...not mere official contiguity...Two places we shall always connect with him especially: one is his study with its reminiscences of quiet talks: the other is his stall in Chapel, from which he- not "preached", they were not set sermons- but spoke to us out of the depths of his heart. These words would be incomplete without some mention of Mrs Chase...We shall always remember her, not only as always ready to dispense tea and coffee to individuals, to societies, or to crews in training, from morning to night,- ready at times even to nurse the sick in the Lodge itself,- but as having welcomed every member of the College with a hospitality that was as charming as it was simple and kindly'.[2]

In 1900, Chase had been chosen to deliver the annual 'Hulsian Lectures', which had been established from an endowment from John Hulse to the University in 1790, to address aspects of Christian theology; but as the original duties had involved 20 sermons each year for five years, the post had remained unfilled until 1819 and, in 1860, the Court of Chancery reduced the workload to a more manageable four lectures during a single year. Chase's lectures were duly published in 1902, entitled: 'The Credibility of the Book of the Acts of the Apostles, Being The Hulsian Lectures for 1900-1901 by Frederic Henry Chase, D.D. President of Queens' College, and Norrisian Professor of Divinity, Cambridge'.[10] (Chase was elected to the Norrisian Professorship of Divinity in 1901; this had been founded in 1777, from a bequest from John Norris, but with a stipulation that the holder should be fined 21 shillings if any student at his lectures had not been provided with copies of the Old and New Testaments and of 'An Exposition of the Creed', published in 1679 by John Pearson). In his preface, Chase states:

'The subject for the Hulsean Lectures 1900-1901 was chosen under the conviction that the credibility of the Book of the Acts of the Apostles is second only in importance to the credibility of the Gospels, and that the final verdict must be based on a rigorous and repeated examination of the main course of the narrative and of the types of Apostolic teaching which the Book professes to embody...Meantime, I may be permitted to say that the study which I have been able to give to the Book confirms my belief that in it we have a truthful and trustworthy history'.[10]

Queen Victoria died on the 22nd of January, 1901, and, as an addendum to his published lectures, Chase writes:

'Little did I think...that this course of lectures would conclude on a Sunday so memorable, so sadly memorable, as this. We know, but we can scarcely realize, that since last Sunday the longest, the greatest, probably the most eventful reign in all English history has ended...if we take a wider view, we remember how the Queen presided over the reorganization and development of England's vast Indian Empire; how she fostered the growth of English colonies, till from little more than straggling and rude settlements they have become mighty commonwealths, bound to each other and bound to the Mother Country by ties of a common loyalty...We pray- for we are sure that the Queen often so prayed, and would have wished us so to pray- for the Empire, that God will make this great national sorrow a wholesome discipline to chasen and to correct our sins and shortcomings in Church and State,- our pride, our waywardness, our luxury, our forgetfulness of God; that, as sometimes, when the sun has set, we are still conscious of his influence in the soft twilight of holy calm, so in her own England and in the world the remembrance of the Queen may be a power making for peace, so that to her very memory may be vouchsafed the blessing of the peacemakers...'.[10]

In 1900, Chase also contributed three articles on St Peter, and on the two epistles of Peter, to the 'Hastings' Dictionary of the Bible', a five-volume Biblical encyclopedia, published between 1898 and 1904,[1] while in 1903 he writes:

'Criticism even of the Gospel records of the Lord's earthly life must among thoughtful Christians be allowed reasonable freedom...(but) no historical evidence can compel men to believe in an event of the past...it can only demonstrate its probability. If the event belongs to the sphere of religion...when historical criticism has done its work, its results become the material with which faith deals. Faith in the living God alone enables us to discern the congruity of the Resurrection, to realize it, to know in our lives its power'.[4,11]

'The Times' of the 5th of January, 1905, notes:

'Mr Balfour's recommendation of Dr Chase as successor to Lord Alwyne Compton, (the 4th son of the 2nd Marquess of Northampton), in the See of Ely will give great satisfaction to the University and Town of Cambridge, where it was fully expected, and will be of benefit to the diocese at large...In 1884...he became the first tutor of the Cambridge Clergy Training School, which Dr Westcott and others were then bringing into existance. He became its Principal in 1887 and...His work at the Training School, though quiet and unobtrusive, was of the highest value, and represents one of his chief claims to his present promotion'.[2]

Chase was consecrated as Bishop of Ely in Westminster Abbey by Randall Davidson, Archbishop of Canterbury, on the 18th of October, 1905, when the sermon was given by the Master of Trinity College, Cambridge, (Henry Montagu Butler), who spoke of:

'The beloved and deeply honoured Professor and Head of a great College, who has won in a rare degree the confidence of Cambridge men, laymen no less than clergy, and will at Ely re-forge and rivet those ties of loyal attachment which still bind us to his venerable predecessor'.[2] Chase was then duly installed in his Cathedral on the 31st of October, after seeking admission by knocking three times on the west door:

'He afterwards preached to a crowded congregation, which included a number of Queens' men and the majority of the clergy in the diocese'.[2] He continued as President of Queens' for just a few months, resigning in 1906.

In 2008, the Secretary of the Ely Diocesan Committee for Family and Social Welfare announced that the Centenary of the Annual General Meeting of the Committee would be held in May of that year in the hall at Queens', after a service of thanksgiving in the College chapel led by the Bishop of Ely. As a contributor to the College 'Record' of 2008 notes:

'In April 1907, the then Bishop of Ely, the Rt Revd. Frederic Chase...gathered together a group of concerned and compassionate people...to discuss his concerns for the destitute young women of the Diocese and how they might be helped "to avoid or escape from the more depraved elements of society". As a result of the meeting, the Ely Diocesan Association for Rescue, Preventative and Penitentiary Work was created. Bishop Chase raised enough financial support to provide a refuge in Ely, a maternity home in Bury St Edmunds, a mother and baby home in Cambridge and a home for training domestic servants in Ely. An adoption service was also started which actually continued until the later 1960s... The services offered...have changed and evolved, but Bishop Chase's original idea of helping and counselling people, empowering them to help and improve their own lives, has remained and has inspired successive Committee members down the years...During the Rt Revd Dr Frederic Chase's time as Bishop of Ely, as well as creating our charity, he also played a major role in the revision of the Book of Common Prayer, the lectionary, (a list of readings to be used for worship), the translation of the prayer book psalter and the office for holy baptism. Bishop Chase took a special interest in the ministrations of women, drawing up a "Form and manner of making deaconesses". His speech in the upper house of the Convocation of Canterbury (in 1920) on an alternative office for Holy Communion was considered a "noteworthy utterance" '.[12]

Chase made a major contribution to revisions of the Church of England's Book of Common Prayer, in a process that began in 1906, following the report of a Royal Commission. This was to take 20 years, but although revisions were eventually approved by the Church in 1927, they were defeated by Parliament the following year, and the version of 1662 remains in force today. However, some of his work was not lost; the revised psalter was incorporated into the prayer book of the Church of Ireland, while the new baptismal office and the service for the institution of deaconesses have both been used in England.[1]

But Chase did not live to see the rejection of the revised Book of Common Prayer. In 1924 his health stared to fail, and he resigned as Bishop, retiring to Woking. He died on the 23rd of September, 1925, aged 72, at the Normanhurst Hotel, Bexhill,

Surrey, and is buried in Brookwood Cemetery, Brookwood, Surrey, (which is the largest cemetery in the UK and a Grade I site in the Register of Historic Parks and Gardens).

His successor at Ely writes:

'I have come to appreciate increasingly the wisdom and soundness of his judgement, the scrupulous care which he devoted to every detail, and the affectionate sympathy and kindness, which he showed to all who sought his advice'.[7]

His memorial plaque at Ely Cathedral reads:

'To the Glory of God
and in loving memory of
FREDERIC HENRY CHASE D.D.
Born February 21st 1853
Died September 23rd 1925
Principal of the Clergy Training School Cambridge 1887-1901
President of Queens' College Cambridge and
Norrisian Professor of Divinity 1901-1905
BISHOP OF ELY 1905-1924
"He that believeth on the Son hath eternal life" '

References

1. Barnes, W.E., revised by Matthew, H.C.G. Chase, Frederic Henry. In: Oxford Dictionary of National Biography. Online. 2004.
2. Queens' Courier No.1 March. 1906. Queens' College, Cambridge. Online. 2020.
3. The Record, 2008. Queens' College, Cambridge. Online. 2020.
4. Twigg, J. A History of Queens' College, Cambridge. 1448-1986 The Boydell Press. 1987. pp 229, 285.
5. Chase, F.H. Chrysostom: A Study in the History of Biblical Interpretation. Deighton, Bell, & Co. Cambridge. George Bell and Sons. London. 1887.
6. Chase, F.H. The Old Syriac Element in the text of Codex Bezae. Macmillan and Co. London and New York. 1893.

7. The Dial No.52. 1925. Queens' College, Cambridge. Online. 2020.
8. Gray, J.H. Queens' College 1879-1909. In: The Dial No.7. 1909. Queens' College, Cambridge. Online. 2020.
9. Queens' House Mission. Queens' College, Cambridge. Online. 2021.
10. Chase, F.H. The Credibility of the book of The Acts of the Apostles. Macmillan and Co. Ltd. London. 1902.
11. Chase, F.H. The Supernatural Element in our Lord's earthly Life in relation to Historical Methods of Study. London. 1903.
12. Le Gallais Redfearn, A.C. CFSU- Something to celebrate. In: The Record, 2008. Queens' College, Cambridge. Online. 2020.

CHAPTER 33

Thomas Cecil Fitzpatrick. President 1906-31.

Summary.

Thomas Cecil Fitzpatrick was born in Bedford in 1861, the youngest son of the Rev. Richard Fitzpatrick, vicar of Holy Trinity Church, Bedford. After attending Bedford School, he was admitted to Christ's College, Cambridge, in 1880, and graduated B.A. in the Natural Sciences Tripos in 1885. In 1888 he was elected a fellow of Christ's, where he would remain for a further 18 years. In the same year he was ordained deacon and appointed College chaplain; he would become the Dean in 1890. At Christ's, and later at Queens', he would attract many tributes for his capacity for friendship, concern for others and actively encouraging collegiate activities.

In 1888 he became an Assistant Demonstrator at the University's Cavendish Laboratory, when Joseph John Thomson was the Cavendish Professor of Physics, (and would become known for the discovery of the electron). For many years, Fitzpatrick made major contributions to the undergraduate teaching of physics, to research into the transport of electricity through solutions, and to establishing standards of electrical resistance. But his last publication was in 1894, when he decided that his talents would be best suited to a career as a 'Man of Affairs', rather than as a 'Man of Science'.

In 1906, Frederic Chase resigned as President of Queens', and Fitzpatrick accepted the unanimous invitation from the fellows to succeed him. He would oversee the College during the Great War and serve as Vice-Chancellor during 1915-17, and again during 1928-29.

During his Presidency, many significant renovations to the College buildings were made, and a new accomodation block, the 'Dokett Building', was completed in 1912. His energy and breadth of activities was remarkable, spanning College, University and many 'outside' boards and committees.

In 1912, Fitzpatrick, then aged 51, married Annie Rosa Cook, aged 29, from Horningsea, Cambridgeshire, who would be a considerable support to her husband in providing the liberal hospitality of his Presidency. There would be no children.

Fitzpatrick's health began to fail in 1928, during his second term as Vice-Chancellor, and he died in 1931. He was a considerable benefactor to the College and is buried in the 'Ascension Burial Ground', in Cambridge.

Timeline.

1861.	Born on the 27th of August, in Bedfordshire. Son of the Rev. Richard Fitzpatrick, vicar of Holy Trinity Church, Bedford.
1878.	Death of his mother.
1881.	Admitted to Christ's College, Cambridge, as a 'pensioner'. Wins a College scholarship for Natural Sciences.
1883.	1st Class in theNatural Sciences Tripos Part 1.
1885.	1st Class in the Natural Sciences Tripos Part II. , (awarded a special mark of distinction for Physics). B.A. .
1888.	Fellow at Christ's. Ordained deacon. Chaplain at Christ's.
1888-1906.	Assistant Demonstrator in Experimental Physics.
1889.	M.A. . Ordained priest.
1890-1906.	Dean at Christ's. Involved in the restoration of Christ's College's chapel by G.F. Bodley.
1895-1911.	An 'Examining Chaplain' to the Bishop of Salisbury.
1906.	President of Queens'.
1907.	Member of Cambridge Town Council.
1912.	Marries Anne Rosa Cook, (1882-1964). Completion of the 'Dokett Building' at Queens'.
1914.	Start of the Great War, on the 28th of July.
1915-17.	Vice-Chancellor.

1915. Military personel begin to be billeted at Queens'.

1917. Death of his brother, the Rev. Nicholas Richard Fitzpatrick. Visit of General Smuts to Queens'.

1918. End of the Great War, on the 11th of November. Death of his sister, Harriet Fitzpatrick.

1920. Death of his brother William Long Fitzpatrick.
Proceeds D.D. . Visit of Queen Mary, (with Princess Mary and Princes Albert, Henry and George), on the 10th of May.

1921. Dedication of the College's War Memorial. Visit of the Crown Prince of Japan. A notorious riot outside Newnham College with damage to the Clough Memorial Gates, after the rejection of a proposal in the Senate to admit women to full membership of the University.

1926. Death of his sister Caroline Fitzpatrick.

1928-29. Vice-Chancellor.

1931. Dies at Queens' on the 28th of October. Bequeathes £10,000 to the College. Is buried at the 'Ascension Burial Ground', Cambridge

Scientist. Priest. Collegiate fellow and President. Administrator. Benefactor.

Thomas Cecil Fitzpatrick was born on the 27th of August, 1861, the yougest son of the Rev. Richard Fitzpatrick, vicar of Holy Trinity Church, Bedford. (This church was built in 1839-40 and is now an annex for the Bedford High School for Girls). Thomas Cecil's paternal grandfather was Nicholas Fitzpatrick, M.D., one of the physicians of the Bedford Infirmary, while his father supported various 'working class' initiatives as a founder of the Bedford Working Men's Institute, a penny bank, and a system of allotments.[1] His father is described by a contemporary as:

'the most generous, good-natured, and imposed-upon person in Bedford'.[1]

The Church of All Saints, Kempston, Bedford, has several stained-glass windows in memory of members of the Fitzpatrick family, the last being given in 1923 by Thomas Cecil, in memory of his brother, William Long Fitzpatrick, who had been High Sheriff of Bedfordshire in 1905. One of Thomas Cecil's grandmothers was the daughter of Sir William Long, c1775-1841, Mayor of Bedford in 1803, 1813, 1822 and 1829, whose portrait can be found at Bedford Town Hall. (He owned a brewery in St Paul's Square and was knighted in 1814. He gave money to build Bedford Bridge, on condition that his carriage should pass free of toll but, shortly afterwards, the tolls were abolished).

Thomas Cecil attended Bedford School from 1869 until 1880, when he was admitted to Christ's College, Cambridge. He obtained first class honours in both the Part I of the Natural Sciences Tripos in 1883 and in the Part II, for physics, in 1885, when he graduated B.A. . In 1888, he was elected a fellow of Christ's, ordained deacon and appointed College chaplain. In the following year, he was ordained priest, and proceeded M.A.; he became Dean of Christ's in 1890.

From 1895 to 1911, he was an 'Examining Chaplain' to Bishop John Wordsworth of Salisbury, (ie helping to select and encourage those seeking ordination). In around 1905, the Bishop invited him to become one of the archdeacons of his diocese, but the offer was declined. (John Wordsworth, 1843-1911, was the Bishop of Salisbury from 1885 to 1911; he was a great-nephew of the poet William Wordsworth, son of Christopher Wordsworth, Bishop of Lincoln, and grandson of Christopher Wordsworth, Master of Trinity College). In 1920, Fitzpatrick proceeded D.D. , 'jure dignitatis', (ie a substantive degree, but awarded without examination). A friend reports:

'I have often quoted what he said to us in Hall the day he received his D.D. degree and had also heard of the death of his brother. He thanked us for being with him "in sorrow and in joy". It was the way it was said that was so characteristic...As an extempore preacher he was simple and direct, and he spoke with an earnestness and transparent conviction that none could fail to recognize...Possessed of good private means, he was as generous as he was unostentatious...he helped many men privately...He was active in the cause of charity and in support of the missionary work of the Church'.[1] (In 1921, he was treasurer of the University Mission to Central Africa).[2]

A friend recalls:

'We were ordained within a few months of each other...I well remember his coming to stay with me for Holy Week and Easter in 1890, and the sermon that he preached on Easter Day. He told us how he had spent the Easter of 1887 in "the isle that is called Patmos". He described his experiences there, and then went on to speak of the testimony of St John to the fact of our Lord's Resurrection. The sermon made a deep impression on all who heard it'.[1] (He had travelled with Joseph Armitage Robinson, his predecessor as Dean of Christ's and, subsequently, Dean of Westminster and of Wells. The Book of Revelation, part of the New Testament of the Bible, was written on Patmos in about AD95 by St. John, believed to be a Jewish Christian prophet, rather than the Apostle John).

Fitzpatrick would be a fellow of Christ's for eighteen years before his election as President of Queens', and a friend recalls:

'In 1895, I was appointed to a College living near Cambridge, and...Fitzpatrick and I met constantly. He talked to me freely about his work as Dean- its opportunities, its joys and its anxieties... undergraduates who had little respect for College rules found the Dean a very unsympathetic and formidable person; to anyone who sought his help and advice he was always most kind and wise in counsel'.[1] Another contemporary adds:

'T.C.Fitzpatrick had a sort of genius for friendship. He was anything but effusive, he could be impetuously impulsive and he had a quality which, in a smaller man, might be counted as obstinacy. Surely this was just natural leadership showing itself much as it used to do on those walks when he would promptly cut the chatter over some disputed turn by setting off on the way of his own chosing. Never was he known to come back and so the rest always followed. So, too, in later days, among the passes and glaciers, and well it always was for us who had the sense to follow him'.[1] This refers to regular mountaineering in his younger days, described in a letter to 'The Times' of the 3rd of November, 1931, by Sir Richard Glazebrook, Director of the National Physical Laboratory:

'Some forty-five years ago he met me by chance in Switzerland, and his first words were, "You have taught me physics for the past three years, I am going to teach you to climb mountains". For the next twenty years or so we met nearly every year, and climbed usually in the district between Arolla and Saas Fee, sometimes wandering as far as Chamonix. On many of these occasions he brought with him as his guests one or more of his undergraduate pupils. He loved the mountains, he would teach others to love them, and he succeeded. Occasionally a novice was somewhat overpowered by the activity of his tutor. Fitzpatrick was a good mountaineer, especially on rocks, very quick and very active, and an inexperienced man found it difficult at times to follow in the footsteps of his guide or to share his enthusiasm for a long expedition every day, sometimes without much regard for the weather...There are many, I am sure, who are grateful to him for their introduction to the Alps and for a wonderful holiday, impossible at the time but for his generous help'.[1] Fitzpatrick's travel destinations also included Greece, Sicily, France, the Lebanon, Jordan, Jericho, Damascus, Jerusalem and, (with his wife), a trip up the Amazon.[1] (One of Fitzpatrick's cousins, William Chandless, 1829-96, had been a distinguished explorer of the Amazon Basin in the 1860s, and is buried in an impressive tomb at St Mary's Church, Paddington, London. In 2003, a Brazilian National Park on the border with Peru was named 'Chandless State Park' in his honour). In 1902, Fitzpatrick travelled to Palestine with three friends. After they had all arrived at 'Beyrout' (ie Beirut), one of his friends recalls that, after three days of quarantine:

'we were allowed to go ashore, so we took our baggage and transhipped to a Russian steamer on which were 700 Russian pilgrims bound for Jerusalem. They were a dirty and odiferous crowd...We sailed at 2.30 pm and woke early next morning to find we were anchored off Jaffa...After luncheon we were taken by our dragoman, Joseph Haddad, to the railway station to catch our train for Jerusalem...we started off...to visit the Church of the Holy Sepulchre. The crowds of pilgrims were somewhat distracting...The sight of an infidel Turk, sitting cross-legged with drawn sword, rather astonished us. We learnt that his duty was to keep the peace between the different Christian sects!...Next morning we visited the Mosque which covers the Rock of Sacrifice on the summit of Mount Moriah...In the afternoon we went to Bethlehem...We found that the mass of tradition that has grown up around these sacred places detracted from the simplicity we had associated with them. We drove to Jericho next morning...In the afternoon we drove to the Dead Sea and bathed in it, enjoying its bouyancy but not its saltiness...At the hotel in Jericho where we spent the night, our rest was much disturbed by the noise of innumerable frogs...Easter Day was a day of glorious sunshine... we went...to the Church of the Holy Sepulchre...numerous processions were walking round and round, singing monotonous chants. The camping part of our tour began next day...Having arrived in Bedouin country it was necessary to have an armed guard to protect us at night. Whether this was really necessary, we could not make out; or whether it was only a way of taxing travellers. Anyhow, the guard did fire off a gun one night. They said that six robbers were approaching the camp from different directions and fled when they fired...We sailed from Beyrout on 15 April and reached London on 24 April. In those days (ie 1902) so much must have been very much as it was in the early days of the Christian era that we were carried back to those times...the peasants travelled in the same way and tilled the soil as they had always done. Small patches of soil between rocks were scratched and corn sown, irresistibly recalling the parable of the sower. Anybody knowing Fitzpatrick will realize how the sights appealed to him...His energy, as usual, was great, and he took imnumerable photographs...which served to bring back to memory a most successful and instructive holiday'.[1] His obituary in the Christ's College Magazine, in 1931, recalls other aspects of his time at Christ's:

'his name brings to many minds happy memories of holidays enjoyed with eager zest; gyps' matches with supper and concert after; a yearly Long Vacation outing in tub-pairs to Wicken Fen, and the hospitality of his rooms to end the day; his yearly visits to the Riffel Alp, where he was known to many men outside Academic circles'.[1]

In 1888, Fitzpatrick became an Assistant Demonstrator at the Cavendish Laboratory of the University, at the time when Joseph John Thomson was the Cavendish Professor of Physics. (Thomson, who was awarded the 1906 Nobel Prize for his work on the conduction of electricity, is known for the discovery of the electron; he was knighted in 1908 and became Master of Trinity College, Cambridge, in 1918). Thomson subsequently recalls:

'I was fortunate enough to induce him to undertake the organization of the teaching of practical physics to medical students...In 1898 Fitzpatrick undertook the lectures as well as the demonstrations to medical students; from that time until he became Vice-Chancellor in 1915 he had the entire management of this department of the Laboratory; he made a great success of it, and his work was of outstanding importance to the progress of the Laboratory. This is far from being the only obligation we are under to Fitzpatrick. Of the many gifts that have been received by the Laboratory, none has been more useful than the apparatus for producing liquid air, which he presented in 1904. Many of the most important researches which have been made would have been impossible without its aid'.[1] Fitzpatick's initial research involved the transport of electricity through solutions and led to several publications; he designed special apparatus and measured the the conductivity of calcium chloride dissolved in water and in alcohol. He also turned his attention to the permanence of the standards of electrical resistance, (which consisted of wire coils), and he co-authored a paper, presented to the British Association in 1866, on a comparison of the temperature coefficients of certain standard coils, (ie changes in physical properties associated with a given change in temperature). (The British Association for the Advancement of Science was founded in 1831 and would make an important contribution to the development of standards for electrical applications: the ohm as the unit of electrical measurement, the volt as the unit of electrical potential, and the ampere as the unit of electrical current). A further paper co-authored by Fitzpatrick in 1888, for the Philosophical Transactions of the Royal Society, contributed to the definition of the ohm.[1] Another of his research interests was the electrical resistance of copper; this was important, as the products of various manufacturers of copper wire differed in conductivity. But he continued his work on solutions and, in 1893, produced his 'Table of Electro-chemical Properties of Aqueous Solutions', consisting of nearly 70 pages. However, he published his last research paper in 1894 and, thereafter, devoted most of his time to College and University business. But while he gave up his post as Assistant Demonstrator in 1906, he continued to lecture at the Laboratory until 1915.

A textbook, 'Solution and Electrolysis', was published by William Cecil Dampier Whetham, then a fellow of Trinity College, in 1895.[3] (He would be elected F.R.S. in 1901 and knighted in 1931 for his services to agriculture, having developed a method of extracting lactose from whey). In the preface, Whetham (later, he would adopt 'Dampier' as his surname) notes:

'A valuable collection of data on the conductivities and migration constants of solutions was made by the Rev. T.C. Fitzpatrick, and published by the British Association in 1893. By the kind permission of the author and of the Council of the British Association, I have been allowed to reprint these tables as an appendix to this book'. In Fitzpatrick's introduction to his tables he states:

'The comparisons of the numerical results of electrolytic observations is rendered difficult from the fact that the data are scattered in various periodicals and expressed by different observers in units that are not comparable without considerable labour. The following table has been compiled with the object of facilitating the comparison'.

In 1910, Fitzpatrick, now President of Queens', would publish 'A History of the Cavendish Laboratory 1871-1910', consisting of chapters from various contributors. He co-authored the first, 'The Building of the Laboratory', with 'W.C.D.Whetham', and notes:

'On December 22, 1909, Sir J.J.Thomson completed the twenty-fifth year of his tenure of the Cavendish Professorship of Experimental Physics in the University of Cambridge...It appeared, therefore, that (this)... might be fitly celebrated by the writing and publication of a History of the Cavendish Laboratory'.[4]

Frederic Chase resigned as President of Queens' in June 1906, and Fitzpatrick accepted the unanimous invitation from the fellows to succeed him. He was an exceptionally active President, both in the College and University. He would oversee the College during the Great War and serve as Vice-Chancellor during 1915-17, and again during 1928-9.

During his long tenure at Queens' a new accomodation block, the 'Dokett Building', was completed in 1912. This had required the demolition of eight alms-houses, built in 1836 to replace those established by the first President, Andrew Doket, which had been sold to St Catharine's College. (While the spelling 'Dokett' is in current use in the College, 'Doket' was chosen in the first Chapter). The architect was Cecil G. Hare, who had been the chief assistant to G.F. Bodley, who had designed the new chapel. Also, Fitzpatrick took a great interest in the fabric of the College; the roof of the hall was replaced by tiles instead of slate and the external rendering of the gallery of the late 16th century President's Lodge was removed, to expose the timbers. The Lodge underwent some internal renovation: the ceiling of the Long Gallery of the Lodge was originally plain flat plaster and a new plaster ceiling was installed in 1923, based on the design of a similar structure at Haddon Hall, Derbyshire. Fitzpatrick was a generous benefactor of the College and paid for various alterations to the Old Court, including the restoration of the south side and southern half of the east side, which was his gift to commemorate the twentieth year of his Presidency.[5]

An article in the 'Cambridge Review' of the 6th of November, 1931, notes:

'As President he knew every man belonging to the College-not merely his name, but his work, his prospects, and to a large extent his habits and character. He was even at pains to memorize the names on each staircase, that he might get some idea of the men's entourage. He took a particular interest in the performance of the College boats...College games in general meant much to him, and he was eager that every man, by the formation of Third Teams or otherwise, should be given a chance to play them...He was Head of the House, and- in his hospitable view as in that of his wife- every member of the Household was reckoned a member of his family'.[1] Also, the Dean of Queens', the Rev. C.T. Wood, writes:

'When Fitzpatrick came to Queens', he insisted that I should lunch with him once a week in the Lodge...He was always deeply interested in every individual man in College, and had an almost uncanny intuition in his judgement of them all. "Something is wrong with so-and-so", he would say; "he is not as happy as he was", or "That man is stronger in character this term". "How do you know?" I would ask; "have you any definite grounds for saying so?" "No", was the usual reply; "but I feel it so"- and in the vast majority of cases he was right...'.[1]

In 1912, Fitzpatick, then aged 51, married Anne Rosa Cook, aged 29, daughter of Alfred Cook and Anna Fincham, from Horningsea, Cambridgeshire. There would be no children. (She died in the Hope Nursing Home, Madingly Road, Cambridge in 1964).[1] They were an hospitable couple, and 'The Times' of the 30th of October, 1931, notes:

'Past and present members of the College were welcomed in the Lodge, not least after the President's marriage to Miss Anne Cook in 1912, and the gallery of the Lodge was in frequent use for the meeting of charitable societies.[1]

However, despite many adulatory recollections, Fitzpatrick was not always easy to relate to, as the Rev. Wood remembers:

'By nature, he had a strong will to carry out his clear views of what should be done, and a strong temper: but his religion and his personal affection combined to put a powerful curb on him...if he had to rebuke anyone, older or younger, however angry he was, his sympathy and affection came through...In some moods, particularly when he was tired, he did not find ordinary small talk with Undergraduates easy: but even then such was their respect for him, that they were glad to be with him'.[1] But although Gilbert Harding, a student in the 1920s, and subsequently a well-known journalist and broadcaster, recalled that Fitzpatrick had hardly any conversation and that his wife was very nervous,[2] Harding would eventually be described by the press as: 'the rudest man in Britain'.

Fitzpatrick played a major part in the administration of the University, as Vice-Chancellor, Deputy Vice-Chancellor for ten years, examiner, Select Preacher, member of the Financial Board, and member of numerous other boards and committees. He also served on the boards and committees of many other institutions and local administrations, including the Cambridge Borough Council. He was instrumental in setting up the 'Workers' Educational Association' in 1903, which is the UK's largest voluntary provider of adult education and one of the UK's biggest charities. Its secretary in 1931 writes to 'The Times':

'Dr Fitzpatrick will live in the memory of working men and women as one of the kindliest and most welcoming men of his generation at Cambridge. As a prominent member of the Local Examinations and Lectures Syndicate he...did all he possibly could to help and encourage the earliest efforts of the Workers' Educational Assiciation in its attempts to bring the University into constructive relatuionship with the organizations of workpeople...'.[1] In a letter to Fitzpatrick's widow he adds:

'He was a great Englishman, a source of strength and power to all who knew him...'. When he was Vice-Chancellor during 1915-17, the University received a visit from the King, and honorary degrees were conferred on General Smuts, Walter Hines Page, (the American Ambassador), and William Massey, Prime Minister of New Zealand.

Jan Smuts, who was born in 1870 in the Cape Colony, South Africa, had won a scholarship to attend Cambridge University to read law at Christ's College, when Fitzpatrick was Dean. He graduated in 1894 with a first class degree, after winning many prizes; in the opinion of the Master of Christ's in 1970:

'in 500 years of the College's history, of all its members, past and present, three had been truly outstanding: John Milton, Charles Darwin and Jan Smuts'.[6] After opposing the British in the Boer War, he was their ally in the First World War, when his forces captured German South-West Africa. From 1917 to 1919 he was a member of the British Imperial War Cabinet and he was instrumental in founding the Royal Air Force. He was Prime Minister of South Africa from 1919 to 1924, and again from 1939 to 1948. He became a British Field Marshall in 1941 and is commemorated by a statue in Parliament Square, London. On the day of his honorary degree, Fitzpatrick entertained him in the hall at Queens', as recalled by one of those present:

'It was odd to think, while he spoke, what his memories of Cambridge must be: first his undergraduate days at Christ's, during which, as the Vice-Chancellor said, he showed unusual ability but scarcely led the College authorities to forsee what a position he would obtain: then a visit to the University after the Boer War, in the course of which, we are sorry to say, the Townspeople at least showed him some hostility; and now this visit, in honour and respect, as the champion of our cause, not of Empire but of liberty...Then he went on to speak with complete frankness of the Boer war and the present conflict. "I did not take up arms now, as you may guess, out of love of Empire, but out of love of what England now fights for". One of the hardest things he ever had to do was to take up arms against us; but he was compelled to do it, because he thought us wrong in coming down with a "heavy hand" on the liberties of a small people,- his own. What (as he believed) he fought for then he was fighting for now. England now stands out as the Champion of liberty against tyranny and of right against injustice: and so he could draw his sword for her in whole-hearted loyalty and devotion'.[7] In 1918, Fitzpatrick gave an address at the Thanksgiving Service convened by the Mayor in Great St Mary's Church, to celebrate the end of the War.

In the autumn term of 1914, the Editorial of the Queens' magazine,'The Dial', reflects:

'...it is no certain doom for which our friends depart: rather there is a strange new prospect of duty and maybe glory for each one of them. Perhaps a "far, far better thing" than the career they interrupt. Some, too will not return, come what may. The "wastage of war" is very great, and we know already of some Queens' men who, in view of the number of vacancies caused, will give their life to the permanent service of the British Army...The Dean of Wells told us that the continuous life of an old college like Queens' is like a bright strand running through the cable of national history.

That strand must not be broken. After all this European War may not last so long as we fear. A new generation will grow up: some, at least, of the men we have proudly sent out to Duty and Service will again live and work and play in Queens'. Let us try and keep going as much of the old collegiate life as is fitting and possible'.[7] At this time there were only 107 undergraduates, just over half the number of the previous year, and the number would decline to 12 in 1917.[2] From the beginning of 1915, soldiers from various regiments were billeted at Queens', and Mrs Fitzpatrick set up a canteen for them, as well as organizing: 'small groups to tea and a game of croquet'.[2] Sadly, relations between the newcomers and the residual students were not always cordial and, in 1916, a resident officer cadet writes to 'The Dial':

'What is necessary is to point out to the modern wartime undergraduate, that we are not outsiders, that we can appreciate this place. How we wish the University would realise this, that in spite of our khaki, our mud and our weird drills, we remain English gentlemen...'.[2] However, the undergraduates were strongly patriotic, as shown by an Editorial in 'The Dial' in 1915:

'If, at this University, men use religion and culture as a stalking-horse to preach peace at any price, Teutonic brotherhood and the "sparing" of Germany...then remember the Lusitania; Remember that our own lads from Queens' were tortured by the foul gas at Ypes. Remember Justice'.[2] In 1917, Fitzpatrick, in similar vein, states:

'No words of mine can express adequately our sorrow for this continued sacrifice, and our thankfulness that Cambridge men have played so noble a part in this long war for right and freedom. How great this part has been is to some extent indicated by the honours that they have won'.[2] When the College's War Memorial was dedicated in 1921, Fitzpatrick was: 'filled with emotion as he read the list of names'.[2] A total of 409 Queens' students, including those who had expected to be admitted in the autumn of 1914, had served in the War; 67 had been killed in action or died of their wounds, seven had died of illness or accident, 121 had been wounded, and 10 taken prisoner.[2] The Editorial of 'The Dial' of autumn 1918 records the solemn mood of the times:

'Never has The Dial appeared in such a momentous era...we are seeing history in the making: and many have had their share in it...we can rejoice at what lies behind, to remain there for ever. And now our hopes are high as the gloomy days recede, and we look forward to the return of those pre-war conditions here which were wholesome. We are to set to work again, chastened, some more, some less. Already our numbers are augmenting and every new term will bring fresh increase. Our real college life will begin anew in its fullness and the broken strands of tradition will be gathered up and interwoven with the fresh and better experience, will form the old fabric, yet new; a thing purged, but not to destruction... there will be one more, and final, War List: a plain record of golden deeds unsung: the key that unlocks the mystery that, whereas we were slaying and being slain, now, though through slaughter and sacrifice, Peace has been brought within sight'.[8]

In 1920, Fitzpatrick had, what must be hoped, a pleasant surprise, as 'The Dial' of 1920 reports:

'On Monday, May 10, Her Majesty the Queen, Princess Mary, Prince Albert, (later George VI), Prince Henry and Prince George paid an unexpected visit to the College, so unexpected that the first information that the President received was that "Her Majesty the Queen is in the Court and wishes to see the Lodge". The President had the privilege of conducting the Royal Party through the Lodge. Her Majesty spent some twenty minutes in the house and even viewed the Hall from the peep-hole in the study... The visitors arrived by the Dockett Gate from King's and so they left by the College Gate. Her Majesty was pleased to say that she was delighted with her visit'.

Another prominent post-war visitor to the College was Hirohito, the Crown Prince of Japan, in 1921. Japan had been a member of the 'Allies' against Germany in the Great War, and the Crown Prince would succeed as Emperor in 1926. In 1921, he made official visits to the UK, France, the Netherlands, Belgium, Italy and Vatican City. In the UK, his extensive itinerary included Cambridge University, where his schedule included a lecture on the 'Relationship between the British Royal Family and its People', the award of an honorary degree, and a visit to Queens':

'On Wednesday, May 18th, a glorious summer day, H.I.H. the Crown Prince of Japan visited Cambridge and our College. He was met at the Docket gate by the President, and conducted through the courts and the Lodge garden to the Lodge. He was accompanied by distinguished representatives of his own country, and of our Foreign Office. He passed through the gallery and the study and the other chief rooms, and showed particular interest in the wig-room, the purpose of which was explained to him by one of his attendants. On passing out of the house, he expressed the sentiment, "Une tres belle maison". In the Cloister Court he was met by members of the College with their cameras, and a similar welcome awaited him in the first court. As he left by the great gate he received a hearty send-off by the College'.[9]

In 1926, Fitzpatrick had completed 20 years as President of Queens', and received a presentation from the College of his portrait by W.G. de Glehn, A.R.A. , with the words of the Vice-President:

'Your loyalty to us has made us loyal to you. You have never spared yourself, you have worked untiringly for all that you deemed conducive to the good of the College. You have given to the College a whole-hearted service. We should indeed be ungrateful if this did not call out our gratitude; and not least important- never for a moment have you forfeited our respect'.[1]

In 1928, Fitzpatrick was elected Vice-Chancellor for the second time, but became ill after a few months and had to rest away from Cambridge. But he returned apparently recovered, and for the last two years of his life:

'his presence on syndicates and boards and at the Council of the Senate, has been invaluable, and many difficult problems have been simplified by his clear memory and acute discernment'.[1] However, in October 1931, he had to be admitted to a nursing home and underwent an operation; although he returned to the Lodge in better health, he collapsed and died on the 28th of the month, aged 70, and his funeral was held on the 31st of October:

'when the College Chapel was filled to overflowing by members of the College and other personal friends of the President. There was a simultaneous memorial service in Great St Mary's Church'.[5]

He is buried in the 'Ascension Parish Burial Ground', near Huntingdon Road, Cambridge. (This was established in 1857, and contains the graves of many eminent University scientists and scholars). He left £10,000 to found one or more fellowships.[2]

He is commemorated by the naming of the 'Fitzpatrick Hall', which is a multi-pupose auditorium in the 'Lyon Court' development in the College, completed in 1989. In 1946, his widow commissioned a new portrait of Fitzpatrick for the College, by Bertram Winterton, in which he is depicted holding a little red book. (As noted on the College website, during the years of student unrest 1968-72, the portrait was defaced by entitling the book: 'The Thoughts of Chairman Mao'). Mrs Fitzpatrick died in 1964, leaving the College £2,000 for a studentship and £1,500 for general maintenance of the older College buildings.

Professor Arthur Cook, a fellow of Queens' from 1900 to 1952, remembers his friend:

'...he belonged to a type, in which the spiritual and the practical are fused in a single warm-hearted personality; and such men have never been common in academic life...The most obvious trait in his mental equipment was, I suppose, sheer business capacity- an almost unerring grasp of the essential data in any given situation and of the right means to employ for making the most of them. This was with him, as with some business magnates, a matter of intuition, not of reasoning...one never heard him argue a point at any length...He told me once that in early days... the choice between two careers had presented itself to him- Man of Science, or Man of Affairs? He had taken stock of his own abilities and deliberately decided that his talents lay in the latter, not in the former, direction. Accordingly, instead of devoting time to Research, he threw himself with zest into the affairs of his College, the affairs of his University, and- to an extent hardly realized even by his friends- into helpful activities at Bedford and elsewhere...any future historian...would be fairly staggered at the number and variety of the Boards, Syndicates, and Committees beneath whose findings appeared the signature T.C.Fitzpatrick... Nothing escaped the Presidential eye. It might be the merest detail- a sow-thistle in the rose-bed, a cigarette-end on the path...The minute defect must needs be remedied, and remedied forthwith... This constant habit of bettering things underlay his really remarkable record of College improvements. There is no court or range of buildings at Queens' that does not bear the obvious impress of his hand...All this genuine interest in Undergraduate life and concerns...would be impossible, had there not been something boyish about the man himself. His frank, unaffected friendliness was a passport to the hearts of all who met him...Of the President's unobtrusive generosity to friends innumerable...nothing can here be said. Nor is there space to dwell on all he did for the encouragement and support of the College Mission...He had spent fifty-five years in Cambridge, twenty-five of them at Christ's, twenty-five at Queens'. In a sense his task was ended and the burden could be laid aside. But in another sense his work is unending. For a life so consistent cannot but be an abiding inspiration to those who shall come after'.[1]

References

1. Rackham, H. Thomas Cecil Fitzpatrick. A Memoir. Cambridge. Privately Printed at the University Press. 1937.
2. Twigg, J. A History of Queens' College, Cambridge. 1448-1986. The Boydell Press. 1987. pp 231, 283, 317-24, 386.
3. Whetham, W.C.D. Solution and Electrolysis. Cambridge. University Press. 1895.
4. Fitzpatrick, T.C. A History of the Cavendish Laboratory 1871-1910. London. Longmans, Green, and Co. 1910.
5. The Record 1939-31. Queens' College, Cambridge. Online. 2020.
6. The Dial. Easter Term 1921. Queens' College, Cambridge. Online. 2020.
7. The Dial. Michaelmas Term. 1914. Queens' College, Cambridge. Online. 2020.
8. The Dial. Michaelmas Term. 1918. Queens' College, Cambridge. Online. 2020.
9. The Dial. Easter Term. 1921. Queens' College, Cambridge. Online. 2020.

CHAPTER 34

John Archibald Venn. President 1932-58.

Summary.

John Archibald Venn was born in Cambridge in 1883, the only child of John Venn, (1834-1923), a fellow of GonvIlle and Caius College, Cambridge. His father would achieve fame when he devised the so-called 'Venn diagrams'.

John Archibald's great-great-grandfather, Henry Venn, (1725-97), a clergyman and prominent social reformer, had been a fellow at Queens' from 1749 to 1757. His great-grandfather, John Venn, (1759-1813), was another clergyman, as was his grandfather, Henry Venn, (1796-1873), who was the second member of the family to have been a fellow of Queens'. Also, John Venn, (1803-1890), a brother of the last-named Henry, had been a fellow of Queens' during 1829-34.

John Archibald Venn was admitted to Trinity College, Cambridge, in 1902. He graduated B.A. in the History Tripos in 1905, after achieving a surprisingly modest third class degree, and, in the following year, he married Lucy Marion Ridgeway, daughter of Professor (of Archeology) William (later Sir William) Ridgeway.

For the next several years, Venn collaborated with his father's historical research into the alumni and colleges of Cambridge University but, during the first three years of the First World War, he served as a lieutenant in the Cambridgeshire Regiment. In 1917, he became a statistician at the Ministry of Agriculture, and, after the War, began an academic career as the Gilbey Lecturer in the History and Economics of Agriculture at Cambridge. His experience in a government department would be a prelude to a parallel career as a public servant, (with the award of the C.M.G.), and he would serve on numerous boards and committees.

In 1927, aged 44, Venn was elected to a fellowship at Queens' and, after the death of Thomas Cecil Fitzpatrick in 1931, Venn, although still the junior fellow, was elected as his successor as President in 1932.

He was to serve as President for 27 years and, as well as contributing to all aspects of the life of the College and University, (he served as Vice-Chancellor during 1941-43), he continued his many local, national and international interests. He presided over the College during the challenging years of the Second World War, but had the satisfaction of welcoming the Queen for the celebration of the College's Quincentenary in 1948.

Venn published 'Foundations of Agricultural Economics' in 1923, but the College 'Record' of 1954 reports on the completion of the work for which he is now remembered:

'The President's Alumni Cantabrigienses, a biographical Register in ten volumes of all known Cambridge men, has been completed after 46 year's work. The 141,000 entries range from the earliest times to the year 1900. The Syndics of the Press marked the occasion by a party given in Emmanuel College on 8 June 1954'.

The 'Fisher Building' at Queens' was completed in 1936 and, in 1956, he launched his second appeal for a new accomodation building for the College. This would be designed by Basil Spence, (the architect of Coventry Cathedral), but, sadly, it was not completed until after Venn's death.

Venn died in March 1958, and his wife died nine days later. His College obituarist notes:

'He was enormously ambitious for the College, not at all for himself'.

Timeline.

1883. Born in Cambridge. (Son of John Venn, logician and mathematician, lecturer in the 'Moral Sciences', and fellow of Gonville and Caius College, Cambridge, who devised 'Venn Diagrams').

1902. Admitted to Trinity College, Cambridge.

1905. B.A. , (with third class honours in the History Tripos).

1906. Marries Lucy Marion Ridgeway, daughter of Professor, (and later 'Sir') Willam Ridgeway.

1909. M.A. .

1911-16. Co-editor of five volumes of an admissions register of Trinity College, Cambridge, and completes- in 1913- the second volume of John Peile's 'Biographical Register of Christ's College'.

1913. Publication of: 'The Book of Matriculation and Degrees: A Catalogue of those who have been admitted to any degree in the University of Cambridge from 1544 to 1659', co-authored with his father, John Venn.

1914. Beginning of the First World War. Serves in the Army as a lieutenant in the Cambridgeshire Regiment.

1917. Works as a statistician in the Ministry of Agriculture.

1918. End of the First World War.

1921. Appointed to the Gilbey lectureship in the History and Economics of Agriculture, at Cambridge.

1922-54. Publishes, with his father John Venn: 'Alumni Cantabrigienses: a biographical list of all known students, graduates and holders of office at the University of Cambridge from the earliest times to 1900'.

1923. Publishes: 'Foundations of Agricultural Economics'. Death of father, John Venn.

1923-32. Advisory Officer in Agricultural Economics, Ministery of Agriculture.

1927. Elected a fellow of Queens'.

1929. D.Litt. .

1930-31. Chairman, Cambridgeshire and Isle of Ely Agricultural Wages Board. Senior Proctor, University of Cambridge.

1932. Death of Thomas Cecil Fitzpatrick. Elected President of Queens'. Adopts a daughter, Elizabeth Avis Venn.

1933-34. Member of the Scientific Council of the International Agricultural Institute, Rome. Member of various committees of the Ministry of Agriculture, the Colonial Office, and the Empire Marketing Board. President, Agricultural Economics Society.

1934-39.	Member of the Council of the British Association for the Advancement of Science.
1934-42.	Member of the Council of the Senate of the University of Cambridge.
1936.	The 'Fisher Building' at Queens' completed.
1937.	Haile Selassie, Emperor of Ethiopia, visits Queens'.
1939.	Second World War begins on the 1st of September.
1940.	Governor and Perpetual Student of the Medical College of St Bartholomew's Hospital.
1941-43.	Vice-Chancellor
1944-45.	Member, Commission on Higher Education in the Colonies.
1945.	The Second World War ends on the 2nd of September, (although this is generally celebrated on the 14th of August).
1945-46.	Member, Hong-Kong University Advisory Committee.
1946.	Findlay Lecturer, University College, Dublin.
1948.	Women become full members of the University of Cambridge and are awarded degrees. The five-hundredth anniversary of the foundation of the College on the 15th of April. The College is visited by the Queen. Marriage of Elizabeth Avis Venn at Queens'.
1948-49.	Chairman of the Commission on the sugar industry in British Guiana.
1949.	The Queen accepts the title of 'Patroness of Queens' College'.
1951.	The President and Mrs Venn visit their daughter in New Zealand, during July-September.
1952.	Death of George VI. Accession of Elizabeth II on the 6th of February. The War Memorial to those from Queens' who gave their lives in the Second World War is dedicated on the 14th of June.
1953.	Queen Elizabeth the Queen Mother visits Queens'.
1956.	Appointed C.M.G. . The Venns celebrate their Golden Wedding. The President launches a College Appeal for a new accomodation building.
1957.	Basil Spence is named as the architect of the proposed new building at Queens', (which will become the 'Erasmus Building' and be completed in 1959).

1958. Dies at the President's Lodge on the 15th of March. His wife dies on the 25th of March.

Agricultural economist. Historian. Public servant.

John Archibald Venn was born at Cambridge on the 10th of November 1883, the only child of John Venn, 1834-1923, a fellow of Gonville and Caius College, Cambridge, and Susanna Carnegie, daughter of the Rev. Charles Edmonstone.[1]

John Archibald's father, John Venn,[2] would achieve fame by devising 'Venn Diagrams', (ie representation of all possible relationships between a finite collection of different sets). His great-great-grandfather, Henry Venn, 1725-97, had been a fellow at Queens' during 1749-57; his great-grandfather, John Venn, 1759-1813, had attended Sidney Sussex College, Cambridge; and his grandfather, Henry Venn, 1796-1873, had also been a fellow of Queens' during 1819-29. John Venn, 1803-1890, (the brother of the above-mentioned Henry Venn, 1796-1873), had been a third member of the family to become a fellow at Queens', during 1829-34. (He had been to India as a cadet with the East India Company before being invalided home and embarking on a clerical career).

The most remote of the above ancestors, Henry Venn, 1725-97, John Archibald's great-great-grandfather, had attended Jesus College, Cambridge, before becoming a fellow of Queens'. In 1754, he was a curate at Holy Trinity Church, Clapham, London, and is credited as the founder of the 'Clapham Sect', a group of social reformers in the Church of England, concerned with the abolition of slavery and with prison reform. They were active during the late 18th century and early-to-mid 19th century, and one of the Sect's most influential leaders was the anti-slavery campaigner William Wilberforce. The group would also include Henry Venn's son, John Venn, 1759-1813, who would become rector of Holy Trinity Church, Clapham, in 1792.

John Archibald's great-grandfather, John Venn, 1759-1813, had attended Sidney Sussex College, and was one of the founders of the 'Society for Missions to Africa and the East' in 1799, (which would be renamed 'The Church Missionary Society' and then the 'Church Mission Society'), as was William Wilberforce and John Venn's friend, the influential evangelical clergyman Charles Simeon. (Simeon was appointed to the living of Holy Trinity Church, Cambridge, in 1783, and befriended John Venn's son, Henry Venn, 1796-1873).

John Archibald's grandfather, Henry Venn, 1796-1873, was an undergraduate at Queens' and then a fellow of the College during 1819-29. He became vicar of Drypool, Hull, and, thereafter, rector of St John's, Holloway, London, and a prebendary of St Paul's Cathedral. He was a leading evangelical in the Church of England and, like his father, he was active in the Church Mission Society, moving in 1841 to Highgate, London, to serve as its honorary secretary until 1872, the year before his death in 1873.

We will now return to John Archibald's father, John Venn. He was born in Yorkshire in 1834, when his father was rector of Drypool, Hull. After the family moved to Highgate, John attended Highgate School, (previously known as Sir Roger Cholmley's School), and the Islington Preparatory School. He was strictly brought up, with the priesthood in mind, and was admitted to Gonville and Caius College, Cambridge, in 1853. He graduated as sixth Wrangler in the Mathematics Tripos of 1857, and was then elected a fellow of his College. He was ordained priest in 1859, before serving as a curate in Cheshunt, Hertfordshire, and later in Mortlake, Surrey. In 1862 he returned to Cambridge as a lecturer in moral science, and taught logic and probability theory. In 1866, he published 'The Logic of Chance' and, in 1881, 'Symbolic Logic'; the latter described what would be known as 'Venn Diagrams', although these had been introduced in his paper: 'On the Diagrammatic and Mechanical Representation of Prepositions and Reasoning', in the 'Philosophical Magazine and Journal of Science', of July 1880. In Chapter V of 'Symbolic Logic', entitled 'Diagramatic Representation', he writes:

'The majority of modern logical treatises make at any rate occasional appeal to diagrammatic aid, in order to give sensible illustration of the relations of terms and propositions to one another...What we ultimately have to do is to break up the entire field into a definite number of classes or compartments which are mutually exclusive and collectively exhaustive'. In 1899, he published a third title in this field: 'The Principles of Empirical Logic'. In 1883, he was elected a fellow of the Royal Society and, in the same year, he resigned from the priesthood because he could not accept the Thirty-Nine Articles of the Church of England. His interests changed to history and, in 1897, he published 'The Biographical History of Gonville and Caius College 1349-1897'. After several further historical publications, he began the Herculean task, with his son John Archibald, to produce a history of the alumni of Cambridge University, which would become: 'Alumni Cantabrigienses: A biographical List of All Known Students, Graduates and Holders of Office at the University of Cambridge, from the Earliest Times to 1900';[3] (this would be published by Cambridge University Press in ten volumes, between 1922 and 1954). In 1903, John Venn was elected as the 'President of Fellows of Gonville and Caius College', a position he retained until his death in 1923. (This has given rise to some confusion, as the holder of this office is often refered to as the 'President of Gonville and Caius College'; however, this 'President' is the representative of the fellowship, while the head of this College is the 'Master'). We cannot leave John Venn without mention of the machine which he built, with the help of his son, for bowling cricket balls; when the Australian cricket team visited in 1909, the machine bowled their leading batsman, (Victor Trumper), on four consecutive occasions.[2]

John Archibald Venn, the future President of Queens', (who will subsequently be referred to as 'Venn'), an only child, was educated as a boarder at Eastbourne College, which had been founded in 1867, with the support of the Duke of Devonshire. In 1902, he was admitted to Trinity College, Cambridge, and studied for the History Tripos, graduating B.A. in 1905. However, he only managed to achieve a third class degree in both parts of the Tripos,[1] a welcome reminder that a modest performance does not necessarily forclose future academic excellence! (He would proceed M.A. in 1909 and Litt.D. in 1929). In 1906, when he was aged 23, he married Lucy Marion Ridgeway, aged 24, the daughter of William Ridgeway, who would become 'Sir William' in 1919, in recognition of his classical scholarship, and who had been elected Disney Professor of Archaeology at Cambridge in 1892.

For several years Venn collaborated with his father's historical research, collecting information on past members of the University and, in 1913, they published: 'The Book of Matriculation and Degrees: A Catalogue of those who have been admitted to any degree in the University of Cambridge from 1544 to 1659'.[1] A further collaboration produced five volumes, published between 1911-16, of an admissions register of Trinity College to 1900. Also, Venn completed and published a second volume of John Piele's 'Biographical Register of Christ's College', in 1913.[1]

Although Venn's career as a future lecturer at Cambridge and government adviser would involve the history and economics of agriculture, he is mainly remembered for his laborious work, originally with his father, on 'Alumni Cantabrigienses...', referred to above. The secretary of the University Press, Sir Sydney Roberts, writing in 1959, notes Venn's:

'immense courage and determination in accomplishing his vast plan'.[1]

During the First World War, Venn was a lieutenant for three years in the Cambridgeshire Regiment and, from 1917, served as a statistician in the Food Production Department of the Ministry of Agriculture. After the War he would remain an adviser to the Ministry of Agriculture and, in 1921, began an academic career as the Gilbey Lecturer in the History and Economics of Agriculture at Cambridge, a post which he held until the University retiring age. In 1923, he published: 'Foundations of Agricultural Economics', which was enlarged for a further edition in 1933. His experience in a government department would be a prelude to an extensive public career, which involved serving on many local, national and international bodies, such as the 'British Association for the Advancement of Science' and the 'Scientific Council of the International Institute of Agriculture'.[1]

In 1927, aged 44, Venn was elected to a fellowship at Queens', as noted in the College's 'Record':

'On July 19 J.A.Venn was elected a Fellow. Mr Venn is a distinguished authority on the history and economics of Agriculture and the editor of that monumental work Alumni Cantabrigienses. He has generously expressed his wish to be a supernumerary, ie unpaid, Fellow'.[4] He was soon put to work as junior bursar and, when Thomas Cecil Fitzpatrick died in 1931, Venn was elected as the next President of Queens', while still the junior fellow. Although Fitzpatrick had died in October 1931, Venn was not elected until the following spring, and Twigg, in his history of the College of 1987, informs us that as Venn was seen as the obvious candidate, the election was postponed because he was travelling abroard.[5] (During his fellowship, Venn and his wife had been regular travellers by passenger ships; in 1928 to Gibraltar; in 1929 to Gibraltar and to Bombay; in 1930 to Sydney, Australia; in 1931 to Egypt; and once more to Australia in 1932). Twigg also notes that the new President was given the responsibility for admissions, which had previously been arranged by the senior tutor, and received extra clerical help for the task.[4]

In 1932, aged 48, he became the youngest head of a College at Cambridge, and:

'with his wife was a hospitable host despite his own teetotalism. He was ambitious for Queens'...His high sense of the traditional dignity of his offices...and of the respect due to them rather than to himself personally meant that those who did not know him sometimes mistook formality for aloofness...',[1] while his wife's social skills are described more generously:

'She inherited her father's Irish outspokenness, his shrewd humour, and his warmth of heart, which endeared her to everyone who knew her. Her meticulous care of the Lodge was worthy of that beautiful house, and indeed a great service to the College, carried out as it was often with her own hands'.[6] Also in 1932, Venn and his wife adopted a daughter, Elizabeth Avis Venn.[1] (She would marry Desmond Sidney Jackson in the Queens' chapel on the 22nd of November 1948, and move to New Zealand).

Venn was to serve for 27 years as President and one of his obituarists highlights his services to the College, among his many activities:

'His care for the fabric of the College was as eager and effective as that of his predecessor in the Presidency. As Junior Bursar he had begun the work of modernising the College buildings; and as President he took the lead in the policy of providing all Queens' undergraduates with two years' residence in College, achieved for a short time before the war... (the 'Fisher Building' was erected in 1935-36, at a cost of about £50,000, and contained 82 two-room 'sets', each originally intended for a single occupant). Before the war, he was solely responsble for admissions to the College, through the period of the slump, when in some years there were hardly enough applicants to maintain a steady intake; yet the level of the College was maintained and even raised during this period. It was on his advice that the College agreed to house the pre-clinical students of St Bartholomew's Hospital during the war; wise advice, indeed, as the College afterwards found when they compared their situation with that of many other colleges...When the Bursar was called away for war service Venn took over his duties, and performed them for many years to the great financial advantage of the College. Yet all this time he was active in University administration. He was on the Council of the Senate from 1934 to 1943, and it fell to him to hold the office of Vice-Chancellor in the anxious middle years of the war; a thankless task, but one for which Venn was particularly well suited, since he was not only experienced in the ways of the Civil Service and of government, but also had little taste for the pomp and ceremony of office, which was in abeyance at the time. But his great days as President came immediately after the war, when the College was filled with a generation of undergraduates of remarkable distinction, and the number of Fellowships had risen to double what it was when he was elected'.[6]

In 1937, Haile Selassie, the Emperor of Ethiopia, (but then in exile), visited Cambridge and, on the 8th of June, he listened to a debate, in French, at the Cambridge Union Society. The following day, he visited Queens', as had been anticipated in the 'Cambridge Daily News':

'Later (on June 9th) at the invitation of the President of Queens' College, his Majesty will visit the college library and inspect the Ethiopic and Amharic books, and will take luncheon with the President and Fellows'. There would be further associations of the Emperor with the College: his youngest son, Prince Sahle Selassie, was a student at Queens' during 1950-51, and a great-grandson graduated from Queens' during the 1970s.

In September 1938, the threat of war prompted the College to prepare air-raid defences. These consisted of trenches in Walnut Tree Court, shelters, and dressing stations. When war broke out the following year, Venn presided over 13 fellows, four of whom would be away on war service for the duration. As noted above, in the pre-war period, Queens' had agreed to host students from St Bartholomew's ('Bart's') Hospital Medical College, and these arrived in September 1939. Luckily, relations between Queens' and Bart's would prove to be: 'extraordinarily happy';[7] Professor Hopwood, Vice-Dean of Bart's, would be elected into an honorary fellowship at Queens', while Venn would be created a 'Perpetual Student' of Bart's. The number of Queens' students was considerably reduced during the war years, but was supplemented by 'Cadets', (ie enlisted members of the armed forces, selected by the Admiralty, the War Office, or the Air Ministry for six-month University courses), who became matriculated members of the University. All students were resident in the College, which meant that two students had to share each set designed for single accomodation. The Bart's students required about 40 sets. The College staff somehow coped with their own reduced numbers and the demands of food rationing and, on one night in 1940, received hundreds of soldiers who had been evacuated from French beaches, (as part of 'Operation Ariel', June 15th-25th, soon after the 'Dunkirk evacuation'). But after Mr William Langley, the College Butler, had organised the feeding of the soldiers, he returned home to 2, Vicarage Terrace and was killed, within an hour, by the first bomb to fall in Cambridge. The late Henry Hart, Dean of Queens', (and fellow, 1936-2004), recalls:

'I have a vivid memory of watching from the Grove, (ie a wooded area next to the river Cam), a German bomber swooping down over King's College Chapel, floodlit in the flares. It was visibly armed to the teeth but did no harm. Perhaps the pilot was an old King's man with nostalgia for his alma mater...There were...about 100 casualties in Cambridge from bombing in the whole war'.[7]

The first post-war issue of the Queens' magazine, 'The Dial', in Easter 1947, displays a dogged determination for life to continue, despite recent events:

'The day of the College magazine is perhaps over. They were mostly founded in those spacious and easy-going times...when one imagines that the intellectual level of the University was generally at a low level. The majority of students were blessed with adequate means and no fears for the future- there was always Parliament or the Church- and the tense atmosphere which is felt in most faculties today was quite absent...These days serious writing is hung about with funeral hatchments for the impending holocaust; comic writing is iconoclastic or else malicious and cruel...There is, too, a growing disparagement of the amateur in all fields...And yet how this wretched universality has drained the virtue out of us! There is no true sympathy left, for how can one sympathise with the petty but real misfortunes of the neighbour, when a thousand people have been killed rioting in the Punjab?... The important facts of our own lives are overshadowed by a paralysis of fear and frustration because, although human, we seem incapable of controlling human affairs. We feel useless and wretched and cynical; the lowest common multiples of the Century of the Common Man...But, however powerless we may feel in the face of "cosmic" events, geopolitics and economic blizzards, there is one sphere in which we still count, and that is in our immediate and personal circle...not in some vast "global" ant-heap, full of problems and stresses...the grave's the end of it, and not all the Foreign Ministers in the world in happy unanimity can alter that. The more we diffuse our sense of responsibility over a sea of troubles, the less use do we become to those for whom we are largely responsible...the 'Dial' is an amateur and homely thing, and as such seems to me to be worthwhile'.[8]

College spirits were lifted the following year, 1948, as this was the Quincentenary of the foundation of Queens' by Queen Margaret of Anjou's charter, which was dated the 15th of April,

1448. Accordingly, on the 15th of April 1948, representatives of the College, University, Town and County met in the College hall for a Commemorative Feast; the Vice-Chancellor proposed the health of Queens' College, and Venn, the 34th President, replied.

This was followed, on the 7th of June, 1948, by a visit from the Queen, as recorded in 'The Dial':

'On Monday, June 7th, 1948, the College was honoured by the visit of Her Majesty the Queen, who was accompanied by her Secretary and Lady-in-Waiting. The ringing of the College bell heralded Her Majesty's arrival to the members of the College, and the Queen's Standard was hoisted at the flagstaff: the Fellows had formed an aisle in the gateway, while the undergraduates lined the Old Court. After the President had been presented to her, he conducted Her Majesty to the Lodge, with the Fellows following in procession. Loud cheering continued until she had left the Old Court, when the time was about a quarter to twelve...At half past twelve the Queen attended a Service of Commemoration in the College Chapel. At lunch in Hall, at which several representative undergraduates were among the guests, the President proposed the health of the Queen, reminding her of the visits of earlier Queens, and greeted her as "our true Foundress by right of succession". Her Majesty began her tour of the College after lunch by a visit to an exhibition of College Treasures which the Librarian, Mr. Seltman, had prepared in the Old Chapel...Her Majesty crossed the river after this...She was next shown a typical undergraduate set of rooms on T staircase of the Fisher Building. On her way to the President's Garden, where several undergraduates from abroad and others were to be presented to her, the Queen showed great interest in a rehearsal of the Bats summer production of "As You Like It", which was being played in costume in the Cloister Court...Walnut Tree and Friars' Courts, as well as the Fellow's Garden, were bright with marquees, summer frocks and scarlet robes when the Queen walked round the assembled company at the Garden Party. About three hundred dignitaries of the University and officials of the Town and Country were present, besides the men in residence, and about four hundred former members of the College, accompanied by their lady guests.

The band of the Black Watch, of which Her Majesty is Colonel-in-Chief, played in Walnut Tree Court...A little before six o'clock she passed through the Old Court, which was now thronged with guests cheering loudly, on the way to her car. As she said good-bye to the President she said she hoped she might be allowed to come again to our College'.[9]

A few days later, Venn received a fulsome letter of thanks from the Queen's Private Secretary, with two signed portraits of the Queen. The celebrations continued with a dinner in a marquee on the 10th of June, for about 385 resident members of the College. In his reply to the toast to 'The College', the President gave an: 'impressive survey' of the College's five hundred years.[9] On the 15th of June the College held its first May Ball since the War, attracting about 300 couples:

'the dancing took place in a marquee in the Bowling Green (ie the fellows' garden). Refreshments, which showed no signs of austerity, were served in Hall and in a marquee in the Old Court'.[10]

The marquee in the fellows' garden was put to further use on the 19th of June, to host the Queens' Club Dinner for about 280 alumni. The President was in optimistic mood; he gave an account of the royal visit and assured the members that the College was in a very healthy state. The series of events continued the following day, with the Commemoration Service in the chapel, and concluded the following month, on the 15th of July, when, after re-erecting a marquee in the fellows' garden:

'a dance was held for the College servants and their relatives, with music, conjuring, and comedy as a floor show'.[9]

A further mark of royal favour was announced by Venn on the 8th of January, 1949:

'The President and Fellows of Queens' College announce that Her Majesty the Queen has graciously consented to accept the title of Patroness of Queens' College, and has thus happily restored the association with the Queen of England which the College was privileged to enjoy during the first century of its existence'.[9] (During the previous year, 1948, the Queen had become the first female recipient of a Cambridge degree, albeit honorary, and women were finally made full members of the University).

The 'Record' of 1942-47 published the College's Roll of Honour, listing 103 members of the College who had given their lives in the Second World War, while the subsequent issue added a futher five names. The War Memorial in the chapel, which records these names, together with the War Memorial Library, (which had been converted from the original chapel), were dedicated by the Bishop of Ripon on Saturday, the 14th of June, 1952.

During the 13 post-war years of Venn's Presidency, he remained active in both College, University, and local affairs. The University appointed him its first honorary keeper of the archives and he was President of the Cambridge Antiquarian Society. Also, he served as a magistrate, a member of the Borough and City Council, (both before and after the Second World War) and, for several years, Chairman of the Agricultural Wages Board for the County.[1] He continued to maintain his interest in national and commonwealth affairs, which included serving on the Commission on Higher Education in the Colonies.[6]

In December 1948, accompanied by his wife, he sailed to British Guiana for several months as Chairman of a commission to investigate the sugar industry.[10,11] He was still absent when the Queen paid an informal visit to Queens' on the 16th of February, 1949.

In 1951, the Venns were away again, from July to December, visiting their daughter in New Zealand.[12]

Elizabeth II acceded to the throne on the 5th of February, 1952, on the death of George VI, so when the Patroness of Queens' visited the College again on the 14th of February, 1953, (when she was inspecting the organization of local flood relief), it was as 'Queen Elizabeth the Queen Mother'; she was entertained to lunch by the President and several of the fellows.[13] Later that year, Venn was one of the 129,051 recipients of the 'Queen Elizabeth II Coronation Medal', struck to commemorate the coronation of Elizabeth II on the 2nd of June, 1953.

The College 'Record' of 1954 records the completion of Venn's major published legacy:

'The President's 'Alumni Cantabrigienses', a biograpical Register in ten volumes of all known Cambridge men, has been completed after 46 years' work. The 141,000 entries range from the earliest times to the year 1900. The Syndics of the Press marked the occasion by a party given in Emmanuel College on 8 June 1954',[12] while the 'Record' of the following year notes:

'The College offers its warmest congratulations to the President on being made a Companion of the Order of St Michael and St George, in the New Year Honours List'.[13] (This order of chivalry was founded in 1818 by the Prince Regent, later George IV. It is abbreviated C.M.G., and is allegedly referred to in the Civil Service as 'Call me God').

In 1956, the Venns celebrated their Golden Wedding and the 'Record' notes that:

'in offering their warmest congratulations, members of the College will also wish to take the opportunity to express their gratitude for all that Dr and Mrs Venn have meant together in the life of the College'.[14]

Although in 1956 Venn had less than two years to live, for the second time during his Presidency he initiated an appeal for a major accomodation building, which would become the 'Erasmus Building'. But this would not be completed until 1959, the year after his death. The appeal was launched on the 16th of June, 1956, and, in the following year, Basil Spence, who had designed Coventry Cathedral, was appointed as architect about two months before Venn's death. (The fellows had rejected initial drawings for a more traditional building by S. Dykes Bower, who had recently restored the interior of the chapel).[5] Spence's first provisional designs provoked some controversy, as would the completed building!

In 1958, the 'Record' contains this brief announcement:

'The President and Mrs Venn were seriously ill while this Record was being prepared, and it is with deep regret that we must record his death on Saturday, 15 March 1958 and her death on Tuesday, 25 March'.[15] He is buried at the Trumpington Parish Extension, Shelford Road, Cambridge. He had made a bequest to the College, which would fund the building of a pavillion at the College Sports Field. His portrait by Thomas Sherwood La Fontaine, (1915-2007), remains at Queens'.[16]

Some of his personal chacteristics are described in his obituary from the College:

'Perhaps Venn's best gift was his ability to delegate responsibility. He trusted the College officers, and never interfered with the details of their work, though he was ready at all times to support and help them if they asked it of him. In spite of his brisk and forthright manner, he was a shy man; he did not seek confidences, but was pleased to receive them. He loved to tell his memories of an earlier Cambridge, and anecdotes of older days, the raw material of the Alumni. And in common with many shy men, he liked to disclose small pieces of odd information about himself; as that he had never possessed a top hat, or that he could not reconcile himself to seeing so mean an animal as a pig being carried by motor transport. His vanities were not about great things, but about small ones; for instance, that though he was one of the earliest motorists, he had never been convicted of a motoring offence. He was unfailingly kind to those it was in his power to do good to, even when he did not like them; but he was apt to respond to hostility with coldness. He had strong prejudices, most of them perhaps deriving from his evangelical ancestry, but never consciously allowed them to affect his conduct of College business. He was enormously ambitious for the College, not at all for himself'.[6]

References

1. Pickles, J.D. Venn, John Archibald. In: Oxford Dictionary of National Biography. Online. 2004.
2. John Venn. Wikipedia. Online. 2020.
3. Alumni Cantabrigienses. Wikipedia. Online. 2020.
4. The Record 1926-7. Queens' College, Cambridge. Online. 2020.
5. Twigg, J. A History of Queens' College, Cambridge. 1448-1986. The Boydell Press. 1987. pp 364, 373, 391.
6. The Record 1957-8. Queens' College, Cambridge. Online. 2020.
7. The Record 1991. Queens' College, Cambridge. Online. 2020.

8. The Dial 1947. Queens' College, Cambridge. Online. 2020.
9. The Dial 1949. Queens' College, Cambridge. Online. 2020.
10. The Record 1947-8. Queens' College, Cambridge. Online. 2020.
11. The Record 1948-9. Queens' College, Cambridge. Online. 2020.
12. The Record 1953-4. Queens' College, Cambridge. Online. 2020.
13. The Record 1954-5. Queens' College, Cambridge. Online. 2020.
14. The Record 1955-6. Queens' College, Cambridge. Online. 2020.
15. The Record 1956-7. Queens' College, Cambridge. Online. 2020.
16. Discover Artworks-Art UK. Online. 2020.

CHAPTER 35

Sir Arthur Llewellyn Armitage. President 1958-70.

Summary.

Arthur Llewellyn Armitage was born in 1916, the elder son of Kenyon Armitage, draper, of Oldham, Greater Manchester. He attended Oldham Hulme Grammar School and was admitted to Queens' in 1933.

He obtained First Class honours in both parts of the Law Tripos, graduating in 1936. He proceeded LL.B. with distinction and spent two years at Yale University on a Commonwealth Fund Fellowship, before being 'called to the bar' at the Inner Temple in 1940. In the same year he married and enlisted in the King's Royal Rifle Corps, in which he served until 1945, attaining the rank of: 'temporary major'.

In 1945, he was elected to a fellowship at Queens' and appointed a University Lecturer in Law. During the 1950s and 1960s, before leaving Cambridge for Manchester, he served Queens' as tutor, director of studies in law and senior tutor, before being elected President in 1958, but he also extended his activities beyond College and University, during a long and distinguished career as a public servant.

As President of Queens', he welcomed Queen Elizabeth the Queen Mother in 1961, when she opened the 'Erasmus Building', (designed by Sir Basil Spence) and, in 1968, made a landmark contribution to the College when, at a feast at St John's College, he attracted the interest of Sir Humphrey Cripps to sponsor, (by a grant from the Cripps Foundation), a new set of buildings for Queens', west of the river. On a less happy note, his last years as President were: 'made wretched' by student unrest, which began in 1968.

In 1970, he was appointed Vice-Chancellor of Manchester University, which faced a number of challenges, but he:

'tackled these problems with vigour in the face of diminishing financial support from central government'.

He continued to be appointed to a variety of public bodies and was awarded a knighthood in the 1975 New Year Honours List. One of his last major appointments was to chair an enquiry into lorries and their effects on the environment, which reported in 1980.

Having resigned from Manchester in 1980 because of illness, he died at his home in Cheshire in 1984. He had kept in regular touch with the College and with Cambridge, and his ashes lie in the churchyard of St Botolph's Church, Cambridge. He was survived by his wife Joan, (who died in 2006), their two daughters, and their families.

His portrait by Ruskin Spear, R.A., which remains at Queens', successfully depicts his prominent bushy eyebrows. His successor recalls Armitage's early years as President:

'The Governing Body was presided over by the President, Arthur Armitage, called Big Arthur, because he was a large man physically, and he sat with his beetle brows bristling as he glowered down the table...'. But this was a very affectionate tribute; he loved the College and had overseen:

'the largest expansion of the College in five hundred years'.

Timeline.

1916.	Born at Marsden, Yorkshire, son of Kenyon Armitage, a draper, of Oldham, Greater Manchester.
1933.	Admitted to Queens'.
1936.	B.A., with First Class honours in the Law Tripos. (He would proceed M.A.; LL.B-with distinction; LL.D.h.c.,- ie 'honoris causa'- Manchester; LL.D.h.c. Queen's Belfast; LL.D.h.c. Liverpool; LL.D.h.c. Birmingham).
1938-39.	Attends Yale University on a Commonwealth Fund Fellowship. (Sails on the 'Queen Mary' in 1938).
1939.	The Second World War begins on the 1st of September.

1940. 'Called to the bar' in the Inner Temple. Marries Joan Marcroft in July, (they would have two daughters).

1940-45. Serves in the army achieving the rank of 'temporary major'.

1945. End of the Second World War.

1945. Elected a fellow of Queens', (he will serve as tutor, director of studies in law, and senior tutor). Appointed a University Lecturer in Law.

c1950. Start of 20 years service as a justice of the peace in Cambridge.

1950s. Edits, with James Turner: 'Cases on Criminal Law', and is an editor of four editions of: 'The Law of Torts. Clerk and Lindsell on Torts'. Chairman of wages councils, (including the committee on the pay of postmen), and of the Agricultural Wages Board for England and Wales.

1958. Elected President of Queens' after the death of John Archibald Venn.

1960. Visits the U.S.A. for a meeting of Canadian, American and British Academic lawyers.

1961. Serves on the Standing Advisory Committee on Grants to Students. On the 5th of June, the new 'Erasmus Building' at Queens' is opened by Queen Elizabeth, the Queen Mother.

1965-71. Deputy chairman of Huntingdon quarter sessions.

1965-67. Vice-Chancellor of the University of Cambridge.

1965-70. President of the Cambridge University Cricket Club,

1966. Armitage's portrait, by Ruskin Spear, R.A., is installed in the College's Combination Room.

1967-70. Deputy Vice-Chancellor.

1967. A member of the University Grants Committee. Serves on the Lord Chancellor's Committee on Legal Education, (the Ormrod committee), and later chairs the committee on legal education in Northern Ireland. President of the Society of Public Teachers of Law for the year.

1968. Armitage meets Sir Humphrey Cripps, who becomes interested in assisting the plans for the development of Queens' by a grant from the 'Cripps Foundation'. Elected an Honorary Master of the Bench of the Honorable Society of the Inner Temple. A member of a UNESCO Mission to the University of the West Indies, in May and June.

1968. The beginning of several years of widespread student unrest.

1969. The Cripps Foundation agrees to sponsor a major development at Queens'.

1970. Resigns as President. Becomes Vice-Chancellor of the Victoria University of Manchester.

1970s. Serves on the Council of the Association of Commonwealth Universities and the Inter-University Council for Higher Education Overseas.

1973-79. Chairman of the National Advisory Council for the Training and Supply of Teachers.

1974-76. Chairman of the Committee of Vice-Chancellors and Principals of the UK Universities.

1975. Receives a knighthood.

1976-79. Chairman of the 'Armitage Committee' to review the rules governing the political activities of civil servants.

1980. Resigns as Vice-Chancellor at Manchester, due to ill-health. Chairman of the Social Security Advisory Committee. Chairman of the committee of enquiry into lorries, and their effect on people and the environment. (The report led to a white paper in December 1981, advocating the acceptance of heavier, but not bigger, lorries, and an expansion of bypasses on lorry routes).

1984. Dies aged 67 in Cheshire. His ashes are interred in the churchyard of St Botolph's Church, Cambridge. He was survived by his wife and daughters.

Academic lawyer. Vice-Chancellor of Manchester University. Public servant. Attracted a major donation to Queens' from the Cripps Foundation.

Arthur Llewellyn Armitage was born on the 1st of August 1916, at Marsden, Yorkshire. He was the elder son of Kenyon Armitage, draper, of Oldham, Greater Manchester, and his wife, Lucy Amelia Beaumont, who is described as a: 'dressmaker' in the 1911 Census. His mother had come from Marsden, and was from a

Methodist background; she had been married in 1915 at the Wesleyan Chapel, Marsden, while her father, Fred Beaumont, is described as a: 'Draper & Wesleyan Local Preacher', in the 1881 Census. Arthur Llewellyn attended Oldham Hulme Grammar School, before being admitted to Queens' in 1933.[1]

He obtained First Class honours in both parts of the Law Tripos, graduating B.A. in 1936. He proceeded LL.B. with distinction, and spent two years at Yale University on a Commonwealth Fund fellowship, before being 'called to the bar' at the Inner Temple in 1940. (The latter is one of the four 'Inns of Court', whose members can practise as barristers in England and Wales). During the Second World War he served in the King's Royal Rifle Corps from 1940 to 1945; he is recorded as 2nd Lieutenant in 1941, but would attain the rank of 'temporary major'.[1]

In 1940, he married Joan, the eldest of three daughters of Harold Marcroft, an Oldham yarn manufacturer. She had met Arthur at dancing classes when they were both 16. Joan worked first as a civil servant and then trained as a physiotherapist at Salford Royal Hospital, which was the beginning of her future involvement in medical work and nursing care.[2] They would have two daughters.

In 1945, Armitage, who was then living in Selwyn Gardens, Cambridge, was elected to a fellowship at Queens', and would serve as tutor, director of studies in law, and senior tutor, before becoming President. He was also appointed as a University Lecturer in Law. With J.W.C. Turner he wrote: 'Cases on Criminal Law', (a second edition appeared in 1958), and was one of the editors of four editions of: 'The Law of Torts. Clerk & Lindsell on Torts'.[1] Also, he was a popular lecturer:

'Armitage's lecturing was noted for both its clarity and its physical vigour; his class watched with fascination as he twisted his body round the podium and often seemed about to crash to the floor...His style became the object of much mimicry among his devoted pupils'. He was active in establishing a department of criminal science, which would become the Cambridge Institute of Criminology.[1]

During the 1950s and 1960s, as well as serving as President of Queens' and Vice-Chancellor during 1965-67, Armitage extended his activities beyond College and University, and would have a long and distinguished career as a public servant. He was a justice of the peace in Cambridge for 20 years and deputy chairman of Huntingdon quarter sessions from 1965 to 1971. He was the chairman of several wages councils, including a committee on the pay of postmen and the Agricultural Wages Board for England and Wales. He was a member of the National Advisory Council on the Training of Magistrates. Also, in the 1960s, he was a member of the University Grants Committee and the UNESCO advisory mission for the development of the University of the West Indies. In 1966 he visited Nigeria for a meeting of the Council of the Association of Commonwealth Universities. Fom 1967 to 1971 he was on the Lord Chancellor's advisory committee on legal education, (the Ormrod committee) and, subsequently, chairman of the committee on legal education in Northern Ireland. In 1967-68 he was president of the Society of Public Teachers of Law.[1]

In 1958, at the age of 42, he was elected President of Queens' after the death of John Archibald Venn. His successor, Derek Bowett, recalls the College in 1960:

'The Governing Body was presided over by the President, Arthur Armitage, called Big Arthur, because he was a large man, physically, and he sat with his beetle brows bristling as he glowered down the table and, with a pronounced Lancashire drawl, summarised the issue before the meeting. "The sum and substance is...", in a few words he would put the issue for decision with great clarity, and with relief we pricked up our ears to have the matter put so clearly, a matter which for ten minutes the Bursar had struggled to clarify.

He was a lawyer, and a very good teacher, not given to much original thinking, but an excellent editor...He was, however, accident-prone. His habit of rocking to and fro as he talked once led him, in the Long Gallery, to step back onto the foot of Joan, his wife- a very handsome woman with beautiful, silver hair- and, with her face pale with pain, she quietly said, "Arthur, you're standing on my foot". One morning he had to leave the Old Schools where he had just finished lecturing to attend a meeting in Sidgwick Avenue. Being late he borrowed a bike from a fellow lawyer, pocketed the key without listening to the advice about the locking mechanism (it was a Raleigh with a lock built into the handlebars which made them immovable). Outside he found the bike, saw no lock and chain, shrugged, and launched himself onto King's Parade. He travelled a few yards before crashing to the ground. Three times he tried, with the same result, before, puzzled, disheveled, and bruised, he returned the bike to its stand'.[3]

On the 5th of June 1961, Queen Elizabeth the Queen Mother visited Queens' to open the new 'Erasmas Building', which was the result of the appeal launched by Armitage's predecessor, John Archibald Venn, and designed by Sir Basil Spence:

'As she entered the College, the Queen Mother was presented to the President, and then, followed by the Fellows in procession, she passed through lines of cheering undergraduates and members of the College staff to the President's Lodge, where Mrs Armitage and her daughters, the Fellows and their wives, were presented.

The Queen Mother then proceeded straight to the Library, where she had a sherry with a company of some fifty undergraduates. This was followed by lunch in the newly decorated Hall with the Governing Body, the Scholars of the College and one or two other guests.

A highlight of the visit was the presentation in Cloister Court of a scene from Richard III, the May Week production...Her Majesty moved to the New Building, where large numbers of undergraduates, (including the present author and his parents), old members of the College and their relations awaited her...'.[4] The text of her speech reads:

'As your Patron I have always taken a particular interest in the affairs of the College...Six centuries of English history are written into the building of Queens'; each one marking a stage in its development. In the past, endowments of the College came from benefactors, sometimes Royal, religious or commercial. Today it must be a source of pride to you that this building has been made possible by the contributions of 1500 members of the

College...In the past 500 years members of Queens' have achieved fame in many walks of life. It is fitting that this new building should be called after the man who, by his passion for learning, became the foremost scholar of Europe at what Froude called the most exciting period in modern history...I now have much pleasure in naming the new addition to Queens' College-"The Erasmus Building" '.[4] (James Anthony Froude, 1818-94, had been Regius Professor of Modern History at Oxford).

However, by the mid-sixties, there was a pressing need for Queens' to provide even more student accomodation, as the Robbins report of 1963 on Higher Education had advocated a major expansion of British universities, while the availability of student lodgings in the town was declining. Also, new kitchens and dining hall were required, as three sittings for the evening hall were needed and the capacity of the hall limited the income from conferences.[3] A Development Committee was set up in 1964, which produced various plans, but warned that:

'...it must be understood that implementation...must depend on the help that the College receives from outside sources'.[5] Luckily for the College, its President would solve this huge problem, allegedly single-handedly, by securing the interest of a sponsor, the Cripps Foundation, a charitable trust created in 1956 by the businessman Sir Humphrey Cripps, which had already funded major developments at St John's and Selwyn Colleges. (Humphrey Cripps had joined the family firm, Pianoforte Supplies Ltd, which had been started by his father in 1919; this made metal components for pianos and also supplied the automotive industry. But during the 1970s he diversified, acquiring shares in Velcro Industries Ltd, which supplied hook and loop fastening systems. He became company chairman, and the company's success enabled him to continue to fund the Cripps Foundation). The resulting gift to Queens' would provide the largest building ever erected by the College. It would be completed in stages between 1974 and 1989, and allow Queens' to offer accomodation for undergraduates on the main College site for three years.[5] As the College's website explains:

'Armitage happened to be Vice-Chancellor 1965-67, during which period the Cripps Building of St John's College was being built. In 1968, at a feast at St John's College, the seating plan placed their alumnus-benefactor Humphrey Cripps next to the recent University Vice-Chancellor. Quite what passed between the two men is now a matter of anecdote, but the result was that Cripps became interested in the Cripps Foundation assisting Queens' with their development plans. That interest soon became a commitment from the Foundation. Cripps took over the Design Team from the successful St John's project to work on the new Queens' buildings...the new building would necessarily have to be erected on the main site. The Queens' Fellows sacrificed their 17th-century walled garden west of the river...The Fitzpatrick Hall, a 1936 conversion of a much older stable block, was also sacrificed...Design work started in 1969'.[6] Also, Armitage's successor recalls:

'Arthur Armitage...met Humphret Cripps...The two men liked each other- they were both big, decisive, blunt men who loved Cambridge. Cripps was sympathetic to the plight of Queens', so he offered to finance the new development, thus making possible the largest expansion of the College in five hundred years'.[7]

On a less happy note, 1968 was the year of the start of an extended period of student unrest, which was a feature of many universities in the U.K., Europe and the U.S.A.[5] In February, an article in the student magazine 'Varsity' claimed that there was a: 'major crisis of confidence' at Queens', and criticised alleged comments about college discipline quoted in another University magazine, 'Granta', which were attributed to the senior tutor of Queens', Dr Max Bull. Dr Bull subsequently said that he had been misquoted but stated:

'I would maintain the value of the phrase "in loco parentis" as a function of a tutor'.[5] As Twigg points out, in his history of the College of 1987, this was the underlying issue of the various complaints about don-student relations, as the idea of a college as a large, heirarchical, family was, in the view of some activists at Queens':

'not...conducive to a real University community. Paternal repression does not produce responsible and aware citizens...The tutorial position "in loco parentis" is clearly unsuited to the creation of a community in which responsible individuals help to formulate the laws circumscribing their own activities...Few parents attempt to legislate for their children in the restrictive manner practised by some colleges...'.[5]

On the 19th of February the President and fellows received a letter from 30 Queens' students, claiming that:

'Certain aspects of the present institutional arrangements seem to have the effect of obstructing the dialogue of communication in the college'.[5]

The saga of demands, disputes and gradual change would continue over several years, and involve many issues including new committees, student representatives attending Governing Body meetings, and extending personal freedoms; the latter particularly related to the hours when the College gate was locked, the wearing of gowns, dress in hall, noise restrictions, rules on the visiting and accomodation of guests, the quality of the catering, and the requirement to take some meals in the College. But concessions often fuelled futher demands; after new gate regulations at Queens' were introduced in January 1969, another student publication comments:

'This time the dons have given in. But whether they will do so again, when faced with demands for representation and the integration of High Table, remains to be seen'.[5] In January 1969, students from various colleges held a sit-in in the Old Schools and passed a demand for:

'the immediate removal of spikes, railings and gates and all other restrictions on free movement',[5] and voted to remove spikes and railings during the night. This led to a rather improbable claim in another student publication:

'Hoses are prepared, gates of colleges all over Cambridge are locked and guarded, rusty firearms are produced and some porters are armed with axes...'.[5] This item also claimed that, at Queens', one of the fellows had organised students: 'whose loyalties are in the right place', to defend its railings. However, if they existed they were not required: no destructive attemps were made. Later in 1969, the issue of guest hours surfaced again and, in November, the students demanded that guests accompanied by a member of the College could enter Queens' between midnight and 2am, and that unaccompanied guests could leave at any time. But this was not all agreed, and a meeting of Queens' students on the 25th of Novenber voted:

'That non-cooperative action on the new rule on guest hours be taken. That this action be non-violent, and should not disturb members of the College not participating in such action'.[4] This led to some students and their guests gathering in the Cloister Court after 2am in defiance of College rules, and Twigg notes that this was the first time that direct action had been approved democratically within a Cambridge college. But the demonstration soon ended after a snowball was thrown through a window of the historic Long Gallery of the President's Lodge. Although the more moderate members of the students' College Union apologised for the damage caused, these events caused considerable alarm and the President and fellows formed a committee to consider:

'the whole nature of the College and the status of its regulations and of the Governing Body in the changing social environment...(and) the possibility that there was within the College a group of people whose object was to disrupt the College'.[5] Also, specific measures to deal with crisis situations were drawn up, which included summoning the police, stopping all service of meals, fines, rustication and expulsion. But nerves were steadied a little during the next few weeks, as, in January 1970, the Governing Body considers that:

'If the College Regulations are enforced firmly and fairly, with the wholehearted backing of the Governing Body, the Committee do not seriously apprehend a total breakdown of law and order within the College. But if this were to occur, the Committee believe that it might be necessary to close the College temporarily'.[5]

In February 1970, student protest in Cambridge involved the so-called 'Garden House riot', which attracted national attention. This involved a student demonstration, with some property damage and fighting, to protest against the military dictatorship ruling Greece at that time. This took place at the Garden House hotel, which was hosting a 'Greek Week' of events organised on behalf of the Greek tourist board. Of the 15 students arrested, four were from Queens' and, while two were acquitted of all charges, the remaining two received the most severe sentences-prison for 18 months and 15 months, although the latter term was commuted to probation on appeal. At Queens', more reforms to the regulations would take place, and, by 1973, the Cambridge University Prospectus, written by students, notes:

'relations with senior members are good, Queens' having arguably the best set of Tutors of any Cambridge college'.[5]

Derek Bowett, who would be elected President in Armitage's stead, and take office in autumn 1970, reflects:

'His last few years, before leaving in 1970 to take up the Vice-Chancellorship of Manchester University, were made wretched by the student unrest which began in the late sixties. Why they targeted a man who so loved the College I never understood, and I found it difficult to forgive that generation...During the student unrest there existed an undergraduate newspaper, The Shilling Paper, which regularly featured attacks on the College, or even on him personally, and one week in particular issue irritated him beyond endurance. He sent for me in his study sitting on his swivel chair before his roll-top desk, he launched into a tirade, waving his arms in his anger. All of a sudden there was a crack, and he went over backwards, banging his head on the floor. The swivel chair lay in pieces around him. I helped him to his feet, fighting to restrain the mirth which bubbled inside me and, eventually, excused myself and went down the spiral staircase into the autumn darkness and back to my rooms in Old Court, giving in to the laughter which I had stifled till then within me. Undergraduates may well have wondered at this gowned figure, quite alone but roaring with laughter, as it crossed Old Court in the darkness of a November night'.[3]

It was in the midst of these trials and tribulations that 'The Record' of the College reports in 1969:

'We congratulate the President on the high honour conferred on him by his election as Vice-Chancellor of the University of Manchester, which has also conferred on him the Honorary Degree of Doctor of Laws. But Queens' will miss him greatly, both on personal grounds and for the guidance that he has given to all the many-sided business of the College. To him and to his family, especially to Mrs Armitage for her devoted service to the Lodge, go the best wishes of all of us'.[8] A subsequent tribute to Joan Armitage notes:

'Everyone who passed through the Lodge received a warm welcome from Joan who also made a point of accompanying Arthur to Chapel twice every Sunday. Joan for many embodied that blend of good-hearted energy with practical good sense, which is said to be archetypical of Lancastrians. Many will recall her readiness to make friends with people of all ages and all backgrounds, her charity work, and her capacity to make her various homes havens of good humour where Arthur and the family and visitors could relax. She took proper pride in her appearance and always appeared elegant, immaculately dressed and coiffured. She had a remarkable capacity for remembering names and would startle Old Queensmen years after they had graduated, "Ah, Mr So-and-so, so nice to see you again" '.[2]

Bowett recalls:

'He had, I believe, already decided that he preferred the excitement of administering a large University to returning to the teaching of law...Yet he hesitated, because his heart was in Queens', and he was anxious lest his departure might in some way prejudice the plans for the new development of the College...He had reckoned without the generosity of spirit of Humphrey Cripps himself, for it was he who both urged Arthur Armitage to go to Manchester as Vice-Chancellor (as he clearly wanted to do) and reassured him that his departure would in no way affect the decision of the Cripps Foundation to support the College'.[9]

The Victoria University of Manchester was the largest non-federal University in the U.K., with a charter from 1904. It was also caught up in the prevailing mood of student protest, and Armitage's appointment as Vice-Chancellor led to over 3000 students occupying the main University building in protest about a perceived lack of consultation.[10] The Archive of the Manchester Vice-Chancellor's office notes that when Armitage arrived, he faced several difficult challenges: dissent from the student body, concerns about the management of departments, and a feeling that Manchester was falling behind in certain areas of research.[10] But Armitage is reported to have:

'tackled these problems with vigour in the face of diminishing financial support from central government'.[11] He would also find time to chair various government committees, under both James Callaghan and Margaret Thatcher, and was awarded a knighthood in the 1975 New Year Honours List. He would chair the National Advisory Council for the Training and Supply of Teachers, (1973-79); the Committee of Vice-Chancellors and Principals of UK Universities (1974-76); the Armitage Committee to review the rules governing the political activities of civil servants (1976-79); the Social Security Advisory Committee (1980); and an enquiry into lorries and their effects on people and the environment (1980). Other appointments included serving on the Council of the Association of Commonwealth Universities, and on the Inter-University Council for Higher Education Oversees.

During the enquiry into lorries and their effects, Armitage, with four assessors, evaluated 1,834 written submissions from individuals and organisations, and conducted 34 oral hearings. The resulting report was published on the 9th of December, 1980, when the subsequent national attention was initially diverted by news of the murder of the singer John Lennon. The enquiry concluded that the economic benefits of heavier- but not bigger-lorries, up to 44 tonnes, should be accepted, while their adverse effects should be reduced by an expansion of bypasses on lorry routes.[1] (However, the legislation which followed in November 1982 did not enact the weight increase proposals beyond 38 tonnes).[12]

After leaving Cambridge, Armitage kept in regular touch with Queens', as his successor recalls:

'Later after he had retired from the Presidency, he regularly came up from Manchester with Joan to attend the Smith Feast, putting up as our guests in the guestroom of the Lodge. Without Joan he was something of a liability. Coming up on his own to chair a meeting of the Governors of the Leys School, he took the guestroom in the Lodge and within an hour he had flooded the bathroom, cut himself shaving, and fallen down the stairs. He was not in the least put out, whereas I nervously watched his every move, awaiting the next catastrophe.

Once, at a dinner for Queens' lawyers in Gray's Inn, he began the pre-prandial Grace: "Benedic domine, nos et dona tua, quae de largitate tua sumus sumpturi, et concede ut illis...Er...Er; or something like that". His memory had failed to recall the exact words, normally spoken by a scholar. He sat down, not the least put out.

He retired early from the Vice-Chancellorship at Manchester, and we were soon to discover why, for he died from cancer. I well remember receiving a phone-call at home one evening about three weeks before his death. It seemed to have no particular purpose and left me puzzled. But when we had news of his death I understood. It was his way of saying "Goodbye"'.[3]

Having resigned as Vice-Chancellor at Manchester in 1980, he died on the 1st of February 1984, at his home, Rowley Lodge, Kermincham, Cheshire, and his ashes lie in the churchyard of St Botolph's Church, Cambridge. His portrait, by Ruskin Spear, R.A., which successfully depicts his prominent bushy eyebrows, remains at Queens'. He was survived by his wife, their daughters Ann and Mary, and their families. (His wife, Joan, died in 2006, having moved back to Cambridge in 1984. She had developed her own interests in Manchester, becoming President of St John's Ambulance for Greater Manchester and president of a variety of University charities and societies, including the Women's Athletic Union).[2]

References

1. Stein, P. Armitage, Sir Arthur Llewellyn. In: Oxford Dictionary of National Biography. 2004. Online. 2020.
2. Holmes, J., Harbury, W. In: The Record. 2007. Queens' College, Cambridge. Online. 2020.
3. Bowett, D. Memories of the Fellowship. In: The Record. 2004. Queens' College, Cambridge. Online. 2020.

4. The Record. 1960-61. Queens' College, Cambridge. Online. 2020.
5. Twigg, J. A History of Queens' College, Cambridge. 1448-1986. The Boydell Press. 1987. pp 406-15, 420-22, 429, 475-77.
6. Cripps Court History. Queens' College, Cambridge. Online. 2020.
7. Bowett, D. Memories of the Fellowship- The Building of Cripps Court. In: The Record. 2008. Queens' College, Cambridge. Online. 2020.
8. The Record. 1968-69. Queens' College, Cambridge. Online. 2020.
9. Bowett, D. Sir Arthur Armitage. The Record. 1984. Queens' College, Cambridge. Online. 2020.
10. Arthur Armitage. Wikipedia. Online. 2020.
11. University of Manchester, Vice-Chancellor's Archive. University of Manchester Library. Online. 2020.
12. Commercial Motor Archive. 11th February1984. Online. 2020.

CHAPTER 36

Sir Derek William Bowett.
President 1970-82.

Summary.

Derek William Bowett was born near Manchester in 1927, the son of Arnold William Bowett, a commercial traveller. His mother died when he was aged 12. He won a place at Manchester Cathedral's Choir School and, subsequently, attended William Hume's Grammar School, Manchester, where he had to pay the fees from his earnings as head chorister.

He enlisted in the Navy in 1945 and, after demobilisation in 1947, he was admitted to Downing College, Cambridge, in 1948, to read law. His First Class honours in the Law Tripos brought him to the attention of Hersch Lauterpacht, the Whewell Professor of International Law, who became his mentor.

In 1951, Bowett became a lecturer in law at Manchester University and, over the decade, developed a reputation as an international lawyer, taking leave during 1957-59 to work in New York as a United Nations Legal Officer.

He had married Betty Northall in 1952; their son Richard was born in 1956 and their son Adam in 1958, in New York. Their daughter, Louise, would be born in 1960.

Bowett had hoped for promotion at Manchester, but this did not materialise and he returned to Cambridge in 1960 as a lecturer in law and a fellow of Queens'. In 1964, he received his first international law brief and, during the decade, he produced many influential publications. In 1966-68 he and the family were in Beirut, where he worked for the United Nations Relief and Works Agency.

When Arthur Armitage resigned as President of Queens' in 1970, Bowett was elected in his stead. His tenure would see major changes in the College: the construction of a major building, (the 'Cripps Court' development), the establishment of harmonious relationships between the fellowship and students after several years of unrest, and the admission of women undergraduates in 1980.

In 1981, Bowett was appointed Whewell Professor of International Law and, because of his new responsibilities and an increasing number of international briefs, he resigned the Presidency of Queens' in 1982.

Over the next two decades he appeared ten times before the International Court of Justice. He resigned as Whewell Professor in 1991 and became a member of the International Law Commission from 1991 to 1996.

Several honours came his way; in 1983 he became a fellow of the British Academy and a C.B.E. . This was followed by a knighthood in 1998.

He died in Cambridge in 2009, after many years of disabling illness. He was survived by Betty, the children, and their families. Recalling his career before international tribunals, he is described as: 'one of the very greatest advocates of his time'.

Timeline.

1927.	Born at Rusholme, near Manchester.
1939.	Start of the Second World War.
1940.	Attends William Hulme's Grammar School, Manchester.
1945.	Enlists in the Royal Navy.
1947.	Demobilised.
1948.	Admitted to Downing College, Cambridge, to read law.
1950.	B.A., (First Class honours in the Law Tripos).
1951.	Proceeds LL.B. . Whewell Scholar in International Law. Represents the University at lacrosse against Oxford.
1951-59.	Lecturer in Law, University of Manchester.
1952.	Marries Betty Northall.
1953.	Called to the bar, (at Middle Temple).

1956. Ph.D., Manchester. Birth of son, Richard.

1957-59. United Nations Legal Officer, New York, working for the International Law Commission.

1958. Birth of son Adam. Publishes: 'Self-Defence in International Law'.

1960-76. Lecturer in Law, University of Cambridge.

1960. Elected a fellow of Queens'. Birth of daughter, Louise.

1962. Publishes: 'The Law of International Institutions'.

1964. Publishes: 'United Nations Forces: A Legal Study of United Nations Practice'. Requested by the government of Somalia to advise it on its territorial disputes with Ethiopia and Kenya, (his first international law brief).

1966-68. In Beirut as Legal Advisor, and then General Counsel, for the United Nations Relief and Works Agency, (UNRWA), for Palestine refugees in the Near East.

1967. Publishes: 'The Law of the Sea'.

1969. The Cripps Foundation agrees to sponsor a major development at Queens', (which will be known as 'Cripps Court').

1970. Elected President of Queens', following the resignation of Arthur Armitage.

1972. Publishes: 'The Search for Peace'. Queens' launches an appeal to complete Cripps Court.

1973-77. Member, Royal Commission on Environmental Pollution.

1974. Part of the undergraduate residential accomodation of Cripps Court is completed for use in October.

1975. Honorary Bencher of the Middle Temple

1976-81. Reader in International Law, University of Cambridge.

1976. LL.D. .

1978. Queen's Counsel. Visiting Professor, Virginia Law School.

1979. The new kitchens and dining hall of the Cripps Court are opened in January. Publishes: 'The Legal Regime of Islands in International Law'.

1980. Women are admitted to Queens' as undergraduates.

1981. Completion of the last staircase on Cripps Court. The first woman fellow of Queens' is elected.

1981-91. Whewell Professor of International Law, University of Cambridge.

1982.	The Queen Mother visits the College on the 28th of January. Resigns as President of Queens' due to the demands of his Professorship. Is elected a (Professorial) fellow of Queens'.
1983.	Fellow of the British Academy. Awarded the C.B.E. . Completion of the second phase of the Cripps Court development.
1988.	Visiting Professor, 'Institute des hautes études...', Geneva.
1989.	Completion of the third (and final) phase of the Cripps Court development.
1991.	Resigns as Whewell Professor. Moves from a 'Professorial' to a 'Life' fellowship of Queens'.
1992.	Elected to an Honorary fellowship at Queens'.
1991-96.	British member, International Law Commission.
1993.	Commander, the Danish Order of Dannebrog. Grand Cross of the Honduran Civil Order, Jose Cecilio del Valle.
c1994.	The start of a disabling illness.
1997.	Co-author of: 'The International Court Process and Procedure'.
1998.	Receives a knighthood.
2000.	Commander, the Slovakian Order of the White Double Cross.
2009.	Dies in Cambridge after many years of pain and impaired movement.

International lawyer. Academic. Respected advocate in international tribunals. President of Queens' during major changes.

Derek William Bowett was born on the 20th of April, 1927, at Rusholme, near Manchester.[1] He was the son of Arnold William Bowett, a commercial traveller, and his first wife, Marion. His paternal grandfather, William Henry Bowett , is described as a: 'Milk Dealer' at his marriage in 1899. In 1928 a sister, Doris, was born, but died the same year. At the time of his birth, the family lived in Ashton Old Road, Higher Openshaw, Manchester.

Derek William's mother died when he was aged 12 and his father remarried; a half-sister Ann would be born in 1950. He had a good treble voice and joined the Manchester Cathedral choir in 1938, selected as one of only three from over 200 applicants. But this was interrupted by the evacuation of the Choir School to Little Thornton, Lancashire, at the start of the Second World War and, again, after the School's return, by the bombing of the Cathedral in December 1940.[2] From the age of 13, he attended William Hulme's Grammar School, South Manchester, whose fees were paid out of his earnings as head chorister.[2]

Early in 1945, just before his 18th birthday, he volunteered for the Fleet Air Arm of the Royal Navy, thinking that, with the imminent defeat of Germany, he might still see some action at sea.[2] He was trained as a radar operator and spent three years in the Navy, some of the time in mine clearance, first in the North Sea and then in the Mediterranean. In October 1946, the destoyers Saumarez and Volage were damaged by mines and Bowett was on board one of the ships towing them to Malta for repairs; but, during the operation, the Saurmarez had to be sunk. In the Far East, he served on HMS Norfolk, when she was the flagship of the Commander-in-Chief East Indies Station.[3] As one of his biographers notes:

'This naval service was also important to him in developing skills of organisation and man management which he carried into his civillian life: it also left him with a capacity to tie knots'.[2]

Bowett was demobilised in December 1947 and, in October 1948, was admitted to Downing College, Cambridge, to read law. He graduated B.A. with First Class honours, which brought him to the attention of Hersch Lauterpacht, the University's seventh Whewell Professor of International Law. He became Bowett's mentor; he encouraged him to stay for the LL.B. degree and, during the following year, he won the 'Whewell Scholarship'. But this did not stop his sporting interests; he was active in several sports and obtained a 'half-blue', representing the University against Oxford at lacrosse.

Bowett was planning a career at the bar, but accepted a lectureship in law at Manchester University in 1951. However, he would be 'called to the bar' at the Middle Temple in 1953 and was able, at Manchester, to get some courtroom practice in the county court.[2] Soon after arrival in Manchester, Bowett had responded to an advertisement for a third tenant to share a house with three women, one of whom was Betty Northall, who had moved to Manchester from Denbeigh, (via Liverpool, where she studied Architecture), to a job as a designer and pattern cutter in a dress-making business.[4] They were married in 1952 at St Asaph, Denbighshire, and she continued in her job until the birth of their first child, Richard, in 1956.

In 1956, Bowett submitted his thesis for a Ph.D, entitled 'Self-Defence in International Law', which was published by Manchester University Press in 1958. Although almost entirely unsupervised, (he reported that he saw his supervisor once and gained nothing from their interchange), the book was still being cited 50 years later.[2] Further involvement in international law came in 1957, when he took leave from Manchester and moved to New York with his family to work for the International Law Commission in the United Nations Codification Division.[2] He was involved in the preparations for the first United Nations 'Law of the Sea' conference in 1956, and he was present in Geneva when the resulting four treaties were signed in April 1958.[3] A second son, Adam, was born in New York; but Betty was unhappy with family life there and with the climate, and they were pleased to return to Manchester in 1959. However, Bowett was hoping for promotion and, as this did not materialise, he was encouraged by Lauterpacht to apply for a University lectureship in law at Cambridge, and was appointed in 1960. In the same year he was elected a fellow of Queens', and moved into College accomodation in Selwyn Gardens. Also in 1960, a daughter, Louise, was born.

Bowett recalls:

'Archie Brown, the Senior Fellow, took me on one side and advised me to keep quiet and listen for the first few years- advice it was not in my nature to follow- but remained friendly despite my disobedience...I recall being interrupted by him, when, in the Combination Room after dinner, we sat drinking coffee and I spoke of the General Election then in progress. "Bowett! We don't talk politics here"...His view of teaching and his contempt for research were well-known. "Research! Bah!" he would snort.

"Fellows should stick to their jobs, and that is teaching undergraduates" '.[5] The new junior fellow was soon put to work as a tutor, and would go on to serve the College as tutor for graduate students and assistant director, and director, of studies in law. He is remembered as:

'an enthusiastic teacher; they remember his habit of emphasising points by making karate-like chops of the hand. As was customary at the time, he had a pipe which required endless- and slightly histrionic- attempts to keep it alight'.[2] One supervisee recalls:

'During one supervision Derek said that he had to take a phone call from the Prime Minister. The phone rang and he went to the phone in another room and said "Hello Harold". To this day I do not know whether he was talking to Harold Wilson or pulling our leg! We were very impressed at the time'.[6] Also:

'Derek maintained an active interest in sport, playing for the college second rugby team on occasion. He was also a rather good cricketer...He proved to be a canny bowler and a resolute batsman; somehow, one could not imagine him being anything else. He was also to be found on the touchline or towpath at important college sporting events'.[2]

As a tutor, he required a certain skill in dealing with inter-personal situations, as well as a sense of humour:

'...Frank Goodyear, a classics fellow who later departed to a chair in London...came to Derek to complain that he had been "shot at" by one of Derek's tutorial pupils whom he named. Somewhat surprised but also alarmed Derek summoned the undergraduate, Phil Norris, later to be a brigadier in the Army and later still a Circuit Judge, who was asked what had happened. Phil, in Derek's own account "confessed that he had leant out of the window of his room in Old Court, pointed a finger at the stout gown-clad figure crossing the court, and said "Bang"...a suitable form of words was agreed and a letter of apology ended the incident'.[6] There was another curious incident in these early Queens' years, which:

'led to Derek's appearance in the dock at Cambridge Magistrates Court. A student at another college complained to the police that Derek had assaulted him when he was leaving Derek's rooms...No-one in authority thought there was any substance in the complaint and no solicitor was willing to take the case, so the student had the summons issued himself. Derek received the summons and in answer to it went along at the appointed time and place. It appears that the student had little idea how to present a case to the magistrates. In due course the magistrates concluded that, by refusing to leave Derek's room, he had become a trespasser and Derek was entirely within his rights to make physical contact with him and had used no more force than was reasonably necessary to eject him. Derek's stay in the dock was brief...'.[6]

He published: 'The Law of International Institutions' in 1962, which: 'set the gold standard',[2] and which he took through four editions. Two further editions were revised by Philippe Sands and Pierre Klein, the second of which was published just after Bowett's death.[1]

In 1964, Bowett received his first international law brief:

'He was asked by the newly independent Government of Somalia to advise it on its territorial disputes with Ethiopia and Kenya. On arriving in Mogadishu he was immediately asked to draft a diplomatic note closing the British Embassy: this was on the basis that her Majesty's Government were refusing to give effect to a plebiscite in the Northern Frontier District of Kenya, which had voted by a large majority to reunite with Somalia. Lacking experience in rupturing diplomatic relations, he asked to see the standard work, Satow's "Guide to Diplomatic Practice". As the Somali Foreign Ministry had no books of any kind, he was told to borrow it from the British Embassy. The book was duly returned, with a note of thanks and another, more formal, note giving the ambassador four days to leave. One wit well versed in legal Latin described it as a case of "persona non grata sed liber gratis" (...but a free book!) '.[2]

From 1966 to 1968, he and the family were in Beirut, where he was Legal Advisor to the United Nations Relief and Works Agency (UNRWA) for Palestinian refugees. (He had been asked to return to New York but, because Betty disliked the city, the UN had agreed to the Middle East placement).[3] The 'Six Day War', between Israel and the states of Jordan, Egypt and Syria, (also known as the 1967 Arab-Israeli War), took place during this time, and led to a major increase in the number of refugees under UNRWA's remit, and caused Betty and the children to be temporarily evacuated back to the UK. Bowett was well-regarded for his work to make UNRWA effective in a situation described by a contemporary as:

'the combination of deliberate neglect as all the States of the region wanted as little to do with the refugees as they conceivably could and, at the same time, the endless, escalating cycle of retribution between Palestinian and Israeli partisans that caused appalling collateral damage to the refugees'.[2] His work resulted in his role being re-titled as 'General Counsel of UNRWA', with a wider remit. But his work made conflict with the State of Israel inevitable, and he would never be briefed to appear for Israel in international law cases.[6] He had a reputation for the clarity of his legal advice, and became known as the: 'Advisor with one hand', as his advice never considered: 'on the other hand'.[2]

Other publications during the 1960s included: 'United Nations Forces' in 1964, in which he argued that these should be developed without waiting for general disarmament- he produced a scheme of over 560 pages for doing so- and: 'The Law of the Sea' in 1967.[2] Later, during his Presidency of Queens', he would publish: 'The Search for Peace' in 1972, a book for students and, in 1979, (having been promoted to Reader in International Law in 1976), 'The Legal Regime of Islands in International Law', based on his experience on a series of cases related to maritime boundaries. This work is still quoted and, in May 2012, it was cited by both parties in a case before the International Court.[2] In 1997, he would write the opening chapter for: 'The International Court of Justice: Process, Practice and Procedure', a report of a Study Group led by Bowett, organised by the British Institute of International and Comparative Law. Also, he would publish many articles during his career.

On the family's return to Cambridge in 1968, he and Betty decided to move from rented College accomodation, and bought a house in Hills Road, which they would retain for the rest of his life. As described in the previous Chapter, 1968 was the start of several years of student unrest, and Bowett was very much involved in the management of the College during the last years of Armitage's presidency. Bowett's leadership, in supporting the more moderate students to achieve a sensible consensus, was one of the factors that led to him receiving many requests to stand for election as President when Armitage announced his resignation to become Vice-Chancellor of Manchester University. Bowett was duly elected and took office in the autumn of 1970. As the new President, he recalls:'

'There were two main attractions to being President. The first was the sense of privilege in heading the College, and the second was living in the Lodge, for the Lodge in Queens' is one of the most beautiful Lodges in Cambridge...The Provost of King's was Sir Edmund Leach, and he telephoned after a Queens' May Ball, furious that his flower bed on the other side of the partition wall on the North side of the Bowling Green had been trampled flat by people climbing out of Queens'. I apologised and later wrote a note apologising again and enclosing a cheque to cover the cost of replacing the plants, but pointing out that people climbed in to May Balls rather than out, so the chances were that people had used his garden as a means of gaining entry illegally. He returned my cheque and apologised for mistaking the situation... Entertaining was one of the duties of the President, and over the year we entertained some two and a half thousand people, most for drinks, but many for lunch or dinner, and a few over the weekend. Our guests included the Queen Mother, Princess Margaret, Humphrey Cripps, Arthur and Joan Armitage, Antonia Fraser, visiting preachers, old Queensmen, the Canadian High Commissioner, Paul Martin and many others...One aspect of entertaining always gave me little pleasure. The British Council would telephone about three times a year to request that Queens' receive a foreign distinguished visitor, invariably over the lunch hour. I suspect this was to minimise the cost of the visit to the British Council. I well recall the visit of a distinguished Bulgarian lady lawyer who was a Professor in an area of law unfamiliar to me, very large, and without humour. We sat in my study, soon very bored and desperate for a topic of mutual interest. In desperation I led her into the Old Library, adjoining my study, for there were some very old fascinating books...I took out the first book and opened it at random. There, facing us on the opened page, was a drawing of a naked lady, with her intestines revealed. Seeing the look of horror on the Bulgarian lady's face, I quickly shut the book, and took out another, again opening it at random. This time there was yet another drawing of a naked lady, even more intimate in its detail. The Bulgarian lady now looked at me very oddly and I, mumbling some apology, quickly quit the Library and took her into lunch...'.[7]

There were other irritations:

'As Derek lived in the Lodge...he might be called out to resolve even a trivial dispute. In one summer vacation the few graduate students in residence were directed to the Bar for dinner as the main dining hall was in use for an outside function. The Chaplain, Dr Jonathan Holmes, happened to be in college looking for an evening meal and the half-dozen or so of them were confronted by three elderly pies on sale and little else. The pies had gone green. As a veterinary surgeon, the Chaplain had some qualification in public health and refused to permit the sale of these pies on health grounds. An enormous fuss ensued and for some reason Derek was summoned from the Lodge to adjudicate. He was (as one might imagine) not happy to be so disturbed and was in irascible mood. He took one look at the pies and said "The Chaplain is quite right", and stormed out, returning briskly to the Lodge'.[2] There are other hints of a capacity for irritability:

'Respect for his colleagues was...conditional; Fellows of Queens' could find themselves re-categorised if they fell short in some way- but not usually for long...he did not always hold all of his Cambridge faculty colleagues in the very highest esteem'.[6] (Later, he would share many of his views on the strengths and shortcomings of his colleagues).[3] However, he may have achieved a respite from the various pressures of life when indulging in his rather eccentric pursuit of fishing in the Cam, often from the steps of the Lodge.[6]

After Arthur Armitage had received a commitment from the Cripps Foundation to finance a major development at Queens', as described in the previous Chapter, the Governing Body established a Development Committee, of which Bowett became Secretary. When he became President in 1970, he would have to deal with the many issues relating to the project, which was not completed until 1989. Bowett remembers that:

'When plans were submitted...We ran into opposition. Sir Nikolaus Pevsner, who had seen the plans when before the Historic Monuments Commission (which approved them), objected to the Minister, and he appointed an Inspector. This meant a delay whilst the College submitted a memorandum to the Minister, but he eventually approved the plans and work by the builders, Laings, began. The work lasted the whole of my twelve years as President, and beyond, and virtually absorbed our lives. A Building Committee of half a dozen members met with Cripps, Moya and Laings every Friday afternoon reviewing progress and deciding matters of detail. It was laborious, demanding work, involving hundreds of hours, but it was necessary...The part played by Humphrey Cripps himself was extraordinary, for he attended every meeting of the Building Committee. Every Friday afternoon he would drive over from Northamptonshire in his Rolls Royce. He knew every detail of the building...he worked as hard as anyone...The furnishing of the rooms and the details of the new JCR were to be financed and settled by the College...Raising the money for this aspect of the project involved an appeal to Old Members and, with the help of professional fundraisers, we held meetings the length and breadth of the country and wrote to every Old Member...memories of this Appeal come to mind...of a meeting in Cardiff, to which both Arthur Armitage and I were invited. We drove over to Cardiff and arrived at a splendid hotel where our rooms were booked and the meeting with the South Wales Appeal Committee was to be held. It was a small, congenial group and, after the meeting, we went in to dine. The meal was sumptuous: five courses, ending with cigars and vintage port, and far more lavish than our usual appeal meeting supper. I commented to Arthur Armitage on this exceptional hospitality. But I had misunderstood, for, two days after returning to Cambridge, I received from the hotel a very large bill covering the whole cost of the meal...I had less to do with Phase Three, since I resigned from the Presidency in 1982, but at last this Phase, too, was completed....The entire building is certainly large, and some find it aggressive. But, given the accomodation needed, it had to be a large building...Queens' will remain an important college in Cambridge, thanks to the extraordinary generosity of Humphrey Cripps'.[8]

We have already noted that, during the years of student unrest, Bowett played an important part in working with the more moderate members of the students' Union to effect various important changes in the life of the College, and it would be on his watch that the nature of the College was transformed by the admission of women undergraduates in 1980. As he explains in 1978:

'The hesitation in some Colleges, and certainly in Queens', arose from the fact that women applicants to Cambridge who were academically competitive with the men were relatively few in number, and certainly below the national average for admission of women to Universities...the effect of a man's College becoming co-residential would be either to attract good applicants away from the women's Colleges- to their considerable detriment- or to dissipate the women undergraduates amongst the co-residential Colleges even further...In Queens' we have carefully monitored the slow but steady increase in the number of good women applicants...The Governing Body has now accepted a Report from the Admissions Committee recommending that...it would be right for the College to admit women in 1981'.[9] But the change occurred a year earlier, in October 1980, as the 'Record' of that year notes:

'For a College founded "...to laud and honneure of sexe feminine...", Queens' must have seemed remarkably remiss for the past 532 years. From next October, our devotion to the wishes of our foundress, Queen Margaret of Anjou, will be more publically apparent...What then, will the 1980 entry contain? About 98 men and 38 women...It will be an interesting year'.[10]

In 1981, Dr Naomi Segal became the first woman to become a fellow of Queens', and was appointed tutor and College Lecturer in Modern and Medieval Languages.[11]

During his time as President, Bowett became a member of the Royal Commission on Environmental Pollution and served until 1977. This involved a number of site investigations, and he would recount how he enjoyed visiting coal mines and oil rigs.[3] He was appointed a Queen's Counsel in 1978.

In 1981, Bowett was elected as the Whewell Professor of International Law, which meant more briefs for his practice and increased responsibilities within the Law Faculty for the many international research students. The College 'Record' notes:

'Dr Bowett's election to the Whewell Chair of International Law from October 1981 gave great pleasure to the College...For the first half of his sabbatical year he has been engaged in a number of international arbitrations and for most of the second half he will be teaching in the United States, resuming the active charge of the College in August 1981'.[11] But as Bowett recalls:

'At the start of my twelfth year in the Presidency approached I knew I had a problem to resolve. I was trying to cope with, in effect, three careers at once: running a College, running the teaching and research into international law...and managing my growing practice as a Silk in international law matters. Something had to go and, with great reluctance, I decided I had to resign from the Presidency...I had twelve years to go to my retirement and I had to think of the financial implications: of all my tasks, it was the Presidency which paid the least...I went to rooms in the Essex building as a Professorial Fellow and tried to keep a low profile, which was easy enough when I saw how capable was my successor, Professor (later, Lord) Oxburgh'.[7] The Bowetts then moved back to their house in Hills Road.

Bowett would remain as Whewell Professor for a decade, but he resigned two years early in 1991, when he became a member of the International Law Commission. (This had been established by the United Nations General Assembly in 1947 to: 'initiate studies and make recommendations fot the purpose of...encouraging the progressive development of international law and its codification'.

It consists of 34 experts in international law, elected by the United Nations General Assembly every five years). He appeared ten times before the International Court of Justice:

Counsel for Libya in Libya-Tunisia, 1982; for Canada in Gulf of Maine case, 1984, (he played a leading role in this arbitration, when two first-world countries settled their boundaries); for Libya in Libya-Malta case; for Honduras in Honduras-El Salvador, 1988-91; for Denmark in Great Belt case, Finland v. Denmark, 1981; for Denmark in Jan Mayan case, 1993; for Australia in East Timor case, 1994; for United Kingdom in the Nuclear Weapons cases in 1996; for Slovakia in Gabcikove-Nagymaros case, 1997; and for Equatorial Guinea in Camaroon v. Nigeria, 2002.[2] Several honours came Bowett's way during these years; in 1883, he was elected a fellow of the British Academy and awarded the C.B.E. . In 1998, he received a knighthood. In addition, he was honoured by the governments of Demark, (as Commander, the Order of Dannebourg), Honduras, (by the Grand Cross of the Civil Order of Jose Cecilio del Valle), and Slovakia, (as Commander, the Order of the White Double Cross). He is described as:

'one of the very greatest advocates of his time', for his appearances before international tribunals.[6]

Sadly, after about 1994, he became progessively afflicted by a painful neurological condition, which, as his colleague the late John Tiley notes, was: 'eventually diagnosed as spinocerebellar ataxia',[2] and was probably a factor in curtailing his career and his ambition to be a judge of the International Court of Justice.[2] In addition, in his later years, he suffered disabling back pain resulting from a fall from a ladder.[6]

At the time of Bowett's death, in Cambridge on the 23rd of May in 2009, six of the fifteen judges of the International Court had studied in Cambridge and three attended his memorial service in the Queens' chapel; two had studied at Queens'.[2] James Crawford, Bowett's successor as Whewell Professor, ended his address at Bowett's funeral as follows:

'We should remember him in his pomp- though "pomp" is hardly the word for such a down-to-earth, practical and unaffected man. I remember him, white hair flowing, in pursuit of a point of law or fact, crisp sentences making his case and at the same time destroying one's own. Above all, there was his laugh, opening up his face, shedding light on the subject under discussion but also putting it into some perspective. It was a wonderful laugh'.[2]

Bowett's portrait, by Andrew Festing in 1977, remains in the College:

'He has caught that slightly impatient- even irascible- look of someone who wonders why a particular fellow is taking quite so long to make a point at a Governing Body meeting- the hands are down, holding the glasses and one can sense the glasses are about to twitch'.[6,12]

He was survived by his wife Betty, (who died in 2019), their three children, and their families.

References

1. Crawford, J. Bowett, Sir Derek William. In: Oxford Dictionary of National Biography. 2013. Online. 2020.
2. Tiley, J. Derek William Bowett 1927-2009. In: Biographical Memoirs of Fellows of the British Academy. XII, 51-75. 2013. Online. 2020.
3. Professor Sir Derek Bowett. In: Squire Law Library's Eminent Scholars Archive. Cambridge. Online. 2020.
4. The Record. 2019. Queens' College, Cambridge. Online. 2020.
5. The Record. 2004. Queens' College, Cambridge. Online. 2020.
6. Tiley, J. In: The Record. 2010. Queens' College, Cambridge. Online. 2020.
7. Bowett, D. In: The Record. 2007. Queens' College, Cambridge. Online. 2020.
8. Bowett, D. In: The Record. 2008. Queens' College, Cambridge. Online. 2020.
9. Bowett, D. In: The Record. 1978. Queens' College, Cambridge. Online. 2020.
10. The Record. 1980. Queens' College, Cambridge. Online. 2020.
11. The Record. 1981. Queens' College, Cambridge. Online. 2020.
12. Discover Artworks-Art UK. Online. 2020.

CHAPTER 37

Ernest Ronald Oxburgh, (Lord Oxburgh, K.B.E.). President 1982-89.

Summary.

Ernest Ronald Oxburgh was born in Liverpool in 1934, where his family remained during the Second World War. After attending the Liverpool Institute he was admitted to University College, Oxford, in 1951, to read Classics, but he soon switched to Geology. After graduating in 1954, he was awarded a Harkness Fellowship to study for a PhD at Princeton University, tutored by one of the worlds' leading geologists, Harry Hammond Hess.

During his time in the US he married Ursula, (they would have three children), and they returned to Oxford in 1960, where he became Demonstrator and Lecturer in Geology, and fellow of St Edmund Hall. Over the next 18 years he developed an international reputation for his work relating to the physical processes affecting the earth's crust and the thermal processes in the crust and underlying mantle. In 1978 he was elected a fellow of the Royal Society.

He came to Cambridge in 1978, as Professor of Mineralogy and Petrology, and became a fellow of Trinity Hall. He was instrumental in the merging of three departments to form the Department of Earth Sciences, of which he became Head in 1980.

In 1982, after the resignation of Derek Bowett as President of Queens', Oxburgh was elected as his successor. He provided successful and energetic leadership until his resignation in 1989, when he was recruited as the Chief Scientific Adviser to the Ministry of Defence. In 1992 he received a knighthood and, in 1993, he was appointed Rector of the Imperial College of Science, Technology and Medicine, London. His tenure of this appointment, which he held until 2001, is remembered for the merging of four institutions to form the Imperial College School of Medicine. He was a member of the committee that provided the 1997 Dearing Report into Higher Education and, in 1999, he was elevated to the House of Lords as Baron Oxburgh of Liverpool.

In 2004 he was appointed to a major commercial role as Chairman of the Shell Transport and Trading Company, which, during his tenure, merged with the Royal Dutch Petroleum Company to form Royal Dutch Shell plc. He bcame an influential advocate of the need to find new energy sources and to reduce greenhouse gas emissions.

In 2010, he chaired an enquiry into the findings of the Climate Research Unit of the University of East Anglia, whose emails had been hacked. He reported that there was: 'absolutely no evidence of any impropriety whatsoever'.

In 2012, he was honoured by the Government of Singapore with an Honorary Citizen Award, for his many years of contributing: 'his time and effort generously to advancing Singapore's Science and Technology interests'.

Oxburgh, an internationally-renowned geologist and geophysicist, has made a major impact not only in the academic world, but also in industry and government.

Timeline.

1934.	Born in Liverpool, on the 2nd of November.
1945.	Liverpool Institute High School for Boys.
1951.	University College, Oxford. Changes from reading Classics to Geology.
1954.	B.A. . Harkness Fellow at Princeton University. Works with Harry Hammond Hess.
1960.	PhD (Princeton).
1960-78.	At Oxford: Demonstrator and Lecturer in Geology, and fellow and tutor for admissions, St Edmund's Hall.
1978.	F.R.S. . Professor of Mineralogy and Petrology, University of Cambridge. Fellow of Trinity Hall, Cambridge.

1980-88. Head of the newly-formed Department of Earth Sciences, University of Cambridge. (He was subsequently asked, in the late 1980s, to examine geology provision in Universities, which led to the 'Oxburgh Review').

1982. President of Queens'.

1983-84. A BBC film crew makes a documentary series about Queens'.

1984. The Queens' Heritage Appeal is launched.

1985-86. On leave, visiting the California Institute of Technology and Cornell University.

1986. The Cripps Foundation is able to begin the third (and final) phase of the Cripps Court development at Queens'.

1988. Visit of Queen Elizabeth the Queen Mother to Queens'.

1988-93. Chief Scientific Adviser to the Ministry of Defence.

1989. Resigns as President on the 6th of January, 1989. Completion of the third phase of the Cripps Court development.

1992. K.B.E. .

1993-2001. Rector of Imperial College of Science, Technology and Medicine; creates the Imperial College School of Medicine, through mergers of four independent medical schools.

1997. The 'Dearing Report' of the National Committee of Enquiry into Higher Education, of which Oxburgh was a member.

1999. Created Baron Oxburgh of Liverpool. Sits as a crossbench peer.

2003-05. Chairman, Trustees of the Natural History Museum.

2004-05. Chairman of the Shell Transport & Trading Company, having been on the Board for several years. Under his chairmanship, the company merges with the Royal Dutch Petroleum Company to form Royal Dutch Shell plc. He expresses fears for the planet and advocates new energy sources and reduction of greenhouse gasses.

2009. Issues a joint statement on carbon capture and storage.

2010. Chairman of an enquiry into research by the Climatic Research Unit of the University of East Anglia.

2012. Honorary Citizen Award, Singapore.

Geologist, whose career has spanned academia, government and the corporate world. Advocate of the issues of energy and climate change.

Ernest Ronald Oxburgh was born in Liverpool in 1934, the son of Ernest Oxburgh, (1897-1980), and Violet Bugden, (1908-2003), who were married in Liverpool in December 1932. His maternal grandfather, John Bugden, is described as a: 'flour miller worker' in the 1901 census. During the second World War the family chose not to be evacuated, and Ronald was a witness to the regular air raids:

'on one occasion, picking his way through the rubble of his grandfather's printing works'.[1]

From 1945, Ronald attended the Liverpool Institute, a grammar school with an excellent reputation, which also educated two of the 'Beatles'; but this would be closed in 1985. Although he had always been interested in science, his headmaster persuaded him to read Classics at Oxford and he was admitted to University College in 1951. But he switched to Geology, and graduated two years later.[1]

He was then awarded a Harkness Fellowship, (financed by the Commonwealth Fund of New York City), and was admitted to Princeton University in 1954 to study for a PhD with one of the world's leading geologists, Harry Hammond Hess, (1906-69). (Hess, together with Robert Dietz of the U.S. Naval Electronics Laboratory in San Diego, are considered to be founding fathers of the theory of plate tectonics, which describes the movement of seven large plates, as well as smaller plates, of the earth's lithosphere- or crust. The theory gained general acceptance after the underlying mechanism of 'seafloor spreading' was proposed by Hess and Dietz, who described movement of the seafloor, carrying the continents with it, due to the formation of new seafloor by volcanic action).

Fieldwork was an important part of Oxburgh's US experience:

'Under the tutelage of this peerless guru of island arc tectonics, Ron got into his stride as an indefatigable field geologist. By all accounts he cut something of an Indiana Jones figure in this period as he swash-buckled his way through the jungles of the Caribbean, on one occasion killing a boa constrictor with a judiciously-wielded geological specimen, on many others running the gauntlet of monkeys, who combined an unhesitating resentment of geologists with disturbing accuracy in their nut-throwing. It was in this same period that he honed orienteering skills which he deployed both for business and pleasure long after. His robust approach to steep slopes was not always appreciated by his students, however, one of whom later commented that "there are two ways to cross mountainous terrain: contouring and Ron-touring"- the latter involving an ultra-direct approach to hill traverses which Hadrian would have commended. In between field forays, Ron acquired a breadth of Earth Science skills which few can match, becoming equally adept at structural mechanics, geophysics, igneous petrology and noble gas geochemistry. Before leaving Princeton, Ron's true love Ursula came over from England, with the marriage being solemnised in the University chapel'.[2] (They would have three children). Oxburgh obtained his PhD from Princeton in 1960, with his thesis: 'Geology of the eastern Carabobo area, Venezuela'.

On return to the U.K., the Oxburghs went to Oxford, where, after an initial temporary appointment, he became Demonstrator and Lecturer in Geology, and fellow, (as well as tutor for admissions), of St Edmund Hall. Over the next 18 years he developed an international reputation in tectonophysics, (the processes that underly deformation of the earth's crust), and the thermal processes in the Earth's crust and mantle. In 1978, his work was recognised by his election as a fellow of the Royal Society, whose biography of him reads:

'As a young researcher in the early days of plate tectonic theory, Ron's extensive field work in South America and the Austrian Alps led to valuable insights into the mobility of ancient geological regions. He has since conducted important studies on the heat lost to the atmosphere through the Earth's mantle, improving our understanding of convection processes on the largest scales'.[3]

In 1978, Oxburgh came to Cambridge as Professor of Mineralogy and Petrology, and became a fellow of Trinity Hall. He is reported to have found that:

'three mutually hostile departments were teaching duplicate classes in geology with no interaction. Beginning first with the establishment of a "committee to investigate the possibility of shared tea-break facilities", Ron's agenda finally prevailed with the establishment of a single Department of Earth Sciences, which he went on to lead to world-class status'.[2] This merger was achieved in 1980, and involved the Department of Mineralogy and Petrology, the Department of Geology, and the Department of Geodesy and Geophysics. Oxburgh then became the Head of the unified Department of Earth Sciences. This experience would lead to the Government's University Grants Committee appointing Oxburgh to chair an 'Earth Sciences Review'; this produced: 'Strengthening University Earth Sciences', published in 1987, and a final report: 'Building for Success in the Earth Sciences', completed in 1989. As this 'Oxburgh Review' involved merging and closing departments with consequent redeployment or loss of jobs, there was some controversy, in particular, relating to the axing of Hull University's Earth Sciences Department.[4]

After Oxburgh had been in Cambridge for four years, Derek Bowett resigned as the President of Queens' in 1982 and the fellows invited Oxburgh to be his successor. He received a suitably learned address in Latin at his installation, which, in translation, reads:

'The Greeks had a phrase to indicate that they had taken a vow of silence: "An ox is standing on my tongue". We recently had an ox on our tongues for several months; and although we have at last been freed from our vow, the ox is still on our lips, for today we are to sing its praises, or rather those of its habitat. There was a town on the Appian Way called Oxburgh (Bovillae). When Alba Longa was destroyed by the Romans, it offered a home to the Alban refugees. Today the roles are reversed, and an Oxburgher seeks a home with us, and we welcome him with our doors and hearts open...He is a real lover of mountains: not only does he climb them for pleasure, but he has also written a learned book about the geology of the Alps. But, most impressive of all, in agreeing to assume the office of President, he has shown that he is equal to tackling Everest. We pray that his path may not be too steep or rugged, and we promise like true sherpas to follow his lead and help shoulder his burdens as best we may.

Senior Fellow, and fellow Fellows of this College, I present to you Ernest Ronald Oxburgh, F.R.S., Professor of Minerology and Petrology, so that he may be admitted President of this College'.[5] In a letter to the next edition of the College's 'Record', Oxburgh gives his initial impressions:

'It is hard to describe the mixture of trepidation and pleasure with which my wife and I viewed the prospect of taking on the formidable task of following in the Bowetts' footsteps; pleasure at the opportunity of joining one of the most distinguished academic institutions in the country, yet trepidation at the thought of undertaking the task as total newcomers to Queens' and with no experience that seemed to be at all relevant.

In the event, we have found ourselves so kindly received by the College that we have begun to feel at home more rapidly than we could have believed possible. Furthermore since October we have been so busy that there has been precious little time to think about anything but the next job to be done.

The College has taken the opportunity of the change in Mastership to inspect thoroughly the fabric of the Lodge... Deathwatch beetle, furniture beetle, various fungi and rots...have all come to light. It is now clear that a fairly expensive job of restoration is needed and that the work on the Long Gallery wing will continue until the end of this year. However, there is a good prospect that our family will be able to move into part of the Lodge during the spring...here we have an institution that is doing its job with enviable success...Yet in two areas it seems to me that we are vulnerable...The College has little in the way of endowments, and depends very heavily on its earned income...we are in a position that makes it more or less out of the question to contemplate new academic initiatives; and for any institution that aspires to the highest standards that is very serious. Furthermore we have no cushion against major unforeseen expense, or sudden changes in income that are beyond our control.

The second area concerns our position as a college within the wider Cambridge community and the relationship of that community to the educational system of the country as a whole... neither this University nor Oxford can take it for granted that... the same selection procedures that have served well over the years will continue to serve without modification for years to come. Our task is to justify the privilege of learning, teaching and researching in Cambridge by ensuring that we attract the best, and that having attracted them, we select between them fairly and effectively, and are seen to do so.

The prospects are challenging; there is plenty to be done; my wife and I look forward to playing our part'.[5]

In the following year, 1984, the President notes:

'Last year I mentioned that our family was shortly to move into the Lodge when the work was complete. In the event the ravages of worm and rot...were as nothing compared with the major structural defects that were subsequently discovered... The whole structure was demonstratably still in motion- joints had opened three quarters of an inch since 1912- and the engineer's report warned of the possibility of collapse. Urgent action was called for...The structure was declared safe once more in October 1983 and the work of restoring the interior could begin...Our family moved into a small part of the Lodge last April and as the work has proceeded we have acquired more rooms...The unexpected major expense...is a long way outside our budget...we shall be announcing a public appeal very shortly...I should like to conclude by saying how much both Ursula and I have enjoyed beginning to make the acquaintance of old members. We have been most touched by the warmth with which, as newcomers to the College community, we have been received'.[6] Subsequently, the 'Heritage Appeal' was launched to raise £500,000 towards the restoration of the older parts of the College.

Meanwhile, in 1983, the BBC had approached Queens' about the possibility of making a documentary film series about life in the College. There was some concern that this could be damaging to the College and University, but many fellows and members felt that the project could help to dispel the air of mystery and the many misconceptions about college life in Cambridge and, after widespread discussions, filming took place between

September 1983 and July 1984. After the resulting series was screened in 1985, an appraisal in 1986 notes:

'There have been many reactions from total disapproval to high praise...many have been adamant that what they have seen confirmed their worst fears (or highest hopes!)...we have attracted a great deal of press coverage: there have been some 97 reviews in the major national papers...many have been complimentary and only a few critical. The most often heard criticism both from colleagues in Cambridge, from students as well as from some members of the press, is that academic pursuits were ignored...No doubt the programmes will have entertained and provoked every one of us in our own particular way...'.[7]

In 1985, Oxburgh was able to provide some positive news for 'The Record':

'As work subsides in one part of the College, however, it begins in another. Our generous benefactor, Dr Humphrey Cripps, has informed us that the Cripps Foundation is now able to begin the third and final phase of the Cripps development on the west side of the river, This phase will include a replacement for the former Fitzpatrick Hall...The new multi-purpose hall will provide a home for many College activities...The work will also involve the rebuilding of the present squash courts that are in a very poor state...'.[8]

The following year, Oxburgh was on leave at the California Institute of Technology as a Sherman-Fanchild Distinguished Visiting Scholar, and at Cornell University as a Snee Distinguished Visiting Professor. Thus, in December 1985, he missed a visit to Queens' by its Patroness, Queen Elizabeth, the Queen Mother; however, in 1987, she made a welcome return, as Oxburgh recalls:

'Her Majesty Queen Elizabeth, the Queen Mother...graciously agreed to attend a Garden Party in July held to mark the success of the Heritage Appeal- to which she had herself made the opening donation. Her Majesty was in sparkling form and spoke to many of the guests as she toured the College gardens...'. He was also able to report good progess on the last phase of the Cripps Development, which would be completed the following year.[9]

However, Oxburgh's time as President was soon to end:

'Professor Oxburgh retired from the Presidency on 6 January 1989 as a result of his being appointed Chief Scientific Adviser to the Ministry of Defence for a period of three years...Although Ron is going to remain part of our Society...it is appropriate to try to express our thanks to him- and to Ursula- for the contribution they have made to the College since October 1982 when he took up his office. When the Fellows had to find a new President following the resignation of Derek Bowett there was a general wish to see someone from outside the College who would build on the successes which it had achieved. Ron offered us energy, vision, leadership and an incisive intellect: he was going to keep us on our toes.

The one thing Ron found hard to find was time. He had hoped to be able to give up the post of Head of Department in Earth Sciences but this proved impossible. Moreover the very qualities we admired made him irresistible to those outside the University who demanded that universities should become commercial institutions and then expect its leading academics to give freely of their time on administrative matters. This led to the Oxburgh Report on the organisation of teaching and research in UK universities. No doubt the rigour of the argument in that report attracted others in Whitehall when they bcame to look for a new Chief Scientific Adviser- and so to our loss.

As we look back, the first thing we see is the extent to which we are the creation of his era- in our community of Fellows no fewer than 21 of our present 54 joined us during this time. This recruitent has owed much to his energy and leadership...Ron- and Ursula- were concerned with more than just academic success. Perhaps because they had children of their own who were going through university at that time, they took great pleasure in the company of undergraduates at teas and that most famous of innovations- breakfasts. They were also concerned with graduate students- the increase in whose numbers and in whose contribution to the life of the College has been so marked. The purchase of Owlstone Croft, (which provides hostel accommodation), in the final year of his time as President is an appropriate monument... However, I suspect that the feature of Ron's Presidency which a future historian will pick out is likely to be his attitude towads Old Members. He always enjoyed the Club Dinners in June and inaugurated the Invitation Dinners...he sets his successor that same high standard we have come to expect from our President and which we have been so fortunate to see fulfilled'.[10]

After his time at the Ministry of Defence, during which he was appointed K.B.E. in 1992, he was appointed Rector of the Imperial College of Science, Technology and Medicine, in 1993. His eight years as Rector is mainly remembered for his role in achieving another amalgamation, to form the Imperial College School of Medicine:

'He succeeded in merging four jealously independent medical schools in west London into a single institution- a Herculean task...'.[2]

The next item of National significance on his increasingly extensive curriculum vitae is his membership of the National Committee of Enquiry into Higher Education, chaired by Sir Ron Dearing, which produced the 'Dearing Report' in 1997. This was the most detailed review of higher education in the UK since the Robbins Committee in the early 1960s, and it recommended a significant change, namely that undergraduate education should be funded by tuition fees, supported by government loans. Also, the 93 recommendations included an expansion of both degree-level and sub-degree level courses.[11] During his tenure as Rector, in 1999, he was elevated to the House of Lords, as Baron Oxburgh of Liverpool, and became active as a crossbench peer on science issues, chairing the Science and Technology Select Committee of the Upper House for four years. Although not so newsworthy, his chairmanship of the Trustees of the Natural History Museum, during 2003-05, demonstrated the increasing breadth of his career.

In 2004 he was appointed to a major commercial role as Chairman of the Shell Transport & Trading Company. (The present company, Royal Dutch Shell plc – known as 'Shell'- is a British-Dutch multinational oil and gas company, the origins of which date back to 1907, when a partnership was formed between the Royal Dutch Petroleum Company and the Shell Transport and Trading Company of the UK. However, although operating as a:

'single-unit partnership', they had a separate legal identity until they were merged to form the present company in 2005).[12] Oxburgh's appointment came at a difficult time for the partnership:

'In November 2004, following a period of turmoil caused by the revelation that Shell had been overstating its oil reserves, (it was forced to restate them four times in 2004, which led to anger amomg shareholders and several resignations from the board of Shell Transport & Trading Company),[13] it was announced that the Shell Group would move to a single capital structure, creating a new parent company to be named Royal Dutch Shell plc...The unification was completed on 20 July 2005...'.[12] Before these events, Oxburgh had been a board member of Shell Transport and Trading, and when its Chairman, Philip Watts, resigned in 2004, Oxburgh became the next Chairman and proceeded to oversee the merger of the company with the Royal Dutch Petroleum Company. When this was completed, he resigned in July 2005, when his responsibilities passed to the CEO and Chaiman of the new company, Royal Dutch Shell. Assessments of his role include:

'Some years later, when an awestruck financial journalist asked him how he could even contemplate managing the merger...Ron was able to smile, shrug and dismiss the task as relatively trivial!...The brutal honesty and integrity of Ron Oxburgh proved the salvation of Shell group when he was hurriedly appointed as Chairman in the wake of the crisis arising from abrupt downward revisions of previously-stated oil reserves. Already known for his independence of thought, manifest in his championing of an uncompromising social responsibility agenda within the Group, he not only put the company back on course but became one of the world's most visible and credible advocates of a fundamental change in thinking over emissions of carbon dioxide to the atmosphere'.[2] Also:

'His tenure was remarkable in that while chairing a fossil fuels giant he expressed his "fears for the planet" because of climate change, sought new energy sources and urged the global community to reduce greenhouse gas emissions'.[14]

Oxburgh served as President of the Carbon Capture and Storage (CCS) Association, which was founded in 2006 to support the development and deployment of 'Capture and Storage' in the

UK, EU and internationally. (This process involves capturing waste carbon dioxide from sources such as industrial and power plants, transporting it to a storage site and depositing it where it will not enter the atmosphere; in 2019 there were 17 operating CCS projects).[15] In 2009, Oxburgh issued a joint statement, with various interested individuals and organisations:

'We urge ministers to ensure CCS is fully integrated within the post-2012 climate change agreement that will be negotiated at COP 15, (The United Nations Climate Change Conference), in Copenhagen in December- which should promote the broard use of CCS technology in both developed and developing countries. This will necessitate the operation of 100 commercial-scale power plants fitted with CCS worldwide by 2020, with a commitment to invest 130bn dollars between now and 2020'.[16]

In March 2010, Oxburgh became involved with events that attracted national and international attention, when he was appointed by the University of East Anglia to chair an enquiry into the research conducted by this University's Climate Research Unit (CRU). A controversy known as 'Climategate', about the work of this Department, began in 2009, when CRU emails were hacked by an external hacker, who copied thousands of emails and files to the internet, a few weeks before the Copenhagen Summit on climate change. This led to claims, by sceptics of climate change, that global warming was a scientific conspiracy and that scientists had manipulated relevant data. There were further claims that the release of emails was a smear campaign to undermine the negotiations at Copenhagen. In the UK, this led to three enquiries: one by the House of Commons Science and Technology Committee, and two by the University of East Anglia. The first of the latter, chaired by Sir Muir Russell, would:

'examine email exchanges to determine whether there is evidence of suppression or manipulation of data', and examine the CRU's policies and practices, while the second enquiry, the 'International Science Assessment Panel', chaired by Oxburgh, (whose members were appointed after consultations with the Royal Society), was asked to reassess key CRU papers that had already been published, and to consider whether:

'the conclusions represented an honest and scientifically justified interpretation of the data'. The panel examined eleven representative CRU publications, selected with advice from the Royal Society, and reported in April 2010. 'The Guardian' summarises the findings:

'The climate scientists at the centre of a media storm over emails released on the internet were disorganised but did not fudge their results, an independent inquiry into the affair reported today. The enquiry...found "absolutely no evidence of any impropriety whatsoever", according to Lord Oxburgh, who led the investigation...Oxburgh said the scientific papers contained the necessary caveats and expressions of uncertainty where required. But he criticised the way these caveats were often stripped away when such research was presented by other bodies... Oxburgh singled out a graph of global temperature used in a 1999 report for the World Meteorological Association, which spliced three different data sets, as an "unfortunate representation of a very complex piece of science"...The Oxburgh review follows a report on the CRU emails last month from the Commons Science and Technology Select Committee, which also cleared the scientists involved of wrongdoing...'.[17] (The enquiry led by Sir Muir Russell reported in July 2010, and also considered that the: 'rigour and honesty' of the scientists were not in doubt). In addition to the three UK enquiries, five others also found no evidence of fraud or scientific misconduct.[18]

In October 2012, Singapore's Ministry of Manpower announces that:

'Singapore will be honouring Lord Ronald Oxburgh, Co-Chairman of A*STAR's (Agency for Science, Technology and Research) Science and Technology Advisory Committee, member of the A*STAR Board and Deputy Chairman of the Board of the Science and Engineering Research Council (SERC) with the Honorary Citizen Award for his valuable contributions to Singapore'.[19]

This award, instituted by the Singapore Government in 2003, recognises the contribution of foreign nationals who have given extensive and valuable services to Singapore and its people. It is the highest form of recognition for a non-Singaporian:

'Lord Oxburgh ...has contributed significantly to Singapore's higher education, science and technology landscape as well as energy policy since 1997...(he) has contributed his time and effort generously to advancing Singapore's Science and Technology interests. Since 2002, Lord Oxburgh served on the Board of the Agency of Science, Technology and Research...Lord Oxburgh has also contributed his expertise to shape other key development areas of Singapore. Since 2006, he has been the Co-Chair if the Environmental & Water Technologies International Advisory Panel to provide counsel on global Environmental and Water issues...Lord Oxburgh assumed the role as Co-Chair of an inter-agency Clean Energy International Advisory Panel in 2007 and led the plan for Clean Energy R & D in Singapore'.[19]

Oxburgh received the twelfth Honorary Citizen Award, (previous recipients had included the Cambridge-based Nobel laureate Dr Sidney Brenner), from the President of Singapore, Tony Tan Keng Yam, at the Istana, the official residence of the President. In his reply Oxburgh said:

'I am both astonished and delighted to have been honoured by Singapore in this way. It is a pleasure and a privilege to work with dedicated colleagues who have done so much to raise the international profile of Singapore's R & D'.[19]

The account of Oxburgh at Princeton pictured someone who relished the outdoors and this continued with orienteering and marathon-running, until knee surgery limited him to mere mountain hikes with Ursula.[14] However, it may have been difficult for him to keep up with his wife, who, at the age of 80 won two bronze medals in the sprint and long-distance events at the World Masters Orienteering Championships in Brazil in 2014. (These championships, which involve both running and navigational skills, are an annual event of the International Orienteering Federation for orienteering runners aged 35 and over). Lady Oxburgh was still a member of the East Anglian Orienteering Association Committee in 2019.

Oxburgh's presentation for an honorary degree, at a ceremony at Liverpool John Moores University in 2006, provides a succinct overview of a remarkable career, even though various achievements and contributions to society still lay ahead:

'Lord Oxburgh of Liverpool, internationally-renowned geologist and geophysicist, has made a telling impact not only in the academic world but also in industry and government, particularly in fields related to energy and the environment. His pre-eminence has been recognised with numerous prestigious appointments and high honours throughout his career. We are pleased to celebrate the achievements of this outstanding Liverpudlian'.[1]

Appendix: Affiliations, appointments and honours not referred to above:

Chairman, investigation into the safety of UK nuclear weapons.
Member, All-Parliamentary Group for Earth Sciences.
Vice-chair, All Party Parliamentary Group on Climate Change.
Chairman, Centre for science and policy, University of Cambridge,
Member, University Grants Committee, Hong Kong.
Member, Science and Engineering Research Council.
Member, Engineering Research Council.
Member, Natural Environment Research Council.
Member, Advisory Council for Science and Technology.
Member, UK Inter-Agency Committee on the Environment and Global Change, 1994-97.
Member, Hammersmith NHS Trust Board.
Member of the National Academies Policy Advisory Group 1995-96.
President, British Association for the Advancement of Science.
Chairman, the Science, Engineering, Technology and Mathematics Network, to promote the subjects among young people.
Director of GLOBE UK, (Global Legislators Organisation for a Balanced Environment, a global warming campaigning network).
National Day Public Service Medal, Singapore, 2008.

Chairman, Falck Renewables, a renewable energy company based in Milan.
Member, Advisory Panel of Climate Change Capital, a specialist investment banking group focused on companies affected by response to climate change.
Chairman D1 Oils, plc., a biodiesel producer, 2007.
Advisor to Climate Change Capital and to Deutsche Bank.
Honorary fellowships at: Queens' College, Cambridge; St Edmund Hall, Oxford; University College, Oxford; Trinity Hall, Cambridge; and Liverpool John Moores University.
Corresponding fellow of the Australian Academy of Science.
Honorary fellow, Royal Academy of Engineering.
Foreign member, US National Academy of Science, and of the Australian and German Academies of Science.
Fellow of the Royal Academy of Engineering.
Honorary degrees from: Paris, Leicester, Loughborough, Edinburgh, Birmingham, Liverpool, Newcastle, Southampton, Lingnan Hong Kong, Leeds, and Wyoming.
Fellow of the Geological Society of London, (founded in 1807), and President, 2000-02.
Honorary Fellow of the Institution of Mechanical Engineers.
Honorary Fellow of the Royal Academy of Engineering.
President of the European Union of Geosciences.
Fellow of the Geological Society of America.
Platts Life Time Achievement Award in 2007. (S & P Global Platts is a provider of energy and commodities information).
Melchett Medal of the British Energy Institute, 2014.

References

1. Lord Ernest Oxburgh. Liverpool John Moores University. 2006. Online 2020.
2. Ernest Ronald Oxburgh DCL. University of Newcastle. 2007. Online. 2020.
3. The Lord Oxburgh. Biography. The Royal Society. Online. 2020.

4. Liston, J. The Earth Sciences Review: Twenty Years On. In: The Geological Curator 9 (6): 363-69. 2011.
5. The Record. 1983. Queens' College, Cambridge. Online. 2020.
6. The Record. 1984. Queens' College, Cambridge. Online. 2020.
7. The Record. 1986. Queens' College, Cambridge. Online. 2020.
8. The Record. 1985. Queens' College, Cambridge. Online. 2020.
9. The Record. 1988. Queens' College, Cambridge. Online. 2020.
10. The Record. 1989. Queens' College, Cambridge. Online. 2020.
11. Dearing Report. Wikipedia. Online. 2020.
12. Royal Dutch Shell. Wikipedia. Online. 2020.
13. BBC News. Profile: Lord Oxburgh. 17 June, 2004. Online. 2020.
14. About Ronald Oxburgh, Baron Oxburgh. British Academic. Peoplepill. Online. 2020.
15. Carbon Capture and Storage. Wikipedia. Online. 2020.
16. Ronald Oxburgh. Powerbase. Online. 2020.
17. Scientists cleared of malpractice in UEA's hacked emails inquiry. The Guardian. 14 April. 2010. Online. 2020.
18. Climate Research Unit email controversy. Wikipedia. Online. 2020.
19. Lord Ronald Oxburgh Conferred Prestigious Honorary Citizen Award. Ministry of Manpower. Singapore. Online. 2020.

CHAPTER 38

(Sir) John Charlton Polkinghorne, K.B.E. . President 1989-96. (Clergymen do not use the title associated with knighthood).

Summary.

John Charlton Polkinghorne was born in Weston-super-Mare in 1930, where his father worked for the post office. When John was aged five, the family moved to Street, Somerset, where he attended local schools but, in 1945, after his father had been promoted to be Head Postmaster at Ely, he attended The Perse School, Cambridge.

He excelled at mathematics and was awarded a major scholarship at Trinity College, Cambridge. After National Service in the Army, he was admitted to Trinity in 1949, graduated in 1952, and proceeded to study for a PhD in theoretical elementary particle physics. He was awarded a research fellowship at Trinity in 1954 and, after completing his doctorate in 1955, he spent a year as an Harkness Fellow at the California Institute of Technology, working with Murray Gell-Martin, who would be awarded the Nobel Prize for Physics in 1969.

In 1956, Polkinghorne was appointed as a lecturer at the Institute of Theoretical Physics in Edinburgh, but returned to Cambridge in 1958 as a University Lecturer and fellow of Trinity. He was promoted Reader in 1965 and, in 1968, was appointed Professor of Mathematical Physics. He became a fellow of the Royal Society in 1974. One of his biographers notes:

'Polkinghorne's contributions to mathematical physics were truly outstanding'.[1]

In 1955, he had married Ruth Martin, whom he had met as an undergraduate. Their first child, Peter, was born in Edinburgh, while Isobel and Michael followed in 1959 and 1963.

In 1977, Polkinghorne made the decision to resign his professorship, (which he did two years later), and train to be a priest in the Church of England:

'I simply felt that I had done my little bit for particle theory and the time had come to do something else...The most fundamental reason for thinking about such an unconventional move was simply that Christianity has always been central to my life'.[2]

After training at Westcott House, Cambridge, he was ordained priest in 1982 and spent the next two years as a curate in Bristol, before being appointed vicar of Blean, near Canterbury. However, two years later, he was invited to apply for the post of Dean of Chapel at Trinity Hall, Cambridge, and, while reluctant to leave his parish after such a short time, he applied and was duly appointed. However, this tenure was also destined to be interrupted, as, in 1989, he was elected as President of Queens', after the resignation of Ronald Oxburgh. He would remain at Queens' until he retired in 1996, aged 66. (His successor would be installed on the 13th of January, 1997).

Polkinghorne had served on, or chaired, several government committees, and was appointed K.B.E. in 1997:

'for distinguished service to science, religion, learning and medical ethics'.[1] In 2002, he was awarded the prestigious, (and very valuable), Templeton Prize; the citation notes:

'John C Polkinghorne is a mathematical physicist and Anglican priest whose treatment of theology as a natural science invigorated the search for interface between science and religion and made him a leading figure in this emerging field...his extensive writings and lectures have consistently applied scientific habits to Christianity, resulting in a modern and compelling new exploration of the faith. His approach...has brought him international recognition as a unique voice for understanding the Bible as well as evolving doctrine'.[1]

Polkinghorne wrote a total of 34 books, 26 of which concern science and religion. He died on the 9th of March 2021.

Timeline.

1930. Born on the 16th of October, at Weston-super-Mare.
1941. Attends Elmhurst Grammar School, Street, Somerset.
1945. His father is appointed Head Postmaster in Ely. Attends The Perse School, Cambridge.
1948-49. National Service in the Royal Army Educational Corps.
1949. Admitted to Trinity College, Cambridge, to read mathematics.
1952. B.A. . Senior Wrangler.
1954. Research Fellow, Trinity College.
1955. PhD, supervised by future Nobel laureate, Abdus Salem. Marries Ruth Martin. Sails from Liverpool to New York to take up a postdoctoral Harkness Fellowship at the California Institute of Technology.
1956. Lecturer, University of Edinburgh.
1957. Birth of son, Peter.
1958. Lecturer, University of Cambridge. Fellow, Trinity College.
1959. Birth of daughter, Isobel.
1963. Birth of son, Michael.
1965. Reader in Theoretical Physics, University of Cambridge.
1968. Professor of Mathematical Physics, University of Cambridge.
1974. F.R.S. . ScD (Cantab).
1977. Decides to enter the ordained ministry of the Church of England and is selected for training.
1978-79. Chairman, Nuclear Physics Board of the Science Research Council.
1979. Resigns professorship. Begins studies for the priesthood at Westcott House, Cambridge.
1981. Ordained deacon in Ely Cathedral. Curate at St Andrew's, Chesterton, Cambridge.
1982. Ordained as an Anglican priest at Trinity College, by Bishop John Robinson.
1982-84. Curate at St Michael and All Angels, Bedminster, Bristol.
1984-86. Vicar of Blean, Kent.
1986. Fellow, Dean of Chapel and chaplain, Trinity Hall, Cambridge.

1989. Resignation of Ronald Oxburgh as President of Queens'. Elected President of Queens'. The Cripps Court development at Queens' is completed.

1993. Visit of Queen Elizabeth, the Queen Mother, to Queens', to mark the benefaction from the Cripps Foundation.

1993-94. Gifford Lecturer, at Edinburgh.

1994-2005. Canon Theologian of Liverpool Cathedral.

1994-96. Chairman, Task Force to Review Services for Drug Misusers.

1996. Resigns as President of Queens'. Life Fellow and Honorary Fellow, Queens'.

1996-97. Six Preacher, Canterbury Cathedral.

1997. K.B.E. .

1999. Awarded an Humboldt Research Award.

2002. Awarded the Templeton Prize.

2006. Death of Ruth Polkinghorne.

2007. Publishes autobiography.

2021. Dies on the 9th of March.

Theoretical physicist. Theologian. Anglican priest. Public servant. Author.

John Charlton Polkinghorne was born in the newly-opened Weston-Super-Mare Hospital on the 16th of October, 1930.[1] His father, George, whose surname originated in Cornwall, was the second child of the 11 children of John's grandparents, Richard and Beatrice. Richard was a stonemason, who helped to build Bodmin Gaol and Truro Cathedral. George's village schoolmaster thought that he was the cleverest boy he had ever taught but, as the family could not afford to send him to the grammar school, he had left school at 14 and joined the Post Office. Thomas Charlton, the father of John's mother, Dorothy, was a head groom and skilled horseman, winning prizes at major shows, while his wife, Harriet, had been a lady's maid before marriage. George and Dorothy, who had also worked for the Post Office, had married in 1920, after George had ignored the fact that, when they met, Dorothy was engaged to someone else.[2]

John was George and Dorothy's third child; his elder brother Peter would be killed while flying in the Royal Air Force in 1942, while an older sister Ann had died aged six months.

When John was aged five, the family moved to Street, Somerset, (where Clark's shoes were made), as John's father had been appointed as the postmaster. John attended the local primary school but, aged seven, he was transferred to a small Quaker school, founded by the Clark family. There was another change in school when John was 11, when he attended the local grammar school, Elmhurst, in Street. Soon after the start of the Second World War, John's father, (who had served in France, in signals units, in the First World War), had been promoted to be Head Postmaster of Wells, Somerset. However, the family stayed in Street, while John's father travelled to work on the bus. In his autobiography, John gives a moving account of his father returning home from the office early, having received a telegram informing him that his son Peter, an RAF sergeant-pilot, was missing together with the rest of his aircraft's crew:

'For a day or two we tried to cling on to the slender hope that their plane might have been blown off course into neutral Ireland, for the night of their mission had been terribly stormy, but that was not to be the case...I was, of course greatly saddened at the time of his death, but recovered in the way that 12-year-old boys do, not because they are heartless but because they live so much in the unfolding present...For my parents, their grief was much more prolonged, though self-contained. They had now lost two of their three children. Neither Mother nor Father ever explicitly imposed on me the burden of feeling that their hopes were now focussed on me alone, but I came to realize that in a way it must be so...'.[2]

In 1945, John's father was promoted again, to be Head Postmaster at Ely, and when he approached the headmaster of the local grammar school at Soham, with a letter from John's previous headmaster, he was advised that John should attend The Perse School, in Cambridge; this was a 'direct grant' school, which charged modest fees. John pays tribute to an inspiring mathematics teacher at The Perse and, in due course, he was awarded a major scholarship at Trinity College, Cambridge. John recalls appearing in the same school production as Peter Hall, the subsequently internationally-known theatre director, in the 'Taming of the Shrew'.[2]

John, (who will now be referred to as 'Polkinghorne', to reflect the end of his schooldays), left The Perse School in 1948, when the family moved to Grantham, Lincolnshire, due to his father's final assignment as a Head Postmaster. He could not be admitted to Trinity until the following year, as he was required to enlist for National Service, and he joined the Army before his 18th birthday. He was to serve for 14 months, initially undergoing three months basic training on Salisbury Plain. This was followed by three months at the Army School of Education, at Bodmin. He was then assigned to the Army Basic Trade Centre, Malvern, as a Sergeant-Instructor, and taught courses in basic mathematics. Polkinghorne recalls:

'I came not to regret having spent a year in this way. It had given me experience of a very different slice of life from that which lay ahead in the next 30 years spent in the academic world'.[2]

As a scholar at Trinity, Polkinghorne had rooms in the College from the time he was admitted in 1949. His fellow mathematics students included Michael –later Sir Michael– Atiyah, (a future President of the Royal Society and Master of Trinity, who would also be Polkinghorne's best man at his wedding), and James Mackay, (a future Lord Chancellor). His first supervisor, (appointed by the College to provide informal weekly teaching, often one-to-one), was Nicholas Kemmer, a Russian-born nuclear physicist, who played an important role in the UK's nuclear programme. In his third year, Polkinghorne was able to concentrate on aspects of quantum physics, (which investigates the nature of the particles that make up matter and of the forces with which they interact). He attended lectures by Paul Dirac, the Lucasian Professor of Mathematics at Cambridge, who has been regarded as one of the most significant physicists of the 20th century, and on a par with Newton, Maxwell and Einstein.[3,4] (He shared the 1933 Nobel Prize in Physics, and predicted the existence of antimatter).[3] Dirac was considered to be an unusual character; Einstein writes: 'I don't understand Dirac at all',[3] however, Polkinghorne reports that:

'...so profound was the material, and so closely structured was the argument, that one was carried along enthralled by the experience. Listening to the mathematical tale unfolded by Dirac was "as satisfying and seemingly inevitable as the development of a Bach fugue" '.[2]

Another inspiring encounter, which would have a major influence on Polkinghorne's life, occurred during his first Sunday as a student, when he went to Holy Trinity Church, Cambridge, to hear a sermon organised by the Cambridge Inter-Collegiate Christian Union (CICCU):

'The preacher was the Revd L.F.E.Wilkinson...We were urged not to miss our opportunity, that very evening, to offer our lives to Christ...and we were invited to come to the front of the church to signify that we had done so. A crowd did come forward, and I was among them. The words of the sermon had powerfully impressed me. I had continued my communicant Christian practice while in the Army, but some other aspects of life away from home had got slacker- not very dramatically so, just things like some bad language and occasionally a pint or two more of beer than would have been prudent...At the time I would have counted that evening as being the moment of my definite Christian conversion... but I would now see it in terms of its being a significant further step in my Christian life, rather than its initiation, for I see that life as already having been begun in the setting of my Christian home'.[2] Polkinghorne also notes a further landmark of his undergraduate days:

'meeting a student from Girton College, Ruth Martin, who was later to become my wife...Marriage still lay some years ahead, but the idea began to form in the back of my mind well before it could seem to be a practical possibility'.[2]

After graduating B.A. in 1952, in the prestigious position of Senior Wrangler, (the top-scoring undergraduate in mathematics), Polkinghorne began work on a PhD in theoretical elementary particle physics, initially supervised by Kemmer. However, the first year proved: 'The most miserable year of my life...I had achieved nothing'.[2] But, in his second year, he submitted some of his work, (which involved a basis for further research into the behavior of elementary particles), in a successful application for a Trinity College Research Fellowship. (One of the other Research Fellowships that year was awarded to Michael Atiyah). Also in this year, Kemmer left Cambridge for a professorship in Edinburgh, and was replaced as Polkinghorne's supervisor by Abdus Salem, who would share the 1979 Nobel Prize for Physics.

The income from his fellowship, although only guaranteed for four years, allowed Polkinghorne and Ruth to get married. The ceremony took place in March 1955, at the church of St James the Great, Friern Barnet, followed by a honeymoon on the Isles of Scilly. Later in the year he graduated PhD, and he and Ruth sailed from Liverpool to New York, as he had been awarded a postdoctoral Harkness fellowship for a year at the California Institute of Technology (Caltech) in Pasadena. They travelled to Pasadena by train, settled into an apartment and began to attend the local United Presbyterian Church, rather than the more distant Episcopalian Church, receiving:

'such a warm welcome...that we decided there and then to become honorary Presbyterians during our stay in Pasadena.'[2] At Caltech, Polkinghorne worked with Murray Gell-Mann, an outstanding theoretical physicist, who would win the 1969 Nobel Prize for Physics, for introducing the term 'quark' and for his work on the quark structure of matter:

'My nine months spent in interacting with him were a transformative experience for me, through which I began to grasp something more about the nature of research in theoretical physics...Many years later, Murray and his wife visited us in the President's Lodge in Queens' College...what seemed to be the high point of the visit came when he spotted an Edwardian collection of stuffed birds, mounted in a glass dome. His eyes lit up as he rushed over to identify all those highly coloured specimens from South America'.[2] Before the end of the year, Polkinghorne had received an offer from Kemmer of a lectureship at the Institute of Theoretical Physics in Edinburgh, where he would spend the next two years.

In 1958, Polkinghorne was invited back to Cambridge, where he would spend the rest of his academic career, becoming Reader in 1965 and, in 1968, the first holder of a newly-established professorship of Mathematical Physics. Also on his return to Cambridge, he became a teaching fellow of Trinity, which involved regular supervision of undergraduates. He recalls two particular students, Martin Rees, (later Sir Martin, Master of Trinity and President of the Royal Society), and Brian Josephson, who shared the Nobel Prize in Physics in 1973 for his work on superconductivity. Polkinghorne remembers:

'Josephson had got a Scholarship to Trinity...he was still unusually young. Perhaps because of this, he was a very quiet student...when I came to write my end-of-term report on him, I did not feel at all sure what to say. I settled for something to the effect that he was an absolute wizard at technique, but I was uncertain about inititive and originality. Within a few years, Josephson had become a Nobel lauteate! I find it a useful spiritual exercise occasionally to recall this spectacular error of judgement'.[2] (In later years, Josephson:

'expressed support for topics such as parapsychology, water memory and cold fusion, which has made him the focus of criticism from fellow scientists').[5]

Polkinghorne's 21 years as a Cambridge academic involved regular visits to the US, particularly to Princeton, Berkeley and Stanford Universities, and to the European Organization for Nuclear Research (CERN) laboratory at Geneva, where he became one of the UK representatives on the CERN Council. His biography, (prepared as one of a series of biographies of mathematicians by the School of Mathematics and Statistics at the University of St Andrew's, Scotland), summarises his scientific career:

'Polkinghorne's contributions to mathematical physics were truly outstanding. Let us look briefly at some of the papers he published. In 1954 he published "An identity for the S matrix for a finite time interval", "Renormalization of the transformation operators of quantum electrodynamics", and "Normal products of Heisenberg operators"...In 1955 Polkinghorne published several important papers:

"Temporally ordered graphs in quantum field theory", in which a graphical representation of the perturbation-theory expansions of quantum field theory is defined, in which the vertices- points at which the interaction operates- are given a definite order in time... also... "On the Feynman principle": The equivalence of the Feynman method of setting up a quantum field theory with the usual canonical formalism is here proved. This is not a new result, but a clear statement and proof of it is hard to find elsewhere in the literature. Also in 1955 he published "Temporarily ordered graphs and bound state equations" and "On the classification of fundamental particles". Then he published "General dispersion relations" in 1956 and "Causal products in quantum field theory" in the following year. Also in a joint paper in 1957 he published "Cauchy's problem in quantum field theory" which explores the relation between the classical and quantum versions of field theories. We give the titles of a few further papers which were fundamental in the development of a mathematical theory of elementary particles: "On Schwinger's variational principle"(1957), "On the strong interactions" (1957), "Causal amplitudes and the Yang-Feldman formalism" (1957)...As well as three papers on analytic properties in perturbation theory, he lectured on that topic at the 1961 Brandeis Summer Institute in Theoretical Physics and these lectures were published in the following year. Polkinghorne continued to publish a remarkable number of important papers...Polkinghorne's group at Cambridge continued developing the so-called "Cambridge program" of formulating and exploiting the concept of maximal analyticity. In 1980, (just after he had resigned from his professorship), he published "Models of high energy processes" which bring the earlier 1966 text (The Analytic S-Matrix) up to date, then set out the achievements of the programme over the following years. Delbourgo writes in a review: "The subject matter is one in which the author has made deep and lasting contributions, and it is easy to discern his expertise from the exposition" '.[1]

Polkinghorne also wrote several books about quantum theory and particle physics for the lay reader, including: 'The Particle Play' (1979), 'Rochester Roundabout' (1989), 'Quantum Theory: A very short introduction' (2002), and 'The Quantum World' (1984), which was the best-selling of these books: 'getting into six figures, including a Japanese translation that has turned out to do remarkably well'.[2]

A significant personal event in Polkinghorne's scientific career was his election as a fellow of the Royal Society (F.R.S.) in 1974:

'When I became a Cambridge professor in 1968, most of my scientific colleagues in the professoriate were FRSs, and I naturally hoped I might join them in the not-too-distant future. In actual fact, it took somewhat longer for this to happen than I had hoped, for it was not until 1974 that I attained this recognition. (It is possible that matters were hindered by a degree of fractionalism then present in the UK particle physics community...)...the ambition to be an FRS was a potent and disturbing element in my scientific life for a good number of years. If you had put to me some curious scheme by which my election would have been assisted by the murder of my grandmother, I would certainly have declined, but there would have been a perceptible pause for mental struggle before I did so'.[2]

The Polkinghornes' first child, Peter, had been born in 1957, in Edinburgh, and two more children were born in Cambridge: Isobel in 1959 and Michael in 1963. Eventually there would be nine grandchildren. Polkinghorne recalls:

'Our life in Cambridge in the 1960s and 1970s followed a pattern that was common for the families of dons at that time. Ruth did not have a job, but she devoted herself to the home and family full-time. Two evenings a week I did my college supervision teaching, staying on to dine in Hall afterwards...At the time all this seemed just the natural rhythm of life, but looking back on it now I can see that it made life pretty easy for the husband and that the present-day style of a greater sharing of parental and domestic tasks has much to be said for it'.[2]

A dramatic career change occurred in 1979, when Polkinghorne resigned his professorship and began training to become a priest in the Church of England. But this was not due to disillusionment with his subject:

'I simply felt that I had done my little bit for particle theory and the time had come to do something else...I was a member of the Science Research Council... I was about to become Chairman of SRC's Nuclear Physics Board (during 1978-79)...I had accumulated a lot of experience of academic policy-making... However, as I considered my future, praying about it and talking with Ruth, my mind turned in the quite different direction of seeking to enter the ordained ministry of the Church of England. The most fundamental reason for thinking about such an unconventional move was simply that Christianity has always been central to my life'.[2]

Polkinghorne made this decision in 1977, two years before resigning his University appointment and, in the same year, was accepted for training for the ministry afrer a selection conference in Sheffield. He then informed his children and his departmental colleagues:

'I remember vividly the astonished silence that followed my announcement'[2] and, after a further 18 months to wind up his academic responsibilities, he began his training at Westcott House in Cambridge, while Ruth also embarked on a career change, starting a three-year nursing training.

During his two years at Westcott House, Polkinghorne recalls:

'Worshipping day by day in its simple but beautiful chapel also taught me what I believe was the most important lesson of my training, the value of the Daily Office, that regular recitation of Morning and Evening Prayer which brings with it the connected reading of scripture and a continuous engagement with the spiritual force of the Psalms as they are read in course (that is, in sequence)'.[2] While he was at Westcott House he retained his fellowship of Trinity and continued providing supervisions in mathematical physics.

Polkinghorne was ordained deacon in Ely Cathedral in June 1981, by the Bishop of Ely, Peter Walker:

'We carried over our arms our white stoles, which after the bishop had laid hands on us in the name of the God and the Church, we would wear "deaconwise", that is, over the left shoulder and tied on the right at the waist...We had been told that we should wear our clerical collars for the first time as we went to the ordination service...Somehow the adoption of this clerical dress code...seemed at the time the most powerful symbol of irreversible change'.[2] As Ruth had not yet completed her nursing training, Polkinghorne spent the next year in Cambridge as a part-time non-stipendiary curate at the parish of St Andrew's, Chesterton. This involved the usual range of duties; parish visiting, preaching and assisting in the Sunday services. A less welcome task was 'crem duty'; this involved a rota system for the crematorium, which he felt was: 'disastrous pastorally', as most of the funerals there were taken by a duty clergyman, who did not know the deceased and had not met the families. Polkinghorne remembers:

'later in my parish ministry, the funerals that I took were on a much more personal basis...It may seem odd to say so, but when eventually I became an academic clergyman...I missed this form of ministry. It gave you the privilege of being with people at a significant and often difficult moment in their lives. The Christian hope of a destiny beyond death, given us by the everlasting faithfulness of God manifested in the resurrection of Christ, is a message that one can seek to share...'.[2]

Polkinghorne was due to be ordained priest at the end of his first year as a deacon:

'an event to which I had been looking forward with eagerness, since I greatly valued the prospect of being given the privilege of presiding at the Eucharist on behalf of the gathered company of believers'.[2] This became a personal occasion, held at Trinity by permission of Bishop Walker, as it was presided over by Bishop John Robinson, who was then a friend and Dean of Trinity. (Robinson had been Bishop of Woolwich until becoming Dean of Chapel at Trinity in 1969. His controversial book 'Honest to God' published in 1963 had rejected the traditional idea of God 'out there', as a kind of 'cosmic supremo', proposing a reinterpretation of God as 'love' and the 'ground of all being').[6] Polkinghorne recalls:

'It was a very happy day for me, for my family and, I believe, for the Christian community in Trinity. I was particularly glad to have John Robinson as my ordaining bishop, as we had become good friends...I loved John for his humanity and faithfulness. He was a man of deep Christian commitment, and the caricature of him as someone on the outskirts of the faith was a mere media image...John was, in fact, the most unreconciled mixture of the instinctively traditional...and the intuitively radical that I have ever encountered'.[2]

The Polkinghornes left Cambridge in 1982, the year Michael left school and Ruth qualified as a nurse, and his next two years were spent as curate at the parish of St Michael and All Angels, Windmill Hill, Bedminster, south Bristol. He enjoyed his time there, gaining experience in the sometimes challenging tasks of taking weddings and performing baptisms, while Ruth worked at the Bristol General Hospital. However, during this time he became seriously ill and required three episodes of abdominal surgery.

Towards the end of his time in Bristol, Polkinghorne received an invitation to become vicar of Blean, a large village a few miles from Canterbury. (He had applied to succeed Robinson as Dean of Trinity in 1983, but was not appointed). The initial meetings with the parish representatives went well, and he accepted the living of 'Vicar in the Blean', whose church's dedication, rare in England, is to St Cosmas, (although in Blean this is idiocyncratically spelt 'Cosmus'), and St Damian, who were 3rd century arab physicians and Christian martyrs. His diocesan bishop was the Archbishop of Canterbury, Robert Runcie, who attended Polkinghorne's induction to the parish in 1984. Recalling his two years at Blean, Polkinghorne came to value: 'a low-key but authentic healing ministry', which had been started by his predecessor and took place once a month:

'People were invited to come and kneel at the altar rails to seek healing by receiving the laying-on of hands, administered alternately by the vicar and by a lay assistant who had been licensed for that purpose by the bishop...accompanied by the repitition of a simple prayer seeking the healing power of the Holy Spirit...In preparatory teaching it had been emphasized that healing is a search for wholeness, which may be given in many ways, ranging from physical recovery to the acceptance of what was happening, including possibly accepting the approach of death'.[2] The Polkinghornes soon settled into village life; Ruth worked part-time as a nurse at the local geriatric hospital and joined the Women's

Institute, while her husband became a member of the Gardeners' Club and a regular visitor at the Pensioners' Club. In addition to his many parish duties, Polkinghorne began writing about science and religion, which would lead to a series of publications, while the University of Kent made him an honorary professor of physics. However this rural idyll, (albeit accompanied by a wish that he could develop his academic interests), was challenged by a 'phone call from a friend at Trinity Hall, Cambridge, informing him that the College would welcome his application to be their Dean of Chapel. Although he was ambivalent about leaving his parish after such a short time, he went for an interview, was offered the job and, after further indecision and discussions, he accepted the post. This involved responsibility for the worship of the College chapel, pastoral care within the College, and acting as the College's director of studies in theology.

After their return to Cambridge after just over four years, the Polkinghornes relocated to the north of the city. As he had become a fellow of Trinity Hall, he had to give up his fellowship at Trinity, but he found that Trinity Hall also took their food seriously! One memorable occasion duing his three years at Trinity Hall was a Roman Catholic Mass held in the College Chapel– the first since the Reformation- to mark the occasion that the Pope was to 'beatify' 40 English martyrs executed in the time of Elizabeth I, one of whom had studied at Trinity Hall. During this time, he continued his writing on science and religion, producing two books, one of which: 'Science and Providence', was dedicated to the Master, fellows and scholars of Trinity Hall. Also during his time at Trinity Hall, he began serving on government committees which were concerned with health and ethics. The first of these followed a 'phone call from the Deputy Chief Medical Officer, who asked him to chair a committee in 1988-89 to review the code of practice for the use of foetal tissue. The resulting proposals were accepted by the Government, and his contribution would lead to further governmental requests.

Polkinghorne was: 'very content' at Trinity Hall, but providence was about to complicate his life once again, when he received a 'phone call asking if he would like to be considered as the next President of Queens'. Although he was uncertain whether such a move would be right for him, he duly accepted an invitation to dine and meet the Queens' fellows and, eventually, he was offered the job. But this was at a time when the College's Governing Body was considering the issue of whether double rooms, with two undergraduates sharing, could become mixed-sex, and as he felt that mixed sharing would:

'give public and institutional endorsement of a moral position with which I would not feel it right to be associated', he stated that he would not be able to accept the Presidency if mixed sharing became College policy. But as the subsequent discussions did not endorse this change, Polkinghorne became President of Queens' in 1989, following the resignation of Ronald Oxburgh. The College 'Record' duly notes:

'The Governing Body is pleased to announce that they have elected The Revd Dr John Charlton Polkinghorne, M.A., PhD., Sc.D., F.R.S., to be President of Queens' in succession to Professor Oxburgh. John Polkinghorne was educated at the Perse School and Trinity College, Cambridge. After a distinguished student career and a Fellowship at the California Institute of Technology, he became a Lecturer at the University of Edinburgh. He returned to a Fellowship at Trinity and a University Lectureship in 1958, and was subsequently Reader and, in 1968, elected Professor of Mathematical Physics. He became a Fellow of the Royal Society in 1974. During that time he was a member of the General Board of the University and served on a number of national committees, becoming Chairman of the Science Board of the Science and Engineering Research Council. In 1979 he resigned his Chair to enter Westcott House and was ordained priest in 1982...Mrs Polkinghorne is a Girtonian mathematician who subsequently trained as a nurse...we wish them every success in the special role they will have in our College'.[7]

He makes his first contribution to the College 'Record' in the following year:

'My Cambridge life has been a slow drift upstream from Trinity... through Trinity Hall to Queens'. As my wife, Ruth, and

I have settled into the splendid President's Lodge we have been able to say with the Psalmist "The lines have fallen to me in pleasant places: yea, I have a goodly heritage". That is certainly true for the College too in relation to buildings, enriched as we are by the provision of past centuries and by the present generosity of Sir Humphrey Cripps...let me express my thanks for the warm welcome I have received and my confidence in the future of the College of which we are all members'.[8] In the following year he notes:

'I spent the Easter Term 1990 on sabbatical leave in the United States, visiting and lecturing at institutions concerned with the interaction of science and theology...the arrangements had been made and the obligations undertaken when I was still the Dean of Trinity Hall, and the Fellows here kindly let me honour them. I was of course, introduced to people as the President of Queens'...I explained that I was not President in a higher executive sense; rather I was a kind of constitutional monarch- albeit of an eighteenth century rather than twentieth century kind for I do not see my role as purely decorative and symbolic, but believe myself to have responsibilities and even modest influence. I was caused to reflect on how fortunate we are that in a curiously English, happenstance sort of way, it has come about that we are the inheritors of the college system, breaking down a large university into convivial academic communities in which authority and opportunity are widely shared...A college is a kind of extended academic family in which all its members matter'.[9] In subsequent years he commented in the 'Record' upon the abolition of the division between universities and polytechnics, the considerable expansion of student numbers, the increasing specialisation of knowledge, the financial pressures on universities, and the increasing pressure for accountability. As well supporting the college system, he defended the value of all forms of learning:

'A particle physicist was once asked by a Senator what his work would do for the defence of the United States. Nothing he said, but it will help to make it worth defending'.[10] In 1993, he notes:

'The immensely generous benefactions which Queens' has received from the Cripps Foundation found a fitting recognition in June when our Patroness, the Queen Mother, graciously unveiled a plaque in Lyon Court in the presence of Sir Humphrey and Lady Cripps and Mr Edward Cripps.'.[11]

Early in his Presidency, Polkinghorne had been asked to give the Gifford Lectures at Edinburgh University for the year 1993-94. These involved giving a series of lectures established in 1887 by Lord Gifford to: 'promote and diffuse the study of natural theology in the widest sense of the term- in other words, the knowledge of God'.[12] Polkinghorne recalls:

'I chose to concentrate nine out of my ten lectures on the discussion and defence of clauses drawn from the Nicene Creed... The argument...was set out in precisely the manner of ... a search for well-motivated belief...After a careful sifting of the New Testament evidence, I find myself persuaded to accept the explanation offered by its writers, that God did indeed raise Jesus from the dead the first Easter Day, however counterintuitive such a belief might at first sight seem to be'.[2] The lectures were published in 1994, under the title, in the UK, of: 'Science and Christian Belief'.[2]

In 1994, Polkinghorne was asked to chair another Government committee, the Task Force to Review Services to Drug Misusers. This met during 1994-96; much evidence was taken, many institutions were visited, and reseach projects were set up. (A million pounds was allocated to the committee for research). The findings were able to demonstrate that, while relapse is a common feature, interventions brought benefits that justified investment, and 79 recommendations were made. Polkinghorne's governmental committee work also involved the ethics of embryo and stem cell use and, for six years, he was a member of the Human Genetics Advisory Commission, for which he chaired a joint working party, (with the Human Fertilisation and Embryology Authority), on cloning.

The Polkinghornes maintained a regular routine of College entertaining during his Presidency; on Saturdays, undergraduates came to breakfast in the Lodge- a dozen at a time, third year students came to lunch on Sundays, and dinner parties for colleagues, friends and visitors took place on Wednesdays. Also, Polkinghorne and Ruth were regular attenders at the College chapel; he recalls:

'This active association with the Christian community in Queens' was very important to me and it confirmed the conviction that I had been right to accept being President'.[2]

Polkinghorne retired as President of Queens' in 1996, aged 66 and his successor was installed on the 13th of January, 1997. He writes:

'This is the seventh and final letter I shall write as President of Queens'. I am immensely grateful for the privilege of serving in this office...My wife, Ruth and I are grateful for the friendship we have received and for the opportunity to live in what is surely one of the finest small great houses in England...A theme I have often touched on...is that the College is a community, in which everyone counts...It is imperative that we preserve the heritage from which we have all benefited, and that we resist to the uttermost those levelling-down forces at work today which threaten to turn Collegiate communities into mere halls of residence. The support of the wider Queens' community is vital to us if we are to fulfil our resolve to hand on intact to future generations what we have ourselves received'.[13]

Soon after retirement, feeling that he should be out of the way of his successor for a while, Polkinghorne travelled to the General Theological Seminary in New York, where he spent a term as a visiting professor and, on returning to Cambridge, he and Ruth became involved in the community of their local parish church. But he was not yet destined for an uneventful retirement as, after less than a year, he received a letter from the Prime Minister proposing to forward Polkinghorne's name to recommend the award of Knight Commander of the Order of the British Empire (K.B.E.). The future knight remembers:

'I was deeply gratified to be recognized in this way and, of course, I immediately signified that I wished to accept'.[2] However, the protocol surrounding this honour decrees that Anglican priests do not use the usual prefix of 'Sir', while, at the investiture, the

Queen does not give priests the usual tap on the shoulder with a sword, but places the order's star on the recipient's chest.

2002 would bring another prestigious award, the Templeton Prize, an annual award with substantial prize money, which is adjusted so that it exceeds that of a Nobel Prize. The recipient is someone:

'whose exemplary achievements advance Sir John Templeton's philanthropic vision: harnessing the power of the sciences to explore the deepest questions of the universe and humankind's place and purpose within it'.[14] (Sir John Templeton, who died in 2008, was a British- but American-born- investor, banker, fund manager and philanthropist, who, in 1999, was described as: 'arguably the greatest global stock picker of the century'.[15] He founded the Templeton Prize in 1972 and, from 2002 to 2008, it was called the 'Templeton Prize for Progress Toward Research or Discoveries about Spiritual Realities').[2,14] Polkinghorne was informed about his good fortune in January 2002, while attending a conference in Rome, in a 'phone call from Dr Jack Templeton, the President of the John Templeton Foundation. His citation notes:

'John C Polkinghorne is a mathematical physicist and Anglican priest whose treatment of theology as a natural science invigorated the search for interface between science and religion and made him a leading figure in this emerging field...his extensive writings and lectures have consistently applied scientific habits to Christianity, resulting in a modern and compelling, new exploration of the faith. His approach to the fundamentals of Christian orthodoxy creation, using the habits of a rigorous scientific mind have brought him international recognition as a unique voice for understanding the Bible as well as evolving doctrine'.[1] In May 2002, he received the award from the Duke of Edinburgh at Buckingham Palace, prior to a reception at the Oxford and Cambridge Club, but soon donated most of the considerable prize money to endow a Research Fellowship in Science and Theology at Queens'. The award was followed by a programme of lectures at English cathedrals organised by the Templeton Foundation; these included an event in Truro Cathedral, which his grandfather had helped to build.

Sadly, 2002 also bought the news that Ruth was suffering from a rare form of leukaemia and, although there were two years of remission, her symptoms returned, and she died in Addenbrooke's Hospital, Cambridge, in 2006. Polkinghorne recalls:

'Her funeral...was an occasion of thankfulness and hope. The large congregation, and the many kind and appreciative letters that we received were a great source of consolation...For the Christian, death is real, and it brings about a real separation from a much-loved companion, but it is not the ultimate reality, for that is the eternal faithfulness of God'.[2] The College 'Record' notes:

'She presided over the Lodge with a quiet dignity, a certain poise and a minumum of fuss. Nothing seemed to faze her- visits of royalty or foreign presidents, shy or difficult undergraduates, small grandchildren, grand receptions, more intimate parties. She was very much part of the life of the Chapel too- a strong Christian faith was the mainstay of her life'.[16]

The above account has not yet included many of Polkinghorne's various appointments, committees and publications. For ten years (1990-2000) he served as the Cambridge University's 'proctor' (delegate) to the General Synod of the Church of England, during which he supported the controversial decision to ordain women to the priesthood, causing him to miss a Governing Body meeting at Queens'. This appointment was followed by membership of the Church of England's Board for Social Responsibility, (chaired by the Bishop of Liverpool, David Sheppard), and Chairmanship of its Science, Medicine and Technology Committee. His meetings with David Sheppard also led to his service, during 1994-2005, as one of the Canon Theologians of Liverpool Cathedral; this involved one or two visits each year, taking part in talks and seminars, and preaching. Another cathedral appointment was as one of the 'Six Preachers' at Canterbury, during 1996-97. (The Six Preachers of Canterbury Cathedral were established in 1541 by Archbishop Thomas Cranmer, on the instructions of Henry VIII. Originally, they were required to preach 20 sermons a year in their own parishes, or in a church dependent on the Cathedral, as well as preaching in the Cathedral). This also involved occasional visits for discussions and preaching. In 1996-97, he delivered the Terry Lectures at Yale University, which had been established in 1905 to address religion in the light of science and philosophy. In 1999, he received an Humboldt Research Award, given to internationally renowned scientists and scholars, to promote and finance international research cooperation. (These are in the gift of the Alexander von Humboldt Foundation, which was established in Berlin in 1860 and re-established in 1953 by the Government of the Federal Republic of Germany). During 1989-95, he served on the Doctrine Commission of the Church of England and, from 1989 to 1998, on the Medical Ethics Committee of the British Medical Association. From 1972 to 1981 he was Chairman of the Governors of The Perse School. During 2002-04, Polkinghorne was the Founding President of the International Society for Science and Religion, which was formed after a four–day conference in Grenada, Spain, and he was one of the founders of the Society of Ordained Scientists. For 18 years he served as a member of the Governing Body of the Society for Promoting Christian Knowledge (SPCK). Also, he was awarded honorary degrees from several universities: Kent (1994), Exeter (1994), Leicester (1995), Durham (1999), Marquette (2003), and Hong Kong Baptist (2006). (The latter involved giving a public lecture and participating in an 'East-West Dialogue' with Yang Chen-Ning, a Nobel laureate in physics). He became an Honorary Fellow of several institutions: St Chad's College, Durham (1999); St Edmund's College, Cambridge (2002); Trinity Hall (1989); and Queens' (1996).

Polkinghorne wrote many books, most of which relate to science and religion, and some of his works have been translated into 18 languages. His books include: 'The Way the World Is: The Christian Perspective of a Scientist' (1984), 'One World: The interaction of science and theology' (1986), 'Science and Creation: The search for understanding' (1988), 'Science and Providence: God's interaction with the world' (1989), 'Reason and Reality: The relationship between science and religion' (1991), 'Science and Christian Belief' (titled 'The Faith of a Physicist' in North America) (1994), 'Quarks, Chaos and Christianity' (1994),

'Searching for truth: A scientist looks at the Bible' (1997), 'Belief in God in an Age of Science' (1998), 'Faith, Science and Understanding' (2000), 'Science and the Trinity: The Christian Encounter with Reality' (2004), 'Quantum Physics and Theology' (2007), 'Questions of Truth: Fiftyone Responses to Questions about God, Science and Belief' (2009), 'Science and Religion in Quest of Truth' (2011), and 'Encountering Scripture: A Scientist Explores the Bible'. (2011).[1,17] (However, Polkinghorne's writings on science and religion have come in for some criticism; one commentator thought that the use of The Royal Society's premises in connection with the launch of 'Questions of Truth...', was a: 'scandal', claiming that Polkinghorne had exploited his fellowship there to publicise a: 'weak, causuistical and tendentious pamphlet', and that Polkinghorne and others were eager to see: 'the credibility accorded to scientific research extended to religious perspectives through association').[18]

Polkinghorne's religious views are reflected in many published quotes:

'As a Christian believer I am, of course, a creationist in the proper sense of the term, for I believe that the mind and purpose of a divine Creator lie behind the fruitful history and remarkable order of the universe which science explores'.[17]

'...the immensely complex information-bearing pattern (memories character, etc) carried at any one time by the matter of my body...is the soul and, although it will dissolve with the decay of my body, it is a perfectly sensible hope that the faithful God will not allow it to be lost but will preserve it in the divine memory in order to restore its embodiment in the great divine act of resurrection...that...will have to be in a new form of "matter", not subject to the drift and decay of the matter of the world...The example and guarantee of this is Christ's resurrection, the seed event from which the new creation has already begun to grow. The tomb was empty precisely because the Lord's dead body had been transformed into the "matter" of his risen and glorious body. Our destiny is resurrection, not spiritual survival, because it is an essential aspect of human existence that we are embodied in some form...Part of the salvific process that awaits us will involve judgement and purgation...This will be painful, but it is a necessary part of our entering fully into reality...As we progressively encounter the divine reality, the life of heaven will be far from boring'.[19]

'Claims for the occurrence of miraculous events will have to be evaluated on a case-by-case basis...but the refusal to contemplate the possibility of revelatory disclosures of an unprecedented kind would be an unacceptable limitation...'.[20]

'I believe that God created this world, this creation, to be other than God's self and that it is allowed to be itself...space and time and matter are all linked together, so that the world is relational in that sense...the discovery of quantum theory...has brought about a number of changes in our thinking...there is a probabilistic character to physical process...Once two quantum entities interact with each other, they retain a very surprising and counterintuitive power to influence each other, however far they separate...the world is not simply objective...In some sense it is veiled from us...can we actually ask God for something?...It seems to me likely (for the world)...to be open to God to act within it. In other words, God's providential interaction with history is not ruled out by what we know about scientific process'.[21]

'God didn't produce a ready-made world. The Creator has done something cleverer than this, making a world able to make itself...There is much cloudy unpredictable process throughout the whole of the physical world. It is a coherent possibility that God interacts with the history of creation by means of "information input" into its open physical process'.[22]

'...a world allowed to make itself is better than a puppet theatre with a Cosmic Tyrant'.[18]

In 2007, Polkinghorne published his autobiography, and considering his own death, he writes:

'For the Christian, it will be the final act in this world of complete commitment into the hands of a faithful God and merciful Saviour'.[2]

But life would continue for many years and, the Queens' 'Record' in 2010 reports:

'At the beginning of the Academic Year the Fellowship had the great pleasure of celebrating the Revd Canon Dr John Polkinghorne's 80th birthday. He and his three children were guests of honour at the termly Fellows' Dinner'.[23] The 'Record' also noted that he had been awarded the honorary degree of Doctor of Divinity by the General Theological Seminary in New York City, and had published a new book, 'Encountering Scripture'.

Polkinghorne's written legacy comprises 34 books; 26 concern science and religion, the last being (with Patrick Miles): 'What Can We Hope For? Dialogues about the future', published in 2019.

Polkinghorne died on the 9th of March, 2021.

References

1. John Charlton Polkinghorne. In: MacTutor History of Mathematics Archive. School of Mathematics and Statistics. University of St Andrew's Scotland. Online. 2020.
2. Polkinghorne, J. From Physicist to Priest. An Autobiography. Society for Promoting Christian Knowledge. London. 2007.
3. Paul Dirac. Wikipedia. Online. 2020.
4. Dirac equation. Wikipedia. Online. 2020.
5. Brian Josephson. Wikipedia. Online. 2020.
6. John Robinson (Bishop of Woolwich). Wikipedia. Online. 2020.
7. The Record. 1989. Queens' College, Cambridge. Online. 2020.
8. The Record. 1990. Queens' College, Cambridge. Online. 2020.
9. The Record. 1991. Queens' College, Cambridge. Online. 2020.
10. The Record. 1992. Queens' College, Cambridge. Online. 2020.
11. The Record. 1993. Queens' College, Cambridge. Online. 2020.
12. Gifford Lectures. Wikipedia. Online. 2020.

13. The Record. 1996. Queens' College, Cambridge. Online. 2020.
14. Templeton Prize. Wikipedia. Online. 2020.
15. John Templeton. Wikipedia. Online. 2020.
16. The Record. 2007. Queens' College, Cambridge. Online. 2020.
17. John Polkinghorne. RationalWiki. Online. 2020.
18. John Polkinghorne. Wikipedia. Online. 2020.
19. Polkinghorne, J. A Destiny beyond death: Heaven. The Society of Saint Francis. Online. 2020.
20. John C Polkinghorne. Goodreads. Quotes. Online. 2020.
21. Divine action: an interview with John Polkinghorne. CrossCurrents. Online. 2020.
22. John Polkinghorne. Wikiquote. Online. 2020.
23. The Record. 2011. Queens' College, Cambridge. Online. 2020.

CHAPTER 39

John Leonard Eatwell, (Lord Eatwell). President 1997-2020.

Summary.

John Leonard Eatwell was born in 1945 and educated at Headlands Grammar School, Swindon, Wiltshire. He was admitted to Queens' in 1964, graduating B.A. in the economics tripos, with first class honours, in 1967. He then attended Harvard University, on a Kennedy Scholarship, where he would be awarded a PhD. Subsequently, he was a research fellow at Queens', before transferring to Trinity College, Cambridge, as a fellow and director of studies in economics. He then became Assistant Lecturer, then Lecturer, in economics at Cambridge, where he would develop a worldwide reputation.

In 1985, he became chief economic adviser to Neil Kinnock, then leader of the Labour Party and, in 1992, he was elevated to the House of Lords as Baron Eatwell of Stratton St Margaret in the County of Wiltshire. In 1988, he was a co-founder, with Clive (later Lord) Hollick, of the New Labour 'think tank': 'The Institute for Public Policy Research'.

He was elected President of Queens' in 1997 and, in 2003, became Professor of Financial Policy at Cambridge. At this time he was also Director of 'The Cambridge Endowment for Research in Finance' (CERF).

He had married Hélène Sappain in 1970; they would have three children. In 2003, after the ending of his first marriage, Eatwell announced his engagement to the Hon. Mrs Susan Digby:

'We are to be married in July. Suzi is a musician. She is a choral conductor and also runs her own music education charity, the Voices Foundation, that promotes the teaching of singing in primary schools'.

As well as serving as President for 23 years, Eatwell produced an acclaimed body of published work in economics and was an active member of the House of Lords. Also, he was on the boards of many companies and of a variety of organisations, including the Royal Opera House, the Royal Ballet School and the British Library. At Queens', he initiated many projects and academic developments, as noted in the College 'Record' in 2020:

'The Fellows, the students, the staff and the alumni, and indeed the wider University, will all wish to pay tribute to the President for all he has accomplished and the way he has led and guided the College through almost a quarter of a century of change and success...A marker (in slate and York stone...) celebrating his Presidency has been unveiled in the centre of the Round...after the unveiling ceremony Professor Weber spoke of the President's involvement with many major projects during his tenure of office and of the many ways in which he has built and enriched our infrastructure, society and academic aims...this marker, together with the newly-endowed John Eatwell Fellowship, are most fitting ways to mark his Presidency'.

Sadly, the last months of his Presidency were blighted by the Covid pandemic. His successor, Dr Mohamed El-Erian, took over the reins of the Presidency on the 1st of October, 2020.

Timeline.

1945.	Born on the 2nd of February, at Swindon, Wiltshire.
1964.	Admitted to Queens'.
1967.	B.A. .
1967-70.	Kennedy Scholar at Harvard University.
1968-69.	Teaching Fellow, Harvard.
1969-70.	Research fellow at Queens'.
1970.	Marries Hélène Seppain.
1970-96.	Fellow and director of studies in economics, Trinity College, Cambridge.
1970.	Birth of son, Nikolai.

1971. M.A. .
1973. Birth of son, Vladimir.
1975. PhD (Harvard).
1975-77. Assistant Lecturer in economics, University of Cambridge.
1977. Lecturer in economics, University of Cambridge.
1978. Birth of daughter, Tatyana.
1985-92. Chief economic adviser to Neil Kinnock, Leader of the Labour Party.
1988-97. A founder (with Clive Hollick- later Lord Hollick) of the London-based 'think tank': 'The Institute for Public Policy Research'. (He would also serve as Secretary, 1988-97, and Chairman, 1997-2001).
1992. Appointed to the House of Lords as Baron Eatwell of Stratton St Margaret in the County of Wiltshire.
1997. Elected President of Queens' after the retirement of John Polkinghorne.
1997. Visit of Queen Elizabeth, the Queen Mother, to Queens' in May. Initiation of the 'Queens' 550' Celebrations and Appeal, which will mark the 550th anniversary of the College in 1998.
1998. Visit to Queens', on the 9th of June, by Queen Elizabeth, the Queen Mother, (her final visit). Chairman of the Royal Ballet.
1998-2006. Board member, Royal Opera House Covent Garden Foundation.
2000. Attends the parade in London, on the 19th of July, to mark the 100th birthday of Queen Elizabeth, the Queen Mother.
2002. Death of Queen Elizabeth the Queen Mother, Patroness of Queens'.
2003. The Queen is: 'pleased to become Patroness of Queens' College'. Professor of Financial Policy at the Judge Institute of Management Studies, (subsequently named the University of Cambridge Judge Business School).
2003-06. Board member, Royal Ballet School.
2005. Visit of Her Majesty the Queen, (her first visit as Patroness), and the Duke of Edinburgh.
2006. Marries Mrs Suzi Digby.

2009. Lord and Lady Eatwell, (with other members of Queens'), attend the opening ceremony, on the 20th of March, of an exhibition in Angers, France, to mark the 600th anniversary of the birth of King René, the father of Queen Margaret of Anjou, foundress of Queens'.

2011. Lord and Lady Eatwell appointed for a semester to the faculty of the University of Southern California.

2012. The cohort of undergraduates is the first to pay annual University fees. Reaches University retirement age. Retires from professorship and as Director of the Cambridge Endowmemt for Research in Finance, but is asked to continue as President of Queens'.

2013. A Deputy Vice-Chancellor of Cambridge University.

2014. As from March, sits in the House of Lords as a non-affiliated peer. Chair of the 'Advisory Board of the Institute for Policy Research' (IPR) at the University of Bath.

2019. Visit of Her Majesty the Queen, the Patroness, to Queens' on the 9th of July.

2020. In March, the Corona virus pandemic initiates restrictive measures. On the 20th of May, Eatwell announces that £2.5 million has been raised to fund the John Eatwell Fellowship. Retires as President of Queens' on the 30th of September.

Eminent and highly-influential economist. Active member of the House of Lords. Public servant. Long-serving and dedicated President of Queens'.

John Leonard Eatwell was born on the 2nd of February, 1945, the son of Harold Jack Eatwell, of Swindon, Wiltshire, (who died in 1998), and Mary Tucker, (who died in 1987).[1,2] He was educated at Headlands Grammar School, which had been formed in 1943 as a selective mixed school for those who passed their 'eleven plus' exam, but became a non-selective 'comprehensive' school in 1964. He was admitted to Queens' in 1964, and graduated B.A. in 1967, having obtained first class honours in the economics tripos.

He then went to the U.S.A. as a Kennedy Scholar at Harvard University, and became a teaching fellow there during 1968-69.

(Kennedy Scholarships had been set up for exceptional students in 1964 as part of a memorial to President Kennedy; British post-graduate students are selected to study at Harvard or the Massachusetts Institute of Technology).

Eatwell came back to Queens' as a research fellow during 1969-70, and then transferred to Trinity College, Cambridge, as a fellow and director of studies in economics. He became a University Assistant Lecturer in economics at Cambridge in 1975, and a Lecturer in 1977. He was awarded his PhD from Harvard in 1975.[2]

On the 24th of April 1970, Eatwell married Hélène Seppain, daughter of Georges Seppain of Marly-le-Roi, France. (They would have three children: Nikolai, born in 1970 and a future partner at the law firm Clifford Chance; Vladimir, born in 1973 and a future software developer; and Tatyana, born in 1978 and a future barrister).[1]

1985 was a pivotal year for Eatwell's career, when he became chief economic adviser to Neil Kinnock, the leader of the Labour Party, which culminated in his elevation to the House of Lords in 1992. In 1988 he was a co-founder, with Clive (later Lord) Hollick of the New Labour 'think tank': the 'Institute for Public Policy Research' (IPPR).[3] This is described (in 2020) as:

'a progressive think tank based in London…IPPR has offices in Newcastle, Manchester, and Edinburgh. Funding comes from trust and foundation grants, government support, and individual donors. The think tank aims to maintain…well-researched and clearly-argued policy analysis, reports, and publications; as well as a high media profile…'.[4] (For example, in September 2018, the think tank published 'Prosperity and justice: A plan for the new economy- The final report of the IPPR Commission on Economic Justice based on two years of research…').[4] In addition to his appointment as a foundation trustee of IPPR, (and a director until 2020), Eatwell served as Secretary during 1988-97, and Chair during 1997-2001. (Clive Hollick became Hambros Bank's youngest-ever director in 1973, was active in business and the media, and was a supporter and donor to the Labour Party. He became a life peer in 1991).[3]

Eatwell was ennobled on the 14th of July, 1992, as Baron Eatwell of Stratton St Margaret in the County of Wiltshire, and was an opposition spokesperson for the Treasury and Economic Affairs during 1992-93, and for Trade and Industry during 1992-96. Also, he was Principal Opposition Spokesperson for Treasury and Economic Affairs during 1993-97 [5] and, during 2010-13, he was again appointed as a Labour opposition spokesperson for the Treasury by the Labour leader Ed Milliband. From the 27th of March 2014, he has sat as a non-affiliated peer.[1] Also, he was a member of several House of Lords Committees: the EU Sub-Committee D, (1993-95); the Financial Services and Markets Joint Committee (1999, March-November); the Economic Affairs Committee (2008-2010); and the Consumer Insurance, Disclosure and Representations, Bill HL Committee, (2011, September-December).[6] He has voted against an equal number of electors per parliamentary constituency, against university tuition fees, against fewer MPs, and for more EU integration.[6]

Eatwell was elected as President of Queens' in 1997, after the retirement of John Polkinghorne. At this point, in addition to his wide-ranging public activities, he had made a significant contribution (which would continue) to the economics literature, with many books, chapters in books, and articles. His books have included: 'The New Palgrave: a dictionary of economics', (with Milgate, M., Newman, P.K., 1978); 'Keynes' economics and the theory of value and distribution' (with Milgate, M., 1983); 'Not Just Another Accession: The Political Economy of EU Enlargement to the East' (as co-author, 1987); 'The New Palgrave: Allocation, information, and markets', (with Milgate, M., Newman, P.K., 1989); 'The New Palgrave: capital theory', (with Milgate, M., Newman, P.K., 1990); 'The New Palgrave dictionary of money & finance', (with Milgate, M., Newman, P.K., 1992); 'Global unemployment: loss of jobs in the '90s', (1996); and 'Global Finance at Risk: the Case for International Regulation', (with Lance Taylor, 2000).

The late Ajit Singh, Professor of Economics at Cambridge University and a fellow of Queens', writes in the 1997 College 'Record':

'In selecting Lord Eatwell as President, the Fellowship has chosen one of the outstanding Queens' men of his generation. He had a brilliant academic record, both at Cambridge (Double First in the Economics Tripos. University's Wrenbury Scholarship in Political Economy) and later at Harvard (Kennedy Scholarship) where he did his PhD. He was a Research Fellow at Queens' before moving to a Fellowship at Trinity, and subsequently to a University Lectureship...He is a highly distinguished economist with a worldwide reputation. The monumental four volume work "The New Palgrave Dictionary of Economic Thought" and its three-volume sequel "The New Palgrave Dictionary of Money and Finance", of which he has been the principal architect, have won him the gratitude of the economics profession. The former publication was included in The Times list of the hundred most influential works published since 1950; the latter won Columbia University's Eccles Prize for Excellence in Economic Writing in 1993. Lord Eatwell has taught at Harvard University, the New School for Social Research, the University of Amsterdam and Columbia University among others...His successful BBC television series "Whatever Happened To Britain?", in the early 1980s, represented a landmark in bringing the profession's ideas to a wide public audience...A glance through Hansard reveals his contributions to the deliberations of the Lords to be no less extensive and lively than those of Lord Kaldor- himself something of a legend in that arena. (Nicholas Kaldor had become Professor of Economics at Cambridge University in 1966).

Lord Eatwell is a man of enormous energy, ability, dedication and resourcefulness...He is also deeply involved with a wide range of other public organisations. He is the Chairman of Crusaid, the national fundraiser for AIDS. In the cultural sphere, he is a Director of the Arts Theatre Trust in Cambridge, and has been Chair of the Board of the Directors of the Extemporary Dance Theatre and Governor of the Contemporary Dance Trust...At a personal level... we...worked together for a number of years as economic advisors to the Government of Mexico...The College is indeed lucky to have him as its leader in a period of growing crisis and potentially far-reaching changes in the system of higher education in this country'.[7]

In his first contribution to the College's 'Record' as President, Eatwell looks forward to the following year, 1998, which will mark the 'Queens' 550 Celebrations and Appeal', planned to mark the College's 550th anniversary of its foundation in 1448:

'...The £5.5 million which is the fundraising target of Queens' 550 will help secure the future of financial support for undergraduates and graduate students. It will fund the College's firm commitment that undergraduate entry to Queens' should be on the basis of ability and potential, not on the basis of financial means...The College faces a number of major challenges over the next few years...I am confident that with the support of the whole College, whether resident or non-resident members, we will meet the challenges and both preserve and develop this unique community...First, there is the challenge to undergraduate funding...Second, there is the necessity to attract and maintain a fellowship of the highest quality...Third, the College must keep abreast of changes in the University. Thirty years ago only about 10% of the student body were graduate students. Now the University is approaching 30%...there is the necessity to provide a new range of accomodation and services geared to a graduate student population...'.[7]

The highlight of the Queens' 550 celebrations was a visit of Her Majesty Queen Elizabeth the Queen Mother on the 9th of June 1998, as described in the 'Record' by Dr Jonathan Holmes, fellow and Dean of Chapel:

'It was her third visit in six years- Her Majesty clearly enjoys coming to Queens' and does not take the title of Patroness lightly...Her Majesty arrived by helicopter at the Barton Road Sportsground...She was then driven to Queens', arriving at the Old Main Gate just before 12.15 p.m. Her first duty after meeting the President and Lady Eatwell and the Senior Fellow, Professor Ajit Singh, was to unveil a plaque on the wall opposite the Old Porters' Lodge to commemorate her visit and her fifty years as Patroness.

Old Court was packed with Fellows and undergraduates... but centre stage there stood a magnificent new rowing eight, presented by Mr John Burton, for the Women's First Boat...and the Queen Mother formally "unveiled" the boat, naming it "The Patroness". Her Majesty stopped to talk to several students... before proceeding...to Cloister Court. Here "A Midsummer Night's Dream"...was in rehearsal. The Queen Mother paused to watch for a short while and met the Director, Zoe Svenson, recalling a rehearsal of "As You Like It" on her visit in 1948... After greeting some of the children from the College Nursery Her Majesty retired into the President's Lodge for a rest....she soon re-emerged...Old Hall was packed for luncheon...Before and during the meal the College Musician and St Margaret Society members played in the Gallery...Scholars and exhibitioners and Q550 Key Members and their guests had been invited to join the Queen Mother in the President's Garden in the early afternoon... Her car was waiting beneath the Erasmus Building, but...she insisted on stopping to shake hands and chat with those who were waiting to see her on her way. In 1948 it was reported that "her interest had been so great" that she was over 20 minutes late in leaving- the same happened in 1998'.[8]

But in the same year, the President writes:

'Unfortunately the year has not been all fun. After much controversy the Government cut the funding for students at Cambridge colleges by a third. This cut in revenue will place a considerable burden on the finances of the College and on the students...That is why the Queens' 550 Appeal is so important... On a personal note, I must confess to being hugely proud to be President of Queens'...we, the Members of Queens', must all play our part in sustaining this remarkable institution'.[8] Financial worries continued and, in 2000, Eatwell reports: 'These are difficult times for the College'.[9] But he has a good excuse to raise the College's eyes to the blue skies above:

'Dr Michael Foale has been once more into space aboard the shuttle, Discovery, and, in a long "Extra-Vehicular Activity". effected major repairs and modifications to the Hubble telescope'.[9] (Colin Michael Foale, C.B.E., is a British-American former NASA astronaut who studied at Queens', receiving a first class honours degree in natural sciences in 1978. He still holds the cumulative time-in-space record for a UK citizen).[10]

The end of the year 2000 marked the formal end of the Q550 Appeal and Eatwell reports:

'At the time of writing the sum raised totals £4.6 million, somewhat short of the £5.5 million target, but of course, very welcome. These new resources will enable the College to make a real difference for students in financial difficulty and to enhance the quality of student life at Queens'.

Now is the time to look to the future...If Queens' is to participate in the growth of the University it will be in the growth of the number of graduate students...the College's first priority must be to improve facilities for them. At present...about 80 (are) at Owlstone Croft, a former nurses' home on the edge of Newnham...The College plans to develop the site into the centre for graduate life at Queens'...such a large-scale development will be a major challenge...It is my job over the next few years to ensure that Queens' has the resources to fulfil this ambition'.[11]

The College's Patroness celebrated her 100th birthday on the 4th of August 2000, and this was marked by a 100th birthday pageant in London on the 19th of July, 2000, attended by members of the royal family, military regiments and many civilian organisations, including Queens'. The Queen Mother arrived in a carriage, escorted by Prince Charles, and enjoyed the hour-long parade:

'When a remarkable Grand Lady celebrates her centenary it is only fitting that those who have received her gift of patronage should pay tribute. So it was that the President, Fellows, Students and Staff of Queens' College gathered to process before their Patroness, Queen Elizabeth the Queen Mother for the QM100 Parade. London awoke to a hot 19th July 2000 with the parade participants pouring into Horse Guards Parade for a rehearsal. They were to be drilled to mititary precision, perfect step and perfect timing...The Queens' "recruits" assembled in their "zone" ...Between rehearsals, the President's Housekeeper opened tempting picnic hampers, the past Dean, Brian Hebblethwaite, was absorbed in the latest Harry Potter book and the President, Fellows, Students and Staff waited in relaxed groups, finding uncommon opportunity to chat with each other...finally all was ready and the Parade began to move forward.

The Head Porter led in the President, the Fellows, Students and Staff to march past the Queen Mother as the airborne salute swooped in from above. There could be no doubt where Queens' was to be found, even amonst the thousands in the Parade. Proudly processing the Queens' flags and blades, their banners streamed out above the crowds. Truly a magnificent day'.[11]

In 2002, Eatwell announces another ambitious building project for Queens':

'a new, very attractive development opportunity has emerged (a brain wave of Dr. Robin Walker, the Junior Bursar). The roof of the Cripps Building has always looked as if the builders downed tools a couple of months before finishing the job...So why not tackle some of Queens' desperate accommodation problems by finishing the job and adding a fourth floor mansard roof? A period of feverish work...has produced an elegant design...Of course all this development costs money...'.[12]

Queen Elizabeth the Queen Mother died on the 30th of March, 2002, as Holmes recalls in the 'Record':

'As soon as news of the death of Her Majesty Queen Elizabeth, the Queen Mother, Patroness of Queens' for 53 years, reached the College on Saturday March 30th, the College flag was raised to half-mast. In addition the Great Gate in Old Court was draped inside and out with black hangings...The President, together with the Dean of Chapel, represented the College at the lying-in-state in Westminster Hall and happened by coincidence to be there when the Prince of Wales, his brothers and his cousin emerged to stand vigil over their grandmother's coffin. The President spoke of the Queen Mother's patronage and special associations with Queens' when the House of Lords met to pay tribute to her memory. The President was also allocated a ticket to the Funeral itself in Westminster Abbey and was accompanied by Mrs Jean Farrington, the longest-serving member of the College staff...Before she died she granted us the right to fly her personal standard on the Great Gate once a year in her memory. The standard was flown for the first time on the first day of Michaelmas Full Term, Tuesday October 8th 2002, and will be flown every year on that day. The President, Dr Callingham and Dr Holmes were present to see the standard raised at dawn'.[13] At the College's subsequent Memorial Service, the President gave the following address:

'Queen Elizabeth the Queen Mother had a very special relationship with this College, and this College had a very special relationship with her. From the very beginning, Queens' was "her" college, and she was "our" patroness- and both sides took a delight in their possession.

It was in 1948 that the Governing Body of Queens' College invited Queen Elizabeth to become patroness of the College, on the occasion of the 500th anniversary of the foundation. This invitation was stimulated by the Queen herself. In her speech in the Senate House in October of that year when she accepted the first degree that Cambridge University ever awarded to a woman, she referred to Queens' College with particular warmth.

The Governing Body took the hint- if hint it was- and so Queen Elizabeth became our fourth patroness. The first two were, of course, our foundresses, Margaret of Anjou, wife of Henry VI, and Elizabeth Woodville, wife of Edward IV. Our third patroness was Anne Neville, wife of Richard III. But from the Battle of Bosworth to 1948 Queens' College had no Patroness. And now we return to that state.

Our new Patroness more than made up for the hiatus. She had visited Queens' before becoming Patroness, and now she took to visiting the College regularly.

On the occasion of her 101st birthday, just before August, I met the Patroness during her birthday visit to the Royal Opera House...the lesson that we can draw from her life and from her association with this College, was that she took a positive view of everything...Queens' College was immensely proud of our Patroness. We will miss her very much'.[13]

However, in late February 2003, Eatwell received a letter from Sir Robin Janvin, the Queen's Private Secretary, informing him that:

'...following the sad death of Her Majesty The Queen Mother...I am delighted to inform you that Her Majesty The Queen would be pleased to become Patroness of Queens' College'. This was announced by the President on the 22nd of February, at the M.A. graduands lunch, when it was: 'received with great applause and acclaim'.[13]

In the President's annual report to the College in the 'Record' of 2003, he notes continuing building works, and the possible impact of the Government's White Paper on Higher Education:

'The important work on Old Hall is described elsewhere in this issue. I am enormously grateful to all those members of the College who have contributed to the funds necessary to return this Hall that we all love to its former glory. Of equal importance will be our medium term plan to add a further floor to the Cripps Building and to develop Owlstone Croft...there will be further growth of graduate education...Queens' intends to be part of this development...The development of Owlstone Croft into a modern graduate "hall" is the very centre of this endeavour.

The impact of the White Paper on Cambridge is likely to be considerable...we are increasing the size of our hardship funds and the range of available bursaries...Already, for someone who comes from a financially disadvantaged backgtound, Cambridge is the cheapest university in the country'.[13]

Also in 2003, the College learned that their President had been elected to a professorship, as described by Professor Ajit Singh:

'When Lord Eatwell was appointed as the President of the College I wrote to the Alumni to say that the appointment was good news, not only for Queens', but also for Cambridge and for the future of higher education in this country. I believe his recent appointment to the Chair of Financial Policy in the University is equally significant. This will give him an opportunity to conduct teaching and research on a subject which increasingly affects the daily lives of millions of people around the globe...Since he became President, Lord Eatwell's dedication and hard work to enhance the social, intellectual and cultural life of our community is widely acknowledged and greatly appreciated. The College rejoices in his achievement'.[13] At this time, Eatwell was also the Director of the 'Cambridge Endowment for Research in Finance' (CERF), established in 2001 at the University of Cambridge, which is:

'devoted to the furtherance of research and study into all aspects of finance, financial institutions, and financial markets, and their relationship with the performance of the economy'.[14]

In 2005, Queens' received its first visit from the Queen as Patroness:

'On the morning of Wednesday 8 June 2005 the College looked its finest...Frogmen who had been searching the river from motor launches that morning had found nothing more unusual than discarded champagne bottles...As midday approached Members of the College gathered in Old Court eagerly to await the arrival of Her Majesty Queen Elizabeth II, our Patroness.

As the Patroness and the Duke of Edinburgh entered into Old Court her standard was raised on the College flagpole. The Patroness...unveiled a plaque to commemorate her first visit as our Patroness...The newly-restored Old Hall was filled with Fellows, staff, students, Old Members and friends of the College... The Patroness seemed very genuinely to enjoy her visit...Lunch ended with a well-received speech by the President, and then the Patroness was further greeted by staff and students as her car departed from the Round'.[15]

After the ending of his first marriage, Eatwell announced his engagement in the following year:

'...in February I was delighted to announce my engagement to the Hon. Mrs Susan Digby. We are to be married in July. Suzi is a musician. She is a choral conductor and also runs her own music education charity, the Voices Foundation, that promotes the teaching of singing in primary schools. I know that she is greatly looking forward to meeting as many Members of the College as possible in the near futute- and encouraging you all to sing!'.[15]

In 2008, Eatwell could inform the Alumni that one of the main building developments during his tenure has been completed, but he flags up his next project:

'The year of the Scaffolding is over, and from the crysalis that enveloped the top of Cripps Court has emerged a beautiful new fourth floor...Now, it's on to the next major project, the Round. Members of the College will be familiar with my complaint that the centre of our College is a puddle-strewn car park. Now at last we are near to doing something about it, Architects have been working on a plan to enlarge the Porters' Lodge, create a cloister linking the Lodge to the entrance to Cripps Court, and landscape the Round...Then all we need to do is to raise the requisite funding![16] The same issue of the 'Record' lists some of Eatwell's recent activities:

'He has advised the government of Brazil and the Congressional Oversight Panel of the US Senate. He has also, with colleagues, written a report on risk management in the European Union for the European Parliament. He is a member of the Economic Affairs Committee of the House of Lords.'.[16]

In 2009, Lord and Lady Eatwell paid a memorable visit to Angers, Pays de la Loire, France, on the occasion of the six-hundreth anniverary of the birth of King René in 1409. (René, the father of Margaret of Anjou, the first foundress of Queens', was Duke of Anjou and Titular King of Sicily. As described by Holmes, he was:

'an extraordinary man, cultured, wise and popular. He spoke several languages, was versed in mathematics and jurisprudence, was an accomplished musician and composer, and a talented painter and poet...Towards the end of his life the French King annexed Anjou and René was forced to retreat to Aix-en-Provence, where he reigned as Count. He chose, however, to be buried in Angers, the capital city of his former Duchy'.[17] Part of the anniversary celebrations was an exhibition of paintings, sculptures and other artefacts in the restored Collegiate Church of St Martin in Angers. This included a section devoted to his daughter, Marguerite d'Anjou, who became Queen Margaret of Anjou, wife of King Henry VI:

'René managed eventually to negotiate the release of Margaret from the Tower of London (see Chapter 1), and she died in retirement in Anjou. She is buried with her parents in the crypt of Angers Cathedral...Lord and Lady Eatwell were invited to attend the opening ceremony of the exhibition and the Chapel Choir to perform at it. The Choir...sang...to a large and very appreciative audience of local dignitaries and invited guests in the lovely Plantagenet chancel of the church. The exhibition was inaugurated by M. Christophe Bechu, President of the Conseil Generale of the Department of Maine-et-Loire, who also welcomed the representatives of Queens' along with other visitors (who included a prince and some princesses, one of whom was a descendant of Le Roi René)...Lord Eatwell replied in impeccable French...The day following...the Chapel Choir also participated in an extraordinary and memorable service in the Cathedral Church of St Maurice in Angers. Before a chancel packed with dignitaries, including the Commander of the Order of St John of Malta... presided over by Monseigneur Delmas, Bishop of Angers... estimates of the total congregation exceeded 1200...the service concluded with a ceremony of blessing the Royal Tombs...During the solemn ceremony conducted by the Bishop with all the clergy, including Dr Holmes, magnificently (and unexpectedly) arrayed in some beautifully embroided Cathedral copes, the "Prayer of King Henry VI", set to music by Henry Ley, was performed for the first time at his wife's grave by the Choirs...The whole ceremony lasted more than two and a quarter hours!...It seemed particularly fitting for the President, the Dean of Chapel and younger members of the College to be present on such an occasion and so honour the memory of our foundress and her father'.[17]

In 2011, the 'Record' informs us that:

'The President, together with Dr Milgate, has written The Fall and Rise of Keynesian Economics, to be published later this year. He was asked to organise a symposium on "The future of international financial regulation" at the annual meeting of the American Economic Association in Denver. Continuing his work in practical financial regulation he has become a Financial Commissioner for Jersey'.[18] Also in 2011, the Eatwells joined the faculty of the University of Southern California for a term:

'Lord John Eatwell, a well-known British economist...and Lady Eatwell (known professionally as Suzi Digby), an acclaimed choral conductor and receipient of the Order of the British Empire for services to music education, have been appointed to the USC faculty for the fall semester...Lord and Lady Eatwell are dynamic leaders and educators in economics and music, respectively...They exemplify the relationship between knowledge and public service that we seek to foster at USC...Lord Eatwell will join the faculty of the USC Dornsife College of Letters, Arts and Sciences, where he will teach a graduate course in the Department of Economics on Classical Economic Theory and its Critics, and an undergraduate course in the School of International Relations... For the latter...he will invite six prominent political figures and experts to give guest lectures...Suzi Digby...will join the faculty of the USC Thornton School of Music, where she will teach an undergraduate course on English choral literature...we feel that she will quickly be recognised as a leader in the arts community of Los Angeles and work to position the Thornton School to better serve the artistic and educational programs of the city...During the last session of Parliament, Lord Eatwell served on the Economic Affairs Committee of the House of Lords, and is currently the opposition spokesperson for treasury within the House. He also is the adviser to several private equity firms and a trustee of the Institute for Public Policy Research...Digby is founder and principal of the Voices Foundation, a music education charity that works to establish sustainable music education programs in the U.K.'s elementary schools. In 1990, she was awarded a Winston Churchill Fellowship, which she used to travel and study...focussing on methods of choral training and music education. In 1993, she was appointed by Yehudi Menuhin to spearhead the U.K. branch of his MUS-E project (to encourage the teaching of the creative arts in primary schools), and in 1998 she launched Singing Schools, a five-year program in South Africa involving 70 schools in Soweto and Johannesburg. She is fellow of the Royal Society of Arts...and the acting director of music at Queens' College...'.[19]

In 2012, after noting that:

'at last the builders have moved into the Round, and the long-awaited refurbishment is under way', Eatwell reports that:

'The autumn was dominated for me by a non-collegiate event: my wife Suzi preparing and then conducting three remarkable performances of Bach's St Mathew Passion, with the Orchestra of the Age of Enlightenment, Sir Willard White as Christus, a wonderful supporting cast and a truly amazing young chorus.

The forthcoming production dominated the summer and the autumn. But it was worth it. The production was part of Suzi's Vocal Futures project, which aims to introduce young people to great classical music, often in unusual spaces (in this case a disused concrete laboratory just by Marylebone tube station)...I reach the Univerity retirement age this year and will stand down from my Professorship. Under our statutes I might have left Queens' too. But last Easter Term the Fellows did me the enormous honour of asking me to stay on as President for a further five years. I was delighted to accept...'.[20]

In 2013, the year in which the development of the Round was completed, Eatwell attended social and fundraising events for Queens' in Hong Kong, Mumbai and Los Angeles, as well as regular London events. On a personal level, Eatwell notes:

'this is the year in which I have been experiencing (partial) retirement. At the end of September I retired from my position as Professor of Financial Policy and Director of the Cambridge Endowment for Research in Finance. But I seem to be as busy as ever. This is primarily because I am determined to devote the next 5 years in placing the College on an even firmer footing, securing its independence into the future, and providing the resources that are needed to fulfil our ambitions.

Suzi has continued her usual whirlwind of choral work... amongst all her classical choral commitments, her most extraordinary experience was performing with Mick Jagger and the Rolling Stones before 25,000 fans at the O2 arena just before Christmas. This event somewhat overshadowed my various endeavours this year!'.[21] Also during this year, Eatwell accepted the invitation to become a University of Cambridge Deputy Vice-Chancellor.

In 2014, Eatwell was appointed Chair of the 'Advisory Board for the Institute for Policy Research' at the University of Bath. This had been established the previous year:

'to bridge the worlds of research, policy and professional practice and enable better collaboration with some of the major policy challenges faced on a local, national and international scale... through our Policy Fellowship Programmes, International

Visiting Fellows scheme, and postgraduate programmes including our Masters in Public Policy and Professional Doctorate in Policy Research and Practice'.[22]

Other appointments during his career have included a director of the Royal Opera House Covent Garden Foundation (1998-2006); Chairman of the British Library (2001-06); Chairman of the Royal Ballet; a director of the Royal Ballet School (2003-06); a Member of the Regulatory Decisions Committee of the Financial Services Authority (2001-06); member and Deputy Chairman of the Enforcement Committee of the Securities and Futures Authority, (1997-2002); and economic adviser to the Secretary of State for Agriculture. He has served on the boards of many companies including: Anglia Television Group (1994-98), ITV Broadcasting Ltd. (1994-2001), National Film Development Fund (1998-2000), European Co-Production Fund Ltd. (1997-2000), Freeway Cam (UK) Ltd. (1997-2000), The Greenlight Fund (1997-2000), British Screen Finance Ltd. (1997-2000), British Screen Rights Ltd. (1997-2000), The Commercial Radio Companies Association Ltd. (2000-04), Cambridge Econometrics Ltd. (1996-2007), I.P.P.R. Trading Ltd. (2000-2011), Newday Cards Ltd. (2007-2011), Newday Ltd. (2010-17), and Newday Group Ltd. (2011-17).[23]

In May 2015, the College 'Record' notes:

'In March 2015 Dr Demis Hassabis was admitted to the ranks of the Fellow Benefactors. Demis read Computer Science at Queens' 1994-97 and shortly after graduating founded Elixir Studios, a computer games company that made pioneering games. He returned to academia in 2005 to study for a PhD in Cognitive Neuroscience at University College, London, and then spent two years as a research Fellow at UCL in the Gatsby Computational Neuroscience Unit. In 2011 he founded DeepMind Technologies which was sold to Google in 2014. He is now Google's Chief Artificial Intelligence Scientist. He has made a munificent benefaction to Queens' which will fund two UTO Fellowships at Queens' in Computer Science and Natural Sciences (the subject read by his wife, Dr Teresa Niccoli, at Queens')'. Hassabis was subsequently awarded the C.B.E. and, in 2018, elected a fellow of the Royal Society and an honorary fellow of Queens'. In 2020, (soon after Dr Mohamed El-Erian had succeeded to the Presidency of Queens'), a scientific breakthrough by DeepMind would receive considerable publicity, and was the subject of the 'Leading Article' of 'The Times' on the 1st of December:

'Artificial intelligence has just resolved a huge scientific puzzle... Scientists have for half a century dwelt on a conundrum often referred to as the "protein-folding problem". Now an advanced AI program known as DeepMind appears to have solved it...The problem involves some of the most basic constituents of life: the group of organic compounds known as amino acids...The protein molecule can coil round itself...The resulting 3D structure is known as protein folding. If scientists can predict how a one-dimensional sequence can form this structure, it should be possible to work out solutions to many problems...The potential practical benefits are immense but the method by which the problem was solved also merits admiration. DeepMind involves not just colossal processing power but the ability to learn...Its ability to replicate, on a much advanced scale, the processing power of the brain is producing dramatic advances for human welfare and understanding'.

Although Eatwell's further five years as President, (after the University retirement age), was due to end in 2017, the fellowship invited him to extend this until 2020, so that it was not until May 2019 that it was revealed that Eatwell's successor would be Dr Mohamed El-Erian who, together with Eatwell, greeted the Queen, when, as Patroness, she visited Queens' on the 9th of July 2019, to be entertained to luncheon in the Old Hall:

'The Queen arrived at the Old Gate and was greeted by the President, Lord Eatwell, who introduced her to the President-elect, Dr Mohamed A. El-Erian. Her Majesty had lunch with more than 80 Fellows, students and staff. The Royal party then departed from Walnut Tree Court, through Friars' Court and out into Queens' Lane. Her Majesty's last visit to the College was in 2005 when she was accompanied by the Duke of Edinburgh who, at that time, was the Chancellor of the University'.[24]

In 2019 it was also announced that:

'To mark Lord Eatwell's distinguished Presidency of the College over the last 23 years, the Fellows of Queens' aim to raise funds for a full College Fellowship. It will be without subject bias, allowing maximum flexibility to apportion teaching where needs arise and will be called The John Eatwell Fellowship'.[24] The funding was soon achieved and, in May 2020, the President was able to inform the College:

'I am delighted to announce that the target of £2.5 million needed to fund The John Eatwell Fellowship has been met. The Fellowship will sustain and indeed, enhance the supervision system at Queens'. In these troubled times the generosity of members and friends of the College is extraordinary...'. The total had been reached several weeks before the June deadline and, in the words of the Vice-President, would be a:

'lasting legacy in honour of his dedication and contribution to Queens'.[25]

In May 2020, Eatwell reflects on his 23 years as President:

'I have lived in Cambridge since I was 19 years old (I'm cheating a little, as three of those years were in Cambridge, Massachusetts). Moving away in the summer, when my tenure as President of Queens' comes to an end, is therefore something more than a "change of scene". Suzi and I have bought a house that is a little over six miles outside Bath, in the direction of Wells. For me it's a return to my West Country roots. I was brought up in north Wiltshire, and spent a lot of time in Bath in my late teens...it's the people of Queens' that I will miss the most. The staff, students and Fellows are quite simply amazing...Of course, there are obvious changes. The student body is notably more diverse than it was 23 years ago. 30% of Fellows are now female compared with 10% when I arrived...The graduate community has grown to near parity with the numbers of undergraduates. And Suzi would never forgive me if I didn't mention that the singing of the Chapel choir is now sublime. There have been significant changes to the estate: the fourth floor on Cripps Building...the landscaping of the Round...the new Nursery at Owlstone Croft and a host of less obvious but, nonetheless, important improvements...For as long as most of us can remember, student welfare was in the hands of the Tutors...Today, this essentially amateur approch to welfare issues is simply inadequate...Queens' is the first college to respond by creating a professional welfare team, working alongside the tutors...Another major change has been the drive to enhance access to a Cambridge education...All the Cambridge colleges are allocated particular areas in which to concentrate their outreach activities. Queens' is the only college that has a full-time schools liason officer in one of our major areas- Bradford...A less positive change in the past 30 years has been a significant increase in the pressures on the Fellowship. The government's research assessment exercises that tie departmental funding to research output, have spelt the end of academia as a contemplative life. It has been replaced by "publish or perish". Many heads of University departments now actively discourage their faculty from taking college fellowships in order that they devote all their time to research...And yet- fundamentally Queens' hasn't changed since as an undergraduate I first walked into Old Court 56 years ago. The change in the gender balance...the growth of the graduate community, the technological changes...all these have been absorbed within that friendly, gregarious community that Queens' was in 1964 and remains today. I don't quite know how the spirit of Queens' endures. It must be something in the bricks'.[25]

But retirement from Queens' did not necessarily predict a life of leisure; in 2020 his activities included adviser to E.M.Warburg Pincus & Co International Ltd., and to Palamon Capital Partners, LLP; Chief Economic Adviser to the Chartered Management Institute; Trustee at the Institute for Public Policy Research; Non-Executive Director for SAV Credit Ltd; Chairman of the Royal Opera House Pension Fund; and Chairman of the Consumer Panel, Classic FM.[26]

The last months of Eatwell's Presidency were blighted by the Covid pandemic and, in August 2020, the Rev.Tim Harling, Dean of Chapel and Head of Welfare, notes in the Record:

'In early 2020 the world was awakening to the fact that CoVid19 and the outbreak crisis was escalating into a pandemic. I think it would be fair to say that in January and February, many of us did not appreciate at all just how much our lives, in College and personally, would be changed...Alongside Trinity...we at Queens' decided very quickly to send the students who could return home back to their families, even though the Lent Term had not quite finished...There was, understandably, criticism from some whose friends and colleagues were still "functioning normally" at other Colleges. However, within a week, the University administration decided all students in all Colleges that could go home should depart...We also decided to shut Owlstone Croft to accommodate all the 50 or so remaining students on the main site...Lockdown started very quickly. Education had to move swiftly to remote teaching via video links and phone calls... the "problem" of imminent exams became very real...each faculty, in consultation with the University, made up its own mind about what to do...So what of the future? We are planning, second guessing, and putting in contingency plans for the new academic year. What will it look like? The honest answer is that, at the time of writing, we just do not know...We will have a new Master to lead us in those decisions and in creating a "new normal"...'.[27]

The 'Record' of August 2020 also notes:

'Although his term of office continues until the end of September, the President will leave Queens' towards the end of July after twenty-three and a half years in office. There were plans for many events, parties, celebrations and dinners to mark John and Suzi Eatwell's departure, but, of course, almost all of these have had to be abandoned or postponed because of the coronavirus pandemic. The Fellows, the students, the staff and the alumni, and indeed the wider University, will all wish to pay tribute to the President for all he has accomplished and the way he has led and guided the College through almost a quarter of a century of change and success. It is more than sixty years since a President has left office after so long a tenure. One tribute from the College was able to go ahead, however. A marker (in slate and York stone, crafted by Lida Kindersley) celebrating his Presidency has been unveiled in the centre of the Round. The project to redevelop the Round was initiated by Lord Eatwell in 2008 as a result of his frustration that the hub of the College, the concourse into which visitors emerged from the Porters' Lodge, was "a puddle-strewn car park". At the Governing Body meeting after the unveiling ceremony Professor Weber spoke of the President's involvement with many major projects during his tenure of office and of the many ways in which he has built and enriched our infrastructure, society and academic aims. The Fellowship believes the Round has a special place in his heart, as does the academic distinction of the College, and so this marker, together with the newly-endowed John Eatwell Fellowship, are most fitting ways to mark his Presidency.' In addition, John, Lord Eatwell, was admitted to an Honorary Fellowship of Queens' in January 2020.[27]

References

1. John Eatwell, Baron Eatwell. Wikipedia. Online. 2020.
2. Eatwell. Burke's Peerage & Baronetage. 2003. Online. 2020.
3. Clive Hollick, Baron Hollick. Wikipedia. Online. 2020.
4. Institute for Public Policy Research. Wikipedia. Online. 2020.
5. www.parliament.uk October 2010. Online. 2020.
6. Lord Eatwell. Non-affiliated Peer. TheyWorkForYou. Online 2020.
7. The Record 1977. Queens' College, Cambridge. Online. 2020.
8. The Record 1999. Queens' College, Cambridge. Online. 2020.
9. The Record 2000. Queens' College, Cambridge. Online. 2020.
10. Michael Foale. Wikipedia. Online. 2020.
11. The Record 2001. Queens' College, Cambridge. Online. 2020.
12. The Record 2002. Queens' College, Cambridge. Online. 2020.
13. The Record 2003. Queens' College, Cambridge. Online. 2020.
14. Cambridge University Statutes and Ordinances. Online. 2020.
15. The Record 2006. Queens' College, Cambridge. Online. 2020.
16. The Record 2008. Queens' College, Cambridge. Online. 2020.
17. The Record 2010. Queens' College, Cambridge. Online. 2020.
18. The Record 2011. Queens' College, Cambridge. Online. 2020.
19. Lord and Lady Eatwell. USC University of Southern California. Online. 2020.
20. The Record 2012. Queens' College, Cambridge. Online. 2020.
21. The Record 2013. Queens' College, Cambridge. Online. 2020.
22. University of Bath. Institute for Policy Research. Online. 2020.

23. John Leonard Eatwell. Companies House. Online. 2020.
24. The Bridge Autumn 2919. Queens' College Cambridge. Online. 2020.
25. The Bridge April 2020. Queens' College, Cambridge. Online. 2020.
26. University of Cambridge Centre for Science and Policy. Lord John Eatwell. Online. 2020.
27. The Record 2020. Queens' College, Cambridge. Online. 2020.

CHAPTER 40

Mohamed Aly El-Erian. President 2020-.

Summary.

Mohamed Aly El-Erian was born in New York City in 1958 to Egyptian and French parents. (His father would serve as Egyptian Ambassador in France and as a judge of the International Court of Justice).

He attended a boarding school in England before being admitted to Queens' on a scholarship in 1977. After graduating with first class honours in economics, he transferred to St Anthony's College, Oxford, and was awarded a DPhil. in economics in 1985.

In 1983, he joined the International Monetary Fund in Washington DC, where he rose to become a Deputy Director. In 1998, he moved to the private financial sector, initially in London, before joining the Pacific Investment Management Company (PIMCO) in 1999 in California, as Managing Director, portfolio manager and head of emerging markets.

In 2005 he resigned to become President and CEO of the Harvard Management Company, (responsible for Harvard University's endowment fund), but returned to PIMCO in 2007 as Co-CEO and Co-Chief Investment Officer (Co-CIO). He became sole CEO in 2009. El-Erian helped to grow PIMCO's assets under management from under one trillion to nearly two trillion US dollars, but resigned in 2014, wishing to spend more time with his family. He was then appointed Chief Economic Adviser to the Management Board of Allianz, PIMCO's parent company and continued writing for the Financial Times, Bloomberg and other publications.

In 2012, El-Erian was appointed Chair of President Obama's Global Development Council.

In 2013, El-Erian was elected an Honorary Fellow of Queens', and Mrs Jamie Walters El-Erian was elected a Fellow Benefactor of the College. In 2015, the El-Erian Institute for Human Behavior and Economic Policy was established, at Queens' and the Faculty of Economics at Cambridge University, by a gift of 25 million US dollars. (In October 2015, the El-Erians filed a Marriage Dissolution/Divorce lawsuit in Orange, California).

El-Erian's extensive curriculum vitae includes many appointments to company boards, committees and a variety of other organisations. He has contributed to many influential conferences and meetings. Also, he has been a prolific author and columnist; he has written two best-selling books on economics, and contributed to many prestigious publications. He has received numerous awards as a highly-influential economist, company executive and philanthropist.

In May 2019, El-Erian was elected as the next President of Queens' and, together with his fiancée, was introduced to the Queen during her visit to the College on the 9th of July, 2019. However, the Covid pandemic blighted the months leading to El-Erian's installation as President of Queens' on the 30th of September, 2020; all his abilities and experience will be needed to guide the College through turbulent times.

Timeline.

1958.	Born on the 19th of August in New York City, New York, the son of Abdullah El-Erian and Nadia Choucri.
1968.	His family moves back to New York, after living in Egypt, when his father takes a post at the UN.
1971-73.	Lives in France, where his father is Egyptian Ambassador.
1973-76.	Attends St John's School, Leatherhead.
1977.	Admitted to Queens' with a scholarship.
1980.	B.A. in economics, with first class honours. Transfers to St Anthony's College, Oxford
1982.	M.Phil. (University of Oxford).
1983.	M.A. (University of Cambridge).

1983-97. Moves to the US, joining the International Monetary Fund in Washington, D.C., (where he will become a Deputy Director during 1995-97).

1985. DPhil. in economics (University of Oxford).

1998. Moves to the private sector; works in London as a managing director of emerging markets at Salomon Smith Barney/ Citigroup.

1999. Joins PIMCO (Pacific Investment Management Company LLC) as managing director, portfolio manager and head of emerging markets.

2005. Joins Harvard Management Company as President and CEO, (managing Harvard University's endowment and related accounts).

2007-14. Returns to PIMCO as Co-CEO (working with Co-CEO Bill Thompson, until the latter's retirement in 2009, when El-Erian becomes sole CEO), and Co-CIO, (Co-Chief Investment Officer), working with PIMCO's co-founder, Bill Gross.

2008. Publishes: 'When Markets Collide', which wins the Financial Times and Goldman Sachs Business Book of the Year Award, and is named a book of the year by the Economist.

2012-17. Chair of President Obama's Global Delelopment Council, providing advice to the President and senior officials on global development policies and practices.

2013. Elected an Honorary Fellow of Queens'. Mrs Jamie Walters El-Erian is elected a Fellow Benefactor of Queens'. Named by Foreign Policy magazine as one of the 'Top Global Thinkers' for four years in a row.

2014. Resigns from PIMCO on the 21st of January, as from mid-March 2014. Remains at the Allianz Group, (a multinational financial services company and parent company of PIMCO), as Chief Economic Adviser to the Management Board. Bill Gross resigns from PIMCO in September.

2015. Admitted as a Companion of the Guild of Benefactors, Cambridge University. Co-Chair of Cambridge University's campaign for £2 billion to support the University and colleges of Cambridge. The El-Erian Institute for Human

Behavior and Economic Policy is established with Queens' and the Faculty of Economics at Cambridge, by a gift of 25 million US dollars. (The Institute will study economics, finance, neuroscience, psychology, politics and behavioral finance). The Chair of the Institute will become a Queens' fellow, and the PhD students and post-doctoral researchers will also be members of the College. The El-Erians file a Marriage Dissolution/Divorce lawsuit in Orange, California on the 1st of October.

2016. Publishes: 'The Only Game in Town: Central Banks, Instability, and Avoiding the Next Collapse', (a New York Times bestseller).

2019. Elected as the next President of Queens'. Senior Global Fellow at the Lauder Institute of Management & International Studies, Philadelphia, USA. Part-time Professor of Practice at The Wharton School of the University of Pensylvania. Senior Advisor to Gramercy Funds Management, an emerging markets investment firm. Is introduced to the Queen, when the Patroness visits Queens' on the 9th of July.

2020. Appointed Non-Executive Director of Barclays, plc. on the 1st of January and serves on the Board of Under Armour. In March, the Corona virus pandemic initiates national restrictive measures. In July, is appointed Chair of Gramercy Funds Management. Installed as President of Queens' on the 30th of September.

Eminent and highly-influential Egyptian- French-American economist, author, and executive in the financial industry. Has published widely on international economic and financial topics. Recipient of numerous awards and accolades for his professional and philanthropic activities.

Mohamed Aly El-Erian was born in New York City on the 19th of August, 1958, to Egyptian and French parents, Abdullah El-Erian and Nadia Choucri.[1] (Abdullah El-Erian, born in 1921, became Professor of International Law at Cairo University and, subsequently, would be appointed Egyptian Ambassador to France and Switzerland. In 1979, he was elected to the International Court of Justice of the United Nations as the representative from Egypt. He died unexpectedly in 1981 from a heart attack, and was survived by his wife and three children).[2] His mother had French nationality and Mohamed El-Erian is a citizen of Egypt, France and the US.[3]

Soon after his birth, the family returned to Egypt, but there would be short periods in Europe when his father attended meetings of the UN law commission.[1] El-Erian returned to the US in 1968, when his father served as Egypt's Deputy Ambassador to the UN,[3] and lived in France during 1971-73, when his father was the Egyptian ambassador. Later, El-Erian said he would:

'credit his sense of perspective to his father- a man of humble beginnings who went from a small village in Egypt to being elected one of the 15 judges on the International Court of Justice, the United Nations main judicial organ, yet never let his achievements go to his head. "My father remained incredibly grounded, refusing any and all sense of entitlement"...That he is like his father is his greatest strength, he said...'.[4]

He attended St John's School, Leatherhead, an independent boarding school in Surrey, founded in 1851 to educate the sons of the clergy. However, he has some reservations about this experience:

'I went to boarding school in England, and I was the only foreigner there. In my year, two of us had made it to Oxbridge- my friend and I- and I had got a scholarship. On speech day, which is when the school highlights its list of achievements, the headmaster said he was proud to report that one of his students would be going to Cambridge. There was no mention of me at all. The school record came out, no mention of me. That was the first time I realised that life is complicated, and you can either get derailed by such issues or you can just say, "It is what it is", and move on. That's the approach I've taken...'.[5]

El-Erian came to Queens' in 1977 as a scholar and, in 1980, graduated B.A. with first class honours in the economics tripos. Also, he had managed to find the time to captain the College's football team.[6] (He is a long-time follower of American football as a New York Jets fan, and has appeared on TV in a 'Jets' jersey).[1] He then transferred to St Anthony's College, Oxford, where he obtained an M.Phil. in economics in 1982, and graduated D.Phil. in economics in 1985. (St Anthony's College was founded for postgraduates in 1950, and specialises in worldwide international relations, development, economics and politics).

In 1983, he began fifteen years of service with the International Monetary Fund (IMF) in Washington, D.C., rising to become a Deputy Director.[3] (The IMF was formed in 1945, and plays a central role in the management of balance of payment difficulties and international financial crises). In 1998, he moved to London, to work in the private sector, as managing director of emerging markets, with the investment bank and financial services company, Salomon Smith Barney/Citigroup. (Smith Barney had merged with Salomon Brothers in 1997, but the company was soon acquired by Travelers Group, which then merged with Citicorp to form Citigroup Inc. in 1998).

El-Erian will have found a contrast between his previous role as a public servant and working in the private financial sector. Salomon Brothers had been the most profitable firm on Wall Street in the 1980s but, like many financial instutions, was associated with a series of financial scandals in the 1990s. Also, perhaps reflecting the working conditions in many hedge funds, private equity firms and investment banks:

'The bank (Salomon Brothers) was famed for their "alpha male" encouragement and "a cutthroat corporate culture that rewarded risk-taking with massive bonuses, punishing poor results with a swift boot". In Michael Lewis' 1989 book Liar's Poker, the insider descriptions of life at Salomon gave way to the popular view of banking in the 1980s and 1990s as a money-focused and work-intense environment...the Salomon bankers...dominated the game of extraordinary profit-making'.[7]

In 1999, El-Erian moved on to join the portfolio management and investment strategy group of the global investment firm PIMCO (Pacific Investment Management Company).[3] PIMCO had been founded in 1971 in Newport Beach, California, by Bill Gross, Jim Mizzy, and Bill Podlich, with an initial $12 million in assets and a belief that bonds should be actively traded to enhance returns. A recent account (in 2020) notes:

'The firm...manages more than $1.92 trillion in assets... PIMCO specializes in fixed income securities. It manages the internationally known Total Return Fund. The company serves institutional investors, high-net-worth individuals, and individual investors with its account services and mutual funds'.[8] In 2000, PIMCO was acquired by Allianz SE, a global financial services company based in Munich, Germany, but has continued to operate as an autonomous subsidiary.[9]

Bill Gross was the initial driving force in the company:

'Bill Gross...pioneered a style of investing that revolutionized bond funds...Through his total return bond strategy emphasizing a bond's price performance as well as its yield, he helped build PIMCO into a $1.7 (in 2019) trillion money manager specializing in fixed income. He was a frequent television guest, expounding on investing, bonds and the economy...Gross amassed a fortune and a global following while riding a decades-long bull market in bonds at PIMCO...The PIMCO Total Return Fund, which he started in 1987, grew to one of the richest mutual funds in the world. Morningstar in 2010 named him "investor of the decade"... Gross became a multibillionaire...'.[10]

However, after seven years, El-Erian left in 2006 to become President and CEO of the Harvard Management Company, which manages Harvard University's endowment. The Harvard Magazine in 2006 reports:

'More than a name and face will change at Harvard Management Company (HMC), the investment organization for the University's endowment, with the arrival early this year of Mohamed A. El-Erian as president and chief executive officer... El-Erian succeeds Jack A. Meyer, M.B.A. 69, who departed September 30 with several senior HMC portfolio professionals and other staff members; they have formed a private money-management firm...Since 1999 El-Erian has been a managing director at Pacific Investment Management Company (PIMCO), the leading fixed-income fund manager, with more than $500 billion in assets...he has been directly responsible for managing more than $28 billion in emerging-market debt investments. He arrived at PIMCO following 16 months in emerging-markets economic research at a London investment bank. From 1983 to 1997, El-Erian worked at the International Monetary Fund, analysing policies on debt and country issues...University treasurer James F. Rothenberg...said El-Erian: "has emerged as a savvy investor with a particular knack for identifying opportunities in complex markets, while developing a reputation as a strong and articulate leader" well equipped with a "perspective on global markets and the role of capital throughout the world"...The widely reported search, he said, underscored just how much "taking a job like this at Harvard puts someone front and center with the media". News interest focuses on the size of the endowment, nearly $26 billion, and the annual disclosure of the compensation paid to HMC investment managers who outperform their market benchmarks: as much as $35 million to one portfolio manager, and $7.2 million received by Meyer in a peak year... El-Erian said he had been attracted to the job by HMC's "very smart people" and by the organization's "core philosophy, which is one of a patient investor" looking for undiscovered opportunities (he cited recent large investments in timberlands) and then waiting for other buyers to catch up. He also valued "a culture of excellence" in which "outperforming is viewed as the norm"... El-Erian intends to keep personally close to the markets by managing money himself: he described himself as a "player-coach", and noted his expertise in emerging markets and other fixed-income assets. (He also intends to teach at Harvard Business School)...Citing his role at PIMCO...El-Erian said, "I've been under the microscope". Of his coming responsibilities representing Harvard, he said, "I can live with it" '.[11]

But in the following year, on the 11th of September 2007, Allianz SE broke the news that:

'PIMCO announced today that Mohamed El-Erian, its former managing director and senior portfolio manager, will return to PIMCO in January 2008, in a newly-created position as managing director, Co-CEO and Co-CIO. In his new position, El-Erian will join CEO Bill Thompson and chief investment officer and company founder Bill Gross, as a member of PIMCO's senior management team..."I am delighted to welcome Mohamed back to Allianz Global Investors. We missed him while he was contributing with great success to the Harvard Fund as the CEO, and we are excited to have an exceptional investor, an international statesman and a good friend back to PIMCO and Allianz Global Investors" said Joachim Faber, CEO of Allianz Global Investors... El-Erian will return to PIMCO from the Harvard Management Company (HMC), where since being hired in October 2005, he distinguished himself as president and CEO of the world's largest university endowment. During his tenure at the HMC, El-Erian rebuilt the professional investment management staff and contributed to outstanding investment results for Harvard... "Mohamed's return to PIMCO creates a powerful and experienced leadership triangle at the most senior level of our firm", CEO Bill Thompson said. "We welcome him home as a proven leader, an exceptional investor and one of the most respected names in the investment world". Thompson added: "Neither Bill Gross not I at this time have any plans to step down, and in fact, have just been elected by PIMCO's managing directors for five-year terms in our respective roles. The demands and complexities of our current positions suggest that the addition of a unique talent such as Mohamed's will enhance both of our contributions going forward". PIMCO founder Bill Gross said El-Erian's return would strengthen an already deep management team, and help position the company for the future. "I am ecstatic to have him join Bill Thompson and me in a top leadership role and help shape our vision for PIMCO's direction in the coming years". El-Erian, 49, said he was excited about rejoining PIMCO after "a stimulating time at HMC where I had the privilege of working with wonderful people...In returning to PIMCO, I look forward to working with a highly talented and skilled group of world-class professionals that are simply the best at what they do, and in helping lead this great company into the future" '.[12] (At this time PIMCO had more than 693 billion US dollars under management).

However, Thompson's plans soon changed and, in September 2008, Allianz SE reports:

'PIMCO announced today that after 15 years as CEO, Bill Thompson will retire at the end of this year. Co-CEO Mohamed A. El-Erian, who returned to PIMCO in January 2008, was elected to serve as the firm's CEO upon Mr. Thompson's retirement. Mr. El-Erian will also continue his role as Co-CIO with Bill Gross...PIMCO is going from "strength to strength" as Mohamed takes the CEO reins from Bill, said Mr Gross'.[13]

This arrangement continued until 2014, when, to the surprise of the financial community, El-Erian announced his resignation from PIMCO in January 2014, (as from mid-March 2014), amid reports of disagreements with Bill Gross.[3] However, he stated that he had decided to leave after receiving a letter from his daughter outlining important events in her life that he had missed,[1] as '9News' reports:

'The head of a $2 trillion investment fund has revealed he quit his job after his 10-year-old daughter wrote him a note listing 22 special moments in her life he had missed. California-based Mohamed El-Erian shocked the financial world when he announced his resignation as chief executive of PIMCO in January 2014. Mr. El-Erian, who made $100 million in 2011 alone, said in a recent essay for Worth that his wife and daughter were at the heart of his decision to quit. The 56-year-old said the "wake up call" happened when he was arguing with his daughter about brushing her teeth and she left to fetch a piece of paper from her room. "It was a list that she had compiled of her important events and activities that I had missed due to work commitments", he wrote. "The list contained 22 items, from her first day at school and first soccer match of the season to a parent-teacher meeting and a Halloween parade. I felt awful and got defensive: I had a good excuse for each missed event! Travel, important meetings, an urgent phone call, sudden to-do. But it dawned on me that I was missing an infinitely more important point...I was not making nearly enough time for her". Mr El-Erian used to leave home for work at 4.30am each morning but since resigning he and his lawyer wife Jamie take turns in waking up their daughter, preparing her breakfast and bringing her to school, he wrote. He said he had taken a "portfolio" of part-time roles, including being chief economic adviser at Allianz, which require far less travelling and allow him more flexibility'.[14] (Mrs Jamie Walters El-Erian, a prominent attorney-at-law, is the daughter of Bill Walters, who was a State Senator for Arkansas for 18 years and who died in 2013. The El-Erians would be the subjects of a Marriage Dissolution/Divorce lawsuit, filed in Orange, California, in October 2015).[15]

El-Erian has repeatedly declined to comment on his relationship with Gross and the situation at PIMCO before his departure, but there is no shortage of speculation:

'Tension increased at Pacific Investment Management Co.'s headquarters here last summer (2013). The bond market was under pressure, losses grew and clients pulled billions of dollars from the firm. Bill Gross, who co-founded PIMCO in 1971 and is largely responsible for building it into a behemoth overseeing almost $2 trillion in assets, struck some of his colleagues as testier than usual. He argued openly with Mohamed El-Erian, PIMCO's chief executive- something employees say they rarely had seen. Mr. Gross- by his own admission, a demanding boss- had long showed respect for Mr. El-Erian and indicated that the younger man eventually would take over the world's biggest bond firm. But one day last June, the two men squared off in front of more than a dozen colleagues amid disagreements about Mr. Gross's conduct, according to two people who were there. "I have a 41-year track record of investing excellence," Mr. Gross told Mr. El-Erian, according to the two witnesses. "What do you have?" "I'm tired of cleaning up your s----," Mr. El-Erian responded, referring to conduct by Mr. Gross that he felt was hurting PIMCO, these two people recall. Later, after Mr. El-Erian told Mr. Gross he needed to change the way he interacted with employees, Mr. Gross, 69 years old, agreed to make adjustments, several PIMCO employees say. But last month (January 2014), PIMCO announced that

Mr. El-Erian, 55, would leave the firm- a surprise to both employees and investors...but will remain on the management committee of PIMCO's parent company, German insurer Allianz SE. Mr. Gross later said Mr. El-Erian wanted to write a second book and spend more time with his family. Interviews with nearly two dozen individuals close to both men and to the firm suggest more important factors in the departure: a high-pressure work environment that turned less collegial over the past year, a deteriorating relationship between the two senior executives and certain decisions by Mr. Gross that confused some employees'.[16]

In 2016, the 'Financial Times' reports on 'Allianz's Mohamed El-Erian on life after PIMCO':

'Mr El-Erian still refuses to take questions on why he left the company he joined 15 years earlier, and what went on between him and its founder, Bill Gross. At the time it was reported that Mr El-Erian departed amid infighting with Mr Gross, who himself walked out of the company eight months later. Whatever did transpire, it is clear the two are now on opposing sides. While Mr El-Erian holds the grand title of chief economic adviser to Allianz...Mr Gross is suing the bond house for at least $200m, claiming that executives plotted to oust him and divide his bonus among themselves...His schedule is full but his days are not as arduous as they were at PIMCO, where Mr El-Erian arrived at the office at 4.30am. He says: "Half of my time is now spent with Allianz, where I chair committees, participate in meetings, speak at various Allianz events and meet clients. I am available as a resource to Allianz. Then a quarter of my time is spent writing (Mr El-Erian writes a column for the Financial Times twice a month) and the final quarter is spent serving Barack Obama's global development council and speaking and meeting with governments". It is clear Mr El-Erian, who chairs the global development council (something he calls a privilege), enjoys his ties with the US president. He only asks to go off the record twice during the hour-long interview- once to recount a personal story that saw him switch into the world of finance from one where he was predestined to become an academic- and another to recall a meeting with Mr Obama that "left a deep impession" on him. It is a nice story. "I like President Obama very much. He is very analytical, he very quickly grasps the main issues and he is very smart. The US will miss him" he says'.[17] (President Obama's 'Global Development Council' was set up with an Executive order in 2012, with El-Erian as the Chair, to inform and advise the President on global development policies pursued by the U.S. government. It was made up of members appointed by the President from a range of sectors).[18]

El-Erian's surprise exit from PIMCO was soon followed by another- that of Bill Gross:

'The bond king heard rumblings of a palace coup. William H. Gross...abruptly quit on Friday for a much smaller firm. The surprising exit came after Mr. Gross learned in recent weeks that top executives at PIMCO and Allianz, the German insurer that owns it, had grown tired of his leadership and were weighing a change. Some executives were pushing for him to be removed as chief investment officer, said two people briefed on the matter. There was concern about his management style and that his increasingly erratic behavior- he appeared at a conference to give a speech wearing sunglasses and wrote an investor a letter that was largely an elegy to his cat- was becoming a distraction...this year has been a rough one for Mr Gross. The giant $221.6 billion bond fund, PIMCO Total Return Fund, which Mr. Gross personally managed, has posted mediocre performance this year. Investors have pulled some $25 billion out of the fund this year and $68 billion over the last 16 months...The resignation of Mr Gross, who is estimated to be worth $2.3 billion, took Wall Street by surprise...'.[19] (Gross was known as a 'quirky' character, who helped fund his MBA by a successful four-month run at Las Vegas blackjack tables. He became a multibillionaire, with a world-class stamp collection, an art collection, and a place on the Forbes 400 list of richest Americans. But, in 2018, he was dropped from the Forbes 400 after an: 'ugly, high-profile divorce that included fights over art, homes and cats').[10]

Soon after Bill Gross had left PIMCO, El-Erian was asked if he would want his old job back. He replied: 'No, I'm really happy with my life':

'...El-Erian had nothing but positive things to say about Gross: "He is a brilliant investor and remains a brilliant investor... the Bill I know is someone who's anchored by three things that you hardly ever find in an investor: Strong fundamentals including economics, a really good feel for the market and strong bond math. And that is what made him so successful" '.[20]

In 2014, the Queens' 'Record' reported that El-Erian had been elected an Honorary Fellow of the College, while Mrs Jamie Walters El-Erian had been elected a Fellow Benefactor[15] and, in 2015, The University of Cambridge Faculty of Economics announces:

'A leading economist has made a major investment in the future of Economics at Cambridge. Alumnus Dr Mohamed El-Erian and his wife Jamie Walters have donated $25 million to create the El-Erian Institute for Human Behaviour and Economic Policy. The donation will be split between the Faculty of Economics and Dr El-Erian's old college Queens' and is designed to examine the many factors that drive human decision making and its implications for economic policy...The donation provides for a Fellowship at Queens' and endows a Chair...as well as linked PhD studentships at the College and an outreach fund. Dr El-Erian...is co-Chair of the campaign for the University and Colleges of Cambridge, which will focus on enhancing the University's beneficial impact on the world'.[21] A report in the University students' newspaper adds:

'El-Erian and Walters' donation comes after a year of careful planning of the unique collaboration between the donors, Queens' and the Faculty of Economics. In forging a partnership between a Cambridge College and a Cambridge Faculty, Lord Eatwell, President of Queens' College, says El-Erian "has stimulated the establishment of new college-university relationships- a new way forward for the collegiate university" '.[22]

In addition to his major appointments with the IMF, Harvard Management Company and PIMCO, El-Erian's extensive curriculum vitae includes many other committees and boards, including board membership of the Carnegie Endowment for International Peace; board membership of the National Bureau for Economic Research, Cambridge, Massachutets; Chair of the Microsoft Investment Advisory Committee; and membership of the Investor Advisory Committee on Financial Markets at the Federal Reserve Bank of New York. In 2019, other appointments included a director at Under Armour, Inc., (an American sports equipment company), and Senior Advisor at Gramercy Funds Management LLC.

He has been, and remains, a prolific author and columnist; he has received many awards and has spoken at many universities, conferences, public institutions and other organizations.

His 2008 book, 'When Markets Collide', was a bestseller, winning the accolade of the Financial Times/Goldman Sachs Business Book of the year, and named a book of the year by the 'Economist' magazine.[3] A reviewer writes:

'The winner of the 2008 Financial Times and Goldman Sachs business book of the year award is a definitive account of the much-chronicled rise of the emerging economies of China, India and the rest...he also throws in a little joke: "There are times that you worry about the return on your capital and times that you worry about the return of your capital" '.[23] His 2016 book, 'The Only Game in Town: Central Banks, Instability and Avoiding the Next Collapse', was also a 'New York Times' bestseller,[24] reviewed as:

'an excellent primer on how we got here. It's also a guide on what to expect as the world struggles to cope with a slower, less equal growth and the resulting populism, nationalism and ugly partisan politics that we see in countries from the U.S. to France and China. At the center of it all is an unglamorous institution: The central bank. Central banks are in charge of controlling the world's money supply and how quickly and easily it can move between countries, companies and the pockets of consumers. In the wake of the 2008 financial crisis...they were forced...to pump unthinkable amounts of cash into the global system...rather than a Great Depression, we got a "new normal" of slower growth... But that New Normal- a term that El-Erian himself coined while at PIMCO- is coming to an end. What replaces it will likely be a period of economic and political volatility...In the 40 or so years leading up to the 2008 financial crisis, the economic policy makers and powers that be focused way too much on promoting and encouraging the financial sector- and the growth of credit- to the detriment of Main Sreet and society as a whole. As El-Erian writes, "Even the common labeling of the industry itself changed- from financial services to just finance". Instead of seeing Wall Street for what it is and should be- a helpmate to business- it became the tail that wagged the dog. "Suddenly, the highest level of capitalistic achievement involved finance," writes El-Erian.... El-Erian focuses on...the growing power of global central bankers over the last several decades...Now, the disconnect between markets and Main Street has become so disconcerting that, in El-Erian's view, businsses are scared to invest and consumers are scared to spend...his most likely "New Normal" is an ongoing era of rocky markets and unpredictable growth...'.[25] Also, El-Erian has contributed frequently to many prestigious publications, including as a contributing editor for the 'Financial Times' and a regular columnist for 'Bloomberg View',[1,3] and he:

'has received numerous awards and recognition for his economics, financial industry and philanthropic activities, including Egyptian Cancer Network's Lifetime Achievement Award for his support of cancer treatment and cures...'.[24] He was named, for four years running (2009-12), in 'Foreign Policy' magazine's list of the Top 100 Global Thinkers and, in 2013, he was counted among the top 500 most-powerful people in the world.[3] He has been a leading participant in many influential meetings and conferences, for example, in 2014, he was the keynote speaker at the CME Conference, attended by Ben Bernanke, (Chair of the Fedreral Reserve 2006-14), and Colin Powell, (the previous US Secretary of State).[1] (CME Group is the world's leading derivatives marketplace).

On the 28th of May, 2019, Queens' announces:

'The Governing Body of Queens' College, Cambridge is delighted to announce the election of Dr Mohamed A. El-Erian as its 42nd (sic) President. He will take up office on 1 October 2020. Dr El-Erian said: "Having experienced the transformational power of Queens' and Cambridge, I am honoured to have the opportunity to work with my colleagues to build on the College's many accomplishments under the 23-year leadership of Lord Eatwell. I am particularly privileged to return to Queens' at a time of great change, not only in social and economic affairs, but also due to exciting technological innovations that influence education and our society in so many ways. Underpinned by our deep commitment to academic excellence, we will work in an inclusive way to continue to broaden access, deepen diversity and promote an ever more supportive environment for intellectual curiosity, deep learning and impactful research'.[26]

Soon afterwards, on the 9th of July, 2019, Her Majesty the Queen visited Queens':

'Dr El-Erian and his fiancée were introduced to Her Majesty the Queen, the Patroness, by Lord Eatwell when she visited Queens' on Tuesday 9 July 2019. Her Majesty was in Cambridge for a visit in the morning to the National Institute of Agricultural Botany for its centenary and to open the newly-completed Royal Papworth Hospital...She arrived at the College about 12 noon and met members of staff and students as she walked through Old Court for lunch in Old Hall. The luncheon was attended by more than 80 Fellows and student and staff representatives. The President made a brief speech and Her Majesty left the College via Walnut Tree Court and the Dokett Gate'.[27]

In August 2019, El-Erian was interviewed for 'Financial News', London:

'More than five-and-a-half years have passed since his shock resignation but El-Erian still refuses to talk about what exactly went on...But he does say he has no regrets about the 15 years he spent at PIMCO, which has been owned by Allianz since 2000. "I had a wonderful time and I have huge respect for Bill Gross. He was one of the most impressive investors I have come across. When the company hit a pothole after I left, I told people not to underestimate how quickly the company would bounce back". It is well-documented that his daughter played a big part in his decision to leave...His daughter is 16 now and attends a boarding school that specialises in theatre and the arts...On leaving PIMCO El-Erian became economic adviser to Allianz in a part-time role.

In 2016 he published the bestseller The Only Game in Town, and earlier this year the 61-year-old joined emerging markets boutique Gramercy Funds Management as a senior adviser...That portfolio is set to get bigger next year when El-Erian becomes president of Cambridge University's Queens' College..."At my age I'm very lucky that I don't need a job for money", says El-Erian, who reportedly earned $100m in one year at PIMCO. "I don't need a job to have a platform, and I don't need a job for fame. Ever since I left PIMCO and decided to pursue a portfolio approach to employment...and spend a lot more time with the family, I haven't been tempted back into a full-time job. Until now...I formally applied for the job at Queens' College once I was told my name had come up," he says. El-Erian will keep his roles at Allianz and Gramercy Funds Management, (an emerging markets investment firm), but will reduce the amount of time he spends working with the German insurer. "I'll just devote less time," he explains. "This is an important opportunity at what couldn't be a more challenging time for the university. Think of a UK university facing the prospect of Brexit, which means less funding from Europe, a UK university facing a general erosion of trust and an anti-establishment wave, and think of a UK university facing technological innovation that impacts not just what people learn but how they learn. The more I discussed this, the more I realised I had the background to help". He says the college's stance on diversity and inclusion particularly interested him. "They do not just carry out initiatives, they actually do things", he says...He was among the final candidates considered for both the role of vice-chair at the Federal Reserve and the job of president at the World Bank. Both eluded him...'.[5] (In September 2019, El-Erian was named a Senior Global Fellow at the Joseph H. Lauder Institute of Management & International Studies and part-time professor of practice at the Wharton School of the University of Pennsylvania, and was appointed a Non-Executive Director of Barclays plc on the 1st of January, 2020. In July 2020 he became Chair of Gramercy Funds Management).

At his installation as President of Queens' on the 30th of September, 2020, his list of anticipated challenges had been dwarfed, at least temporarily, by the Covid pandemic, and the historic traditions at the ceremony were witnessed by only a handful of the fellowship. The President-elect was met at the Gatehouse by the Vice-President (Professor Marie Edmonds, Ron Oxburgh Fellow in Earth Sciences) and the Praelector (Dr David Butterfield) who escorted him to the chapel. The Praelector introduced the President-elect to the Senior Fellow (Professor Richard Weber), who was seated. After taking the oath of office, the President was then led to his seat at the west end of the Chapel. The few fellows who had been permitted to attend then left in order of seniority, bowing to the new President on their way. The Senior Fellow then gave the President a copy of the Statutes.

The new President takes office at a critical time for Queens', and indeed for all universities. The College will need all his ability, energy, experience and optimism during his tenure. In his first email to the College, on the 11th of October, 2020, he writes:

'As we enter the first full week of lectures and supervisions for most of you, I would like to thank you for all the efforts, and sacrifices, you have made in contributing to a relatively healthy start to term...We have all been getting used to new ways of walking around College, of getting food and of interacting. We welcomed our largest ever intake of students...We dealt with a very small number of positive Covid-19 test results...Anna and I have loved being in College but deeply regret not being able to host you in the Lodge which is also having its "health and safety" adjustments (i.e. repairs). As soon as we can, we will have you over where, should you wish, you can also meet Bosa. For a dog that never left California, Bosa is adjusting remarkably well (though she is yet to get used to rain, something that she rarely experienced in the first nine-plus years of her life). Looking forward, the public health outlook remains uncertain, especially with infection cases and hospitalization going up in an increasing number of areas in Britain...Whether it's the world class teaching, the welfare resources and/or the additional student support funds that have been raised, the College is here to support you as you pursue your transformational educational opportunities and make friends for life...'.

At the time of concluding this account, (March 2021), the UK remains in a period of pandemic-related restrictions in a second 'lockdown', although the success of the vaccination programme allows us to anticipate a degree of normality later in the year. It will be for future historians of the College to document the inevitably challenging times ahead.

References

1. Mohamed A. El-Erian. Wikipedia. Online. 2020.
2. Judge Abdullah El-Erian. UPI Archives 1981. Online. 2020.
3. Clark. J.H. Mohamed El-Erian. Britannia. Online. 2020.
4. Mohamed El-Erian: The 2013 1A 25 Extended Profile. AdvisorOne. Online. 2020.
5. Newlands, C. An audience with Mohamed El-Erian on his move from high-finance to academia. Financial News, London, 2019. Online. 2020.
6. The Bridge, Autumn 2019. Queens' College, Cambridge. Online 2020.
7. Salomon Brothers. Wikipedia. Online 2020.
8. Kenton, W. PIMCO. Investopedia. Online 2020.
9. PIMCO. Wikipedia. Online 2020.
10. Heath, T. A look back at Pimco founder Bill Gross. The Seattle Times, 2019. Online 2020.
11. El-Erian for the Endowment. Harvard Magazine, January-February 2006. Online 2020.
12. Mohamed El-Erian to rejoin PIMCO as Co-CEO, Co-CIO. Allianz, 2007. Online 2020.
13. PIMCO Co-CEO Bill Thompson to retire at end of 2008. Allianz, 2008. Online 2020.
14. High-flying CEO quits. 9News September 2014. Online 2020.
15. The Record, 2014. Queens' College, Cambridge. Online 2020.
16. Zukerman, G., Grind, K. Inside the showdown atop PIMCO. The Wall Street Journal, February 2014. Online 2020.

17. Newlands, C. Allianz's Mohamed El-Erian on life after PIMCO. Financial Times, June 2016. Online. 2020.
18. O'Sullivan, H. The President's Global Development Council's Second Report 2015. Participating Local Democracy. Online. 2020.
19. Goldstein, M. Bill Gross, King of Bonds, Abruptly Leaves Mutual Fund Giant PIMCO, September 2014. Online. 2020.
20. Belvedere, M.J. Gross gone, but El-Erian just says no to PIMCO. CNBC, October 2014. Online. 2020.
21. Faculty of Economics Receives USD 25m gift. University of Cambridge, 2015. Online. 2020.
22. McCullagh, S. 'Yours, Cambridge' receives $25m gift. Varsity, October 2015. Online. 2020.
23. The best business books of all time. Independent, December 2008. Online. 2020.
24. Mohamed A. El-Erian. SALT, 2019. Online 2020.
25. Foroohar, R. Book Review: Mohamed El-Erian's 'The Only Game in Town'. Time. 2016. Online. 2020.
26. Dr. Mohamed A. El-Erian elected as new President. Queens' College, Cambridge, 2019. Online. 2020.
27. The Record, 2019. Queens' College, Cambridge. Online. 2020.

Index.

www.ingramcontent.com/pod-product-compliance
Lightning Source LLC
Chambersburg PA
CBHW020409100426
42812CB00001B/262

* 9 7 8 1 8 3 9 7 5 8 8 9 8 *